# THE FILMS OF AKIRA KUROSAWA

# THE FILMS OF AKIRA KUROSAWA

by
DONALD RICHIE

with additional material by JOAN MELLEN

UNIVERSITY OF CALIFORNIA PRESS
Berkeley, Los Angeles, London

University of California Press
Berkeley and Los Angeles, California

University of California Press, Ltd.
London, England

First published in 1965; revised edition 1984; expanded
and updated 1996.

The essays on *Dodesukaden* and *Dersu Uzala* were written
by Joan Mellen for the 1979 Japanese edition of this book
(Kinema Jumpo-Sha, Tokyo); she also made additions to the
final chapter.

1 2 3 4 5 6 7 8 9


Richie, Donald, 1924–
    The films of Akira Kurosawa / Donald Richie.—3rd ed.,
expanded and updated.
        p.    cm.
    Filmography: p.
    Includes bibliographical references and index.
    ISBN 0–520–20026–8 (pbk.: alk. paper)
    1. Kurosawa, Akira, 1910–    —Criticism and interpretation.
I. Title.
PN1998.3.K87R5    1996                         95–47804
791.43'0233'092—dc20                           CIP

The paper used in this publication meets the minimum
requirements of American National Standard for Information
Sciences—Permanence of Paper for Printed Library Materials,
ANSI Z39.48–1984 ⊗

Stills on title-page are from *Sanjuro,* courtesy of Toho Co., Ltd.

A fishing spot along the Tamagawa River.

Kurosawa and Chiaki are fishing.

It is during the shooting of *Seven Samurai:* only half the film is finished, the budget is all used up, shooting is interrupted.

*Chiaki:* So what's going to happen?

*Kurosawa:* Well, the company isn't going to throw away all the money it's already put into the film. So long as my pictures are hits I can afford to be unreasonable. Of course, if they start losing money then I've made some enemies.

Money is found, shooting is begun again; money is used up, shooting is interrupted. Kurosawa and Chiaki go fishing again.

*Kurosawa:* (Dangling his line with some satisfaction.) Now that they've gotten in this deep, they have no choice but to finish it!

And, indeed, *Seven Samurai* finally got finished; it took over a year and was a big hit.

Chiaki's house.

He and Kurosawa are drinking; both are rather drunk.

*Kurosawa:* Hey, Chiaki. You probably got more for appearing in the picture than I got for directing it. You're too expensive!

*Chiaki:* (Frowning silence. Then his inner-voice speaks, though no one hears:) It isn't that I'm too expensive; it's that you're too cheap.

At the golf course.

Kurosawa and Chiaki are playing golf. Kurosawa hits the ball. It goes off to one side. Chiaki hits the ball. It goes high and straight—a beautiful shot.

*Kurosawa:* (Dejected.) Why is it I'm so lousy?

*Chiaki:* When you are making films you are a demon of strength; when you can't hit the golf-ball you are like some little girl. Where is this strength; where does it go?

*Kurosawa:* It is quite enough if a human being has but one thing where he is strong. (As though to console himself.) If a human being were strong in everything it wouldn't be nice for other people, would it?

Written by Minoru Chiaki upon being asked for a word-portrait of Akira Kurosawa.

# TABLE OF CONTENTS

**Acknowledgments**   In preparing this new edition I remain particularly grateful to Nagamasa and Kashiko Kawakita for long and valued assistance. In addition, I am indebted to the Kawakita Zaidan as well as to Toho, Shochiku, and Kurosawa Productions.

DONALD RICHIE
TOKYO
1996

# Akira Kurosawa

Akira Kurosawa was born in Tokyo in 1910. "I had three elder sisters and three elder brothers, so I was the last of seven children. I was also both a crybaby and real little operator. At the same time I was backward. Just after the war I saw Hiroshi Inagaki's *Forgotten Children* [a 1945 film about a retarded child] and there was a lot in it that reminded me of myself. It wasn't so much that I was really backward, perhaps, but that I was unusually gentle, unusually obedient.

"We were Edokko [third generation in Tokyo, with the implication of being a real Tokyoite] and my mother was a very gentle woman, but my father was quite severe. He was a graduate of the first class of the Toyama School [a school for training Army Officers] and after that he went into the Army. When he got out he became interested in physical education and was a member of the Japan Physical Education Association. He was extremely active—helped make Japan's first swimming pool.

"When I was little he was a teacher at the Ebara Middle School, more famous for graduating sportsmen than bright pupils—it was known for creating the strong in body and its methods were quite spartan. Since I was born and brought up at Tachiaigawa which was quite near, I remember often going to father's school and watching them play baseball from behind the net. I wasn't allowed to play. My two elder brothers had both gotten pleurisy by devoting themselves entirely to sport. Anyway, I wasn't very strong as a child and really couldn't have competed. At the time, however, I remember that what I had decided to be was the captain of a merchant vessel.

"When I was in the second year of primary school my family moved and I was transferred to the Kuroda Primary School at Edogawa. Keinosuke Uegusa was in the same class and we became friends —I was the class president and he was the vice-president."

Of this period, Keinosuke Uegusa, now a script-writer, has said: "When he first came, I remember, no one paid much attention to him but from his second year on he became class president. He has said that he was a crybaby when he was little. I don't remember any indication of this. He certainly was not the little-genius type who merely gets good grades, but neither was he the bully boy-leader type. I remember that he never chose favorites—he was always just as friendly with the bad boys of the class.

"We used to go together a lot to the banks of the Edogawa, a place called Kuseyama, and play there. He was good at *kendo* and usually had his bamboo sword with him. What he said, how he acted, were commanding. He had prestige. Without his even trying to, he became popular. Maybe it was because he came from the old samurai class, but even back then I remember he hated anything crooked or underhanded.

"He was fond of spelling and painting—and he was good at both. That all of us children were attracted to art was the doing of our teacher." Kurosawa has said that this teacher was the first important influence in his life. "From my second year on, the teacher in charge was named Tachikawa. He was really ahead of his time, as a great advocate for art education for the young. Also he was progressive and believed that the brightest children should get the most opportunity. I remember that on Sundays five or six of us would go invade his house, then sit around talking. It was he who introduced me to the fine arts—and through them, films.

"In this, my father—though an inflexible military man—encouraged me because he had an understanding of the new age. But I remember that when I entered the Keika Middle School, what I hated more than anything else was the military education. The instructor was an ex-military man, had been a captain, would make the boys [between twelve and seventeen years old] carry rifles and march around while he scolded and shouted. I always managed to get away and never once carried a rifle or a bayonet. Naturally, not once did I turn up for shooting practice with real bullets. I was always given a zero for the course.

"Around the time of my graduation from middle school, about 1927, I decided to become a painter and enrolled at the Doshusha School of Western Painting. During that time I became rather proficient and twice something I'd done was selected for the big Nika Exhibition. At the same time I decided to earn my living by painting, since all the money we ever had was my father's income, and would paint pictures for the cooking supplements of ladies' magazines, or illustrations for love stories. I would knock myself out doing this. But you can't make a living this way.

"My family was poor, I couldn't really study because I had to work so hard; even a tube of red paint was usually too expensive for me, there was no question of my going abroad to study. And, then I thought: Even if I could make my living by painting, who would look at my pictures?"

Uegusa had gone to a different middle school but "nevertheless, we met occasionally. Several years after graduation, Kurosawa and I both entered the Japan Proletariat Artists' Group. He was in the fine arts section. I was in the literary section. We signed up not because we were in love with Marxist theory but because we felt such a strong resistance against things as they were and in this group at that time we could study the new movements in art and literature. We were both much interested in the latter—particularly in nineteenth century Russian literature." Kurosawa remembers: "I was a great reader—we would talk for hours about Tolstoy, Turgenev, Dostoevsky, etc . . . particularly of Dostoevsky. I was very fond of him, and have remained so to this day. He was a great influence.

"Another influence, and someone I will never forget, was my elder brother Heigo. He was the third brother—that is, the one directly above me, and after Tachikawa he had the greatest influence on my life.

"He was artistic, and he loved films. During the end of the silentfilm period he was a *benshi* [film narrator-commentator] appearing under the name of Teimei Tsuda at the Musashino Cinema. He specialized in foreign silent films and used to fascinate his listeners with his detailed psychological descriptions.

"In father's eyes Heigo was always wrong. His way of life was too much for him because father was a former soldier and retained a soldier's outlook. Heigo liked to play around with art and it looked frivolous—that is why father always had it in for him. When Heigo said that he wanted to go and live with his girl, father got furious and threw him out of the house."

Shinbi Iida, the film critic, remembers this brother: "I knew him. When I was working for Shochiku at the Teikoku Theater in Asakusa we had a kind of letters-to-the-editor column in our program. Someone named Kurosawa used to write in all the time. His handwriting was excellent and the letters were so good that I would frequently publish them. He started coming to see me, would come to my place, and we would talk. He was a very tall, very pleasant young man. He didn't seem sad in the least, nor at all the kind of person who would do what he did."

Kurosawa remembers: "He went to live with the woman anyway and I used to go and see him, hiding it, naturally, from our father. I was always welcome. He would take me to *yosé* [traditional Japanese vaudeville] and to *kodan* [a story-telling entertainment where traditional samurai tales were told] and to the movies. He had a pass, since he worked for a theater, and I used to use it to go the movies free. We used to talk a lot too. I remember once we walked all the way from Ushigome where he lived to Asakusa [formerly the largest entertainment district in Tokyo] and back again, talking all the way. I learned a very great deal from him, particularly about literature.

"Then, one day, he went into the mountains of Yugashima and killed himself. I clearly remember the day before he committed suicide. He had taken me to a movie in the Yamate district and afterwards said that that was all for today, that I should go home. We parted at Shin Okubo station. He started up the stairs and I had started to walk off, then he stopped and called me back. He looked at me, looked into my eyes, and then we parted. I know now what he must have been feeling. He was a brother whom I loved very much and I have never gotten over this feeling of loss.

"In 1936 I knew that I would have to make my own living. Accidentally I happened to see a newspaper advertisement from the P.C.L. Studios—they wanted people to try out for assistant directorships. At that time, though I certainly did not dislike films, and went a lot, still I had no desire at all to make my name in the movies. What I mainly felt was that I could not be dependent on my parents. I had to make my own living and this seemed to offer a way.

"The ad said that I was to send in an essay pointing out the basic defects of Japanese films and how they could be remedied. I thought to myself, if the defect is basic, how do you remedy it?—but I wrote something and sent it in. Shortly thereafter I was called out to the studio. About five hundred people must have turned up. We were shown a newspaper clipping about a laborer who fell in love with a dancing girl and told to do a treatment of it. I remember writing something along the lines of a contrast between his black factory area and her bright Nichigeki-like environs. [The Nichigeki is the main Tokyo entertainment palace with movies, stage shows, and strip tease.]

"Afterwards we were taken to the studio restaurant and given curried rice to eat. That was the first time I saw Kajiro Yamamoto. He had hurt his foot, I remember, and didn't strike me as an imposing figure at all—later, when I saw him, I didn't even recognize him."

Yamamoto, who became Kurosawa's only teacher, remembers that "the first time I saw him was at these examinations. Most of the entrants were disqualified on the basis of the treatment they had written and only a few were given the oral examination. What I liked about Kurosawa's answers were that they showed that he knew a lot about things other than movies. In particular, he knew a lot about art—but he was no dilettante. When you asked him his favorite artists, he mentioned Ikeno Taiga [an eighteenth century landscape painter] and Tessai and Tetsugoro Urozu—and the reasons he gave for liking them were convincing. The kind of people we wanted at the time were those who could be trained by P.C.L., who showed promise. Kurosawa seemed to fit our qualifications and I recommended him."

Kurosawa remembers that "there were about seven people who took the orals. There were the examiners, all lined up. One of them kept asking about my family and I got angry and asked: Is this a criminal investigation? After that I was certain I had failed but I wasn't upset. I had already seen actresses thick with greasepaint and it made me feet slightly ill. Then I received notification that I'd been taken on. I talked with my father about whether I should go. He said: Well, isn't everything an experience? This decided me. I entered P.C.L.

"I didn't like it. Several times I just got fed up and tried to quit. Each time, though, those I was working with talked me out of it. Then I became attached to Kajiro Yamamoto's group and thereafter everything changed. He was a real teacher and it was due to him that I settled down and made movies my life work.

"He never made a film without involving everyone in it—we were all drawn directly into the experience of making a film. When I became one of his assistants, he would talk over everything with me, and gradually I caught his enthusiasm. He taught me in the most graphic way all about the various stages of production, about scenario writing, about editing, the whole a-b-c of directing. He used to let us substitute for him, letting us put all of these theories into practice."

Yamamoto remembers: "From the day he came I knew I was right about him. He was quite able to get along with people but he was also firm with them. I told him, I remember, to write some scenarios and by the time he had done two or three he knew how. He was so full of ideas. Assistant directors are kept pretty busy but somehow he always found time to turn up with yet another scenario—he is completely creative.

"He is the inspired rather than the buckle-down-and-get-it-done type. These scenarios were absolutely superior, both in content and in expression. And I remember, when I taught him about editing, he learned it at once. He had natural talent.

"He learned more than just the tricks of the trade. If we had time we talked about art, or about women. Talking about it often enough is just not the real thing and sometimes he and Senkichi Taniguchi and I would go over to Tamanoi which was then one of the biggest of the whorehouse districts. We'd go after work to one of the small bars there and the girls would come over and sit around and talk. There were occasional airraids and people were rushing around with gas masks slung over their shoulders, and there we would sit, more or less free among ourselves of the great burdens of being at war. In a way ours was a tiny little resistance against the times.

"Assistant directors are kept extremely busy," remembers Kurosawa," and it was about that time that the sheer labor started building me up and I got much stronger. Also, assistant directors are supposed to write scripts. I remember that one of the producers made me do one about a *naniwabushi* singer and I thought the script was really lousy and then it turned out they paid me a lot for it. But the real reason that I was turning out one script after another was that I wanted to be a director myself and they wouldn't let me. Whatever I brought them, they never said: Fine, go out and direct it. So, then I would say: All right, what about this one then?

"Among these early scripts I particularly like *A German at the Daruma Temple*. The chief character was based on Bruno Taut. The original was stolen by someone but I was so full of it that I had no difficulty rewriting it. All of these scenarios were full of images, I remember—much more so than now—and I always wrote them as though I were going to direct them. Another one I liked was *Three Hundred Miles through Enemy Lines*. I would really have loved to have directed it. [It was finally filmed in 1957 by Daiei, with Issei Mori directing.] I remember I wrote it in three days and had von Suppe's *Light Cavalry Overture* on the phonograph all the time. It is rather fast music, you know, and the film was all about Cossacks. Three days—my head was so full of wonderful images I could hardly put them all down.

"One of the Yamamoto films I worked on was *The Loves of Tojuro* and it starred Takako Irie [whom Kurosawa later used in *The Most Beautiful* and who played the refined old lady in *Sanjuro*]. It was about an Osaka actor, a period-piece, there were lots of extras. It was my job to select these and keep them together. I noticed one of them. I went up to him. It was Uegusa."

This schoolboy friend of Kurosawa remembers: "All the time he was being an apprentice at the studio, I was studying drama and I never had enough money. So I decided to be an extra for a while. I went out to the Toho studios and turned around, and there he was. He gave me a five-yen note."

"I said," says Kurosawa: "This is all I have on me so take it and go home. He was terribly moved but my real feeling was that if he stayed around the set we would both be so embarrassed that we couldn't work. But he didn't go home. He worked there and made the day's wage and then went home."

Later, Kurosawa and Uegusa made a number of films together. The first was *One Wonderful Sunday*. "After it was released," says Uegusa, "we got a letter. It was from our old teacher, Tachikawa, and he was filled with the joy that any teacher would feel when he found out that two of his pupils had made their way in the world, had done something together." Kurosawa remembers: "I was delighted to find he was still alive. We hadn't heard anything at all about him during or after the war. But he was even more pleased than we were—two little boys whom he had led by the hand were doing something adult together. We decided to invite him out." They did so, and Uegusa remembers: "That was a time when no one had very much, so we decided to ask him to the Toho dormitory where we were staying. We had sukiyaki which during those years was just about the biggest treat you could give anyone. And I remember that teacher's teeth had gotten so bad he couldn't eat anything. There he was, the teacher we remembered as so healthy, so strong, sitting there before us, and we both realized what a very long time it had been. He seemed really pleased though, and after that we have sometimes heard from him. It

must make him proud to have been Kurosawa's first and most important teacher."

"I remember Kurosawa learning to direct," says Yamamoto. "When we were making *Horses* he was still called my assistant, but he was much more than that, he was more like my other self. He took responsibility for the second unit work in this semi-documentary about farmers in the Tohoku district. I could come down to Tokyo and work on a musical comedy knowing that things were going fine up in the country.

"If there was any discrepancy between the script and the rushes, it was he who saw it and worked at it until it was right. Even when I felt like passing it, it was he who would say: No, Mr. Yamamoto, this won't do. In fact, he would always hold out much more than I would, and I remember how surprised the staff, the light people, the costume people, were at this. We all had to admit he was right, however. The Kurosawa view was always the correct one. As this process repeated itself again and again, everyone began to realize how enormously talented he was. People began to talk about him and his brilliant future."

"When I remember those days I think of Yamamoto," says Kurosawa. "There were quite a number of us at Toho who were educated under him. We don't all make movies the same way but each one of us reveals something. If we are able to reveal something of ourselves in our films, it is due to Yamamoto and what he taught us. When I think back, the reason I am today what I am is simply because I was very fortunate. At every crisis in my life there was someone—Tachikawa, my brother, Yamamoto, to help me, to teach me, to pull me along. I really believe that no one has been as lucky as I have been."

"From the very beginning," Yamamoto has said, "Kurosawa was completely engrossed in separating what is real from what is false. He is intensely concerned with this, and holds out until everything is just the way that he sees it. This is terribly important in a director and I think it shows much of him as an artist. He undoubtedly had it as a painter, and he has certainly kept it as a director. He was ready for *Sanshiro Sugata* when his chance came."

# Sanshiro Sugata

## 1943

"*Sugata* was my first film as a director," says Kurosawa, "but in films like *Horses,* I had been so much in charge of production that I felt like the director. Somehow I didn't feel as though it were the first time. I thought I knew what it was all about. Still, those around me told me that when I first shouted *camera, action* my voice sounded quite strange.

"I remember how it came about that I got to be director. I had heard of a new novel by Tsuneo Tomita called *Sanshiro Sugata* and I decided that it was for me. I went to Iwao Mori's house—he was the producer then—and asked him to buy the rights for me. 'Have you read it yet?' he asked. 'It hasn't come out yet—how could I?' I asked. When it finally appeared, I bought a copy, and read it in one evening, then went to his house and said: 'This I can do—please let me do it.' He bought it and two days later every major studio was after it. It was ideal as an entertainment film and that was about all we were allowed to make back in 1943."

One of the reasons that Kurosawa was allowed to direct had to do with the novel itself. Two of his scripts had been printed and one had won the Education Minister's prize but none were made because, in the language of the time, "they failed to meet the government-specified requirements of a wartime film." It was said that the reason none of his early scripts were filmed (until after the war) was that they showed too much American influence.

Tsuneo Tomita's novel was considered quite safe. It was about something martial, the rivalry between judo and jujitsu; it was extremely "Japanese"; it was reassuringly period and it was, above all, popular—belonging to that genre of historical novels which in the West has produced *Anthony Adverse* and the works of Kenneth Roberts. Toho had, for some time, been considering using Kurosawa in a more creative way and his own enthusiasm for the novel decided them.

Kurosawa has said: "When I think of this picture I remember mostly having had a good time making it. It was wartime and you weren't allowed to say anything worth saying. The information bureau was being extremely troublesome, saying you can't film this and you can't shoot that. All the directors had to make films in accordance with national policy. Back then everyone was saying that the real

Japanese-style film should be as simple as possible. I disagreed and got away with disagreeing—that much I could say. I decided that, since I couldn't say anything very much, I would make a really movie-like movie."

# STORY AND TREATMENT

Even now *Sugata* is a surprising picture. That it was the debut film of a thirty-three year-old and was made in 1943 is astonishing. From the very first sequence the director is fully in command in a way that very few directors ever are—particularly in Japan—and the film as a whole has directness, economy, and a superb athletic beauty.

The opening sequence begins with the title: 1882—under which is a typical Meiji-period street-scene. Susumu Fujita playing Sugata—his first major screen role—walks down the street and turns into an alley. A group of young girls are playing and singing.

Girls: "Where does this path lead?
It leads to the shrine of the heavenly gods.
May I get past?
No, those without right may not pass."
Sugata: But I have the right.
Girl: To pray?
Sugata: No, I am looking for the jujitsu teacher.
Girl: "It is easy to go but hard to return."

In this initial short scene, Kurosawa has suggested the theme of the film, the education of Sugata, who learns not only about judo but also about himself. The song (the first four lines and the last given above) also suggests the story: those without the need never know themselves but knowledge makes difficulties. This is what Sugata will discover during the course of the film and Kurosawa suggests this so subtly in this opening that it is only afterwards that one understands what he had done.

At the end of this scene, Kurosawa first used the punctuation which will be his favorite throughout all of his work. It is the wipe, a punctuation mark much less common than the cut, the fade, or the dissolve. The new image pushes off the old, as one lantern slide pushes off the other. The device is relatively uncommon in modern cinema and yet is so consistently used by Kurosawa that it seems to have a definite meaning for him. Perhaps it is its finality that appeals, this single stroke cancelling all that went before, questioning it, at the same time bringing in the new. It is often used after an important scene, as though he calls attention to the fact that it is over, that it was important.

It is rarely used, however, to indicate the passage of time (like most other directors, for this he uses fades or dissolves) and here the following scene is one which chronologically follows—Sugata finds the house of the jujitsu master and offers himself as a pupil.

The master and his men are talking about judo—a variant form of self-defense which has just come to their notice. It is new, untried, seemingly complicated with ritual, rich in spiritual overtones. The jujitsu master makes fun of it, the men laugh. Then Sugata, in all innocence asks: "What is judo?"

Judo will become Sugata's life, it will be his identity, yet he does not know what it is. And one of the points of judo is that one never knows what it is until one has done it. It is, above all else, a spiritual discipline and his question is both pertinent and child-like. To ask a group of jujitsu experts this is like asking the Shinto priest: What is zen?—or like asking the protestant minister: What is the holy ghost?

The jujitsu men laugh. But, after all, they do not know either. Sugata kneels on the *tatami* and looks first at one and then the other. They tell him that judo is a fraud and the teacher is an impostor. Another says that this new kind of jujitsu is dangerous, that they cannot allow it, particularly since they have finally gotten the police to start learning old-fashioned jujitsu. Yet another says that Sugata is fortunate for this very evening they intend to have a showdown.

Sugata looks at them, open, innocent. This scene, too, has its hidden meaning, hidden until we have seen the entire film. Sugata starts his career when he asks: What is judo? Further, if the picture is about education, then it is also about initiation—for, as it turns out, Sugata's education is one long initiation.

This follows at once, and shows a form which Kurosawa later uses in most of his pictures: first, theory; then, practice. We are told about judo and then, during the fight that follows, we watch it. In addition, and more important, however, practice and theory in the world of Kurosawa almost always also means reality versus illusion. What we have just heard about judo is not true. We watch judo and we know it is not true.

The fight takes place at night on a deserted pier. The moon illuminates the scene. The judo expert is stopped, challenged. With his back to the water he silently and efficiently disposes of one man after the other, throwing them over his shoulder into the bay. Yet, each throw is different. The entire battle is an explication of judo and each throw is

revelatory of a different technique. When one compares this with all of the battles to come in Kurosawa's films—with sword, spear, gun, knife—one sees that all of his fights are intensely concerned with technique and with making this technique clear and understandable.

The battle is silent. There is no music, nothing to detract from the combat. Opponents face each other, neither moving, time passes, then with a cry the attacker leaps, is surprised, flashes through the air, and there is yet another splash in the water. All of Kurosawa's battles are like this. They begin with immobility, then spring into action. Often—as in the later fights in *Sugata*—the real battle is before the grappling, when the two, perfectly matched, stand silent, unmoving before the other. The struggle is so intense that both are sweating without having once moved. Kurosawa's picture of confrontation in all of his later films is this. The battle is spiritual—action is the outcome of a spiritual tension.

Finally all of the jujitsu men are in the bay, Sugata stands nearby, an observer, and the judo teacher looks about him, unruffled, and says: "It is a shame that all of this feeling wasn't put into developing jujitsu."

This is the end of the first reel. Only ten minutes have elapsed and yet Kurosawa is not only deep within his story, he has also, with great art, indicated the theme and presaged the conclusion. This first reel has become famous in Japanese cinema, as indeed it ought, because here is something which the Japanese film had not until this time known. One might compare it with the ordinary period-film, to see the many differences.

It might well have begun with the fight, full of shouts and screams, action all over the screen with comic touches from the jujitsu men floundering in the water. Or, if it had begun as does Kurosawa's film, the opening song would have been merely decorative and Sugata might have stopped to pat one of the children's heads to show how gentle he essentially is. With the jujitsu men, one would have seen at once that they were villains (rather than individuals who actually have a very good reason for disliking judo) and only Sugata—limited if gentle—would have failed to realize this. Or, Sugata—gentle and very bright—would have joined the judo expert and thrown his share of jujitsu men into the water, thus instantly establishing himself as hero. All of these possibilities are seen hundreds of times in the average period-film—they are accepted attitudes. Even more likely, Sugata would never have gone to the rival's school. He would have called on the judo man, become his student, and the first reel would have ended with his revealing his prowess. Kurosawa is not interested in Sugata's prowess, however. He is only interested in Sugata's education—which is a much more interesting subject.

This, the next sequence illustrates. Some time has passed. Sugata has apparently gotten very good indeed and we watch him break up a village festival. He is using all of the correct judo procedures, besting one man after the other. All of this is shown with fast cutting at its most seductive. It is an exhilarating passage. It is like something from the ordinary Japanese fight-picture, only much more skillfully done. We—not yet guessing what the picture is about—think: that Sugata is a real man, a real hero. The crowd thinks so. There are cries of how wonderful he is, how marvelous. Sugata, carried away, attacks one man after the other, always winning.

There is a cut to the judo teacher's room. Everything is still. He does not move, there is no movement on the screen, and after the furious motion of the sequence directly before it is like an admonition. He sits there, as though waiting, the seconds pass. Then Sugata, his kimono torn, comes in.

*Teacher:* Well, you must feel good after having thrown so many people around.

*Sugata:* I'm sorry.

*Teacher:* I rather wanted to see you in action. You're very strong, really very strong indeed. Maybe you are even stronger than I am now. But, you know, there is very little similarity between your kind of judo and my kind of judo. Do you know what I mean? You do not know how to use it, you do not know the way of life. And to teach judo to someone who does not know that is like giving a knife to a madman.

*Sugata:* But I know it.

*Teacher:* That is a lie. To act as you do, without meaning or purpose, to hate and attack—is that the way of life? No—the way is loyalty and love. This is the natural truth of heaven and earth. It is the ultimate truth and only through it can a man face death.

*Sugata:* I can face death. I'm not afraid to die right now, if you order it.

*Teacher:* Shut up, you're nothing but a common street-fighter.

*Sugata:* I'm not afraid to die.

*Teacher:* Then go and die.

Then Sugata does an extraordinary thing. He opens the *shoji* and without a look backward or below he leaps.

This extraordinary leap, right out of the house, lands him—as it did the jujitsu men—in the water, only this water is the lotus pond and we see that the teacher has been living in a temple. The nuances and hidden meanings in this sequence are worth investigating. Death is introduced as the great adversary, and this is something Sugata will discover at the end of the film where he is almost killed. What saves him then is a remembered vision of this scene with the teacher and later, in the pond. It is there, if anywhere, that he comes to realize "the way of life." At the same time, now, his teacher has thrown him into the water just as surely as he did the jujitsu men. Water is always a purification, a baptism; and, as in Christian baptism, it is also an initiation. That the teacher has been living in a temple is no accident for a temple

is the home of initiation, and of faith, and Sugata's extraordinary leap can be understood as that—a leap into faith. The *shoji* opens—there is the lotus pond, he chooses to leap.

After the leap comes the trial. Sugata has gotten himself into the water, it is up to his shoulders, it is cold. The teacher may have thrown him but he himself chose to be thrown. He had thought to prove that he was not afraid to die but, once in the pool, it becomes apparent that all he can prove is that he is not afraid to live.

This sequence, Sugata in the pool, is of a beauty that even now, a whole war and over two decades away, can move almost to tears. He grasps a post, holding himself to it, and—clinging there—stares. Lost, confused, afraid, unsure, he can only cling to this post, the cold waters around him. Later one of the priests points to the post and tells him that that was his staff of life—and so it was. Without it to center himself upon he might have climbed out of the pond, it was easy enough to have done. But he does not. He clings and waits. The priest tries to

talk with him. Sugata, unsure, shows defiance, refuses to answer, and the priest says: "Judging from the fact that you refuse to answer, you still have not received enlightenment. All right, you can spend the night looking at the moon."

The camera watches Sanshiro. He stays in the water, holding onto the post, looking up at the moon. There is a particularly beautiful transition as the last light of evening fades from the *shoji* of the teacher's room and the light appears—he is there, just on the other side of the paper. Outside it is night. Sanshiro looks at the moon.

There is a close-up of the moon, and over it the sound of frogs, followed by a direct cut to Sanshiro in the pond, faintly lighted, mists around him, and the distant call of a rooster. It is dawn. He turns, then looks. Before him a lotus is open. There is a short scene of Sugata looking at it, uncomprehendingly, the look of an animal. Then —and the beauty of the scene is such that no description can suggest it—Sugata understands. He has seen truth and beauty and this he shows. He races from the pond, he pounds on the teacher's door—it opens at once, the teacher was not asleep. The priests and other students appear. Sugata has understood, the trial is over.

If this film were about boxing or wrestling, or almost any other kind of sport, such mystical overtones would seem irrelevant and ostentatious. But there is a mystique about judo and judo is a discipline just as much as zen is. It is not accidental that so many young enthusiasts are given to lives of meditation and self-denial. The way of life is a known route.

And it is precisely this which appealed to Kurosawa in the original book and which he underlines in his film. The entire lotus-pond passage did not appear in the book. Kurosawa wrote it. As later in *Rashomon*, he adds to a literary conception something of which only film is capable. Sugata's vigil is something to be seen, to be lived through, and to be remembered. And it is, tellingly, this image which —above all others—remains alive in the memory long after the film has been experienced. That is, after all, what remains of all films— these separate images, alive in the mind long after the film itself may be forgotten. When Kurosawa said that he wanted to make a really movie-like movie this is what he meant. The construction is superb, the cutting is marvelous—but it is the inexplicable, the unexpected, the truly moving which remains behind.

# CHARACTERIZATION

Kurosawa was very interested in judo, just as he is very interested in sword-fighting, but this interest is here, as always, incidental to the question about the way men fight. He is not too interested in any of his films in *why*—he is continually interested in *how*.

His interest is in a certain kind of character. Since all men have much the same reasons for action, their only differentiation can be in how they act. The Kurosawa hero is a very special sort of person and since he (from film to film) shows the same characteristics, it is well to examine the first of the line.

Sugata seems to be average in all ways. His only difference is that he wants to be different from what he is. It is he who searches for a teacher and, having found one, persists in learning. The path to inner wisdom, according to Kurosawa, is a very difficult one, so difficult indeed that very few are those who even manage its beginnings—and no one, of course, ever discovers its ending. Yet, difficult though it is, the Kurosawa hero is distinguished by his perseverance, by his refusal to be defeated. His victories are neither easy nor apparent and often the final bout occurs without audience, with no spectators to record the event. They are not necessary because the struggle is always an inner one. It is like the real judo bout, the real sword fight, where the outcome is determined before the first movement, where effort makes sweat start on men who have not yet begun to move. This effort is spiritual—and all of Kurosawa's films have as their turning point a spiritual crisis. It is here—in the mind—that resolution takes place. The action which follows is usually the outcome of this resolution. It is, again, the practical aspect of the theoretical. The detective in *Stray Dog* lives in anguish because it is his pistol which is killing others. His crisis is his finally accepting this seemingly absurd responsibility and his action results in his catching the murderer. The hero of *Ikiru* knows not only that he is to die, he also knows when. This is his crisis and he must in a short time vindicate his life. The park which he creates is symbolic action. Because he has finally accomplished something he may now die. In *High and Low*, the moment of anguish occurs when the manufacturer must pay a ransom which will ruin him, and do it for a reason which is completely peripheral to himself. His action comes at the very end of the picture when he must confront the man responsible for his ruin and to realize that he was responsible for that man. The young hero of *Red Beard*, like Sugata, also searches for and finds a teacher. His crisis occurs when, far from finding someone to take care of him, he is given someone to take care of himself.

Sugata is a much less involved hero than some and his trials take the form of direct bouts, feats of skill and strength. Likewise, his picture is without the metaphysical complication of *Record of a Living Being* or, above all, *High and Low*. Nonetheless, this heroic pattern which Kurosawa evolves fits Sugata very well. His trials are all predicated upon the strength which he showed first in leaping into the pond, and then in remaining there, keeping himself deaf to the seducing councils of self-preservation, propriety, and common sense.

In the final trial he must face the villain. Since most Kurosawa films have no villains (because we understand them all too well and this, in fact, is the main problem of the hero: he understands his opponent, he sees in him merely another man, and he feels compassion) and since

absolute evil does not exist in Kurosawa's world, this ur-opponent is very interesting.

He is a man of the world—which Sugata is certainly not. He is well dressed, wears a moustache, is even slightly foppish. Also, he obviously knows what he is about. He is so good that he need never show his strength. He would not, one feels, ever resort to throwing people around as we know Sugata has done. And yet something is missing in him. Sugata may not know the "way of life" but at least he is learning. This man will never know it. He shows it in little ways. At one point, smoking a cigarette—the mark of a dandy in Meiji Japan—he does not bother to look for an ashtray. Instead, he disposes of his ash in an open flower, part of an arrangement on a nearby table. Sugata would not do that because it would not occur to him to do it. Flowers—the lotus—mean something else to Sugata. And later, when they are locked in battle on the moor, it is the vision of the open lotus (seen in superimposition) that gives him strength, that lets him break the strangle hold. One may cavil at all of this symbolism but the idea is sound enough: strength is to be found through gentleness, respect for yourself is found only through respect for other things.

Kurosawa remembers: "Ryunosuke Tsukigata was playing the villain. The critics all said that in his portrayal he influenced me too much, got out of hand. That is not true. If it looked as though he overacted it was because I told him to. I was much more interested in his character than in the hero's."

This is, in a way, a typical remark and Kurosawa has often preferred his villains. His preference, however, should be understood in a particular way. The hero is man actively engaged in becoming himself —never a very reassuring sight. The villain, on the other hand, has already become something. Everything about Tsukigata suggests that he has arrived. There is not a wasted gesture, not an uncalculated movement. He has found what is to his advantage and acts accordingly. Sugata, by comparison, is all thumbs.

Kurosawa's preference is the preference we all have for the formed man. In the ordinary film this man would be the hero. But he is not and, despite his admiration, Kurosawa has told us why. One of the attributes of all of his heroes, beginning with Sugata, is that they are all unformed in just this way. For this reason, all of his pictures are about education—the education of the hero.

The first meeting of the hero and the villain makes this difference clear. We see Sugata, head and shoulders. He is doing something odd but we do not know what. He seems to be marching up and down in the same spot. The villain appears, suave, self-assured, and the two have a short talk, commonplace but for the intensity of Sugata's instant antagonism and the cold interest of the villain in the hero. The camera dollies back. There stands the villain, immaculate; and there stands Sugata—he has been doing his laundry by treading on it. One can no more imagine the villain doing his laundry than one can imagine a foppish Sugata smoking a cigarette. The latter is almost a boy by comparison with the former—and it is boys who must learn, have initiations, and be educated.

The villain insists upon fighting Sugata then and there. He is refused. The teacher says that Sugata will not fight, that he is still training. When they finally do, at the end of the film, the villain says: "If you had allowed Sugata and myself to have fought each other at first, it would not have been necessary for us to fight now."

The implication is that the formed man always sees the unformed as a challenge, precisely because he is unformed. He always feels possibility a threat and he seeks to destroy it. This theme is a continual one in Kurosawa's pictures and the unformed hero is, likewise, ready for the trial when it comes. Here Sugata says: "You can laugh if you want to because what we are going to do is absurd—but, nonetheless, it is our destiny."

Destiny, however, is something Sugata is in the process of making. Every day he has a new destiny. The villain, on the other hand, has achieved a destiny. In other words, he has become what he thinks he is. He is truly self-made, but the fact that he thinks the job completed reveals his weakness. He is—as are so many of the bad men in Kurosawa—a completed sum. He might as well be dead. And it is just for this reason that the unformed but living Sugata is a threat, an object of hatred for him.

Sugata does not know who he himself is. He has become interested in a girl and then learns that her father is his opponent. His reaction is the decent one—he won't fight, and if he must then he will purposely lose. He and the priest have some talk about this:

*Sugata:* That girl is innocent and pure. I cannot fight her father.
*Priest:* Then you should become as innocent as she.
*Sugata:* I'm not. I cannot . . .

*Priest:* You were once. In that pond Sanshiro Sugata was born.
*Sugata:* . . .
*Priest:* What are you, Sanshiro Sugata? Who are you?

This is the question. Like any athlete he has tried to realize himself, to prove his identity through his body. Now he has a problem where it is just this identification which is not enough.

It is, however, all that he has: He goes to the fight. He faces the girl's father. And he throws him, time after time, his face contorted with distress, with pain, yet he continues to throw him until he has won. He has, indeed, become as pure as she. And it is this resolution which later saves him. He has purposely blinded himself to the seductive call of decency, compassion, love. At the end of the fight he is the winner, but he is profoundly shaken, shocked—shocked by his own possibilities, by what the kind, gentle, compassionate Sugata is capable of.

The last of the trials of the flesh occurs high on the plains of Ukyogahara where he finally meets the villain in combat. The field, filled with tall standing rushes, is so high that the clouds rush overhead with an almost incredible rapidity. Kurosawa has prepared his climax with extreme care. Two sequences earlier, when Sugata is eating with the girl and her father, all having become friends, the villain enters. As he stands there looking at them there is the sound of wind rising. There is a direct cut to the villain's letter of challenge and his voice reads it. Only the letter is visible and the sound of wind rises. At the end of the letter (" . . . in passing, it is also hereby announced that the fight may be to the death.") there is a cut to a close-up of the *shoji* in the teacher's study (just off the lotus pond) and the shadows of the bamboo, lashed by the wind. There is a direct cut to the plains and the tossing bamboo are replaced by the streaming clouds, by the rushes rippling in the wind like a river. There is Sugata, standing in the middle of this fantastic landscape. He is reciting:

> In his right hand he held a sword,
> And astride a horse rode the youth.
> Do not weep, do not weep, dearest Ao,
> Though it is not love that he thinks of tonight.
> The rain is falling and his armour is drenched
> And though he must try
> He cannot climb the pass at Tawara.

A number of parallel transitions have brought us here, from the domestic supper scene to the wild setting for the duel, done it in less than half a minute, and done so with such tact and skill that we are already prepared. The wind motive has continued throughout, a crescendo; the letter has become poetry read and then poetry spoken; the single flower arrangement in the girl's house has become the bamboo, become this great flowing plain. And the song—a very early poem of the sort associated with classical aspiration, with spiritual meditation—is the story of Sugata until now.

There is another, and even more subtle transition. It has become night. The meal was supper, the *shoji* scene was the last of sunset, and this fantastic plain is now illuminated by the moon. Thus this final duel is, like the first, nocturnal. Like Sugata's meditation in the lotus pond, it occurs at night. From this debut film on Kurosawa has shown himself fond of the extended cyclic form—things returning to their beginnings but with a great and inalterable difference. More, here—as in *High and Low*—night, when everyone else is sleeping, when one is truly alone, is where the greatest struggles occur, unobserved, unrecorded.

This fight scene which follows has become the most famous in all Japanese cinema and its influence continues until now. The fight on the moor at the end of Kobayashi's excellent *Harakiri*, for example, owes everything to this night-time battle. It is silent but for the rushing wind and the sound of reeds trampled upon. It is motionless for almost a minute and then erupts into action so swift one can almost not follow it. As in the sword-fights in *Seven Samurai* and *Sanjuro*, we see two men, opposed, still as statues. Then the action is so sudden, so furious, that the two men become fused, welded into the very image of battle. There is none of the wary circling of the ordinary *chambara* swordsmen. Two men are apart, and then suddenly—with no transition—they are one. And this what battle really is. Hate welds together just as strongly as love; only indifference separates.

After this superb battle—one which Sugata barely and only with the greatest difficulty wins—one might expect the picture to end with some kind of statement that he has at last grown-up, that he has arrived, that he has *become* something—the great judo champion. This would be the logical Western conclusion to a film about the education of a hero.

Kurosawa, however, has seen that this cannot be true. A hero who actually *becomes* is tantamount to a villain—for this was the only tangible aspect of the villain's villainy. To suggest that peace, contentment, happiness, follows a single battle, no matter how important, is literally untrue—and it would limit Sugata precisely because of the limitations suggested in the words "happiness" or "judo champion." After the battle we would expect to see him with the girl and her father preparing

20

for maturity. Instead we learn from the priest that he has decided to take a trip—that he is no longer here.

> Priest: Well, someone should tell him that when he gets into trouble again he should come and look at that post in the lotus pond.
> Deacon: I don't think that will be necessary. He has finally grown up.
> Teacher: Oh, no, not yet, not yet. He is still just a little boy.

Cut to a train, one of those charming Meiji-period trains, all engine and smoke and rattling cars covered with ormolou and gingerbread. Inside sit Sanshiro and the girl, each embarrassed, saying very little to the other. She has come to see him off and will return from the next station. Sugata's big capable hands hang loose in his lap. He is blushing. He shows a mixture of pain and pleasure, bashfulness and pride. He is uncomfortable but pleased. Now he is very good at judo indeed, but the ways of life are many and he doesn't know what to make of the girl. She suddenly gets something in her eye and we leave them there, he

insisting that he must help her get it out but, at the same time having no idea how to go about it.

The absurd and lovable train chugs around the corner carrying them away.

# STYLE

A director's style is often an accumulation of details, various short-cuts he has devised, various preferences appearing in picture after picture, a certain predilection for a certain kind of story, the fondness for a particular kind of image. In this Kurosawa is no different from anyone else. What is unusual is that from his first film onward the elements

of his style should be so visible. He himself has said that he knew just how to film this debut film. This is completely true: most of the elements of his style are as visible here as they are in *Red Beard*.

Besides this fondness for a certain kind of story, a certain kind of hero, for cyclic form, for theory and practice in parallel scenes, for the resultant implications of illusion and reality; and besides his liking for such punctuation marks as the wipe—there are many other elements of the Kurosawa style which are visible in *Sugata*.

Most important, since his craft is based directly upon it, are the various short-cuts, the many telescopings, the extraordinary economy of the way in which he shows his story. The Kurosawa film lacks any extraneous scenes, is without longueurs, and all unimportant transitions are missing. His craftsmanship and his economy are one. This efficiency, as rare in films as it is in anything else, accounts for much of the compelling interest generated by a Kurosawa picture, by the immediacy of its action, and in his debut film some of the devices through which it is realized are worth examining.

After the first fight all of Sugata's jujitsu acquaintances are floundering in the bay. The judo teacher, who came by rickshaw, stands looking at him—the only person left, the rickshaw puller having fled. Sugata stands up, goes to the rickshaw, the teacher steps in. Then Sugata steps out of his wooden clogs and, since there is no place to put them on the rickshaw itself, and since he must run barefoot if he is to pull, he looks at them, then puts them down in the middle of the road. There is a Japanese phrase, *geta o azukeru*, which literally means to hand over the wooden clogs but has the figurative meaning of putting oneself in the hands of others. Perhaps this was in Kurosawa's mind when he constructed the sequence which follows. Sugata, having put himself in the hands of the judo teacher, and made himself barefoot to do so, pulls the rickshaw off down the road. The camera, however, turns toward the forgotten *geta*. In a series of short cuts we see: broad daylight, the *geta* on their sides; evening, a puppy chewing on them; morning, one of them high on a fence post, where a child perhaps put it; in the rain; in the stream leading into the bay, caught against a rock; floating free and going down to the ocean. In this fifteen-second bridge we see what has happened to the *geta*. At the same time we see that this is another presage. Sugata himself, after various adventures and complications "floats free." At the same time—and this is the ostensible reason for the bridge—we see that time is passing.

However, from the last image of this sequence (the *geta* floating down to the sea) to the first sequence of the next (Sugata fighting with the crowd) there is only a direct cut. Consequently there is no way of seeing that these are two separate sequences. One flows into the other and we only know that time has elapsed. The fight-sequence is made of the same kind of short shots and the implication is unavoidable. The *geta* is only presage—Sugata is by no means floating free as yet. And this is shown in the most natural and simple way.

The *geta* floating is shown in close-up. The next cut shows the river itself, the *geta* floating along it. The camera pans up from the *geta* to show the bank, people running, and then a pan to show what they are running to. The pan stops at Sugata. In other words, both elements in these two sequences are shown within the same cut—a device which registers the strongest possible immediacy. We can now guess that presage and actuality are far from each other. The next cut shows Sanshiro fighting the crowd.

As in the beginning, Kurosawa later uses songs both as presage and as bridges from one sequence to the other. After his first fight, Sugata becomes very famous, particularly among the children, and they make up a song about him:

> Here comes Sanshiro,
> Don't get near him, that's Sanshiro.
> Keep away, don't touch him—
> Let's run away.
> Be careful, be careful. That's Sanshiro.

The children are never seen, only heard in the distance. Upon the first occasion the villain is speaking with the girl and uses this song as transition for talk about Sugata—this dangerous man who will be fighting her father. After the fight the children are singing their song again. They run past in the distance. Then he and she are seen walking. There is a slow fade to a single lamp. It is evening—then another fade to her house. He is sitting by her father.

This short passage shows both the economy and the nuances of which Kurosawa from the first was capable. To the children Sugata is a kind of sacred monster. So he was to the girl who feared for her father. The worst has happened. She walks silently with him. He goes and sees her father. This seems to contradict the song, which is fading into the distance as he sits by the older man. Again, as always, illusion (bad Sugata) and reality (good Sugata)—and, again, these suggestions are woven into a passage the ostensible reason for which is bridging between two sequences. The middle image, the lamp, is completely abstract, a turning point, like a pillow-word in Japanese poetry. Yet such is the economy of Kurosawa's style that it is not arbitrary. In the context of this ten-second bridge it shares the immediacy of the images on either side of it.

Economy at its most daring is seen in the introduction of the girl. Sugata and his teacher are walking near a shrine. They see a girl praying. The teacher says: "Look—isn't that beautiful? Sugata—do you know why? It is because right now she has forgotten all evil. She is praying. She has forgotten herself and is in harmony with god." Over his words are a series of cuts, each one nearer to the praying girl. Next—with only a straight cut as punctuation—the girl is walking and Sanshiro is behind her. It could be the next day, or the following week. Her *geta* thong breaks and it is Sanshiro who comes to her assistance. (The *geta* theme reoccurs here and his fixing it for her would seems to

suggest that she—in some future time, after the film has ended—will put herself in his hands.) He fixes it with the short towel which most kimonoed Japanese still carry with them. The next sequence is a series of tiny scenes, each about two seconds long, with the girl meeting him —apparently every day— and trying to return the towel. She is wearing a different kimono each time, the weather is each time different, her inflection is always different, and each time Sugata (having discovered that she is the daughter of the man he must fight) finds some excuse to run away. The telescoping of action is extreme, a whole week collapsed into fifteen seconds, but the continuity is kept. Not until films such as *Marienbad* and *Vivre sa vie* was such extraordinary brevity seen again and its presence in a Japanese commercial film in 1943 is completely surprising.

It certainly surprised the critics when the film was released but in drab wartime Japan such invention was exhilarating. Later when he experimented even more freely in *No Regrets for Our Youth* the critics took exception to such extreme freedom, calling it confusing and, in particular, complaining about the extremely rapid cutting.

But, in *Sugata* Kurosawa is first seen as "the world's greatest editor" (which is what his staff still calls him) because the impact of these short scenes, and the continuity of both the story and its implications, depend entirely upon his sense of timing and his feeling for tempo. That he knew what he was doing is indicated in his editing of the 1965 Toho remake of this film, directed by Seiichiro Uchikawa. He put whole scenes together in the same way in both films—and Kurosawa is not a director who will follow a precedent (even his own) if he sees a better way of doing it.

The cut in any Kurosawa film is never arbitrary. There is always a place to begin, and a place to complete the action, and this he searches for until he finds it. The meeting scene between Sugata and the girl is typical.

> The girl on the steps coming down.
> The camera pans with her, Sugata
> behind her. A wipe, but a wipe
> down from the top of the screen,
> catching up with the downward pan.
> In the new scene it is later, it
> is snowing, pan downward continued;
> she breaks geta. Cut.
> Both seen from top, both
> carrying umbrellas. His closes,
> and he becomes visible. Cut. The
> temple gate seen as still life,
> then the camera dollies back to
> include both of them, he still
> fixing her geta.

This sequence takes ten seconds and Kurosawa has chosen to use the wipe, the cut, the pan, the dolly and the held shot. It is difficult to describe the effect but each has its own emotional component and in this particular combination they give the feeling of (1) time having passed (2) the peace of the temple compound (3) the continuity of a simple action and (4) the continuity of the larger story. The pan down is considerably reinforced by the wipe down, and one of its effects is a physical immediacy. The held shot of the temple gate, though seemingly out of context, reinforces the incident precisely because it breaks it. The backward dolly always gives the feeling of something accomplished, of something done. We now know they will be interested in each other. In addition to all of the above, the tempo—the simple amount of time each image is on the screen—is perfectly calculated. The first shot is the shortest, the last is the longest. It is a decelerendo and a growing of interest. Since we must look longer we look more closely.

In an early fight-scene this effect is brilliantly described. Sugata is fighting the head of the jujitsu house, the man he met before he met his teacher at the beginning of the film. The match itself is superbly edited and its conclusion is this:

> A face in the crowd watching.
> Sugata throws the man.
> Another face.
> The man flying through the air (12 frames).
> Face in the crowd (sound of body crashing).
> The man still rolling (slow-motion).
> His daughter's face.
> The man, rolling (slow-motion) and a shoji frame,
> jarred loose by the impact, falling (slow-motion).
> A slow pan (normal motion) of the faces in the crowd.
> Long close-up of daughter showing her hatred.
> Over it the sound of a voice saying: But, he's dead.

This unusual combination of fast cutting and slow-motion (seen also in the beginning fight with the kidnapper in the uncut *Seven Samurai*), each short section of film precisely the right length, each adding to the emotional effect, here creates a short sequence of the greatest power. The final long close-up is by contrast with what went before much more powerful than any single close-up usually is. And thus is should be because the girl's hatred must be impressive.

(This girl is, of course, different from the temple-girl though the story obviously parallels these two daughters. Since all existing prints of *Sugata* are mutilated and sections of the original negative are missing, she disappears after an aborted attempt on Sugata's life. The negative was only reconstructed in 1952 and this also accounts for the lavish use of titles in existing prints. The later editors decided to explain everything while they had the chance and many of the major sequences are separated by needless continuity titles telling us that so many months have passed or that such and such has happened.)

One other element of the mature Kurosawa technique is also present in this film and this is his peculiar use of the flash-back—seen in its perfection in *Rashomon*. Unlike many directors, Kurosawa does not favor extended flash-back, perhaps because it is too easy, and too expected. However, in many of his earlier films, there are looks backward which are really flashes and nothing more. They remind but, more than that, they are used either to establish plot points (as in *Stray Dog*) or—more important—to indicate emotional states, as in *No Regrets for Our Youth* and here.

On the day of the big fight with the temple-girl's father, Sanshiro is sitting before the *shoji* reciting a poem, a classical poem about bravery and grandeur, Mount Fuji, and so on—just the sort of thing that athletes meditate upon before their bouts. There is a curious cut to the *shoji* itself to show its texture and pattern. This is followed by a shot of kimono material, a distinctive arrow-pattern which seems familiar. The kimono material is plainly in a bolt, however. Another cut, and this time we see the kimono and a girl inside. It is the temple-girl, and we remember that her kimono on that first day was made of this arrow-patterned material. She smiles. It is one of the towel-returning scenes we are re-seeing. Another cut, and this is of her praying—the first shot we had of her. Another cut to Sanshiro startled because he has been hit on the head (blow not seen but heard over the shot of the girl praying) by the priest because we are back in front of the *shoji* and the latter is saying: "What do you think you are doing? Daydreaming like this before an important match."

At first this looks like a simple and old-fashioned device to show what is going on in Sanshiro's head, and so it is, in part. In addition, however, we have seen that the *shoji* pattern makes him think of the kimono pattern and this prepares us for the final reel where the cloud pattern (Sugata, his neck held in the vice of the villain, looking up at the sky) makes him think of the opening lotus. In addition, it is later seen that the villain has bought the bolt of kimono material for the girl, knowing she likes the pattern. We do not learn this until much later and this flash is therefore also a flash forward. It is like that isolated shot of the turret window in *Hiroshima mon amour*, presented to us long before we could possibly know that the girl associates it with her German lover, with her own imprisonment. Yet, though we do not know, we remember, and a context may be prepared in the past or in the future since any film is always continuous present. Back then, and from now on are always *now* on film.

All of these innovations were, even in 1943, peculiar to Kurosawa and they make *Sugata* an extraordinary debut film—doubly extraordinary in that, a quarter of a century later, the picture is emotionally valid (which is more than one can say for some of the pictures in between) and still almost as surprising as the day it was released. In it, Kurosawa showed fully the profile which the entire world would come to know.

# Sanshiro Sugata Part Two

## 1945

Though this film was made a year later, and another intervened, it is convenient to discuss it now, not only because the story and cast are the same, but also because, as a film, it is so very bad that its deficiencies will further explain the excellences of the 1943 picture, and those to follow.

Kurosawa has said: "This film did not interest me in the slightest. I had already done it once. This was just warmed-over." It is considerably worse than merely warmed-over. In it we have what the original *Sugata* might have been had an ordinary director done it.

The character of Sanshiro might be interpreted in a way different from the way I have. He is a diligent, solemn, serious young man who is bent upon realizing all of his forces, spiritual as well as physical. He is down-to-earth, has no grandiose ideas about himself, but—on the other hand—is naturally strong, naturally proud, defends the weak, subdues the strong, does not smoke, nor drink, is very proper, suffers, is something of a prig, and is frightfully moral. Another side of his character or, rather, another view of his character becomes visible. A comparison of the opening sequences in the two pictures shows that the later film prefers the latter view.

A title tells us that it is 1887 (five years after the beginning of the first film) and Sugata comes across a bad American sailor tormenting a poor Japanese rickshaw boy. He attempts to protect the boy without harming the sailor. The latter, however, grows abusive. Sugata topples him into the water and the rickshaw boy looks up at him with shining eyes.

It is a parody of the waterfront fight in the first film, done in middle-shot, long-shot, completely unexciting. It is reminiscent of the original fight only in that someone is thrown into the water.

We see at once what kind of hero Sugata is to be in this film. Since the picture is a completely conventional picture, he will be a completely conventional hero. There is more, however. It escaped no one in the 1944 audience that the hero was protecting a poor, helpless Japanese from a big, brutal foreigner. The first *Sugata* managed to avoid all of the cliches of the wartime Japanese film; the second subscribes to most of them.

This is seen in the second sequence. Sugata is taken by the Japanese interpreter of the American legation (a foppish Japanese in Western clothes, given to smoking cigarettes, who talks about "we Japanese" as the camera dollies back to reveal him dressed up like an organ-grinder's monkey) to a match between a worn-out jujitsu man and a foreign boxer. The crowd is almost entirely foreign, screaming blonde ladies, grim cigar-stub chewing gentlemen, parodies all. Sugata, offended, turns to leave, then returns to let everyone know how much he dislikes this sort of thing. The beaten jujitsu man says he does it to eat. Sugata stops, thinks. Yes, he decides, it is all his fault. Since judo is the proper way it is natural that jujitsu men should go hungry. However, it is all for the good of the glorious martial arts of Japan, etc.

This view of things foreign and things Japanese quite agreed with the aims of the Japanese wartime propaganda department and particularly grateful was the inference (seen at the end of the picture) that the subtle, agile Japanese judo will always win over massive, mindless American boxing. This Sugata sets out to demonstrate and his line of reasoning is pure Japanese war department. Foreigners must be made to recognize not only the glory of the Japanese martial arts, but also that Japan's attitude is entirely benevolent. Japan is the kindly elder brother who chastizes only because he must.

Actually the difference between the two Sanshiro's is not this great. It is possible to see the hero of the first picture as the war department hero (though extremely difficult to see the hero of the second as sharing with the original any of his spirtual anguish, any of his realization of identity). The significant difference is that between an interested Kurosawa and one completely disinterested.

Not that the film does not have its moments. The education of the rickshaw boy (who naturally takes up judo) is seen in a series of small scenes (somewhat like the celebrated breakfast-scenes in *Citizen Kane*) where he performs an identical action (kneeling before a bout) a number of times, each time becoming more assured, more raffish—it is a very funny series. Something like it occurs when the girl is talking about her father (dead, though not apparently through Sanshiro's beating) and for each line of dialogue there is a new cut. There is another charming scene where Sugata and priest practice the austerity of *zazen* sitting up all night, meditating. The two of them are sitting in front of the *shoji*. There is a long dissolve to morning. Sugata is flat on his back—obviously he failed to get *satori*. Ashamed, he quickly sits up and glances at the priest who appears deep in meditation. But then, as he looks, he hears the faint sounds of snoring. They have both failed.

Such moments are, however, very few. Like all Japanese two-part films you have to see the first to understand the second. Otherwise one would not understand: the teacher's being pulled by Sugata, bending over and saying: "Remember the first time?"; the bolt of arrow-patterned kimono material in the villain's house—apparently she returned it; and the final fight.

This is a copy of the marvelous fight in the first film and like a copy it is smudged and much erased. Again Sugata sings (this time in the snow rather than in the wind) but he has no particular reason for doing so. Then the villains (two of them—brothers to the now bed-ridden villain of the first film) appear and the fight takes place in the winter mountains.

These brothers are straight from the average period-film. One is plain bad and the other is insane. To make certain that audiences realize this, the latter is made to wear his hair long and to carry the bamboo branch which symbolizes the mad woman in the Noh drama, and Kurosawa much amuses himself with various Noh steps and Noh inflections. After they are beaten, the script insists that they spend the night in the snow. Sugata paternally puts his judo robe over the fallen karate champion—which is a bit thick even for one so benevolently stupid as Sanshiro is shown in this picture—and then falls asleep himself. Sure enough the mad brother (in a series of slow dissolves, like those much better used at the end of *Rashomon*) takes out a knife and approaches the sleeping hero. Just then, on the sound track is heard the voice of the girl, warning. Sugata smiles in his sleep and this unnerves the madman who puts back the knife and the sun comes up. Sugata (who does not know what nearly happened) gets up, rubs snow on his face, gives a big Rin-Tin-Tin smile, affirms that life is worth living, and the picture suddenly ends.

The ending is particularly bad because the fight that went before seemed to indicate something different from melodrama. It is almost entirely long shots with snow piling (as in *The Idiot*) on head and chest, all back-lighted, with the mad howls of the karate brothers echoing among the mountains. A karate-chop misses, hits a tree, and the tree slowly falls. Everything is slow, and the howls bounce back and forth. It is like a fight under water. (In the boxing match scene Kurosawa also showed that a fight usually brings forth his best: here he intercuts the two sides—white and yellow—in the Eisenstein-manner, and then, during the fight, inserts still photographs, using movie-camera-taken scenes in which no one is moving as bridges—and the effect is splendid.) The men wade about almost invisible in the snow while the score screws itself from one climax to the next, the shouts bounce back from the mountains. Pictorially it is quite fine, if a bit meaningless.

It is just this ultimate meaninglessness, however, that makes a comparison with the fight in the first film impossible. There Sugata is a real person, struggling to find himself, and doing so through the terrible ordeal of the fight on the plains. Here he is a stock hero who will win no matter what and the fight is merely something striking to look at.

This lack of meaning pervades the entire picture and the reasons that this should be so reveal something about Kurosawa as a director. Kajiro Yamamoto has said that he is the "inspirational" type of creator, and this is true. He sees things clearly and whole upon the moment of conception and the making of a film is therefore the battle to regain the initial vision. He, as director, is never satisfied, but what he considers only a partial success becomes, for us who do not know the original vision, the picture itself, which is often near perfection. When, as in *The Idiot*, he makes himself rewrite too much or, as in *Record of a Living Being* and *Scandal*, there are other reasons for revision, the initial vision fades away. The film becomes extended, overwrought, uneven. In this second part of *Sugata* there was no original vision to sustain since it is the only film he has made without wanting to. What is surprising is that it is not worse than it is.

It, then, is the nearest that the director has ever come to the ordinary commercial Japanese films and its similarities and differences are worth noting. It is a propaganda picture—utterly the opposite from a personal picture; it is an entertainment film—quite different from an entertaining film. Kurosawa's lack of interest was a lack of interest in the content because what a picture is about remains for him the most important thing about a picture.

# The Most Beautiful

# 1944

After the success of *Sanshiro Sugata,* Kurosawa was encouraged to make another picture which would both satisfy the requirements of 'national policy' and, at the same time, make money. His answer was the script for this film. "It was my own story but followed national policy and had a very strong wartime coloring. In it I wanted to portray women in a group—a kind of everyday documentary of their lives."

## THE STORY

A group of girls work in a precision-optical-instruments factory, making lenses, binoculars, etc. Since this is wartime they are volunteers who live under almost military conditions, leading lives almost as impersonal as those of soldiers. They are cared for by the head of production (Takashi Shimura) and his associates who are concerned for the girls but, at the same time, are equally worried about keeping up the required output.

The film is episodic, made of the various stories of the girls, their happinesses, their sorrows. One (Takako Irie) becomes ill and has to go home, which she does much against her will, but finally comes back, strong again. Another falls from the roof and breaks her leg but insists upon going on with the work. Yet another has a persistent fever (perhaps TB) which she attempts to hide and enlists the sympathies of their girl-leader who is then accused of partiality to the sick girl. Finally, there is the story of the girl-leader herself (Yoko Yaguchi) who knows that her mother is dying back home but who decides to stay on at the factory, and who (because of squabbles about her supposed favoritism) mislays a lens and must hunt for it through all the thousands of boxes of finished lenses, but who eventually emerges as a kind of production-line heroine.

## TREATMENT

Kurosawa wanted to make a "documentary" and that is precisely what the film is. It opens with the head of production making a speech and we are shown the lines of employees, standing like soldiers, as they listen. It is a real factory, with real workers, and we are shown it in real documentary fashion.

The real documentary fashion that Kurosawa knew was a combination of Russian and German techniques. The British documentary was unknown at the time and even now has had almost no influence on the Japanese documentary. The documentary style is therefore something like the German prewar *Kunstfilm,* something like the Russian 'dynamic' documentary. During the speech scene, for example, one shot of Shimura talking into the microphone is followed by a series of five or six shots (all beautifully back-lit in the German manner) showing the standing listeners, reverting again to Shimura, then again to the listeners. Each cut of the standing workers is slightly shorter than the one which went before, making for a gradual but noticeable acceleration. When the girls play volleyball, the technique is "analytical montage" with very short scenes of faces, arms, the ball flying, legs leaping, all cut together. Occasionally, as in *Triumph of the Will,* long shots of still-life (people or objects) are used to stop the flow of a particular sequence or to heighten its effect. At the same time, much use is made of the machines (lens-polishers, etc.) themselves and as we follow the various stories, we are shown how to polish lenses, etc.

All of these various elements are very well integrated and, as a documentary, the picture is beautifully carpentered. Following the Russian example Kurosawa devotes the camera to people. Rarely do we a see a background, only occasionally is a room or a section of the factory examined. Usually, he fills his frame with girls, and a typical scene is one which occurs early in the picture. This is the dining hall shot where the camera is so high that the back wall is invisible and we are shown a field of girls receding into the distance. A shaft of sunlight illuminates the middle distance where the girl-leader and her friends sit talking. The effect is that nothing but these girls exists; hundreds of them seen, the few in the foreground demanding our attention. One thinks of *Berlin;* one thinks more of *Arsenal.*

At the same time that Kurosawa was creating Japan's best documentary, he wanted more. Specifically, he wanted a kind of empathy which the documentary technique cannot usually afford. In order to achieve this he did a number of things not common in the documentary. He used actresses, he allowed himself drama, and he sought for more subtle ways to show emotion. Consequently he invented techniques, and many of these involved the rudiments of a grammar which was later to become peculiarly his own.

One of these was the short-cut. Though he could milk a scene dry of tears (as in the interminable sequence where Takako Irie has to go home and all the girls say goodbye and then burst into sobs), he was equally concerned with shortening, a concern which later grew into one of his major technical innovations. There is a scene for example, of the girl-leader reading alone at night. The director must get her into the corridor, to encounter the teacher and exchange some dialogue necessary for the plot. The problem is solved in three cuts: *She is seen from the back, turning a page, then she closes the book / cut.*

*A close-up of an alarm clock / cut.*

*A big close-up of a door swinging open to reveal her face, in close-up, as she moves into the corridor.*

This only takes five seconds and moves us about quite efficiently. At the same time the closing of the book and the opening of the door are so put together (since the alarm-clock shot is very short) that they seem part of the same action.

In another sequence Kurosawa becomes (for 1944) extremely daring. The girl with the fever puts the thermometer under her arm and we have to wait for it to register. We are shown the girl-leader waiting / cut / same girl but entirely different position / cut / again, same girl, same background, but position, expression is different /cut / same thing—on for six cuts. When the cuts are over we discover we have not been waiting for the thermometer after all but for the arrival of the lady teacher whom she may or may not tell of the girl's illness. Such extreme condensation (used again in *No Regrets for Our Youth*) was not generally seen in commercial cinema until after *A bout de souffle* and here, as there, it has the effect not only of cutting across time but also of defining character (by surprising it, as it were) in an extraordinarily forceful manner.

Another grammatical invention already seen in *Sugata* (and present-ed amplified and finished in *Ikiru*) is Kurosawa's peculiarly personal use of flash-back. The girl-leader has been wrongly accused of favorit-ism and the other girls are very contrite, particularly when they learn that it was through them that she mislaid the lens. When their teacher returns they tell everything and we see the missing scenes (laying the lens to one side, etc.) as well as, over again, several short scenes we saw previously. What is peculiarly Kurosawa-like, however, is the extreme brevity of these past scenes. They last three, four seconds at the most, and are inserted into the present only at the dialogue points to which they refer. The past is *used* rather than indulged by Kurosawa and he—interested here only in cause and effect—cuts in this visual explanation as briskly as though it were dialogue. In *Ikiru* the wake sequence is a sustained example of this, with dialogue beginning, image continuing, and dialogue concluding an explana-tion. In *Rashomon* the technique is also used with superlative effect,

and the police-methods of *High and Low* are explicated in the same manner. In *Red Beard,* on the other hand, the flashbacks are used more conservatively, though no less concisely.

There is another interesting pre-echo of *Ikiru* in the picture. The girl-leader is in bed. She is troubled. She turns, with a gesture just like Watanabe's, pulls the covers over her head and begins to weep. Wipe to a military parade (parades are often used in this film as links from one sequence to the next) and then a fade, the sequence is over. There is no logical reason for the parade at this point but there are some very good irrational reasons. She is alone, crying; this is contrasted with a parade, that symbol of togetherness, banners flying, band play-ing. Consequently one image reinforces the other and we feel her isolation the more. Simultaneously, we know that this particular girl is the most dedicated of the group and so the parade-shot is in a way a presage of what will come (that is, she will overcome her feelings and struggle on to make more and better lenses). At the same time—and most irrational of all—the cut of the parade *seems* right and it does so because Kurosawa's context in this picture is the docu-mentary, even the sociological document. The placing is right because throughout the film, though its national-policy theme is insisted upon, Kurosawa keeps reminding us that the life is very hard, and so the tone of the film is honest—it is very dark. One is reminded of *Ikiru*—both lonely person and military band, one image succeeding the other, and the effect is much the same.

The theme of the film shares something with *Ikiru*. The title refers not to the most beautiful of the girls but (as a scene where they recite their morning poem—an inspirational-type creation—indicates) to the girl who has the most beautiful *kokoro* (a word which defies translation but which might be called 'spirit') and so, like *Ikiru*, the picture is about spirit, about what a person is made of.

The title obviously refers to the girl-leader. It is she who quiets the others when they begin chattering in school-girl fashion and forget the importance of their wartime task; it is she who is continually exhorting the others on to further efforts (and who would seem, given the montage-sequences that always follow such scenes, responsible for the rise in the production-graph we are then shown); and it is she whose motto, repeated endlessly, is: "Keep on trying, do your best," etc. Her test comes (as it must to every major Kurosawa figure) when she mislays the lens and has to find it again. This she must do with a microscope and we already know (a big scene is planted near the beginning of the film) that she is subject to headaches.

The task is enormous. She must examine hundreds of finished lenses to find the (numbered) one she mislaid. We are shown all of this and it lasts all night and into the next day. Dissolves are much used—dissolve to the clock, dissolve to her, dissolve to numbed fingers reaching for another lens, dissolve to the clock, etc. It is a bit much because we know it is only a lens and because we resent having our sympathies manipulated in this way. At the same time, however, we know that, like the detective in *Stray Dog* who faces the impossible task of finding his gun in teeming Tokyo, she is admirable because she is practicing precisely what she has preached. She is persevering in an almost impossible task. Common sense alone would indicate its impossibility, yet there she is ruining her eyes at the microscope and making herself stay there (as did Sugata in the pond), though everything in her tells her to forget about it and go to bed. This attribute Kurosawa finds very attractive—though usually he makes the object one of greater importance and hence enlists our sympathies as well. As it is, her perseverence strikes us (like that of the girl who wills to believe in enchantment in *One Wonderful Sunday*) as almost disagreeable. The impression is further enhanced in the coda which follows. There she is, stern, dedicated, working at her microscope—just like the doctor in *Quiet Duel*—giving her life to her duty, but doing so with little grace and no apparent contentment.

Twenty years later it is almost impossible for us to think a lost lens this important. Even at the time, however, one might have questioned the weight, and sentimentality, of these sequences. The object just doesn't seem worth all of this concern.

Kurosawa, however (at the time), thought differently, and this is seen in a number of these early films where "uplift" becomes important. He knows from the first that the solitary way is the true way and the hardest. His love of individuality (and even the national-policy films are full of it) is predicated upon the extreme difficulty of anyone's attaining it. At the same time (as in *One Wonderful Sunday, The Quiet Duel*, sections of *Drunken Angel*, the Christmas-eve sequences of *Scandal*) merely the fact of being together, of doing something in a group, seems to be a palliative and we are never shown it as anything but almost deliriously comforting.

This is very Japanese. No other people are so compulsively gregarious, and no others flock to safety in numbers with such acute frequency. So, it is only in later films, *Ikiru* and *Seven Samurai* in particular, that Kurosawa sees through this chimera, and becomes un-Japanese enough to disbelieve it. In *The Most Beautiful* it does not once occur to him (as it would now) that the girls are being exploited, that part of the brain-washing consists of playing upon this purely Japanese need for being a part of something larger than themselves.

Though few facts of Kurosawa's spiritual biography are known—and he is very careful that they not be—one that *is* known is how he became aware that collective social action is not the answer. In 1946, after making *They Who Step on the Tiger's Tail* (which was not released until 1953), he was approached by the very powerful and very new Japan Motion Picture and Drama Employees Union to make an anti-company, anti-*zaibatsu*, anti-capitalist film to be called

*Those Who Make Tomorrow (Asu o Tsukuru Hitobito)*. It was to be directed by Kurosawa along with the (then) better-known directors, Kajiro Yamamoto and Hideo Sekigawa. Kurosawa has repudiated the film: "It is not mine—and it's not the other two's either. It was really made by the labor union and is an excellent example of why a committee-made film is no good. I did my part in a week and it wasn't too bad for a week's work." There is little indication in the finished film as to who did what, Kurosawa doesn't say, and there is no visible sign of him anyplace in it—except that the "uplift" is so strong that it remains even now, embarrassing. Those who make tomorrow are, naturally, the workers, and those who stubbornly refuse to make tomorrow are, naturally, the employers. The togetherness in the picture is little short of suffocating—and scenes of everyone working happily together, scenes of emotional community action, scenes of masses of workers rushing to make tomorrow are so frequent that they seriously interfere with the plot. It is singular that Kurosawa ever got mixed up in such a picture (not so singular for Yamamoto who went on to make a number of "Communist" films, or Sekigawa who, after the Americans left, embarked on a string of anti-American pictures of a vilification unexampled even in Japan), but, at the same time, he believed—along with everyone else—in the positive joys of everyone doing something together.

He had no control over the script (about two sisters, one a script-girl, the other an actress; their father opposes unions, being an upper-class white collar worker; finally, through the efforts of the daughters, he sees the light and heads a striker's parade) and none over the editing, and this was disturbing, but even more disturbing was that he, as director, had become embroiled in something much larger than a motion picture.

The film was intended as propaganda material because, as actually occurred later in the year, the Communist-led Congress of Industrial Unions decided that a test of strike tactics was in order, and that the Japan Motion Picture and Drama Employees Union should do the testing. This led to prolonged strikes and, in 1948, considerable violence. Kurosawa, now embroiled, had to go to the Tokyo District Court to "explain" the union's stand, and a number of incidents (including American tanks at the gates of Toho) occurred. One that Kurosawa remembered and which seems to have been conclusive, was that some policemen were captured, stripped naked, and decorated by having insulting words and phrases scribbled over their flesh before they were released.

This sort of action is quite different from the pure uplift of everyone pushing together and making a better world and yet there is a definite connection, one which Kurosawa never again forgot. The townsfolk in *Yojimbo*, the malefactors in *Sanjuro* are members of a community in which a community action has taken just this kind of turn. After his union experiences, after his brief flirtation with Communism, he was cured of ever again believing that all that this world needs is for us to get together and make a better one. From this film on he ceased to believe in people, but he had the strength to continue to believe in persons, in individuals.

This was a change that few Japanese critics have ever been able to forgive because a direct and positive disbelief in the efficacy of community action is really and truly un-Japanese. One might point out that, to the Anglo-Saxon, the Japanese seem to have less community spirit than any people but the Greeks. Nonetheless, the belief continues that, somehow, being together will solve everything. Thus when the critics accuse Kurosawa of being "too Western," they are accusing him of being too individual, too self-sufficient. Kurosawa answers this by saying (in reference to the 1946 film): "I don't know why but when I hear the band music on May Day, I feel very, very sleepy."

In *The Most Beautiful,* Kurosawa still believed that human beings could solve their problems together. At the same time, however, he shows in his treatment of the girl-leader, that he also believed in the individual. It is this balance which is interesting in the film. In his next, *They Who Step on the Tiger's Tail,* it was the individual for and to whom he spoke.

# PRODUCTION

*The Most Beautiful,* nonetheless, is extremely likeable and one of the reasons, certainly, is that Kurosawa's documentary is so enriched by the kind of beauty which only truth can give. The plot line is manipulated to a degree but, oddly, the characters are not. In this context of presumed actuality, of beautifully captured wartime stringency (the very conditions of which—not enough film, not enough lights, not enough sets—might account for the extreme economy and directness of the picture), the performances ring with a kind of truth that one finds usually only in real documentaries. "I told all the actresses not to use any of their professional idiosyncracies. I told them to play it like amateurs. And I really made them live together in a dormitory during the filming, and made them do lots of things—running for example—which they had never done, in order to remove their polish, their hesitations in these roles which were so different from any they had ever played before."

One remembers from this film mainly wonderful vignettes of character which are so right, so beautifully placed: the dumb sorrow on the face of the girl who has to go home; a fine moment where the girl who did the accusing goes at night into the vegetable garden to look at the moon, hears the distant whistle of a train, and bursts into tears; the despair on the face of a girl who has accidentally ruined a lens-polisher; the hands of a girl bored by her work; young, healthy, girlish faces hidden behind field microscopes which act as fearsome masks; the sick girl, well again, romping like a child, and so on.

In this film Kurosawa showed that he was able to extract performances that few other Japanese directors could; that he was able, with patience and tact, to make real tears flow, real screams sound. This experience was intense—both for him and for the girls. "It is interesting that, after the film, one after the other got married and all, I understand, became exemplary wives...I too married after the picture was over. I married Yoko Yaguchi."

In this picture Kurosawa again sounded the major theme that had become his (as in *Sugata:* the problem of becoming oneself, the necessity of realizing this, the difficulty of persevering) but did so within the framework of the present (and, even now, he feels the present, the contemporary-life-film, to be the more important genre; feels, even now, that its actuality, its life-likeness makes it more important than the "period" genre) and, further, sounded it within the context of actuality itself—the documentary. Just as one may trace from *Sugata* many of the elements in the later films, in *The Most Beautiful,* can be found the beginnings of that intense concern for actuality which animates so many of his pictures.

It is the only one of these earlier films for which he now has a kind word. "You know, I still like it myself."

# They Who Step on the Tiger's Tail

## 1945

# THE SOURCE

This is a film version of a medieval episode which also forms the basis for both the Noh drama *Ataka*, and the Kabuki play *Kanjincho*. Yoshitsune, one of Japan's most famous generals, is fleeing from his brother, Yoritomo. He is accompanied by his retainers and by Benkei—all of whom are disguised as mountain priests. At Ataka is a *sekisho* or check-point through which they must pass on their flight, but it is in the hands of Yoritomo's forces. The false monks must convince the commander, Togashi, that they are real and **Benkei** reads an empty scroll pretending that it is the *kanjin-cho* or subscription-book of their temple. When they are leaving, Yoshitsune—dressed as a porter—is recognized. Benkei averts the discovery by finding this porter too slow and by beating him. The beating of a lord by his retainer is directly contrary to the ethos of Japanese feudalism and, though Togashi suspects, he is so moved by this that he not only allows the party to proceed but sends a train of bearers after them with saké. Benkei formally begs pardon of Yoshitsune, receives it, and then gets drunk on the saké and dances. Though the Noh is not so popular —no Noh is—the Kabuki is perhaps the most famous in the repertoire and every child knows all about the exploits of Benkei and Yoshitsune. The story is much more famous than that of, say, the disguised Edward II in the West. If the story of Robin Hood had happened to be also a famous play we would have a more exact parallel.

Kurosawa had not particularly wanted to make this film but the military authorities were, naturally, all in favor of it. He had wanted to make a costume picture but horses were not available, so he sat down and wrote the script for this film in one night.

It is ostensibly a straight film version of the historical anecdote (including additions from both the Noh and the Kabuki versions) with but one change. But that change alters the entire meaning of the play. Kurosawa added one character, an extra porter, and gave the part to the comedian Kenichi Enomoto, better known as Enoken—a bit like adding Jerry Lewis to the cast of *Hamlet*.

# MUSIC

Kurosawa, remembering both Noh and Kabuki, included much music and some dancing in this film. The hour-long picture came out very like a musical—the other musical that Kurosawa has done is *One Wonderful Sunday*—but the music is of three separate kinds. First, there is Noh music, particularly in the first transformation scene which takes us from the forest to the barrier-camp. Benkei turns his back to the camera and begins a line straight from the Noh version about going to the barrier. Before this the dialogue has been fairly colloquial. Now his inflexion changes, the vowels are lengthened. The late Denjiro

Okochi, who plays the part, manages the gutterals of the Noh actor, and there is a horizontal wipe (just like a curtain going up) and we are at the barrier station. This entire scene, which includes the reading of the scroll and also a disputation on Buddhist principles, is accompanied by Noh music. Second, there is music from the Kabuki version, particularly at the end. One of the most famous moments in all Kabuki is the exit of the drunken Benkei, and it is this music which occurs at the end of the film. Third, there is Western music. The credits and opening scenes are accompanied by a full orchestra and chorus. This chorus takes the place of the chorus in Noh and Kabuki and gives the story but does so to the square rhythms and block harmonies of Japanese film music at its most Western. The hymn-like chorus is heard from time to time, and at the end of the film, after the Kabuki music, the orchestra manages a full Western C-major cadence.

It is as though, in music as in treatment, Kurosawa remains aware of the various levels of his story: the historical, that of the Noh, that of the Kabuki, and that of this modern version which he is creating. That the score does not at all appear a mishmash of styles is because the picture itself keeps these levels clear of each other, yet manages to use them all.

# CAMERA

The conclusion of shooting all but coincided with the conclusion of the Pacific War and it is not suprising that Kurosawa was allowed, in those stringent times, only a single set—the barrier-camp. All the rest of the picture had to be shot on location. "This was an order," remembers Kurosawa: "But the picture was much easier to shoot this way."

In another way it made it more difficult because Kurosawa, remembering that both dramatic versions are quite static, had to find a way of keeping the camera moving within confined spaces, had to lend motion to a very talky script. This he did in a number of ways.

The opening sequence is in the forest, a dolly showing the tops of the trees (much like those in the later *Rashomon*), finally a tilt down one of the trees to show the party small in the distance. Following this is a series of nearly identical scenes, each separated by a wipe, each panned, showing the new porter trying to strike up a conversation (about the weather) with the grim and devoted followers. This makes the opening of the film quite lively, as does the scene a bit later when Yoshitsune is being dressed as a porter. Here Kurosawa uses a kind of analytical montage. The face is not seen (we do not see Yoshitsune properly until the final reel); instead, portions of the body are shown: a carrying case being put on the back, an arm slipping out of a sleeve, a large straw hat being fitted to the back of the head. There is also some very odd cutting, done to enliven and to prepare for the static scene at the barrier. At one point Benkei turns his head to look at someone over his shoulder. This is done in two shots. The first is taken full face and the second is taken from beside him. The cut occurs halfway through his turning his head. It is the boldest kind of jump cut but quite acceptable in the general activity of the scene. At the end of the film—after the barrier scenes—the camera picks up the tempo again. Benkei's getting drunk is managed in a series of dissolves (like those at the end of *One Wonderful Sunday* and *Rashomon*) which telescope time and offer a kind of short-hand interpretation of the action. The final dance, too, is all motion—though here it is in the object photographed, Enoken trying vainly to imitate Benkei's famous exit.

Another way in which Kurosawa increases interest is by varying his camera viewpoint. At the start of the film the warrior retainers are seen from beneath and their ugly and dangerous aspects are emphasized. This is complimented by our usually viewing Enoken slightly from above. As the film progresses, however, as both we and Enoken begin to understand why it is that the priests are so forbidding, the camera rises more and more level with the face. By the end of the film we are quite on equal terms with Benkei, with his men, and even with the new porter.

The slowest part of the film is the middle section, in the barrier-camp. But it is just here that Kurosawa can rely on the story to carry interest. The longest scene in the picture is therefore the full scene of the camp with soldiers standing about, the Buddhist invocation and the following religious talk between Benkei and Togashi. It is broken in the middle by a pan—the first half centers on the speaking Benkei, the later half on the listening Togashi. It is almost five minutes long and is the still heart of the picture just as the like scene is the heart of the Noh.

Shortly thereafter, however, Kurosawa begins to pick up tempo. He frames the two in their further scenes using a composition taken plainly from the Noh—as he was later again to do in *The Throne of Blood*. When the attendant to Togashi (wearing a villainous Western-style moustache—a touch for which perhaps the producers rather than Kurosawa were responsible) suspects the scroll of being blank, he edges forward. We are shown Benkei reading and glancing up and the camera slowly dollies toward him just as the attendant would be moving. At the end of the sequence, in order to intensify the panic that all must be feeling, the need to escape, the improbability of doing so, Kurosawa resorts to probably the most extreme and experimental cutting of his entire career.

The set used was quite small but in editing—in the manner of the plate-breaking scene or the steps sequence in *Potemkin*—Kurosawa made it much larger. The fugitives start out and the camera dollies along beside them. There is a cut and the same actions are repeated from halfway, therefore going half again as far as in the first shot. This crab-like progression is insisted upon and at the same time the

off-screen chorus has the line: *Tora no ō o fumu otokotachi*—from which the title of the film is taken. They are men on a tightrope, men softly treading on the tail of the suspicious but yet reclining tiger. It takes a length of time for them to get to the gate and just then they are told to stop. After that Benkei, tears in his eyes, must beat his master.

Kurosawa was probably never more conscious of his camera than in this film but his reasons were so good that viewing it we are not conscious of the camera. He avoids longueurs which would so strike us in a film, though they might not on the stage; yet, at the same time, he gives dramatic action its due. It is an almost perfectly photographed film.

The director apparently thought so. Despite its cool reception (it suffered the irony of being banned by the American Occupation Forces because of "the feudalistic idea of loyalty expressed in the film," and was not released until 1952) Kurosawa has always been fond of it and has said: "I wanted to remake this film with more sets, lots more technique." He spoke of this with Fumio Hayasaka, his composer who was also his best friend and his closest associate, "but we never did anything about it. Then he died—and his death ruined this as well."

# CHARACTERIZATION

Apparently Kurosawa shares the belief entertained in some Kabuki circles that the really interesting character in *Kanjincho* is the barrier-captain, Togashi. This is a touchy point in the Kabuki and different actors play it differently. Did he truly know that it was Yoshitsune? Therefore, knowing, does he allow him to escape? This is the one psychologically interesting explanation, but for years a controversy has been raging in the Kabuki as to just how the role should be interpreted. Kurosawa had no such doubts. For one thing, this is the only interesting explanation of Togashi; for another he has since *Sugata* had an especial fondness for his villains. Yet, his conception of Togashi does not stop there—he creates one of his most interesting, and most enigmatic film characters.

The part was given to Susumu Fujita (the young hero of *Sugata*) who was youthful, boyish, athletic—indeed, just the opposite of the usual Kabuki actor. Since Fujita was far too young to play the part (the opposing Okochi was twice as old), there is something very disarming about his intelligent silences, his obvious self-command. He is a bit like the youth-leader of the boy-scout samurai in *Sanjuro* —a film which shares much with this one. At one minute he is a severe young man with a problem on his hands, the next finds him bursting with good nature and boyish laughter. He knows a good bit about Buddhist liturgy but, during the long reading of the scroll,

he almost falls asleep. One feels that discipline has been imposed entirely from the outside, that at heart he is twenty, rather lazy, enthusiastic, outgoing. He is a boy wearing a full set of feudal armour.

He is by no means stupid, however, and one of the most disturbing elements in Fujita's superb interpretation is just the intelligence which he brings to the part—his sudden shifts from laughter to comprehension, from suspicion to understanding. There is no doubt at all that he knows—he guesses when the new porter almost gives away that Yoshitsune's armour is in the big basket which also contains the scroll. And in the end he makes it clear that he knows and is allowing them to escape.

It is just here that the Kabuki quarrel centers. If Togashi lets them go, knowing, then that means that they fooled no one and it makes Benkei less the hero. It even throws some doubt on the usefulness of the unthinkable tableau of retainer beating master. Kabuki, being Kabuki, is often content to sacrifice psychological interest to the interests of feudal glory—and the interests of the actor playing Benkei. Kurosawa, being Kurosawa, is only interested in the curious psychology of both Togashi and Benkei.

This he insists upon by showing that Benkei knows that Togashi knows. There is no dialogue to cover these points and Kurosawa relies entirely upon his actors, the delicate half-smile hovering on the lips of Togashi, his sudden resolution to let them go—almost as reward for their fine performance. Okochi suggests the ruefulness of a man seen through, mixed with the satisfaction of a man who, his pride in tatters, has nonetheless managed to pull something off.

Even the messengers who come bearing the saké know what has happened. It is an open secret. The other priests know and are of several minds about it, the more fierce inclining to the Kabuki reaction of having had their heroism snatched from them. And all of this is shown plainly on the faces of the actors. The scene with the saké is a triumph of ensemble acting the like of which Kurosawa did not again create until *The Lower Depths*.

The other character of major interest is that of the new porter—Enoken. "The general idea," says Kurosawa, "was to make the encounter between Benkei and Togashi the center of the film but to have the Enoken role go all the way through. I'd seen something of him in my assistant-director days when he'd appeared in a Yamamoto film, and when I wrote the script for this picture the idea was that he would make the picture come alive. We had to do something. No sets, couldn't move the camera around very much, yet had to give the picture an interesting form, had to make it lively. It was very hard work." The comedian was at this time at the height of his popularity. His stock character was that of an ordinary neurotic Japanese who over-reacts to everything—including the war. He was a parody of the anxious ordinary man. This is precisely his role in this film.

In the opening sequence, he seems mere clown. We first hear his laugh—an aimless, meaningless, self-depreciating and irritating laugh. It brings down the wrath of the disguised priests who will have nothing to do with him. We agree—he is completely ordinary and our interest therefore is in laughing at him. As the film progresses, however, its very sophistication suggests that more than a clown is present. The antics of Enoken are so very much those of a spectator—told to shut up he sits on a rock, looks around appreciatively, listens, applauds—that we soon identify him with the audience. Not *us*, of course—we are brighter than that; but, perhaps, the man sitting next to us.

Enoken reacts to just everything. Scolded, he cowers; spoken to, he beams and struts; noticed, he simpers; when he is terrified that Yoshitsune will be discovered he all but gives the whole thing away himself; when they finally leave, the charming way in which he attempts to placate suspicion is enough to rouse doubts in the most trusting guard.

At the same time, he is common sense itself—and common sense is at a complete loss in a world where everything is ruled by ritual and precedent. He has not the faintest idea of the code which controls Benkei, Yoshitsune, and Togashi alike. All of the subtle interplay between the retainer and the barrier-captain is utterly lost upon him. No wonder the encounter at the barrier so unnerves him. He is obviously interested in what is happening but his interest is expressed in the most elemental and inelegant ways: will they escape? will he get any saké to drink? what will happen next? In the meantime all the profundities of the story, all of the subtle revelation of character find him looking the other way.

At the beginning of the picture he attempts to entertain the warrior priests with a story he has just heard. It is that a band of bloody warriors, disguised as priests, are trying to escape to the north. Isn't that dreadful? Well, he certainly hopes they won't meet them. They don't sound like the sort one would like to meet. He is giving the story of *Kanjincho* all right, but his emphasis is scarcely that of the Kabuki version and his commiseration over the degree of wickedness in this world is only equaled by his thrill-struck horror when it is finally made clear that his companions *are* the bloody warriors.

The contrast between the porter and everyone else in the picture could not be greater. Their faces habitually show absolutely nothing

—we must guess from the minor movement of an eyelid, the inflexion of a certain word. The face of the porter is an open book, literally everything, all the fleeting notions, all the discarded ideas, all the sudden hopes and fears are there for all to see. They are the heroes, the demigods. He is a parody of us.

Yet it is he who is truly traditional and not they. He may bungle badly during his final Kabuki dance but in things that count he is completely conservative. It is he who stops the beating that Benkei is giving his lord. He enters the action for the first time and stops Benkei's arm. He, a porter, lowest of the low, simply cannot tolerate the idea of a retainer's beating a lord—the sublimity of the motivation is, of course, lost upon him. His act is one of superstition, compassion, and—if there is any such thing—abject bravery. Yet it is, actually, just this act which saves them. The barrier guards think that he, himself a porter, could not bear to see another porter beaten. Here Kurosawa's irony is almost as fine as that in *Kanjincho* itself—and is certainly more subtle.

One would not expect Kurosawa to uphold the feudal thesis of *Kanjincho* and he does not. But neither does he denigrate it. What he

does is to uphold the drama, the story, the fable—and to show us its strength. Both Benkei—the demigod—and the lowly porter find it in themselves to think the unthinkable, to perform the unperformable: both surpass themselves. None of the other warriors could rise to the height of Benkei, or to the height of the porter. Togashi cannot conceivably see through the actions of the porter and thus heroic status is rescued—by this parody of the common man.

Not that the heroes thank him. They remain unaware of what he has done. They are much more taken by the spectacle of Benkei begging his lord's pardon and among them are many restrained tears and much gruff clearing of congested throats. Nor does the porter know what he has done. The saké comes and he gets a bit of it—which is all he ever wanted: a good time and reasonable freedom from worry.

The best irony is reserved for the end. The porter falls asleep and there is a dissolve to his waking up. He is alone, covered by Yoshitsune's rich robe, a purse in his lap—presents from the perhaps contemptuously grateful heroes. The wind rises, the moor-grass bends. He sits there, huddled up, the robe around him. He has been deserted.

During the drunken scene there has been indication he would be. After his dance the porter makes a remarkable Chaplin-like fall into the lap of the most fierce of the warriors who suddenly laughs—for the first time they laugh with and not at the porter. Surprised, pleased, the porter looks at the demigod, eyes shining with love and gratitude, then—he is quite drunk—he curls up, there in the lap, for a little nap. He is finally secure, comfortable, loved. The warrior, outraged at the familiarity, picks him up and drops him on the ground.

This might well be what the porter is remembering, alone on the moor, huddled under rich brocade. The sound track suddenly begins the famous exit music of Benkei from the Kabuki version of the play, and the porter stands up. He begins to impersonate Benkei in this most famous moment in Kabuki.

On the stage it is called the flying-off-in-all-directions dance and the idea is that it expresses not only Benkei's prowess (to be able to do this difficult balancing dance with a hangover), but also his joy at having left the trials behind. At the same time—since Kabuki is, above all else, an actors's theater—it is a solo cadenza, a tour de force for the actor, a 'high-light' like an aria.

It is this dance (one of the many famous moments in Kabuki) which is given to the porter who is hopelessly unable to cope with its demands. His hangover is all too real and he never could balance very well. He falls down, he tries again, falls down again. The parody is delicious but at the same time it is disturbing. The porter is just an ordinary man, he is merely human, what business has he doing this? —and, at the same time, for the first time in the film, Enoken ceases to be a comedian. He is really trying to do the dance, and really failing. His eyes are large with effort, an expression of real rather than mock anxiety appears, he begins to perspire.

We see that the porter had realized himself through these adventures with his betters. He is merely human—a virtue it is true, and one which Kurosawa insists upon in such anti-heroic films as *Yojimbo* and *Sanjuro*—but now he has tasted more. He was engaged in a great adventure and now he is again only himself lost on the moor—the going-off-in-all-direction dance has, for once, a literal meaning. What —the film seems to ask in this final image—will happen to this poor human porter (whose very humanity was the reason we finally came to accept and love him) who has adventured with demigods and who has seen such great things? And what then becomes of us—poor humans all—when confronted with the glorious exploits, the bold deeds of all the heroes? We are only human. They are not for the likes of us.

And the film ends on this dance (we do not see the conclusion, the dance is painful, we are allowed a slow fade-out in the middle of it), the very symbol of search and of uncertainty. Being human is quite enough—the message of *The Idiot*—but what about those of us who have been led astray?

# No Regrets for Our Youth

## 1946

Kurosawa thinks of himself as a socially-minded rather than as a politically-minded man. *Those Who Make Tomorrow* and *Drunken Angel* are comments on society though the former, thanks to its multi-director-ship, comes close to political polemic. Because he wants to see a social problem whole and in all of its parts, Kurosawa has rarely lent himself to politics since this presumes a choosing of sides, and this is just what he is unwilling to do. Not, however, that his view is dispassionate. He gets angry, and both *Record of a Living Being* and *The Bad Sleep Well* were created from a deeply personal sense of outrage. In these films, however, he is angry at the stupidity of human beings as a whole and not at the stupidity of a certain segment. When Imai or Sekigawa become angry they presume that their side is heroic. Kurosawa is unable to do this. He finds it impossible to be partisan. Like the de-tective hero of *Stray Dog* he sees too clearly, he understands the other side too well, and he cannot completely condemn.

It is because of this that even those pictures which are intended as social documents emerge as much more than merely that. *Scandal, Record of a Living Being, The Bad Sleep Well* were all to have "some social significance" and yet this turns out to be the least impor-tant aspect of these pictures. Kurosawa's talent is stronger than his wish to be socially useful. This is one continuing aspect of all of his films and is seen at its strongest in *No Regrets for Our Youth.*

The picture is based upon the famous Takikawa Incident of 1933 which forced the resignation of Professor Yukitoki Takikawa from the faculty of Kyoto University for his supposed "Communistic thought," and caused a sensation among the nation's intellectuals. One of his pupils was Hidemi Ozaki, who became involved in the fa-mous Sorge spy case, and was executed in Tokyo in 1944. What appealed to Kurosawa in the story was not the suppression of a certain kind of political thought, but the fact that thought of any kind was suppressed; not that a possible leftist was executed but that any man was executed.

His sense of injustice and outrage provided the initial decision to make the picture. At the beginning of the film there is a terse title which tells us that both before and during the war such militaristic excess was common; a title toward the end states that the war is now over and "we have regained our freedom." Yet, in the picture itself, there is very little direct emphasis upon either militaristic excess or lost freedom. This is because, as is usual with Kurosawa, he is so inter-ested, is so engrossed in *how* something such as lack of freedom affects a person, how a living character reacts in all of its richness and humani-ty, that he forgets the social issue or, better, finds it irrelevant. Such-and-such has occurred to so-and-so. Kurosawa's interest is entirely in the reaction, what the person makes or does not make of this new condition. He is not at all interested in what forces have made people what they are; he is completely interested in what people make out of what the forces have made of them.

It is for this reason that the people in films of Sekigawa and Imai are cardboard and their pictures are forgotten; it is for this reason that long after the social event has become history, the people in Kurosawa films continue to live.

# THE STORY

Kurosawa has said: "The original script was a lot better than the one we had to use eventually. Eijiro Hisaita wrote it and told what really happened to Hidemi Ozaki, how he was suspected of spying, and how he died in prison. The trouble was that there was another script which Kiyoshi Kusuda wanted to use and there was a certain amount of resemblance. The scenario committee asked me if I 'wanted to stand in the way of a young director.' Naturally, I didn't want to do that but I pointed out that simply because two directors were involved the films would be different. That is the way movies are. The difference comes from the director, not the story. In fact, I said, I wanted to make a better film than he would. This they didn't like. So I had to change the whole second half of my script. Hisaita initially refused, I begged, and somehow or other we started shooting."

In the finished story, the professor-father (Denjiro Okochi) is relieved of his post. His daughter (Setsuko Hara) does not realize the meaning of this. She is still a girl, particularly friendly with two of her father's pupils (Susumu Fujita and Akitake Kono). She is in love with the former and his being put into prison is the first indication she has of the kind of world she lives in. When she goes to Tokyo to work as a secretary, Kono shows her an article that Fujita, now out of jail, has written. She goes to see him, and they live together. He is arrested, accused of being a spy, and executed. She goes back to Kyoto and then makes an extraordinary decision. She will take his ashes back to his parents in the country, and will stay there. So she does, this well-bred Kyoto girl, working in the rice-fields like a peasant. Her life is particularly hard. The animosity of the neighboring farmers, all of whom know about the case, is extreme, yet she will not give up. The war over, she returns home, but realizes she has no place there. At the end of the picture she returns to the peasants.

Even in resumé, it is apparent that the picture is not about Ozaki or Takikawa. It is about the girl. The clash of liberal and militaristic beliefs is far away indeed. As always when Kurosawa expresses the intention of making a socially significant picture, the director's true interest lies not in ideas as such, but in the way these ideas affect life, in this case the life of the heroine which we follow from 1933 to 1946. Other directors may be interested in personifying political ideas in terms of character; Kurosawa is interested only in character for its own sake and he makes very clear indeed that the girl's going to the peasants is not motivated by political considerations (she has no political considerations) but, rather, is something like personal salvation for her. "At that time," he has said: "I believed that the only way for Japan to make a new start was to begin by respecting the 'self'—and I still believe that. I wanted to show a woman who did just that."

# CHARACTERIZATION

Setsuko Hara is the center of the picture; everything that happens is in relation to her. While we do not see things through her eyes (we are shown, for example, the student riots—something she could not have seen), we are so closely associated with her during the course of the film that it is her interpretation of things which we accept. Initially, however, she has no interpretation. She is the well-brought-up young Japanese girl who plays the piano and studies flower-arranging. The world of political dissent seems far away.

The first sequence shows her and her school friends in Arashiyama, near Kyoto. First we hear them singing in the forest, their school song; then we see their feet (in these early pictures Kurosawa was using the American technique of introduction through feet—*Sugata, One Wonderful Sunday,* etc.) and finally see the three of them, Setsuko and the two boys, as they cross a stream and climb a hill. At the top they recite poetry (a common enough occupation, still enjoyed in the innocent promiscuity allowed college students) but are interrupted by machine-gun fire. She runs to look and finds at her feet a wounded soldier (wounded perhaps in target practice) and shows not only horror, but also disbelief that this could occur in her secure world.

Her father's dismissal does not touch her nearly this deeply. When they are talking about the dismissal she continues to play the piano, the Mussorgsky *Pictures at an Exhibition,* played with all the mechnical prowess and lack of understanding exhibited by most Japanese girls who have learned how to play hard pieces on the piano. Besides, she has something else to think about.

It is her father who first calls attention to her state. He says to his wife: "I'm worried." She, thinking of the dismissal, of the university, says: "Oh, students! They are—"He interrupts with: "No, I'm talking about her." The wife glances up–cut–there, in an entirely different part of the house, stands Setsuko, not doing anything, just standing, but the abstracted expression, the droop of the shoulders, the carressing touch of her fingers on the bannister, the sad, bemused eyes—this, in context, is the very picture of the young girl in love.

Later (much later—1938) we see her arranging flowers at class (she has presumably graduated and is teaching others, as many Japanese girls do) and suddenly she begins tearing the flowers apart. It is an extraordinary act, sheer perversity. A bit later she is playing the piano again—those hard scales at the end of *The Great Gate of Kiev*—and suddenly she stops and pounds the piano. Her mother comes in. She turns, and almost shouts at her: "I'm going to get married. I'm going to get married." Instantly, she continues and the only change of expression is a smile which might be guilty, might be joyous: "No, it's a lie. It's a lie. I'm not. I was lying."

These mercurial moods, these sudden emotional changes of direction are so true, so real, and yet (for good reason) so seldom seen on the screen, that at first one almost disbelieves them, particularly when Kurosawa—supremely confident—cuts one on top of the other. Given their absolutely right context of closed family life, however, given her love for Fujita (and shown Hara's marvelously detailed and delicate performance), one has no choice but to believe.

In one extremely fine sequence we find her busy in her room, see only her face, and then the camera, after a time, draws back, to reveal what she is doing (just as it drew back to show Sugata doing his laundry after we had enjoyed the mystery of a human face intent on something we could not even guess). She is packing. Her father comes in and his first words are not what are you doing or where are you going but: "Oh—you must think of your mother." This tells volumes about the household and the answer tells at least chapters about her: "Why? She has never thought of herself?" They argue—a muted argument. He is a gentle, liberal man, and it is just his gentleness, his liberality, which has been in part responsible for her raging need for change, for her violence, for her protean emotionality. She turns toward the window (here as in *Drunken Angel* a window means the outside, the foreign, the different, freedom) and says what she has kept secret for years: "I want to find what it is to live."

Fade—then the title: 1941. She is in Tokyo leading her own life. Her hair is cut short, she wears fashionable new clothes, she is a secretary, she is violently unhappy. Freedom is not so pleasant as she had hoped it would be. Consequently she is really pleased to meet Kono on the street. He has changed and anyone who knows Japan sees that Kurosawa here, too, is not afraid to tell the truth. We last saw this student friend idealistic, ready to fight for ideas, fresh-faced, staring defiantly into the future; and here he is with that half-cynical smile, that shrug when he remembers idealistic days, that worn, grey, tired look which is the reward that workaday Japan has for its intellectual youth. It turns out that Fujita still lives by his earlier ideals, that he is editing a magazine highly critical of the regime. Kono's job is just the opposite, he is working for the government. Yet, this does not make him a villain, in her eyes nor in ours. She accepts it.

But she also goes to see Fujita and there is a superb psychological development when she finally (in his darkened office) forces herself to ask him about his work. There is only silence for reply. Silence and the two of them unmoving in the dark for twenty seconds, an enormous amount of screen time. He never does answer. She wavers, then turns, flees, and would never have seen him again, if he had not gone after her, caught her in a collision which knocks both off balance and would be comic were it not so deeply concerned with showing two people so powerfully affected by each other that each becomes awkward. The psychology is superb in that Kurosawa risks silence rather than explanation. One shudders at what, given this opportu-

nity to explain the cause, Sekigawa or Imai would have done.

Kurosawa's interest, however, is entirely in the couple as human beings and not as personification of political ideas. In particular it is in her, because Fujita has seen, and we are beginning to see, that she is just the opposite of the common denominator of the ordinary protest picture, the usual socially-significant film. She is extraordinary.

When he dies she is put into prison and, as so often in Kurosawa, it is constraint, imprisonment, the vision of death, which brings out this nascent greatness. At home again, after prison, she is no longer as she was. She looks at the piano, tenderly, as one might look at an old friend. She touches it. Then she plays, but it is not Mussorgsky, it is Schumann, and she stops in the middle.

Her father is worried about her, he talks of responsibility and his meaning is the usual well-intentioned fuzzy meaning that most liberals have when they talk about it. She looks at him, one adult look, and he is reduced to silence. She knows what responsibility means. It is then that she takes the white-cloth-covered box of ashes (all that remains of the single person she has loved) and decides to take it to the country, to his peasant parents.

Just as the many critics who have said that Kurosawa does not understand women have obviously forgotten about this superb portrayal—so fine that one had to wait for Monica Vitti in *L'Avventura*, Jeanne Moreau in *Jules et Jim,* and Anna Karina in *Vivre sa vie* for anything at all comparable; so, the critics who have said that Kurosawa was to be numbered on the left have obviously never noticed his treatment of the proletariat in this film.

Kurosawa has the strength (and in Japan the strength needed is enormous) to say that the poor are not necessarily the better, that the life of poverty is not somehow more *real* than the life of wealth. The sentimentality necessary to find farming more noble than other oc-

cupations, however, is not at all foreign to Kurosawa, but (like Buñuel, especially in *Viridiana*) his compassion is so extreme that he guards against this excess to which many another director has fallen instant and easy prey. He has the courage in this film (and it took courage in 1946, a time when Communism was the new hope, when the proletariat was the new ideal) to tell the truth: that poverty may make brutes of men, but that the men themselves are no less responsible for their own brutishness.

The peasants (her in-laws excepted) are awful: they are mean, malicious, destructive, crafty, petty, perverse—they are the opposite of what Rousseau thought they were, they share nothing with the noble George Sand peasants, they are (and this is heresy to Japanese Marxists) not even worth saving.

Kurosawa's political uninvolvement is nowhere better seen than in these farm sequences. The military, the heroes of the right, are monsters; the peasants, heroes of the left, are also monstrous. The world and both of its extremes are not good enough, and how can simple striving humanity exist in such a place? This question, which reverberates throughout all of Kurosawa's later films, never remains unanswered. In this picture, he gives an answer through simple example.

Here is a well-born, even aristocratic girl from Kyoto, home of Japanese culture, up to her thighs in the mud, planting rice, back-breaking labor; her hands, which used to play Schumann, used to arrange flowers, are now cracked, torn, swollen; her face, which should have the pale Kyoto complexion still considered the most beautiful, is dark with the sun, grimed with dirt. She has *become* a peasant. And, on the other hand, here are peasants: cruel, selfish, crafty, continually shouting "spy-spy" after her, setting their children on her, trampling down the rice which she has labored so hard to plant. They have *become* nothing at all. They simply are.

As in *Sugata,* in many of the later pictures, the finished, the accomplished, things and people as they *are*—these are the lesser. Sanshiro's adversary thinks, feels, acts, as though he is fully formed; Setsuko's adversaries—the peasants—are those who have accepted their limitations, who are quite ready to explain away their state with references to god, to history, to politics. The single person—Sugata, this girl—who decides to change, to become, becomes the more in any Kurosawa film, and consequently becomes the focus of interest in that film. Setsuko performs the impossible, just as Sugata and the detective in *Stray Dog* perform the impossible. How this is done is shown in a very short scene toward the end of the farming-sequences. The peasants have with an all but incredible malice trampled down the entire field of rice which she and her husband's mother have so laboriously planted. We have watched them work and we know what it was like—the peasant's lot is one of the hardest that can befall a human being. When she discovers what has happened, the mother simply sits down and cries for she, too, is a peasant and this is an act of god, nothing can be done, it cannot be helped. Setsuko is also near tears. Then she shows in what way she is different. Wearily, almost with indifference, she picks up one trampled rice plant and sets it in its place again. She is going to start over.

Her act shares much with the try-and-try-again philosophy seen in so many of Kurosawa's pictures but in this one it is particularly poignant. The sound track carries her voice and she repeats what she said to her parents when she made her initial decision to leave Kyoto and go to the peasants: "But, I am his wife."

This has supported her during all the arduous rice-planting, during her mistreatment both by the right (the militarists) and the left (the peasants). She had thought that she knew what responsibility was. She would be responsible to the memory of her husband. But now—when she discovers that, far from ending, the labor is to be eternal, that she will forever be planting rice, that the next crop will follow this one, that in planting as in life there is no rest, no secession from the struggle—now she realizes where her responsibility lies.

It was she who made this astonishing choice to become a peasant (a choice very like Sugata's instant choice to jump into the pond) and though she could leave just as easily as he could have climbed from the pond, she, like him, refuses. Her responsibility has been recognized. She will be responsible to herself and to the tasks she has taken upon herself.

Back in Kyoto, after the war, after "we have regained our freedom," she is alone in knowing precisely what her freedom consists of. Her father is back at school again, her mother is busy, happy around the house, Kono is occupied, presumably with some Allied Occupation job. She looks at the piano once again. She touches it—but no Mussorgsky, no Schumann; she idly plays, with one finger, the school-song we heard at the beginning of the film. This fine single stroke of characterization seems to suggest that she has been so honed, so sharpened, that all externals have been planed away, that never again could she be the little girl in love who banged out hard passages on the piano, who either fixed the flowers beautifully or else pettily tore them apart.

She is again in Arashiyama, at the river which she and her friends had once crossed. A group of students comes by. They cross the river, jumping from stone to stone, just as she did, so long ago. She watches them; the only sound is the rush of the stream, the distant summer-sound of the cicada, and her eyes slowly fill with tears. Then she again packs.

Her parents do not say much. They no longer recognize her, she is no longer the daughter they knew. She tells them that she thinks she will go back and help on the farm, explaining that farm women have a hard life, that she is going to help them. But it is uncertain that she is really thinking about farm women. Rather, it is as though she knows what she must do—and she must do it for and by herself.

Kurosawa has said that the only way for Japan to make a new start was by respecting the "self," the individual, that "I wanted to show a woman who did just this." And so he has, but what he has shown is so much more serious, so much more truly responsible than anything we are used to seeing in life, let alone the movies, that the very hardness, the difficulty of what he is suggesting, almost repels.

It is as though he knew this. In the last scene of the picture we see her, her face serene but almost entirely without hope, climbing onto a farmer-filled truck, and being carried away from the camera, away from us, into a sunset landscape of an almost unearthly beauty, distant romantic mountains, sun-drenched fields. It is as though he wanted to insist upon the hopeless self-responsibility of the heroine and at the same to time to suggest that beauty (which so often seems to insist upon hope) exists quite regardless of what we do or do not do, that our resolves are accomplished in the very face of an irrelevant beauty. The last second of the picture shows the truck, the heroine, disappearing, being swallowed by the perfect beauty of this landscape.

Kurosawa shows us that beauty, like truth, consists in giving yourself to yourself. This is where the film has been leading us, this is where her character, growing, fulfilling, has been pointing. In a way, it is an apotheosis—a strange one to be sure, a lumbering truck disappearing into a back-lit landscape, a long road leading nowhere but into the sunset—and yet it is absolutely right. It is a very moving scene, a fitting conclusion to an intensely moving film.

And a very difficult film as well, because it is extremely personal and because it offers so little comfort. Belonging to the left or belonging to the right, these are comforting; *being* a peasant, *being* a well-off Kyoto girl, these too are comforting. They comfort because they suggest security, and Kurosawa in this film—as in *Ikiru,* as in *High and Low* —is insisting that there *is* no security, that all fancied security is only a form of blindness. Hence the picture moves, unnerves, and repels.

It repelled the Japanese, particularly the intellectuals, and especially the critics, who were unanimous in their dislike of the "unlikely" heroine. Kurosawa has said: "The critics were ferocious about the character of the woman . . . but it was only here and in *Rashomon* that I ever fairly and fully portrayed a woman. Of course, all of my women are rather strange, I agree, but this woman I wanted to show as the new Japan. I was right, I still think, to show a women who lived by and was true to her own feelings. The critics hated her as though she were a man. But she wasn't—and that was the point. If it had been a man those critics who so attacked the character would either have said nothing or else they might have thought what she did good."

Her choice (difficult enough for a Japanese man, or any man at all) certainly becomes magnified: a Japanese woman would have to be even stronger than any man to make this kind of choice. Even so, however, it seems likely that the critics would have continued to hate the picture precisely because it is so very hard-boiled, and gives so very little hope, and because its honesty is so extreme, so completely free of the comfortable corner-cutting which all of us find so congenial. What the critics and public alike resented most deeply was Kurosawa's daring to state that most fundamental and disturbing of all truths: the road to yourself is the hardest road of all and it is the only road which can justify life, since we humans believe justification necessary; the only road which can vindicate, since we insist upon vindication; the only road which—since we are living beings—allows us to live.

This is shown us so sternly, so uncompromisingly (for he had not yet learned how to sugar-coat the pill as in *Yojimbo* and *Sanjuro*) that the film infuriated precisely because it reached its audience so directly and involved them so deeply. If the critics hated the character of the girl it was because rarely in the history of cinema has a woman's character been shown in its fullness, its contradictions, its perversities, and its strengths—and almost never has it been suggested, as Kurosawa has in this picture, that (stronger than most men) she has the strength to disregard training, society, her "place," and, instead, realize herself, forge herself, make herself into an intensely living human being. "I want to find what it is to live," she says. This is just what she does.

## CAMERA AND EDITING

Since the picture is about the girl, about her character, Kurosawa's techniques in this film are to some extent determined by the nature of that character. Just as the various sections of *Rashomon* are filmed and edited according to the content of the section (for example, the woodcutter's story, the 'funny' section, uses long shots so that we can observe cause-and-effect in the terrified duel; uses very fast cutting so that we can see the action and reaction one directly following the

40

other) so both filming and editing in this picture are devoted to the explication of the girl's character. Since this character is mercurial, given to violent and almost simultaneous extremes (in the first half of the film at any rate), Kurosawa has invented a kind of grammar to show this to us.

Kono has come to dinner. Setsuko is sulking, at the same time behaving like a little girl. One second she is near tears; the next she is giggling and reaching across to take a tidbit off her mother's plate. The talk turns to Fujita. She says she never wants to see him, doesn't want him to come. This last sentence is heard over a new image: a close-up of her but she is in another part of the house, looking sad. Dissolve to her smiling (new location) and on top of that another dissolve (another location) looking angry. No sooner have we seen this then there is dissolve back to the dinner table, only it is much later. Fujita is there and she is looking at him. This tiny bridge takes about four seconds. It takes us forward in time, moves us from one dinner scene to another, but the way in which it is done shows us much about her character. Directly following this (she barely speaks to Fujita, just looks at him, or looks out the window) are five dissolves of her at the door (first the door to her room; then the door to her house) and in each dissolve her position is slightly different. There is no one else in the frame but at the end she looks down and mumbles: "Come again." She has been talking to him we now understand, though he is not visible. These dissolves have perfectly indicated her moods, her unsureness, her fears, her love.

In Tokyo there are five identical scenes (cut directly together rather than dissolved into each other) which perform the function of bridging time, indicating the strength of her emotions and, since they are rather amusing, commenting upon her. The camera is set up behind a great plate glass window, obviously some store front. Across the busy street are other windows and stores. Setsuko appears on the sidewalk, looks carefully around, and we understand (in context) that this is Fujita's office. Then, with an abstemious biting of the lips, she hurries on. Cut—same scene, it is raining. Setsuko appears with an umbrella protecting her. She lingers a bit longer, then squares her shoulders, tosses her head, marches off. Cut—it is autumn, the wind is blowing dead leaves along the street, she appears again, looking rather wan. She hesitates, can barely drag herself away, but does. And so on —each new scene (each one about four seconds long) adding to what we know of this girl's character. At the same time (as in the apprentice's training scenes in *Sugata, Part Two*, as in the opening wipes of *They Who Step on the Tiger's Tail* where Enoken tries to make friends with the priests) the fact that the scenes are identical, that we (watching time telescoped) are able to watch and compare as the characters themselves are not able to, makes them amusing. Setsuko appears, this time more determined. She stops, looks in; this time she is going to go to see him. She turns to enter the building and collides with a man. It is Fujita. He has been outside also, and is just returning.

Their life together is seen in a series of fragments. The sequence is built like a mosaic, little scenes sometimes no more than two seconds long placed among slightly longer ones.

*A big close-up of Setsuko's face, she is apparently sewing. Another one, she is crying. A third, she has picked up the scissors and thrown them, apparently at Fujita. A fourth, she is kissing him. He is leaving, she smiles. They are at a movie: he is laughing, she is crying. She is looking at a picture of his parents (whom we get to know rather well in the second half of the film); then she is looking out of the window. She is in his office, looks up at the sky, and says: "Oh, look at that cloud. Do you remember!" He whistles a tune—it is the school song. Cut—there they are in Arashiyama again, lying on the grass. One instantly thinks: a flashback. But it is not. In extremely abbreviated form, the continuity is hurrying us forward. They have apparently made a trip there, perhaps because she saw the cloud, perhaps because he remembered. There is a close-up of him but the music is now a rhumba. He is slapped with enormous force and his glasses are knocked off. The glasses on the floor, crushed. Two seconds of frenzied movement on the screen, impossible to see what is happening except that a hand is seen for an instant. He is being carried off. She (new location) looks up. It is their house and police are walking on the tatami with their shoes on. An entirely new character (Takashi Shimura) picks his teeth and looks at her. She is standing, her picture is being taken, a number under her face. Her face again —it is a photograph. Her face again, she is being slapped. A voice says: "Well, you think it over. You have lots of time to think." Over this is dissolved a picture of a pendulum swinging, and under it (in double-exposure) is Setsuko in prison. She faints, dissolve, prison-bars and sky, dissolve, clouds, against them (double-exposure) the first scene of the film, with the students in the woods, dissolve, her face, dissolve, her face again but she is washed and clean—she is back home.*

This has been their life together, this apparently disconnected series of tiny scenes leading from marriage to catastrophe, seen with none of the connecting links usually observed in classic screen grammar. One of the reasons for this extreme form of short-hand might be that Kurosawa, after all, had to show twelve years in two hours, but certainly the more important is that, by showing us in this way he not only telescopes the actions, moves the story, but, at the same time, and most important, shows how things appear *to* her. This kind of expressionism (if that is the word for it: at any rate, this view of the world as subjective) was not commonly seen until *A bout de souffle* and *Hiroshima, mon amour.* One is struck by the similarity in feeling between those scenes of Setsuko Hara at the door, and those of Delphine Serig on the bed in *Marienbad* and the similarity is not surprising because the reasons for their being there are the same. Both directors are presenting a subjective view of character.

This occurs very rarely in the work of Kurosawa. Usually an examination of character takes the form of repeated action (in *Rashomon* and *Ikiru*), or an investigation (the second half of *Ikiru*) or, as in the majority of his films, the orthodox method of a character's revealing himself through language and action. But then in no other film, not even *Ikiru*, was Kurosawa so concerned with a single character.

The expressionistic use of camera, cutting, and dialogue (showing us things as she herself sees them) continues during the farm scenes. When she walks down the lane we hear the voices of the children whispering "spy-spy" although actually there are no children there. When she has become ill from overwork she looks at the forest, and the camera reels. At the same time we (she) hears the sound of laughter, as though the forest is laughing. She turns to a field of standing rushes, rippling in the wind, and the sound of laughter again sweeps over her. Later in the picture, she is working again, working like an animal, eyes to the ground, hearing nothing, seeing nothing, and she hears laughter. Startled, she looks up. This time the laughter is real. It is her mother-in-law, laughing with pure pleasure at seeing the paddy almost fully planted. Shortly after this (the next day apparently) the peasants destroy the crop. As she stands, dazed, looking at the havoc, the sound track carries the noise of a village celebration; laughter, high flutes, drums, shouts, cries.

There is an extremely beautiful passage (particularly beautiful in context, perhaps because all the planting scenes have been shown almost too extensively, with the full paraphernalia of double-exposure, and optical printing, very Dovzhenko, insisting upon the epic note: beautiful therefore because it is so simple) where she has begun once again to replant the paddy.

*Dissolve from her bent figure to her hands working in the mud.*
*Dissolve from her muddy hands to her hands, soft, clean, playing the piano. A phrase of the Schumann is heard, but is swallowed by a sound which we do not at first recognize except that it sounds clean, refreshing.*
*Dissolve to her cracked hands in the stream. The sound we heard over the Schumann was that of rushing water.*
*Dissolve to her face, looking at her hands, an expression bemused but not self-pitying, an expression reminiscent of that when she played the piano, years ago, but now subtly changed, adult, knowing but not tragic.*

This extraordinary picture (just as extraordinary as was *Sanshiro Sugata* but in an entirely different way) was naturally roundly abused

as cinema. Kurosawa has said: "Actually, it wasn't much of a production—the labor union got in the way for one thing. Still, it was the first film in which *I* had something to say and in which *my* feelings were used. Everyone disagreed. They said I should go 'back' to the style of *Sugata*. Look, I said, if I could have had my complete say on *Sugata* I wouldn't have made it in the way that I did. What did I have to go back to? Then they said that *Sugata* was technically the more proficient which just isn't so. It is just because a director has something to say that he finds the form, the skill, the technique, to bring it out. If you are only concerned with how you say something, without having anything to say, then even the way you say it won't come to anything. Besides, technique is there only to support a director's intentions. If he relies solely on the technique his original thought won't appear. Techniques do not enlarge a director, they limit him. Technique alone, with nothing to support its weight, always crushes the basic idea which should prevail."

This is an extremely cogent statement of Kurosawa's ideas on style, and one which he himself has observed throughout his career. In 1963 he said: "Nothing could be more difficult for me than to define my own style. I simply make a picture as I want it to be, or as nearly as it is possible for me to do so. And I've never thought of defining my own particular style. If I ever did a thing like that I'd be doing myself a grave disservice."

One of Kurosawa's strongest attributes as a director is that he knows not only that the style is the man, he also knows that the man is continually changing, growing, and that therefore, style itself grows, changes, and it is this metamorphosis, this continual adaptation which is most necessary, most interesting, and most rewarding.

If he never returned to the style of *No Regrets for Our Youth* with its extraordinary freedom, its enormous power of evocation, it was because other stories demanded other styles. His remarks on *Sugata* are interesting for they suggest that, by 1946, only three years later, he had discovered other ways to show the story (and to circumvent other people's intentions), other ways of expressing this "basic idea" which is for him the heart of the film.

And it is for this reason that each of his films, though bound to the others by reason of certain stylistic affinities, by a continuing interest in a single and basic story, are at the same time completely different from each other. This gives his work a variety which is very rare in contemporary cinema. But equally rare is the perfection of those of his pictures which are perfect. *No Regrets for My Youth* is the first of these.

# One Wonderful Sunday

## THE STORY

Kurosawa has said: 'I got the idea for this film from an old D.W. Griffith picture about a couple just after the first war who plant potatoes. First crop is ruined, second crop is stolen—but they don't give up. They try again. Though this film won me a prize for the best director of the year I don't think I made it nearly freely enough. I had a lot of things to say and I got them all mixed up—it certainly is not my favorite film. But I remembered, and in *Drunken Angel* I kept my eyes open."

A young factory worker (Isao Numazaki) and his fiancée (Chieko Nakakita) spend their weekly holiday together. It is a Sunday in spring and they have just thirty-five yen. They meet at the station, they go see a model house, they play baseball with some boys and the ball lands in a cookie-seller's display. He is forced to buy two crushed cookies. They go to a cabaret but spend no money, go to the zoo, meet a war orphan. It rains. They decide to go to a concert but the cheap tickets have all been bought by scalpers. He tries to get them to sell at the legal rate. They beat him up. The two go to his room. He wants her; she is afraid and runs away. Then she returns and they go to a coffee shop where he has to leave his raincoat because they haven't enough to pay for the coffee. They wander in the ruins, pretend to own their own coffee shop; they sing and play on the swings. Later they go to a bandshell and pretend to have a concert. Then he takes her to the station. She leaves. They promise to meet again next Sunday.

The film is episodic, as is *Stray Dog;* held together by the young couple themselves and by the gradually diminishing thirty-five yen. The theme, as in so many of Kurosawa's films, is try-and-try-again. A similarity of attitude is the reason that the films of Griffith appealed to him so at this time and why, even now, he thinks highly of Frank Capra. The theme is reflected in the character of the girl.

Her's is an extremely well-drawn character, beautifully played. From the very first we know that she is good—in the way that Japanese girls so very often are. She is truly generous, truly unselfish. She likes to pretend that things are better than they are—the model house, the imaginary coffee shop, the imaginary concert—and this helps make them so. At the same time she knows her own failings. Her very

compassion is apt to catch her. After she has seen the war orphan she is quiet, withdrawn. Then she turns and, visibly, gets herself under control. With a little shake of the shoulders, she turns again, says to herself: All right now, stop it—and turns back to him, smiling. At the same time she is very innocent. In his room, the pass he makes terrifies her and she runs away, but has the bravery to come back, to bravely try again. She could be a sister to the girl in *Ikiru*—an older, wiser sister.

It is also her character which underlines the construction of the film, which is unusually rich in parallels and reoccurring actions. The opening shot shows her on the train, and the final scene is her departure by train. In the model house she plays the wife and he—who doubts throughout the film—says: Stop it—be more realistic. To which she answers: If you don't believe in dreams you can't live properly. And he—the voice of common sense: Dreams don't fill the stomach. At the end of the film they are in another house, a ruined one, and pretend to be in a coffee shop; he is the waiter and she is the customer. After he has served an imaginary cup of coffee she suddenly bursts into laughter and says: Who was it said that dreams don't fill the stomach? She likes music and it was at a concert that they originally met. In the middle of the film they attempt to go to a concert and they fail. At the end they have their own concert. It is also she who continually underlines the assumptions and meanings of the story—she, in fact, who creates it. They are talking about the difficulty of life. He is sunk in despair. She shakes her head, looks grim, says stoutly: And it isn't even our fault. Then, in the next instant, she is smiling and saying: Want some tea? Tea makes you feel better.

## MUSIC

Kurosawa, from the first, has taken a great interest in the music of his pictures and in this film has created a kind of musical—at least it is his nearest approach to the genre. Much of the music is Schubert because that is the young couple's favorite composer. The credit titles carry an orchestration of the most famous of the *Moments musicaux*. It is later used to accompany the race to the concert, and the cutting is designed to synchronize with the phrases of the Schubert. The first movement of the *Unfinished* is heard complete—when he conducts it during the imaginary concert. The second movement begins under the final sequence at the station and is concluded (much shortened and with a new coda) at the end of the film.

There is lots of other music, however. In the model-house sequence the sound track carries *My Blue Heaven*, played on a radio far away. During the baseball game it is *Twinkle, Twinkle Little Star*. He marches up to the cookie-seller to the strains of the march from *Carmen* and assorted tunes-of-the-day are usually somewhere on the sound track.

There is a very imaginative use of one—an American tango—when he is in his room during the rain storm. She has left. He decides to take a nap. Just then the loudspeaker across the way begins blaring the tango. He cannot sleep. She comes back. There is no dialogue. She weeps. The strains of the tango, all in the minor, occur and reoccur. She finally moves to the window, looks out, says: Oh, the sun is shining—and, at the same time, the tango shifts to major. It is a magical and very simple effect, precisely as though the sun had come out. After this the tango accompanies them to the real coffee shop (where it is revealed as radio music) and later to the imaginary coffee shop.

The most imaginative use of sound, however, is not musical. The first is in his room. The roof is leaking. She puts his wash-pan under the leak and thereafter the sound of the drop hitting the metal pan, at an interval so slow that one never comes to expect it, contributes much to the atmosphere of building tension and strain. The second is after the imaginary concert. The first movement of the Schubert sweeps to a close through a series of dissolves which leaves the couple on the railway station, still bemused by the music, waiting for their train. The train whistle sounds and they look down the track. Only it is not

a train whistle. It is the A of the oboe—the tuning pitch of the orchestra. Directly, the second movement of the Schubert begins. The third is at the bandshell where he is feeling silly about pretending to conduct. She is in the audience, waiting. Knowing it is absurd, he waves his arms. There is sound, but it is not the Schubert. At that moment a wind rises and scatters the dead leaves in the shell and their rustling progress with the whisper of the wind makes her start, makes him drop his arms. It is a magical effect—much mitigated, it is true, by the fact that, eventually, the Schubert begins.

# CAMERA

Given the year, the handicaps of making films in 1947, even now the film looks splendidly made. The opening shot is stunning—the kind of shot that all directors want but which is extraordinarily difficult to capture. The camera is very close to the edge of the station platform. A train is rushing by at fullspeed and the image is blurred. Then it begins to slow down, the windows are discernable, then the doors, as they rush past. The train slows down, one by one the windows go by. Finally it stops and there, perfectly framed in a single window, is the girl—looking out.

Following this we watch feet in the station, marching this way and that, all looking oddly impersonal and undirected since we cannot see the bodies they are attached to. It would be, perhaps, too clever a comment on aimlessness if there were not another reason for it. The young man has been eyeing a cigarette butt which someone has thrown away, wondering whether to pick it up or not. He has just decided to when the camera, following her feet, comes upon his hand, then pans up to her looking at him, disapproving. (Later on, at the end of the film, the feeling of cyclic form is further intensified by his finding, after she has gone, a cigarette butt. There is then a close-up of his foot crushing it. Formally, beginning and end join; thematically it indicates, of course, that he has learned something—at least he has learned not to smoke thrown-away cigarette butts.)

The focus continually emphasizes her, which is proper. Particularly in his room there are many scenes where he is in the foreground and she in the background, or vice versa. Since deep focus was out of the question both because of inferior lenses and inadequate lighting, Kurosawa turned this limitation into a virtue and conspicuously favors her with the sharp focus, allowing him to slide out of focus. The visual implication is that she is the more interesting—which is quite true.

In this picture, more than in many of the period, Kurosawa made much use of lateral motion. There are scenes of people walking into (and out of) the frame—a trick then not so clichéd as now; and there are numerous scenes where action is begun in back of the camera and the characters then advance to visibility in front of it. When the baseball crashes into the cookie-seller's display there is, first, the ball in the cookies, then the sound of the march from *Carmen* and finally, the hero advancing from behind the camera to go to the cookie-seller and the effect is comic. When they are on the swings, the camera is placed midway between the two and at the place where the swings would hang when unused. Thus, both zoom out from behind the camera, sail into middle-distance, then return to invisibility behind the camera. Since they do not appear at the same time, there is a constant motion on the left side of the screen, then on the right—the entire effect considerably enhanced by a fine full moon (later shown in close-up as transition to coffee shop, a shot unfortunate in that the wires holding the moon are plainly visible) and his singing a children's song he has suddenly remembered. Here the effect is poetic, the two of them up in the air, sailing free, singing the songs of childhood.

Kurosawa in this film began to take real care of his compositions —they are no longer of an obviousness that shows how much care he took; rather, they seem casual but are perfect. When the two eat the cookies they are standing near an open section of an enormous concrete sewage pipe which is lying on its side in a vacant lot. Each new shot, using the movement of the actors, the shape of the pipe, the fact that she sits down in it, that he leans over it—is precisely right. Yet they are moving about and the sequence is made up with many cuts so that the composition is always shifting and changing. From a technical point of view it is very daring, very free—and Kurosawa did nothing quite like it again until the splendid diagonal compositions, of *The Lower Depths* and *The Bad Sleep Well*.

The punctuation in the film is mostly the standard cut—there are no wipes in this picture. But there are some interesting dissolves, particularly at the end. The first movement of the Schubert ends accompanied by a dissolve which takes us from the bandshell to the train platform. There, in the distance, sit the couple. They do not move, they are happy, bemused. Rather than dolly up, Kurosawa uses four dissolves to get us there. It is very much the same as the final dissolves in *Rashomon* where five are used to draw us to the woodcutter and the the priest. The effect of these advancing dissolves is one of great care. It is as though we are stealing upon them, unwilling to break their mood, to disturb them. We do not advance, we hover, then melt nearer. It is precisely right for the mood of the moment.

# INFLUENCES

When Kurosawa says that his three favorite directors are Ford, Wyler, and Capra, he is saying what he has said since 1947—though nowadays he will also include Antonioni. He continues to mention the triumvirate because this is what he told the press once, and what the press thinks and writes is of little relevance to him. If he gives the expected Ford-Wyler-Capra answer then he will not have to explicate— the press will think it understands. Also, at the time he was deeply influenced by Capra.

This is obvious in *One Wonderful Sunday*. The whimsicality of the later scenes, the jaunty optimism of the girl, the right-you-are-if-you-think-you-are story, the humanism which is always threatening to curdle into sentimentality—this is the legacy of Frank Capra. Even the acting style is influenced—the way that she (a plucky Jean Arthur) is always reaching up to him (a rueful James Stewart) to fix his hat properly. Kurosawa had seen *It Happened One Night, Mr. Deeds Goes to Town,* and *Lady for a Day*—and the film shows it.

There are other American influences, however. The final reels (night—studio-built Tokyo) are seemingly out of von Sternberg. The foggy station platform looks like something from *Docks of New York*— but might have come either from the many UFA productions Kurosawa saw or, more likely, strained through Mamoulian.

At the same time, there are strong Japanese influences in the picture. The scenes in his room are all *echt* Japanese—almost to the point of parody. The longueurs of this sequence are so extreme that even the Japanese audience—the most attentive and permissive in the world— always show signs of restlessness and fidgeting. Minute after minute goes by and nothing happens. When she returns her weeping is painfully and minutely recorded. And it all seems quite pointless, given the generally sunny context of the film. It is right here, also, that the film starts to fall apart.

There is nothing Japanese about the concert-finale—it is straight from Henry Koster's *One Hundred Men and a Girl,* a great prewar Japanese favorite. There sits the good little girl, pulling for her young

man just as Deanna Durbin pulled for Stokowski—same polished cheeks, same tear-filled eyes. At the same time the camera pulls rapidly away and the scene is revealed as an elaborate crane shot. The entire sequence stands revealed as a production number with the crane swooping about, the obviously studio-built bandshell and park standing there in all of its expensive and badly-lit splendour. It is all supremely irrelevant to the film.

Schubert washes over the couple. He cries, she cries, mixed in with lots of shots of her handbag (attention drawn to it when she left it behind in his room) with her little mascot—cute little furry toy dog—just peeping out. Then, all of a sudden, inspiration falters. He has not only realized how silly it is—he has lost his faith in the impossible. Schubert grinds to a halt.

In an unbelievable and all too unforgettable moment, the girl turns to the audience and (just like Wendy) cries out, tears running: "Oh, if you believe . . . show it by clapping your hands, applause, applause, applause!" She herself sets an efficient example, the audience squirms (no one to my knowledge has ever clapped), and eventually he gathers

courage and the Schubert begins again.

This is, of course, enough to ruin the entire picture and that it does not says a good deal for the strength of Kurosawa and the extreme skill of Chieko Nakakita—she almost makes this riot of kitsch believable. The main trouble with it is that it is a parody of the philosophy of the film. One can only experience the good when it takes a form both complicated and profound, as in *Red Beard*. This we have been shown by the girl in the first two-thirds of the picture. Now, deeper feeling turns into whimsey and the sentimental for its own sake. Kurosawa's 'humanism' suddenly becomes shallow and our feet drag on the bottom.

This is always a danger for him. His films are as concerned with uplift as are those of Griffith but Kurosawa is much the cleverer director and feels just as deeply. When the feelings run riot as in sections of *The Idiot,* the end of *Record of a Living Being,* and in this film the audience can do little but reject the simplicity of the rationale. Kurosawa himself, of course, knows of this danger, of the ease with which the deeply felt becomes the sentimental. He seldom made this kind of mistake again.

# Drunken Angel

Japanese critics have agreed that this picture is to Japanese cinema as *Paisa* or *Bicycle Thieves* is to Italian, that it perfectly epitomizes a period, its hopes, its fears; that it marks the major "breakthrough" of a major directorial talent who has finally "realized" himself. Kurosawa is just as suspicious of that word "realized" as would be Rossellini or De Sica. "I have undergone no major change," he said at the time: "the only difference is that in earlier films I was never allowed to express myself properly." Nonetheless, *Drunken Angel* remains, for most Japanese, Kurosawa's "first picture" and its evocation of the early postwar years, both their misery and their freedom, has made it one of the director's most revived films. Kurosawa himself remains fond of it because, as he says: "In this picture I was finally myself. It was *my* picture. I was doing it and no one else."

## THE STORY

Under the opening credits the scummy surface of a pond appears, a filthy sump in the middle of a city, perhaps an enormous bomb crater, perhaps the flooded ruins of some burned mansion. Around it are the jerry-built false-front shops of the postwar era, plywood festooned with neon. Gas bubbles to the surface of the pond on which floats garbage, half-burned wood, a single shoe—the debris of war.

This pond becomes the center of the film, its core, and on its banks occurs the anecdote. Dangerous, filled with disease, it is experienced daily by the hundreds and thousands who live around it. It is like a a huge cancer, alive, bubbling—both a reminder of a moral state and, at the same time, symptom and symbol of a very sick society.

As an example: the neighborhood is completely run by gangsters, young toughs who have come of age since the war. They live by extortion, intimidation; they are bragging, stupid, malicious, and dangerous. One of them (Toshiro Mifune) is wounded, and goes to the local doctor (Takashi Shimura) to have a bullet removed from his hand. The doctor discovers he has tuberculosis as well and insists upon treating him. Their relationship is the story of the film. Toward the end, Mifune—displaced by the return from prison of his boss, a prewar gangster, a hard, brutal, experienced man—turns and, partially

to save the nurse (who had been connected with the gangster), tries to kill him. He himself is killed, and his funeral expenses are paid by a bar girl who has long loved him.

The pond remains, there is one hoodlum less, and ostensibly nothing has changed.

## CHARACTERIZATION

The picture is an exhaustive, even occasionally exhausting accounting of and for the relationship between doctor and gangster. Each has something that the other needs. On the simplest level, any doctor needs disease and any gangster needs health.

Mifune has told the doctor that he has a nail in his hand. Shimura, instead, finds a bullet.

*Doctor:* This is a nail? Look I'm expensive. I always am for no-goods like you.
*Gangster:* Won't you even give me a shot when you take it out?
*Doctor:* Not for your kind I won't.

The battle starts with the first dialogue because, no matter how the doctor needs the sick, he hates the hoodlums. He equates them with the sump, the poisonous pond which he equally hates. The gangster's reasons for hating the doctor are simpler. Anyone who is not intimidated is a threat.

The doctor discovers that the gangster has tuberculosis.

*Doctor:* Naturally, you don't feel anything at first. When you do it is too late. Are you afraid?
*Gangster:* Afraid? Look, I hate doctors. They always lie to make money.
*Doctor:* Sure, sure. Five TB cases and a doctor is made.

When the doctor tells him he won't last long, Mifune's reaction is fury: he attacks the doctor, and beats him up. The idea of a serious illness is something which the gangster cannot tolerate and so he must attack the very person who discovered it. When he leaves, the doctor turns to the nurse and says:

Well, there is hope for him. His kind really hates to get

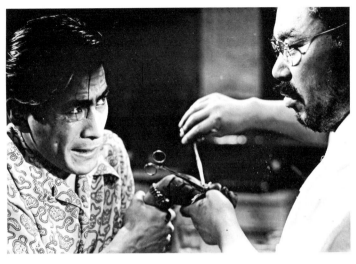

sick. Now, he's worried. And he got mad. That proves he hasn't sunk too low.

The doctor's attitude toward disease is shown in the scene which follows directly. Some children are playing around the sump. He storms out with an enormous and truly frantic energy, one quite incommensurate with the sight of a few children standing on the edges of a dirty pond. He waves his arms, he shouts, he screams, and bellows. He truly hates disease.

In the next sequence we see why. It is because he himself is diseased. He is an alcoholic. He stops at a small bar and there finds a patient. Instantly he is transfixed with fury—imagine that, a patient drinking! The poor man creeps away and the doctor sits down to toss off several himself. While drinking he asks the bar girl about Mifune, and she asks: "Are you in love with him too?"

The question is thrown away, almost unheard in the general conversation, but it is completely relevant. He and the gangster already hate each other with such intensity that one must suspect love as well. Love is very often based upon need and each needs the other. After being thrashed by the gangster the doctor goes back to the clinic and says to the nurse:

> It's his own funeral. He doesn't understand, doesn't appreciate kindness. He's better off dead. I'm not going to see him any more.

*Nurse:* Oh, yes, you will. You always do. Your patients are more important to you than anything else.

We see, however, that he is motivated by something much stronger than the doctor's oath, a disinterested benevolence, a desire to do good. He is possessed by the need to do *something*. Like Watanabe in *Ikiru* he feels his life has been worthless, that he must somehow vindicate it. Later he says:

> This gangster. He reminds me of myself when I was young. He acts tough but he is lonely inside. And he cannot kill that feeling.

Perhaps this feeling is the reason that the doctor chooses the gangster as the person he most wants to help, as though he were really helping himself when he does so. When he tells the gangster what he thinks of him, he might be speaking of himself.

> You're afraid of being sick? Idiot. I'm not laughing at you for being afraid. That's natural, and nothing to be ashamed of. But you think that that's courage. You're wrong. You're a coward, you are all cowards. Strutting around, all that big talk, the tattoos. That little girl that just left here has more courage than you will ever have. You—you're afraid of the dark.

The little girl, recovering nicely from tuberculosis, is naturally the contrast he needs for both himself and the gangster. She is very young, very innocent. She is not yet ill with all of the illnesses that maturity can bring.

Mifune is so furious at this encounter that he goes out and attacks the first person who crosses his path, a student whom he leaves dazed with one blow. The reaction is quite appropriate. Evil of this sort exists through fear. He attacks because he is afraid he will be attacked. Mifune could scarcely attack the disease. Hence he leaves an anonymous and astonished student reeling in the street. He has punished, but he has only punished himself.

Shimura, too, goes to his punishment. He runs into a friend, a fellow-student in their intern days, one who is now wealthy, has a car—is, in fact, what Shimura might have become.

*Doctor:* Well, how are you making out? Killing a lot?

*Shimura:* Do you have any surplus alcohol?

*Doctor:* For you to drink?

*Shimura:* No. For my patients.
*Doctor:* What about your own ration?
*Shimura:* I drank it.

He has another favor to ask. He wants this doctor to look at Mifune, to take an x-ray picture, to confirm what he has found. It is as though he is asking a better, more dispassionate self. For he is certainly not dispassionate. He is intensely involved with the gangster. He fights and struggles to save but it is not clear whether he is trying to save the gangster or to save himself.

The nurse sees this. After yet another of their battles in which the doctor and the patient throw things at each other, even hurt each other, she says:

> Look. Being a doctor is silly in the first place. They all need sick people. But you . . . you try to cure them. In a way, Doctor, you are too honest. I don't mean you have to lie, but there are other ways of telling the truth.

Other ways of telling the truth—a presage of *Rashomon*. But the doctor is too much concerned with his personal salvation to see the wisdom of her remark. Instead he insists upon flinging himself on the gangster, wrestling with him as though he were the angel of the title.

He is not, however.
*Gangster:* You are really pretty nasty.
*Doctor:* No. I'm here out of kindness. I'm a sort of angel.
*Gangster:* A dirty, nasty angel.
*Doctor:* Oh, you think that angels are nice and clean and pretty? They're not. They're just like me.
*Gangster:* Shut up.

Indeed, the doctor *is* a kind of angel because he is absolutely determined to do good, the way that other men might be determined to do bad. Like the title-hero of *Red Beard,* he knows precisely wherein good lies and nothing will stop him. But Mifune is a kind of angel too, though of a darker breed. He is the kind of angel one wrestles with and Shimura must play Jacob to this dark, unknowable power.

Men, angels, and devils are all one, however—any man encompasses all three. Good or bad—these two men are angels to each other. Mifune has had a bullet in his hand. He fights with the doctor. He pushes him, knocks him down. When the doctor gets to his feet he finds that *his* hand and arm are hurt. Mifune storms out. The doctor dresses his own wound, muttering the while. It may appear a simple accident, a coincidence. But something more important has occured. It is a meaningful act. It is like the rites of blood. It is like a declaration of brotherhood.

# TREATMENT

Kurosawa has said: "I made the film to denounce the way of gangsters, and to show how silly they are as human beings." If this feeling were stronger in the finished film one might see a protest in it. As it is, however, the invariable silliness of all gangsters is a minor theme. Part of this is due to the performance of Mifune. Though he had been seen in films before, this was his first starring role and it resulted in instant fame. "Shimura played the doctor beautifully but I found I could not control Mifune. When I saw this, I let him do as he wanted, let him play the part freely. At the same time, I was worried because, if I didn't control him, the picture would turn out differently from what I'd wanted. It was a real dilemma. Still, I did not want to smother that vitality. In the end, though the title refers to the doctor, it is Mifune that everyone remembers."

"I had seen him before—in Taniguchi's *To the End of the Silver Mountains*—but had no idea he would be like this. Just as an example, his reactions are so very swift. If I say one thing, he understands ten. He reacts extraordinarily quickly to the director's intentions. Most Japanese actors are the opposite of this and so I wanted Mifune to cultivate this gift."

If Mifune was one dilemma successfully resolved, the character of the doctor was another. "Uegusa and I rewrote his part over and over again, and he still wasn't interesting. We had almost given up when it occured to me that he was just too good to be true. He needed a defect, a vice. That is why we made him an alcoholic. At this time most film characters were still either all black or all white. We made the doctor grey."

Keinosuke Uegusa remembers that "while we were working the weight shifted toward the gangster and the doctor got weaker and weaker. We decided that the gangster simply could not be the hero . . . and I remember we decided that the mistake was about halfway through. So we rewrote from then on.

"Kurosawa's way of working is so relentless that, once the place was discovered he felt no compunction at all in cutting through all the attractive bad spots. He always does this—with neither regrets nor compromises. His attitude is a fine, cutting sword. He not only has the strength to go directly to the foundations of any idea, he also has the strength to throw things out. Come to think of it, it is probably this combination which makes him an artist."

The halfway point in the film comes when the gangster goes to the doctor in the middle of the night. He is dead drunk and he brings the x-ray negative of his chest. It is almost as though he got drunk so that he could come, as the doctor told him to—something he might have refused to do had he been sober. For once the doctor is completely sober and so the roles are reversed. He complains about the thoughtlessness of some people, waking other people up, but is as pleased as can be. Mifune, his careful gangster's hair-do all undone, is all but out on his feet. He looks at the doctor, asks: "Then, will I really get well?" —and the doctor knows he has won. Mifune passes out and the camera dollies over him, then turns and continues, out of the door, and over the sump.

It is a splendid linking of cause and effect, the sick gangster, the fetid pond, all in one smooth and economical movement. But this is not all. Kurosawa's camera rarely editorializes in this direct manner. The camera turns, looks, and on the far side of the pond sits the guitar player who so often is there of a summer evening (who, in fact, opened the film) but he is not alone. We move nearer and see that with him is the gangster's boss, returned from prison.

This is an admirable transition, suggesting as it does a metaphysical and then an actual reason for the gangster's condition, but—more— since we know that Mifune is on the verge of reformation, it suggests complications. It is as though we have turned a corner and suddenly glimpsed the future.

Mifune leaves, the doctor has told him not to drink any more, he has agreed. He takes a flower from the florists' shop as is his habit, and they bow and smile at him, as is theirs. He grins and the music on the soundtrack swells with hope. He stands by the edge of the sump, looking at it. The camera pans down to see what he is seeing, the filthy, bubbling pond, and it seems a mere indication of what he is seeing, thinking about, until we notice that his shadow is stretched across its surface. This seems some kind of visual symbol—he came from the sump but is triumphing. Then we see why we are shown his shadow. Another shadow has moved beside it. The camera moves swiftly back to the gangster and there is the ex-boss with him. But, more important, we are shown a gangster completely different from the one who was there a few seconds before, proudly looking at his reflection. Instead, Mifune is bowing, cringing, suddenly reduced to the cheap hoodlum he had been. The boss tells him to come with him. Mifune smiles, ducks his head, nods, trots after him, and, with a gesture of embarrassment and disgust throws the carnation into the pond. The camera turns to look because this is important, a straight symbol, the white carnation floating on the liquid filth—for Mifune has thrown himself away.

Like the vengeful young husband in *The Bad Sleep Well*, like the actor in *The Lower Depths*, the gangster's downfall begins at the very moment when he had decided to reform. This is ironical but, more, this is the first of the many suggestions in Kurosawa's pictures that no single person is as good as the world is bad; or, that the virtues of compassion, understanding, are precisely those which insist that the guard be lowered; or, that the person who attacked first through fear that he would be attacked, finds once he has given up attacking, himself attacked. At any rate, despite or because of his choice, Mifune goes rapidly down from here. He loses his position, his mistress, his

money. What he does not lose, however, is something he has just recently gained, his sense of himself.

The doctor has decided to really work over saving Mifune now. He says: Your lungs are just like this place, filthy. And it isn't enough to clean them, we have to get you out of here

At that point the ex-boss comes to the clinic to get the nurse, his former girl. The doctor refuses.

*Boss:* You want to die?

*Doctor:* Don't brag about killing people. I've killed a lot more than you have.

Mifune, very ill now, appears. He asks the doctor not to go to the police, that he will take care of it somehow, that if he goes to the police he himself would lose face.

*Doctor:* Stupid. Babies and patients never lose face.

*Gangster:* But we have a code of honor.

*Doctor:* Your code of honor is a security pact. It is all about money.

Scenes such as this wear the gangster down or, better, they hone him, cleanse him. Every one of the reasons that a gangster has for being a gangster is taken away from him. Further (as the carnation scene and others have indicated), he would be only too happy to escape from himself into some kind of false identity.

In this he is very much like the nurse (Chieko Nakakita of *One Wonderful Sunday*). The difference is that she resists her ready-made role, moll to the gang boss. She hates the idea, and yet it strongly attracts her: it would be so simple.

*Nurse:* But, my life is ruined . . .

*Doctor:* Don't be afraid, now. That is, if you really mean to break off seeing him.

Nurse: Oh, you don't know how I hate him. But, he has ruined my life.

Doctor: Only half of it.

Kurosawa has shown us the relationship between gangster and nurse, that they much resemble each other, in this beautifully conceived and very meaningful bit of continuity:

> A scene where the gang recognizes the nurse as the ex-boss's girl-friend—cut.
> The pond, oily, muddy—a child's rag doll floating on it—dolly back to show:
> Mifune on the bank, looking at the sump—cut.
> Garbage being tipped into it—cut.
> The doll, floating—cut.
> A close-up of Mifune, looking—cut.
> A close-up of the doll.
> Dissolve to the sea.

Dissolve to the sea because it is at this point that Mifune's has a dream. In this sequence we have been given a deliberate contrast and comparison between the girl and Mifune. When she reacts with fear at being recognized we identify the doll with her. But it is Mifune who is looking at the doll—not she. And it is the thought of the doll, the thought of the sump, which leads directly to the open sea—escape itself, since both of them want to escape.

Mifune's dream is, naturally, only about himself. He is in a black suit and wearing a white scarf—respectable at last. The waves wash a large box ashore. He takes an ax and chops it open. It is a coffin. Inside is himself, dressed in the bright sports-shirt he wore in the first part of the picture. The former Mifune gives chase to the new Mifune—the latter is shot in slow-motion, the former at ordinary speed.

There are no cuts at all in this sequence; only one dissolve after the other. Mifune runs, pursued, barely able to drag one foot after the other—the gangster gains on him.

The meaning of the dream is perfectly clear—so clear that Bergman used something like it over again in *Wild Strawberries* (or perhaps it is that both directors had seen *Vampyr*). From the very first of the picture we have understood that Mifune does not want to be what he is. *Therefore*, he is a gangster. He wears his clothes badly, he hasn't a gangster's body; his shoes pinch him, he can apparently barely squeeze his feet into the fashionable models the well-dressed hood must wear; and he doesn't carry his new authority very well; also he doesn't govern his men in the proper way. His illness makes him confront himself. A sick gangster is no gangster—it is one of the few professions where illness is not tolerated. What he thinks he is, what he wants to be, in no way corresponds with what he is capable of becoming. This is what the doctor perceives. And in the dream, Mifune himself perceives it—in the frightening and thoroughly convincing form of the *doppelgänger*.

(This dream sequence has been argued against on stylistic grounds —that in a film this realistic, you cannot have fantasy. Leaving aside the questionable point of a person's dreams being fantasy, the main defense for the sequence is that it is necessary to the film. Actually, there are more serious errors in *Drunken Angel* than that. One of the technical errors is a scene in deep summer with Shimura slapping imaginary mosquitoes left and right, talking to the nurse, and with each sentence his breath condensing in front of him because of the cold when the scene was shot. An error of judgement is the big production number, a night-club act brought in for no apparent reason, whole minutes of *The Jungle Boogie*, which in itself is perhaps all right—seen now it is a wonderful evocation of Tokyo, 1948—but showing the gangsters tripping about with the precision of chorus boys was certainly an error—one repeated, one might add, during the fire-festival in *The Hidden Fortress* where the entire cast, it appears, just happens to know the highly involved choreography. If the dream is an error it is a necessary one.)

It is necessary and convincing because it is the only indication of the profound change that overtakes Mifune when he finally realizes who he is. Illness, here as in *Ikiru*, acts as a catalyst and when he leaves his bed he is a changed man. He is what perhaps he would have been had he not accepted the false role of gangster, just as Watanabe in *Ikiru* becomes at the end of the picture what he would have been had he not accepted the false role of civil servant. Watanabe nearly wrecks the bureaucracy and Mifune nearly wrecks the gang.

He walks onto the *tatami* with his shoes on—a sure sign a Japanese is upset—and at that moment it is decided that he and his ex-boss will have it out. The continuity of this sequence makes entirely clear that the gangster—like Watanabe—is out to redeem his life.

*He is walking the sordid little street. The loud-speakers are blaring a particularly vapid piece of music:* The Cuckoo Waltz. *He goes to a bar for a drink but what was once security is now poison. The bar girl at long last declares her love, pleads with him to go with her into the country, where he can get well. He refuses, passes the florist, takes a flower. The shop girl runs after him, asks for thirty yen. Obviously his days of power are past. The sump, a wind (possibly autumnal) ruffles it, just as it would a secluded pond in a forest or among the mountains. Mifune's girl and the boss. They are living together. The hallway outside. Mifune lurches (not drunk, sick) down the hall, past ladders and buckets which some painters have left, and goes into the room. The camera waits and watches. A scream is heard; the girl runs out. Inside the room. Mifune, breathing heavily, is moving toward the boss. His reflection is seen in the three-panel vanity mirror. It trebles—three reflections spread across the screen. The camera dollies around the two. The silence is broken only by their breathing. They fumble over the knife. Mifune backs up and suddenly has a hemorrhage. Blood on the floor. His back to the wall; he slides slowly down to the floor. He knows he will die. He looks at his boss, blood flowing down his chin, he seems to be supplicating. The music begins. There is a direct cut to the doctor. He has bought some eggs—the symbol of nascent life itself—and is going home. The hallway. Mifune rushes out but so does the boss. It is difficult to say who is chasing whom. They bump into the ladders and buckets. White paint is spilled over the floor. Both of them, with comic gestures that are grisly in this context, slip and slide on the paint. First one falls, then the other. They grapple. Both of them fight; only now (as at the end of* Stray Dog) *it is difficult to tell which is which, both are covered with paint, and both are white, white as angels. Mifune stands, reaches the doors to a small balcony and pushes. At that moment the boss stabs him in the back. This extra push causes the doors to open. The camera follows as though by inertia and we are suddenly outdoors, on the roof, Mifune staggering, falling before us. As in* The Hidden Fortress, *escape has been made palpable, the confines disappear behind us, we are under the open sky. The camera (as though knowing this) shoots the next scene from a very high position, a flying crane. Mifune has come to rest on a laundry platform and there, among the freshly starched sheets and in the sunlight he dies, stretched out. The camera waits, then moves slowly forward, then rests again and the scene fades.*

We have, until this time, been given the gangster's character only in terms of what he says (and such hints as we can get from the way he dresses and behaves); but in this final battle we are shown only what he does and are given none of his reasons, though we may deduce them.

The last reel of the film—pure coda—is given over to these deductions and to a continuation of one of the major themes of the film. The doctor stops by the sump. The bar girl is sitting there, it is winter. She has a small white-cloth-wrapped package with her.

*Doctor:* Don't try to kill yourself here—it's too dirty.

. . .

Anyway, he's to blame.

*Bar girl:* Don't talk bad about the dead.

He looks at the small white package. It contains the ashes of the gangster, all that is left of him.

*Doctor:* A dog is a dog. You can't change that.

*Bar girl:* It's not that easy. He was convinced.

. . .

*Doctor:* Don't cry. I know how you feel. That is why I cannot forgive him.

The doctor believes, apparently, that the final fight was just another gang fight. He does not see that the struggle was not actually with the boss but was inside Mifune himself. He and the bar girl become a chorus commenting upon the gangster and their deductions are wrong, or at least incomplete.

(It is in *Drunken Angel* that Kurosawa first uses this device of the commenting chorus. In an earlier scene it is the dance-hall girls who talk about Mifune. We listen and learn. In later films, the chorus has a much more important part. The newspapermen of *Ikiru, The Bad Sleep Well,* and *High and Low* comment directly upon the action, explain and distort or clarify it; the servants in *The Throne of Blood* say such things as "The Lady Asaji must be very happy." Next we are shown a scene in which she is anything but happy. These choruses often have the function of contradiction, they underlie appearances and neglect the truth.)

Thus, the gangster's fight, like Sanshiro's battle, was performed without witnesses and it is ironic that the very man whose ideals were responsible for the enormous change in the gangster's character should now so completely misunderstand the reasons for the fight. Even the girl who said she loved him misunderstands.

But then, how could they understand? They did not see the dream, they could not have known that the fight was not about power. Everything that the gangster had done before indicated that he would die a violent death. And he did. The difference is (as always in Kurosawa's films) that how he died is the most important aspect of his death. He died fighting what he finally identified as evil, he died fighting his former self.

All is not lost, however. The doctor admits his love—for the first time. He tells the bar girl that he knows how she feels. At the same time—love and hate being brothers—he shouts that he will not forgive the dead. Directly after this, he turns and begins heaving rocks at the sump. As he stands there shouting, waving his arms, attacking the pond, music begins. It is the hopeful music which we first heard when the gangster left the hospital.

(Originally, Kurosawa wanted to use the suite from *Die Dreigro-schenoper* for this picture, "particularly the Mackie Messer music, but the rights were too expensive, so we used this cheap guitar music as a substitute. This was the first picture that Hayasaka worked with me, and from the first we agreed on everything. Like using that vapid *Cuckoo Waltz* for the saddest part of the film. We thought of it separately . . . and after inspiration had struck both of us, I remember we shook hands." For the hopeful music Kurosawa wanted some-thing like Debussy's *Clair de lune*, which is just what he got.)

The camera turns and the reason for the hope is seen. It is the little girl (Yoshiko Kuga in one of her first pictures—she was later to appear in *The Idiot*) who has successfully recovered from tuberculosis. Earlier in the film, they have said:

Doctor: Just remember, in TB, it is will power—
Girl:  It is will power that is important. You've already told me that ten times.

She joins the other two at the edge of the pond and the meeting is seen from a crane shot, very like that used to show the last of Mifune. She turns to the doctor:

Girl:  Will power can cure TB, can't it?
Doctor: It can cure all human ailments.

So it probably can, but this as final dialogue would seem a bit sticky if we did not remember that in his final battle Mifune showed more will power—which he might have called guts—than either the doctor, or the girl have shown. As we come to comprehend this, the camera on its crane flies higher and higher. The two turn into a street, they are on their way to the candy shop. They are lost in the crowd and we are left staring at a small, crowded alley, filled with people, all of them anonymous, all of them unknown.

Kurosawa was worried that the gangster took over, that he became the hero. So he does, thanks in part to a fine performance by Mifune, thanks mostly to the way that the character is conceived. But the reason we remember the gangster best in the film is that by the time he becomes a hero he is no longer a gangster. He has become something else, an avenging angel, out to vindicate himself, for himself, anonymously, with no hope of being understood. We understand. His beloved enemy does not. This—says Kurosawa—is enough. We have watched naked heroism, as impersonal as that in *Ikiru*, and as necessary.

It is indeed Kurosawa's "first" picture, ("I was doing it and no one else"), for this theme becomes that of all of his best later pictures.

# The Quiet Duel

This is Kurosawa's only film based upon a contemporary Japanese play—*They Who Step on the Tiger's Tail, The Throne of Blood,* and *The Lower Depths* are from various classic theaters—and it is perhaps the single picture in which the director thought first of the actor, then of the film. At any rate, he says: "Originally, I saw the stage play [starring Chiaki Minoru who did not enter the Kurosawa troupe until he played the girlie-show art director in *Stray Dog,* and who is best remembered as the larger of the two bumpkins in *The Hidden Fortress* and the ex-samurai in *The Lower Depths*] and I thought it would be good for Mifune. He had been the gangster [in *Drunken Angel*], and now he could be the doctor." Another consideration was that "it was the first production of an independent unit I had formed and it was the kind of film that a young production company could more easily do," though he now adds: "The people working in movie studios are pretty much the same and I have certainly never lacked confidence."

The considerations then were somewhat different from what they usually were. Since it was the unit's first production, and was to be released by Daiei rather than Toho, a popular play was chosen as vehicle; this play was chosen rather than another because it offered a new kind of part for Mifune; anything more difficult might have been beyond the young talents of the director's unit. Kurosawa never used these criteria again. In choosing *Macbeth* as basis for *Throne of Blood* thoughts of creating chances for Mifune did not play much part. When he again organized an independent unit, in 1959, he deliberately chose a non-popular theme and, further, one very difficult to film.

## THE STORY

During the war, on a South Pacific island, a young doctor (Toshiro Mifune) operates on a soldier, accidentally cuts his finger on a scalpel, but completes the operation. A few weeks later he learns that the patient is syphilitic, and that he has also contracted the disease.

After the war he returns to private practice with his father (Takashi Shimura) in the family clinic. He also returns to his girl (Miki Sanjo) who has waited for him during six years of war. He does not tell her the reason for his coldness, for his unwillingness to marry.

One of the nurses (Noriko Sengoku—who played the bar girl in love with Mifune in *Drunken Angel* and the girl arrested for pistol-selling in *Stray Dog*) sees Mifune giving himself treatment and later overhears him telling his father the truth.

Asked by the police to attend one of their number, he discovers that the man who had attacked the policeman is none other than the man who originally infected him. He learns the man is married, indeed that a baby is expected. Mifune insists upon the wife's being examined and the husband unwillingly agrees.

The wife (Chieko Nakakita—the girl in *One Wonderful Sunday*) bears a deformed and still born child. The husband, drunk and abusive, loudly accuses the doctors of turning his wife against him—since she is now determined to divorce. Nurse Sengoku at once recognizes in him the man who nearly ruined her life by forcing her to have an abortion. He rushes into the delivery room and collapses when he sees his dead child.

Mifune's girl has decided to marry someone else and recover from her love. The nurse is impressed by Mifune's character and determines to be serious in her nursing. The wife recovers and the husband is sent to a hospital. Mifune determines to be a splendid doctor, working together with his father.

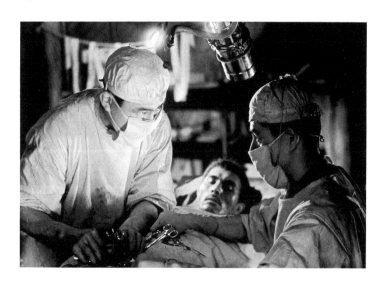

# TREATMENT

A film is to be seen and not read, hence a plot outline usually does it an injustice. In this instance, however, such is not the case. The finished film is no more interesting than the synopsis would indicate, and the harsh plot lines which such précis must insist upon are completely visible in the finished picture. Kurosawa has said: "When I remember this film, it seems to me that only the early scenes in the field hospital have any validity. This is because I didn't describe things too well in this picture. When the locale moved back to Japan, somehow the drama left the film."

There was another reason for the departure of the drama. In 1949 all directors still had to submit their story-outlines to the American Occupation Civil Information and Education Section—always on the look out for what was then called 'feudal content.' There was nothing particularly feudal about this outline but it was sent to the Medical Section at G.H.Q. where the doctor told Kurosawa that the ending would have to be changed, that it would terrify people and no one would come for medical aid. In the original ending Mifune went mad with spectacular results.

Kurosawa was in the same position as when earlier he had written a script about a race horse only to be told—by the Daiei president, the late Kan Kikuchi, who happened to be an expert in such matters—that lineage was decisive in horses and the script as he wrote it simply could not happen. He took the story of *Quiet Duel* to a number of Japanese doctors and they all agreed that it was un-medical. "If you show a man going insane from syphilis, they said, it would simply not be true. Anyway, the script was approved up to that point and so it couldn't be helped—Mifune did not go insane in the end."

Though Mifune was later allowed to go insane in two films—*Record of a Living Being* and *The Throne of Blood*—these changes not only took away a part of Kurosawa's interest, since any director who had chosen a vehicle solely for his actor would want the role to be as expressive as possible, they also changed the film. "We had many script problems. I decided to make it a tragic love-story, and that, tellingly, was the most difficult part of the picture to make."

When Kurosawa said that he did not describe things too well in this picture what he might have been saying was that he did not feel things too deeply. It is true that the opening scenes have a validity which the others lack. Under the credits are details of a tropical downpour: rain pouring through reed-matting, a discarded boot, palm fronds, washing on a line, a painted hospital red-cross—all these images accompanied by a single drum. The last image—the cross—is illuminated by a passing truck. The truck stops, wounded are brought out. In the field hospital two doctors are sleeping sitting up. Mifune, sound asleep, has his hand in the air, his arm resting on the elbow, as though to call attention to what is going to happen to that hand. During the operation scene which follows, one of the soldiers is fanning the doctors and the camera is so placed that the fan cuts off the view, its motion confusing the attention of the spectator (as does the electric fan in several scenes in *Record of a Living Being,* and one of the scenes in *High and Low*). At the same time the roof starts to leak and to the irritation of the fan is added the maddening ostinato of the sound of dropping water (as in *One Wonderful Sunday.*) In this film, as in the others, these aural and visual ostinati are used because they irritate. They irritate us, convince us of heat and discomfort, and they irritate Mifune. This is why he drops the scalpel, cuts his hand, and starts the plot moving.

There is another reason, however. If he had not finished the operation he would not have touched the patient after he had cut himself and would not have contracted the disease. Though it is difficult to read very much into this, one might say that Mifune was dedicated from the beginning and his consequent sufferings only rendered him more so—which completely nullifies the plot. Or, one might say that he is an innocent—like the heroes of *High and Low* and *Red Beard* to whom something happens, whose ideas of themselves are shattered—in which case the plot is useless because he ends up no different than he was. Just more so.

These scenes in the field hospital have an especial validity because they are deeply felt and are hence well described—and also because they are at the beginning. In this, the early Kurosawa is little different from any director. The initial scenes of a film are generally better than later ones precisely because the director is still deeply interested and the routine of making a picture has not as yet dulled the initial enthusiasm.

Kurosawa has remarked that when the locale removes to Tokyo the drama leaves the film and this is true—only it is not to Tokyo that the locale removes, it is to the studio. Among all of the director's pictures this is perhaps the most studio bound. There is a single set—the clinic—which, large as it is, does not begin to suggest the spaciousness of that single room in *The Lower Depths*. The reason is that, though the clinic set is much more detailed than the field hospital set, it is not used creatively. The actors are allowed to move around the clinic as though they are on the stage. In the field hospital, on the other hand, there was rain and flickering light, fast cutting, and a minimum of talk. The remainder of the film contains little of the imagination that went into the field hospital cut which contained the moving fan and the dropping water. Once in the clinic we are forced to interest ourself in plot.

The plot is about a social disease and its consequences but the emphasis is much more upon the *disease* than upon its *social* aspect. In *Drunken Angel* the pond is symbol; in *Quiet Duel* the disease would seem to be nothing more than itself, something to move the plot along, something to make Mifune an interesting acting assignment. Not that the film does not have symbols. We see Mifune and his girl walking along a wall outside. Later it is used—as was the sandal in *Sugata*—to show time passing: wall in autumn, dissolve, wall covered with snow, dissolve, wall in rain storm. Like the low wall in the love scenes of *The Bad Sleep Well* it has symbolic connotations—a wall is something which separates. Mifune and his girl are viewed through the grill of the wall. Later Mifune looks at the wall and thinks of the girl.

It might be thought that the husband, the man who gave Mifune VD, who ruined the loyal nurse, who kills his own child, and almost his wife—that he might be society since he is the one who has the

disease and the disease is, after all, social. Mifune seems to imply as much when he tells the man: "It's your crime—you know." But if that is so then the collapse of the husband, his screams and resultant little-theater mannerisms could only mean a collapse of society and this is certainly not the director's intention.

Instead, and with some reluctance, one must forego the search for higher meaning. The picture won't stand it. On the other hand, it is interesting to see what Kurosawa does when he is not too interested in what he is doing. The set-ups in this film are meticulous—the composition is precise and the balance is miraculous. It is also lifeless—the vitality of the diagonal compositions of say, *The Lower Depths,* is missing because their meaning is predicated upon the characters, our interest in their predicament diminishing according to their distance from the camera. The artistry here becomes purely formal. And—as consequence—the film becomes extremely slow.

Mifune cannot let the girl know that he has this disease, since her impulse would be to sacrifice more years in waiting for him. At the same time he suffers from not being able to tell her. Of course he *could* have let her know but in that case we would not have the "tragic love-story" that Kurosawa compromised to have. This makes the hero an *homme aux camelias* who must not confess love because he loves so entirely. One could say this shows an excess of delicacy—but it seems more like cant and even dishonesty.

And Kurosawa obviously did not see it this way. Yet, whenever he (or any other director) attempts to milk emotion directly, he fails. We cry when Watanabe cries because he is *not* making a bid for our sympathy; when this young doctor, however, carries on about his own nobility—for in essence this is what he does—all eyes remain dry. Empathy is possible only if the reasons for happiness or unhappiness are in themselves valid. Watanabe is going to die, he has no way out. The doctor in *Quiet Duel* has a number of ways out.

Not, however, the expected one, for in 1945—which is the time of the Tokyo hospital scenes—there seemed no cure for the disease but a long and drastic process. In fact, if the film had been seen abroad in 1949, its only possible message—"stamp out VD"—would have caused a sensation, so much more frank is it than the pussyfooting *Dr. Ehrlich's Magic Bullet*. Yet, if the film is now antiquated it is not because VD has become curable but because the motivations of the leading character were antiquated long before Dumas made use of them.

As in *The Idiot* and the final scenes of *The Bad Sleep Well*, we are invited to suffer for inadequate reasons. Since the director knows perfectly well that the given reasons are inadequate, he attempts to compensate by deepening the pathos and lengthening the exposure time. In *Ikiru* some of the most affecting moments must be caught in a second or two. Kurosawa is sure of his material and he can afford the enormous tact of apparently throwing a revelation away. In *Quiet Duel* he is not so sure and there is an enormously long sequence which proves this point. His girl makes a speech the content of which one can easily guess by this time. He turns to kiss her. Then he stops (as Mifune does again in *The Bad Sleep Well*) and pulls away. Cut, snow on the fence—i.e. not only separation but cold separation. Cut, the two of them, talking again, this time with organ music in the background to enforce the pathos. And so on. Finally he tells her to go. She does, but nurse comes in immediately. She has heard all. Then, a big scene, rather like an aria, during which Mifune cries and says how dreadful the world is. Then he becomes angry and throws things. (Interesting and very valid observation of Kurosawa that when people learn they are ill—or when they finally admit it—they become angry and throw things. The gangster in *Drunken Angel,* the husband in this picture, and now Dr. Mifune, having finally understood how ill he is: all pick up something and heave it.) Then he quiets down, controls himself, gives a few terse orders to the nurse (who is also crying as Japanese women will) and turns. Cut to big close-up of Mifune; cut to floor, there lies his stethoscope, dropped or knocked off his desk during the passion; cut, Mifune seeing it; cut, he picks it up, turns, leaves. The sequence represents all it is supposed to: his renunciation, his agony, his renewed dedication—but the lack of tact, the inordinate length, the atrocious acting, all point to Kurosawa's basic lack of interest.

The picture, naturally, has its moments. Besides the opening sequence and the pure beauty and ingenuity of the compositional set-ups, there is a tender moment when his girl first comes to see him. He is, naturally, not looking forward to the meeting, is staring into space. The background-music at this point is a trumpet tune carried over from field camp scenes and is thus psychologically apt. She stands beside him, looking up at him, then softly says his name. The music stops. It is as though she had brought him back to reality. She asks what is the matter. Mifune stops, as though to think, then says: "Oh, I guess it's just that I'm getting old." The scene is very delicate. He is thinking of death and disease but only mentions getting old. She, too, is subtle, she merely addresses him by name. There is a constraint, based on true affection, which makes them both believeable and loveable. Later, when Mifune tells Shimura, he is playing with a musical cigarette-box. It opens and so his revelation comes to the accompaniment of the innocent, tawdry, childish, celesta-like sound which means safety and security to almost everyone in the civilized world. In the final scene, the uplift is considerably underplayed. The wife is still in bed but the sun is shining and fresh linen is hanging outside the window. She and the nurse have a little talk the upshot of which is: you *can* get well, and by implication, get well after everything, including syphilis. Then Shimura is shown carrying a baby with its unavoidable implication of new life (as in *Rashomon* and *Record of a Living Being*); and then the wife, now happy, looks at some flowers and we are treated to a big close-up of one (which, after the flower close-ups of *Sugata* and *Drunken Angel*, brings this particular phase of

Kurosawa's career to an end: we will never again have to look at a close-up of a flower, unless it plays a definite part in the plot, as does the camelia in *Sanjuro*); after which we glimpse Mifune working away, operating on someone, dedicated.

If this final sequence seems a bit much, still, it *is* underplayed and quite delicate compared with some of what went before. Hindsight is, of course, notoriously easy to come by. Still, there were certain points during the picture where more could have been made of a particular scene. A whole new—and better—film is suggested by the nurse's saying, when she finds the doctor giving himself an injection: "You're such a great humanist ... yet you got VD." This is passed off, however. It is as though the "humanist" side of Kurosawa, always a danger to him when he manipulates ideas rather than feelings, when he thinks of this "humanism" (babies, flowers, do-gooding) as a concept, refuses the implications of a true social disease, preferring the shallower way of reassurance, uplift, and the bright side of things.

It is interesting that, in speaking of this film, Kurosawa made one of his most revealing statements, though his reasons for associating it with this particular film become evident only upon thought: "I am the kind of person who works violently, throwing myself into it. I also like hot summers, cold winters, heavy rains, and snows, and I think most of my pictures show this. I like extremes because I find them most alive. I have always found that men who think like men, who act like men, who most *are* themselves are always better...." *The Quiet Duel* takes the middle road.

# Stray Dog

## 1949

The story of this film is based upon something which really happened. "The anecdote is quite true," says Kurosawa: "The original idea for the picture came when I heard about a real detective who was so unfortunate during those days of shortages as to have lost his pistol." Taken with the idea, and seeing its possibilities, Kurosawa decided to write a novel about it—and did so, though the novel remains unpublished. "I am very fond of Georges Simenon," he says: "And I wanted to do something in his manner."

## THE STORY

A young detective named Murakami (Toshiro Mifune) has his pistol stolen in a crowded bus. Afraid of losing his job—since pistols were very scarce in 1949—he decides to look for it, though the task seems impossible. Hunting for a thief in one of the largest cities in the world, he has the enormous luck of instantly spotting in a suspect-file the woman who leaned against him on the bus. Nothing can be proved (and, in any event, she was only an accomplice—he knows the thief was a man) but she tells him to investigate the pistol black-market. Disguised as a returned soldier, he walks Ueno and Asakusa, asking people, and eventually is approached by one of the pistol black-marketers. One clue leads to another, from one person to the next. Eventually, Mifune and his section chief (Takashi Shimura) go to the thief's home, then to the girlie-show where his girl-friend is working. Each clue leads them further but, in the meantime, there has been a robbery and a murder. Mifune, apprehensive that it is his gun which is being used, remembers that during pistol practice he hit the stump of a tree behind the target. He digs out the bullet, has it calibrated—and this proves that indeed the weapon used was his. Shimura arrives at the hotel of the murderer who, realizing that the police are close, shoots him and escapes. Mifune learns from the girl (Keiko Awaji in her first screen appearance) that the murderer has made a rendezvous with her. Mifune goes instead, chases him, retrieves his pistol, and captures him.

## CHARACTERIZATION

What most appealed to Kurosawa in the original anecdote was its adaptability, its possibilities. Many of his films take the form of the search. Criminals are hunted for in *High and Low* and *The Bad Sleep Well;* the quest for truth is the subject of *Rashomon;* gold is the object in *The Hidden Fortress;* and the meaning of life is sought in *Ikiru.* One of the reasons, perhaps, that Kurosawa has been so fond of the films of John Ford is that they, like his, are about moral battles and often incorporate all the elements of the great quest. When he heard the anecdote, Kurosawa first thought of Simenon for all detective stories are variations of the quest.

Further, the detective searches all over downtown Tokyo, and Kurosawa has always liked closed worlds, microcosms. The whole world is included in the *Rashomon* triangle, in the family of *Record of a Living Being,* in the underworld jungle of *Drunken Angel.* Mifune's search is a pilgrim's progress, as is Watanabe's in *Ikiru.* He harrows hell and he endures purgatory. Kurosawa originally had intended to film the search in four representative sections of Tokyo: Asakusa, Ueno, Shinjuku, Shibuya—that is, from the "lowest" circle to the "highest." He and De Sica had the same idea at the same time. *Bicycle Thieves* is the more complete allegory (and is a picture which so impressed Kurosawa that he mentioned it in his speech accepting the 1951 Venice prize for *Rashomon*) because the extraordinary typhoons of 1949 made it impossible for him to film the Shinjuku and Shibuya sections. As social allegory *Stray Dog* stays in "hell."

This, as it turns out, suits the picture. Always fond of extremes, Kurosawa began his novel with: "It was the hottest day of the year . . ."

Thereafter there is not an image that is not drenched in sweat: perspiration is beaded upon brows; armpits are sticky; shirts cling to backs; the girls come off the stage and at once collapse, their breasts heaving, sweat running down their temples, sweat caught in their mascara. The screen is continually fluttering with the motion of fans, folded newspapers; handkerchiefs are worn around the neck to catch the sweat; one of the men carries an electric fan in front of him. Everyone is wearied, snappish, exhausted by this great and unnatural heat.

The manager of the dancing troupe says to the girl: "Where were you yesterday?" She says: "I wasn't well . . . ." He answers, indicating that this is no excuse: "No one is in this heat." Later Mifune asks Shimura why the girl cried when she was being questioned and the older man answers: "She was tired . . . we all are."

It is interesting that Kurosawa again uses extreme heat when he again wishes to show a whole city exhausted, fearful, defenseless, in *Record of a Living Being*. His comment, in both films, is that people are prostrated: in the 1955 film by fear of atomic disintegration; in the 1949 picture by the long war and the new carpet-bagger civilization.

It is too hot to even move, much less walk, much less run. Yet, though Mifune sweats as much as the rest, he is continually running. He has to, for he is the man who is searching, and he is searching for much more than his lost pistol.

The character of the detective (the only living among the dead) is extremely interesting. When he loses the pistol he feels unmanned—worse, he feels unidentified. A detective is not a policeman. He has no uniform. His only identity is his pistol. If you take that away from him you take away everything.

*Policeman:* Do you think you'll be fired?

*Mifune:* Yes.

*Policeman* (Laughing): You won't be fired.

Mifune already believes that he will lose his job. Actually, the danger of this is not great—though he goes on half pay—and later in the film he is given another pistol. The point is that he thinks it is. If he loses his position, he has no place in society. He becomes a stray.

This is the beginning of the purposeful confusion between cop and robber, between Mifune and the criminal, which so enriches this film. We have taken for granted that the title refers to the criminal and the policemen often so describe him. Shimura says: "Stopping his next crime is important. Once does not make a habit, but twice . . . a stray dog becomes a mad dog. Right?" Later, when Mifune is feeling the strain, the older detective turns to him.

*Shimura:* Cops who are all nerves are no good.

*Mifune:* I feel like I'm about to break down.

*Shimura:* It looks as though you already have. Look, killers are like mad dogs. You know how a mad dog acts. There is even a saying about them: 'Mad dogs can only see what they are after.'

This, ironically, applies to Mifune as much as it does to the killer.

Mifune can only see his lost pistol and what it means to him. The reason he is about to break down (and he actually does go "mad" when Shimura is shot—that is, for a time he loses all restraint, weeps, slides into a deep depression) is that he takes upon himself the crimes of the criminal—because it was his gun which was used.

Early in the film he reacts in an exaggerated manner when reading of a hold up.

*Mifune:* Look, this article is about a hold up—

*Shimura:* And that surprises you these days?

*Mifune:* No, but what if it were my gun. . . .

He has already begun to attribute the crimes to himself. When his superior chides him for failing to have rounded up the pistol black-marketers since he was so intent upon his single weapon, he does not understand. When he hears about the murder his instant reaction is: "Was it my gun?" And when the calibrating technician, not knowing what has happened, smiles and says: "Yes it was, congratulations!" Mifune turns and runs away. He says to Shimura: "It is my fault . . . it was my gun," and Shimura answers: "That doesn't matter—stopping the next crime is the more important."

But it does matter to Mifune. In the house where the murder occurred Mifune breaks in with: "Was it my gun?" The answer is the common-sense: "What if it was?" But he does not even seem to hear this: the mad dog sees only what it is after.

This confusion between cop and robber, however, is based upon something much deeper than Mifune's feelings of guilt. The detectives visit the house of the murderer (a completely squalid room, like that of the kidnapper in *High and Low*) and find part of a journal where he writes that he had killed a cat simply because the cat's mewing annoyed him. Then he adds that the cat was worthless, just as he himself is worthless.

The detectives see him as a mad dog; he sees himself as a worthless cat. Dogs chase cats and cops chase robbers. By association, Mifune is the dog. Later, when they finally meet, the recognition is mutual and instant. The criminal does not even stop to look closely. Animal-like, he *knows* and the chase that began the film thus ends it. It is as though Mifune knows too, and—further—knows that since both are human the fact that each assumes the identity of dog or cat, cop or robber, is accidental. That, in fact, they are not different.

*Shimura:* My house isn't much, but his place was horrible. No place for a person to live.

*Mifune:* You mean bad surroundings make bad men?

*Shimura:* 'There are no bad people in this world—there is only bad environment.'

*Mifune:* I've heard that someplace. In a way I'm sorry for him.

*Shimura:* You cannot afford to feel sorry for him. We all tend to feel that way because we're always chasing them. But we mustn't forget how many sheep get hurt by just one wolf.

After all, we are the guardians. Let the writers analyze the criminal mind. For me—I have to hate it. Evil is always evil.

*Mifune:* I can't think that way yet. During the war I saw how easily good men turned bad. Perhaps it is the difference in our ages, yours and mine—or perhaps the times have changed, but...

*Shimura:* You understand him too well.

As indeed he does. He understands him so well that he identifies himself with him. And so does Kurosawa and so—therefore—does the viewer. There have been indications of this mutuality before.

During the first chase—which is shown as comedy—Mifune follows the lady-pickpocket all over downtown Tokyo and this very funny sequence ends with them side by side but carefully ignoring each other, gulping down soda-pop because they are both human and hot chases make people thirsty. Later, she gives up and tells him about the black-marketeers. They are sitting on a bridge. Then she leans back and there is a single short scene shot from beneath, showing the two of them and the star-filled summer sky. The woman, who has been shown so brutish as to be amusing, leans back, looks up and says, in a soft, even girlish voice: "Oh, look. How beautiful. For twenty whole years I've forgotten how beautiful stars can be." One is reminded of that lovely scene in *Ikiru* when Watanabe stops on the bridge, looks at the sunset and says: "Oh, how lovely—I haven't seen a sunset for thirty years." In both pictures these scenes show nature as appealing to lives which have been closed; in *Stray Dog* it also insists upon the identical humanity of all humans.

This last (the theme of the picture) is brilliantly visualized in the final reel, the end of the chase. It is about six in the morning in a small suburban railway station. The sun is rising. Mifune chases the murderer down the tracks and into the woods.

*The murderer turns. There is a house in the distance. Distant sounds of a Mozart sonata being played. Mifune faces his own pistol. The criminal fires. Mifune is hit in the arm. The blood runs down his hand. A single drop falls on a flower by his feet. In the distant house a young girl stops playing the piano at the sound of the shot, then begins again. The murderer looks at Mifune; Mifune looks back. The sound of the Mozart. The criminal fires again and misses. The gun is empty. He turns to run, then throws the gun at Mifune, who gives up the chase for a second in order to retrieve the pistol. They both emerge in a flowering field. A rooster is heard in the distance; the Mozart fades. Mifune catches him; they struggle among the flowers; they fall into a stream; they grapple in the mud. Finally Mifune handcuffs him. He feels in his pocket to make certain that the pistol is safe, is his again. Then he collapses. The camera looks at cop and robber, both so mud-covered that it is difficult to tell which is which. They look identical. The sound of distant children singing is heard. It is a group of school-children on their way to classes. The murderer listens, looks up and sees the nodding blossoms in the sun. There is the sound of a lark. He begins to cry. Mifune sits up and looks at him. The murderer cries like a little child.*

In this profound and beautiful sequence all of the elements of the film come together. The images are those of love and hope: sunrise, rooster, flowers, children, lark, Mozart—yet here are two grown men trying to kill each other. The battle finished, they are revealed as identical. And it is then that the confrontation occurs. Mifune's quest is done and he turns to look at what this did to him—and he finds a frightened man who realizes he may never again hear a lark or see a flower or listen to Mozart. Men are not cats and dog—whose hatred is instinctive. Man's fight against evil is artificial, man himself is both hero and villain, in himself.

But Kurosawa is too wise to leave it at this. Earlier he has us discover that this particular man went bad after all of his belongings were stolen (the same provocation that De Sica used in *Bicycle Thieves*—theft) when he was returning from the war. Shimura says: "Look, *my* knapsack and money were stolen too. I felt outraged. I too could have stolen. I knew that this was a dangerous point in my life. But what did I do? I chose this work." Shimura, then, is like the pyromaniac who becomes fire-chief. He retains the original impulse but directs it. Indeed, he cannot *afford* (as he admits) to "understand" the criminal impulse because he knows it very well indeed. What saved him and made him a detective was just that moment of choice.

And that, in turn, was predicated upon his feeling that he had the power to make this choice—in other words, that he had a chance. In this he and Mifune are much alike. The young detective is faced with the hunt for a needle in a human haystack. His finding the pistol at all is based on pure luck. If he had not accidentally discovered the lady-pickpocket in the files in the first minute of looking (we are shown that the files themselves are so numerous as to fill a whole room) he might not have had the faith and strength to continue. But the point is that he had the strength to begin and the faith to continue in a search which most of us would not even have attempted. We would have thought it useless.

In this the detective is a real Kurosawa hero. Watanabe, too, faces hopeless-seeming odds, so do the seven samurai, so do the heroes of *Yojimbo* and *Sanjuro*. The Kurosawa hero is a man who continues in the very face of certain defeat. He refuses to give up even after everyone else is convinced he has already lost. This is the reason that he is always alone. And seemingly certain failure is not all. Even more subtle temptations lie in wait.

In *The Bad Sleep Well* Mifune discovers that you cannot fight evil without you yourself becoming evil. He has fought the good fight but what kills him is his feeling of love—for his wife. A continued feeling of hate might have saved him. In *High and Low* Mifune would not have been ruined had he refused to pay the ransom. It is this "better" nature which does the Kurosawa hero in. In *Stray Dog* it is Mifune's compas-

sion and understanding, his acknowledging the identity of cop and robber which almost paralyzes him. Kurosawa seems to be saying, in this film as in all of his others, that the "better" nature is not only the truly human but that it is too good for this world. The ones who prevail (the peasants in *Seven Samurai,* the cynical gambler in *The Lower Depths,* the two bumpkins in *The Hidden Fortress*—or the older detective in *Stray Dog*) are either those who do not understand the struggle and are not involved in it, or those who know it and, even knowing it, dedicate themselves to one side.

Complete compassion, complete understanding, the knowledge that warring sides are identical; that black and white are really the same; that there is no high, no low; no heaven, no hell—this knowledge brings about the downfall of the hero. There is often a single scene which illustrates this: Sugata suddenly sees judo as meaningless if it means he must fight the father of the girl he is beginning to love; Togashi sees what Benkei is doing and lets him go—and was later forced to commit suicide; the gangster in *Drunken Angel* finally understands the doctor, turns and tries to kill his own boss, and is killed; the doctor in *Quiet Duel* equates—through the disease—himself and the man who gave him syphilis, thus gives up his girl; the actor in *The Lower Depths* gives up drinking, gets money for the journey by working, is suddenly overcome by knowledge, kills himself; the vengeful Mifune in *The Bad Sleep Well* brings flowers to his wife, determines to be a good husband, is killed; even Sanjuro in *Yojimbo* is almost undone by the compassion that he feels for the abducted wife and her husband; and the Prince Myushikin character in *The Idiot* is, of course, the prototype of this hero.

What saves a man, and makes him less a hero, is the knowledge that he must compromise his own virtue, his own understanding, his own compassion. Shimura in *Stray Dog* understands this. He speaks of the criminal as though he were someone Mifune had loved (as indeed, in a very special way, he did)—the final dialogue in the picture is:

*Mifune:* The whole case was my fault . . .

*Shimura:* Still thinking about that gun. Actually, thanks to you, we have collected over a thousand illegally owned pistols.

*Mifune:* But, sometimes I feel that he—

*Shimura:* Yes, I remember I once felt like that. It is hard to forget one's first case. But, you must remember that there are many more men like him than you think. Don't worry. In time you will forget about him.

# PRODUCTION

Kurosawa does not think well of this film. "I wanted to make a

film in the manner of Simenon, but I failed. Everyone likes the picture but I don't. It is just too *technical.* All that technique and not one real thought in it. Shimura is quite good but I didn't see very deeply into his character—nor anyone else's for that matter. If I saw into anyone at all, it was the murderer. This was played by Ko Kimura, and it was his first part in a film. [Kimura was also the young doctor in *Ikiru,* the love-struck samurai in *Seven Samurai,* and the youngest of the

he gave up narration completely), an intrusion further unwarranted in that, at the end of the film, the off-screen voice has turned into Mifune's ("Which could the criminal be ... let's see ... twenty-eight years old, left-handed ... oh, it is all my fault") and so there is basic disagreement between narrations. Kurosawa has noticed this. "I remember that the first scene in the film was to have been the opening scene in the police station. We saw the rushes and they were no good for the opening. I reread my novel and finally understood why. In the novel it explained itself, this scene. In the film there was no context for it. The book had begun with a number of details, that it was the hottest day of the year, for example. After I had taken this into account, it all worked." But the way he took this into account was to have an anonymous narrator speak up with: "It was a very hot day...." Then, during the flash-back pistol-stealing scene on the bus, he continues, in *benshi* fashion (for once having spoken he must continue for a time) to tell us what we are seeing as we are seeing it: "Sweat was in his eyes ... a woman was leaning heavily against him, etc." Next is included a very clumsy flash-back showing target-practice, simply to account for the bullet's being lodged in the stump, something one line of dialogue in the proper place could have covered equally well. In other words, since the context did not arise from the initial situation, and from the first impulse of Kurosawa's imagining the scene (for he was writing a novel rather than a script), all further attempts merely blurred the image. This is always true of his pictures, and his failures (*Quiet Duel, The Idiot, Record of a Living Being*) are those which he, for one reason or another, was forced to rewrite. "I thought it would be easy to make the script from the novel. Not at all. Writing the script took just as much time as it always does. Time was a problem in another way, too. Movies have their own internal time—motion time. In writing a scenario one is always surprised at how much longer it takes than the actual filming does. Yet, that is the way it is. You write a scenario with a different part of your mind, as it were. And you have to remember the context of each shot and make use of it."

*Stray Dog* is full of temporal miscalculations. One of them is the endless montage sequence of Mifune disguised and searching Asakusa and Ueno for his gun. It is a full ten minutes of double-exposure, dissolves, fades, multiple images. The atmosphere is caught, to be sure (which was the reason for the montage), but it is so long that one expects summer to be over and autumn begun by the time it finally stops. There is further clumsy scripting when Shimura asks Mifune for his pistol and goes off alone to check the criminal's address. How did Mifune get the gun? This is not explained. If he had another gun and still so single-mindedly pursued his own, then this is something which should be examined because it shows something about him, something which would further have elucidated his character. This second gun he later gives to Shimura—thus Mifune does *not* have it at the showdown with the criminal, since Kurosawa relished the idea of Mifune

detectives in *High and Low.*]" The director, since he is the creator, of course is the one person who knows what his intentions were. Apparently he intended more with *Stray Dog* and his comparison is one between this ideal and the finished film.

His remarks on technique are interesting, however, because technically the picture is rather clumsy. One of the most glaring miscalculations is the use of a narrator in the beginning of the film (after *Ikiru* having to face his own pistol defenseless. But in that case why insert the new pistol at all?

As always with Kurosawa, true technique illuminates. Leaving aside such excellences as the music, the photography, and the acting, there is in the beginning a short scene where Mifune chases the pickpocket and comes to the corner, streets stretching in all four directions. It is very like a similar scene at the beginning of *Yojimbo* where chance determines action. Mifune can now go in any direction, the choice is his, (Sanjuro throws a stick into the air and follows where it points) and it is pictorially realized. Too, suspense is engendered by a device similar to that used in *One Wonderful Sunday*. Just as the sum of thirty-five yen is the chronological link which determines our interest (how far are they from nothing?) so, in this film, the number of bullets left keeps up the suspense. There were seven originally, Mifune used one in target-practice, then one was used in the murder, two were used on Shimura. How many are left for Mifune during the confrontation? Sometimes, Kurosawa uses technique to play jokes on us. There is a scene where we have investigated hovels and squalor and misery and Shimura says somewhat mysteriously. "Well, there is one more house we must go to." Cut to a deserted yard, silence, a broken gate hangs ominously, danger seems in the very air. Then we hear children crying: "Welcome home, daddy." It is Shimura's house, perfectly ordinary but, in the context, completely sinister and there follows the beautiful and relaxed supper scene with the sun hanging low over the hazy fields in the background, and the tough head-detective is revealed as a fine father, the perfect family man.

One of the most magical moments in the film is also one of the most irrational. We have seen the heat, even seemed to feel it. Over and over, people say: "I wish it would rain." The detectives go to see the tough little girl-friend of the killer. She argues with them, then argues with her mother, and then—quite suddenly—begins to cry. This time the tears are real (before, she cried merely to get rid of the cops) and as she cries there is thunder, the heavens open, and there is a cloud-burst. Everyone, everything is instantly drenched. The heat is truly off because just after this the criminal is discovered. It is as though someone needed to break down and admit humanity before the heavens would open and the reign of evil be over.

It is interesting that Kurosawa would feel that he only saw into the character of the murderer. Even discounting his well-known predilection for his villains, this character is completely anonymous—much more anonymous than the kidnapper in *High and Low*. We do not even see him until the final reel. Yet, Kurosawa is absolutely correct. He saw into him completely but the way in which he did so was by so defining the characters of Shimura, Mifune, the girl, and others, that the character of the criminal was what was left over, so to speak—his character was the quality not yet accounted for. The criminal then is evil and his character is evil. But we have already seen that evil is merely the wrong choice at the moment of truth.

Kurosawa is so exclusively concerned with this problem (and with its corollary: why is it that the truly human and the truly good are not identical?) that it is not surprising that he sees the character of the criminal as most interesting. By suggesting that good and evil, cops and robbers, are one, he has shown us that we are in ourselves both good and evil, both cop and robber. The difference among these is not one of essence. It has to do merely with identity. The character of the murderer is indeed the most important because it is only he (among all the others in film) who made the choice not to hunt, not to find himself, not to persevere, not to believe. It is through him that Mifune himself decides and comes to realize that compassion and understanding are not enough. One must act, one must oneself choose.

# Scandal

## 1950

Kurosawa has said: "This was a protest film—it was directly connected with the rise of the press in Japan and its habitual confusion of freedom with license. Personal privacy is never respected and the scandal sheets are the worst offenders." As *Drunken Angel* is anti-gangster, and *Record of a Living Being* is anti-bomb and *The Bad Sleep Well* is anti-graft—this film is anti-yellow-press. There is, however, perhaps another reason for its having been made.

Kurosawa is personally very cool to the press and always has been. He remains the only Japanese celebrity never televised, he dislikes giving press-interviews, and does not like to read even favorable criticism of his work. He has been found a man-of-mystery for just these reasons, and he usually does not tolerate photographers and journalists either on the set or in his home. Nonetheless, or perhaps for this very reason, after the war more than one magazine linked him romantically with Hideko Takamine—who had been the actress in *Horses*. These stories spoke of a doomed romance and insinuated that Kurosawa was more loving than loved. Leaving aside whether or not these tales were based on anything more than the opportunistic imagination which the director so castigates in this film, they proved very long-lived. Even now one hears them repeated and heads are wisely nodded.

Feeling as he does about privacy, this intrusion would have been extremely distasteful to Kurosawa—particularly when he noticed that it was happening not only to him but to many others as well. 1950 was a year of scandal and many were the skeletons, real or imagined, that came tumbling out of closets. The Occupation was coming to an end and for the first time in the history of Japan people were beginning to be allowed to say, do, read, write anything that they pleased. The stream of vilification that flowed from the press at this point was extraordinarily wide and few were the celebrities that did not at least get their feet wet. Kurosawa thus had two reasons for making the film: a personal one, and also an impersonal one—the state of the press was fast becoming a social issue. "I felt outraged," the director has written and this outrage in part at least produced the picture.

## THE STORY

A young painter (Toshiro Mifune) goes off into the mountains to paint and accidentally meets a well-known young singer. He gives her a ride on his motorcycle and they stay at the same inn. Photographers, however, have been shadowing her. She had refused an interview to a *Confidential*-type magazine called *Amour* (ironic name), and they are out to get her. A picture is taken which the magazine publishes, along with a faked-up story about a romance: *The True Love Story of Miyako Saijo: Desire on a Motorcycle*. Both of the young people are much upset. He decides to sue but his lawyer, (Takashi Shimura), anxious to buy nice things for his bedridden daughter, takes money from the magazine to throw the case. At the last minute the lawyer decides to confess all, though he be disbarred, and does so. The reputation of the two is saved, *Amour* is restrained by a court injunction, and the daughter dies.

It is interesting that Kurosawa here—for the only time—makes his ostensible hero a painter. To be sure we never see what he paints (once he sketches the girl's features while he is supposed to be painting his model) but it is made clear that he is well enough known that this accidental scandal might hurt him. He is successful, something which Kurosawa as a painter was not. Such easy identification of director and hero is probably meaningless but it might indicate the degree of personal involvement Kurosawa might have felt in this film, since he never again made any hero a painter.

Also, it is interesting that the film breaks in two. Mifune is ostensibly the painter-hero and we follow his adventures for the first half of the picture. When Shimura as the lawyer appears, Mifune is largely forgotten. The girl, Yoshiko Yamaguchi, has only a nominal role anyway, and so the hero of the picture turns out to be the lawyer. Kurosawa experienced some difficulty in writing the scenario and has said: "The script wouldn't work right and no matter how hard we tried, it did not satisfy us. Then I thought of the character that became the lawyer in the film and that solved the problem."

If it did not solve any problems, it at least created a very interesting character. Kurosawa has told how he happened to create this particular role and it is an interesting example of how his mind sometimes works. "It was about ten years before—about 1940—that I was in a small bar in Shibuya and this man next to me got talking. He had a sick daughter in the hospital and he talked and talked on and on about her. It got late but still he continued—and I stayed, listening. He adored her, there was no one in the world like her. And for some reason or other this impressed me. I stayed a long time drinking with him. Later, when I was working on this picture, I suddenly thought of just the kind of man we needed. I told Shimura and we created him. When we had finished and looked at some of the rushes I saw what I had done. I had created in the lawyer, the very image of this man in the bar. He walked like him, talked like him, acted like him—it *was* him."

Shimura's role is that of man who is not very good at what he does and knows it. He is apologetic and at the same time belligerent. Easily cowed, he tries to be very fierce. When he presents a brief he tries to bluff, fails; tries to curry favor, fails; and is finally reduced to sitting, eyes downcast—the very picture of moral confusion. He loves his sick daughter with a passion and she has become the only reason for his continuing to live.

The lawyer is a bit like the doctor in *Drunken Angel* and the civil servant in *Ikiru*. His character in this picture might be considered the

first sketch for the finished portrait in the 1952 film. Shimura plays him with a blending of fear and bluff, hopeless enthusiasm and resignation that is an occasionally painful pleasure to watch. Kurosawa has said that he thinks this character is much more interesting than that of the doctor in *Drunken Angel* and adds that "I think this because the doctor was someone I'd thought up but the lawyer had been living in the back of my head waiting to come out." Another reason for the preference, too, would have been the performance of Shimura—of all his fine interpretations only that in *Seven Samurai* is better than this.

# REALIZATION

The picture looks like a more than usually well-made Japanese programmer and few of the excellences of *Stray Dog* or *Rashomon* are visible. That the creator of *No Regrets for Our Youth* could make a film as shallow as this makes one share Kurosawa's concern when he says: ". . . if it had not been for *Rashomon* . . . I don't know what kind of slump I would have gone into." The opening for example

> Titles—title background is the rear wheel of a speeding motorcycle. When the director's name appears the music fades and the cycle noise is heard.
> Long-shot of Mifune on motorcycle.
> A mountain top, long-shot, Mifune painting, surrounded by three farmers. They examine the painting, then look at the mountains.
> Shot of the mountains. Over it the sound of a girl singing something from Puccini.
> Mifune and the farmers, reacting. Pan to a rock: around it comes Yoshiko Yamaguchi singing Puccini. Close-up of Yoshiko covered with confusion.

Obviously the concern here was to get the plot started as soon as possible. How Yoshiko got to the top of the mountain, what the farmers were doing there—these questions are not even asked, much less answered. In the entire first half (until the appearance of Shimura) everything is shown without art—that is, tact—and the happenings are either obvious or inexplicable. Heroines always wander over mountains singing; farmers are forever on the heights looking for painters rather than tilling their fields in the valleys.

Of course, suddenly appearing or disappearing heroines can sometimes be pleasant enough, but their use does not apply to the kind of film that *Scandal* became. Everything else in the film is so painfully plotted that such arbitrary assumptions appear merely bad film-making. There are other things more seriously wrong with the film, however.

If Kurosawa set out to blacken the yellow-press then he did it in the direct, obvious, and unsatisfactory way of making journalists villains.

He allowed Eitaro Ozawa not only to overact but also gave him the dark glasses that, in 1950 at any rate, were the legacy of all villains in Japanese films. The journalists' point of view is never given. They are bad, bad, bad. To be sure, the director's attitude to the press (in his films) has always been ambivalent. In *The Bad Sleep Well* and *High and Low* the press corps becomes useful because they can act as chorus. In *Ikiru* they are even more than neutral because they suspect who really made the park. Even so, they are shown as cold, ruthless, not after the truth but after their story. This last, one might think, would be an interesting theme to follow, the willful manipulation of objective reality. But, in *Scandal* at any rate, Kurosawa was only interested in making journalists as black as possible.

It is unfortunate that we must judge their badness through the goodness he insists upon in the other characters. Strictly speaking Mifune and Yamaguchi have no characters. They are merely people to whom something happens. Their reaction is anyone's reaction: he hits the editor; she cries. Goodness is seen in the bed-ridden daughter and there is a very maudlin sequence which attempts to indicate this.

Christmas Eve, father out drinking, Mifune brings a decorated Christmas tree on the back of his motorcycle. Fade. Inside, there is Mifune pedaling the harmonium and skillfully fingering *Silent Night*, and there is Yoshiko singing it, and there is the girl's mother crying in a corner, and there is the girl, sitting up, beatific, big white teddy-bear in her arms. And there is the father creeping in drunk. He sees the simple scene, lets out a great cry, crashes through the *shoji*, runs away.

If this is seen as good, the next sequence then shows us that we can all be good. Father rushes out, Mifune follows and they end up in a low night-spot where everyone is drunk and un-Christian. Bokuzen Hidari (making his debut in the Kurosawa group—he later played the old clerk in *Ikiru* and the travelling priest in *The Lower Depths*) gets up and makes a speech about just that. These are father's sentiments as well. Together they begin to sing. They sing *Auld Lange Syne*—a tune ubiquitous in Japan, one freighted with sentimental associations, one which all Japanese are convinced the Scots have unkindly appropriated—and soon all the whores are crying, the band is crying, the

drunks are crying, all roaring out the lyrics. The horror of the situation (for this is plainly the genesis of the harrowing night-town sequence of *Ikiru*) does not occur to the director. Rather, these are good and simple people and this is their moment of truth. Most of one's embarrassment at this sequence is because—as in the final sequence of *One Wonderful Sunday*—one is already convinced that people are good and simple and for that reason the director should not be so lavish with moments of truth. He should choose them with care and present them with concern.

Besides the character of the lawyer, there are a number of interesting technical aspects. Here, again, Kurosawa proved that he can make a bad film but that it is difficult for him to make a dull one. The reason is the sheer carpentry of the picture: the matter of short-cuts, for example. Mifune up on the mountain says to Yoshiko: "I'll be going down soon, I'll take you." Wipe, followed by a long-shot of the two of them going down the mountain on the motorcycle. Again, the bad magazine boss says: "Oh, we don't have anything to be afraid of," and in the act of saying it he hears Mifune's motorcycle stopping outside the building. Or, in the short scene that follows: he hits the editor, there is a close-up of his hand grabbing his scarf and goggles, followed at once by a short shot of his riding away through traffic. Later, the bad man says to Shimura: "Let's have a drink." Cut. Scene of lawyer being brought home in *Amour* truck, plastered. Also, the bad man will not accept a leaflet from the Salvation Army-type Santa. Santa nonetheless says: "Merry Christmas." Cut. Christmas tree ornaments dangling from branch, branch is jiggling. Cut. Mifune comes roaring toward camera, fully decorated Christmas tree on the back of his bike.

Besides cutting out the extraneous, Kurosawa often intensifies. One such moment is when the father looks into the room where the three of them are happily celebrating Christmas. The camera, from inside the room, sees him looking through the small square glass window in the *shoji*. At the same time, we see, superimposed upon his face, the reflection of the face of his happy daughter. Amid the general meaninglessness of this sequence the effect is wasted. For one thing, we already know how deeply the father loves his daughter, and this insistence upon identification between the two is not so impressive as it might be. For another, it is on the screen for so short a time that it appears merely decorative. Kurosawa remembered and used it again with astonishing and devastating effect at the end of *High and Low*.

Another moment of intensification occurs when Mifune goes to see the lawyer. We already know what kind of man he is but as yet know nothing of the daughter or of his various troubles. Mifune finds the office and Kurosawa presents the lawyer in terms of where he works. No one is there and as Mifune walks around the room the camera peers and hovers, making its dispassionate survey of a man's environment. The floor is dirty, the wastebasket overflowing; the table is loaded with unfinished work and the ashtray is piled high. It looks more like

the den of some animal than the office of a lawyer. About three minutes are used in this sequence, Mifune and the camera just looking. It is the method of the Russian novelists, or of Dickens: a description of a man through his habitat. We are convinced the lawyer is a pig. Then Mifune—for all the world like a Dostoevsky character—looks at the single picture on the wall, a tiny snapshot. It is the daughter, smiling. At once both he and we know something more, something important. The lawyer is not an animal. The lawyer loves. As in *Stray Dog* (the visit to the head detective's home), and in *Red Beard*, we have been led to expect one thing and are given another. Tricked into believing the worst, we have been shown that we believed the worst too soon, believed it all too willingly.

This is again stated in the most intense moment in the film, the trial scene, which is so good—or perhaps it is that it suggests so many possibilities—that one wonders at Kurosawa's never again taking his camera into the courtroom. This particular kind of scene would lend itself well to his continual preoccupation with illusion versus reality. The crime would be the latter; the trial, the former. He does, to be sure, use this form. In *Rashomon*, for example, the entire action is seen through interrogation, the principals in the act are also the witnesses, and the story is made up of their interpretations and/or falsifications of reality. In other films as well, *Ikiru*, for instance, characters appear, one by one, in front of the camera (as in the opening sequence where the housewives' committee is sent from one section to another) stating their case, incriminating themselves.

Yet *Scandal* is the only Kurosawa picture to contain a courtroom scene—and he makes the most of it. We have already seen, in life, what has happened. Then, at the trial, we are shown what is made of these happenings, how they are falsified, how they are turned into lies, how they are made illusion.

And here we are shown (at the end as at the beginning) that we have misjudged (though it is Kurosawa himself who forced the judgement) and that the lawyer saves himself by losing himself. Just as the picture of the daughter is intended to redeem his disorderly den, so the final action of the lawyer (telling the truth no matter the cost) redeems him, though it means, in effect, the end of his career. He will certainly be disbarred.

This means little to him for this is one of the moments of truth of which Kurosawa is so fond. Just as Watanabe in *Ikiru* and the detective in *Stray Dog* finally reach a point where their own life becomes a matter of indifference to them, so the lawyer having lost the only thing he loved, his daughter, now sees no reason for lying (the original purpose of which was to obtain money for her) or for continuing. By telling the truth he can not only vindicate the innocent, he can also deprive himself of the very means to go on living.

Mifune waits impatiently for him to begin his case. Shimura sits, eyes downcast. The judge looks at him. The villain smiles and lights a cigarette. Yoshiko turns, stares. Still, Shimura sits, silent, while the witnesses, the audience begin to whisper at this unheard-of turn of events. The silence grows, minutes pass. The scene becomes uncomfortable even if one has found the daughter a goose and Toshiro and Yoshiko one of the most uninteresting young couples in all Japanese film. It becomes uncomfortable because, as one watches, one becomes aware of what is going on inside of the lawyer. It is a silent struggle but a struggle nonetheless.

The camera turns from one person to another in great wide pans reminiscent of those in the interrogation scene of *They Who Step on the Tiger's Tail*. There is silence except for the whisperings in the court room audience. Then Shimura stands, sways, fumbles in his pocket for the guilty check, and slowly, painfully, begins his confession. The entire sequence takes almost fifteen minutes and is the most fully intensified section of the film. There are no short-cuts. Everything is watched. It is literal enactment. And as the lawyer speaks, struggling with words, with ideas, his mind numbed but determined, we see that we have misjudged, that we, too, have played judge and jurors, and that we have been wrong.

# MORAL

Kurosawa himself has said that this a "protest film," and any protest film has a moral. The ostensible one here is that innocent people get victimized but, if lucky, are proved guiltless. The accidental one is that everyone has to make a living, even the kind of people that run *Amour*. This is what comes of Kurosawa's using the same kind of black and white standards that he accuses his villains of using. Yet another moral is that scandals come and scandals go. This is underlined by the final shot.

During the publication montage we have seen an entire wall plaster-ed with pictures of the "guilty" two and advertisements for the magazine. Mifune has raced by it on his motorcycle and was thus informed of what had happened. At the end of the picture, the two of them—spotless—walk past the wall on their way to probable happiness. Now time has passed, it has rained, the posters are torn and ragged, one cannot tell which is Yoshiko, which Mifune. The final shot continues this, a close-up of the wall, with normal Tokyo traffic in front of it. The suggestion is that things come and go, which is a singular way to end a protest film. On the other hand, perhaps the intention is ironic, perhaps Kurosawa wanted to indicate that, after all, all this fuss had been over very little. This would agree with the proposition that the true moral of the film has very little to do with hero or heroine—rather, that the true hero of the film is the lawyer.

*Scandal* had script trouble. When the lawyer enters he takes over the picture. The result is a curiously unbalanced film with first and second halves in different focus, as it were. Kurosawa usually loses interest when an initial idea is tampered with—even thought it is he himself who does the tampering, as in *Quiet Duel*. In *Scandal*, he appears not to have so much lost as changed interest. Half-way through shooting he became concerned with the character of the lawyer. Those who have called this picture "the first of Kurosawa's movies in the Dostoevsky manner" can only have been thinking of the last half of the film and, in particular, of the character of the lawyer.

The picture is a protest film all right but its protestations are not aimed at the world of the yellow press. They are aimed at the world itself, at this world which takes what is loved, which forces impossible decisions, which insists upon a choice among evils. It states, however, that moral dilemmas may be cut if not untied; that the truth, reality, seeing things as they are, goes a long way toward saving.

In this case, the lawyer saves himself, thought he loses everything that belongs to him. In *Rashomon*, the picture that directly followed this one, Kurosawa goes one step further and questions reality itself.

# Rashomon

Kurosawa had for some time wanted to make the film that eventually became *Rashomon*. A scenario was written, a budget was determined, and then (in 1948) the picture was cancelled because the small Toyoko Company, which was to have financed it, decided it was too much of a risk. Toho—Kurosawa's company off and on for a number of years—was against it. Then Daiei signed a one-year distribution and production contract with Kurosawa. He and his associates left Toho to form the short-lived Motion Picture Art Association, and one of the director's hopes was to be able to make this picture.

After making *Scandal*, Kurosawa showed Daiei the script which became *Rashomon*. "It was a bit too short ... but all of my friends liked it very much. Daiei, however, did not understand it and kept asking: But what is it about? I made it longer, put on a beginning and an ending—and they eventually agreed to make it. Thus Daiei joined those—Shochiku for *The Idiot*, Toho for *Record of a Living Being*—who were brave enough to try something different." This is a very charitable statement. Actually Daiei was adamant in its refusal to understand. Masaichi Nagata, head of the studio and standing somewhat in relation to Japanese film as Darryl Zanuck once stood to American production, walked out on the first screening and, until the picture began winning prizes abroad, was very fond of telling the press how little he understood *his* film—his, since he, in the manner of a Goldwyn or a Zanuck, or a Wald, often signs his own name as executive producer. Toho never gave adequate foreign distribution to *Record of a Living Being* and Shochiku butchered *The Idiot*.

## SOURCE

The beginnings of *Rashomon* lie in the stories of Ryunosuke Akutagawa, that brilliant and erratic stylist who died, a suicide of thirty-five, in 1927. His position in Japanese letters, though secure, has always been special—as special as that of Poe in America or Maupassant in France. He has always been extremely popular and also critically well-thought-of, almost despite his popularity. Yet he has never been considered in the "main stream" of Japanese literature. His defenders point out his inventive style; his detractors call him "Western" in his orientation. He *is* "Western" in the same way as Kurosawa: he is concerned with truths which are ordinarily outside pragmatic

Japanese morality and, being concerned with them, he questions them. This he does with an involuted, elliptical style, the essence of which is irony. In translation he sounds very fin-de-siècle, a better Beardsley, a less involved Lafcadio Hearn—though there is no trace of this in Kurosawa's film.

It is based, loosely, upon two of Akutagawa's hundred-odd short stories: the title story, *Rashomon*, and *In a Grove*—which gives the film its plot, or plots. The title story has little in it that Kurosawa used, except the general description of the ruined gate, the conversation about the devastation of Kyoto during the period of civil wars and the atmosphere of complete desolation. The story, like the film, begins in the rain. A discharged servant shelters himself under the gate, then decides to wait in the loft for the weather to clear. There he finds an old woman who is stealing hair from the corpses left there. She pleads that she only steals to make a living by making wigs from the stolen hair. The servant, who has decided to become a thief, knocks her down and takes her clothes saying that her defense has proved his own. He runs away and that is the end of the story.

*In a Grove* opens abruptly with the testimony of a woodcutter before the police. This is followed by various testimonies: that of a priest, a police agent, an old woman who turns out to be the mother of the girl the bandit raped, the bandit himself, the girl herself, the murdered man through a medium, and there is no conclusion: the reader is presented with seven testimonies and given no indication of how he should think about them. Akutagawa's point was the simple one that all truth is relative, with the corollary that there is thus no truth at all.

Kurosawa's most significant addition (beside that of the abandoned baby in the last scenes) is the introduction of the character of the commoner, a cynical yet inquisitive man, whose questions and disbelief act as a comment upon all the various versions of the story. The commoner talks to both priest and woodcutter—since all three are found under the gate at the beginning of the film—and in a way acts as a moral (or amoral) chorus. He is the single person in the cast of eight (the medium herself is involved because she speaks for the dead man) who is essentially uninvolved. He alone has no story, no version to tell. It is through his questions that the film evolves.

First the woodcutter tells how he went into the forest and found the woman's hat, some rope, an amulet-case, and then went to the police. There he recounts how he found the body. The priest's testimony follows directly. He tells how he saw the murdered man and his wife some time before. This is followed directly by the story of the police agent who tells how he managed to capture the bandit. His story is broken into by the bandit who tells the apparent truth of his capture and continues to give the first version of the tragedy.

He was asleep under a tree when the man and wife went past; the wind blew her veil and he saw her and decided he wanted her. He tricked the husband into following him, tied him up, went back, got the wife, raped her in front of the husband, and then turned to go when she stopped him saying that her honor demanded that they fight. In the resulting duel the bandit killed the husband and the woman ran away.

The second version is the woman's in the police court. She takes up the story after the rape, says that the bandit went away and that her own husband spurned her because she had been (presumably so easily) violated. Wild with grief she apparently kills him, then runs away and is finally found by the police.

The third version is that of the dead husband himself, speaking through the lips of a medium. He says that after the rape the bandit made overtures, wanting to take her away with him. She agrees and then insists that he kill the husband. This angers the bandit who spurns her and goes away. The man finds the woman's dagger (which has been mentioned in all earlier versions of the story) and kills himself. Much later, after he has been dead for some time, he feels someone taking the dagger away.

The fourth version is that of the woodcutter who is prevailed upon to correct his first story. He says that after the rape he found the bandit on his knees before the woman, pleading with her to go away with him. The woman says that she cannot decide, that only the men can. They are reluctant but she insists. They fight and the bandit kills the husband. She runs away and eventually the bandit also leaves. The woodcutter—whose own veracity is questioned when it transpires that *he* might have stolen the dagger, either from the ground or from the chest of the dead man—says: "I don't understand any of them —they don't make sense." To which the commoner replies: "Well, don't worry about it—it isn't as though men were reasonable."

This is more or less the point of the Akutagawa story and this is where the original stops. Kurosawa, however, goes on. Having invented the character of the commoner, having chosen to frame all of his stories within the general story of the three conversing under the ruined gate, he now invents a further incident. They hear a baby crying and the commoner finds it. He takes its clothes (a suggestion perhaps from the original *Rashomon* story), an act which horrifies the other two and which, in turn, makes him culpable. Throughout the picture he has not once acted, merely asked questions—now he acts and his act is immoral. The woodcutter picks up the naked child, saying he will take it home. The priest says that this single act has restored his faith in men and the picture concludes with the rain stopping, the sun breaking through, and the woodcutter going off with the baby.

Akutagawa is content to question all moral values, all truth. Kurosawa, obviously, is not. Neither anarchist nor misanthrope, he insists upon hope, upon the possibility of gratuitous action. Like the priest he cannot believe that men are evil—and, indeed, if Kurosawa has a spokesman in the film it is probably the priest: weak, confused, but ultimately trusting.

# THE STORY

There is, however, much more to the film than this. There is an apparent mystery, an elliptical intent, which has fascinated audiences all over the world. Daiei was quite right to ask what the picture was about, though its dismissal of the picture as being a kind of mystification was ill-judged. One of the most fascinating aspects of the film is just that it is extremely difficult to determine *what* it means. It shares with other modern art (abstract painting, free-form sculpture) an apparent lack of ostensible meaning which (in painting) returns to us our ability to see form and color, which (in sculpture) gives us our original vision—that of children—and lets us observe rock as rock, wood as wood, and which (in films such as *Rashomon, Muriel, Paris nous appartient*) allows us to examine human action undistracted by plot, undisturbed by ostensible reality.

The central section of *Rashomon* is an anecdote presented four times, in four different ways. Each member of the triangle (bandit, woman, husband) tells his version, and the fourth is that of the only witness: the woodcutter.

At first he says only that he found the body of the husband but at the end he confesses that he saw the entire thing. Thus, it is he who might be lying. He is the only eye witness—that is, we hear the testimony of the other three only through the priest and himself, both of whom were present at the prison questioning. We never once see the others directly. Everything is history—and the story is told by the two to a third, the commoner. Further, the only link between these two sets of three people is the woodcutter himself. The husband is dead, wife and bandit are either in jail or executed for murder. In any case, all are unavailable to us. The priest only knows what he has heard wife, bandit, and husband say. So, it comes down to the woodcutter. He is the only one who saw anything. He lied once. He may lie again.

There is a further difficulty in that we are never quite certain *who* is telling some of these apparently varying stories. A break down of the various recountings of the anecdote gives:

1. The discovery of the body. — Told by the woodcutter.
2. Man and wife seen in the forest. — Told by the priest.
3. Tajomaru's capture. — Told by the police agent.
4. Tajomaru's version of the story. — Told by Tajomaru, the bandit.
5. The wife's version. — Told by the wife.
6. The husband's version. — Told by the husband through the medium.
7. The woodcutter's version. — Told by the woodcutter.

The only first-person stories are therefore those of the woodcutter and the priest, and the latter only happened to see the two of them (alive) in the woods. This means that he saw them before the time of the anecdote and before the woodcutter says he saw them. That his story and the woodcutter's agree means little since the priest actually saw nothing of the action that followed. However, it is presumed that the third-person recountings (the versions of Tajomaru, the wife, and the husband) are to be accepted as substantially true because in the court-scenes we see the woodcutter and the priest kneeling in the background and listening. Thus, they have been there to hear what the three have said, and if there were any differences in this third-person version they give the commoner, one might be expected to contradict the other. This, however, must be inferred by the viewer, and given the character of the priest, it is not at all certain that he is the kind of person who would contradict even if he saw that the stories were being falsified by the woodcutter in the re-telling.

To say this, however, is to presume that it is the woodcutter who is doing the re-telling and this is by no means certain. It could equally well be the priest who is recounting—or it could be both of them. Since these three stories are mutually contradictory (or at least seem to be) we are initially given the choice of disbelieving the priest and the woodcutter, or disbelieving one and/or all of the original triangle of bandit, husband, wife.

Kurosawa gives us no reason at all for disbelieving the priest. At the same time we are given very little for disbelieving what is said by any of the original three because their stories, if lies, are not the kind of lies which one tells to escape punishment, and this would seem to be the usual reason for lying. The bandit admits to killing the husband; the wife admits to killing the husband; the husband admits to killing himself. There is no shifting of blame. Each pleads guilty.

There is, on the other hand, a reason for the woodcutter's lying. He is the only person who has something to gain from falsehood. First, as he says, he did not want to become involved with the police (then as now a dangerous alternative in Japan); second, it transpires that he might be a thief (the dagger) as well. One might understand his lying to keep clear of the police but under the gate with an all-forgiving priest and the kind of man who steals clothes from abandoned infants there seems little motivation for falsehood. If he stole the dagger the other two could not care less—though the commoner might covet it.

It would seem that someone—more than one—is lying. Yet there is no reason. At this point the thought occurs: is it not possible that no one is lying and that the stories can be reconciled?

The disagreement in the stories is only over the murder. All the stories of attack and rape agree. Kurosawa helps us very little in sorting out the different versions and their possible agreement, but he does help some. The bandit, for example, says that they fought because she insisted and at the end of his version he backs the husband into a thicket and kills him. The woodcutter agrees with the bandit: they fought because she insisted. At the end of his version, Kurosawa is careful to show us that it is the same thicket into which the husband is backed and killed. There are many differences (emotion, intention) but the actions in the first and fourth versions agree.

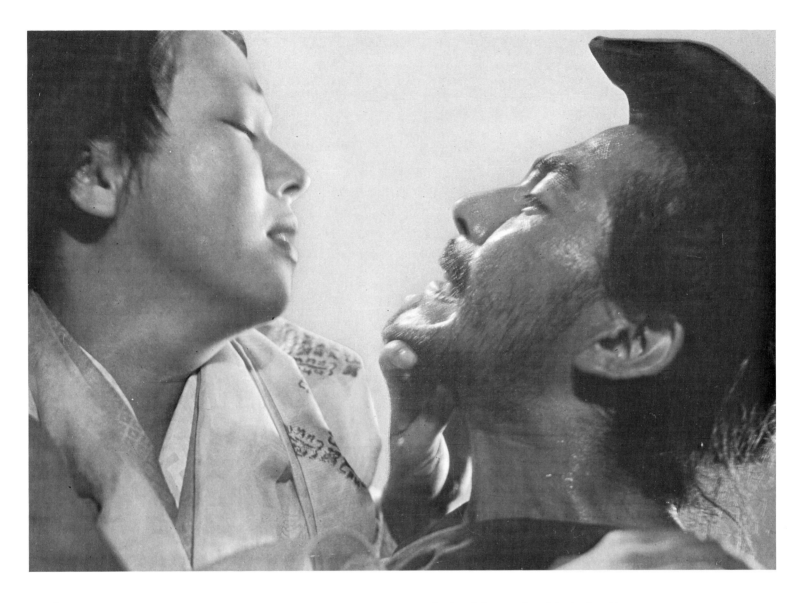

The problem becomes one of having to reconcile the other two. The third version, that of the husband, may be hastily disposed of. He is dead. The dead do not speak—through the mouths of mediums or otherwise. That the three under the gate happen to believe in spirits does not mean that we must. Rape, murder, these are physical facts; the talking-dead are not. The poor, demented woman called upon by the magistrates, obviously terrified by her position, makes up her own version which (though she may believe it) is not, *can* not be true. (That one need not be so cavalier with both an important section of the film and Kurosawa's express intentions will be demonstrated later: there is perfectly good reason for believing in both the speaking-

dead and the veracity of the husband.)

This leaves the story of the wife. Hers is more difficult to reconcile but not impossible (if you cheat a bit). Apparently, after the rape, there was a lapse of some time—recounted in the woodcutter's story as well—when the bandit was not there. During this time her husband shows her how he has come to hate her. (This point is agreed upon in all the stories—leaving out the husband's which we, for the present, have agreed is no story at all. The implication in both the woodcutter's and the bandit's version is that it was she who suggested the duel, and so some amount of hate between the spouses is necessary.) She remembers that he looked at her with the greatest scorn. She cuts his bonds, offers him her dagger, asks him to kill her, then faints. When she revives, her husband is dead and the dagger is in his chest.

Now, if only it were not for the dagger, all the stories would more or less agree because she could just as easily have either fainted or lost her reason during a duel which followed and of which she would have known nothing. However, the dagger remains (as well as a number of other loose ends). Further, at the end of the film it transpires that the woodcutter might have taken it. He has now a very good reason for lying. Not only may he have stolen the dagger, he might also have crept up during the wife's swoon and stabbed the husband himself. Leaving aside the extreme unlikelihood of a simple woodcutter daring to stab a noble, however, what would have been the motivation for such an act? Robbery? But then a number of their belongings would be missing and the police do not mention this nor does the wife. The only missing objects are the horse and sword (which the bandit took) and the dagger (which the woodcutter might have taken). But, let us presume that this is what happened—that either the wife or the woodcutter killed the husband.

One can do this because the woodcutter now has a reason for lying (possible murder) and this makes his story (both parts of it) falsehood. Then one remembers that his version happened to jibe particularly well with that of the bandit. Where is the bandit now? His head has probably been cut off. At any rate he can tell us no more than the husband could. And who told us the bandit's story? Why the woodcutter, of course. And he lied about it, even taking care that it match and thus lend credulity to his own. If he has been the one who has told us all these stories, then they are all lies. But, in that case, why include two (husband's and wife's) that would weaken his own case? Perhaps it is because the priest tells some and the priest (though he has perhaps heard the bandit's story) does not presume to correct. Then, one solution to the *Great Rashomon Murder Mystery* would be:

| | | |
|---|---|---|
| 1. | The discovery of the husband's body. | A lie told by the woodcutter. |
| 2. | Man and wife seen in the forest. | The truth told by the priest. |
| 3. | Tajomaru's capture. | Told by the police agent. | The truth told by the woodcutter or the priest. |
| 4. | Tajomaru's version of the story. | Told by Tajomaru. | A lie told by the woodcutter. |
| 5. | The wife's version. | Told by the wife. | The truth told by the priest. |
| 6. | The husband's version. | Told by the husband through the medium. | Accepted as true and told by the priest. |
| 7. | The woodcutter's version. | | A lie told by the woodcutter. |

There is some (not much) reason for the validity of this arrangement given in the context of the film itself. At the end of 4., the commoner is speaking to the woodcutter—as though he were responding to something which the woodcutter had told him. He says that he thinks Tajomaru probably killed the woman as well.

*Priest:* But this woman turned up at prison too, you know. It seems she went to seek refuge at some temple and the police found her there.

*Woodcutter:* (Breaking in) It's a lie. They're all lies. Tajomaru's confession, the woman's story. They're lies.

*Commoner:* Well, men are only men. That's why they lie. They can't tell the truth. Not even to each other.

*Priest:* That may be true. But it is because men are so weak. That's why they lie. That's why they must deceive themselves.

*Commoner:* Not another sermon. I don't mind a lie—not if it's an interesting one. What kind of story did she tell?

*Priest:* Well, hers was a completely different story from the bandit's. And, speaking of differences—the bandit talked about her temper. I saw nothing like that at all. I found her very pitiful. I felt a great compassion for her.

Then follows the wife's version which, in this context, seems very much as though retold by the priest who, having no reason for lying, would himself tell the truth as he heard it.

It would be convenient if, at the end of 5., the woodcutter would have again said it was a lie but he unfortunately does not. He says nothing, merely states that the next story, the husband's story, is a lie. There is here no indication as to who tells 6. because the last word before it begins belongs to the commoner. Besides, at that moment (perhaps to prepare for the supernatural to come) there is a great flash of lightning, followed by thunder. At the end of 6., the woodcutter is walking about and then stops and says that it wasn't true. If he had been telling the dead husband's story he would not have said this. It must have been the priest. He goes on to say that it wasn't a dagger that killed him anyway. It was a sword. Now, we know that the bandit stole and sold the sword, but we do actually know how the husband was killed. The woodcutter is telling us. Since he has lied about the dagger there is no reason to believe this remark about the sword. And it is here that the priest decides he doesn't want to hear any more—almost as though he can no longer countenance such lying from the woodcutter. It is now revealed that his having said he found the body was a lie and even the commoner becomes suspicious. At the end of 7.:

*Commoner:* And I suppose that that is supposed to be true.

*Woodcutter:* I don't tell lies. I saw it with my own eyes.

*Commoner:* That I doubt.

*Woodcutter:* I don't tell lies.

*Commoner:* Well, that is just what you'd say, isn't it?—no one tells lies after he has *said* he is going to tell one.

*Priest:* It's horrible—if men do not tell the truth, do not trust one another, then the earth becomes hell indeed.

*Commoner:* Absolutely right. The world we live in is hell.

It might be assumed then the woodcutter is consistently lying, that the priest knows it but for some reason (fear, compassion) restrains himself. Therefore the only correct version is the woman's—which is given by the priest. Further, the woodcutter may have murdered the husband as well. The commoner says: "You say you don't lie. That's funny. You may have fooled the police but you don't fool me." Then the woodcutter attacks the commoner—perhaps not the act of an innocent man—and the two fight. Then:

*Priest:* (Seeing the woodcutter pick up the baby and misinterpreting his intentions). What are you doing—trying to take what little it has left?

*Woodcutter:* I have six children of my own. One more won't make it any more difficult.

*Priest:* I'm sorry. I shouldn't have said that.

*Woodcutter:* Oh, one cannot afford not to be suspicious of people. I'm the one who is ashamed. I don't know why I did a thing like that.

A thing like what? Is he confessing, indicating his guilt to this priest who refused to expose his lies in front of the commoner? Is this a kind of covenant between the two? Then this final gesture, the saving of the baby, might be a mark of contrition. The woodcutter will save a life and make amends for the life he either himself took or else did not prevent the wife from taking. And if this is true the final dialogue in the film is double-edged and profoundly ironic.

*Priest:* I am grateful to you. Because... thanks to you, I think I will be able to keep my faith in men.

But what if it were the priest who had told Tajomaru's story? What then? Well—what then indeed? The question, like this murder-mystery aspect of the film, is really irrelevant. It is only meaningful if one thinks that the picture is about relative truth. And if that were what it is about, would not Kurosawa have made the stories a bit less reconcilable than they are? If the film is about relative truth (which on one level it is, to be sure) then it is also a partial failure because, judging merely by externals—who did what to whom—the actions are not enough at variance to make a point which one might suppose that he (like Akutagawa) was making.

One doubts very much that Kurosawa was deeply interested in objective truth in this or in any other film. This is because the *why* is always implied. And in none of his pictures is Kurosawa even slightly interested in the why of a matter. Instead, always, *how*. This offers a clue. The level of objective truth is not the truly interesting one. Much more interesting is the level of subjective truth. If the truth searched for becomes subjective, then no one lies, and the stories are wildly at variance.

Truth as it appears to others. This is one of the themes, perhaps the main one of this picture. No one—priest, woodcutter, husband, bandit, medium—lied. They all told the story the way they saw it, the way they believed it, and they all told the truth. Kurosawa therefore does not question truth. He questions reality.

Once asked why he thought that *Rashomon* had become so popular, both in Japan and abroad, he answered: "Well, you see... it's about this rape." Everyone laughed but the answer is not, perhaps, so cynical as it sounds. *Rashomon* is *about* an action as few pictures are *about* anything at all. We can turn the object this way and that, look at it from various angles, and it resembles a number of things but *is* only one thing, the object that it is. The film is about a rape (and a murder) but, more than this, it is about the reality of these events. Precisely, it is about what five people think this reality consists of. How a thing happens may reflect nothing about the thing itself but it must reflect something about the person involved in the happening and supplying the how.

Five people interpret an action and each interpretation is different because, in the telling and in the retelling, the people reveal not the action but themselves. This is why Kurosawa could leave the plot, insofar as there is one, dangling and unresolved. The fact that it *is* unresolved is itself one of the meanings of the film.

In all of Kurosawa's pictures there is this preoccupation with the conflict between illusion (the reactions of the five and their stories) and reality (the fact of the rape and murder). To do something is to realize that it is far different from what one had thought. To have done something and then to explain it completes the cycle because this too is (equally) different from what the thing itself was. Given a traumatic experience, one fraught with emotional connotations (murder, falling in love, bankruptcy, rape) reality escapes even more swiftly.

One can now assign various reasons for the five having seen and heard the things that they thought they saw and heard. All the stories have in common one single element—pride. Tajomaru is proud to have raped and fought and killed; the wife is proud to have (perhaps) killed; the husband (for now there is every reason to believe that the dead talk) is proud to have killed himself; and the woodcutter is proud to have seen and robbed. They are proud of these actions and we know because they insist upon them. One confesses only what one is openly or secretly proud of, which is the reason that contrition is rarely sincere. But the reasons for the pride, as Parker Tyler has indicated in his fine analysis of this film, are not those commonly encountered.

Each is proud of what he did because, as he might tell you: "It is just the sort of thing that I would do." Each thinks of his character as being fully formed, of being a *thing*, like the rape or the dagger is a thing, and of his therefore (during an emergency such as this) being capable of only a certain number of (consistent) reactions. They are *in character* because they have defined their own character for themselves and will admit none of the surprising opportunities which must occur when one does not. They "had no choice"; circumstances "forced" their various actions; what each did "could not be helped." It is no wonder that the reported actions refuse to agree with each other. As the commoner has wisely remarked: "Men are only men . . . they can't tell the truth—not even to each other." One of the points of the picture then is not that men will not but that men *can* not tell the truth. The priest sees this: "It is because men are so weak. That's why they lie. That's why they must deceive themselves."

If one is going to agree that one is a certain kind of person one also agrees that one is engaged in self-deception, in bad faith. We know

what Kurosawa thinks about this. From *Sugata* on, his villains have been in bad faith, that is, they see themselves as a kind of person to whom only certain actions, certain alternatives are open. In the effort to create themselves they only codify; in the effort to free themselves (by making action simpler and therefore easier) they limit themselves.

It is interesting that *Rashomon* should have been an historical film—Kurosawa's second (since the Japanese tend to think of the Meiji period—the era of *Sugata Sanshiro*—as being somehow modern), because this limitation of spirit, this tacit agreement (social in its scope) that one *is* and cannot *become*, is one feudalistic precept which plagues the country to this day. This was as useful to the Kamakura Government as it proved to the administration during the last war. In *Rashomon*, as in *They Who Step on the Tiger's Tail* and *Sanjuro*, Kurosawa is presenting an indictment of feudal remains. That he sets the scene in the Heian-period is merely due to Akutagawa's having used it, and where

the director follows the author in this film, he does so literally. The people, and their way of thinking, are—twelfth century or present day—completely feudal. It is as though in this film he is holding up a mirror.

In more ways than one. *Rashomon* is like a vast distorting mirror or, better, a collection of prisms that reflect and refract reality. By showing us its various interpretations (perhaps the husband really loved his wife, was lost without her and hence felt he must kill himself; perhaps she really thought to save her husband by a show of affection for the bandit, and thus played the role of faithful wife; perhaps the woodcutter knows much more, perhaps he too entered the action—mirrors within mirrors, each intention bringing forth another, until the triangle fades into the distance) he has shown first that human beings are incapable of judging reality, much less truth, and, second, that they must

continually deceive themselves if they are to remain true to the ideas of themselves that they have.

Here then, more than in any other single film, is found Kurosawa's central theme: the world is illusion, you yourself make reality, but this reality undoes you if you submit to being limited by what you have made. The important corollary—you are not, however, truly subject to this reality, you can break free from it, can live even closer to the nature you are continually creating—this occurs only in the later films.

# PRODUCTION

The visual starting point remains the Akutagawa stories. The author's description of the gate and medieval Kyoto is literally followed by both the script and camera. There is, for example, no reason at all for the bandit to be discovered by the police agent near a small bridge (seen in the film) except that this is where Akutagawa says it happened. What turned out to be an excellent cinematic device, all the testimonies being given to the audience, questions answered by unheard questions being repeated as a question and then answered by those testifying, is taken directly from the author. Likewise, in the original script, all the characters' names are retained even though, in the case of husband and wife, they never appear in the dialogue. Given the eventual difference between story and film—which is extreme and which the Japanese critics complained of when they said the director had been false to the spirit of the tales—such literal fidelity is remarkable.

The acting style, however, owes nothing at all to Akutagawa or any of his suggestions. It springs from a different source. "We were

the glint of sunlight on the ax. Again, during the rape scene, the camera seeks the sky, the sun, the trees, contrasting this with the two, wife and bandit. When the rape is consummated and just before we return to the prison courtyard for the conclusion of the bandit's story, the sun comes out from behind a branch, dazzling, shining directly into the lenses: a metaphor. Just as much a metaphor certainly as the scene shortly before where she drops her dagger and it falls point first to land upright, quivering in the ground; or the celebrated scene where Mifune is asleep and the two pass. He has mentioned the breeze in his testimony. Now we see it (accompanied by the cooling celesta on the sound track) as it ruffles his hair. He opens his eyes and sees it raising her veil. It is an extended metaphor, like a two-line poem. In Kurosawa's later films, this impressionism is not often seen though there is a fine example at the end of *Sanjuro* where, after all the camellias

staying in Kyoto," says Kurosawa, "waiting for the set to be finished. While we were there we ran off some sixteen mm. prints to amuse ourselves. One of them was a Martin Johnson jungle film in which there was a shot of a lion roaming around. I noticed it and told Mifune that that was just what I wanted him to be. At the same time Mori had seen a jungle picture in which a black leopard was shown. We all went to see it. When the leopard came on Machiko was so upset that she hid her face. I saw and recognized the gesture. It was just what I wanted for the young wife."

Cinematically the style is made of various parts, all of which work admirably together. Perhaps the most noticeable is a kind of rhapsodic impressionism which from time to time carries the story and creates the atmosphere. Take, for example, the much-admired walk of the woodcutter through the forest. This is pure cinema impressionism— one literally receives impressions: the passing trees overhead, the sun,

have been sent off down the stream there is a pause and then, as the bad man falls, a single blossom falls, all by itself, and is carried away— the perfect classic metaphor for the cut-short life.

Kurosawa in this film, and more than in any other, makes use of contrasting shots. A shot of the woman is held for a certain length of time. This is matched by a shot of the bandit, held for the same time. He intercuts these, back and forth, matching the timing so delicately that one does not notice the number of repeats while watching the film—and is surprised upon reading the script to discover that there are so many.

In the same way he uses single close-ups to emphasize the triangular nature of the story. A shot of the woman is followed by a shot of the bandit is followed by a shot of the husband, and this process continues, going round and round as it were. Mostly, however, he insists upon the triangle through composition. The picture is filled with masterful triangular compositions, often one following directly after another, the frame filled with woman, bandit, husband, but always in different compositional relationships to each other. When the Japanese critics mentioned Kurosawa's "silent-film technique" they meant his great reliance upon composition—which with this film became, and still remains, one of the strongest elements of his film style.

Kurosawa's use of cinematic punctuation is always imaginative and, as we have seen, he is one of the few directors remaining who can intelligently use that most maligned of punctuation marks: the wipe. There is a fine use of it when the woman is waiting, during the bandit's story, and it (as always with Kurosawa) gives the effect of time, usually a short period of time, having elapsed. Here, as in *Ikiru,* the wipe is masterfully used. In *The Idiot,* on the other hand, Kurosawa was so unsure (because he was filming his favorite novel, by his favorite author, and doing it mainly for a then-uncooperative company) that he uses the wipe within a single scene, not once but many times, and the time indicated as having passed can only be a matter of seconds. An experiment, it remains in *The Idiot* entirely uncontrolled and very mannered—something which cannot be said of its use in *Rashomon.*

Kurosawa does not usually use fades (either in or out) tending to be suspicious of the softening effect they produce. Certainly the ending of *The Lower Depths*—it ends on an unexpected cut—would be far less effective with a fade-out. He uses it only, as in the opening and closing of *The Throne of Blood,* when he deliberately wants the effect of distance and uninvolvement. For Kurosawa the fade usually means the elegiac.

The dissolve on the other hand usually means time passing. The end of *Rashomon* is a beautiful example of this. The three men are standing under the gate and there is a series of dissolves moving closer and closer. This is almost a rhetorical device since, in actuality, not much time could have passed. It is a formal gesture, a gesture which makes us look, and makes us feel. If the purpose is merely to indicate passage of time, however, Kurosawa has even simpler ways of doing it—one of the most imaginative in this picture is where the husband is waiting and his voice tells us that he waited a very long time. Here the effect is given through three long held shots with no dissolves or wipes at all—simply a long-shot, followed by a far-shot, followed by a medium close-up. These are used so consummately that one does not question that hours have passed.

Kurosawa's preoccupation with time (*the* preoccupation for any serious director) began with *Rashomon.* There are two kinds of time which concern him—and any other director. One is ostensible time—the time the story takes. The other is a certain kind of psychological time, the time that each sequence, and that each shot within this sequence takes. The first kind is the kind which is appreciable to the audience as well. *Rashomon* is a series of flashbacks, all of them both true and false; *Ikiru* on the other hand is a film in which flashback

leads into further flashback—the scene where the father finds the baseball bat, remembers the ballgame, remembers the operation, remembers the hospital, remembers the son going off to war. The second half of *Ikiru* is a series of flash backs, in the *Citizen Kane* manner (a film which Kurosawa had not yet seen), which reconstructs the hero's life. The second kind of time is the kind of which no audience is aware—this is created in the alchemy of the cutting room, and it is telling that Kurosawa takes almost as long to cut as he does to shoot a film.

In *Rashomon* one remembers a series of seemingly actual, or at least realistic, actions. And yet the film—extraordinarily so, even for Kurosawa—is a mosaic. The average of the shorter cuts is 2 ft. (1 1/3 seconds) and, though there are several shorter cuts, and though scenes also last for minutes (the dialogue scenes under the gate), still, the average length of each shot is shorter in *Rashomon* than in any other of Kurosawa's films. This always has the effect of reality on the screen. As Naoki Noborikawa has noticed: "In *Rashomon* there is a scene where Tajomaru takes Takehiro [the husband] into the woods, then runs back and tells the woman that her husband has been bitten by a snake. The scenery through which the two together run to where he has left the husband tied up, is full of great natural beauty but the camera passes by it in one flash. I had thought that this was one shot, a swiftly moving pan. Seeing the film for the second time, however, I noticed that this was not so, and when I counted, on seeing it for the third time, I was surprised to discover that there were seven cuts in this small scene." As Kurosawa knew full well, one cuts fast and often for fast sections, slow and seldom for slow. But another reason for the extreme brevity of the *Rashomon* shots might be that the director knew he was asking his audience to look at the same material four or more times. He could not rely upon the novelty of the pictorial image to help sustain interest.

In addition, and maybe for the same reasons, he probably never moved the camera more than in *Rashomon.* The shooting script is full of directions to pan, to dolly in and out, etc. He used a favorite device of a dolly shot directly attached to a pan shot to get a continuity of action, and he was unusually careful of action continuity. This great mobility never calls attention to itself but gives the effect of continuous movement which we remember as being part of the style of the film.

All of these shots, stationary or moving, are superbly calculated as to their time on the screen and their effect there. There are few other directors who know so precisely the proper length for a given section of film. The shot of the dog carrying the human hand at the opening of *Yojimbo* is an example. One second less and we would not have known what he was carrying; one second more and the scene would have been forced, vulgar. In *Rashomon* the dagger drops into the ground and is allowed to quiver not often but just twice. All of the images are handled in this imaginative and economical manner.

Kurosawa rarely makes a mistake in his timing, and the inner or psychological timing of *Rashomon* is perfection. There are 408 separate shots in the body of the film (with 12 more for titles making a total of 420). This is more than twice the number in the usual film, and yet these shots never call attention to themselves—rather, they make it possible for us to feel this film, to be reached with immediacy, to be drawn into it, intellectually curious and emotionally aware. In a very special way, *Rashomon*—like any truly fine film—creates within its audience the very demand which it satisfies.

For a director as young as Kurosawa—he was then forty—and particularly for so young a Japanese director, the film is remarkably free from influences. Though some scenes owe much to Dovshenko's *Aerograd,* they owe nothing at all to Fritz Lang's *Siegfried* (an ostensible "influence" often mentioned) because the director has never seen it. The structure may owe something to *The Marriage Circle,* that Lubitsch film which Kurosawa—like most Japanese directors—remembers with affection and admiration, but the debt is very slight.

Of the style, Kurosawa has said only: "I like silent pictures and I always have. They are often so much more beautiful than sound pictures are. Perhaps they had to be. At any rate, I wanted to restore some of this beauty. I thought of it, I remember, in this way: one of the techniques of modern art is simplification, and that I must therefore simplify this film." Simplification is also one of the techniques of Japanese art and long has been. Those who noticed a "Japanese" look about some of the scenes (mainly their composition, aside from temple architecture, sand gardens and the like) were right though the director had perhaps reached this through his own knowledge of simplified painting techniques in the West—those of Klee and Matisse for example. Otherwise there is little "Japanese" influence. In fact the film is the complete opposite of the ordinary Japanese historical film in that it questions while they reaffirm; it is completely realistic, while they are always romantic; it is using its period as a pretext and a decoration while the ordinary period film aims at simple reconstruction. Despite foreign commentators on the subject, there is absolutely no influence at all from classical Japanese drama. Only the sword-fighting techniques owe something to the modern Japanese stage. Anyone who has ever seen Kabuki will realize the enormous difference between its acting style and that of *Rashomon*. The acting in the film is naturalistic, in the Japanese sense of the word. It is apparently unrestrained, and it is in the grand manner which the West once knew but has now almost lost. Indeed, Mifune as the bandit was so "grand" that even Japanese critics complained of overacting. There is another debt to the stage, however, though the stage is Japanese modern theater—the Shingeki. Since the budget was small the sets (there are only two—both studio sets—the gate and the prison courtyard) are deliberately stylized, deliberately simplified in the manner of modern stage scenery (again, not Kabuki scenery, which is flamboyant, detailed,

and very nineteenth century to the eye). Likewise, the costumes owe much to modern stage costumes, with their simplicity, their lack of ornament. Too—the music owes much to incidental-music methods on the modern Japanese stage.

That the music owes even more to another source is so notorious some critics (Western) have admitted that the film was partially spoiled for them. This is not the fault of the composer. The late Fumio Hayasaka was one of Japan's most individual and creative composers and it was Kurosawa himself who said "write something like Ravel's *Boléro*" —a work which in Japan had not yet become as clichéd as in the West. The composer complied and the results, as a matter of fact, do detract—particularly from the opening scenes.

Again and again in the films of Kurosawa one notices his musical tastes. Like most liberally-educated Japanese he has tended to like the chestnuts. He has already written how he once composed a thrilling scenario about cossacks while under the influence of *The Light Cavalry Overture*. Likewise one has noticed the strains of *Clair de lune* in *The Drunken Angel* and an orgy of Schubert in *One Wonderful Sunday*. This continues, though as a music-lover he has grown considerably more sophisticated and has recently spoken of his liking for Haydn, much in evidence in *Red Beard,* as is his new liking for late Brahms. Still, if one listens to the *Yojimbo* and *Sanjuro* scores one finds not only the *Boléro* again (this time on the English horn) but also that the big "Sanjuro" theme bears more than a close family resemblance to the opening melody of the Liszt *Second Hungarian Rhapsody*.

The shooting time for the film was unusually short (it was completed within a matter of weeks because most of the pre-production work had been done for some time) and is one of the few Kurosawa pictures that did not go over its budget. Daiei, though loudly announcing that it had no idea what the picture was about, nevertheless exhibited it with some care. It was given a formal premiere in what was then one of Tokyo's best theaters; the press was invited and it was given an initial run of two weeks (even now the usual run is only a single week) at all the theaters in the Daiei chain. Contrary to later legend, it was not a box office failure—it ranked fourth in 1950's Daiei listings of best money-earners. Nor did the audience seem to have trouble understanding it—though occasionally an apprehensive theater manager would hire a *benshi,* a lecturer-commentator, to talk throughout the film, giving hints as to what it was about.

Daiei, though more pleased than not with its second Kurosawa picture, made no attempt to detain him when he returned to Toho, and after the second and third runs were completed, shelved the picture. There it would probably have remained to this day had it not been for a series of fortuitous circumstances which led to its becoming the best-known Japanese film ever made.

Venice sent an invitation to Japan asking that a film be entered in the film festival. This was before Japan became as well-acquainted with film festivals as it is now, and there was consternation as to what to send. *Rashomon* was not even considered. In the meantime, at the request of Venice, Guilliana Stramigioli, then head of Italiafilm in Japan, had viewed a number of Japanese films, had seen *Rashomon,* and had liked it. When she recommended it, however, the suggestion was met with much opposition—particularly from Daiei which had neither hope nor faith in the film. It was with the greatest reluctance that they agreed to sending the film to the 1951 Venice Festival, where it won first prize.

Its winning what was then the best-thought-of cinema prize came as a profound shock to Japan. For one thing, it had not been made for export and there remains a long-standing Japanese prejudice that things not especially constructed for foreigners will not be understood by them. For another, the Japanese critics had not liked the film. Tadashi Iijima thought the film failed because of "its insufficient plan for visualizing the style of the original stories;" Tatsuhiko Shigeno objected to the language, saying that no robber would ever use words that big. Other critics thought the script was too complicated, or that the direction was too monotonous, or that there was too much cursing. What perhaps most surprised the Japanese however, was that an historical film (and they continued to think of *Rashomon* as "historical" in the "costume-picture" sense of the word) should prove acceptable to the West. This eventually led to a rash of Western-aimed "historical" films—of which *Gate of Hell* is the only surviving example—but initially critics were at a loss to explain its winning the Venice prize and its consequent popularity in most other countries. Eventually, they decided that it was because *Rashomon* was "exotic" (in the sense that *Gate of Hell* is truly exotic—and little else) and that foreigners like exoticism. Even now it is the rare critic who will admit that *Rashomon* could have had any other appeal to the West.

Once the rare critic is found, however, he will say—as several have—that the reason the West liked it was because the reasoning in the picture was "Western," by which is meant analytic, logical, and speculative—processes which are indeed not often found in pat-

terns of Japanese thought. Recognizing that the film questions reality yet champions hope, the critic says that this is not the Japanese way and, in a sense, he is right. Actually, of course, what had happened is that in this film (though not for the first time in Japanese cinema history) the confines of "Japanese" thought could not contain the director who thereby joined the world at large. *Rashomon* speaks to everyone, not just to the Japanese.

Kurosawa has said: "Japanese are terribly critical of Japanese films, so it is not too surprising that a foreigner should have been responsible for my film's being sent to Venice. It was the same way with Japanese woodcuts—it was the foreigners who first appreciated them. We Japanese think too little of our own things. Actually, *Rashomon* wasn't all that good, I don't think. Yet, when people have said to me that its reception was just a stroke of luck, a fluke, I have answered by saying that they only say these things because the film is, after all, Japanese, and then I wonder: Why do we all think so little of our own things? Why don't we stand up for our films? What are we so afraid of?"

Though Daiei did not retain the director, it followed the usual maxim of film companies: if you have a success, repeat it. In the following year Daiei's Keigo Kimura made *The Beauty and the Bandits* which was taken directly from *Rashomon,* and the much better *Tale of Genji* by Kimisaburo Yoshimura. Kurosawa himself, his reputation enormously enhanced by the international success of the film, went back to Toho to make *Ikiru.* Show-biz decided that Japan had made an unexampled breakthrough into the "foreign market," and the man on the street was as delighted over the Venice prize as he would have been had a Japanese athlete won an Olympics medal. Thus, in a way, the worth of *Rashomon* was partially obscured by its own success. It is only now, fifteen years later, that one realizes it is one of the few living films from Japan's cinematic past. Its frequent revivals in Japan, its frequent re-showings in other countries, its constant appearance in retrospectives, the fact that it is still talked about, still discussed, makes one finally realize that, along with *Ikiru* and *Seven Samurai,* it is a masterpiece.

# The Idiot

"I had wanted to make this film long before *Rashomon*," Kurosawa has said. "Since I was little I've liked Russian literature, and have read the greater part of it, but I find that I like Dostoevsky the best and had long thought that this book would make a wonderful film. He is still my favorite author, and he is the one—I still think—who writes most honestly about human existence. There is certainly no other author who is so attractive to me, so—well, so gentle.

"When I say gentle, I mean the kind of gentleness that makes you want to avert your eyes when you see something really dreadful, really tragic. He has this power of compassion. And then he refuses to turn his eyes away; he, too, looks; he, too, suffers. There is something which is more than human, better than human about him. He seems so terribly subjective, yet when you have finished the book you find that no more objective author exists.

"Anyway, this more than human quality, this compassion, this near godlike quality . . . this is what I admire in Dostoevsky, and what I love terribly in his Prince Myushikin."

## SOURCE

Like the novel, the picture opens with the return of the hero (Masayuki Mori, the husband in *Rashomon*, in the Myushikin role), and his meeting with the Rogozhin-character (Toshiro Mifune). Dostoevsky makes use of the Swiss upbringing of his hero to present—through his eyes—a picture of fashionable Russia. Kurosawa has his hero returning from tropical Okinawa—where he has been in an asylum—to the snow-country of Hokkaido. Myushikin thus goes from the provinces to the capital; Mori goes from one outpost to another. It is apparent that the social criticism of the novel—St. Petersburg seen through innocent eyes—is to have no place in the film.

Kurosawa's choice of Hokkaido as locale seems due to its long contact with Russia; it might be thought closer to Dostoevsky's milieu than any other area in Japan. In this northern island the traditional modes of Japanese living are not common. Chairs and tables are widely used, for example. At the same time the people have some of that peculiarly inward quality which one finds in snow-countries.

He made elaborate use of these differences. Much of the location work was done during the winter in Hokkaido and even in those portions shot in the studios near Tokyo he had snow falling in almost every scene. Since the Hokkaido people are historically more "Western," their differences were presumed to explain the extremely un-Japanese quality of the characters. Kurosawa must have thought this necessary because, though the differences between the Russian and Japanese character are great, the differences between the Dostoevsky character and the average Japanese are even greater. And, such was the director's fidelity to his favorite author, he did nothing at all toward adapting the characters to their Japanese milieu. They exist just as they do in the novel—except that they consequently appear misplaced.

The story continues with remarkable fidelity to the original. Mifune is in love with Nastasya Filippovna; Mori is in love with both her and Aglaïa. She in turn falls in love with Mori. He, however, is more drawn to Nastasya, learns she is someone's mistress, and offers her money. She, touched, throws the money which was to have bought her freedom into the fire, and gives herself to him. The men argue about the girl; the girls argue with each other. Then Mifune, seeing that he has lost her, stabs her. At the end both he and Mori (in a departure from Dostoevsky) go insane together.

The characters are recognizable, much of the dialogue is from the novel and yet the film is neither Dostoevsky nor Kurosawa. It is something like a French play in a New York production (or an American play in a Paris production) in that lines and characters are there but the spirit is entirely missing because the transposition has been literal.

A novel is more than its story and the film, by insisting upon fidelity, remains only story. Reduced to plot, anything which stood in the way of plot had to go. A telling and ambivalent line from the novel, such as: "You say you love two women at once? Then most likely you have never loved either of them,"—finds no place in this film because it suggests a psychological complication that only a much less literal film could have contained. In the same way, richly ambivalent figures in the novel (such as Aglaïa's father, here played by Takashi Shimura) are cut down to almost nothing.

In later adaptations (*The Throne of Blood* and *The Lower Depths*), Kurosawa was much less personally involved with his material and did not feel it necessary to be literal. Macbeth could rise and fall in medieval Japan, Gorky's characters could be made to fit an Edo Period tenement. In *The Idiot* all the characters must inhabit a compromise country—Hokkaido; Mifune must talk anarchism, and Mori, Christianity—issues not burning to the Japanese; Kurosawa must take a nineteenth-century novel and lay it in contemporary Japan, hoping that this would preserve the immediacy of Dostoevsky, and—instead—obscures it.

# TREATMENT

Kurosawa's refusal to tamper with Dostoevsky gave him endless problems. By insisting upon a complete respect for his author, he found that he had a lot of explaining to do. The first reel is almost entirely compounded of explanatory titles and a very verbal commentator, feverishly filling in the spectator, trying to give the past history of the main characters and their mutual relations. Naturally, this is done in terms of a précis and so the richness and perception of the original disappears.

This desire to "preserve" Dostoevsky weakens the film at every turn because Kurosawa's faith in his author was so strong, and so blind, that he seemed to feel that the mere act of photographing scenes from the novel would give the same effect on the screen as they do on the page. What occurs, however, is merely a devastating simplification. Aglaïa's mother, a very important and imposing figure in the novel, turns into the usual, complaisant Japanese film-mother. No longer is Aglaïa tormented by the goodness of her betrothed. She becomes a little Japanese girl who simply cannot make up her mind. All trace of grandness has left Nastasya. She is merely hysterical.

Just as Kurosawa's failure with character is complete, so—for the only time in his career—is his failure with the actors. Mori, one of Japan's most intelligent actors, is given an incomprehensible role

and reacts by trying to play everything with his face. It is a very intelligent face but alone cannot reproduce Myushikin. In an effort to produce the compassion he is supposed to be feeling, Mori sacrifices something even more important—dignity.

Mifune is given to overacting when unsure. Kurosawa usually restrains him or else, as in *Rashomon,* turns this occasional hamming to good account. In *The Idiot,* Mifune was encouraged to play Rogozhin as he "felt" and the results are embarrassing. The Aglaïa of Yoshiko Kuga (who played the young girl cured of tuberculosis in *Drunken Angel*) is merely petulant because the actress is given very little to do. Likewise, such talented actors as Chieko Higashiyama and Minoru Chiaki, as the mother and the secretary, merely appear.

The worst acting flaw is the casting of Setsuko Hara in the Nastasya Filippovna role. Though excellent as the young girl in *No Regrets for Our Youth,* she had, by 1951, become the "women's woman" of Japanese cinema and casting her in this film was like casting Joan Crawford in *The Brothers Karamazov.* Matters were made worse in that either she or Kurosawa had seen and been impressed by Cocteau's *Orphée.* Her make-up, her hair-style, her cape, her whole manner, is that of Maria Casarés and, right as that is for the Cocteau picture, it is absolutely ludicrous in the Kurosawa.

It was not that the actors did not try hard, it was that they tried so hard that it is wearing to watch them. And Kurosawa was so wrought-up over his feelings for Dostoevsky, so respectful of them that he allowed things in this film he never allowed before or after. He allows Setsuko Hara to make grand gestures with her cape, allows Mori little-theater mannerisms, allows Mifune to scream and roll his eyes, allows the art department to make a Frankenstein-type dungeon for Mifune to live in; allows the music department a field-

day among the light classics with long cribs from Grieg ("The Hall of the Mountain King") and unmerciful repetitions of *A Night on Bald Mountain.* Kurosawa had never allowed himself to be so indulgent with himself and with others—but now it was, somehow, all for Dostoevsky.

The interest in the film, then, is that despite its excesses (extreme even for a Japanese film: the first part of the picture, for example, has the grand title—*Love and Agony;* the second, the only slightly less grandiloquent *Love and Hatred*) or because of them, it shows the Kurosawa style evolving.

What we recognize in later pictures makes a first and often tentative appearance in this one. Kurosawa, who had long preferred action to talk, here forced himself to make room for talk in his cinematic vocabulary, and in this picture we see the extremely skillful movement of characters within the frame which became part of the visual style of *The Lower Depths* and *The Bad Sleep Well.* In a scene at the secretary's house, for example, he has Setsuko Hara in the middle and looking past the camera, flanked and balanced by Chiaki on one side and Mifune on the other, with Bokuzen Hidari (the priest in *The Lower Depths*) breaking the symmetry of the composition. When she stands, Chiaki sits down, thus presenting a new composition. This, to be sure, calls attention to itself in this film, but when Kurosawa used the same technique in *The Bad Sleep Well* it had become so much a part of the fabric of the picture that one does not consciously notice.

When Mifune pursues Mori through the snow, we are given another draft of the night-town sequence from *Ikiru.* Kurosawa, cutting very fast, opposes direction, purposely confuses left and right entrances into the frame, creating with only snow and two actors the feeling of real pursuit, of real danger, of real confusion.

Likewise, the party scene—where, as in Dostoevsky, the hero speaks of the execution he witnessed—is the first pale sketch for the magnificent wedding dinner that opens *The Bad Sleep Well*, the brilliant party which closes *The Lower Depths*. The same methods are employed: a great number of varied camera set-ups, the skillful moving of large numbers of people; the use of composition to indicate the person of interest. It is all very tentative in *The Idiot*, but is also already a part of the director's style.

The nocturnal ice-festival, apparently intended for ironic contrast (happy skaters, unhappy principal characters) does not come off at any level but it contains the germ for the fire-festival in *The Hidden Fortress*. The wipe—Kurosawa's favorite punctuation mark—is much misused in this film in that its use is excessive, occurring as it does even within scenes; nevertheless, it more than occasionally appears in the precisely right place—as it invariably does in, say, *Seven Samurai*.

At the same time, in bondage to Dostoevsky though he insisted upon being, Kurosawa—being himself—illuminates many passages of this film. A piece of accidental good fortune is turned to good account very early in the picture. Though *hakuchi* is Japanese for 'idiot,' it is not often used. It is a medical word and carries little of the everyday connotations of, say, *l'idiot*. But the word for "fool" (*baka*) is heard every day. It is a favorite with the Japanese who may use it affectionately (with children or animals), or with each other and really mean it. *Baka* has a use in Japanese which 'fool' or 'idiot' have never had in English. This allows for a number of scenes in which ordinary conversation has a most unfortunate effect on the hero. He seems to hear *baka* everywhere, as indeed he would. In the film this has the odd and enriching effect (unobtainable to Dostoevsky) of making him live continually with his foolishness, his idiocy, his madness. Mifune uses it playfully in the first scene of the film, Mori reacts, and though we are later told much, much more, we are already in possession of all we really need to know.

There are other indications of Kurosawa. At one point the girl's parents are talking and are disturbed by the sound of snow sliding from the roof, a minor avalanche, common enough perhaps but something which in the context of their conversation makes them look apprehensively at each other. It is like the call of the crow in *The Lower Depths*. What it means is not explained, and an explanation is not necessary because we feel its effect.

When Mori is talking about the execution (in the film it is a firing squad and not a guillotine) the sound track carries the flashback. That is, we hear the tread of the squad and then the volley. The scene is brilliant precisely because here Kurosawa gives us the actuality of memory and spares us direct explanation.

Kurosawa also telescopes time in this very long picture. For example, the secretary is waiting for a reply to a letter sent to the daughter. We see her reading, hear her voice, and this sound continues over the scenes of his waiting. Her own answer (her own voice) follows at once, and we see Mori giving him this letter. He opens it in time for the sound track to carry his own voice reading the final and most telling sentence.

The courtship between the hero and the daughter is handled very imaginatively. The opening scene of this sequence finds them at the piano. She picks out a little tune. A number of short scenes follow, all variations on the first one. The music is a set of variations which uses as a theme the tune she first picked out. This is not done incisively and the sequence is too short to make its full effect but this is the beginning of such musico-dramatic insights as those which we are given in *The Bad Sleep Well*.

The final sequence is quite different from the Dostoevsky. Nastasya is dead, having been stabbed by Rogozhin-Mifune. Mori enters and finds the room cold. "Can't we have a fire?" he asks. Mifune says no and turns to look at the stove. It is cold. The meaning of this shot is explained in that earlier Nastasya's great explosive scenes were intercut with shots of the stove burning so fiercely that flame and smoke were escaping from the top. Now it sits, iron cold. Mori asks: "And her—is she asleep?" Mifune does not look at the stove again. He turns and looks at the camera, at *us*. This is unnerving. His look is an accusation and, at the same time, it recalls the only other scene in the film where a character looked at the camera: when Nastasya first realizes that she loves the hero. It is a very powerful moment precisely because it is not logical.

The best scene in the film has no counterpart in Dostoevsky and indicates what the picture might have been had not respect paralyzed Kurosawa. Mifune and Mori have been arguing. In the following scene Mifune will stalk Mori through the snow. In between, however, and for no logical reason, but apparently because it felt right, Kurosawa inserts an invented scene, a very lovely one where Mifune takes Mori to have tea with his mother. She is very deaf, very religious, realizes that she has no cakes and so, with the most gracious and charming of smiles, takes the offering from the family altar and they together eat it. Intellectually, this tender scene has no place in the film; emotionally, it is just right. It is so good and so strong that it even carries and for a time we "believe" the chase through the snow which follows.

Such interpolated scenes become more common in later Kurosawa (as in the fine scene—not in Shakespeare—where the cutting of the forest drives the birds into the castle in *Throne of Blood*) but this one remains one of the most beautiful. It is both ironic and telling that the best scene in *The Idiot* should be the single scene that is not in the novel. It is perfect for Dostoevsky and perfect for Kurosawa.

# PRODUCTION

Kurosawa has spoken of the seeming subjectivity of Dostoevsky, and contrasted it with his real objectivity. He might have remembered this when making the film because Kurosawa himself became so "subjective" that the film fails to communicate what was intended. Not that Kurosawa believes it failed. "I think I succeeded pretty well in doing what I wanted to do. I distorted to be sure, but I don't think I have ever put more of myself into any other picture."

He certainly never put so much labor into a film and has spoken at length about it. "Making the film was very hard work. It was extraordinarily difficult to make. At times I felt as though I just wanted to die. Dostoevsky is very heavy and now I was under him. I knew just how those enormous *sumo* wrestlers feel. All the same it was a marvelous experience for me."

The film was very badly received. "People complained about being bored . . . but then Dostoevsky's world *is* boring. *I* got so tired of it that I thought I just couldn't go on. . . . Dostoevsky's novels are, well, like subjecting the human spirit to a scientific experiment. The people are put into an extreme situation, a pure situation, and then he watches what happens to them. . . . If I do say so myself I think that after making this picture my own powers increased considerably."

The experience of making the film was so subjective that it was as though Kurosawa had placed himself in this extreme situation and then watched himself. "All the same, it was a marvelous experience for me," is a statement which Kurosawa has several times stressed in speaking of this film. It is as though the experience counted more for him than the film.

At the same time: " . . . people have said it was a failure. I don't think so. At least, as entertainment, it is not a failure. Of all my films, people wrote me most about this one. If it had been as bad as all that, they wouldn't have written me. I trust my audience. They understood what I was saying. It was a new kind of melodrama [in Japan the word 'melodrama' has no nuance of the derogatory; we should perhaps use the term psychological drama with the understanding that the psychology is shown by action] and this the audience understood. That is why I wanted to make the picture at Shochiku." [Shochiku had a reputation for making action-films of the melodrama variety.]

Perhaps because the film was so intensely personal, Kurosawa reacted to Shochiku's suggestion that this extraordinarily long two-part film be cut, not with his customary firmness and tact but with real anger. Yamamoto, his teacher, has remembered: " . . . they wanted to cut the film because it was too long and he sent me a long letter in which he literally poured out his anger [with them]. It seemed as though he could not control it. He went so far as to write that if they wanted to cut it, they might as well do so lengthwise—from

beginning to end. When it was finally released—in its cut form—I have literally never seen Kurosawa so furious."

"The reviews were terrible [and those from America where it was shown in its cut form in 1963 were equally bad] and if I had not made this film perhaps the critics would not have so had it in for me afterwards. Still, on thinking it over, I suppose that any director ought at least once to have been attacked and embarrassed to this extent. One should be brave enough to make this kind of 'mistake.'

"Directors are too smart. They avoid this kind of 'failure.' Yet, to make a failure is no disgrace. Still, I would have been happy if at least one critic had admired *something* about it."

And there are many admirable things about *The Idiot,* but the single interesting thing about it is Kurosawa's attitude toward it and toward Dostoevsky. He himself called *Drunken Angel* and *Ikiru* "films in the Dostoevsky manner," which they certainly are. *Red Beard* is the most compassionate, the most "Dostoevskian" of them all. Oddly, in *The Idiot,* the "Dostoevsky manner" is nowhere in evidence. It is as though in this single picture he did not take that necessary step away which brings artist and material into perfect focus. That he did not, indicates his extreme reverence for Dostoevsky but, more than this, it makes one wonder if any artist can ever do real justice to that in which he himself is deeply and personally involved. The paradox is that disassociation is necessary for creation.

In *Ikiru,* which appeared a year and a half after this picture, the quality which Kurosawa finds essential to Dostoevsky—compassion—appears in a picture of unparalleled power. Without the trials, disappointments, mistakes, and uncertainties of *The Idiot,* it might not have appeared at all.

# Ikiru

**1952**

"Sometimes I think of my death," Kurosawa has written: "I think of ceasing to be ... and it is from these thoughts that *Ikiru* came." The story of a man who knows he is going to die, the film is a search for affirmation. The affirmation is found in the moral message of the film, which, in turn, is contained in the title: *ikiru* is the in- transitive verb meaning 'to live.' This is the affirmation: existence is enough. But the art of simple existence is one of the most difficult to master. When one lives, one must live entirely—and that is the lesson learned by Kanji Watanabe, the petty official whose life and death give the meaning to the film.

# THE STORY

Kurosawa's example is an extreme one. Watanabe not only knows that he is to die, he also knows when. He says to the doctor: "Be honest with me . . . . Tell me the truth . . . tell me it is cancer." When he leaves, the doctor asks the intern: "If you were like him, with only half a year to live, what would you do?"

The film answers the question, and we are shown the snares and delusions to which man in crisis is subject. Watanabe's first reaction is fear. In bed that night he cries, huddled under his blanket. His second is to lose himself in his family. He cannot. His son—the person closest to him since his wife is dead—has married, become different, alienated. Finding no solace there he begins, for the first time in his life, to doubt; and to doubt means to feel, to begin to live. He doubts the office, doubts his twenty-five years of faithful service, and—most difficult of all—doubts his son.

Awakened by knowledge of his death (for, as the narrator has observed, "he is like a corpse, and actually he has been dead for the past twenty-five years"), it is approaching death which makes him realize for the first time that freedom is his, life is his, has always been his, and that he cannot avoid it. He is alone and free. All of his habits, those regular comforts which made life bearable, the empty eight hours at the city office which seemed to give meaning, the presence of a son which seemed to indicate companionship, all of these no longer offer solace.

He decides to live for himself, to spend his last months in pleasure; draws his money from the bank and goes out for a good time.

He meets a writer and eventually tells him he has gastric cancer.

*Writer:* Then, you shouldn't drink like this . . . it's like committing suicide.

*Watanabe:* Oh, no. It's not that easy. I had thought it would be a quick death, but it's hard to die. And I can't die just yet. I don't know what I've been living for all of these years.

. . .

*Writer:* Does it taste good?

*Watanabe:* No, it doesn't. But it makes me forget. I'm drinking . . . now because . . . well, because I never did before. I know it is like drinking poison. I mean . . . it seems like poison. But it's so soothing.

. . .

*Writer:* I see that adversity does have its virtues and that man finds truth in misfortune . . . having cancer has made you taste life. Man is such a fool. It is always just when he is going to leave it that he finally discovers how beautiful life can be. And even then people who realize this are rare. Some die without ever once knowing what life is. You're a fine man because you are fighting against death, and that is what impresses me. Up to now you've been life's slave but now you are going to be its master. And it is man's duty to enjoy life. It is against nature not to. Man must have a greed for life. We are taught that that is immoral, but it isn't. The greed to live is a virtue.

They decide to go out on the town, to really live, to have a good time. They first play pin-ball.

*Writer:* See this little silver ball. That is you. That is your life. This is a marvelous machine. A wonderful machine that frees you from all the worries of life. It is an automatic dream machine.

In the street a girl snatches Watanabe's hat.

*Writer:* Oh, to try and get it back would cost you more than it is worth. Come on . . . we're going to buy you a new hat to say good-bye to your old life with.

In a bar, they talk to the hostess:

*Writer:* Take a good look at him. See? He's god and he's carrying a cross called cancer. Most people die off the minute they learn this. Not him. He's different. From that moment on *he* started to live.

They go to a dance hall, a beer hall, a strip show.

*Writer:* Oh, that's not art. A strip tease isn't art. It is too direct. It is more direct than art. That woman's body up there— it's a big juicy steak, it's a glass of gin, it's hormone extract, streptomycin, uranium!

And, in the early hours, in a bar, we find Watanabe singing, having asked the pianist to play this song which he remembers:

*Life is so short,*
*Fall in love, dear maiden,*
*While your lips are still red,*
*And before you are cold,*
*For there will be no tomorrow.*
*Life is so short,*
*Fall in love, dear maiden,*
*While your hair is still black,*
*And before your heart withers,*
*For today will not come again.*

Pleasure (like fear, like family solace) is empty. He does not again attempt the experiment of artificial happiness. Rather, he decides, he will devote himself to someone. He chooses a girl from the office and for a short time he is happy with her. They are like children, playing childish games together. She, for example, makes him guess the nicknames she has for everyone in the office.

*Girl:* I gave you a nickname too but I won't tell you. It wouldn't be nice.

*Watanabe:* Please do. I don't mind. Anyway, I'd like it if you did.

*Girl:* All right . . . the mummy.

Watanabe: . . .
Girl: I'm sorry.
Watanabe: That's all right.

    . . .

    For these past thirty years . . . I've been just like a mummy. Oh, don't misunderstand. I'm not angry you called me a mummy. It's true. But the reason I became like one is . . . it was all for my son's sake. But now he doesn't appreciate it.
    He—

Girl: But you can't very well blame him for that. After all, he didn't *ask* you to become like a mummy. Parents are all alike. My mother says the same thing. She says: I have suffered because of you. But, if you think of it . . . well, I appreciate having been born. I really do. But I wasn't responsible for it.

    The son and his wife quite misunderstand this friendship and when the father tries to tell him about his cancer the son jumps to the conclusion that he wants to speak about the girl and forbids him. Instead, and with a cruelty completely unintentional, he begins talking about rights and money. As the narrator says: " . . . all these rumors, all these surmises came to a single conclusion: that Mr. Watanabe was acting very foolishly. Yet, to Watanabe, these same actions were the most meaningful of his entire life."

    And his friendship with the girl is also delusion. He has forgotten that she, too, is a human being, that she cannot exist simply as an object for his own passion to live. With the best will in the world, she cannot allow him to live through and for her. The last time they meet he tries to explain:

Watanabe: I have less than a year to live. When I found that out . . .

somehow I was drawn to you. Once when I was a child I nearly drowned. It is just that feeling. Darkness is everywhere and there is nothing for me to hold on to no matter how hard I try. There is only you.

Girl: What about your son?
Watanabe: Don't even talk about him. I have no son, I am all alone . . . . he is far away somewhere. Just as my parents were far away when I was drowning . . . .
Girl: But what help am I?
Watanabe: You . . . just to look at you makes me feel better. It warms this . . . this mummy heart of mine. And you are so kind to me. No, that's not it. You are so young, so healthy. No, that's not it either. You are so full of life. And me . . . I'm envious of that. If only for one day I would like to be like you before I die. I won't be able to die, somehow, unless I can be. Oh, I want to do something. Only you can show me. I don't know what to do. I don't know how to do it. Maybe you don't know either, but, please, if you can, show me how to be like you.
Girl: I don't know . . .
Watanabe: How can I be like you?
Girl: All I do is work—and eat. That's all.
Watanabe: Really?
Girl: Yes, really. I just make toys like this. (She puts a mechanical rabbit on the table in front of them—she works in a toy factory now.) And that is all I do, but I feel as though I am friends with all the children in Japan. Mr. Watanabe, why don't you do something like that, too?

*Watanabe:* What could I do at the office?
*Girl:* Well, that's true. Then resign and find something else.
*Watanabe:* It is too late. . . . No, it isn't too late. It isn't impossible . . . . I *can* do something if I really want to.

This marks the point of Watanabe's resolve and it is right here that Kurosawa deliberately breaks the film. The narrator simply tells us that Watanabe is dead. We have been shown that there is no hope and no solace for the soul in crisis. Watanabe has run from one shelter to the next and found each to be no shelter at all. Going blind, he at last sees; dying, he finally discovers what we all know but forget, because we are unable to live with the knowledge: that we are naked, alone, and alive. *Since* he cannot return to mindless comfort, he at last knows what it means to live. Having gained this knowledge, he dies. But he has gained more—and in the second half of the picture we discover what it is.

# TREATMENT

As with *The Drunken Angel* and *High and Low,* Kurosawa choose to break *Ikiru* in half. In the 1948 film the reason was that he was tracing a parallel between doctor and gangster; in the 1963 picture, he was concerned with practice and theory (and illusion and reality) on a very large scale. In *Ikiru* it is important that the second half becomes posthumous because much of the irony of the film results from a (wrong) assessment of Watanabe's actions made by others after his death. Or, to put it another way, we have seen what is real—Watanabe and his reactions to his approaching death. Now, in the second half, we see illusion—the reactions of others, their excuses, their accidental stumblings on the truth, their final rejection of both the truth and of Watanabe.

Perhaps for this reason Kurosawa insists so much upon the 'reality' of the first half, and uses all cinematic techniques to make certain that we become absolutely convinced of this reality. Not that he insists upon the literal, far from it. He, along with the writer whom Watanabe meets, knows that "art is not direct." Rather he uses a variety of styles (expressionistic, impressionistic, etc.) in conjunction with almost all of the techniques of which the camera is capable.

The picture begins with plain lettering, white on black (a bit like that of *Citizen Kane* which this film in more than one way resembles but which Kurosawa had not yet seen) and under it is what becomes the main musical theme of the film. It is a fugue or, to be more precise, a *ricercare*. Whether this (*ricercare* means to search for again, to hunt for, or to follow) was intentional or not, it was certainly a happy thought because this, after all, is what the film is about. The first scene is a close-up of an x-ray. We are thus shown Watanabe's inside before we are shown his outside, and we are shown the cancer (literally) as defining the man. In the same way, throughout the first half of the film, we are shown his body and what he does; in the second half the body has disappeared and we are shown—through the conversation of others—his soul, what remains of him. As we see the x-ray the narrator begins. Narration is unrealistic but it is at the same time necessarily dispassionate. And an anonymous third-person, as Kurosawa knows, gives a credulity that very often a simple exhibition, a mere showing, does not. The narrator is completely straightforward, refers to the person we will know as Watanabe as "our hero" and informs us that he himself knows nothing about the cancer. There is a direct cut to Watanabe—the cut is from the inside of the man therefore to his outside, and he is shown at the municipal office revealed in a habitual gesture (one which will later have much meaning for him)—looking at his watch.

Having shown us the hero, Kurosawa shows us his habitat. The camera cuts back to reveal the typical Japanese governmental office: piles of paper everywhere and no one doing any work. It is the picture of bureaucracy.

The girl in the office (Miki Odagiri) suddenly begins to laugh. When reprimanded, she says she was laughing at a joke in a magazine. Commanded to read, she unwillingly does so:

'You've never had a day off, have you?'

'No.'

'Why? Are you indispensable?

'No. I don't want them to find out that they can do without me.'

No one laughs, but Watanabe (Takashi Shimura) looks up. He, it turns out, has, as a matter of fact, never taken off a single day. It is as though he has not heard. He goes back to stamping papers while the narrator says that he has been dead for a quarter-century but that "before that he had some life in him. He even tried to work." This is accompanied by Watanabe looking for something to clean his seal with. He opens a desk drawer full of old documents. The top one reads: *A Plan to Raise Office Efficiency*. He tears off the first page, cleans his seal, throws the paper into the basket and goes on working. He looks up, abstracted, frowns, then takes some medicine, while the narrator says:

Is this right,—being busy, oh, so busy, yet doing nothing at all? Well, before our hero thinks seriously about this, his stomach must get a bit worse and some more useless hours must accumulate.

Having shown us the municipal office, Kurosawa next shows us how it works—or rather how it doesn't. A group of housewives comes with a complaint (a sump in the neighborhood is making their children sick—a reminiscence from *Drunken Angel*—couldn't something be done about it? a playground perhaps?) and they approach the window plainly marked:

*THIS IS YOUR WINDOW. IT IS YOUR LINK WITH THE CITY HALL. WE WELCOME BOTH REQUESTS AND COMPLAINTS.*

What happens is that the housewives are directed from one department to the next (shown in a series of short, wipe-punctuated scenes in which each department head speaks directly to the camera as though to the housewives) until they have made a great circle and are back where they started. (At the end of the picture this useless cycle is started again when—despite all the vows made during the wake—the clerks, who have not changed, not reformed in the slightest, send a group of housewives off to the next department.) It is a real *ricercare* in itself—and one leading nowhere.

In the next sequence the second-in-command (Kamatari Fujiwara) looks toward Watanabe's desk but Watanabe is not there. He is at the hospital. (The punctuation is very interesting here. It is: Fujiwara looking at desk / cut / empty desk / cut / Watanabe in the hospital corridor / dissolve / Watanabe at the hospital drinking

fountain. One would have expected the dissolve to occur between the desk and the corridor scenes, after all it is a new location and presumably time has elapsed. Kurosawa, however, thinks of it in another way. He is saying that Fujiwara, desk, and Watanabe are all of a unit, that they belong to the office. However (dissolve), something odd, something important, will happen to Watanabe in the hospital; in a way, in the hospital Watanabe is a different man). (Scenes of crisis are interpreted by directors in various ways. For Antonioni, for example, the scene is usually one of travel: the island, the strange town, the villa in *L'Avventura*; the known-place revisited, the villa visited for the first time in *La Notte*; the long walks in new surroundings, the boy's house explored in *L'Eclisse*. For Kurosawa, the place of crisis is often the hospital. In *Drunken Angel, The Quiet Duel, Red Beard* all important scenes are in the hospital. In *Record of a Living Being* the final agony is in a clinic. In *High and Low* the finale begins in a hospital and the kidnapper is an intern. In *Stray Dog* Mifune's vigil and break down is in a hospital. Here, in *Ikiru*, the crisis begins in a hospital—ironic in that a hospital is, by definition, a place in which to get well.) He has indeed become different because a talkative patient, talking about cancer, happens to describe Watanabe's own symptoms, even describes what the doctor will say. And it happens just as he has said it would. Watanabe knows that he will die and he is crushed.

We are shown this directly (his expression) and indirectly. The final scene in the hospital sequence has been, again, a close-up of the x-ray and the only sound has been that of the buzzing of the fluorescent light. There is a direct cut to Watanabe walking along a busy street. As we watch, we feel that something is wrong with the scene, though we do not know what it is until, with a great roar of sound, a truck nearly runs the dazed Watanabe down. Then we see that until the noise of the truck, the scene had been completely silent, despite the cars and people in it. It is as though we, like Watanabe, had become deaf through shock. This is the first of many techniques which Kurosawa uses in this picture to make us view through Watanabe's eyes, to empathize completely with him.

The strongest of all of these is toward the end of the night-town sequence when he is singing. This is shown in full close-up and Watanabe is gazing straight into the camera, tears running down his cheeks as he sings this song he remembers from his youth and which now has such meaning for him. It is like gazing into a mirror, and rarely has feeling of empathy been so strongly evoked.

One of the most involved of these subjective-making devices, and one of the most beautiful sequences in any of Kurosawa's pictures, is when he goes home, discovers that his son will not understand, and prepares for bed.

It opens with a casual inspection of the room. It is an anonymous room with a shrine in an alcove, some clothes hanging on a hook, a clock on the table. The camera inspects it much as it does the room of the lawyer in *Scandal* (a character much like that of Watanabe). This definition of a person through his surroundings is insisted upon in the former picture where the camera stoops, peers, turns, gazes, and finally lights on the picture of the daughter, where it pauses. In *Ikiru,* the definition is much more precise. We are given a short look at the room and then Watanabe himself enters it. The following sequence is so magnificently made that it must be quoted in full.

Watanabe kneels and opens the shrine. Inside is a picture of his dead wife. Close-up of the picture. Close-up of Watanabe looking at it. Big close-up of the picture. Dissolve to scene of a hearse being driven away, shot through the rain-flecked windshield of a moving car.

Cut to inside the car, the back seat, where sit a much younger Watanabe, his brother and sister-in-law and a child, his son Mitsuo. They are apparently going to the funeral and the elders are talking about her youth, about how hard it must have been to leave this child behind. Cut to the hearse. It is turning a corner. Cut to the child, watching it. Cut to hearse (always seen through the windshield, its image always cut by the wipers). Cut to the child who suddenly says:

Upstairs, in his son's room, the radio is on. It is playing a song that the couple was humming earlier: *Too Young to Love.*
At the close-up, the song fades and the sound-track carries a hesitant, very Mahler-like oboe theme which is derived from the opening fugue.
The sound of windshield wipers is added, below the music.

*Hurry. We must hurry. Mother is leaving us behind.*

Cut to the back-seat. Watanabe is holding the child. Cut to Watanabe's room.
He is in front of the shrine. At the sound of laughter, he looks up at the ceiling. Cut to another room. He, much younger, is at his

*The song, Too Young;* sudden laughter from above; it would seem the son and his wife are making love.

brother's and they are talking about his remarrying. Watanabe is idly listening then looks up as though to answer but on the sound-track we hear his son's grown-up voice:

Under their talk, the oboe melody.

*Father.*

Cut to Watanabe's room. He rushes to the stairs and is half up them, so great is his sudden affection for his son. Cut to Watanabe as seen from the top of the stairs while his son (in another room) says:

*Goodnight. And lock up, will you?*

Watanabe rests his head against the top stair, then slowly backs down into the darkness. He whispers:

*Mitsuo!*

Cut to the entryway. He slowly closes it, locks the door. From the corner he takes a baseball bat and jams it tight, as is apparently his nightly habit, against the sliding door so that it cannot be opened from the outside. Cut to a close-up of the bat.

At the same time, the sound of bat hitting a ball, the roar of a crowd cheering a home-run. At the same time, the oboe tune, under the crowd noises.

Cut to Watanabe at a baseball game. He turns to the man next to him and begins to tell him that the batter is his son. Cut to the young Mitsuo running for home base. At the same time Watanabe's (old) voice calling:

*Mitsuo!*

Cut to Watanabe in the stands, the man next to him saying:

*What's that guy think he's doing?*

| Image | Sound |
|---|---|
| Flash-pan to the ball game, something has gone wrong, perhaps it was Mitsuo's fault. | |
| Cut to Watanabe in his room. He was standing, now he sits and the camera elevators down with him. Halfway through this action, cut to the ball game where Watanabe is sitting down, and camera elevators down with him, thus completing the act of sitting begun years later in his room. But the action is not fully completed before there is a cut to Watanabe and his son in an elevator (the entire scene this 'elevatoring' up), the boy on a stretcher, he is ill. He tells the boy that an appendix operation is nothing (and this perhaps was what happened at the ball-game: Mitsuo became ill). He asks his father if he isn't going to stay.<br>His father says: | The oboe tune continuing.<br><br>*I . . . I have some things to do.* |
| Cut to the entryway. Watanabe's lips are not moving but over the music we hear: | *Mitsuo! Mitsuo!* |
| Cut to his room—he is standing there, not moving. | The sudden blast of a train whistle. |
| Cut to the railway station. It is full of people and flags and banners. Young soldiers are being seen off to war. Cut to Mitsuo, now older, in his army uniform. He is frightened and grave but | A military march, but over it the melody of the oboe, hesitant, constrained, yet very expressive. |
| he salutes. The train begins to move, suddenly he makes a gesture of supplication: | *Father. Father!* |
| Watanabe, standing beneath him, moves, then stops. The train is gathering speed. Cut to the train pulling out, Watanabe standing. His lips do not move. | The oboe melody is drowned by sound of the train.<br><br>*Mitsuo! Mitsuo!*<br>The noise of the train suddenly fades and it departs in silence except for Watanabe's saying the name of his son over and over again.<br>The final *Mitsuo!* occurs when he stops, midway on the stairs. |
| Slow dissolve from this scene to the stairs as he climbs them, then stops half way. Dissolve to his room. He hangs up his kimono. He puts his trousers under the pallet to press them, as he has apparently always done. | |
| He winds his pocket watch and puts it on the table. He reaches for the alarm-clock, then drops it. He does not move. Seconds pass. Then, as though in terror, he suddenly crawls under the covers, pulls them over his head. | The sound of Watanabe's weeping. |
| Cut to further away, Watanabe and the wall. On the wall, high up, is a framed citation. Cut to the citation, which reads: *Letter of Commendation. Mr. Kenji Watanabe is hereby given recognition for twenty-five years of devoted service. April 10, 1946. Signed: Chairman, National Mayor's Association.* | The sound of weeping continues, slowly fading. |

This magnificent sequence, besides being one of the most compelling in modern cinema, is, at the same time, directly relevant to both Watanabe as we know him and Watanabe as he will be revealed in the second half of the film. He is a man who has no present and he certainly has no future. Therefore, he lives in the past—as we have seen. At the same time, his apotheosis (the word is not too grand) is also revealed to us *in the past*. The entire wake sequence is a raking through time just as this sequence has been evocation of time.

Kurosawa is showing us something else as well. Here we have been shown the past, and in the night town sequences we are shown the immediate present, and in the final wake sequence (though we seem to be viewing the past again, since we have made a chronological jump of half a year) we are shown the future because what we are told and shown has *become* Watanabe's future. He has become much more than simply dead. Just as, dying, he learns to live; so, dead, he becomes more alive for others than he ever was before.

First, however, having shown the past as fallacy, Kurosawa must do the same for the present, and this he does in the celebrated night-town sequences, a *tour de force* of cinema which brings the immediate immediately before us. It is so full of things that outside printing its scenario (and even then one misses much of the subtlety: in the sequence given above, for example, there is no indication of cut length, nor of camera position, though these two components are essential to the power generated by what we are shown) one may only indicate some of them.

Enormous use is made of mirrors, reflecting surfaces, the shiny tops of automobiles, prisms—all those things which reflect (distort) reality. Since one of the points is that Watanabe is trying to escape into the present, into masses of other people, there is one tremendous scene of a packed dancehall, hundreds of people milling around in the frame (very cleverly cut so that each entrance of the 'rhumba' band—trumpets standing, trombones standing, saxes standing, begins a new scene and the cut occurs on the cadence of the music), the very image of packed humanity.

There is music everywhere, most of it ironic in its context. In the bar, it is *J'ai deux amours* (the old Josephine Baker recording); while Watanabe is vomitting, the music is *Music-Mambo—Take it Away;* the whores in the auto sing *Come on 'a My House.* (The entire sequence is like that in *Scandal*—though much more accomplished—where, over the cries of the drunks, *Buckles and Bows* rises and falls; and the next image—whores, writer, Watanabe, in the neon-flecked car—is much like that after the sentimental orgy where Mifune and Shimura sit by a pond and look at the stars reflected in the water.) At the same time score and sound-effects also comment. The pin-ball is introduced with a "magical" passage on the celesta, and the entire adventure begins with a faint train-whistle in the distance, that really magical sound which seems to promise opportunity,

adventure, romance. Again, when Watanabe has returned after having (presumably) vomited blood, there is another train sound. But this is no dim, romantic whistle. It is the hurtling, brutal, tearing sound of a train passing directly overhead.

There is also constant motion: flash-pans, elevators, elaborate dollies, all enforcing the idea of the living, the actual. There is even a literary reference: at the beginning, the writer fancifully refers to himself as Mephistopheles ("but a good one, who won't ask to be paid") and then notices at his feet a black dog—familiar to the devil himself—thus enforcing the Faustian element that others have noticed in this film. And indeed it would be possible to build a like morality around the night-town scenes, each as one of the deadly sins (strip-show as lust, for example), each also as one of the stations of the cross along Watanabe's way, "carrying his cross called cancer." All are welded into a sequence of the most superb brilliance, filled with visual irony, and musical ridicule. And it does not end—it slides directly into the next sequence. There is, at the end of the night-town scenes, a left-to-right dolly of the moving car / cut / a left to right pan showing Watanabe on the street (the morning after) still in his new hat. The reason why the sequence leads directly into the next is that this (relations with the girl) is also a part of the present, the *now,* its serious rather than frivolous face. We must be shown that it, too, is no refuge.

The scene where he learns the falseness, the impossibility, of love for another, is treated with the most refined irony. He and she have their last meeting in a coffee shop, traditionally the haunt of the young in Japan. The phonograph is playing *Poupée valsante* (arranged for violin and piano), just the sort of thing one hears in "artistic" coffee shops, just the sort of thing its young customers like. While Watanabe is struggling with his confession there is much bustle on a further balcony which the girl looks at enviously (all people her own age) from time to time. The music has changed. It is *The Parade of the Wooden Soldiers* and over its jaunty strains Watanabe tries to explain himself. At the moment of truth, when he sees that it is not yet too late, there is a great commotion among the far youngsters and a cake is brought in. Watanabe grabs the rabbit and rushes for the stairs. At that moment a young girl, pretty, well-dressed, comes up the stairs and the others begin *Happy Birthday*—it is a surprise birthday party. As in *Record of a Living Being,* youth goes up the stairs, age goes down and the song which all of us recognize as connected with our happiest childhood days rings in our ears as it does in Watanabe's.

And it continues, for in the next scene we see him doing something no public official ever does. He is rummaging in his desk and finds a long-neglected petition, asking that some wasteland be turned into a playground. He takes the petition, and rushes out of the office, followed by the baffled Fujiwara. *Happy Birthday* rings like a fanfare on the sound track. The glass door swings to and fro. It is raining outside.

On this simple cut Kurosawa ends the first half of the film. The evidence about past and present is all before us now.

Next is a picture of Watanabe on the funeral altar and the narrator says: "Five months later our hero died." From now on we will delve into this past which has become Watanabe's future, the future he made for himself in those last five months. Just as he and we together have unscrambled his past, so we must alone now unscramble his future.

The second half of the film is almost all in Watanabe's room (now practically unrecognizable in its funeral trappings) and consists of the all-night wake. Here, all is still, there is very little movement and nothing of the visual prodigality of the first half. It is like *High and Low* in this way (though the final half of that film is the busy one)—and the reasons are the same: we have seen various kinds of reality, now we will see illusion—and compare.

But we must see it in context and consequently the entire office force is gathered for the wake, complete with all the petty jealousies and ambitions which are so much a part of a government office. Little by little we are given the story. Watanabe died in the snow. He froze to death, he committed suicide. No, it was cancer, but he didn't know he had it. No, he knew he had it—and further, he made the park. What nonsense, everyone knows that the Department of Parks made the park—how could one man make it? Between this present and the recent past we shuttle back and forth, and see what indeed really happened. Watanabe with a patient insistence one would not have thought possible, forces his way through the bureaucracy, sitting, humbly waiting, refusing to move, until he gets what he wants. He strength is incredible—even the local gang does not intimidate him, even the mayor does not intimidate him. Like the detective in *Stray Dog* he struggles on, hopeless yet believing, devoting all of his life, all of his energy to the park and getting it completed.

What he goes through (and we see it all in flash-back, told by the office-workers who are very often unconscious of revealing what they do) is so extreme that it offers a severe indictment of Japanese municipal government (completely deserved) but the point is not so much what he fights, as that he *continues* to fight. Fujiwara is astonished at what Watanabe puts up with and asks: "Doesn't it make you angry to be insulted like this?"

*Watanabe:*   No, I can't be angry with anyone. I don't have the time to be angry.

He grows more and more ill, and yet his face becomes more and more determined. He carries the look of the girl in *No Regrets for Our Youth* when she said: "I want to find out what it is to live." We follow the discussion as one piece of evidence leads to the next. (There is only one repeated scene, his initial departure from the office into the rain, the office door swinging—though Kurosawa is careful never to lose us in time. One of the later scenes, for example, is in the rain, and we may surmise that this occurred the same day that he first took up the project and rushed from the office.) Finally the last piece of the puzzle slips into place. The policeman, who has brought Watanabe's battered new hat from where he found it, tells of seeing him on the night of his death, in the park, sitting on one of the swings in the snow, swinging, and singing the song that we heard him sing six months ago in the bar. He died then, and presumably died happily.

Like Sartre's Roquent, like Camus' 'foreigner' (who also knows he is going to die), like Kafka's Gregor and Dostoevsky's Prince Myushkin, Watanabe has discovered what it means to exist, to be—and the pain is so exquisite that it drives, it inspires him. He conceives the plan which will save him, though in the simplest of terms it is a form of insurance against having "lived in vain." He rescues the petition from certain oblivion and turns wasteland into a park. He has flung himself onto this one thing which will keep him afloat. He forces the park into being.

During the wake and its successive revelations it has become gradually clear that Watanabe has found his vindication through action. The park was only a pretext for this action. It makes no difference that now the department of parks or the deputy mayor claim credit for the finished park. Even the small voice of the one fellow-worker who stands up for the dead Watanabe has no real meaning.

The meaning is that Watanabe has discovered himself through *doing*. Perhaps without even grasping the profound truth he was acting out, he behaved as though he believed that it is action alone which matters; that a man is not his thoughts, nor his wishes, nor his intentions, but is simply what he does. Watanabe discovered a way to be responsible for others, he found a way to vindicate his death and, more important, his life. He found out what it means *to live*.

The office-workers (at least when drunk at the wake) seem to believe this. They are loud in their sobs of repentance and their praise of the dead (this wake is not in the slightest overdone—Japanese wakes are always like this: drunk, full of back-biting toward the deceased, to end in an orgy of praise and fellow-feeling around dawn) but—sober—they have forgotten their moment of truth. Only one—the one who first spoke up for Watanabe at the wake—remembers. He is reprimanded. He sits down and Kurosawa has so placed the camera that he disappears behind his piles of papers as though he were being buried alive. He has—in his way—*become* Watanabe. And the final scene also suggests this. This clerk is on his way home. It is evening. Below the bridge where he stands is the park which Watanabe made. He stops and looks at the sunset just as Watanabe has in an earlier scene when he stopped, at the same place, looked and said: "Oh, how lovely—I haven't seen a sunset for thirty years." It is as though this single clerk might remember Watanabe's lesson—a man *is* what he *does*.

On the other hand, it is quite possible that Kurosawa would disagree with this interpretation of his picture. He certainly does not think of himself as an existentialist. Still, throughout his films there runs a moral assumption which has much in common with the existential thesis. The same thing occurs in Dostoevsky, a disaffiliate whom the existentialists have claimed, and it is telling that the Russian author should be the director's favorite.

Of course, one of the fine things about *Ikiru* is that, like other great films, it is a moral document and part of its greatness lies in the various ways in which it may be interpreted. Here, as in the novels of Dostoevsky, we see layer after layer peeled away until man stands alone—though what the layers mean and what the standing man means may vary with the interpretation. Personally (as I have indicated) I think it means that man is alone, responsible for himself, and responsible to the choice which forever renews itself. This interpretation has never been better put than by Richard Brown, when he wrote:

"*Ikiru* is a cinematic expression of modern existentialist thought. It consists of a restrained affirmation within the context of a giant negation. What it says in starkly lucid terms is that 'life' is meaningless when everything is said and done; at the same time one man's life can acquire meaning when he undertakes to perform some task which *to him* is meaningful. What everyone else thinks about that man's life is utterly beside the point, even ludicrous. The meaning of his life is what he commits the meaning of his life to be. There is nothing else."

# PRODUCTION

The genesis of this film, Kurosawa has said, was in his own meditations upon death: " . . . I think—how could I bear to take a final

breath? While living this life, how could I bear to leave it? There is, I feel, so much for me to do. I keep feeling I have lived so little. Then I become thoughtful, but not sad." Another reason for making the picture is seen in the speech he made upon accepting the Venice prize for *Rashomon*: "Everyone likes to receive prizes and so I'm happy . . . but I'd be even happier if I were getting it for having shown something of contemporary Japan." He, in other words, wanted to show his country as it is and, at the same time, wanted (finally) to make a film directly about one of the themes which has occurred in most of his earlier work—the problem of identity, the problem of living.

Modern Japan has perhaps never been so fully exposed (in both senses of the word) as in this film. It is an extremely powerful indictment not only of official bureaucracy but also of the world as it exists. Those who see *Ikiru* as a social statement have their reasons for doing so, though to see it only as statement, is to do it an injustice.

For here, more than in any other of his pictures, Kurosawa has managed an (uneasy) truce between the part of him (*Scandal, Record of a Living Being, The Bad Sleep Well*) that says social endeavor is the answer and the other part of him (*Rashomon, The Lower Depths, High and Low*) which knows perfectly well that it is not. This has unbalanced some of his pictures (*The Quiet Duel, Scandal, The Bad Sleep Well*) but here these two concerns sustain and fructify each other.

Kurosawa has told how he wrote this script. "I usually write with someone else. If I work by myself it tends to get lop-sided; but if I can work with someone else then he has a chance to make his debut, and if the two of us discuss things as we go on, then things—to a certain extent—go better. The way we work is that we all sit at a big table but a bit away from each other. Uegusa, or Hashimoto, or Oguni, and myself, we all write. Then we show each other what we've written. It is a real competition. Then each takes the other's and rewrites it. Then we talk about it and decide what to use. Even for a talented scenarist, this is very hard work."

"In *Ikiru* it was Oguni who had the best ideas—and he wasn't even writing. He sat in the middle [between Hashimoto and Kurosawa] and gave suggestions and asked for more copy. One gets angry writing this way, to be sure. That is necessary. Lots of times he'd say things like: 'No, it has just got to be like this or it's all wrong,' or: 'You simply cannot do that,' or: 'Ah-hah, you're cheating in this spot.'

"In my case, I never write the script as though it were a closed or finished form. I start by visualizing just the first scene. There is a certain kind of character, with a certain kind of potential, and he is in a certain kind of position. Then if this character has it in him, he begins to move by himself. [In this regard, Kurosawa has already told how the character of that ur-Watanabe, the lawyer in *Scandal*, was formed.] And until he starts to move, it is very hard work. It may take months of thinking about. When he finally begins to move, then we all talk it over. 'If he does that, then what would she do?' etc. . . . Of course, we're only human, and so it is dangerous for us to try to see everything right up to the end, the last scene. Thanks to a bit of dialogue a character going, for example, to the right can end up on the left. One never knows what will happen. Therefore, I leave it all as free as possible when I write. When the first scene is finished I have an approximate idea of how the film will end it—but the first question is always the same: how long will it take before this character starts to move?

"Naturally, it was in this way that the character of Watanabe was created. Actually, I cannot say I was completely satisfied with Shimura's interpretation. From his point of view, he gave all he could, but—if you ask me—his image of Watanabe was not the same as mine. He played the part with all stops out and I would have preferred something a bit more relaxed. Of course, here both the scenario and myself were also at fault. Still, I would have wanted something a bit more largely conceived, something not quite so strained.

"Shimura always says that he is no good. That is certainly not the truth. He grows with every film. If he did *Drunken Angel* with the power he has now something very different would have happened. Shimura is the kind of man who is always making things difficult for himself and so he strains too much.

"Of course, in this film, *I* was a bit stiff too. *Ikiru* has something both stagey and literary about it. You cannot call it out-and-out cinematic. But then what I really like to do is just something like this. Take something not entirely cinematic, even literary—and then when you've finished it, you look at it, and it has *become* cinematic.

"As a matter of fact the film wasn't difficult to make . . . the wake scenes went particularly well because I was relaxed during them. When a director gets stiff, nothing good can come from it. But, maybe the reason it didn't seem difficult to make was because it came right after *The Idiot*. I'll never make a film that difficult to make again—and in any case Shochiku would probably never allow me to. Once in a while though, one has to do something like that, get mixed up in something which demands *all* of your strength.

The picture was an outstanding success, popular as well as critical. It was even placed first on the 1952 *Kinema Jumpo* "Ten Best" list—a poll ordinarily as indicative of merit as the Academy Award—though one heard and still hears voices complaining of extreme length, particularly in the latter half. This complaint had a curious echo during the Kurosawa Retrospective in Berlin in 1961. I was in charge of it and word came through that the David O. Selznick 'Golden Laurel' was to be given to *Ikiru*—which thus outclassed *Pather Panchali, Wild Strawberries,* and other worthy entries. Mr. Selznick's representative called upon me and told me the news, then added: "It is a great film, one of the best films ever made—after all it is going to receive Mr. Selznick's own 'Golden Laurel'—but Mr. Selznick is of the opinion that it drags a bit, particularly during the funeral scenes. Don't you think we might shorten it a little?"

# Seven Samurai

# 1954

Kurosawa had long wanted to make a real *jidai-geki,* a real period-film. Though, at this time, fully half of all Japanese films made were *jidai-geki,* the "real" ones were very rare. Most of them were (then as now) *chambara,* simple sword-fight films. Japanese critics are fond of comparing the *chambara* with the American Western (the *seibu-geki*) and the comparison is appropriate. But, just as there are meaningful Westerns (*The Covered Wagon, Cimarron,* and *Stagecoach*), so there are meaningful *jidai-geki.* One can, in fact, trace the development of the "real" Japanese period-films from the early pictures of Daisuke Ito and Mansaku Itami, through Sadao Yamanaka and Kenji Mizoguchi, to Masaki Kobayashi, and Kurosawa himself. These latter are "real" because they do not stop at simple historical reconstruction, inhabited by stock figures (which is true of costume-pictures all over the world), but insist upon the validity of the past, and the continuing meaning of the historical. That the rule should be otherwise in Japan (so famous for its being a museum in which nothing is thrown away, almost notorious for its regard for the past, practically infamous for its historical sense) is surprising, but otherwise it is. The ordinary *jidai-geki* has no more vital connection to the past than does any Steve Reeves epic.

Kurosawa, then, wanted to present the past as meaningful, but do it within the framework of the *jidai-geki* (something he was to do again in *The Hidden Fortress,* in *Yojimbo,* and particularly in *Sanjuro*); at the same time, he says, he wanted to make a picture that was also completely entertaining. (He did not consider *Rashomon* either a *jidai-geki* or entertaining.) This is what he meant when he said: "Japanese films all tend to be *assari shite iru* [light, plain, simple but wholesome], just like *ochazuke* [green tea over a rice, a dish the *assari* connotations of which are so celebrated that Ozu—'the most Japanese of all Japanese directors'—used it as a film title once] but I think we ought to have both richer foods and richer films. And so I thought I would make a film which was entertaining enough to eat, as it were."

Entertaining it certainly is: convincing, thrilling, meaningful, compelling. It remains (along with *Ikiru*) the director's own favorite. At the same time it is completely serious. Most film-makers believe that to be entertaining you also have be amusing, just as most musicians believe that to play fast you must also play loud. Kurosawa knows otherwise. He also knows that nothing compels (particularly in a film) more than immaculate realism, and that this is even more true

in a historical film where the reality has long vanished, and we are used to seeing only the slipshod reconstructions and interpretations of others—something the director particularly holds against the ordinary period-film. In this regard Kurosawa's remarks on Mizoguchi are interesting.

"His greatness was that he never gave up trying to heighten the reality of each scene. He never made compromises. He never said that something or other 'would do.' Instead, he pulled—or pushed—everyone along with him until they had created the feeling which matched that of his own inner image. An ordinary director is quite incapable of this. And in this lay his true spirit as a director—for he had the temperament of a true creator. He pushed and bullied and he was often criticized for this but he held out, and he created masterpieces. This attitude toward creation is not at all easy, but a director like him is especially necessary in Japan where this kind of pushing is so resisted.... Of all Japanese directors I have the greatest admiration for him but, at that same time, I can't say that everything he did was equally good. If he portrays an old merchant you get marvelously successful scenes, like those in *A Tale from Chikamatsu,* but he was no good at samurai. In *Ugetsu,* when you get to the war scenes it just isn't war. A long time ago he did *Chushingura* and he left out the last scene [the great vendetta with much fighting and sword-play] which isn't surprising at all. Our historical worlds are actually different. His central figures are women and the world he describes is largely either that of women or of merchants. That is not my world. I think I am best at delineating *bushi* [warriors, samurai] .... But, in the death of Mizoguchi, Japanese film lost its truest creator."

Certainly the realism of the Mizoguchi historical film (a realism shared with Yamanaka and Itami) is enormously compelling but of equal importance is Mizoguchi's almost continual insistence that history be regarded as contemporary in that its problems were no less unique, no less personal, than are ours, and further—given the perspective of history—we are more likely to appreciate something of ourselves when it is given us out of our own historical context.

This, to be sure, *does* happen in the ordinary *jidai-geki,* just as it happens in the Kabuki, but the perspective we are offered is all too often that of the single, set view, the ordinary "historical outlook." It is acknowledged that the past gives perspective; at the same time it is decided for us just what that perspective is, and it is invariable:

the Kabuki, like the ordinary *chambara,* has decided *for* us. All past Japanese problems were about the conflict between love and duty. A lord loves a lady but he, alas, is a lord with a lord's responsibilities, so he gives her up; father loves his son but must also take care of his lord's son, enemy comes demanding head of the latter youngster, and—after what visible agonies only the Kabuki-goer can imagine—the man lets his own boy be decapitated; and so on.

But, as E. M. Forster, in another context, has wisely remarked: "The contest lay not between love and duty. Perhaps there never is such a contest. It lay between the real and the pretended." Indeed, there never is such a contest, and one of Kurosawa's concerns, both as a thinker and as a film-maker is with myriad ways in which he indicates just this. The way of the Kabuki, the way of *chambara* is much too facile for him. At the same time the fact that it exists (and is believed in, even now, by a great number of Japanese), is a continual spur, a continuous thorn in the side, a constant pain in the neck. He resents the pretended—that is, the illusion. And he delights in revealing it as illusion. Reality is much more difficult to deal with, of course, and consequently a major theme in any of his films is just this search for reality. That it often results in failure tells much about us and, perhaps, something about the nature of reality itself.

The important thing, therefore, is that his people concern themselves with this search for meaning and do not allow themselves to be too misled by illusion. Kurosawa knows perfectly well that illusion is necessary and one of his pictures (*The Lower Depths*) is about just that. At the same time, he would invite us—in the very face of apparently certain defeat—to pursue the real in so far as we are able, to face life, and to settle for nothing less.

This is, of course, what *Ikiru* is about, and the interest continues throughout all of his films until now. In *Seven Samurai,* we have a particularly impressive example, however, because, since it is a historical film, we can see more clearly, we can see freshly. We have become so used to our own epoch that we don't even see it any more. We are blind to it. The period of civil wars, the presumably exotic and distant sixteenth-century, however—that is another matter. Things become clear and in a way the problem becomes simpler. Since it becomes simpler, Kurosawa may go further in his explorations than he has done before. He can, as it were, go beyond reality and try to find what is there.

Needless perhaps to add, he has said none of the above nor has he ever himself given me any reason for believing that he would ever say it. He is much less dogmatic than I am here making him seem. Rather, as Kajiro Yamamoto had noticed years before, he would be "completely engrossed in separating what is real from what is false," at the same time, never once forgetting that he was making an entertaining film.

# THE STORY

A small village is yearly invaded by bandits and the farmers lose their crops and sometimes their lives. This year the elders decide to do something about it. They have heard of a village which once hired masterless samurai and was saved. They decide to do the same and send some of their number to search for willing samurai. Since there is no pay, merely food, a place to sleep, and the fun of fighting, the farmers are fortunate that they first meet Kambei (Takashi Shimura), a strong and dedicated man who decides to make their cause his own. A young *ronin,* Katsushiro (Ko Kimura) joins him, then he accidentally meets an old friend, Shichiroji (Daisuke Kato). He himself chooses Gorobei (Yoshio Inaba) who in turn chooses Heihachi (Minoru Chiaki). A master swordsman, Kyuzo (Seiji Miyaguchi) joins, and so, eventually, does Kikuchiyo (Toshiro Mifune), a farmer's son himself, who has been following them around for some time, attracted—as all of them are—by Kambei.

Once in the village they prepare for war. Not waiting for the first attack, they storm the bandits' fort, burn it and kill a number of the bandits—though Heihachi is also killed. The bandits attack the village and they repulse them, though Gorobei is killed. Then they hit upon the plan of allowing a few in and spearing them to death. In the final battle both Kyuzo and Kikuchiyo are killed—but the bandits are all dead.

It is spring, once more the rice-planting season has come. Of the original seven samurai, only three are left and they soon will go their separate ways.

As the précis indicates, the picture is about three groups of people: the farmers, the bandits, and the samurai. There are over a hundred farmers, forty bandits, and just seven samurai. Kurosawa keeps these three units apart in various ways. The first sequence shows the bandits, and then we do not see any more of them until an hour and ten minutes (in the "standard" export version of the film) has elapsed. The second sequence shows the village as a group (gathered together in a closed circle), and it is not until the final battle that they mingle with samurai and bandits. The third sequence is about the selecting of the samurai and they, too, form a unit which is not broken into until the battle. The music also insists upon differentiation. The credit music is low drums and this becomes associated with the bandits; the farmers' music is folk-music, flute and percussion; the samurai music is a low humming (male chorus), the main "theme" of the picture, and fanfare-like horn calls. These three kinds of music may be heard in conjunction but are never heard together.

Those who want to see *Seven Samurai* as social epic in the Soviet manner (the "Soviet manner" of the 1930's) have excellent reason for doing so. The picture *is* about groups of people and their social actions. But to see it only as a Russian-style social epic is both to ignore the ending (something no Russian in the 1930's would have filmed) and to neglect the fact that the film is not only about people—it is also, and mainly, about persons.

It is about the seven samurai as individuals (though Kurosawa does not so individualize the bandits, and there are only a few of the farmers who are given personal profiles) and, as an adventure-story, is entirely about *their* exploits and how *each* reacts to this great adventure. For these are no ordinary samurai, and no ordinary men.

We first see Takashi Shimura having his head shaved. This usually means either punishment (for a samurai to lose his top-knot means that he is declassé and no longer a samurai) or that he is going to leave the world (to become a priest). As the watching Mifune discovers, however, it is neither. In what seems to be return for two balls of rice, he will save the child of a farmer, kidnapped and held prisoner by a madman. Shimura is given a priest's robe and the rice balls. He approaches the house where the madman is holding the child, impersonates a priest, catches the kidnapper off guard, kills him and saves the child. The parents are happy, the local farmers are full of congratulations. Then they all go away, back to their work.

The farmers searching for samurai to help them, decide that this is one they want. But he is also being followed by young Kimura, who begs to become his disciple, and by Mifune who can make nothing whatever of such apparently unmotivated goodness. Finally one of the farmers kneels in front of him and pleads. Shimura sees that one or two samurai would be useless—seven would be needed, and besides:

"It isn't easy to find that many reliable samurai ... particularly when the only reward would be three meals a day and the fun of it. Besides I'm tired of fighting. Maybe I'm getting old."

The farmers are so disappointed that they begin to cry. A laborer makes fun of them, saying:

"I'm certainly glad I wasn't born a farmer—rather be born a dog than a farmer. Take it from me, a dog has a better life. Look, why don't you just go hang yourselves—all of you farmers. You'll be much better off. . . . And you, samurai. You know what these wretches eat? Millet! Because they'll be saving all their precious rice for you. They'll be giving you all they have—their very best."

This decides Shimura because he is the kind of man who makes decisions in this way. In the same way he allowed himself to be shaved and to save the child, for no reward at all. It is as though by personal example he will set the world right, and this is what so captivates Kimura and intrigues Mifune.

Just as Shimura knows himself, so he also knows other men. He devises a test for his future fellow-samurai. Kimura is to hide behind the door and bring down a stick on the head of the applicant. If the man senses something amiss and manages not to get hit, he is good enough for the task. He sees Inaba in the street and says to try him. This samurai does not even enter the door, but can see something is wrong even from the outside. He joins them:

"I know that farmers suffer but that is not why I am joining you. I'm accepting because your character interests me very much."

Kato, Shimura's old friend, is found by accident. Kimura stands by watching, and the leader asks:

"Are you tired of fighting?"

Kato is not and joins them. Eventually, all seven are gathered and go to the village.

The farmers dislike the military life very much and several attempt to revolt:

*Farmer:*    All of you who live beyond the bridge, come with me, put down your spears. It's useless to carry a spear to protect someone else's house when you can't protect your own.

*Shimura:*    Wait. Pick up that spear and return to your unit . . . . There are only three houses beyond the bridge and in the village there are twenty. We cannot endanger twenty because of three. And if the village is destroyed those three will not be safe anyway. Do you understand? War is like that. If you defend for all, each individual will be protected. He who thinks only of himself destroys himself. From now on, any such desertion will be punished.

Shimura's intentions are social—that is, he will save the village. At the same time, as leader, he never makes the mistake to which leaders are prone. He continues to view men as individuals and to make allowances for their individuality. In a wry way he even makes allowances for whatever individuality the bandits possess:

"Most probably they'll attack here in the morning. This time we'll let them in. Oh, not all of them, just one or two. As soon as they are in we'll close our spear line. Then they will be helpless. We'll get them all this way—one by one."

He makes careful distinctions, however. When the swordsman returns with a gun, Mifune is jealous and goes out, has a very funny adventure, and comes back with a gun himself. To do so, however, he had to leave his post.

*Shimura:* You fool, why did you leave your post?

*Mifune:* I don't deserve to be talked to like that—look, I got the gun and the post is safe enough.

*Shimura:* Your going off like that merits no praise at all. Listen carefully—in war you never fight individually.

At the same time, the swordsman who, after all (and Mifune is right) did the same thing, is only praised for his action. Like any true leader, Shimura knows his men—knows that the swordsman can safely do this, and knows that Mifune cannot, that his getting the gun and returning alive is only luck.

At the end of the film when the villagers have forgotten the samurai who saved them, have turned their attention to the rice-planting, Shimura (of the three surviving) is the only one not hurt or disappointed. After the battle he has said to his old friend Kato, said with wonder and awe: "Again we've survived." At the end of the film he turns to his friend and says, philosophically: "And again we've lost."

Few things surprise Shimura. He is like the pilgrim-priest in *The Lower Depths* because he knows better than to hope. All a man can do, he seems to say, is to do his best. If he does his best for himself that is one thing; but it is better to do your best for others: even if the task is dangerous and without reward; even if (as here) it is absurd. Still, it is better to have done it. The farmers are saved (whatever that means); the village still stands (whatever that means); and these three are alive (whatever that means). Something has been accomplished, and if it is meaningless then that is small concern of ours.

This is heroism, and of a kind that particularly appeals to Kurosawa. It is stoic, hopeless in the strongest possible sense, and generous. It is for this reason that Shimura has become a leader, and it is why his character so interests his men that they are willing to die for him. He knows that men are individuals; he knows that all social actions are collective; he recognizes the gulf that exists between these two—and he still chooses to act.

The other samurai share something of this. Obviously, or they would not have been attracted to the pointless adventure. Inaba most closely resembles Shimura and it is he who becomes second-in-command; and it is he who finds Chiaki. Finds him chopping wood, an occupation unheard of for a samurai.

*Chiaki:* Yah! (Giving the samurai-cry as he brings down the ax as though it were a sword, neatly chopping the log in

half. After a bit he becomes irritated that Inaba is watching.) Haven't you ever seen anyone cut firewood before?

*Inaba:* Yes, but you seem to enjoy it.

*Chiaki:* I guess I'm just made that way. Yah! (Slices firewood.)

*Inaba:* You're very good.

*Chiaki:* Not really. It is a lot harder than killing enemies. Yah!

*Inaba:* Killed many?

*Chiaki:* Well, you see. Since it is impossible to kill them all— yah!—I usually run away.

*Inaba:* A splendid principle.

*Chiaki:* Thank you very much. Yah!

*Inaba:* By the way, you wouldn't perhaps be interested in killing twenty or thirty bandits?

*Chiaki:* Yah! (But he is so surprised that he completely misses the log.)

Minoru's ideas on war are very close to those of Kato who at one point tells what he thinks:

"All right, now remember. (To the farmers.) War is mostly *run*. We are going to run, both in offensive and defensive. When you can't run in a war—that is when you get killed."

At an extreme from such practicality is the swordsman, Miyaguchi. He is a complete professional; we know this because we have seen him fight. He says very little, is closed, and—like his sword itself—only uses himself when he needs to. We know that he is lethal, though peaceful, and there is one beautiful scene of him alone in the forest where he carefully picks a single flower and looks at it. He incorporates the true spirit of *bushi*—something which none of the others do. He is killed, ironically, by a bullet.

The youngest samurai, Kimura, has an enormous veneration for the swordsman, even more than for Shimura. When the latter comes back with the gun, strolls into camp, and prepares for sleep, Kimura approaches him, eyes shining, and says: "You are a wonderful person,"—at which, for the only time in the picture, the swordsman smiles.

He, too, is attracted by the boy and the only time he displays any curiosity is when the boy meets and gives his rice to a girl. Kimura had originally met her in the forest while he lagged behind picking flowers. Since she has had her long hair cut short by her father, he takes her for a boy—which was the father's intention, since he mistrusted the samurai. She is also picking flowers and they accidentally meet:

*Kimura:* If you're a boy, why aren't you out drilling with the rest? Picking flowers at a time like this! (He suddenly remembers that he too has flowers in his hand.)

The others treat Kimura as the child they think he is, though there are some indications that he is growing up. Shimura and Inaba are going out for night patrol. Kimura is sleeping beside them.

*Shimura:* Well, shall we go?

| | |
|---|---|
| *Inaba:* | Shall we wake him? |
| *Shimura:* | No. Let the child sleep. |
| *Kimura:* | (In his sleep.) Shino! |
| *Shimura:* | What's that? Shino is a girl's name, isn't it? |
| *Inaba:* | Yes, indeed. Not a very childish remark for a sleeping child to make, is it? |

Later, he makes love for the first time, and the very next day, kills his first man. He himself has become a man. Yet, when the swordsman is suddenly killed by a stray shot, he kneels into the mud and weeps as though his heart is breaking. Shimura looks at him. The boy remembers to ask if there are any more bandits. No, there are no more. Then he flings himself to the ground, sobbing, while Shimura looks. The child is not quite yet a man."

It is, indirectly, through the swordsman and the boy that Mifune dies. Like all the rest of the samurai he wants the regard of Shimura, and he also (like the swordsman) enjoys the adulation of the youth. When the latter begins telling him how wonderful the swordsman is, Mifune is sarcastic, but it is just after that that he goes out and gets the gun. And when he sees the boy weeping, it is he who goes after the bandit chief, and kills him—though he himself is killed in the attempt.

And bravery is not at all natural to him. To be sure, it is to no one, it must be acquired, but Mifune has acquired little enough of it. A buffoon, a standard joke to the rest, it is nonetheless he who kills the final and most important bandit—as though, by this action, he will vindicate himself in the eyes of both the leader and the boy.

Unlike the others, he is no warrior. Indeed, if things had happened differently he might just as well have been one of the bandits. But his parents were killed by bandits, and he was orphaned. This is shown in a single scene where, during the burning of the mill, the dying mother gives her living child to him. He holds it in his arms, aston-ished, up to his thighs in the stream, the burning mill behind him, then suddenly sits down in the water and bursts into tears:

| | |
|---|---|
| *Shimura:* | She was speared. What enormous will she had to come this far afterwards. Well, bring the child, let's go back. What is the matter with you? |
| *Mifune:* | (Looking at the baby in his arms, crying.) This ... baby. It's me. The same thing happened to me. The very same thing! (Sobs, holding the baby.) |

Mifune is also a farmer's son, and though he has come a long way from the soil he has never forgotten the enmity traditional not only between farmer and bandit, but also farmer and samurai. At one point he hopes to please his comrades by bringing them armour which he has found hidden away in the village. The others are solemn be-cause they know that the armour was stolen from samurai whom, perhaps, the villagers themselves murdered.

| | |
|---|---|
| *Miyaguchi:* | I'm beginning to want to kill every farmer in this village. |

| | |
|---|---|
| *Mifune:* | What do you think farmers are? Saints? They are the most cunning and untrustworthy animals on earth. If you ask them for rice, they'll say they have none. But they have. They have everything. Look in their rafters, dig in the ground, you'll find it. Rice in jars. Salt. Beans. Saké. Look in the mountains, hidden farms everywhere. And yet they pretend to be oppressed. They are full of lies. When they smell a battle they make themselves bamboo spears. And then they hunt. But they hunt the wounded and the defeated. Farmers are miserly, craven, mean, stupid, murderous beasts. (Tears in his eyes.) You make me laugh so hard I'm crying. |

But then, who made animals out of them? You. You

did—you samurai. All of you damned samurai. (He picks up a handful of arrows and throws them at the wall.) Each time you fight you burn villages, you destroy the fields, you take away the food, you seduce the women and enslave the men. And kill them if they resist. You hear me—you damned samurai? (He begins to cry.)

Shimura: (Quietly, with great sincerity.) You're a farmer's son aren't you?

He is a farmer's son but he dies as a samurai. And it is perhaps he whom the others will miss the most, precisely because he was so weak, so very human. Shimura appears almost superhuman, but Mifune is completely human. And it is he who therefore sees the dilemma that even Shimura has missed. Aren't, then, samurai and bandits to be equated?—aren't the actions of each equally absurd? —and don't they really do much the same things?

It is a startling question. One which Kurosawa has asked in *Stray Dog* and will ask again in *High and Low*. Good and bad might be identical. The farmers would find it so. They are almost as distrustful of the samurai as they are of the bandits. For them it is plainly a choice between evils. We are thus prepared for the final scene.

The opening sequence with Shimura has shown a gratuitous action, one for which he expects neither reward nor acclaim. The laborer, and now Mifune, have indicated that one need not expect to find generosity, gratitude, or other such civilized luxuries among the peasants. And at the end, therefore, when the three remaining samurai are ignored by the farmers who are, obviously, only waiting for them to leave (and in a scene carefully prepared since it was just these three—Shimura, Kato and Kimura—who were present when the leader asks Kato: "Tired of fighting?"), Shimura may say:

*Shimura:*     And again we lose.

*Kato:*     . . . ?

*Shimura:*     We lose. Those farmers . . . they're the winners.

What did Shimura hope to win? He knew the entire venture was quixotic, he knew it would be without reward, he knew that its only profit was in the "fun of it." To be disappointed in the farmers was to have hoped, and this is something which, until now, he has not allowed himself. Yet he had hoped to win, and further had hoped that this winning would somehow change something. He has become human enough to confuse ends and means and forget that everything is means and that there is no end. The true wisdom (cold, comfort-less) would have been to enjoy the "fun" while he had it, to (put in a way which Kurosawa would never be guilty of saying) realize that *being* is the sole end, and that *becoming* turns into snare and delusion if looked for, hoped for.

This does not mean, of course, that *becoming* is impossible. Indeed, it is impossible *not to become.* Nor does this mean that wishes and will have no power—indeed, they have considerable power, as *Ikiru* has indicated. But what disappoints is when one allows the illusion (the unfulfilled wish) to supersede reality (ungrateful peasants, dead comrades).

Kurosawa made *Seven Samurai* because, in part, he deeply resented the facility of the ordinary *chambara* with its specious conflict between inclination and duty. Yet—at the end of this film—he shows us that, beyond illusion (duty), inclination becomes truly lonely, truly fright-ening. What will they do now, now that the work at hand is finished, proved of no particular value, now that they see themselves perfectly equated with the very enemy against whom they fought? Their only choice is to go on and have another unprofitable adventure and, perhaps, to remember this time that it is the adventure itself that counts, not its hoped-for consequences.

*Seven Samurai* is an epic all right—it is an epic of the human spirit because very few films indeed have dared to go this far, to show this much, to indicate the astonishing and frightening scope of the struggle, and to dare suggest personal bravery, gratuitous action, and choice in the very face of the chaos that threatens to overwhelm.

# TREATMENT

Like the Russians (Eisenstein, Dovshenko) to whose epics *Seven Samurai* has often been compared, Kurosawa—here perhaps more than in any other single film—insisted that the motion-picture be composed entirely of *motion.* The film opens with fast pans of the bandits riding over hills, and ends with the chaos of the battle itself, motion so swift we can almost not see it at all. There is no shot that does not have motion, either in the object photographed, or in the movement of the camera itself. The motion may be small (the quivering nostrils in the long-held image of the village elder) or it may be great (the huge, sweeping frescoes of the charges) but it is always there.

At the same time, another kind of motion is present. Kurosawa, always an economical film-maker, uses a number of short-cuts which hasten the pace of the story itself. When the farmer first approaches Shimura the continuity is:

*Farmer, face down in the dirt, Shimura looking / cut / new location, an inn, and Shimura is saying to the farmer: "It's impossible."*

All obvious retelling is left out, all obvious continuity linkage (the two of them walking to the inn, for example) is rigorously excluded. Again, Inaba (sensing that Kimura is waiting with the stick just inside the door) stops outside.

*He says: "Oh, come now. No jokes," / cut / inside the inn, he and Shimizu are sitting down and he is saying: "Well, it sounds interes-ting."*

Sometimes scenes are telescoped and put into one. There is a beautiful example of this during the funeral of Chiaki. All are gath-ered around the mound and Mifune dashes back to get their banner (which Chiaki had made) and climbs a roof to put it on the ridge-pole—a gesture of defiance. He suddenly looks at the hills and there, as though in answer (a marvelous image), come wave after wave of bandits, riding down on the village, heralding the first of the major battles. As Mifune looks, there is a wide pan which moves from village to hills. At the same time the sounds of weeping turn to cries of alarm from the villagers, to cries of exultation from the samurai—who now want to fight. Within this single scene not only has action been carried foward but—as though the pan had caused it which, in a way it did—the entire mood has been changed, in just two seconds, from abject sorrow to the most fierce joy.

Another means of telescoping is through the interlinking of very short (usually funny) scenes, connected with wipes, that Kurosawa has used from *They Who Step on the Tiger's Tail* onward. It is seen at its funniest both here and in *Sanjuro.* The samurai are being taken to the village, and their journey is seen in a mosaic of tiny scenes the point of which is that they are being followed by Mifune who, taciturn, apparently stupid, wants to join them, and at the same time cannot bring himself to. The entire sequence (covering

a seemingly enormous journey) takes just three minutes and at the end Mifune, looking down at the village, utters his ironic and prophetic remark which (in retrospect at any rate) makes him appear much more human, much less of the clown: "Whew—what a dung pile. I'd certainly hate to die in a place like that."

All of these short-cuts and telescopings, all of this motion on the screen, means that the picture moves very fast indeed. It is so swift that Kurosawa has availed himself of at least several devices to insure that he does not lose his audience. The first of these is the banner and, at the same time, a list which Shimura draws up in which the number of circles indicates the number of bandits. Like the bullets in *Stray Dog,* like the money in *One Wonderful Sunday,* the viewer keeps score, as it were, by seeing how many down, how many to go. Each scratched circle means one less bandit.

Another way in which Kurosawa keeps his audience up to the pace he has set is by a full explication of the visual surroundings. In the original version of the picture, this is even stronger, but even in the cut version (which is all that other countries ever see of this picture) this explication is very strong. He begins with a map (as he does in *Stray Dog,* in *The Hidden Fortress,* and in *High and Low*)—a map which Shimura has drawn and which is a bird's-eye view of the village. Kurosawa loves bird's-eye views, and he is particularly fond of anything which will show all the ingredients of a certain situation, which will allow you to spread them all out before you and try to put them together. It is like the watchmaker's interest, the cook's interest—the finished thing is all very well but how it got finished is the most interesting thing. Consequently we learn all about the various sections of the village and (as with the room in *The Lower Depths*) we get to know it extremely well, better perhaps than most places we actually visit. In the same way we watch the samurai, first hear of their plans, and then see them in action (much as we, fascinated, watch the police force in *High and Low*) and then judge the results. As always, Kurosawa is particularly careful to show us *how* a thing happens.

Finally, in the last reel, we are shown *how* a battle occurs. It resembles what we have been prepared for, but at the same time it is entirely different. Shimura speaking in measured tones and pointing to his map is one thing; this inferno of men and horses, rain and mud, is quite another thing. Reality is very different from illusion.

Even on a technical level, quite removed from the context which gives it its final meaning, this last reel is one of the greatest of cinematic accomplishments. It is chaotic but never chaos; disordered but orderly in its disorder. The rain pours down; bandits dash in; horses neigh and rear; Shimura poses, bow ready; Mifune slashes; an arrow thuds home and we glimpse it only for the fraction of a second necessary; riderless horses rear in terror; a samurai slips; Mifune grabs another sword. All of these images and literally hundreds more are crowded into a final reel which galvanizes the screen. (Having already given us plenty of excitement in the earlier battles, here Kurosawa does himself one better and uses telephoto lenses—a rarity in 1954—to bring the action directly into the laps of the audience. The first of these telescopic shots is a horse-fall which seems to occur directly where the camera is and rarely fails to evoke a gasp from the audience.)

At the same time, in the final reel, we again see that what keeps this film (and all of Kurosawa's films) so completely vital is, after all, the cutting, and consequently the tempo. We have had indication of this before in the film. In the hunting-for-the-samurai section, a set piece like the journey-to-the-village which follows, Kurosawa shows us the four farmers in two pairs, each searching through the same town. In between each image of a pair of farmers looking from right to left, or left to right, their eyes following the samurai, sweeping pans of the samurai themselves are intercut. Thus the sweeping pans are answered by sweeping movements of the eyes of the peasants. The delight of this sequence (the delight of the hunt, of the unknown, accompanied on the sound track by music unmistakably of that intent), lies in the very brevity of each shot. Each is no longer than two seconds. Thus, even in a simple sequence such as this, expectation and excitement are generated through the cutting.

Mifune's fine scene with the armour is another example of Kurosawa's editing. It plays so very well and is so powerful that it is only on re-seeing that one notices, first, that Mifune acts directly into the camera (which is one of the reasons for the power—as in the final

close-up in *The Lower Depths*) and second, that each shot of Mifune is a bit shorter than the one which went before. The tempo is accelerated by the cutting, and these long scenes become shorter. The next to last (Shimura) and last (Mifune) are the conventional one-two shots, each lasting for a conventional amount of time.

Another example of creative cutting is the raid on the bandits' fort. There is a broad downward pan. First we see mountains, then below it the road along which the three horsemen are galloping. The pan does not turn sidewise with the horsemen, however, nor does it stop (as one might expect)—rather, it continues on down, leaving the road (and the action) behind. At the same time, as the road disappears at the top of the frame, a slow lateral wipe (left to right) begins. This is the waterfall scene, and the samurai are already at their destination. The effect on the screen is, oddly, diagonal. Two essentially unrelated scenes have been perfectly connected, and we accept cause and effect though there is actually a great and purposeful lapse in the continuity. This fine effect of continuous movement is achieved entirely in the editing, since it would be impossible to obtain it photographically.

Sometimes sound enforces the cut. On the first day of the battle, there is a good example:

> *The samurai, all asleep / cut / enormous close-ups of horses running, the bandits approaching, hoofs thundering on the sound track / cut / all asleeep, but the swordsmen has heard (though we hear nothing) and stands up / cut / racing horses and hoofbeats / cut / all the samurai are standing and waiting; we hear hoofs very faintly and then, in the far distance see the dust raised by the horses.*

These are only four shots and each is slightly shorter than the other. By the time the battle begins, we are quite prepared for it, and the editing has done it.

Besides technique, however, there is something else about this film (and about most of Kurosawa's pictures) that defies analysis because there are no words to describe the effect. What I mean might be called the irrational rightness of an apparently gratuitous image in its proper place, and the image that I always think of is that wonderful and mysterious scene in *Zéro de conduite* where it is apparently Sunday,

Papa is reading the paper, and the boy's little sister moves the fishbowl (hanging on a chain from its stand) so that when her brother removes his blindfold he can see the sun touching it. The scene moves me to tears and I have no idea why. It was not economical of Vigo to have included it, it "means" nothing—and it is beautiful beyond words.

Part of the beauty of such scenes (actually rather common in all sorts of films, good, bad, and indifferent) is just that they are "thrown away" as it were, that they have no place, they they do not ostensibly contribute, that they even constitute what has been called bad film-making. It is not the beauty of these unexpected images, however, that captivates (plenty of films, particularly Japanese films, are filled with irrelevant and beautiful scenes which completely fail to move) but their mystery. They *must* remain unexplained. It has been said that after a film is over all that remains are a few scattered images, and if they remain then the film was memorable. That is true so far as it goes but one must add that if the images remain, it means only that the images were for some reason or other memorable. Further, if one remembers carefully one finds that it is only the uneconomical, mysterious images which remain.

Kurosawa's films are filled with them, and if I have not spoken of them before it is because I have been trying to make certain similarities among the films clear, to trace a general family likeness among them. Actually, these isolated images are his most beautiful, and (because so mysterious) his most profound.

For example, in *Drunken Angel* there is a scene where Mifune lies ill in the room of his mistress. Shimura comes in and does not

wake him but sits by the bed. He opens the girl's powder-box. It has a music-box inside and plays a Chinese tune. While it is playing, he notices a Javanese shadow-puppet hanging on the wall. While looking benevolently at the sleeping Mifune (and this is the first time he has been nice to him—when he is asleep and cannot know about it), he begins to move the puppet this way and that, observing its large shadow over the sleeping gangster. While one might be able to read something into the scene, it is so beautiful, so perfect, and so mysterious, that even the critical faculty must hesitate, then back away.

Its beauty, certainly, is partly that in the closely reasoned philosophical argument which is this film, it is a luxury—take it away and it would never be missed. It gives no information about plot or character. Kurosawa's films are so rigorous and, at the same time, so closely reasoned, that little scenes such as this appeal with the direct simplicity of water in the desert. There are many more (a mysterious shot of the tinker in *The Lower Depths* all alone, outside, huddled up on the ground, devouring a piece of candy; a completely unmotivated scene of Mifune in *Scandal* roaring his motorcycle—only the motorcycle is in his studio, where he brings it for the night, and it is up on its stand, going no place; etc.) but in no other single film are there as many as in *Seven Samurai.*

What one remembers best from this superbly economical film then are those scenes which seem most uneconomical—that is, those which apparently add nothing to it. There is a short cut during the burning of the bandit's fort where we watch a woman awake, see the fire, and yet refuse to warn the others. (She is the wife of one of the farmers, raped and carried away by the bandits.) The scene is beautiful enough, this hopeless farm woman, clothed in stolen silk, half obscured by the wisps of smoke—but Kurosawa renders it utterly mysterious (and completely right) by inserting beneath it the sound of the Noh flute with unearthly effect—a trick he later repeated, less gratuitously, in *The Throne of Blood* and *The Hidden Fortress.* Again, there is the short scene where a prisoner has been caught, and the oldest woman in the village—she who has lost all of her sons—is called to come and murder him. She marches slowly forward, a hoe in her hand, terribly old, terribly bent, a crone. And though we sympathize, the image is one of horror—it is death itself because we have seen, and will see, men killed and think little of it, but here is death itself with a hoe, mysterious, unwilled. Or, those several shots of the avenue of cryptomerias, and two bonfires, one far and one near. This is where the bandits will come but we do not yet know this. Instead, the trees, the fires, the night—all are mysterious, memorable. Or, that magnificent image which we see after Mifune has rescued the baby and burst into tears. The mill is burning and Mifune is sitting in the stream, looking at the child and crying. The next scene is a simple shot of the water-wheel turning, as it always has. But the wheel is on fire. Or, that curiously long close-up of the dead Mifune. He has stolen some armor but his bottom is unprotected. Now he lies on a narrow bridge, on his face, and the rain is washing away the dirt from his buttocks. He lies there like a child—all men with bare bottoms look like children —yet he is dead, and faintly ridiculous in death, and yet he was our friend for we have come to love him. All of this we must think as we sit through the seconds of this simple, unnecessary, and unforgettable scene.

Or, my favorite among all of these magical images, that following Shimura's saying that the bandits are all dead, and Kimura's sinking, weeping, into the mud. The screen slowly darkens. It is as though the end has come, and one hopes it has not, because this, somehow, is not enough and because, even more strongly, we do not want to leave these men yet. The screen gets darker and darker. They are lost in the gloom. We sit in the darkness and then we hear music. It is the music of the farmers, and the screen lightens to reveal one of the most delightful and heart-breaking of sequences: the rice-planting.

It is seen as dance, which indeed rice-planting is in Japan. A small orchestra (flute, drums, bells, singer) accompanies the girls as they plunge the new shoots into the wet earth, all in unison. Since this is the way rice is actually planted, we accept it as real. At the same time, after the uproar, pain, horror, grief of the final battle, we had not expected a divertissement. Strictly speaking, the entire rice-planting sequence is unnecessary to the film; not speaking strictly at all, it is vital—perhaps because it relaxes, with its very beauty and its anticlimax. Nerves have been played upon and wrought up to an extent completely unusual in an action-picture, and suddenly— childlike beauty. When tears flow in *Seven Samurai,* they flow here.

Then comes the great final scene with its reminiscence of the opening scene, followed by Shimura's profoundly ironic remark, and the picture ends on the splendid image of the high grave-hill with four naked swords stuck into the top, and three mere men standing below. And, under this, the child-like music of the peasants fades and is replaced by the music associated with the samurai.

Kurosawa has given us beauty in the midst of knowledge, a kind of reassurance while questioning all reassurances. At the same time that he questions deeds, hopes, thoughts, he has purposely played upon our emotions and we, too, have become open and child-like. More, in this profoundly subtle and mysterious final sequence (samurai and peasants; fighting and rice-planting; silence and music; darkness and light), he has indicated hope. We are all, after all, human; we all feel the same—we are all peasants at heart.

# PRODUCTION

The production difficulties of *Seven Samurai* have become legend. Long before it was released it had become very widely discussed. It had taken well over a year to make and already it had become the most expensive film which Toho had ever undertaken. By the time it was finished, it had become the most expensive picture ever made in Japan. The company, afraid, tried to get Kurosawa to come back to Tokyo (most of the picture was made on location which was one of the things which made it so expensive), and he retaliated by threatening to quit. He afterwards spoke of the "intense labor" of making a really entertaining film. "Something always comes up. We didn't have enough horses; it rained all the time. It was just the kind of picture that is impossible to make in this country."

It was perhaps this film which gave Kurosawa his nickname of *tenno* or "emperor" because of his alleged dictatorial mannerisms. It is telling, however, that no one of his staff has ever used the word and that, on the contrary, it is the Japanese press which is so fond of it that it still uses it. However, Kurosawa could indeed be very dictatorial to his company—because this was just the kind of pushing which he so admired in Mizoguchi. At the same time, he deeply resented the bad press that the film was getting before it was even finished. In answer to the charge of wasting time he snapped back: "And why not. I was only location hunting. The location must be perfect and a director may spend months hunting for just the right one. Why not—it doesn't cost money." When told he was spending too much he launched an attack himself. "You try to give a film a little pictorial scope and the journalists jump on you for spending too much money. That is what I really hate about them—they are only an extended form of advertising. They talk big and make pictures sound important to make themselves seem more important. The more they try the greater they lie. For instance, one of my aims—as it is with every director—is to stay inside the budget. But something always happens and I go over it. How the journalists pounce on me and say I am squandering precious resources. Yet, right now, Olivier and I are both making *Macbeth* [this was in 1957; the reference was to *The Throne of Blood*; Olivier's film was merely projected, never completed] and I bet I could finance my whole film just for the cost of one of his larger scenes. Japanese films are made too cheaply."

Once released, the film had great box office success but evoked little critical enthusiasm even though Kurosawa had prepared a manifesto which said, in part, "*jidai-geki* faces a dead-end, there are no talented *jidai-geki* producers," and something must be done about it—the implication being that he had. The critics, while realizing that the film was indeed in the line of Yamanaka and Mizoguchi, almost wilfully misunderstood. One of them complained that it was not very democratic of him to condemn the poor farmers; another, that he was saying the farmers were not worth saving. (An interesting remark, though far removed from the point of the film—and one which Kurosawa may have remembered when in *Sanjuro* he gave himself the handicap of creating in the kidnapped chamberlain a very nice incompetent who *really* is not worth the saving: thus the entire reason for the whole adventure evaporates and Kurosawa leaves

us free to draw conclusions from this.) Another critic wondered about the wisdom of such emphasis on what was, in effect, civil war in these present troubled times. (A hint which Kurosawa took full advantage of: *The Throne of Blood, The Hidden Fortress, Yojimbo, Sanjuro* are directly—and *Record of a Living Being* and *The Bad Sleep Well* indirectly—about civil war.) There were, to be sure, some perceptive judgements but it is only now, over a decade later, that the critics speak in measured terms of "this epoch-making masterpiece."

Still, as Kurosawa consoled himself "it was released uncut—in Japan at any rate. [The original version was two hundred minutes in length and was shown, in 1954, only in the key major cities. A shortened version played second and third runs. A second shortened version was made for export and this one-hundred-sixty minute film is the one most people have seen. A third was made for the Venice festival. The American version (called *The Magnificent Seven* until John Sturgis' remake caused all prints to be recalled—in America at any rate) was an RKO-butchered edition of this second version. The German version is also cut from the second Japanese version but less damage has been done. There are no prints of the original in Japan and even negatives of the cutouts have disappeared.] But we had to shorten it for Venice. Naturally no one understood it. They all complained about the first half's being confused. It certainly was. The second half the Venice people liked well enough because that only had a few minor cuts which, as a matter of fact, helped it."

Nevertheless, *Seven Samurai* has, outside Japan in 1954, never really been seen. This is one of the major cinematic tragedies—just as lamentable as those better known ones of *Greed, The Wedding March, The Magnificent Ambersons,* and *Ivan the Terrible.* It is not only Kurosawa's most vital picture, it is also perhaps the best Japanese film ever made.

# Record of a Living Being

While making *Seven Samurai* Kurosawa went to see his best friend, the composer Fumio Hayasaka, who was very ill, indeed dying. "He was a fine man," Kurosawa has said: "We worked so well together because one's weakness was the other's strength. It was as though he—with his glasses—were blind; and as though I were deaf. We had been together ten years and then he died. It was not only my loss. It was music's loss as well. You don't meet a person like that twice in your life."

1954 was a somber year in Japan. With Hiroshima and Nagasaki less than a decade in the past, the Japanese regarded the experimental nuclear explosions staged by Russia, America, and Great Britain with great suspicion. During the Bikini experiments a Japanese fishing boat wandered into the area and its crew was exposed to fallout. One died (though the later diagnosis was that the death was caused by hepatitis) and the Japanese—with excellent reason—became worried and concerned.

A massive and popular peace movement was formed, civic groups went out on the street to collect signatures to register opposition to nuclear testing, the Japan Council Against Atomic and Hydrogen Bombs (Gensuikyo) was formed, literally millions signed petitions, and when radioactive rain began to fall (as it did over most northern countries during 1954–55), press and public reached near-hysteria. A number of films (most of them sincere) were made on the subject and Kurosawa went to see his dying friend.

"He was quite ill . . . and just before we had had word of the Bikini experiments. When he said to me that a dying person could not work, I thought he meant himself. But he didn't, it turned out. He meant everyone. All of us. The next time I went to see him, he suggested we do a film on just this subject. He was quite taken with the idea and that is how the film began.

"We decided together, and then talking to other people, that a satire would be the best way of saying what we wanted to. This followed more or less what I had wanted to do—make a satire. But how do you make a satire on the H-bomb? This was the problem I kept running into when I tried to write the script. When one is as involved as we were, it is very difficult to keep one's distance; it was very hard to keep it satirical.

"As we [Shinobu Hashimoto, Hideo Oguni, and Kurosawa himself] worked on the script it became less and less satire and more and more something else. We really felt that we were making the kind of picture that, after everything was all over and the last judgement was upon us, we could stand up and account for our past lives by saying proudly: 'We are the men who made *Record of a Living Being*.' At any rate, that is the kind of picture it turned out to be.

"And this [turning a satire into a tragedy] would be the reason why the film might be thought incoherent—even chaotic. Still it was good we made it. Anyway, the way we felt—how could we have made a satire?"

## THE STORY

A dentist named Harada (Takashi Shimura) is a volunteer-worker in the Domestic Relations Department of the Tokyo Family Court. He is a quiet, sober, serious man who is unusual only in that he takes his civic responsibilities seriously. At the beginning of the picture he receives a phone call and goes to help at the court.

A family squabble of more than usual size is in progress. Nakajima (Toshiro Mifune), an elderly man, wants to make his family emigrate with him; his reason is that Japan has become too dangerous to live in. He feels that he is under the constant threat of atomic extinction and, for some reason, thinks that South America is safe. He has attempted to persuade his large family (including mistresses and their children)

and they retaliate by trying to get the family court to judge him incompetent. Their application reads, in part:

*I demand that Kiichi Nakajima be certified quasi-incompetent on grounds that the applicant, wife of said Kiichi Nakajima, finds that since June of last year he has become suddenly, extremely, and inexplicably fearful of atomic and hydrogen bombs and of the radioactivity thereof, and, seeking to evade radioactivity from the south did, despite the opposition of his family, purchase property in Akita Prefecture, and did begin to build an underground shelter. Further, upon learning that radioactivity was coming from the north as well, he stopped this construction thus causing his family the meaningless loss of seven million yen. His conduct has now continued and, stating that safety lies only in South America, he has willfully planned his family's emigration, declaring that he will invest all funds he possesses in order to realize this aim. Unless he is declared quasi-incompetent and is placed under a guardian, not only his own but the lives of his entire family will be in jeopardy, and the family will be ruined. Therefore, the court is requested to take this procedure.*

The Family Court, including Shimura, are rather upset by the case, not only by the earnestness of the old man and the patent and callous unconcern of his family (except for his wife, who—though coerced into making the petition by her children—would willingly go wherever he would be happier) but also by their own fears—the fear that he is absolutely right, right to be afraid if not to emigrate. Shimura voices their concern when he says:

"I agree that he has gone too far but, after all, we're as worried as he is . . . only we don't build underground shelters nor try to get to Brazil. But that doesn't mean that we can fail to understand how he feels. It is, after all, a feeling that all of us Japanese know all too well. He has gone too far, perhaps, but we cannot for that reason take his fears any the less seriously."

Shimura himself begins to worry. He speaks with his son about it, he reads *Ashes of Death* and says, after his son has flippantly asked if he too wants to go to Brazil:

"Well, here. Read it. If birds and animals could read, they would get out of Japan as soon as they could."

Mifune has, in the meantime, gone outside his immediate family and tried to convince the other members: the son of a mistress who has died; the second mistress and her daughter; the present mistress and her baby. All refuse for various reasons and when the legal family hears of what he has done they are particularly angry. Their relations with these unofficial members of the family and their own half-brothers and sisters have never been good. The Family Court finally decides against Mifune. One day Shimura accidentally sees him in the street car. He is considerably aged. He says:

"Look at me, you who made that decision . . . look at me now. I am afraid, hopelessly afraid, and I am helpless before my fear. I can do nothing and my life has become a living hell."

Shimura, impressed, goes back to the judge whose opinion is:

"But, was it possible for our decision to have been any different? I too have thought a lot about that man since then. And there is really no way to save him. After all, his misfortune is no one's fault—H-bombs happen to exist. And he feels, I must say, so strongly that one must blame, I suppose, his disposition. Too, his mind, you know, doesn't seem to know where to stop. He was just born to go too far into anything."

Now thoroughly frightened, Mifune makes an extraordinary decision. He will do what is very difficult for an old-fashioned Japanese father to do. He will beg rather than command. He calls a grand family council with the new mistress and her baby, and says:

"Please. I beg you. Come to Brazil. All of us together—as one family. You may think me insane—maybe I am. But the bombs actually exist. War may break out at any time and if that happens then it is too late. We can still make it. We still have time. Let us flee while we can. This baby—I must spare him. I cannot let the bombs kill him. If I could save even this little child it would be enough. But you—you who are my flesh and blood—I can't leave you here. Please come with me."

He prostrates himself on the *tatami*—an act unheard of in the traditional Japanese family. His wife breaks down and tries to prevail upon her children. The youngest daughter begins to cry, saying that she will go. And at that point Mifune collapses—exhausted.

Mifune next does something equally extraordinary. To force his family to go and knowing that the family money might be the strongest reason for their staying, he purposely sets fire to his own foundry and burns it to the ground. He has thought that this would make the family go.

But he had forgotten about his workers, now jobless. This is perhaps what causes him finally to become completely irrational. He is confined to a mental hospital. Shimura comes to see him because, as he says: "You see, I feel . . . well, a sort of guilt. I feel that perhaps the court gave the wrong decision."

The psychiatrist says: "This patient, I must admit, does disturb me. It is the first time this has happened—he is the first one to make me feel that maybe *we* are not sane. And so I wonder, who is mad: he or me?" Shimura goes to see Mifune, who says:

"Come in, come in, I'm very glad to see you. You see, here you are completely safe. So, rest assured. And by the way, whatever happened to the earth? Still many people there? Oh, that's bad. I don't like that. They had better get away soon or they'll be sorry. Why don't they wake up? They must escape quickly. Now *this* planet is perfectly safe—but they had better hurry. Oh, look! (He has glimpsed the setting sun.) Oh, my god. It is burning. The earth is burning. Burning. At last, finally, it is burning."

# TREATMENT

Just as the next-to-final image in the film is a great telescopic-lensed shot of the setting sun, so—throughout the picture—great emphasis has been given the extreme heat of late Tokyo summer. The opening credits are seen over street-scenes, people hot and sweating, creeping along the scorching pavements. A street-car moves past, filled with perspiring people. The camera pans to follow it, then stops and looks at a window, moves forward, enters the window and we are in Shimura's dental clinic. This brilliant opening (all studio made, with the most accomplished of smooth, gliding pan/ dolly/ elevator shots) with its creeping camera captures the very atmosphere of a city prostrated by heat. Just as the extraordinary summer-heat of *Stray Dog* indicated a city parched by war, so here the endless brilliance of the sun, the windless confines of a sweat-drenched city, suggests fear and the apocalypse. In the courtroom scenes everyone, shirts sticking to backs, is fanning himself. Electric fans are buzzing in corners. In the scene where the family is bickering at the beginning, their nervous movements with the fans, and the steady hum of the electric fan in the corner, set up an irritation to the eye and ear (somewhat like that in the beginning of *The Quiet Duel*) which grows and continues until the blazing eye-scorching image of the sun itself with which the film ends.

During one brilliant scene, Mifune has gone to see his latest mistress, his baby, and the girl's father. The dialogue does not reassure him (nor us) and further, Kurosawa has placed at the very bottom of the frame a magazine (lying on the the *tatami* and hence very close to the camera, placed so low that the figures seem to loom above us) the pages of which are ruffled by an electric fan so that the dialogue is continually accompanied by the distraction of irrelevant movement, a constant

and meaningless fluttering which irritates and adds considerably to the feeling of discomfort the scene is intended to convey.

> *Father:* Isn't the weather strange? The newspapers say it is because of the H-bomb tests. Of course you know a lot more about this than I do, but they say that the radioactivity is bound to reach Japan no matter where the bomb itself explodes. I'm no scientist, mind you, but it's something about some atmospheric currents and Japan is in some sort of valley—and anyway all the radioactivity is bound to flow down on us. Wonder what will happen. Our hair will fall out, I guess, and then our bones will get rotten, I hear. Well, it's not very nice to think about, is it? Just the other day I saw in a magazine something about Hiroshima. It was a pretty gruesome sight—they had pictures too, but I imagine you already saw it. Anyway, they had a picture of a baby—it was just about this big and—
>
> *Mifune:* Shut up!

A bit later in the scene there is the sudden scream of jets overhead. It is obviously a group on maneuver but Mifune instantly scrambles to the baby, trying to protect it. As he cowers on the *tatami* there is a terrific clap of thunder (as though in answer to the jets) which wakes up the child. It screams (as though in answer to the thunder) and—suddenly (as though in answer to the child) there is a cloudburst. One second it is dry, hot insufferable summer. The next, the world is awash. The effect of this apparently fortuitous happening is (given both the dialogue and the visual irritation which went before) most upsetting and the rain itself is not (as in *Stray Dog*) a sign of relief. Just the opposite, because this might be the radioactive rain which all so fear.

Besides the heat itself there is much talk of fire. Since Mifune owns a foundry, the yards are filled with smoke and coke and coal, flames bellow from the forges, and the interiors look like infernos. One of the amusements of the youngest daughter (the nice one who makes friends with the mistress at the end) is to take the garden hose and when the workers emerge, smoked, begrimed, dripping with sweat and looking much like survivors from some local Hiroshima, give them a good cold dousing. Early in the film Mifune has warned his workers to be careful of fire—ironic in that it is he who finally sets the blaze himself. Too, he learns from his friend (the man who is going to sell him a farm in Brazil) that what actually motivated his initial emigration was a fire through which he lost his business. This, in turn, may have been what motivated Mifune to destroy the foundry.

Mifune's character is given very careful consideration in the picture. It is as though Kurosawa knew he was working with something which could very easily turn into the grotesque. There was the further handicap of having an actor (though an extremely good one) play a character twice as old as he actually was. For this reason, the character of the hero is purposely allowed to be contradictory. He has none of the edges smoothed off (as do some of the members of the family whose sole function is to oppose him) and is presented in all his richness and complication.

He is an old-fashioned, rigid, paternal, traditional Japanese father. At first we are inclined to think him something of a monster because our introduction (like Shimura's) is through the official family request. Here (as is common in most of his later films) Kurosawa purposely gives us first an illusion (the father as seen by his family, a prejudiced view) later corrected by reality (the father as we see him ourselves). Just as the judges are of two minds about his character and his fears so—insists Kurosawa—must we ourselves be.

He is a monster who in the most heated of the arguments when father and sons are barely speaking, remembers to go out and buy cold drinks for his family, thrusting them into their reluctant hands with all the brusqueness of the family-head who knows his duty, and who also truly loves his family but doesn't often show it.

He could, of course, escape at any time that he wanted. Nothing is stopping him. His great problem is his concern for the others, for the family, and it is *this* which is, in a way, irrational. We are never shown that any of them deserve to be spared the fate he fears probable. In this he is like a number of other Kurosawa heroes, weakened and eventually damned by his own humanity. Mifune the cop in *Stray Dog*, Mifune the swordsman in *Yojimbo* are almost done in by their compassion; Mifune the avenger in *The Bad Sleep Well*, Mifune the father in this film *are* killed by it.

Again, as in other films, the final problem set before the audience becomes: what then is reality? The psychiatrist thinks that Mifune's madness may be more concerned with actuality, with things as they are, than is his own sanity. Shimura has, apparently, become heir to the fears of Mifune who, it would seem, has escaped into madness. The question is not so much answered as postponed. This is indicated in the final scene of the picture.

The mental ward is apparently somewhere near the top of the hospital. At least it is between floors. The screen is divided in half and directly in the middle is the bannister. At the right are stairs leading away and up; at the left are stairs leading away and down. Shimura comes down the stairs. At the same time the young mistress and the baby come up the stairs. They do not stop because it so happens that they are the two members of the cast who have never met each other and so they cannot know each has a definite bond with Mifune.

The implications of the scene are inescapable. Shimura (already old and now perhaps fearful) is going down. The baby, on the other hand, is going up. This would seem to say that there is always room for hope. Perhaps the elders will not be saved, but perhaps the young will be; the experienced are doomed, but the innocent may yet escape.

This statement shares much with that in *Rashomon* (abandoned baby saved), with *Drunken Angel* (little girl cured), with *Ikiru* (a memorial left for children), with *Seven Samurai* (simple farmers prevailing). and with *Red Beard* (child saved). At the same time, the statement somewhat militates against the "message" which is that we had all better do something about the situation if we don't want to get killed. The final scene seems, at the last moment, to imply that there is some hope anyway, while the rest of the film has been telling us there is no hope at all.

That the confusion is not serious is because, since the character of Mifune is so rich and complicated and contradictory, the "message" (for it would be his) is by no means simple. We are not presented with an answer; we are presented with a question, a problem with which it would be wise to concern ourselves. It is thus possible to see Mifune's final disintegration (if that is what it is) as melodrama, as wisdom, as allegory, or as symbol.

Kurosawa himself finds confusion in the film. "When we made it, the entire staff sensed our confusion. No one said very much and everyone worked hard and it was very hard work indeed." He kept remembering, he says, the composer's words: "The world has come to such at state that we don't really know what is in store for us tomorrow. I wouldn't even know how to go on living—I'm that uncertain. Uncertainties, nothing but uncertainties. Every day there are fewer and fewer places that are safe. Soon there will be no place at all."

Then, in the midst of production, Hayasaka died—of tuberculosis. Kurosawa has said: "It was during the filming of the scenes after the fire in the foundry—it was just then that Hayasaka died. This was a great shock. I no longer had the strength to work, to work well at any rate, and that is why these scenes are so weak. And the ending, that is very weak too. Finally, it was over. After *Seven Samurai* we were all tired but happy. After this film we were exhausted."

"I remember that we had a party to celebrate, afterwards. Noriko Sengoku [the girl who was the nurse in *The Quiet Duel*, the model in *Scandal*, and the bar girl in *Drunken Angel*—and who has a rather mysterious part in this film: as the wife of one of the sons she is in almost every family scene and has but one line of dialogue, one which would seem to indicate that she too is on Mifune's side] came up to me and said: 'Well we worked hard, didn't we? But from now on living our parts will be the more difficult.' I agreed with her and would still agree. Yet, at the same time, after I had made this film, I felt as though I had put down a heavy load. I felt as though I had gone through a lot of things, had gotten rid of a lot of things."

Hayasaka's death affected not only this picture; it also affected Kurosawa. "I was completely overwhelmed," he said. "It went so far that I wondered if this loss would not incapacitate me, ruin me. Truly, at that time, I was like a person half of whom is gone. Hayasaka was indispensable to me. It is of course generally known that he had great talent as a composer but beyond that he was such a fine human being. And he was a wise man—he had really fine opinions about film-making, and about the combinations of image and sound he had such excellent ideas that I listened with the greatest interest. There are many experiments in my films which are the result of the two of us talking things over and most of them are good.

"I remember when we were making *Stray Dog* he and I went from one used-record store to the next trying to find just the right music for the scene where the radio is playing and they are talking to the show-girl. The record had to be old and scratched, and the music had to be right. I remember we were so happy when we finally found that ancient rendition of *La Paloma* which we actually used.

"And in *Scandal*. There, we had the sick daughter die. The lawyer tells us. At that point Hayasaka insisted we use a trumpet. A trumpet? —I wondered, and until I saw the scene with sound I didn't know how very right he was. I still remember the scene—image and sound had become one. This taught me an enormous amount.

"And I remember *Ikiru* too. Originally we had wanted music all under the long wake sequence and so Hayasaka went ahead and did the score. Yet, when it came time to dub, I thought that the scenes and the music simply did not fit. So, I thought about it for a while, and then took all the music out. I remember how disappointed he was. He didn't say anything, and spent the rest of the day trying to be cheerful. I was sorry I had done it, but I guess I was right. At any rate, there is no way of telling him now how I felt. He is gone.

"Actually, I think it was our work—his and mine—which set a kind of precedent, at least in Japanese films. We showed that sound effects, dialogue, music when put under the image do not simply add to it—they multiply it. It is as though a three-dimensional effect is created.

"Oh—we had so much more work to do together. There were just lots of things I would have liked to have done had he lived. He never was very strong, but he was far too young to die."

(I knew Hayasaka very well during the Occupation years, though I did not at the time know Kurosawa. He was an extremely gentle, extremely intelligent young man with thick glasses, wild hair which he always wore in the manner that students wear theirs, and a wife and family for the support of which, mildly grumbling all the while, he would make dance-band arrangements or scores for movies he did not like. He used to come to my billet to listen to new records I would get from America and I still remember his extreme pleasure and excitement when he first heard the Berg *Violin Concerto*. His own serious music was highly adventuresome, and I remember the premiere of his *Concerto for Piano, Tympani, and Orchestra*, a very striking work which stunned its 1947 audience. Once he took me to the Toho studios and we watched them make a film and I was introduced to the director. The film was *Drunken Angel* and the director was Kurosawa.

I have often thought that the reason Kurosawa has always been patient with me, kind to me, allowed me to watch when he might have forbidden others, and has always welcomed me was simply because I was first introduced to him by Hayasaka.)

# PRODUCTION

Perhaps because he became so personally involved in the film, perhaps because he felt it (therefore—maybe) to be a partial failure, he has spoken more about its production than he has about many of his other films.

"This film is again about a social problem. And one of the reasons that I like social problems is simply that by using them I can make a question better understandable to my audience. Indeed, there is something topical about films. If they don't have topicality, they are not meaningful. Films are not for museums." This 'documentary' frame of mind is very strong in *Record of a Living Being*. The wipes are as terse as those in newsreels, the photography is particularly contrasty with very black blacks, very washed-out whites, and a noticeable amount of grain; there are also huge and impersonal close-ups of machines (fans, typewriters—an interest continuing in the machines of *The Bad Sleep Well*—tape recorders, etc.—and the full machinery of the police department in *High and Low*); there is even the no-comment type of humour one sometimes sees in Japanese newsreels— the business-deal between the escaping Mifune and his Brazilian friend is carried on at a plateau with all of 'sacred' Mount Fuji looming in the background.

Here (as in *High and Low*) Kurosawa became extremely interested in the techniques of film—certainly interested enough to talk about them afterwards. "There is a lot of talk about multi-camera technique but it seems to me that everyone completely misunderstands. They say that efficiency may go up but that the amount of raw stock used goes up too—this is rubbish. In the first place, I didn't start using a number of cameras at once merely to become more efficient myself. In the second place, just because we get good results this way doesn't mean we're going to shoot every scene this way. Actually, I'd like never again to use more than one camera. I get exhausted. Even if we only do a single shot a day, we get so tired doing it we can hardly go on.

"To say that three cameras wastes three times the amount of raw film is amateur talk. Actually—and this surprised even me—there is no waste at all. One of the reasons is that no [between-scene] leader is used, and another is that the amount of retakes necessary drops tremendously. If we had shot *Record* in the standard way, I think we'd have used up another thirty or forty thousand feet. Actually, we did not exceed our allowance very much. In fact, if you do use this technique you rarely exceed your budget.

"Naturally not all scenes deserve this method and you cannot tell much about its advantages and disadvantages taking *Record* as an example. I used telescopic lenses in *Seven Samurai* and sometime in the future I'd like to do away with artificial lighting, but not all the time. In *Record* the newsreel look came out just as I'd planned but I still don't think this method is the one to apply in every case.

"I discovered, for example, that three cameras going at once are not too good for static scenes with people sitting around. The impact of simultaneous ensemble acting seems to disappear.... When Mifune bows before his family I took the scene from three angles, simultaneously. When I cut it, though, I used just one of the shots, did it as one full scene seen from a single angle.....

"Sometimes, though, it works admirably. For one thing, the actors are very aware of three cameras looking at them, and one of the results is that unexpectedly real-looking expressions and postures appear. For another, you can get all sorts of interesting pictorial effects and compositions which would be impossible using only a single camera.... Of course, one camera or three, what really counts is to have something good in front of the camera to photograph. That is why rehearsals are so important to me. When we made *Record* I ordered twenty days of full rehearsal before I shot a single foot of film. The point is to immerse the actors completely in the characters they are to portray. In this picture I wanted a real family atmosphere. I wanted to feel (and to have them feel) that they were really brothers and sisters, parents and children. I even told my staff never to call the actors by their real names but always to use names like Sué or Yoshiko [names of characters in the film] because creating this atmosphere both in front of and behind the camera is the most important thing about putting a film together. If you don't have that then it makes no difference whether you have one or three cameras."

When the film was released, during the fall after an exceptionally hot summer, there was surprisingly little popular response. In fact, this film lost more money than any picture that Kurosawa has directed. For one thing it *had* been a very hot summer, for another there had just been a radioactive tuna scare in Tokyo and the Japanese were (for the only time in their history) fishless, and—in general—the problems of the film hit too close to home. Kurosawa has said: "It was my biggest box office loss. After having put so much of myself into this film, after having seriously treated a serious theme, this complete lack of interest disappointed me. When I think about it, however, I see that we made the film too soon. At that time no one was thinking seriously of atomic extinction. It was only later that people got frightened and that a number of films—*On the Beach* among them—were made."

Another way of thinking about it would have been that the timing had been too good, and that the Japanese people were so actively concerned that their main interest was to escape from having to think. Now, ten years later, the dusted fisherman has died of hepatitis; the Gensuikyo is a political organ which insists that nuclear testing by "the socialist camp" (China, that is) should not be equated with testing by "imperialist" forces; the yearly signature campaigns (designed to coincide with the Hiroshima anniversary) collect mere thousands, and *Record of a Living Being* is (ironically) a "museum-piece" which is only occasionally revived. (This is, one must add, only the Japanese view. The film was first seen abroad as a part of the Kurosawa Retrospective at the 1961 Berlin Filmfestspiele where it made a much greater sensation than it had in 1955 Tokyo.)

Yet, indeed, if the film had been merely a "social" document it would not continue to live in the memory, and would not—with all of its flaws—remain truly the "record of a living being." The reason is that Kurosawa (as in *The Quiet Duel,* as in *Scandal,* as in *The Bad Sleep Well*) became more interested in the "living" aspect of his subject than he did in its "social" aspect. In doing so he created in the old father a kind of everyman, a modern Lear even, who sees what may happen and who fears it. This is the reason that the message gets lost but through this loss something much more important is gained.

The spectacle of fear has something in it (as all dramatists have known) that makes us less afraid. Perhaps it is because few things compel our compassion more than do the fears of another. It is (as *The Hidden Fortress* suggests) our mutual fears which keep us together, and all civilization has its root in our completely rational fears and insecurities.

One might say that the father's fears are irrational and, further, nothing can be done. This is just what one of the characters does say: "H-bombs, eh? That's a foolish thing to worry about. Let the Prime Minister do the worrying. If you're so worried why don't you just move off the earth altogether?" One is then free to find the hero intensely neurotic and finally 'insane.'

Kurosawa's point would be different. He is directing our attention to a curious but central problem. If it is our insecurity which has created our civilization, how very ironic, then, that we—so highly civilized—should be (presumably) on the verge of destroying what we have created by succumbing to the very fear (for the cause of war is fear) which was originally responsible for the now threatened civilization. The father might well then be afraid, might with even more reason be afraid of that fear itself, since he is every one of us.

In this way, the picture becomes very "social" indeed—social in the deepest possible sense. And the "record" becomes the case-history of history, and the "living being" becomes myself.

# The Throne of Blood

**1957**

Kurosawa had wanted to make this film for some time. "After finishing *Rashomon* I wanted to do something with Shakespeare's *Macbeth*, but just about that time the Orson Welles' version was announced and so I postponed mine." He had long been fond of the play, once called it "my favorite Shakespeare," and—beyond this—had another reason for making it. "I've always thought that the Japanese *jidai* film is historically uninformed. Also, it never uses modern film-making techniques. In *Seven Samurai* we tried to do something about this, and *The Throne of Blood* had the same general feeling behind it."

Most Japanese, and Kurosawa is no exception, think of films as being divided into two major categories: the *jidai-geki*, or period-pictures, and the *gendai-mono*, or modern-story films—an attitude we share in our conception of the crime-film, the thriller, and the Western. The *jidai-geki*, however, has long degenerated into the romantic costume-picture. Except for the exceptional period-films of Mizoguchi, Kobayashi, and Kurosawa, the genre has no vitality. The pictures become highly colored but meaningless historical excursions, such as Inagaki's *Samurai* and *Chushingura*, or Kinugasa's *Gate of Hell*.

This attitude one would not expect in Japan, of all places, where the past is so important, where the historical consciousness is so developed. Yet, it is only a handful of historians, novelists, and film-makers who ever avail themselves of the living past. The ordinary historical novel, the ordinary historical film is content to repeat the cliché, to commemorate the meaningless gesture.

Pictures such as *Ugetsu*, *Harakiri*, and *Seven Samurai*, however, share in common an attitude which, first, tries to show history as it probably was and, second, attempts to give the characters both individuality and a contemporary psychology. This intent is quite different from that of the standard *jidai* film. It is like the difference between opera and operetta. Mathis, Tom Rakewell, Moses, Duke Bluebeard are real people who feel as we do. The student prince and the gypsy baron, the merry widow and the medium are stock characters with stock responses—we cannot even remember their names.

In *Macbeth*, Kurosawa saw a contemporary issue—a parallel between medieval Scotland and medieval Japan which illuminated contemporary society; and, further, a pattern which is valid in both historical and contemporary contexts. Once asked—none too acutely it is true—if he wanted to ask philosophical questions in his films or whether he was merely making entertainment, he answered: "I look at life as an ordinary man. I simply put my feelings onto film. When I look at Japanese history—or the history of the world for that matter—what I see is how man repeats himself over and over again."

For Kurosawa the pattern of repetition is destructive and it is this pattern which his free heroes attempt to destroy—as in *Ikiru*, for example. This is not the only possible attitude. Ozu celebrates patterns and his characters sometimes acknowledge that it is pattern, their knowledge of it, that gives them the strength to continue. In the pictures of Naruse, on the other hand, the eternal patterns of Japanese life—just as strong in reality as they are on film—are unacknowledged and his people bang their heads against the wall, losing freedom in their attempts to achieve it. One may either wholly accept, as in *Tokyo Story*; or wholly reject, as in *Ikiru*. Anything else—as *The Throne of Blood* and the entire output of Naruse suggest—leads to death.

The fable of Macbeth held a especial attraction for Kurosawa. The hero—cousin to Sugata—tries to realize himself. His fault—not ambition nor pride, as such—is his failure to realize himself completely. Instead, he wants merely to rise in the world, he wants something as conventional as power. Naturally, one murder leads to the other, because this is the pattern of power. The play had the attraction of being an exemplary or cautionary tale, of being the obverse of *Ikiru*. One, further, as true now as then.

It is perhaps because he is here exclusively concerned with limitation, negation, death, that Kurosawa—for the first time—created a formal film. He himself has called it an "experiment" and in it has created a balance, a roundness, a unity, a compactness, which one cannot help but admire even knowing just what this finished-aspect means to Kurosawa. It is a *finished* film with no loose ends. The characters have no future. Cause and effect is the only law. Freedom does not exist. Those who complained that the film was cool were only half right. It is ice-cold. Here, Kurosawa is making his point by allowing no hope and no escape. The inner richness of Sanshiro, the heroic gesture of Watanabe—these cannot exist in this lunar half-world which is the one most of us inhabit.

115

# THE STORY

The single source is Shakespeare and the film follows the play very closely, though there are a number of minor differences from the original. General Washizu and his friend, General Miki, are lost in the forest and meet a witch who prophesies that Washizu will reign but that Miki's heirs will prevail. They are rewarded for valor but Washizu kills, first, his lord, and then, Miki. A second visit to the witch tells him that he is safe until the forest moves. Miki's son attacks the castle using as protection and camouflage the trees of the forest. Washizu's son is still-born, his wife goes mad, and he is immolated by the arrows of his own men.

Other than the differences above, Kurosawa has included a number of new scenes (in particular that magical scene where the birds flee the ruined forest and invade the castle) and has further simplified the characters. His Macbeth is not grand. Rather, he is possessed from the beginning, he is compulsive, he is so profoundly afraid that he kills to insure that he himself is not killed. He is a little man, lacking in grandeur precisely because he is not torn between desires. Rather, he is ruled by ambition and we watch his rise and fall unmoved. At the same time, Kurosawa has so prodigiously illustrated this fall, so subtly indicated the parallels, the hidden meanings, so artfully prepared the traps and pitfalls and—in so doing—so fully explained the pattern, that this cautionary tale truly cautions.

# TREATMENT

The films begins and ends with the same image, post stones, the ruins of a castle, fog drifting, over which the camera moves. It is very like the opening and closing scenes of Mizoguchi's *Sansho the Bailiff*, a picture which Kurosawa much admires. It suggests (in both films) the transience of all earthly things, the end of all ambition, the grave which is our lot. At the same time—differing from the Mizoguchi—at both the beginning and end, a chorus is heard intoning the moral of the film. At the beginning, the story is told. Here, says the chorus, once stood a mighty fortress where—

> *Lived a proud warrior*
> *Murdered by ambition,*
> *His spirit walking still.*

The final chorus, at the end of the film, repeats the story and strengthens the moral:

> *Still his spirit walks, his fame is known,*
> *For what once was is now yet true,*
> *Murderous ambition will pursue. . .*

As in *They Who Step on the Tiger's Tail*, Kurosawa is using a known story and in both pictures he repeats the story under the opening credits—in the same manner, and for the same reasons that Cocteau repeats the myth before both *Oedipus-Rex* and *La machine infernale*. Further, and as in the 1945 film, he is using a Japanese theatrical convention: the chorus—which is one of the elements of the Noh, understandable enough in a film version of *Kanjincho*, but rather surprising in *Macbeth*. Surprising, at any rate, until one realizes that various elements of the Japanese theater are to be directly used in the film itself.

There are several reasons for this but one of them is that Kurosawa is very fond of the Noh. "Essentially," he has said, "I am very Japanese. I like Japanese ceramics, Japanese painting—but I like the Noh best of all. It's funny though. If you really like something like this, you don't often use it in your films. At any rate, I've never much cared for the Kabuki, perhaps because I like Noh so much. I like it because it is the real heart, the core of all Japanese drama. Its degree of compression is extreme, and it is full of symbols, full of subtlety. It is as though the actors and the audience are engaged in a kind of contest and as though this contest involves the entire Japanese cultural heritage." Further, "in the Noh, style and story are one. In this film the problem was how to adapt the story to Japanese thinking. The story is understandable enough but the Japanese tend to think differently about such things as witches and ghosts." The idea of a vengeful ghost is common enough, as in the innumerable *kaidan* films. There are, in fact, no motiveless ghosts, as in the West. But the idea of a trio of malevolent witches is far from the Japanese imagination. The witch, the warlock, are really priests, embodiments of a nature which is neither good nor evil. They are diviners and fortune tellers who attempt to pierce the future but the gratuitous evil of Shakespeare's witches is impossible.

Still, in the Noh, spirits are common and ghosts abound. "I wanted to use the way that Noh actors have of moving their bodies, the way they have of walking, and the general composition which the Noh stage provides." Besides, such reasons as the director's tastes and the need for explaining the witch, there is another reason for using the Noh in this picture. The way the actor moves, the way he uses his body, is prescribed, conventionalized. It is ritual drama, and the world of the Noh is both closed and artificial. It is the limitations of character which interested Kurosawa in this picture; the Noh offered the clearest visual indications of these limitations.

If that is true, it is interesting that in the picture the Noh elements are mostly associated with Asaji—the Lady Macbeth role—for she is the most limited, the most confined, the most driven, the most evil. She moves, heel to toe, as does the Noh actor; the shape of Isuzu Yamada's face is used to suggest the Noh mask; her scenes with her husband have a very Noh-like composition, and her handwashing is pure Noh drama.

Other borrowings from Noh are concerned with the other "evil" person—the witch. Her reed hut closely resembles a Noh property and her make-up suggests the ghost-mask of the Noh drama. Her prophecies

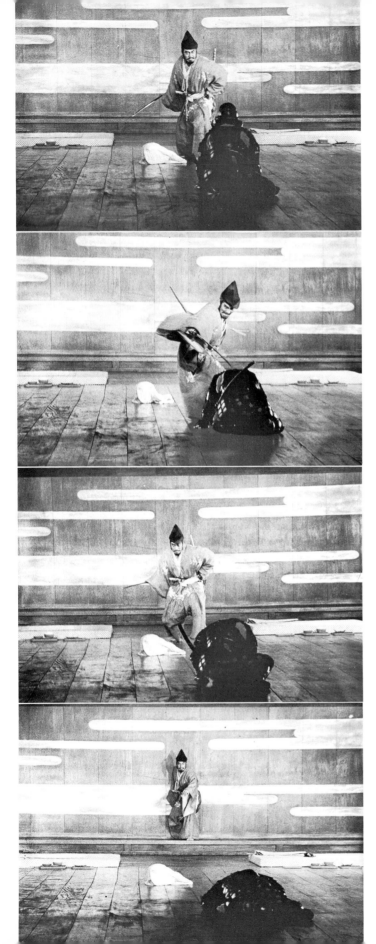

are voiced in the husky and unintonated voice of the Noh actor, and the sounds which both women make—the squeak of Asaji's *tabi*, the sound of her kimono dragging, the slight clatter of the witch's spinning wheel, her rustlings in her reed hut—are sounds which one strongly associates with the Noh.

The formal, closed, ritual, limited quality of the Noh is thus associated with the two women in the picture. The appearance of the ghost—that of Miki, former friend to Washizu, is not seen Noh style. Rather, he is suddenly there—in the manner of film ghosts. Even the finale, with Washizu transfixed by arrows, so amenable, one would think, to the accelerated tempi of the final moments of a Noh drama, that most theatrical of moments when rite turns to act—even here, there is no influence from the Noh. Rather, it is the two women who live in this stylized and ritual world. And it is they, who, after all, are the movers of the plot and who, in Kurosawa as in Shakespeare, are firmly on the side of evil.

In the Lady Asaji, Kurosawa has created his only villainess. In the majority of his pictures women are better than men (*One Wonderful Sunday, Ikiru, Drunken Angel, No Regrets for Our Youth*) or are, at least (as in *Rashomon*) stronger. He, to be sure, has Shakespeare's precedent, but Lady Asaji is a good deal more evil than Lady Macbeth. Or perhaps it is merely a matter of degree. Just as Nastasya in *The Idiot* possesses a power which leads to personal affirmation, so Asaji—equally strong—embodies the spirit of negation. These women are more capable of extremes than most of the men in Kurosawa's films. Asaji has gone the whole way. Washizu wavers.

The witch notices this when she tells him that he will be lord and Washizu is shocked to his feudal depths. He cannot be. The lord is the lord. The witch replies: "You humans! Never will I comprehend you . . . . You are afraid of your desires. You attempt to hide them. She might have said: "You men!" One feels that she and the lady Asaji would have gotten on well together. Washizu himself sees something of this when he says that he feels he has had a frightening dream and Miki innocently voices his own thoughts with: "We dream of what we wish." This does not mean, however, that Washizu comprehends, though he does come to understand a bit more than is good for him. Actually, he does not have the equipment to carry ambition. He is too afraid. This is what Asaji means when she taunts him with: "You who would rule a kingdom are yet afraid of a ghost."

She, being a creature of extremes, would go all the way and be damned to everything else. She would have her way. This is not necessarily the thought of a villainess but it indicates the direction. She will realize herself no matter what. Self-realization usually means stepping on others and this she is quite prepared to do.

In a way, she rather than Washizu is the protagonist because she shares many attributes with Kurosawa's heroes: like Sanshiro she wants to realize herself; like Gondo in *High and Low* she is none too careful about how she does it. If one of the problems in any Kurosawa film is how to realize yourself without making life too impossible for others, how to gain self-mastery without gaining power over others, how to resist and yet retain compassion and understanding—she is a fine example of one possible answer: self-realization is the more important, one may therefore sacrifice compassion, understanding, love itself. She believes that: "This is a wicked world. To save yourself you often first must kill . . . . Children kill their parents for less." This last is ironic in that it is her own child who, still-born, will kill her. In the face of all this Washizu can only answer that somehow or other "we must have faith in our friends."

It is a weak answer but it is, after all, the only one. It is the kind of remark that the girl in *Ikiru* might have made. True, it may be a wicked world but we are lost if we do not trust. It may be true that you must realize yourself but perhaps it will, after all, not be necessary to kill others in order to do so.

In equating Asaji with both the witch (who also believes in a wicked world, as in: "If you choose ambition, then choose it honestly, with cruelty . . . if you would make a mountain of the dead, then pile it to the sky; if you would shed blood, then let it run as a river,") and with the Noh, Kurosawa suggests that the rite, the ritual, man's idea of the world, the rigid, the formal, the pattern of life endlessly the same—that this is the opposite of the free, the human. The static, the full-formed, is negative. The only positive is that which chooses faith, which chooses to believe and does so in the face of reason, history, experience and the world as it seems.

Which is what some of Kurosawa's heroes usually do—Watanabe in *Ikiru*, the leader of the seven samurai. Sometimes, however, we are shown examples of what happens if they do not. Unable to escape, the heroes of *Record of a Living Being* and *The Idiot* go mad; the actor in *The Lower Depths* kills himself—a rare alternative in a Kurosawa film though there is both an attempted and a successful suicide in *The Bad Sleep Well*; the kidnapper in *High and Low* is executed, as will be the murderer in *Stray Dog*; the gangster in *Drunken Angel* dies. All these men share in common that they refused to believe, they refused to commit themselves to faith in the seemingly impossible. They are men of the world who live by worldly rules and do not see that these rules are only made to be broken.

Not only is this refusal to believe the first step into something worse (madness, prison, death) but also, this belief is its own end. It can lead to nothing other than itself. It is true that Asaji wants to realize herself through power and thinks that she will better her condition by killing. This, we are shown, leads to madness and death. But it is also true that if there were a way of achieving this power without harming others, this would not necessarily lead to the happiness she ostensibly desires. And it is also true that if she had faith, if she did not kill and did not goad her husband into killing, she would not have *attained*

anything at the end because this belief can have no goal. It is the opposite of ambition. Belief is a way of living and it exists from second to second. Ambition is always in the future, and its flickering intensity always leads into the morass.

Asaji has made up her mind. She knows what she wants. Consequently she denies herself the freedom to change her mind. She is as rigid as the Noh mask which her face imitates. She gives herself over to cause and effect because she believes in it. Sugata continually surprises himself. How could he know that beating up the father of the girl he likes—an act abhorrent to him—would lead to a degree of self-realization he could not otherwise have attained? Asaji never once surprises herself, she has a plan. She thinks she knows her nature and she acts as best she can upon her assumptions. How could she know that this would not only make her evil—for this much she guesses—but also that it would lead to failure?

Of course all this talk about good and evil and success and failure is far from what concerns Kurosawa. While this picture was being made, I was at the Washizu mansion location in Izu and, knowing the story, asked Kurosawa what the picture would become, what it would mean. He answered: "I keep saying the same thing over and over again. Why—I ask—is it that human beings cannot get along with each other, why can't they live with each other with more good will?" *The Throne of Blood*, he added, was to show several of the reasons.

One certainly is that people—particularly intelligent, sensitive, feeling people—learn the rules of the world and then, unfortunately, believe them. This naturally precludes a belief in goodness. It is only with a great effort that a man can unlearn this lesson and then proceed alone and naked as does Watanabe in *Ikiru*.

And another reflects a dilemma which is very close to Kurosawa himself—the conflict between self and the world. What, one wonders, has the man's life been that he sees the problem so steadfastly, views it with such integrity, and so rigorously spurns any compromise, any easy answer? Whatever the reason it is irrelevant because he has chosen to ask this question, to state this dilemma through his work, and whatever answer may be found is to be found only here. We are all Asajis, driven, wanting to be ourselves yet not willing, unlike her, to sacrifice others to gain this. Perhaps our error is in pretending to know what *ourselves* consists in.

In any event, Asaji never entertains the slightest doubt. She knows who and what she is, or thinks she does. If Miki gets in the way of her ambition, it is too bad for Miki. She sees her future much more clearly than she does her present—for she too is a kind of witch—and she has made a choice of and for herself. Unlike Watanabe she does not want to realize herself *through* anything, she wants to realize *herself* and these are two different things. Like the villain in *Sanshiro Sugata,* she is fully formed, she has cut off her own future, she can never become anything more than she is. She is dead.

This is one of the reasons that the lunar world of the Noh fits her so beautifully and that Kurosawa, loving this world as we all love it, as we always love the absolute, the perfect, the finished, be it this most subtle of dramatic forms, or the perfect beauty of a person, has created in this picture a like world—a formal, enclosed, and stylistically perfect confine.

Visually, the film is a marvel because it is made of so little: fog, wind, trees, mist—the forest and the castle. There has rarely been a blacker and a whiter black and white film. He purposely restricts himself. The only punctuation he allows is the simple cut and the simple wipe. There are no fades, no dissolves, nothing soft, nothing flowing, nothing amorphous. Everything is rigidly either/or. Washizu's banner carries the totemic emblem of the predatory centipede; the flag of the innocent Miki holds a rabbit. Things are as they are, preordained, named. There is no escape, limitations are everywhere, and forest and castle alike are labyrinths.

There is a visual sameness which enforces the visual style. It always rains. There is always fog and wind. The only two scenes where the sun is allowed to shine are, first, at his mansion where Washizu still has a chance, and—second—when he is leading his men, and may still turn back. Also, action turns back upon itself in the form of parallel and repetition. The original rebel, from whom Washizu defended the lord, becomes Washizu himself. The dead lord's lady kills herself as Asaji will in turn commit suicide. During the banquet the entertainment consists of a *kyogen* dance and the singer sings:

> *All of you wicked. Listen while*
> *I tell of a man, vain,*
> *Sinful, vile—*
> *Who, though ambitious, insolent*
> *Could not escape his punishment.*

Thus this entertainment becomes comment. The past warriors—the ghosts which the witch raises—all have had the same career as Washizu, and he will end as they have. The chorus at beginning and end, the battles during the first scenes and the last, the two views of the ruins of the castle—all of this suggests repetition and the same actions endlessly, mindlessly repeating themselves.

A now famous example is when Miki and Washizu are lost in the woods near the beginning of the picture and we watch them—in the uncut version of the film—gallop out of the fog and into it, not once nor twice, but for twelve whole times. Part of the reason is that, as Kurosawa has said, he has always liked the idea of a samurai galloping in and out of the fog. But another reason is that this repeated action suggests futility just as certainly as do the repeated actions in the full *L'Avventura*.

The restriction of image is matched by the restriction of technique. There are, for example, almost no close-ups. Kurosawa has said that

this was because of the Noh influence where, naturally, everything is seen full. "There are very few close-ups. I tried to do everything using full-shots. Japanese almost never make films this way and I remember I confused my staff thoroughly with my instructions. They were so used to moving up for moments of emotion and I kept telling them to move back."

Another reason, besides that of the Noh influence, might have been that alienation is one of the effects of moving the camera back, just as moving it forward suggests empathy. The full-shot reveals everything, which is one of the reasons it is so effective in comedy: it disengages the viewer and allows him to see cause and effect. In *The Throne of Blood* the camera is always furthest away from its characters when they are undergoing the most strain. Washizu sits, struggling with his conscience, with his wish to kill his lord, and Asaji glides behind him. His face is contorted and he is sweating. The scene calls for a close-up but this is rigorously denied. It is as though we had no wish to involve ourselves with them. Only at the end of the film, during the immolation of Washizu by the arrows of his own men, do we get close-ups.

This splendid, indeed almost operatic finale—where Macbeth becomes Verdi's rather than Shakespeare's—is a protracted death agony. Washizu panics, the arrows thud into the wood around him, stick into his armor, then into his flesh. Slowly, tottering, he descends from the ramparts—a human porcupine. He advances upon his enemies, his own men. He stands before them, he is confronting them. It is as though only will keeps him alive. Then, before our eyes, an arrow transfixes his neck. He falls, rolls, lies still. The swirling mist covers his body.

What, one wonders, was Washizu intending to do—to merely confront? punish? or to reach out, to believe, to love? His motions have become inhuman, his face expresses nothing. It is too late. The camera peers very closely during this last scene and we realize that it is not sympathy which impels the closer view, it is cold curiosity. As we watch he falls, dies. The mists cover him. The chorus is heard insisting that what once was true is yet true, that he walks as a ghost. This is fitting. All ghosts share this theme: endless repeated actions, souls caught forever, fixed in their identifying act.

Since Kurosawa is showing us a causal world not only are his people caught by their own acts, they treat their future as magic and consequently live lives rich in prophecy, augeries, and presage. Asaji and her lord plan the first murder. He is unable to sleep, he says. The camera looks at him. Past him, past the *shoji* in the courtyard of the castle, a horse is running, round and round, galloping wildly, unable to stop, racing in a circle. Again, Asaji tells her husband that she is with child. The scene is cut short and the next shows a horse, wild, whinnying, kicking and scattering the servants. It is an evil omen, they say, but which do they mean?—the horse or the child?

Again, after the death of Miki, and after the hired assassin is killed, a great wind rises, shaking the castle. Again—one of the most brilliant scenes Kurosawa has achieved—the servants are gathered together and they speak of the rats leaving the castle. They know that Washizu is going to fight and they do not think he will win. He is having a war council in the upper chambers when, suddenly, the rooms are invaded by birds. Wood doves, grouse, larks, hop and flutter. Trapped, they swoop at the astonished courtiers. In the silence, broken only by the hundreds of fluttering wings, the distant sound is heard of wood being cut. The enemy is destroying the forest and the birds have fled. The courtiers see this as an evil omen. Washizu stands, says it is omen indeed, a good omen, for it means that the enemy is trapped in the forest.

He has long had faith in the forest. It will protect the castle which has become his citadel. It is, as Miki says at the beginning of the film: "... a maze, for here the enemy would lose his way and never find us." Washizu has equal faith in the castle: "No one could defeat the man who planned this place. They cannot see us here inside, while we can see them all." This fortified castle, as labyrinthine as the palace in Olivier's *Hamlet*, is the burrow, and it is thought safe. The forest is not safe (it harbors a witch and her ghosts, is very easy to be lost in) but its function is to protect the castle. Yet, it does not. At one point the witch says: "It is a natural labyrinth if you follow the trails. Therefore avoid them. Go straight ahead and do not let the trails deceive you." This is excellent advice, and fine philosophy as well. But Washizu trusts to the trails in all things, including those well travelled highways that presume to lead to good and evil.

Hence his terror and wonder during that fine scene toward the end of the film when he leans from the ramparts of his safe castle and sees the wood advancing upon him. It is alive and moving, the trees are marching down the hill. It is a cataract of foliage. Kurosawa shows us this scene using slow motion and long-distance lenses. The screen seems to dissolve, serrated from top to bottom, grass, men, trees, grass, trees, the entire hillside flowing, the forest seen as a waterfall, one which will deluge the very castle Washizu thought safe.

The magical forest is powerless to save him now for what are paths, even false ones, when the trees are gone? The forest has become a plain and the castle, the very center of Washizu's being and ambition, stands naked and exposed. And it is here that he finally recognizes his enemy. It is the castle itself, it is this edifice which has become himself and which "no one could defeat." It is true that the enemy could never take it but there is always more than one enemy. An arrow thuds into the wood beside him as he stares at the streaming forest. The true enemy is himself, his own men. A crow caws—poetic presage of death, as in *The Lower Depths*. He turns to face the arrows.

One remembers something which Asaji has earlier said: "Without ambition, man is not a man." This is true, and this is where ambition leads, man immolated upon himself. To be human means to realize yourself, to realize yourself means ambition, ambition is what others call evil. This indeed is why "human beings can't live with each other with more good will." They cannot because they are human.

# PRODUCTION

Kurosawa did not intend this film for himself. "Originally, I wanted merely to produce the picture and let someone younger direct it. But when the script was finished and Toho saw how expensive it would be, they asked me to direct it. So I did. My contract expired after these next three films anyway." Perhaps if he had written the script with himself in mind he might have written it differently. He has said that the scripts he does for others are usually much richer in visuals than those he does for himself—and *The Throne of Blood* is visually extremely rich. But what occurred, he says, is that he often visualized scenes differently from the way he had written them. Not that he improvised, or invented on the set. "I never do that. I tried it once. Never again. I had to throw out all of the impromptu stuff." What he did do, once he knew he was to direct the picture, was to begin a study of the traditional Japanese *musha-e*—those early picture scrolls of battle scenes. At the same time he asked Kohei Esaki—famous for continuing this genre—to be the art consultant.

The designer, Yoshiro Muraki, remembers: "We studied old castle layouts, the really old ones, not those white castles we still have around. And we decided to use black and armored walls since they would go well with the *suiboku-ga* (ink-painting) effect we planned with lots of mist and fog. That also is the reason we decided that the locations should be high on Mount Fuji, because of the fog and the black volcanic soil. But . . . we created something which never came from any single historical period. To emphasize the psychology of the hero, driven by compulsion, we made the interiors wide with low ceilings and squat pillars to create the effect of oppression." Kurosawa remembers that "first, we built an open set at the base of Fuji with a flat castle rather than a real three-dimensional one. When it was ready, it just didn't look right. For one thing, the roof tiles were too thin and this would not do. I insisted and held out, saying I could not possibly work with such limitations, that I wanted to get the feeling of the real thing from wherever I chose to shoot." Consequently, Toho having learned from *Seven Samurai* onward that Kurosawa would somehow get his way, the entire open set was dismantled.

"About sets," Kurosawa has admitted: "I'm on the severe side. This is from *Ikiru* onward. Until then we had to make do with false-fronts. We didn't have the material. But you cannot expect to get a feeling of realism if you use, for example, cheap new wood in a set which is supposed to be an old farm-house. I feel very strongly about this. After all, the real life of any film lies just in its being as true as possible to appearances."

After a further argument with Ezaki, who wanted a high and towering castle while Kurosawa wanted a low and squat one, the set eventually used was built—to Kurosawa's specifications (which were extreme: even the lacquer-ware had to be especially made, from models which he found in museums). "It was a very hard film to make. I decided that the main castle set had to be built high up on Fuji and we didn't have enough people and the location was miles from Tokyo. Fortunately there was a U.S. Marine Corps base nearby and they helped a lot. We all worked very hard, clearing the ground, building the set, and doing the whole thing on this steep, fog-bound slope. An entire MP battalion helped most of the time. I remember it absolutely exhausted all of us—we almost got sick."

Actually, only the castle exteriors were shot here. The castle court-yard (with volcanic soil brought all the way from Fuji so that the ground would match) was constructed at Toho's Tamagawa studios in the suburbs, and the interiors were shot in a smaller Tokyo studio. In addition, the forest scenes were a combination of actual Fuji forest and studio in Tokyo, and Washizu's mansion was miles away from anywhere, in the Izu peninsula.

I remember this set particularly. Like all the others it was completely three dimensional and was, in effect, a real mansion set in the midst of rice paddies in an almost inaccessible valley. I remember it particularly because I was there when Kurosawa visualized a scene. Though it was in the script, there had been little indication as to how it would be seen and, after some thought the night before, Kurosawa had decided. The scenes included those where a messenger comes announcing the arrival of the lord and his hunting party.

Washizu, already thinking of murder, rushes out of his mansion, astonished that fortune should at this time direct that the lord appear for the night.

The first camera was on a platform inside the mansion gates, and the second was located in the rice-field outside, the two cameras hidden from each other by an angle in the wall. Kurosawa was on the platform, looking through the finder, and selecting the angle he thought best.

There was one rehearsal and then the take. From the far distance, the messenger galloped up on horseback and announced the lord. The castle retainers rushed out of the gate and the scene was stopped because one of them slipped and fell down. "A little too much atmosphere," said Kurosawa, everyone laughed, and the scene was re-shot.

The main camera was taking this scene from inside the gates, while the auxiliary camera was taking it from the side. The next scene, a continuation of the first, shot the messenger giving his message and the main camera was equipped with long-distance lenses. After this was shot, the two cameras, both with long-distance lenses, shot the distant hunting party (complete with deer and boar, an enormous procession) advancing. The next shot in this small sequence was to show Mifune rushing out as the distraught Washizu. Mifune practiced running back and forth to get himself properly winded, and the take was made, with both cameras panning with him, one with long-distance lenses. Then more scenes were taken of the advancing hunting party, its number now swelled by all the neighborhood farmers that the production chief could find costumes for.

Particularly fine were those rushes of the advancing hunting party, both the long silhouette shots and, later, the advance, taken with long-distance lenses which flattened the figures out and looked like a medieval tapestry. After they were taken Kurosawa said he was pleased. "I have about ten times more than I need."

In the finished film this morning's work takes ten seconds. Gone are the living tapestries ("they only held up the action"); the wonderful turning shots of the messenger ("I don't know—they looked confused to me"); a splendid entrance of Mifune skidding to a stop ("you know, Washizu wasn't *that* upset"); and a lovely framing shot of the procession seen through the gate ("too pretty").

I still think of Kurosawa that morning, up on his platform, direct-

ing everything, always quiet, suggesting rather than commanding, looking through the view-finders, getting down to run through the mud to the other camera, making jokes, getting just what he wanted. And then—having the courage, the discipline to choose from that morning's richness just these few frames which contained what would best benefit the film. And, all the time, making the definitive statement on man's solitude, his ambition, his self-betrayal.

# The Lower Depths

"I'd always wanted to make Gorky's play into a movie," Kurosawa has said: "…into a really easy and entertaining movie. After all *The Lower Depths* isn't at all gloomy. It is very funny and I remember laughing over it. That is because we are shown people who really want to live and we are shown them—I think—humorously. People are just supposed to relax and enjoy this picture as they would any programmer." Another interpretation of the play is that it is one of the great sob-stories of the stage. And it is this desperate and pathetic aspect that is insisted upon in both the Mosfilm 1952 version and in the film scenario which Gorky himself wrote in the early 1930's. It is possible but not likely that Kurosawa intended his remarks to be ironical. It would be just like him see the affirmation rather than the negation. It would be equally possible for him to see *Paradise Lost* as ending happily. (Indeed, he almost did so in *High and Low*.)

Elsewhere, Kurosawa has mentioned another reason for turning Gorky's play into a film. "I wanted to make a stage play. I wanted to see what I could do." He did, indeed, so splendidly that one wonders what he could not do if he (like Visconti and Bergman) occasionally worked for the stage.

"Gorky's period was Imperial Russia but I changed it to Japan, the Edo period. [Here, perhaps, Kurosawa's choice *was* ironic. Most Japanese look back to the Edo period with some romantic nostalgia—period of the great courtesans, the great actors, the great woodcut artists. Kurosawa, on the other hand, here thinks of life at that time as comparable to the miseries of nineteenth century Russia.] In Edo [now Tokyo] during this period, the Shogunate was falling to pieces and thousands were living almost unendurable lives. Their resentment we can still feel in the *senryu* and *rakushu* [satirical poems and entertainments] of the time. Anyway, I wanted to show this atmosphere, to reveal it—though whether I really did or not, I don't know."

## THE SOURCE

The transformation to film is literal. If one compares the play with the scenario, one is surprised how little is added, how little removed. It is as though Kurosawa so agreed with Gorky (as he did with Dostoevsky) that he could find little to change. The picture then is, in this sense, an adaptation—much more so than *The Throne of Blood* (where *Macbeth* is made into a psychological *jidai-geki*) or *They Who Step on the Tiger's Tail* (where *Kanjincho* turns into an indictment of the very things it stands for). Kurosawa is in such basic agreement with Gorky that whole pages of dialogue and action remain the same. The difference is one of interpretation—action and dialogue may remain the same but Kurosawa's emphasis is different from Gorky's which is why the film may be seen as a comedy although the play is usually seen as something different from that. This is more clearly seen in Kurosawa's precise delineation of the major characters.

## CHARACTERIZATION

As is well-known, Gorky's play is no star vehicle. It is for a repertory company and it is only repertory companies which continue to give it. This aspect was one which appealed to Kurosawa because he has never liked the idea of the "star" and, besides, had already formed what remains the best repertory company in Japan, stage or otherwise. Thus (as in the films of Bergman) well-known stars (Kyoko Kagawa, Isuzu Yamada, Ganjiro Nakamura, Toshiro Mifune) were given non-starring roles and the emphasis was (here more than in any other Kurosawa film) upon the ensemble rather than upon the actor.

This interest has always been visible in Kurosawa's films and something could perhaps be made of his preoccupation with the group-hero—the warrior-priests in *They Who Step on the Tiger's Tail*, the groupings of warriors, bandits, and farmers in *Seven Samurai*, even the boy-samurai in *Sanjuro*). His interest in the various problems of ensemble acting, however—the meshing or clashing of various moods or intentions, the playing off of one character against another, usually within the same frame—began with *Record of a Living Being* and continued in this picture. It is perhaps for this reason that he saw in Gorky's play a collection of *individuals* and consequently failed to be saddened or disturbed by the sense of misery and waste which comes if you see the play as group-message or social comment or something of the sort.

As in Gorky, the character that talks the most is the gambler (Satin in the original; here called Yoshisaburo and played by Koji Mitsui) and it is he who has both the first and last words—though this does not make him the most important of the characters. He is, however, the most cynical: he does not hope. When someone says to him that he'd better watch out, he'll end up in hell, he calmly turns and says that he already lives in hell. (Dialogue which is written by Kurosawa, not Gorky, voicing a thought common in many of his films—the same thing is said in *Rashomon, Record of a Living Being,* and *High and Low.*) Since he knows the worst, he can sit back and enjoy things (just like the hero of *Yojimbo*), taking neither side, simply commenting on the spectacle. When the thief and landlord have a fight, he shouts out: "Fine—end of act one." (This line belongs to the actor in Gorky but Kurosawa here gives it to this amoral gambler —and does much the same thing in *The Bad Sleep Well* when the same actor, playing a newspaperman, comments on the action by saying: "What do you mean—one-act play? This is only the prelude.") Consequently the gambler amuses himself at the expense of others. He tries to get the actor to spend the few coins he earned in order to go to the place where he thinks he'll be cured of his passion for saké; he is pleased when the old woman dies because he won't be disturbed by her coughing any more; he delights in refusing to believe that the ex-samurai was a samurai at all. At the same time, since he is so uninvolved in any of the action, he can see more clearly than the others. When they insist that the old pilgrim lied when he said there was still hope left in the world, it is the gambler who says: "Of course he lied, but he only lied in order to encourage you. The world is full of people like you, and the old man merely supplied what you needed—what you can't live without." The implication is that he, the gambler, can live very well without hope and he thus becomes the single person who is not deeply involved either with the others or with himself. He consequently becomes the only one we can trust. It is for this reason that his final words have such an effect.

All the others are untrustworthy because each has an idea of himself which does not correspond to the reality of his situation. This is, of course, the genesis of all comedy and is probably the reason why Kurosawa originally found the Gorky play funny. Indeed, the ragged samurai living on dreams of the past; the whore living on dreams of an impossible love; the tinker fancying himself a craftsman; the thief thinking himself redeemed through love—all of this is very funny because it is so inappropriate to the situation, and it amuses the gambler exceedingly.

Having rid himself of hope he rids himself of compassion. It is not so easy for us (nor for Kurosawa), because our laughter would indicate that we are not like them at all (as indeed the gambler is not), when in actuality we are all so very like them that their various disappointments and miseries become real to us.

Their illusions and delusions are various and share in common only that they are completely necessary if life is to continue. The craftsman, for example (called Kletsch in the original; here called Tomekichi and played by Eijiro Tono) needs to believe that he is a craftsman though all he does is mend, first, an old pot that no one wants, and finally, a drum (taking the place of the accordion in the original). He can stand the death of his wife easily enough but he cannot stand being forced to face that he is not what he thinks he is. The samurai is speaking of the facts of life: "I take things as I find them and I face facts." The tinker has been brooding and suddenly bursts into a great rage: "You and your 'facts.' Here are your 'facts'—no money, no work, and the only thing you can do is to starve to death. Does facing facts like this help you at all?" (It is interesting that Kurosawa here completely neglects one of the points Gorky stresses when he has his locksmith take violent exception to someone's remark that nobody has a good life, and shouts: "Nobody? That's a lie. Some people have it all right. If everyone suffered it would be all right and you wouldn't feel that life had been so unfair." It is as though Kurosawa felt that social criticism was much less important than this painstaking—and occasionally painful—exploration of human motive and desire.) For himself, the tinker has arrived at a truth and one which cruelly exposes his own identification of himself because a craftsman who makes no money and starves is, by his own definition, no craftsman at all.

The landlady (Vassilissa in the original; here called Osugi and played by Isuzu Yamada who was 'Lady Macbeth' in *The Throne of Blood*) does not vaccilate in this manner and consequently has no such moments of naked despair. Earlier she has decided what she wants to get and how she wants to get it. It is a dog-eat-dog world and so she wants power. She married for this reason and she has played up to the thief for the same reason. To be powerful, in her sense, however, means that you must have power *over* someone. She has her younger sister, she has her lodgers, she has her husband, and she has the thief. Greedy, she tries to get the latter to kill her husband but when he actually does she sees that this will lead to yet more power if she can have him sent to jail for it. She has, in other words, chosen evil. Rather than rising above the rules of the world (as does the gambler) or trying to live patiently within them (as does the craftsman), she decides to use them. There is a special punishment for people who do this. At the end (much more certainly in the Kurosawa than in the Gorky), she is probably punished by the law for being an accomplice in the very crime to which she so urged her robber-lover. By choosing to identify herself as evil she has brought what she would call evil down upon herself.

Her sister (Natasha in the original; here called Okayo and played by Kyoko Kagawa, who was later the wife in both *The Bad Sleep Well* and *High and Low*) has not advanced nearly so far into evil, perhaps because she suffered at the hands of her elder sister. Still, distrust and suspicion are sometimes the beginnings of a dedicated badness, and these she certainly has. Though she admits that she is just waiting for something nice to happen (much as the whore is waiting for the same thing), when it finally comes and the thief honestly and sincerely proposes to take her away, she distrusts and, at the debacle, when he kills her uncle, she instantly believes the worst, thinks the whole thing was a plot to get *her*, and more loudly than anyone else denounces the man who truly thought he loved her. If her sister believed too strongly in the illusion that she was all-powerful, this girl believes too strongly in the illusion that she is powerless.

Her uncle (Kostylyov in the original; Rokubei in the film and played by the Kabuki actor Ganjiro Nakamura) is a combination of wife and niece. He has (like the former) decided to play the game with the world's weapons but (like the latter) has become powerless. At the same time he insists upon his long-vanished power and uses this illusion to keep what little self-respect *he* finds necessary for life. At the same time, knowing his power is going, he is trying to find a new role for himself and that is the role of philanthropist. This is not surprising when one considers that power over others is often predicated upon doing wholly bad or doing wholly good. His mistake is that he vacillates between them, as in the following passage.

*Actor:* (To the tinker). I put your wife out in the sun.

*Rokubei:* Ah, you have done a good deed. Your kindness will one day be rewarded.

*Actor:* When?

*Rokubei:* Oh, in the next world.

*Actor:* I'd rather have it in this one. How about canceling half of what I owe you.

*Rokubei:* You are joking. It is no joke. Kindness is very precious. Kindness is something you cannot buy. Besides (*thinking*) kindness is one thing. Debt is another. Don't mix them up.

As a landlord I'm like a father to you. You are all my children.

*Gambler:* Yes, indeed. The devil's own brood.

Naturally, the landlord is hypocrisy itself but, after all, what we call hypocrisy is only the result of two (unsatisfactory because mutually contradictory) images which one has of oneself. Later, the travelling priest looks at him and says: "No matter how bad a man is, he must have someone to love him. If no one loves you, that means that your days are numbered." This is shown as literally true. In the very next cut we see the old landlord pottering about, suddenly feeling a chill, suddenly hearing the caw of a crow—presage of death. He pulls his kimono closer about him and in the next sequence he is murdered. Like the actor, he perhaps tried to change (he wanted to become a

paternal tyrant) and it was this which killed him. Either strongly evil (like his wife) or strongly good (like the pilgrim) or above it all (like the gambler) and he would have had more time. But, selfish as all the others, and incapable of loving, he naturally had no one to love him.

The sister dimly realizes that perhaps love will solve her problems, and the whore is convinced of it (to the point of going around and telling everyone the story of her great love affair—true in that she thinks it is, though she gets the name of the lover confused from one telling to the other). The only one who really feels the great opportunity which love seems to offer is the thief (Vassily in the original; here Sutekichi and played by Toshiro Mifune—so beautifully played that this is not only Mifune's finest single role but also one of the great pieces of acting in Japanese cinema). He falls in love.

*Sutekichi*: Let's leave, together.
*Okayo*: To jail?
*Sutekichi*: Don't you believe me? I'm not a thief any more. I swear it. I'll work hard but I just can't go on like this. Lots of thieves never get caught and this used to make me feel a lot better but not any more. I'm troubled. I don't regret what I've done. I'd have died if I hadn't stolen. But there must be a better life than this. I can't go on living like this.
*Priest*: You're absolutely right.
*Sutekichi*: Let's look together ... it is easier to look together than alone.
*Okayo*: But I can't trust you—I can't trust anyone.
 ... What about my sister?
*Sutekichi*: Who cares about her?
*Priest*: She meant nothing to him. She just happened to be there when he needed someone.
*Sutekichi*: Needed? It was like stepping on a rotten board.

He therefore (like everyone who falls in love) needs someone. The older sister did not support him—indeed, she threatened to upset him completely. Now he has again fallen in love. This time with a girl who would, indeed, not be too weak nor too strong for him if she but trusted him. But she does not and that is ironic because, as the priest says, they are "made for each other."

Of all of the various snares, love is the most attractive, and the most dangerous, because it seems to offer such security and, at the same time, such hope. The ex-samurai ('the Baron' in the original; the 'Tono-sama' here and played by Minoru Chiaki, the priest in *Rashomon,* etc.) lives on his past and keeps remembering former glories which were (perhaps) actually real. But he is alone in his delusion, just as the whore (Nastya in the original; Osen here and played by Akemi Negishi who was the mistress in *Record of a Living Being*) is alone and both live on memories. They are relatively secure—

memory can curb if not keep off reality. Sutekichi and Okayo *are* rather than *have been.* He believes in the reality of the promise, in the actuality of the hope. And it is here that he gets caught. Like the actor, like the hero in *The Bad Sleep Well,* he 'reforms' too late. Perhaps if he had not reformed ... ? But then, as he himself has said, he could no longer go on that way.

The actor (played by Kamatari Fujiwara, one of the bumpkins in *The Hidden Fortress,* the stoker in *High and Low,* etc.) also tries to reform. An alcoholic, his last hope is a temple the priest tells him about where he can get cured. At one point he tries to remember a passage from the Kabuki that he was particularly fond of, but his memory is gone.

*Actor*: I can't remember a word—and they were my favorite lines.
*Priest*: That is bad. You should never forget what you have loved. The things you love are the things to live for.

The actor finally decides. Even when (drunk) he remembers his lines (though there is no one to hear them now so he does them alone) he still decides that he will go and be cured. He works all day to get money. He stays away from saké. He is dead sober. The sobriety kills him. He takes a drink to stiffen his nerves, goes out and kills himself, which is a thing he would probably not have done drunk. As with the thief—resolve undoes him.

Then, as Okayo asks, "Is no one happy in this world—are we all like this?" Is there no escape at all? There is, perhaps, one way, but it is like the temple in the mountains that the priest speaks of. It is very difficult to reach and even he has forgotten the name of the place. Still, such a place (such a way) ought to exist.

The one person who has rid himself even more of delusion than has the gambler is the priest (Luka in the original, Kahei in the film, played by Bokuzen Hidari who was the old clerk in *Ikiru,* etc.). He knows what the world is like ("Oh, the way that people live here," he says twice in the film, and both times with great pity, with great compassion) and he knows that hope is necessary for others, if not himself. In this he differs from the gambler who believes that hope ought to be unnecessary for everyone—and acts accordingly. The priest knows that hope is, however unfortunately, necessary—even in the face of death. The dying wife speaks to him:

*Wife*: I'm afraid. Lonely and afraid.
*Priest*: That's right. You feel like that when death is near. Don't be afraid. Everything will be all right. Once you are dead, everything will be all right. No more pain. You will enjoy your rest in blessed peace.
*Wife*: Really? Are you sure?
*Priest*: Now why should I lie to you? ... Buddha will bless you and show you mercy.
 ...
*Wife*: But suppose ... suppose I get well again.

| | |
|---|---|
| *Priest:* | What for?—more suffering? |
| *Wife:* | Even though it hurts, I want to live. Just a little longer. Just a little. If there is no sorrow in the next world, then I might be able to stand it a little longer down here. |

Even the thief, who has made fun of the above exchange, needs hope.

| | |
|---|---|
| *Sutekichi:* | You are very smooth—you liar. You say that paradise is anywhere except here. Well, I don't believe it. |
| *Priest:* | Then go and find out for yourself. You say you hate lies. Yet lies are not always evil. Nor is the truth always good. Think twice before the truth makes them hang you. |
| | . . . |
| *Sutekichi:* | Tell me straight, now. Does paradise really exist? |
| *Priest:* | . . . |
| *Sutekichi:* | Tell me. |
| *Priest:* | It does to those who want it. |

The answer is similar to some advice that the priest gives the actor.

| | |
|---|---|
| *Priest:* | It's a temple. I don't remember its name but I will soon enough. First, you must make up your mind to get well, and not to drink. Then, when you are well, you can start all over again. |
| *Actor:* | All over again? That's a nice thought. But . . . do you think I can do it? I am weak. |
| *Priest:* | Of course you can. A person can do anything he really wants to. You can do anything. |

This is the truth but what the priest refrains from mentioning is that while everything is possible if you want it enough, just wanting it enough is the real problem. Man is very weak and it is almost impossible to want something enough to make it happen.

This solution to life's difficulties (wanting something enough) has been one of the major themes in Kurosawa's work and his finding it in Gorky might have been one of the things that decided him to eventually film the play. Kurosawa's characters sometimes not only want something but they want it sufficiently: Sugata stays in the pool; Yukie goes and works with the peasants; Murakami finds his gun; Watanabe builds his park; Kambei wins the war for the peasants; Rokurota gets both princess and gold through the enemy lines. They all wanted something so badly that they were ready to undergo all sorts of difficulties to achieve it. (The "failures" such as the heroes of *The Bad Sleep Well* and *Drunken Angel* fail, first, because what they wanted was not truly enough; second, because they see it is not enough and attempt to change. In *The Lower Depths* both actor and thief fail because they do not want enough what they want—both lack that completely irrational faith that Murakami showed when he began to search for his pistol, that Watanabe showed when he built his park.)

The priest knows this. After he leaves, everyone in the tenement is changed; not for the better, simply changed. As the gambler said: "Of course he lied, but he only lied in order to encourage you . . . the old man merely supplied what was needed." And earlier he has voiced what might be the major theme of both play and film when he says: "Blessed are those who can believe in something even if it is nothing."

Belief and hope are answers but both gambler and pilgrim have put themselves beyond them. Yet the gambler's cynical insistence upon his own freedom from hope is in itself a kind of hope, and his belief is just that he is beyond belief. The pilgrim is different and, of all the people in both the play and the film, it is fitting that he should therefore be the only one who came into this tenement of his own free will and who leaves of his own free will. He is, in fact, the only one who *is* free.

He carries this freedom about with him as he carries his pilgrim's pack and, since it has become *his*, he is free to move as he will. He does not, as he says, know where he is going. And consequently he is not afraid. He needs nothing since he is sufficient to himself and for this reason he need not be consistent. This is why all the others are so attracted to him. He seems to be a part of themselves because he so easily leaves himself and becomes them. The whore has quite fallen in love with him, the actor is entranced, even the gambler is impressed. But none of these impress the priest. At the end of the first act in the Gorky the dying wife says: "You remind me of my father—just as kind . . . and soft." And he replies: "I've been thoroughly trampled upon. That's why I'm soft." Kurosawa's emphasis is entirely different.

| | |
|---|---|
| *Wife:* | You are a nice old man . . . very nice. |
| *Priest:* | Oh, I'm like a pebble in the river . . . washed down from the mountains, polished smooth all over. |

Mountain pebbles are hard, not soft—and the priest is not soft in the slightest. He is, like a rock, of indeterminate form and it is possible to find all kinds of shapes in a single stone. But, find what you will, the rock remains the rock. As the thief has said, he is very smooth—in both senses of the word. He, it would seem, is the only person in the film then who knows what reality is and who is not afraid to face it.

The picture is, along with *Rashomon,* Kurosawa's major statement concerning his continual preoccupation with illusion versus reality. The other characters insist upon one illusion or another. Only the priest can endure naked reality. And this is why Kurosawa makes him comic—because the priest is very funny (and indeed—as in *They Who Step on the Tiger's Tail*—the part is played by a fairly well-known comedian; having Bokuzen Hidari play the part in this Japanese production would be somewhat analogous to having Smiley Burnette play the part in some American production). Comedy is certainly one of the results of believing in illusion to the point of incongruity;

but another cause of high comedy, as Kurosawa will again indicate in *Yojimbo,* is being free of illusion. The glimpse of reality which all of us achieve from time to time can result either in suicide or in laughter.

If the result is laughter, then life becomes a kind of divertissement, serious but a show nonetheless. The gambler refuses to take it seriously because he knows it is a show. The priest, knowing it to be a performance, nevertheless allows himself the luxury of—at the same time—half believing it. And this is important because it means that he may not only observe, he himself may also live. The gambler does not live so much as he observes. Consequently he judges the quality of the performance, something that the priest would not do.

At the very end of both play and film, a kind of play within a play has begun, and the inmates have started to sing and caper about. Then comes the news that the actor has hung himself. The whore is fearful—she feels perhaps that she will be next. All of the others are uneasy. Death is near. The gambler, however, has seen only another performance—he does not see that the alternative to suicide is laughter —and so, even a bit petulantly, he says: "The idiot . . . just as the fun was beginning."

His personal pleasure has been spoiled, and it was he who allowed it to be. After the curtain has come down, after the screen is darkened, it is not impossible to imagine all of them sitting there, their thoughts turning to the vanished priest. Reality (suicide) has spoiled their fun. How would the priest have reacted, what would he have done, would not he perhaps have been able to make a kind of sense from this chaos?

# TREATMENT

Kurosawa has never been one to allow himself indulgences, but only in *They Who Step on the Tiger's Tail* has he been more rigorous than here. There it was through outside influences (the war, lack of equipment, etc.) but here it was through choice. There are but two sets. Three-quarters of the film is in a single room; the other quarter is in an adjoining courtyard. Not once do we see beyond the confines to the town.

Confinement is suggested from the first image onward. The film opens with an almost three hundred-sixty degree pan, shooting upward to show the cliffs that enclose the tenement, a pan which explicates the confines and shows that there is no escape. It begins at a small temple, makes its circle, and when it returns two acolytes are there, emptying baskets of leaves into this deep and small valley where we are confined. Not only is it a hole from which there is no escape; it is also the kind of place where others dump refuse. In a single cut we are then inside that room we will come to know so well and the action begins.

The room is chaos: dirt, filth, people lying here and there; no sign of any order—and the noise! Throughout the picture people shout and scream and to this is added the irritatingly irregular sound of the tinker banging his pot. As in other pictures (*One Wonderful Sunday, Record of a Living Being, The Quiet Duel*) Kurosawa makes wonderfully maddening use of both visual and aural ostenati. By the time the pilgrim-priest arrives he is to us (as to them) something like respite in this clangorous hell in which they live.

At the same time, Kurosawa is continually reminding us (as the priest reminds them) that this is a *performance* we are watching. He does this, first, by being literal, by adapting Gorky; second, by insisting upon the same act divisions that the original uses (the only fades in the film are here; and the following scene is a short placing shot: leaves on the roof, or rain pouring down the eaves—there is no punctuation other than the straight cut); and third by insuring that the actors themselves give great *performances,* which is a completely different thing from great interpretations.

As he himself has said: "We worked steadily and well, and the shooting did not take long . . . . We had many rehearsals and worked out all the choreography (actors, camera, etc.,) well in advance. Maybe that was why it was so easy to make." He had, in fact, a forty-day rehearsal period in which all the cast and technicians assembled on the set in full make up and costume, with cameras running though empty. At the end of this month and a half any "interpretation" with its suggestion of "feeling the part" and so on, had long evaporated. The actors were so immersed in their roles that they could *only* perform.

The performances they give are great. Singly, each actor rises to heights of professionality (rather than inspiration) he had rarely reached before; together, the production is a miracle of ensemble playing—each pause, each delivery, is so superbly timed, so properly gauged that it becomes a word-ballet, a pantomime of spare and meaningful gesture.

One might single out Mifune's performance. His mimicry is flawless: every one of the recognized details of the *yakuza* is there; the mock-toughness, the little-boy angularity of gesture, the abrupt shift of his kimono skirt, the calculated vulgarity of his squat, the sudden warmth of his smile—the nastiness, the sexiness, the innocence, the danger. All of this is continually before us; yet, as in any great performance, it is varied by the person with whom he is acting. Here Mifune's timing seems almost miraculous. The reactions take precisely the right amount of time—not one second more nor less than required. One is thoroughly convinced that he is absolutely right for the character but, at the same time, there is little that is realistic about it. Real *yakuza* are never (could not be) this *yakuza*-like. At the same time his emotional range is very wide. With the landlady he is a petulant little boy; with her sister he is the ardent lover; with the landlord he is danger itself; with the priest he is an unwillingly curious schoolboy. Mifune shifts from one to the other with never a misstep. He has been talking with the priest about the after-life when he is suddenly aware that the tinker's wife has died. Instantly he is up on his feet, his lips in a little grimace of distaste, making a tiny, angular skip as though to remove himself from the body, admitting—with a boyish grin—that he is afraid of the dead, following this instantly with a look of such real horror that it is almost frightening. His is a superb performance and its whole point is that it *is* a performance. One applauds it as one would that of a solo dancer, an acrobat, an athlete.

The camera continually insists upon the fact that, in this film, acting is presentation rather than interpretation. Stanislavsky would perhaps not like what happens but, for the film, it is superbly right. (So right that, for me at any rate, Renoir's naturalistic *Les bas-fonds* suffers by comparison though, as has been pointed out, it may have been Kurosawa's having seen the Renoir that in part motivated his desire to film the play himself.) For many of the scenes two or three cameras were used, thus sustaining action, performance, and continuity. The scenes of the argument between the thief and the tinker,

131

for example, were shot with two cameras, facing but hidden from each other. The finished scene alternates between positions, dialogue often being given the person seen from the back.

The use of the actor's back (seen in finished form in *Yojimbo*) heightens the feeling of performance because we cannot see his face while he is speaking (something which Godard used impeccably during the opening reel of *Vivre sa vie*). When the thief talks about Buddhism with the priest the camera is behind him, yet he does most of the talking. It is *because* we cannot see his face that (alienated, unable to empathize with a man's back) we look for performance details, and find them everywhere: in the way he pulls back his sleeve, in the way he turns from time to time to show us he is picking his teeth while speaking, etc.

The camera is rarely used for close-ups but when it is the close-ups are usually silent. At one point landlady and thief are embracing and the landlord is watching. They are seen in middle-distance, but the sudden glimpse of the husband is seen in close-up. There he is, peering through the *shoji,* his face half obscured by the torn paper blown by the wind, his lizard-like eyes glistening. Their dialogue continues over this single, still, large image which becomes, still though it is, pantomime: we are watching an actor watching himself watching.

At the same time, the image itself comments. One of the ways it does so is through lighting. When thief and landlady talk about her husband, they move to a darkened corner and are seen black against the light of the room; when the men carry out the body of the tinker's wife they, too, are seen back-lighted, moving dark in front of us; when the actor suddenly remembers his lines, the wind blows out the single candle and he suddenly becomes a silhouette—his speech over, death near.

Another way that the image comments is by use of the architecture of the place. The walls are lined with bunk-beds, each with its own curtain. Thus they (like so many things about Japanese architecture) share something with the stage. A favorite camera position is in front of a pair of such beds, one above the other. The gambler, below, opens his curtains and looks out, or the actor, above, peevishly jerks his shut. It is somewhat like the double stage, used in Japan as well as in Europe, where action occurs both above and below. At the end of the film, the frame itself becomes the stage. The four men dance —grotesque, like something from Gogol, singing and dancing, an apotheosis to futility and to innocence—and the camera, by moving very slightly keeps their heart-breaking 'performance' in the perfect center, framed only by the proscenium lines of the camera-opening. Rather than limiting and making the action appear stagey, this has the opposite effect. It is as though by insisting upon the limitations of the screen itself, we are given a feeling of freedom, freedom at any rate to work within these limitations. This, of course, is precisely

*what* we are being *shown:* human beings, now drunk and carefree, living within an extreme limitation which they continue to feel.

The major way in which image comments (in this film as in many others of Kurosawa) is by working what is photographed into a meaningful and balanced composition. Such images are numerous in the film and the majority of them are both unexpected and subtle. Symmetry is rarely found here. Instead, each is carefully asymmetrical; a far figure somehow balancing someone near; two near figures, one half-obscuring the screen, somehow leading our eye to someone else, tiny in the distance, almost invisible. The most beautiful and meaningful of these is also the most famous. Some of the characters are in the courtyard and the screen is boldly cut by the diagonal of a log which has been placed as a buttress against the house. This diagonal (or others like it) appears throughout the succeeding scenes.

Since the interiors have no diagonals (all is straight up and down—as in all Japanese houses) this sudden diagonal refreshes the constricted eye. Equally important, however, it leads the eye to the apparently fortuitous arrangement of the people themselves. Nearest the camera sit those who speak first, the priest, the whore, the sister, the ex-samurai. On a ledge at some distance sits the man who will speak next. And huddled into the corner in the far distance is the tinker who will speak last. Thus what our eye sees first, directed by composition and also by the dialogue since we always look at people who speak, is the foreground. Dialogue leads us further into the scene but the composition, strengthed by the diagonal, has also prepared us for this. A feeling of naturalness, even reality is the result. Finally, when the tinker speaks, our eye is led into the furthest recess of all. He is so far away that we must look well to distinguish him, must strain our ears to hear him. At the same time, the meaning of the scene, what they say, is given us in reverse-order, as it were. We listen to the whore's love-story (and the composition is enriched, as is usual with Kurosawa, by having people move about, thus changing it) and the probable meaning of what she is saying is revealed by the man sitting further back. But *his* true meaning is only revealed by the tinker who stands up and shouts his speech about the true facts of life. The nearness to the camera is therefore in inverse ratio to the (philosophical) importance of what is being said.

This long, very beautiful, extremely subtle single shot, is so very successful that one can only believe in it as performance—which is just what Kurosawa intended. Its subtlety is so extreme (and Kurosawa's painter's-eye was never put to better use) that one cannot call it arty because it does not draw the kind of attention to itself which makes one realize that it was put there merely because it was pretty. At the same time it is so anti-naturalistic (though it appears perfectly "natural") that one must feel it on two separate levels: emotionally, one sees it as real and satisfying; intellectually, one sees it as a *coup de théâtre.*

Kurosawa enhances this theatrical aspect of the film by using both sound-effects and music in a completely original way. "I used *bakabayashi* [the flute, drums, clappers traditionaly associated with travelling entertainments, with shrine fairs] because we always think of this music as being joyous and festive, and I wanted it to suggest precisely the opposite, something dark and tragic. . . . Also, once, to get everyone in the proper mood, I invited onto the set one of the few remaining old men who could still do Edo *rakugo* [humorous, highly satiric stories] and we never had more fun than on that day." (Another example of Kurosawa's intentions is that "I wanted Mifune to play his part in the style of Nezumi-kozo [a fictious and romantic robber who saves maidens and steals from the rich—the hero of a hundred films. He is naturally a figure much looked down upon by the intelligentsia and only children, farmers, and laborers crowd into his frequent film appearances. A bit like Robin Hood, he is too near in time to have acquired any antique patina and Kurosawa's intentions were personal, interesting, and almost dogmatically un-fashionable] but that didn't work. Mifune is simply too well-built, he has too much presence. He can't help but bring his own dignity to his roles.")

The opening 'music' is highly controlled (performed) in that it consists only of five strokes of a temple bell, and the first stroke coin-cides with the (superimposed) main title. All of the other music, except for the sound-effect at the very end, is made by the cast itself, and there are various snippets from folksongs and from the Kabuki (the actor, when he takes the dying wife into the sun, does so with a line—wry indeed in its context—from the Kabuki, from a *michiyuki* where the two young lovers defy the world and rush off to find hap-piness together); and at the very end there is a full-scale *bakabayashi* with the actors hooting, humming, cackling, crowing, banging on glasses, dishes, and bottles the while.

Then comes the end—one so completely theatrical, so much a presentation itself that it surprises by being so extraordinarily right. The dance has been broken off by news that the actor has killed himself. There is silence, followed by a close-up (rare in this film) of the gambler. His next line, and the last in the film, is directed not to the others, but to us, since the gambler speaks directly into the camera.

Even used for comic effect (as in Laurel and Hardy), this is an unnerving experience. Given the context of death, despair, and chaos, it becomes even more upsetting. Then he says—in effect—that the actor's death has spoiled not only his fun, but ours as well. He is therefore insisting upon our being spectators, upon our having seen a performance, neither more nor less. It is like the epilogue in *Don Giovanni* where—moved, impressed, near tears—we are suddenly asked to view the whole thing as a comedy and nothing more.

At the same time Kurosawa makes *his* comment. The last three seconds of film are:

1. *Gambler:* The idiot . . . just as the fun was beginning.
2. A cut to complete darkness (black film) accompanied by a single sharp, percussive stroke from the *hyoshige,* the clappers used to begin and end traditional Japanese theatrical entertainments.
3. The end title (appearing in silence), glowing briefly (white against black) and swiftly fading away.

A number of things have happened. The gambler, who has been acting as chorus, as *our* spokesman, suddenly turns and, as it were, accuses us; the *hyoshige* insists (along with him) that what we have seen is not real, that it has all been illusion, a purely theatrical presentation; and suddenly it is all over. The final song and dance have been intensely moving as only the sight of unknowing innocence can be moving in a world shown as hopeless. Then, like cold water dashed in the face, we are told to come out of it, to come off it, the show's over.

The ending is very shocking. It certainly shocked the Japanese, the majority of whom disliked the film; the critics were particularly strong on what they innocently called Kurosawa's "negative" attitude. His attitude is, of course, nothing of the sort. Unlike his audience, Kurosawa prefers to take life straight, to see illusion as illusion. No more positive attitude can be imagined, nor any attitude more dif-ficult. It is, indeed, so difficult that it becomes funny. He was right: *The Lower Depths* is a very funny play, and the film is a very funny film. If life is not something to cry over, then it must become something to laugh about.

# The Hidden Fortress

## MATERIALS

It is the sixteenth century, a period of civil wars. A princess, with her family, her retainers, and the clan treasure is being pursued. If they can cross enemy territory and reach a friendly province they will be saved. The enemy knows this and posts a reward for the capture of the princess.

She is being guarded by one of her generals and it is he who leads her on the long and dangerous journey that follows. They take along with them the sixteen hundred pounds of gold and also two farmers whom the general has captured.

All are caught at the barrier-station, within sight of safety. Their captor, however, is revealed as a warrior whom the princess' general once defeated and who thereupon suffered great disgrace. He joins their

escape and the entire party eventually finds refuge in the friendly province where the two farmers are rewarded for their help.

In synopsis, this sounds like any of the hundred-or-so period pictures which the Japanese industry annually turns out—and that is just the point of the film. Kurosawa here—as in *Sanjuro*—purposely uses the very stuff from which the sword-fight costume-pictures are made: coincidence, loyalty, disguised princesses, lost treasure, the flight through enemy lines. He also insists upon the production numbers which are so much a part of the costume-picture: see the revolt of the slaves, wonder at the fire-festival, thrill at the great escape.

If *Seven Samurai* and *The Throne of Blood* were, in part, a criticism of the standard period film, *The Hidden Fortress* takes the bigger step of beating it at its own game. It is as though Buñuel had made *The Mark of Zorro*. At the same time, Kurosawa himself is by no means immune to the charms of this particularly mindless genre—of which the West received a very typical example in the Academy-Award-winning *Samurai*. Though he admires greatly what Mizoguchi, Yamanaka, and Itami did to make the period-film meaningful to contemporary audiences, and though he himself has done the same thing in *Seven Samurai,* he is also fond of the never-never land of the *chambara* where might is right and the hero sings as he chops. *The Hidden Fortress* does the *chambara* one better.

If the ordinary period-film is an exercise in empty heroics, he would have reasoned, then this film will have even more heroics and they won't be empty; if it is a disguised operetta with songs and dances, then I will undisguise it; if it is an unrealized fairy-tale, then I will realize it. The result is what they call an action-drama in the trade, but one so beautifully made, one so imaginative, so funny, so tender, and so sophisticated, that it comes near to being the most lovable film Kurosawa has ever made.

# TREATMENT

It starts off big with a stirring march under the credits, full orchestra, full percussion, big, empty phrases, grandiloquence itself—it sounds like spectacle-music, like the march in *Quo Vadis?* Under this, however, the title background shows merely two men, slowly marching, back to the camera. After the titles are over, and the men get a bit farther from the camera, we see that they are mere farmers and, further, not very happy ones. The leaden sky presses down on them, the dust rises. They are obviously lost, obviously hopeless. *Quo Vadis?* indeed.

Still, from the back at any rate, they retain a kind of dignity. When they turn and start bickering with each other, they lose even that. They are ludicrous, scratching monkeys, completely impotent, whose

rage only makes each the more hideous. This then is civil war, this is the glorious sixteenth century with its honor and its gallantry—reduced to these two simian shapes jabbering and gesticulating on an empty plain.

Mounted samurai appear chasing another soldier. They kill him. The farmers are not worth killing. The samurai merely look at them as though they were animals and ride off. Afraid, the two forget to bicker for a time, then start quarrelling again and decide to part, which they do, hurling imprecations at each other.

They are both made slaves and their separate slave-gangs pass. The farmers recognize each other. Instantly they are wild to be together again; they struggle, they call out to each other, they weep with chagrin when carried away. The point is made. This, indeed, is the pattern of civil war. One may bicker until danger comes; then mutual need is stronger than mutual dislike.

The ordinary period-film would scarcely have begun with these two scruffy characters. Instead, there would have been the general and the princess and their troubles, taken very seriously indeed, and the farmers would have been comic relief, inserted among the general seriousness. Kurosawa has turned the pattern upside down. We must follow the farmers all the way through the picture and it is the princess and her general who are interspersed. The only reaction we are allowed to all of their varied and thrilling adventures is that of the farmers, alternately incredulous and terrified.

In this they are like the porter in *They Who Step on the Tiger's Tail*. General and princess are impassive, their faces are like masks; the farmers show everything on their faces. They over-react—they are like the audience at the *chambara* and they are therefore us. Sly, cowardly, greedy, they include all the vices. But vice in itself is petty. Between them they have not one scrap of dignity. They are bad men.

The Japanese title, however, is *Three Bad Men in a Hidden Fortress.*

There is only one other man in the major cast: the general. He looks and acts like the *chambara* hero, is properly impassive, properly loyal, properly active with the sword. There seems no indication of badness at all.

Yet he is bad, and the princess knows why. If the farmers are bad it is because they are all too human, the general is bad because he is inhuman. In truly traditional fashion, he substituted his own sister, who died in place of the princess. Now, the princess turns on him: "Kofuyu was sixteen. I am sixteen too. There is no difference between her life and mine.... You killed your sister and didn't shed one tear. Only that loyal look of yours. I hate it."

The code of honor, such abstract concepts as fealty and obligation, are quite taken care of in this speech. Villains and heroes are, as always in a Kurosawa picture, equated. All three men are bad. Later on a fourth is added, and yet another feudal precept is cheerfully broken. The general—Mifune—fights with his old enemy—Susumu Fujita. Mifune wins, Fujita is humiliated for having lost and so, when Mifune and the princess and the farmers are captured by him, he lets them escape and quite sensibly decides to run away with them—something unheard of in the usual loyalty-to-the-last *chambara*. So all four men must be judged to be bad but when the majority is bad, something happens: the balance must be readjusted. Any majority adjusts the norm and it was our accepted morality that was at fault at the beginning. By the end of the picture we are calling the men good. The title, then, is to be understood as so many of Kurosawa's titles must be—ironically.

General Fujita suggests Togashi in *They Who Step on the Tiger's Tail*, just as General Mifune suggests Benkei. The situation is very reminiscent of *Kanjincho*. The princess, just like Yoshitsune, is disguised as a porter and must carry her share of the wood in which the gold is carefully hidden. The two farmers, now saddled with the gold they coveted, divide among them the Enoken role of the former film and their own apprehensions of being apprehended almost get the whole party captured. There is even a scene where Mifune apologizes to the princess—as Benkei did to Yoshitsune and is forgiven, though the princess' reason are the more interesting: "I do not mind dying, Roku-rota. I have enjoyed a happiness which I could never have known in the castle. I have seen people in their true form, and beauty and ugliness with my own eyes. I thank you, Rokurota. Now I may die without regret."

The resemblance to the 1945 film is heightened by the use of Noh music. This is often connected with the princess. When she first appears, high on the rocks surrounding the hidden fortress, there is a piercing call in the Noh *fué*. Later, she is given a dagger with which to kill herself if captured and the Noh flute is again heard. At the fire festival the music is folk-music but when the princess in captivity sings the festival song, she gives it Noh intonation—and the same thing occurs when Fujita is making up his mind to join the fugitives. At the

end of the film the farmers (certain they are to be executed) raise their eyes and see the princess and the two generals now in full regalia, revealed as royal heroes. The music is pure Noh, delicate little rattlings from the drums, a ravishing obligato for the flute, grand punctuation from the great *taiko*—and the tableau is seen as a ballet, it looks just like Noh.

The Noh music is particularly apt in that, first, the structure of the story is rather Noh-like. The princess is disguised (just as the god or demon is disguised in the first half of the Noh play) and the farmers think she is merely a mute servant (and one of the most delicious sections of the film is where, to *kyogen*-like music, the two engage in a pantomime to convey to her that the horses need water, at the same time trying to hide their intention of stealing horses and gold). At the end—as at the end of the Noh play—she is revealed as her goddess-like self. The farmers, like the porter in *They Who Step on the Tiger's Tail* come to

realize that they have been adventuring with demigods.

Too, the use of Noh structure and Noh music is particularly appropriate because the Noh story is very close to myth and, as the film progresses, it becomes apparent that Kurosawa is telling a fairy-tale. The farmers' accidentally discovering the gold (accompanied by percussive and Noh-like sounds on the sound-track) is the first indication, and Mifune's splendid entrance is another. They are rummaging around the rocks, pushing and pulling each other, each trying to find the next piece. The camera pans with them and as they continue to scramble we see, in the furthest distance, perfectly framed by a cleft in the rocks, Mifune standing—tiny in the distance—looking at them. It is an entrance for a tenor, it is like the entrance of Ivan in *L'Oiseau de feu*: mysterious, glamorous, the very image of heroic possibility.

Later in the film, Kurosawa makes his intentions very clear. The general and the farmers sit around a fire next to a stream and Kurosawa purposely uses dry ice to create that low-lying mist whose presence is so notoriously indicative of the supernatural in the ordinary Toho science-fiction or fairy-tale film. The royal family is living in a cave behind a waterfall, not so much for safety one would guess—rather, to give the camera an opportunity of filming very striking entrances and exits. The forest pool is straight from *Green Mansions,* a paradise on earth, almost impossibly lovely. When the enemy troops advance they do so through misted pines, conch-shells blowing—it is like an attack of the trolls. Both the revolt of the slaves and the fire-festival are done on a very grand scale—so grand that these scenes look like something from an early UFA production; one thinks of a better *Siegfried,* a meaningful *Metropolis.* Perhaps this is what Kurosawa meant when he said: "I liked *Henry V* very much and wanted to capture some of its spirit in this picture." At the end of the film there is a glorious image of the three horses, saddled with gold, clinking as they gallop, running

free into friendly territory. They leave the princess and the generals far behind. The camera follows them as they race along the roads. They come upon the two farmers (arguing as usual) and they stop. These are magical horses.

Kurosawa has said that he wanted to remake *They Who Step on the Tiger's Tail* with many sets, with more music, with much more technique. Without advertising the fact, he has done so in *The Hidden Fortress.* It is, in fact, a fairy-tale seen as a musical—there are arias, big production-number ballets, pantomimes. Thematically, too, it is again a criticism of the *Kanjincho* premise, but this time—since it is, after all, a fairy-tale, a romance—all ends happily with the demigods back in place and the squabbling farmers given as reward one single piece of gold, something they cannot fight about simply because it cannot be divided. For once then, it is good fortune rather than danger which brings them together. They are pleased, they even try to get the other

to carry it, take care of it. This might be unlikely but, after all, the picture is a fairy-tale and fairy-tales always end happily.

The moral of the film—since fairy-tales also have morals—is given by the princess, for this down-to-earth and sensible young lady is the only one who keeps her head throughout the film. She finds what she believes in the song of the fire-festival and—as she later explains—it is an exhortation to be yourself, to be what you are, to realize yourself.

> *"Kindle your life and burn it away,*
> *Live with all of your might.*
> *Kindle a blaze in this dark world,*
> *For life's dream lasts but one night."*

# PRODUCTION

This was Kurosawa's last film for Toho, the company with which he started, and for which he had done the majority of his pictures. With it his contract was fulfilled and he was able to form his own production unit. It would probably be unfair to compare the jubilation of this film with the despair of the two preceding it, and attempt to find some correlation with the fact that, together, these represented a three-picture contract after which the director would be free. Nonetheless, there is, in this picture, a fluidity and freedom which are much different from the calculated restraint of *The Throne of Blood* and *The Lower Depths.*

One of the reasons perhaps was that in this picture Kurosawa for the first time used the wide-screen process, and used it superlatively—used it so well that he never returned to the standard-format screen. This is apparent from the first scene on. There is only the leaden, pressing sky, the apparently endless plain, and the two black figures, fighting, grumbling, lost. In these middle-period pictures Kurosawa always uses the image frame itself to comment upon the action—the carefully constricted framing in *The Lower Depths,* for example. Given the new freedom, and the new challenge of wide screen, the first image he creates is—tellingly—agoraphobic. The very means of seeing comments upon what is seen.

Kurosawa exploits the uses of wide-screen throughout. There is a very interesting sequence in which the action occurs most of the time at the extreme edges of the image. The two farmers are being made to dig a hole and the sequence begins with them in the middle of the screen, down in the hole (along with the camera) fighting. Disgusted with each other, they climb out, one on each side of the hole, and the camera tilts back to watch them. They begin walking forward, each far on his own side of the hole, far on his own side of the screen, and the camera (still in the hole) dollies back. They walk back, but the camera does not follow—for the reason that they join and walk away, at which point the camera elevates itself, and pans to follow them. Why Kurosawa chooses to film a certain scene in a certain way is always interesting. In this case he chose a method which precludes cutting. Instead of moving the camera around and cutting together the resultant images, he prefered to put the camera in the hole and dolly and pan. One of the reasons is that any image held for a long time on the screen intensifies the feeling of the place—that is, the atmosphere. In this sequence he was concerned with the blinding white rocks, the heat, the dust, the desolation. Another reason, however, was that the wide screen adapts itself particularly well to feelings of isolation, of enmity. Even a simple close-up, if seen on one side of the wide screen, suggests solitude because it is balanced by an almost equal extent of blank screen. In the same way, two men, each on his own side of the screen, must gaze across the void at each other. They are visibly separated.

On the other hand, when he wants to, Kurosawa cuts the film very freely, successfully breaking one of the rules of the new aesthetic that the wide-screen image cannot lend itself to swift montage. He even uses his favorite excitement-generating device of very swift, wide pans, linked one to the other (seen also in Mifune's motorcycle ride up the mountain in *Scandal,* in the climb up the hill at the beginning of *No Regrets for Our Youth,* and in the forest scenes of *The Throne of Blood*). In one sequence Mifune must chase three escaping horsemen who have recognized them. The setting is a narrow road in the forest. The camera is placed at the side, looking down the road, and along come the four, the camera panning swiftly to keep them in the center of the image, and following them as they rush past and away. This is repeated four times (and each time the camera is further along the road) and then the four pans (each about one second long) are edited together. The effect, exhilarating enough in the standard format, is overpowering on wide screen.

These four seconds build up momentum of which, in the last cut, Kurosawa takes extremely clever advantage. The last horseman killed, the camera movement established in our minds, the last pan starts and suddenly there is the gate to the enemy camp. Mifune cannot curb his horse in time; we have hardly time to see what has happened when the momentum, both of horse and of camera movement, carries him directly into the enemies' hands.

The final escape—using the same method of repeated shots—is one of the nicest bits of sheer movie-making in contemporary cinema. The action is as follows:

*The captives are bound, in the background the distant hills of the friendly province seen through the gate. The horses are turned, they are to be taken in the opposite direction.*

*General Fujita is humming—oddly. He is humming the fire-festival song that the princess sang. Suddenly he decides and lashes the gold-laden horses which take off through the gate. His men are astonished. With his sword he slashes the bonds of Mifune and the princess. Their horses rear*

*and start toward the gate. Mifune sees the girl they had saved in an earlier section of the picture, scoops her up from horseback, swings her around and sails through the gate, the princess following.*

*Fujita turns on his own men with his sword, leaps onto a horse. The horse springs toward the gate—the other three already in the distance. A fanfare, and the music begins. It is the march from the beginning but it is now double-time, a real gallop with percussion and snare drums. The gate flies past and the horses gallop away. The three horses gallop around the hair-pin curves, toward the border and the friendly province. The music races, the horses' hoofs pound the sound-track. At a rise the princess stops, then Mifune joins her, then Fujita. They are free, they have passed the boundary. Fanfare, and in the silence, broken only by the sound of distant birds, they look and laugh. Far below, we see the three horses, carrying gold, and the sound of the jingling metal fills the screen.*

This marvelous moment takes just fifteen seconds. Yet in it Kurosawa does not once lose us, explains the inexplicable—Fujita's desertion—celebrates it, and—at the same time—creates in the spectator, through motion, music, sound, the precise psychological equivalent of an escape. The confines of the gate race past the camera and there is only free sky; the music matches the emotion, heightens it. The screen turns from black to white and the distant sound of birds is freedom itself. It is one of those rare moments where effect is so delicately calculated, and so brutally carried out that the assaulted spectator can only gasp. One knew it would all end happily but one could never have guessed that it would be so glorious.

Another of the reasons for the exhilaration is that, by this time, though we know it is only a fairy-tale we are watching, we have come to believe. By insisting that the picture is about civil war, based on historical reality; by treating us to massive set pieces (the revolt of the slaves); by making the sets as realistic as possible (whole towns built, the marvelous set for the barrier-station constructed in full), and by making all of the reactions completely contemporary, Kurosawa has made us believe in the unbelievable.

At one point, one of the princess's advisers questions the motives of the farmers for it is they who have suggested the escape plan. Mifune says: "I trust their greed. They will do anything if they are saddled with gold." And they do. They toil and labor without one word of complaint because it is gold they are carrying. Mifune is later offered gold (the last thing in the world he needs) for his horse, and he is forced to sell. And so the two farmers, even more burdened, labor on, hating but still bearing what they most wanted—gold. Later still, the gold hidden among the wood, they escape by way of the fire-festival. But fire burns wood and they must pile their precious faggots onto the roaring blaze. There is the delicious feeling (as in the wedding sequence of *The Bad Sleep Well*) of a ritual gone wrong. Later, the farmers' capture two soldiers and make them carry part of the gold. In just following the theme of the gold, itself, one sees that all the

reactions are quite commonly human, the gold itself is not magical, and the people are not fairy-tale people. We believe in them because they are just like us. And it is our belief which, as Kurosawa has confidently and cleverly foreseen, makes this fairy-tale something more real to us than the naturalistic reality of the ordinary contemporary-life film. We no more think of disbelieving in the magical horses than we think of questioning the voice of the dead husband in *Rashomon*. We are too deeply involved to question.

The Japanese audience, often common-sense itself and usually al-lergic to fantasy, did not question. As Kurosawa has said: "It was an enormously difficult film to make. Typhoons came and chewed up our scenery . . . the weather at the base of Mount Fuji is completely changeable and I remember, at one point, we waited over one hundred days for good weather, and so our film was considerably over its three-month production schedule. . . . But, no matter how hard it was to make, it was an enormous hit [and remained Kurosawa's biggest finan-cial success until *Yojimbo*] and the company was delighted. It was very expensive but the books balanced out most comfortably in the black."

# The Bad Sleep Well

"This was the first film of Kurosawa Productions, my own unit which I run and finance myself. From this film on, I was responsible for everything. Consequently, when I began, I wondered what kind of film to make. A film made only to make money did not appeal to me—one should not take advantage of an audience. Instead, I wanted to make a movie of some social significance. At last I decided to do something about corruption, because it has always seemed to me that graft, bribery, etc., at the public level, is one of the worst crimes that there is. These people hide behind the facade of some great company or corporation and consequently no one knows how dreadful they really are, what awful things they do. Exposing them was, I thought, a socially significant act—and so I started the film."

## THE STORY

The daughter (Kyoko Kagawa) of the president of a government housing corporation (Masayuki Mori) is married to her father's secretary (Toshiro Mifune). At the ceremony itself there are upsetting references to the death five years ago of one of the former employees of the corporation—a death officially designated "suicide." Before long other things start occurring within the corporation. There is a police inquiry about bribery of the corporation officials by a construction company, in connection with public tenders, and the various corpora-

tion heads are worried. The police are given several scapegoats. One of them, told to commit suicide by his superiors, actually kills himself. The other (Kamatari Fujiwara) is saved by Mifune. Saved for his own purposes, because Mifune turns out to be the son of the man murdered five years before and engaged in a vendetta against his father's murderers. Eventually, he is recognized but has already kidnapped the vice-president (Takashi Shimura) and finds where the stolen funds are hidden. All would have ended well but that his wife, whom he loves and who loves him, believes her father, believes that her father's character has changed, trusts him. The father has both Fujiwara and Mifune murdered.

## TREATMENT

As in *Scandal*, Kurosawa here wanted to expose. He wanted this film to be, like *Record of a Living Being*, "a movie of some social significance." As early as *Drunken Angel* "the critics had started calling me a 'journalistic' director, meaning that I interested myself in 'timely themes.' Actually, I have always thought of film as a kind of journalism if journalism means a series of happenings, usually contemporary, which can be shaped into a film. At the same time, I know that a timely subject does not make an interesting film, if that is all that it has. One ought to make a film in such a way that the original idea, no matter where it comes from, remains the most important thing, and the feeling that one felt at that moment of having the idea is important. Timely, then, in my sense, is the opposite of sensational."

Since he wanted to expose in this picture, he and his script writers (Shinobu Hashimoto, Ryuzo Kikushima, Hideo Oguni, and Eijiro Hisaita) decided to tell the story of an exposure. Just as Mifune seeks to expose the cruelty of the murderers of his father, so Kurosawa wanted to expose the corruption of those in the highest places in Japan. The form of the revenge-tragedy came naturally. Much traditional drama and many Japanese period-films use the formula. If they knew it, the Japanese might make *The Spanish Tragedy* one of their favorite plays. As it is, they have long felt a great affection for *Hamlet*.

The parallel between this picture and Shakespeare's tragedy has been noted. Mifune-Hamlet's father has been killed by the man who becomes his own second father (father-in-law rather than step-father in the film) and the hero's initial motivation is simple revenge. He loves Kagawa-

Ophelia in his own way but his relationship to Mori-Claudius is of such strength that she is sacrificed and her Laertes-like brother's attempts to avenge her are instrumental in bringing about the hero's downfall. Mifune has a Horatio-like friend and even a Polonius-like mentor (Fujiwara) whose advice he carefully disregards. He even arranges a kind of play (the opening wedding-sequence) in which to trap the conscience of the corporation president. The ending of both film and play is suitably Elizabethan with many corpses and much scenery-chewing.

Though Kurosawa himself has said nothing about this parallel to *Hamlet* (he once told me that it and *Macbeth* were his favorite Shakespeare), the prince's dilemma might have suggested itself to him at the time when he was trying to recapture "the feeling that one felt at the moment of having the idea. . . ." Further, there is another, more subtle parallel to Shakespeare's play.

Hamlet vacillates (in at least several interpretations of the play), because he has caught his own conscience as well as the king's. Hamlet is not afraid of doing bad (murder) because it seems good to him. He is mortally afraid, however, of *being* bad. This strain wears on Hamlet. Precisely, it *tires* him and so the final murders are more or less accidental —nothing would have happened without Laertes. Mifune—like Hamlet—fights to keep revenge glowing in his breast but he is, after all, only human. The spark of vengeance is never very strong. The flame wavers, dies, goes out. Mifune decides to give it up. It is as though Hamlet has decided not to send Ophelia to the nunnery after all. Mifune, significantly, decides to be a real husband. But the effects of past actions, the effects of a sustained vendetta, are not easily disregarded. Actions always live longer than the intention which created them. Mifune, like Hamlet, is ensnared in what he himself has done. He who fights fire with fire will get burned.

Story, exposition, and the eventual fate of the hero are all presaged in the opening sequence—twenty minutes of a brilliancy unparalleled even in Kurosawa. A wedding ceremony, very formal, a major ritual, held amid the nineteenth-century opulence of one of Tokyo's great halls, *gagaku* in the distance. The elevator doors open, the ushers bow, guests appear, in kimono or morning-dress, dignity itself, good manners elevated to rite. The elevator doors open a second time, the ushers bow, then straighten, surprised, because here are the newspapermen, cameramen, shouting, pushing, no dignity here—having scented scandal from afar they now arrive. Thus the earliest image in the film presents the front which monied dignity assumes; the second shows human beings as they sometimes also are, pushing, pulling, grasping, out to know the worst. The film is about falseness in high places and this is what Kurosawa initially suggests.

The ushers make way, bride and groom are appearing. Kagawa first, Mifune second, the procession passes. The bride is lame, one of her *zori* is inches higher than the other. The newsmen see this, stare. She

feels their hostile curiosity. She stumbles; the march (Wagner) stops. There is a moment of horrified silence and then it is her brother (Tatsuya Mihashi) rather than Mifune who rushes forward, catches her, helps her to her place.

A limping bride is bad enough; a bride who stumbles is even worse. The guests are horrified because, at any ritual, any breaking of the rite seems a bad omen, in Japan as elsewhere. At this solemn moment such a break seems freighted with evil presage. Too, in Japan there is an aversion toward the physically disabled, and there is even a saying about a bride who stumbles. Kurosawa has purposely used this popular suspicion just as in *The Lower Depths* he used the equally popular superstition that the cry of the crow presages death. In both instances, the superstitions are upheld: the man who heard the crow dies; the marriage is doomed. At the same time, however, we see that it is the brother rather than the groom who rescues the bride, and this establishes a pattern we will see elaborated upon throughout the rest of the film.

Music begins again, this time the Strauss *Voices of Spring*—an ironic choice given what has just happened—and the wedding party continues. The camera stays behind with the reporters and we listen to them (for they are chorus in this film) talk about the financial scandal which is about to break. Over their talk we hear applause in the distance; cut, the applause is very loud, we are at the banquet and the various people concerned are, as is the Japanese custom, being formally introduced.

These introductions have a triple function. First, this is just what happens at Japanese weddings and consequently they deepen the feeling of reality; second, we as audience are introduced to most of the characters, and hear something of their history; third, and most important, we are shown that the truth is something different from what we are hearing.

This is accomplished in two ways. The first is through a conscious comment by the camera. The master of ceremonies is speaking of Mifune and uses the phrase " . . . a most promising young man." At

that instant, however, the camera shows us not Mifune but the brother. He is toying with a champagne glass, has been casting cynical glances about the table, is obviously not a promising young man at all. Yet the "promise" is also contained in the apparent irony because it is the brother who is going to cut short the promising career of Mifune. The second is through the chorus of cynical newspapermen. The word "auspicious" is used by the master of ceremonies—cut to the head newspaper man saying: "'Auspicious'—that's the word all right," using the word in a difference sense, meaning that the scandal is about to be uncovered, that the police are due to arrive at any moment. And just then the chief of Criminal Investigation (Susumu Fujita) does arrive. A second ritual begins—the ritual of arrest. These two rituals are incompatible and for the remainder of the sequence there is the delicious sensation of a ritual gone wrong. Almost everyone knows what is happening, with police standing in the halls, waiters busy carrying messages to the high-placed culprits, and yet the mask-like faces of polite Japanese attending an important function indicate nothing of it. It is only later that we will see these same faces laughing, crying, screaming.

Yet even a mask is not truly impassive and Kurosawa delights in showing human fears lurking in the bitten underlip, while the eyes stare impassively ahead. As always, he is showing the human beneath the inhuman; the heart unruly, the head determined. At the same time that we see these masks, false-faces all with false smiles, false politesse, we hear about what the people are actually like because, as each is introduced, the newspapermen comment. We learn not only who is who but also what evil they have done.

Here, more brilliantly than ever before, Kurosawa has again insisted upon the difference between illusion and reality. Each man, face impassive, is fulsomely introduced and (as in the remarkable funeral-watching sequence which occurs later in the film) he is, at his moment of full social dignity, stripped bare by what the reporters tell about him.

The exception is the brother. His speech is direct, to the point, honest. He asks Mifune to treat his sister well and, as though he knew what was going to happen, says: "And if you don't . . . I'll kill you." The guests agree to find this a joke, but it is no joke. He feels responsible for her for it was he who accidentally lamed her in their childhood. Too, he feels that Mifune may be an opportunist. He is right—for the wrong reasons—and one of the many ironies at the end of the picture is that it is he who is accidentally instrumental in Mifune's death. Directly after this the camera looks at his sister, the bride. The camera is placed low so that she appears to be sitting amid a formal bouquet, surrounded by flowers. It seems as though the camera, by showing us this in context with the previous shot, is insisting that we later recognize that she, too, is responsible since Mifune, in love, finally decides to give up revenge for her sake,

and in token of this, brings her a bouquet which looks much like this one. And it is she who, as we discover, unwittingly allows her father to have him killed.

It is time for the toast. Shimura, thoroughly shaken by the scandal hanging over them, is about to speak. Behind him the waiters open the champagne bottles and the sound is that of gun-fire. He falters—the very picture of a guilty man. The signal is given for the cake to be brought in. Polite applause. The Mendelssohn wedding-march, festive, even triumphant is heard. All eyes turn.

Shimura gasps, for the cake being wheeled ceremoniously down the aisles by waiters who understand nothing and are only doing what someone has told them to do, is in the shape of an office building, and in one of the miniature windows, at the top, is a single rose. We know that one of the corporation employees, five years ago, mysteriously fell from this building, from this very window. Ritual is forgotten, the cake-knife falls from nerveless hands, the bad men openly gape. It is like that moment in *Hamlet* where the king calls for lights, where court protocol, even decorum vanishes; a court ritual—the king viewing a play—is forgotten, and the scene turns into a rout.

The cake is wheeled directly behind Mori, an accidental justice in that it was he who was responsible for the murder. Mendelssohn trumpets on: happiness assured; the perfect ending, marriage in sight. One newsman turns to the other, and says: "This is the best one-act play I've ever seen." The other, settling himself comfortably in a chair, eyes shining with anticipation, says: "What do you mean—one act? This is only the prelude." Under this exchange Mendelssohn fades and in its place we hear the throbbing rhythm, the chromatic bass clarinet tune which we first heard under the titles. The music marks the end of this completely brilliant sequence and continues building, for what follows is three minutes of the most inventive montage that Kurosawa has ever created.

Just as we have seen the wedding in full detail, rich in its implications, have seen it in the amount of time it would actually have taken —twenty minutes; so we now see the next two months in Kurosawa's striking short-hand. Newspaper headlines unfold across the screen, arrests are glimpsed, something is rotten in the state of modern Japan indeed and we see the culprits as though in a newsreel, one after the other apprehended. The police discover they have been using an elegant tea-house for the scenes of their collusion and we see this tea-house for a second's flash before its photograph appears in grainy newsprint. The owner, a large woman of comfortable means, is seen as though on TV: she looks at the camera—at us—coldly as she passes. A flash-bulb explodes and there she is again but gross, retouched. It is her picture in the newspaper. The music grinds away and the last image is a greatly retouched newspaper blow-up of the face of Fujiwara. Silence, suddenly; then a cut; Fujiwara's face, only now it is individual, alive; he is at the police station; he is being questioned.

Until now the film has been one of the most dense, the most brilliant, the most incisive, in Kurosawa's entire output. These twenty-three minutes are staggeringly good cinema and splendid philosophy (when seen in context of the film itself)—but then something happens. Kurosawa himself has said that the film does not live up to its beginnings, and this is quite true. As a "movie of some social significance" it is a failure. This failure, however, is much more interesting than many successes. As always (*Scandal, The Quiet Duel, Record of a Living Being*), Kurosawa moves from the social to the individual and this changes the focus of the film. Yet, in this film more than in any of the others, his richly detailed and rigorously ambiguous presentation of the individual caught up in social action is so pregnant with philosophical meaning that the picture is by no means ruined by this social failure. Kurosawa has explained why the "message" is weak. "But even while we were making it, I knew that it wasn't working out as I had planned and that this was because I was simply not telling and showing enough. Like the final scene with Mori on the telephone. This is the last of several calls, all apparently to the same person, someone very high in the Japanese government. That suggests, but it is not explicit enough. An even worse man is at the other end of that telephone line but in Japan if you go any further than that you are bound to run into serious trouble. This came as a big surprise to me, and maybe the picture would have been better if I had been braver. At any rate, it was too bad I didn't go further. Maybe I could have in a big country like America. Japan, however, cannot be this free and this makes me sad."

## CHARACTERIZATION

The bad men of the title (Mori, Shimura, etc.) always get away with murder, precisely because they are so thoroughly bad. They sleep well because their consciences are so bad that they are serene. The implication seems to be that they are naturally bad. This is insisted upon in the final minute of the film where Mori (on the telephone) says good-night to the party at the other end and then corrects himself because it is only afternoon. The touch is awkward but the reasoning for it is not. The very bad share with the very good a like serenity. Too, the title might also be translated as *The Worse You Are the Better You Sleep*, which rendition gives more of the feeling of the Japanese, and at the same time suggests more strongly Kurosawa's assumption that pure evil, like pure good, is a non-reflective state, a state with few tensions, a state that allows you—for example—to sleep extremely well.

Certainly none of the villains (as deep-dyed as any in Kurosawa's films since *Scandal*) suffer a moment's indecision. They are convinced of the validity of their actions. Bribery, blackmail, murder?—why, of course. These are the facts of their lives. This calm acceptance is precisely what so alarms us in this film. These are not men of passion; they are men who have a certain way of life and, on their terms, a very successful one. Being a murderer does not preclude one's being a good father (which Kurosawa shows us in a rather touching scene where Papa Mori complete with funny apron is preparing a patio-supper for his family and his son says to Mifune: "It is hard to believe that he is really bad"). Even in his moments of temper, the bad man is so consistent that one cannot believe a single doubt has ever touched him. Just before the patio-scene we have seen him at a meeting with fellow robber-barons. The object of discussion is whether and how to murder one of their too-dangerous underlings. Mori loses his temper and shouts: "A superior must be broad-minded." The bourgeois remark coming from a completely evil man who does not for a moment believe he is anything but broad-minded has an extremely ironic effect. Mori does not realize that he is bad. It is just this which makes him such a powerful adversary. He has sound moral reasons for every-thing that he does. That his morality is different from ours does not disturb him. He has tested his time and again.

This theme of the world as a very wicked place indeed, sounded in *The Throne of Blood* and in *The Lower Depths*, here becomes a major melody—a great cantus firmus over which the rest of the film is built. None of us can be as good as the world is bad. The innocent perish and the bad sleep well.

But who sleeps the best, after the film is over and we are thinking about it? Why, the dead sleep best. And Mifune is dead. His is the central character and he has been introduced as virtue (revenge) against vice (the original murderers) but just as in *The Hidden Fortress*, in *High and Low*, one must stop and consider. Perhaps, after all, the title refers to him.

The character at first seems simple, single-minded. He blurts out his function at once. We watch Fujiwara climb to the top of a volcano, prepare to throw himself in, when out of the fog and steam (just like the ghost of Hamlet's father) steps Mifune and his first question is an uncomprehending: "But, don't you want revenge?" Bit by bit we discover who Mifune is and what he is after.

He allows nothing to stand in his way. He is absolutely ruthless in his pursuit of evil. He must convince Fujiwara of the extent of the villanies and so takes him to his own funeral—the newspapers having printed that he has committed suicide. They watch from their parked car and, at the same time, Mifune plays a tape he has surreptitiously made of the two—whom they now see bowing before the funeral altar—when they decided to force him to commit suicide. The irony is extreme. We see one thing and hear another. There are the Buddhist priests banging their drums at the funeral but we hear the mambo-rhythms of a night-club band. There is Shimura lighting incense and praying while we hear his voice saying: "Well, there is no choice—we'll have to kill him." There they are, both in deep mourning, bowing to the

bereaved wife and daughter while we hear one say to to the other: "Well, come on. At times like this . . . a young girl is always best." Illusion and reality collide in this brilliant sequence, the main point of which, however, is to demonstrate to what lengths Mifune will go to demonstrate the evilness of others. He is a man obsessed.

Later in order to break down the underling (Akira Nishimura) he has Fujiwara play ghost to frighten him; later he pretends he is going to push him from the same window his father was pushed from; again, he makes him drink supposedly poisoned whiskey. The very variety of these means should make us suspicious of Mifune. That we are not (and indeed most of any audience sees him as the virtuous if unfortunate hero to the very end of the film) is because he fits so perfectly into a film-type, a role that we know—we are quite familiar with revenge-seekers on the Japanese as well as the American screens.

Kurosawa, however, has no interest in film-types and has never dealt with them. If Mifune resembles one it is because Kurosawa is in this film is not so much interested in what bad men are like as in how (always in Kurosawa's films—this continual *how*) they get that way. Mifune shows us.

Fujiwara notices it first. Mifune is looking at a photograph of his father's body, lying crumbled after having been pushed from the window. How awful, how sad—he says. In the next minute he is trying to push Nishimura (not even the murderer) out of the same window. This would be equally awful, equally sad—Mifune's father, after, all, was one of the corporation, one of the gang. And this man too, Fujiwara insists, also has a wife and child. But Mifune does not see it that way.

Later he and his friend (Takeshi Kato) capture Shimura and hold him in the ruined air-raid shelter of an abandoned factory. They are unnecessarily cruel to him. To be sure, they have good reasons for everything they do. But then, so did Mori and the rest of them. Shimura, a villain, brought to bay, is a pleasing sight and one rejoices. At the same time, however, Mifune is going too far.

Kurosawa underlines this by having a theme associated with Mifune (first whistled by the hero during the funeral sequence, later heard under the love-confession scene) decked out with "funny" bassoon noises, piccolo, celesta, and played as a rollicking march during these "revenge" sequences which are in actuality torture-scenes. Then, in a very important scene (cut from prints shown abroad) he shows what he is doing. (The "foreign" version of this film differs from that released in Japan. The reasons given included the extreme length of the picture—it is two hours and thirty-two minutes uncut, just eight minutes shorter than the cut *Seven Samurai*. Besides the above scene, also missing are: an extremely interesting sequence showing the under-ling at the bank; a scene of Fujiwara's wife and daughter with Shimura after they have heard their husband and father is alive; the crucial scene where Mifune is identified by Shimura from an old photograph—and without which nothing becomes too clear; an ironic scene where the friend buys flowers for Mifune to take home to his wife; and all the love scenes.)

After they have tired of torturing (taunting, not feeding) Shimura, the hero and his friend leave the air-raid shelter and walk amid the ruins and during their walk talk about the days just after the war where, it turns out, they did precisely what the big bad bosses had done. They bought and sold, they parlayed, they were not too scrupulous about where their money came from. The difference is that the bosses are spectacularly successful at this and they are not. Fujiwara in his own way tries to point this out. At once the friend turns on him with: "Look, that man's a bastard—it is either him or us." There is a cut to Mori sitting alone in his room. It is a very short cut but completely enigmatic. Is this the "bastard" or is this a lonely old man? Who *are* the heroes in this picture? Are there any?

Yes. Mifune shows us that evil begets evil, that the revenger is as bad as those he wants to be revenged upon, that murder is contagious. At the same time, however (and here lies the ambivalent meaning of the film), he is an unsuccessful revenger. In an earlier scene he has admitted to loving his wife and yet does not dare show her that he does (a complication reminiscent of the love-plot of *The Quiet Duel*). His reasons are that he married her only to get that much nearer to her father. Now he surprises himself at feeling the way he does.

Mifune:   I'm not tough enough. I should have pushed him out of that window. Then the papers would have printed it all up, the bosses would have gotten it. I don't hate enough.

Fujiwara:   No, you're wrong. It's unnatural . . .

Mifune:   Oh, it's hard to hate evil. I have to hate and become hateful myself.

Fujiwara:   You can hate evil all you like—but to sacrifice innocent people . . . like your own wife. What if she found out?

Mifune:   Shut up.

Kato:   What are you two shouting about? Say—you haven't fallen in love with her have you?

Mifune:   Unfortunately.

Kato:   Well, what's so bad about that? It's a fine thing. Go on then and love her. So, she's your enemy's daughter —so what? But don't let it mix you up. If you do, you're soft.

Mifune:   On our wedding night—it is hard for her to get around, we didn't go on a honeymoon—she just lay there and waited for me in the bedroom. Her face was pale, she was trembling, her eyes were closed. I couldn't bear to sacrifice her, so—

Kato:   Idiot. That was a worse sacrifice for her.

Mifune:   I know. I was wrong. After that I began to change. I really tried to do cruel things, anything to make my hate burn bright. It wasn't just to avenge my father, I know that now. I just wanted to punish . . . . But all that determination I had when I changed identities with you, where is it now?

Kato:   Well, let's start all over again.

Mifune looks at the picture of his father's body, then tears it up and burns the fragments.

Mifune:   I don't need this.

Kato:   That's the spirit. Now what will we do?

Mifune:   It will be dynamite. I'll get to the bottom of this, then bang!

This scene is set in the loft of the automobile company run by the friend with whom Mifune has changed names. In back of him, outside the frosted window, is the line of the roof, creating that diagonal which Kurosawa so likes using (as in *The Lower Depths*) when motivation is changing. The same things may happen (Mori exposed, the triumph of justice) but the manner, the *how* will be different. Mifune will be acting as an efficient, uninvolved agent. He no longer wants to see them dead. He wants to see them in jail.

This change of attitude is extremely important for it is here that Mifune makes peace with the world. This way he can see justice done. At the same time he can do justice to himself as a human being. He is done with being hard, cold, calculating. No longer will he fight with the weapons his adversaries have used.

And, as in *Stray Dog*, it is here that his troubles really begin. He who feels compassion is lost in this wicked world. He brings flowers home to his wife; the brother (having overheard Mori and Shimura

145

discover who Mifune actually is), lets out the secret, tries to shoot him. Mifune kidnaps Shimura, hides him. Fujiwara, fearing the worst, brings the wife to persuade Mifune. She is tricked into leading her father to the air-raid shelter. The father's hired henchmen (in a scene re-enacted by the friend since we do not see the actual killing) first inject alcohol into Mifune's veins, then arrange that his car—with him and Fujiwara in it—is hit by a train.

The bad men all escape. To be sure, Mori's children turn against him but it is difficult to believe that this is punishment for him. The daughter is mad (which accounts for the alternate English title, *A Rose in the Mud*, used in early American and European showings) and Mori feels that he must resign from the corporation but, considering the gravity of his crimes, he gets off lightly.

Indeed, everyone escapes except Mifune. In the final scene between him and his wife (which is cut from prints shown abroad), we learn more about his character. He and she are standing in a corridor of the air-raid shelter and a low wall is (fittingly) separating them from each other.

> *Kagawa:* When I think of your father, I cannot blame you for hating mine. But I can't hate him. Tell me. What shall we do?
>
> *Mifune:* Life is ironical . . . so is our relationship. And it was the same between my father and myself. Let me tell you about him. I learned I was illegitimate when I entered high school. I thought my father was dead. Then he turned out to be the man I had always called uncle . . . . I hated the sight of him, then. I left the house when he came. About five years ago . . . I don't know how he found out, but he came to where I was living. I think he wanted somehow to make it up to me before he died. He cried. I insulted him and left. Next day I heard that he had committed suicide and had left me a lot of money. It couldn't have been honest money, there was too much of it. Then I began to regret what I'd done—I remembered the way he'd looked at me when I was little, what he'd said to me. He had loved me so and I'd been cold. So . . . that is why I did what I did. I used up all the money working on it. It seemed the only way.
>
> *Kagawa:* I will make father make up for what he has done.
>
> *Mifune:* That is impossible.

> *Kagawa:* What shall we do then?
>
> *Mifune:* If you really want to help, then leave things to me. It may be hard for you that he must be exposed for what he is, but it's the only way.

Mifune's father was bad, Mifune's wife's father is bad, Mifune himself is bad. But he, himself, will somehow put a stop to this chain of evil. He will content himself merely with exposure. He will not kill. To agree not to kill in this world is the same thing as suicide. By his willing to do justice and not to do evil, he unchains those forces which will kill him. This truth is completely unpalatable, unsavory. It is also highly undramatic.

The drama rapidly turns to melodrama because the denouement now insists upon tragedy—including a final tragic irony—since Mifune has changed identities with his friend (to cover his tracks when revenge was his sole motive) it will appear that he *was* the friend. The friend remains alive but (and the case is much aggravated in Japan where everything about a person is carefully noted down in various official registers) is now without any identity. It also turns to melodrama because Kurosawa can rarely resist screwing irony a bit tighter and in some part destroying the effectiveness of the scene he has prepared. In this picture he allows the final scene with the friend to turn into ranting and raving; even melodrama, let alone tragedy, must be allowed to generate its *own* emotion. Kato's overacting, and dialogue which is intended to be pathetic, beg us to donate our feelings. Consequently, few tears are jerked.

The ironies are complete, perhaps even too complete (the newspapermen bow respectfully to Mori at the end, convinced of the actuality of his feigned sorrow, thus showing us that illusion has triumphed) and only we, the audience, know what really happened, only *we* have seen *how* it happened. After the final scene of Mori on the telephone, the screen darkens, and once more, before the end title, the main title of the film appears—*The Bad Sleep Well*—as though insisting upon the unfortunate truth we have been shown.

What remains afterward, however (beside a number of stunning images, a number of proofs of the phenomenal security of Kurosawa's technique in this picture), is the idea of Mifune—the hero who must die because he admitted love, hope, compassion. The after-taste of this film is bitter, but bitter as medicine is bitter. It seems inevitable, Mifune's fall—though one had hoped for something different. Perhaps, on this level, Kurosawa really *did* create "a movie of some social significance."

# Yojimbo

"For a long time," Kurosawa has said: "I'd wanted to make a really interesting film. It finally turned into this picture. The story is so ideally interesting that it's surprising no one else ever thought of it. The idea is about rivalry on both sides, and both sides are equally bad. We all know what that is like. Here we are, weakly caught in the middle, and it is impossible to choose between evils. Myself, I've always wanted to somehow or other stop these senseless battles of bad against bad, but we're all more or less weak—I've never been able to. And that is why the hero of this picture is different from us. He is able to stand squarely in the middle, and stop the fight. And it is this—him—that I thought of first. That was the beginning of the film in my mind."

## THE STORY

Into a small town strides the hero (Toshiro Mifune), a masterless samurai who goes from place to place earning his living with his sword. This particular town is in the midst of a civic war which has completely divided it. On one side is the silk merchant (Kamatari Fujiwara) and his henchman (Seizaburo Kawazu); on the other is the saké merchant (Takashi Shimura) and *his* henchman (Kyu Sazanka). Both sides have hired various ruffians and the entire town lives in a state of terror. Mifune at once sees an opportunity to make money out of the situation and, initially, hires himself to the silk merchant, thus ousting the former *yojimbo* (a word which means body-guard, *bravo,* or bouncer) who (Susumu Fujita) is quite happy to leave this dangerous, if lucrative, position. From the first, however, it is apparent that Mifune has a plan. He has discovered a way to do very little and still collect. He will allow each side to exterminate the other while he enjoys the spectacle.

In the meantime Sazanka's younger brother (Tatsuya Nakadai) comes home. He is different, much more dangerous than the rest of the gang. Furthermore, he has a pistol—the only one in that part of the country. Mifune pretends to join this side of the conflict and manages to kill quite a few of their men. He had, however, also attempted to help a farmer (Yoshio Tsuchiya) and his wife (Yoko Tsukasa) and child to escape from the town. Nakadai sees a letter they injudiciously sent Mifune, and captures, beats, and imprisons him. With the help of the saké-seller (Eijiro Tono) Mifune escapes and turns up just in time for the big fight which will decide the quarrel once and for all.

It does. Almost all the men are killed, including Nakadai. The coffin-maker, who before was complaining that there were so few killings that he was over-stocked, now complains that there are so many that no one is bothering with coffins. Mifune, having thus settled the fight and made a bit of money as well, leaves as he came.

The resemblance of this picture to the American Western has often been mentioned. Kurosawa himself has said: "Good Westerns are liked by everyone. Since humans are weak they want to see good people and great heroes. Westerns have been done over and over again and in the process a kind of grammar has evolved. I have learned from this grammar of the Western."

The town is very much like one of those god-forsaken places in the middle of nowhere remembered from the films of Ford, of Sturges, from *Bad Day at Black Rock* or *High Noon.* Mifune (just like Alan Ladd or Gary Cooper) is the outsider who wanders in and then wanders out—as in *Shane,* a picture extraordinarily popular in Japan. The townspeople (like those in *High Noon*) are not worth saving and so the hero's actions become absurd, gratuitous—except that Mifune, unlike Cooper, is quite willing to take money.

Like Cooper, however, Mifune feels that bad people are bad,

that they should not be allowed to get away with what they do. Cooper is moralistic on this point; Mifune is rueful, cynical, amoral. The former awaits the testing with trepidation if not fear; the latter looks forward to it with the calm fatality of the professional sword-slinger. What they do is the same: they both clean up a nasty, unwholesome little town. Their reasons and *how* they do it, however, are different.

Zinnemann keeps shaking his head over his awful people and Cooper's face grows solemn with the importance of his act. Kurosawa seems to say: look how dreadful they are, and then he smiles. Mifune is engaged in nothing larger than the cleaning up of a nasty town, and no great moral purpose looms in back of him. Kurosawa refuses to be portentous about an important matter—social action. For this reason he refuses first tragedy, then melodrama. He insists upon making a comedy.

*Yojimbo* (along with *Sanjuro*) is comic Kurosawa. No Kurosawa film, even *Ikiru,* has been entirely lacking in humor but this was his first "full-length comedy." It shares much with *They Who Step on the Tiger's Tail* and *The Hidden Fortress,* and Mifune's character shares something with that of Kikichiyo in *Seven Samurai* and Sutekichi in *The Lower Depths.* Yet the conception was new to Kurosawa.

An indication of this is the townspeople. They are a gallery of grotesques, a congress of monsters. The saké and the silk merchant are bad, bad, bad (as are the great unseen powers looming behind the villains in *The Bad Sleep Well*—which they much resemble), but they are also ludicrous. Kawazu's wife (Isuzu Yamada) is a termagant, a virago. Their son (Hiroshi Tachikawa) is absolutely craven. Sazanka's second brother (Daisuke Kato) is a ferocious little animal with boar's teeth. Both sides are composed of the brand-marked, the tattooed, of dwarfs and giants. Evil—finally—becomes grotesque.

This horrid assortment, then, is the world. This is what we have been shaking our heads over in *Ikiru*, in *Record of a Living Being*, in *The Bad Sleep Well*. Look at them! There is almost no one in the whole town, who is for any conceivable reason worth saving. (The exceptions—the farmer and his wife—almost result in the hero's downfall, however.) Watanabe faced this problem, so did the doctor in *Drunken Angel*, so did the detective in *Stray Dog*. People are so dreadful; the world is not good enough; people will not be happy together (or apart). But, in this picture, there is suddenly no dilemma. Mifune's only problem is how to get enough to eat and find something interesting to do. Quite suddenly (and just after *The Bad Sleep Well*—that most painful of Kurosawa's searches for good) evil ceases to matter.

One can see what has happened. If these monsters appear Dickensian to us it is because, like Dickens, Kurosawa is almost exclusively concerned with human dignity, beauty, and freedom. He has his *Bleak House*, his *Great Expectations*—he has even, upon occasion, been so carried away that he has given us his own version of Little Nell. There next comes a time in one's struggle with the world when everything becomes clear. It is not a crying matter at all—it is a laughing one. If the reason that the world so confuses us is that it is made up of angel-demons, then it won't hurt to insist for once upon the demonic, to phrase the eternal question in another way, to turn the

argument inside out, to cut right through the knot, since it so persistently resists being untied.

People who care about the world (a minority) reach the point of laughter. It is all so senseless, so hideous, that (quite suddenly) Renoir slyly shows us the rules of the game as they are, the tortured Buñuel joyously proclaims that the meek are by no means blessed, Bergman happily turns his world upside down and gives us *Smiles of a Summer's Night*.

Too, just as *The Hidden Fortress* is, in part, a trouncing of history on its own terms; so *Yojimbo* is a thrashing administered to the world using its own weapons. Disinterest, selfishness, suspicion—these are weapons used by the bad world. Very well. Then Kurosawa will make a hero in which just these three unattractive characteristics are outstanding. He'll show us. Two can play this game!

Mifune is just as monstrous as any of the monsters. In *The Bad Sleep Well* the hero is torn apart by the thought that he might *be* evil himself. Such concerns are far from the world of *Yojimbo* where Mifune is naturally bad, just as the townspeople are naturally bad. And why not? Kurosawa seems to ask. Let us, just for one film, face the fact that we are also animals and that, just as we are faintly amusing walking about on our two hind legs, so our pretentions to the good are also fairly ludicrous. Let us have a hero whose only virtue is a negative one: he is not actively concerned in being bad. For reasons entirely non-moral (he is quixotic, he is easily bored, he likes a good time) he decides to help the bad destroy each other. This accomplished, still unmoved, by no means a samaritan, without a civic thought in his animal-head, he can walk away and forget about the whole thing.

This role resembles that of the god in Greek plays. He descends, makes an end, ascends again. The drama, the pathos, the morality,

none of these touch him though he may be responsible for all three. The affairs of men bore him (Giraudoux's Zeus rather than Sartre's) though they may occasionally divert. It is because he is so supremely uninvolved that he can view the doings of the world as high comedy. This is Mifune's position when he climbs the town fire-tower and settles down, eyes shining with anticipation, to watch the amusing spectacle of the battle to death which he himself has engineered. The hero's sole qualification for lending himself to anything is whether it is *omoshiroi* (interesting, amusing) or not. His attitude during the battle is the attitude of an ordinary man during a dogfight. It might not be fascinating but it is something to watch.

There is a wariness here. The refusal to be involved, the affectation of omnipotence, is—like sentimentality, like cynicism—a question of balance, and Mifune upon his fire-tower is surely unbalanced. In order to play god one must, like Don Quixote, like Lear, be at least a little mad. Mifune, however, is only human. One major human problem (as Kurosawa is never tired of pointing out) is that it is almost impossible to remain uninvolved with other humans and at the same time (though the dying Watanabe is an exception) it is almost impossible to be enough involved. Mifune is eventually caught off balance. The farmer and his wife arouse his lurking sympathy. He helps them escape and attempts to do so in the same manner that he arranged the fight—dispassionately, for his own amusement. The difference is that they are worth saving, in his eyes, and this involves him. He blusters when they threaten to overcome him with their gratitude ("Shut up—I hate grateful people. If you cry I'm going to kill you right now"), and tries to get rid of them at once. He, in fact, behaves as though his human generosity is a weakness. Having done the

'right' thing he is then (as is common in the later Kurosawa) punished for having done it. The human sentiment, as in *Stray Dog*, as in *The Bad Sleep Well*, as in *High and Low*, has its consequences.

It is just these consequences that Mifune finally evades and this is one of the things about him which appeals to us so strongly. His single encounter with the good therefore gives the same thrill that in other pictures we get when the hero dabbles with the bad. He confronts good and gets away with it. In the gloriously upside-down morality that Kurosawa has created for *Yojimbo*, the hero resolutely spreads death and destruction and at the end can say with calm satisfaction: "Now it will be quiet in this town."

And so it will. Everyone is dead. The only ones left are the saké-seller, the coffin-maker, and the watchman. These people will always be around. As in *Seven Samurai*, the ones who do not fight prevail. The two bosses who began it—one is mad; the other dazed. They too did not fight. They hired fighters and now, ruined, they are identical with saké-seller and coffin-maker. Mifune looks around at the dead: Nakadai with his precious pistol in his hand, all the others. Then he shakes his head with impatience but not disgust—the grown-up sorrowing over naughty children, but not too much—turns and leaves.

# TREATMENT

The picture begins (as did *Sugata*) with a very short scene which serves to characterize the hero and, at the same time, to present the theme of the film in miniature. Under the credits we see the back of the hero's head as he walks. Next we see his feet, sandals in the dust—it is the walk of a swordsman. The camera pans up and he stops. There is the sound of wind and, in the distance, the caw of the crow. Someone will die, but this does not disturb the hero. He picks up a stick, throws it into the air. He is at a crossroads. The stick lands and he turns to follow where it points.

Having left everything to chance, benevolent or otherwise, his first adventure presents the film's theme in minuscule. A boy runs past Mifune pursued by his father.

*Father:*    Idiot. You'll only get killed. I want you to stay home here on the farm. Who wants to go and waste his life?

*Son:*    And who wants to spend his life around here eating rice-gruel? I want a short, exciting life.

*Mifune:*    Excuse me, may I have a drink of water?
(The son runs off down the road.)

*Father:*    Why didn't you stop him?

*Wife:*    He wouldn't listen to me. All the young people have gone crazy these days.

*Father:*    It's not just the young ones. Everyone is after easy money these days.

The theme is then civil disorder, even civil war—father against son, neighbor against neighbor. The social problem (since *Yojimbo* is predicated upon one) is the breakdown of a traditional society.

At the end of the picture Mifune, who has remained more or less uninvolved in the social implications as well as the actual battles, takes his stand. After the final fight—during which a farmer's son (perhaps the same one) has died calling for his mother, Mifune says, to no one in particular: "Yes . . . a long life eating rice-gruel is the best."

This then is the "message" of the film, a singularly conventional one in that its context within the picture is complete social anarchy. Yet, Kurosawa has said many times that he considers his only audience to be that of the young Japanese: that is, it is these young people he is trying to reach, trying to counsel. Didacticism is certainly not one of the director's strong points, but here the message is both loud and clear. The dreadful town in *Yojimbo* is contemporary Japan and the choice of the farmer's son is one which confronts young people today.

Not that there is too much to choose among. Kurosawa makes this clear in a very funny scene where father, mother, and son, go into the bedding closet (for privacy) to have a conference. Family conferences are common and unavoidable in Japan and the young never become quite inured to their horror. Hence the point of this fine parody of a family *sodan*—on what to do about Mifune.

*Mother:* Of course, we could kill him ourselves and save all the money.

*Son:* That's not very nice.

*Mother:* You just shut up. You'll be head of the family one day. Don't you forget that.

*Father:* Yes, remember, you can't get ahead in this world unless folks think you're both a cheat *and* a killer.

*Mother:* Now you, son—you kill him. Do it from behind, and it'll be quite easy enough.

*Father:* Your mother is right. After all, you have to kill a few men or folks won't respect you.

*Son:* But I already killed one.

*Mother:* Only one. (With great scorn.) That's a fine thing to brag about.

In fact, the choice would seem to be the choice that Mifune himself makes: to be a part of this wicked world and, at the same time, to withhold yourself from it. What Mifune likes best is to arrange something and then sit back and watch it. When he himself must become involved he does so with regret. He, for example, meets one of the gangs—monsters all.

*Mifune:* What sweet faces.

*Men:* . . . ?

*Mifune:* When you're angry you look even nicer.

*Man:* Look here. See this tattoo? I wasn't in prison for nothing.

*Another:* The law's after me. I'll hang if they catch me.

*Another:* Me too, me too! They'll cut off my head!

*Another:* There's nothing bad I haven't done.

*Mifune:* No objections to fighting then?

*Man:* You just try and kill me!

*Mifune:* It'll hurt a little.

*Man:* Bad men like us can't be cowards.

*Mifune:* (Sighing.) Then, it cannot be helped.

Snick-snack—the sword is out, an arm lies on the ground, one of the men lies doubled, cleft from chin to groin, and Mifune is with quiet dignity replacing his sword in its sheath. This, says Kurosawa, is the way to deal with the world. If possible, avoid the encounter, warn even of the consequences, but if worst comes to worst, then do your worst. A long life eating rice-gruel may be best but if you cannot do that then fight the world on its own terms.

That the picture was an enormous hit (Kurosawa's most lucrative and one of the biggest box-office successes in the history of Japanese films) seems to indicate that the point got across. Kurosawa has said: "The other companies all insisted that it was because of the sword-fighting. That isn't so. The reason was the character of the hero and what he does. He is a real hero, and when he fights he has a real reason for fighting, and he really does. He doesn't just stand around and wave his sword in the air."

Throughout the film, Kurosawa illustrates his thesis. The introduction to the town is through a dog carrying a human hand down the street—this is the kind of world the hero lives in. In the saké-house Mifune looks out of the window and watches the visits of the officials. As he looks the saké-seller explains that the tea is really spiked (and we see saké being poured into the tea-cups of the officials) and that they are really being bribed (and we see them given folded paper containing money) and that the town is really run by the big businessmen (and we see the silk merchant and the saké merchant bow formally to the officials). It is like watching a play because (as in the funeral sequence and the wedding scenes of *The Bad Sleep Well*) we see that illusion and reality are not the same. We watch one thing, are told another, and by looking carefully we see it. Later, the headman's wife tries to seduce Mifune with girls. But (since we see things through Mifune's wide-open eyes) all we see is sweat, false gaiety, and duplicity. The world as it is has become completely visible. The watchman whose duty it is to announce the time, claps his sticks together, announces that all is well, and then runs for his life. It is that kind of world.

And we are shown it precisely as it is. Consequently, the hero has something to fight and consequently he does. Fortunate hero—Kurosawa seems to be saying—who has reason to fight, and who can see clearly who is bad, who is good, who deserves to die, and who does not. It is for this reason that that the picture is a comedy.

The world is so awful it becomes funny. When dogs carry human hands through the streets about all you can do is laugh.

And this is indicated in a splendid moment toward the end of the film. Mifune (just like Burt Lancaster, or Kirk Douglas, or Alan Ladd, or Gary Cooper) is all alone, with only a knife in his hand. The wind is blowing the dust, the street is empty, and he is advancing alone for the showdown. During this slow march, death itself seems in the air. The houses are empty or barricaded, it is deep autumn and dry leaves scatter in the wind. The town is half-ruined and fires still smoke. Mifune walks slowly down the empty street and pauses, for there in the distance, lined up, is the enemy including the most deadly of all, with a gun.

Then—a magnificent moment—he suddenly straightens his shoulders, there is a burst of music on the sound track, he moves forward with the swinging gait we have seen, and he smiles.

This is in such complete contradiction to the scene, the setting, the context, that it is astonishing. More than that, it is joyous—it is, for the first time in the film, an affirmation. Climax, high-point, the moment when the singer reaches the highest note, the dancer his greatest leap, it is the moment when all roles are cast aside, when motive becomes action. And Mifune's action is a joyous one. In the face of something so horrid that it becomes ridiculous, in the face of death itself, what can one do? One can smile.

# CAMERA

*Yojimbo* is the best-filmed of any of Kurosawa's pictures. Kazuo Miyagawa had worked with the director just once before, on *Rashomon,* and the director has spoken of his admiration. "The thing that surprised and pleased me most about that picture was the camera work. Miyagawa, I learned, was worrying about whether it was good enough. Shimura had known him from way back, and told me about his fears. When I saw the first day's rushes, I knew. He was absolutely perfect." One of the reasons that they had not done further work together was that they were employed by different companies (Miyagawa usually worked with Daiei—which had produced *Rashomon*—and the director had been with Toho).

Kurosawa had so liked the *Rashomon* photography because Miyagawa had completely understood what he wanted and, at the same time, had himself brought ideas (the low-angle photography which enforces the 'comic' aspects of the woodcutter's version, the long shots which make the entire duel slightly ridiculous) which benefited the film. In *Yojimbo,* Miyagawa—who had in ten years become Japan's best cameraman, no small honor—brought more than this. He brought a finished style which peculiarly suited the picture.

Miyagawa's style, (seen in pictures as otherwise dissimilar as Mizoguchi's *Ugetsu,* Ozu's *Ukigusa,* and Ichikawa's *Kagi*) consists of almost perfectly balanced framing, though this framing is rarely symmetrical; the creation of a pattern which is often based upon the lateral (objects and or people) which lends a two-dimensional aspect somewhat like a stage-set; the insistence upon an unusually deep focus which brings the very near and the very far into visual alignment; and a fondness for the kind of lighting which will fill (or even obscure) a portion of the wide screen with a dark, partially lighted object

(usually a person) against a fairly light background, thus directing our interest to two planes at the same time. In addition, Miyagawa and his crew have one of the most secure techniques in the business.

His style plus Kurosawa's intentions created the individual world of *Yojimbo* just as surely the style of Gregg Toland contributed enormously (if not wholly) to the individual look of *Citizen Kane.* One of the effects of this merger of intentions is that *Yojimbo,* while it does not have the look of the stage in the slightest, purposely insists upon the two-dimensional, the foreground and the background. With

Kurosawa's careful choreography, the effect becomes even more striking and, in a way, even more reminiscent. Just as *The Hidden Fortress* is reminiscent of the operetta, of the film musical, so *Yojimbo* is reminiscent of the ballet, or the Japanese dance.

The setting (aside from the framing scenes in the country at beginning and end) is the town itself. It is one long street with houses on either side and at the end. This is a long rectangle, something like a football field. In the middle is a cross street and it is here that the fire-tower stands. This is the entire set (and the houses were carefully

made in all three dimensions and were so completely realistic that "the night-watchmen on the set could sleep there at night"—though what night-watchmen were doing sleeping we are not told). It was, in other words, something like a stage.

The way that Kurosawa deployed his cameras (he used three in the fight scenes) was so that they are almost always at right angles to what they show. Thus they either face a facade of houses (those on either side) or else they are in the middle of the street (looking at one end or the other). There are very few diagonal shots across the

set. Likewise, inside the houses (particularly the shop of the saké-seller where much of the action occurs) the camera faces the street side (and much of the action occurs outside the windows, on the open set itself) or it faces the inside to show what is happening there. One of the results is a uniform geometry which presents the eye with continual right angles. That this does not result in a feeling of rigidity is due to the extreme skill of the various compositions—among the most skillful Kurosawa has created. That one of the results is claustrophobia is completely intentional. Because *we* almost never view the world at right angles, at least not consistently since most of our movements insist upon the diagonal, there is a feeling of artifice (though not artificiality) which makes (in conjunction with the realism that the set insists upon, the atmosphere that its very size makes possible) for the impression—here more than in most Kurosawa pictures—that this is a *presentation.*

Something of the sort was present in *The Lower Depths* where the literal, the enclosed set, the careful compositions, contrived to give the feeling (as was indeed Kurosawa's intention) of the stage. In *Yojimbo* the actual feeling of the stage is not there but, at the same time, one thinks of open-air drama or, better, dance.

The music, choreography, and cutting enforce this impression. The picture has more music than any other Kurosawa film. The beginning and end are like overture and postlude—they even carry a musical theme which one is to associate with the hero. Also, music is used in a ballet-like way. When Mifune initially calls on one of the bad leaders he climbs the stairs, slowly. After each step, in the silences between each footfall, there is music. It is like *secco recitatif* for the dance. Mifune's movements are not specifically ballet-like but the music gives the impression that they are. Again, there is a scene where Nakadai and his men are going to confront the rival gang for an exchange of prisoners. They advance straight into the camera, then stop, and Nakadai makes a flourish with his pistol—cut. It is like the end of an ensemble; the finale of a dance for the *corps de ballet.* Again, Mifune has finally gotten both sides to fight each other and he climbs the fire-tower. The camera is very low so that not only Mifune but also each side in the battle will be visible. They emerge therefore, from either side of the wide screen, just as they would on the stage, and their movements (hesitant due to cowardice and caution) are pantomimic. The scenes inside the saké-shop looking out are also seen as pantomime and here the choreography (inside and outside the shop) is augmented by Miyagawa's superlative use of architecture (both inside and outside) to create an entire series of compositions which depend upon windows opening and closing, the camera dollying forward or sideways, the actors turning their heads (both Mifune and the seller inside; the officials and the servants outside) this way and that, obscuring a line of vision or allowing one to see, creating an enormously subtle interplay of movement and visible

form which it is impossible not to see as ballet. There are other indications as to how Kurosawa thought of this aspect of the film. One is the
use of the wipe as punctuation. He has always been fond of this particular visual effect but in few other films has he used quite so many
and in no other does he so carefully place them. The effect is therefore
just like a curtain (the Japanese theatrical curtain which moves at
right angles across the stage) and the wipes separate the action into
scenes.

Too, there is the first entrance of Nakadai. We look straight down
the main street, perspective perfectly balanced on either side. A
gust of wind blows the dust, obscures the scene, and through it we
see figures moving. The dust settles, and it is Nakadai in his striped
kimono, waving his little pistol. He has been brought on just like
a *premier danseur* and one of the underlings is sufficiently awed to
remark: "...see, even the winds welcome you." Again, there is
a very fine sequence where Mifune attacks the side to which he is
ostensibly attached, dispatches all the men with little or no difficulty,
and then proceeds to arrange the setting to look as though it was the
work of a whole group of men. He wrecks the *shoji*, he cuts the rice-
bags, he rips up the *tatami*, cuts the rope that holds the kettles—and
all of this he does with a second's reflective pause between each action
which seems to suggest: Let's see now, what shall I do next? He is
literally *arranging* (much in the same way that the mediocre director
arranges the ordinary *chambara* scene—an inside joke not in the least
lost on the movie-conscious Japanese) and it is therefore like a great
solo dance. The movements seem fraught with passion and emotion
but there is no need for feelings because, after all, all the men are dead.
Instead, the emotion is just that much needed to cut a stubborn rope,
to slit a *shoji*. Mifune is performing rather than acting. And then,
at the end, there is a delicious two-second scene where (dance over)
Mifune looks around to make certain that he has forgotten nothing
and notes off the items by nodding his chin, counting to make certain.
Coming directly after all the spectacular (and needless—for such is
its point) leaping and cutting, this matter-of-fact accounting is one
of the funniest things in this very funny film.

There are other indications of intended theatricality, including
another private joke. When Mifune escapes from his torturers he
crawls under the house, and there is one scene which has him crouch-
ing under the foundations while on the veranda above the villains
stand and discuss—which is a deliberate take-off on the famous letter-
scene from *Chushingura* in the Kabuki, a joke which never fails to
delight perceptive Japanese movie-goers. Also there is a splendid
production number (done in the grand style of the fire-festival of
*The Hidden Fortress*) in which the great casks of saké at the rich merchant's storehouse are unplugged, and the liquor gushes and inun-
dantes while the camera (precisely in the middle—the proper place
for spectacles) records it all. Also—and this is an effect upon which

almost everyone has commented—there is Mifune's walk.

As we were shown in the first cut (after the titles) this is the walk of a swordsman and this in itself makes it ballet-like—Japanese sport and Japanese dance are very close indeed. Too, it is a walk which the composer has delighted in *synchronizing* so that the hero appears to move to music. Asked about this walk, Kurosawa has said: "It is Mifune's own, but to stress it I carefully selected camera framings and lenses." In other words Kurosawa took advantage of natural choreography to stress it. He did the same thing with other attributes of Mifune.

In any of the Kurosawa pictures in which Mifune has appeared, one notices a small number of mannerisms (changing from picture to picture) which help to characterize the respective hero. In *Drunken Angel,* it is a servile bow coupled with an arrogant toss of the head, occasionally a hand to the temple to make certain that the elaborate gangster-style hair-do is still in place. In both *Rashomon* and *Seven Samurai* the distinguishing style was based upon a very interesting combination of the exuberant (leaps and capers) and the rueful (hand to chin, a pulling at the corners of the mouth.) In *Record of a Living Being*—a tour de force of acting—it was a bending of the neck, quick turtle-like motions of the head, and claw-like clutchings with the hands. In *The Bad Sleep Well* (a different kind of tour de force) it was a single gesture, the pushing of the bridge of the glasses higher on the nose. In *Sanjuro* it consisted mainly of unshaven-chin in hand, various scratchings, and a runny nose. The hero in *Yojimbo* shares like mannerisms but here they are much more heavily accentuated than in any of the other pictures. First there is the walk, then there is the hand on the chin, and finally there is the toothpick. This last is a splendid idea. A man who continually munches on a toothpick cannot help but look reflective, and at the same time informal. Most Japanese-movie samurai would curl up with shame at the idea of something so plebeian as a toothpick—it would be like giving chewing-gum to Gary Cooper. Yet it is precisely right for this particular hero and, further, becomes a major *gesture* in Mifune's ballet-like interpretation of the role.

One of the reasons that *Yojimbo* is so satisfying as a film—and it has become the most popular that Kurosawa has ever created—is that its cheerfully anarchistic philosophy is presented with a stylistic unity which (far from merely realistic) is the product of that rare kind of art that hides itself. Mifune beats the world by seeing through it, and he beats it on its own terms. Kurosawa shows us a seen-through world, one where 'reality' as such has ceased to count just as for Mifune the world's idea of 'reality' is unimportant. It is because Mifune sees through and re-orders the moral world that we feel delight. It is because Kurosawa has seen through and re-ordered the 'actual' visible world in terms of dance, spectacle, movement, composition, that we feel beauty.

# Sanjuro

"Originally, this was a story by Shugoro Yamamoto [who also wrote the novel upon which *Red Beard* is based]. I'd changed it around and finished the script before doing *Yojimbo*. In my first version the hero was not very good with the sword but was smart enough—he fought with his head. After *Yojimbo* was such a success, however, our company decided to make something like it, and so this not-so-strong samurai became the hero, Sanjuro. I rewrote the script and was going to give it to Hiromichi Horikawa to direct but, again, the company decided that I'd better do it. So—I wrote it over yet again. And each time Sanjuro was getting more athletic, better with the sword. Eventually we used only a third of the original script, and included lots of action not in the original."

## THE STORY

The chamberlain's nephew (Yuzo Kayama) and his young friends—serious samurai all—are having a secret meeting in a deserted shrine. His uncle, in charge of civic matters while the lord is in Edo, has just infuriated the youngsters by refusing to take seriously their petition to clean up graft and corruption within the city.

*Kayama:* And so I asked why he overlooked corruption among the junior chamberlains and the clan elders. (The other eight young samurai earnestly nod.) He smiled and said: 'Perhaps I'm behind it all, you never know. After all, people aren't what they seem to be. *You* have no idea which the bad ones are. It's dangerous, very dangerous,' he said. Then he tore up our petition! (Sensation. Show of indignation.) So, I gave up, went to see the superintendent. (Close attention, meaningful glances.) He understood . . . he thought for a while and then he said he'd help us. (He smiles; the others nod, impressed.) He wants to have a good, long talk with us. (The others bob in eager agreement.) So he said to get all of you here as soon as possible for the meeting. And that's how it went.

The young men laugh with relief, anticipation. Laughter continues and they look around in consternation for none of them are laughing. Out of the inner sanctuary ambles Sanjuro (Toshiro Mifune), yawning, scratching himself, thumping his shoulders, stiff with sleep. The youngsters reach for their swords. He barely glances at them.

The contrast between the spick-and-span boy-samurai with their terse nods, their meaningful glances, and Sanjuro, a real samurai, a real man, could not be greater. This opening scene is irresistibly funny because the two are so incongruous and this incongruity is one of the things that the film is about. They ask, in approved samurai fashion, words clipped, hands on swords, glaring, why he is there. He scratches a bit more before he answers that it was because it didn't cost anything to sleep in a temple. The young men stare at him in amazement because they had always thought such concerns far beneath a samurai. This is what they have been taught, and this is what they believe. Later, after he has saved them by guessing that the superintendent has called the meeting merely to get rid of them, that the superintendent is indeed the villain, the young samurai are compelled by their own etiquette to bow before him and to say the conventional if meaningless phrase:

*Kayama:* We do not know how to thank you.

*Mifune:* You needn't. How about giving me some money?

The youths are dumbfounded, aghast. This man has saved their lives and according to the feudal code they are bound to him. Yet, he is obviously a man who cares nothing for codes. What self-respecting samurai (such as themselves) would ask for something so common, so vulgar as money? They are confused, disturbed, and apprehensive as well. The leader places his money-bag in front of him. Mifune again surprises them by not taking the whole thing, but merely as much as he needs. They quite obviously expect people to be completely virtuous (to refuse all money) or completely bad (to take it all). The first are obviously like themselves (all of whom would die before accepting, much less demanding money); the second are (equally obviously) like the corrupt junior chamberlains whom they are attempting to expose—or the superintendent himself, who has so recently been revealed as their real adversary. For them, the world is a very simple place, made up of the black and the white, the bad and the good.

Mifune has already warned them of the dangers of this view when he speaks of the chamberlain:

"I don't know because I've never met the gentleman concerned—that is one of the good things about eavesdropping . . . outsiders can judge a lot better. He's ugly, I hear. Well, that's a good thing.

At least he seems honest. He told you he didn't mind being called a fool, is that right? Well, any man who says that isn't likely to be entirely bad. Now the superintendent. You say that he is honest and sincere. That must mean he is a fine-looking, handsome man, right? But people are not what they seem. The chamberlain told you that you didn't know who the bad ones were, didn't he? And you don't. I think the superintendent is behind the whole thing."

He gives his reasons for thinking so, and the young men are abashed and amazed because they have so judged these men on their mere appearance, and because they have therefore been fooled.

At the same time, while realizing this, they continue to judge Mifune on *his* appearance (dirty, unkempt, sloppy—the very opposite of the clean-cut samurai) and it is not until the end of the picture that, finally, at least several of them are temporarily cured of judging by illusion.

Again, the theme of the picture, as in many of Kurosawa's films, is illusion versus reality; things as they seem, things as they are, and the muddle that comes from confusing them. The boy-samurai, however, have, as yet, learned nothing. Remorseful over having misjudged the chamberlain, they swing from insubordination to allegiance—without stopping at any of the more likely emotions in between:

Kayama:   You have opened our eyes. We have learned our lesson. We will apologize and ask my uncle for orders.

Mifune:   (Wryly) Very obedient. Good boys.

Kayama:   I was a fool! I am to blame!

Others:   No, no. We are all to blame! We are all in this together. .

Another:   Yes. Live or die, just we nine men—

Sanjuro:   (Sighing) Oh—make it ten. It's too dangerous standing around watching you.

And so the adventure begins, for it turns out that the chamberlain has been kidnapped and the task is to rescue him from the superintendent and his men. First, however, it is necessary to rescue his wife and daughter. These ladies (Takako Irie—who had one of the leads in *The Most Beautiful*—and Reiko Dan) are very great ladies

indeed. They—like the boy-samurai—have their own code of behaviour and the most exquisitely funny scenes in the film come from
the incongruity of this behaviour, the fact that—given their peril-
fraught situation—their well-bred politesse is completely inappropriate.

The ladies enter the barn where all have taken refuge—enter,
pursued. The mother with a little sigh sinks down onto the hay:

"Oh . . . I have never run so fast in my life. Now you must let me
rest for a bit. Oh. (Patting her bosom, fanning herself with her
kerchief. After she has revived a bit she looks around with interest.)
Well. This must be our barn. I have never been here before. And
this is hay. My, but it smells nice. (The daughter confides that she
and her young cousin have often come to the barn and that once
she fell asleep with "his arm as my pillow." The mother shakes
her head, then smiles.) My, my, what bad manners. But, it really
is a nice smell, you know."

There they sit, two perfect Japanese ladies, talking about nature
in the very midst of their various emergencies, nodding gently and
agreeing, anxious to find the pleasant, the agreeable, while the boy-scout
samurai dash about importantly. Finally, side by side, feet under them
like the true ladies that they are, they fall asleep in the hay.

Later the mother sees Sanjuro (who has kept well away from the
ladies) and politely asks, with the patronizing air of which only the
great are innocently capable:

Lady:        And who is this person?
Kayama:      Well . . . it is hard to explain. But, he's our friend.
             Matter of fact, we owe our lives to him.
Lady:        Well! (With an expression of polite interest but not
             thinking to enquire further into the particulars of this
             life-saving.) Is that so? (Polite concern at what must
             have been a difficult and doubtless laudable endeavor.)

Thank you, very much. (Sweet smile.)

A spy (Keiju Kobayashi) is brought in and the question is what
to do with him. Sanjuro says that he must die.

Lady:        (With some show of spirit.) No, that you must not do.
             (Gently enquiring.) And did you kill the other guards?
Mifune:      Had to. To save you.
Lady:        I'm sorry to say this (pursing her lips, looking severely
             but kindly at Sanjuro), particularly since you were so
             very good to have saved us, but (shaking her head with
             gentle emphasis) killing people upon the slightest excuse
             is really a bad habit, you know. (Then she gives both
             the moral and poetry.) Yes, I can see ... you are like
             a sword without a scabbard.
Mifune:      A sword without a scabbard?
Lady:        Precisely. (Carried away by the beauty of the image.)
             A sword without a scabbard! And you cut well. But
             swords, you know, really good ones, should be kept in
             their scabbards and not used at all. (She relapses into
             dignified and self-satisfied silence while her daughter nods
             in gentle agreement.)

These scenes are completely amusing (as are the following scenes
where the lady, in order to escape over a garden wall, cannot bring
herself to step on Mifune's back, and finally, only after he has said
he'll run her through with his sword if she doesn't, can she bring
herself with the most fulsome of apologies, the most formal of language,
to take the necessary climb; where the boy-scout samurai are trying
to decide whether red or white camellias should be the attack signal,
and the ladies help, but their criteria are completely aesthetic, and they
soon enter into gentle dissent as to which is the more beautiful of the
colors; where, finally, at the end of the picture, the camellias sail down
the stream and the samurai jump into bloody action at the same time
as the ladies, in the very midst of danger, are clapping their hands
with girlish delight at the sheer beauty of the spectacle of the flowers
on the water), but, beyond being amusing, they are comic in that the
great lady intimidates Mifune just as he intimidates the boys.

And at the end of the film, he sees that her wisdom was greater
than his own. He has killed the villain in a spectacular sword fight
and the boys are tremendously impressed. He turns on them:

"Shut up. What was so great about that? He was exactly like
me—a drawn sword. Your old lady was right. Really good swords
are kept in their scabbards. Yours better stay in yours. And don't
try to follow me or I'll kill you. Goodbye."

These are the last words in the film. And it as though Mifune,
having taught the boys not to judge by appearances, to carefully
separate illusion from reality, to judge only after the evidence has
been examined, has himself learned something further from the
adventure—a higher wisdom.

It would seem that he too, as he now understands, had confused what is illusory, what is real. He had accepted as real an illusory situation. He had become involved in a battle which he treated as meaningful. Even though his thoughts on it were a bit more realistic than those of the boys, that he found it necessary to fight indicates the extent to which he was involved with the illusion that the world matters at all.

The lady's advice is to own a sword, to carry one, but not to use it, to keep it clean in the scabbard. This means to treat the visible world of illusion with the contempt that it deserves. And she herself, in her own way, does this. She insists upon finding beauty in everything. It is funny, it is touching. It is the opposite of common sense but (and this is a theme which many Kurosawa films have in common) common sense never gets us very far anyway. The merely pragmatic (in *Stray Dog, Ikiru, Rashomon, High and Low*) is no answer. It is only another way of phrasing the question. Sanjuro is looking for answers and the lady has taught him a valuable one: to be most yourself, take charge of and responsibility for your surroundings—do not allow things to happen to you, act as though they do not occur, and find what is necessary in what occurs; what counts is not what life makes of you but what you make of what life has made you; if necessary subscribe to a code, but make it a good one (not like that of the young samurai) by making it solely and wholly your own, and for that very reason do not draw your sword; keep it, like your essential self, the self you are trying to find, inside of you.

# TREATMENT

In making *Sanjuro* Kurosawa was relaxing between the rigors of *Yojimbo* and *High and Low* and has himself said that he had great fun filming it. Certainly it took less time to make than any Kurosawa picture except for the earlier ones. He did not think of it as a philosophic block-buster (*The Idiot, Ikiru, Record of a Living Being*) and it is perhaps for this very reason that its singularly complicated and elliptical message should emerge so clearly. Or perhaps it is that its genesis is (unlike that of, say, *The Idiot*) so uncomplicated. Stylistically, it is based upon only two factors: *Yojimbo*, and the ordinary Japanese *jidai-geki*. The resemblances to *Yojimbo* are extreme, superficially at any rate. Not only is the hero again called Sanjuro, not only are many of Mifune's mannerisms the same (with many subtle differences, of course), but the two pictures share even a scene in common.

This is the scene where Mifune is asked what his name is. In *Yojimbo* he looks out of the window, sees the mulberry field, and says Kuwabatake ('mulberry field'), that his first name is Sanjuro ('thirty years old') adding: "Going on forty, though." In *Sanjuro* the same scene occurs.

| *Lady:* | Now, I place my trust in you, but please, I beg you, do not use *too* much violence. And, by the way, what is your name? |
| *Mifune:* | Uh . . . (he looks around the room, then into the garden where the camellia—*tsubaki* in Japanese—are in bloom). Tsubaki . . . Tsubaki Sanjuro. Going on forty, though." (Music.) |
| *Lady:* | My—what an interesting gentleman. |

There are other similarities to *Yojimbo* as well. In order to avert suspicion he pretends in both pictures to a greed he does not feel, and tries to get money for giving information. The villain (again—Tatsuya Nakadai) is around for the first fight, admires Mifune, tries to get him to join his side, and is, in the end, killed by him.

Again (though this is true of all his films from *Seven Samurai* on) Kurosawa gives a very great importance to the actual location. *Yojimbo* in a seaside town is hard to imagine—one needs the plains, the winds, the whirls of dust. Likewise (since Sanjuro has moved up in the world and is now consorting with his betters), the location in *Sanjuro* (a castle city; in particular, two adjoining mansions) is full of grand Tokugawa architecture, splendid rooms and luxurious gardens. The result is that locale becomes very real—atmosphere is created. Further, the location must do its share of the work. Just as Mifune's map in *The Hidden Fortress* informs us of all future locations; just as the maps in *Stray Dog* and *High and Low* show us where we are before we even get there; just as we get to know the town in *Yojimbo* so intimately that we are never lost, know just where danger lurks and where not—so, in *Sanjuro*, the two gardens, connected by a stream, not only lend atmosphere but also are responsible for the plot itself since, at the end, it is this stream which will carry the camellia signal from one garden (where Mifune is imprisoned) to the next (where the boy-samurai wait).

The use of setting as plot motivation (the shaky bridge, the cabin filled with dynamite, the earthquake, fire, flood for which we have been painfully prepared) is thought of as being bad dramaturgy—but that is just the point in this film. Streams that carry messages are rife in Japanese literature. One hears about them in the *kodan*, those spoken stories of feudal chivalry, one sees them in the Kabuki, and there is certainly no dearth in the ordinary period-film.

Which is precisely why Kurosawa uses such a stream and makes it so important. The major stylistic influence in *Sanjuro* is just this ordinary *jidai-geki*. While, on one hand, in *Seven Samurai* and in *Yojimbo* one of the major considerations was a renovation of this particularly tired genre, both here and in *The Hidden Fortress* the very stuff of *jidai-geki* is used as is. There are many scenes in *Sanjuro* which could have come straight from a standard period sword-slinger. The boys (precisely the sort of clean-cut Japanese youths which are used in romantic spectaculars) dash about, valiantly doing a man's job and doing it well; they hitch up their skirts and pull back their sleeves in the best movie-samurai fashion; they scramble up and over walls; intensely suspicious they challenge everyone; they respect their leader, will die if necessary, and are just the sort of persons that most adolescent Japanese males (and some a bit older) would like to become.

If a number of separate scenes could have come from the *chambara*, however, their context is anything but *chambara*-like. The purpose of using such scenes (and of using a *jidai-geki* style itself throughout the film) is that they lend themselves so well equally to satire and to ridicule. The philosophy of the film is so un-feudal that such feudal remnants become funny.

All of the cliches are here: the notes, the signals, the good side, the bad side, the needless sword fights, the fortuitous stream. They are used because the boy-scout samurai are *stupid* enough to use them. When the boys bustle about making plans, they are really making up *jidai-geki* plots. Nothing is too unlikely for them to believe, no idea too lavish for them to entertain. Since they obviously believe in *jidai-geki*, they hoist their skirts, pull their sleeves, ready their swords, and are then dumbfounded when nothing turns out the way they had expected.

Mifune, of course, knows better. He knows that the world of the *jidai-geki* is not real. One of the most hilarious passages in the picture underlines just this. He is trying to sleep. They, however, intensely excited, are bustling about, racing in and out of the room, intent on their various plans. In a series of very short cuts, each separated by a wipe (a technique used for comic effect in many of Kurosawa's films from *They Who Step on he Tiger's Tail* on), we watch Mifune becoming more and more irritated.

*The door bangs open, Mifune awakes with a jolt, scowls, the excited youths exchange confidences, rush out again / wipe / bang, the door is thrown open, the boys run, Mifune looks up, frowns, scratches himself,*

*closes his eyes / wipe / crash—the shoji is flung open and the boys, full of important messages for each other, crowd in; Mifune glowers, a big, disturbed, rueful, resentful tom-cat—for Mifune is very feline in this film, both superb and sleepy, while the boy-samurai yap, growl, and worry.*

A number of scenes explicate the differences between the play-samurai and the real. In order to test whether men are indeed hidden in a room Mifune resorts to the well-known device of tossing a rock into a pool in which he has first ascertained that there are fish. Sure enough, the men rush out, think the noise only that of a carp, and go back. Later, one of the boys having approved this thoroughly traditional method, has occasion to call the attention of another. He heaves a rock though he could just as easily have gone and tapped the other on the shoulder. Mifune is pained. Again, the boys never once get to actually fight. They spend all of their time carrying messages back and forth to each other. When Mifune fights, it is for real. The rescue of the ladies is an example. It takes just four seconds on the screen and included (all visible in two cuts and three fine sweeping pans) are three men dead and two ladies safely rescued.

The effect of this use of *jidai-geki* is, naturally, a superb parody of the *jidai-geki* itself. When Kurosawa shows us all nine boy-samurai obediently paddling after a disgusted Mifune, he is saying that the weakness of samurai is that they must always join something, must always follow someone. And Mifune continually embarrasses *them* as well because, though they know he is a fine swordsman, he does not look in the slightest like the beau-ideal they have always envisioned. A samurai who needs a shave, who is dirty and scratches, who drinks and gets drunk, who sleeps all the time, who calls their great lady an old woman—a fine samurai indeed! When they come up with a splendid plan, the man who saved their lives and whom they must follow never does anything but ridicule.

*Leader:*      There . . . how does that sound?
*Mifune:*      Not spectacular—but it may keep us awake.

Yet, despite their self-importance, they are only boys, and try as they will they cannot but show this. They capture the spy (this role, along with that of the lady, are the only two characters unchanged from the script which Kurosawa initially wrote) and cannot understand why Mifune is not jubilant. After all, in *jidai-geki* spies are *always* captured. Nor can they understand the lady who insists upon giving him a fine kimono (her nephew's best) and treating him as a guest. (Her inadvertent wisdom is seen when they finally ask the spy why he didn't escape and he answers: "It was hard to when it didn't even occur to the lady that I might.") At the same time, when they hear some particular good news, and are jumping up and down and congratulating each other, they naturally include the spy who, being a very poor spy, is just as delighted as they are. Then there is the telling,

touching, and very funny moment when they suddenly remember that he is on the *bad* side, that they have forgotten their stern, dedicated samurai spirit, that they have neglected their *bushido*.

Even more clearly than in *They Who Step on the Tiger's Tail,* Kurosawa here shows just what he thinks of what passes for *bushido* in our time. Its true ascetic spirit is shown in *Sugata,* in the swordsman in *Seven Samurai,* where it is truly a way of the spirit. In its *chambara*-corrupted form, it is heroics which would be empty if did they not at the same time subtly corrupt the spirit by insisting upon inflexibility in a world where the merely inflexible will invariably bring grief. The boys themselves seem to realize this (though with approval) when they, busy making up *jidai-geki* plots, prophecy that the superintendent will end up committing hara-kiri, which is just what he does. But this, in turn, only proves that *he* as well thinks in terms of *jidai-geki.*

Ironically, what brings the boys around and really impresses them (for they have begun to distrust Mifune, to think him a *traitor* to their side simply because he uses his head in fighting) is precisely the wrong thing: a sword-fight.

This splendid final duel between Nakadai and Mifune *is* terribly impressive to be sure. They meet outside the city and Mifune is forced to fight though he does not want to. They face each other. Both being fine swordsmen there is no bluffing offensive, no strategic retreat, no slashing. Swords still in scabbards they confront each other and there is a long wait—a very long one, fifteen whole seconds, an enormous amount of time at the climax of a film. Then, in a single movement, both draw and (at the same time) strike. What follows is so grand that it is beyond the dreams of even the most avid *chambara* fan. Mifune

has slashed so quickly and so deeply that he has sliced into the heart of his opponent. There is an explosion of blood, a great spray (a vat of chocolate syrup and carbonated water under thirty pounds of pressure, triggered by a lever and hidden under Nakadai's kimono) which gushes out like a geyser, accompanied by the most blood-curdling of sound-effects.

The boys are impressed beyond expression. When they recover themselves a bit the leader remembers he is after all a samurai and says the proper thing: "Splendid!" and this occasions Sanjuro's tirade and departure. They stand, confused, elated, dejected, impressed, unsure—the same attitude in which Kurosawa perhaps in this picture hoped to leave the young Japanese audience to which, as he has often said, his films are directed.

"Personally, I think this film very different from *Yojimbo.* In Japan the audience does too. The youngsters loved *Yojimbo,* but it was the adults who liked *Sanjuro.* I think they liked it because it is the funnier and really the more attractive of the two." Also, it is one of his most didactic films (though so amusing, so cleverly constructed, that this is not at all apparent), and while the satire was certainly not lost upon the adult audiences in Japan and (surprisingly) in the West, the effect upon the young was a bit chastening.

That final fight, that single heroic slash, followed by the spectacular demise of Nakadai, contains Kurosawa's comment. He gives his audience its cake and at the same time lets them eat it (very rare in an entertainment), but in the very midst of the horror-struck thrill he shows what it is really made of. That grand *splaaaaat* at the end is a lethal thrust indeed—straight into the heart of conventional *jidai-geki,* and all of the more stupid feudal remains it so appeals to.

# High and Low

## THE STORY

The story, with major revisions, is taken from a novel by Edward McBain. Gondo (Toshiro Mifune) is production head of a shoe company who, having trouble with the directors, is planning a coup whereby he will gain control of the stock and thereby the company. He mortgages his home and belongings to get enough money to make the initial payment. Just then he receives word that his son is kidnapped and the criminal asks for an exorbitant amount—very near that which he has just raised. A bit later the boy returns and it is discovered that his playmate, the chauffeur's son, was the one who was kidnapped.

The question becomes: is a chauffeur's son worth as much as an industrialist's? At first Mifune says no, refuses, particularly when the kidnapper calls, admits the mistake, but insists that he be paid anyway. After much thought the industrialist, upon the advice of the police, agrees to pay. The rendezvous is on a speeding express-train. The money is handed over, the boy is returned and the first half of the film is over. Mifune is ruined but now the police start trying to get back the money. This occupies the second half of the film.

One clue leads to another, and eventually a young intern, Takeuchi (Tsutomu Yamazaki), is implicated. He is also guilty of selling heroin to addicts and, eventually, of killing his accomplices in the kidnapping. He is captured, confesses and in the final scene in the prison asks to meet Mifune.

*Yamazaki:* Ah, Mr. Gondo, thanks for coming. You look very well. What are you doing these days?

*Mifune:* Making shoes, just as I always have. It's a small company but they've been kind enough to put me in charge of production. I hope someday to be able to build something even better than National Shoes was.

*Yamazaki:* Why do you keep *looking* at me like that? In a few hours I'm going to die but don't think that frightens me. It doesn't. And don't think I called you here because I wanted your pity...why should I spend the last few moments of my life listening to slop like that? You see, I'm concerned with the truth, no matter how ugly... But, how about it—now that I'm going to die, are you happy?

*Mifune:* Why do you talk like that? Why are you so convinced that it is right that we hate each other?

*Yamazaki:* I don't know about that...it is just that...from my dirty little room, too cold to sleep in the winter, too hot to breathe in the summer, I could see your house and it was like looking up at heaven. I looked up at your house every day and somehow began to hate you. After a while it was hating you that kept me going.

And you know something? I found out that people like me can have a lot of fun making people like you miserable.

*Mifune:* Were you that miserable?

*Yamazaki:* Want the story of my life? Not a chance. Your sympathy doesn't interest me, Mr. Gondo, and I really don't have that much time.... It will soon be over and I'm glad of it.

*Mifune:* If that is the way you feel why did you send for me?

*Yamazaki:* I didn't want you to think that I died begging for mercy...

He suddenly clutches the wire-screen, his hands shaking.

You think my hands are shaking because I'm scared. Look—I've been in solitary for two weeks now—it is a common physical reaction. When a man is taken out of solitary he starts to shake—that's the truth. A death sentence means nothing to me. I've been living in my own private hell for a long time. So I'm not afraid of going to hell.

He stands up, anguished, shouts:

Now, if someone were to tell me I was going to heaven, then I guess I'd really start to shake, wouldn't I?

He begins to cry, to laugh, to shout. The guards rush in and take him away. The iron shutter falls over the glass and wire between them. Mifune is left sitting alone in front of the closed prison shutter, and the film ends.

## TREATMENT

The title of the film in Japanese is *Tengoku to Jigoku* (or *Heaven and Hell*) and this suggests an extreme opposite that merely *High and Low* does not. The first half of the picture takes place in heaven—that is, in Mifune's apartment, high on a bluff in Yokohama and visible

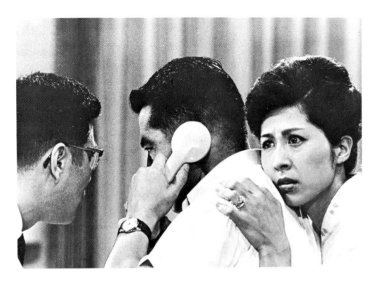

from most of that section of the city. Even the background for the credit titles is scenes of Yokohama taken from high up. These include the harbor, Chinatown, the trains and factory chimneys which later become important to the action, and all are seen as Mifune himself sees them—from above. The second half of the film takes place in hell—in Yokohama itself, and eventually descends to the lowest circle: the alleys around Chinatown where in a warren of cheap hotels and bars the heroin pushers are found.

Formally, the film is designed to break into two. At the end of the first, the ostensible story is over—the boy is back, we are consequently no longer emotionally involved. The second half is an elaborate hunt and our interest becomes intellectual. As in *Stray Dog* we are presented with a puzzle and then watch it worked out, step by step.

As in the 1948 film (and oddly, *Un carnet du bal*—a film much admired in Japan) the audience is given evidence bit by bit.

Kurosawa plainly shows what *he* thinks is important. It is not the kidnapping itself (done off screen) nor the fate of the small victim (the return is purposely done in extreme long-shot as though to rob it of all emotion), nor is it Mifune's moral dilemma. It is the search, the capture, and the confrontation. The form would indicate this—or else why have the boy returned half way through the film?—and so does the way in which the two parts are filmed.

If the first half is statement and exposition, then the second half is development and conclusion; if the first is theory, then the second is practice.

The first half—it takes one hour and five minutes—not only takes place entirely in Mifune's apartment, but the action is so static that it is very close to theater. Several cameras are used but the takes are enormously long—some run to ten minutes and would probably have run longer but this was the capacity of the camera's magazines.

I was present during the filming of the early morning scene where the detectives have stayed the night: Mifune comes in, opens the windows, is asked to close them, eventually refuses to pay and goes out. During the rehearsals one of the lights fused. It was an arc simulating early morning sunlight outside the window from which Mifune was to pull the curtain. Even though it was only a rehearsal Kurosawa said: "Let's wait until they fix the light . . . we might as well do it right."

This is typical of the meticulousness which went into these static-appearing scenes. We know they are static, even feel a mild claustrophobia, but we are never bored, we remain interested. And when things happen, they happen fast: the chauffeur comes in with a sweater for his son, asks for him, the wife goes to look in the garden, the telephone rings, it is the kidnapper, and we get the first close-up: Mifune on the phone.

There are only three indications of passing of time in the first half. They are all wipes. The first is the second phone call, the detectives already there, wipe/the next scene is everyone listening to a taping made by the police some time after. The second leaves the chauffeur pleading with his employer, in full obeisance on the floor, with Mifune walking out of the room, wipe/next morning Mifune coming downstairs. The third is the call, wipe/the family listening to the taped call while in the background the detectives are following the kidnapper's taped instructions, putting the money into briefcases—cause and effect included in the single shot. There are many other short-cuts used in this first half. "Is that the police?" asks the wife. "No," says the chauffeur, "only a department store truck." "Funny time for it to come," says Mifune and instantly the chauffeur is announcing the police, and there is not another word explaining that they came disguised as truckers.

The train sequence, which is the visual center of the film, is given the amount of time it would actually have taken, about four minutes—but four minutes of an action so furious that after the stillness of the first hour, the effect is overwhelming.

The second half begins at once and here the leisurely method of the story-telling chronicle is abruptly changed—using the freely-cut train sequences as link—to an essay-like, analytical narration (a bit like that in *Ikiru*) where past and present are seen at the same time. First, however, Kurosawa makes certain that we understand we are now in hell. Detectives are checking phone boxes. They look up and there is Mifune's house. One says to the other: "Looking up at his place from here it *does* sort of seem he's looking down his nose at everyone." The camera looks at the scummy canal and in a distance the radio is heard playing the theme and variations movement of Schubert's *Forellen* quintet, the camera pans up and follows a new character, a young man. He is followed through alleys until he reaches his room, turns on the radio, starts searching the newspapers. It is the kidnapper.

Here, Kurosawa purposely throws away mystery and suspense. Not only do we know that the boy has been returned, we also know what the kidnapper looks like, which is more than anyone else does. We are forced to become as analytical as the detectives. We can savor their getting nearer and nearer because we now know what the criminal looks like and we discover something about his life.

We are not allowed to look too long, however. At once we are taken on the chase which includes almost every technique in the cinematic repertoire.

> *First we see the eight millimeter shots taken from the train, then a blow-up of a single frame, there is a man with a cow. It was he who says he saw a man running with two brief-cases and driving away. From this they get tire-marks and some paint scrapings. The little victim has in the meantime drawn a picture of what he saw: Mt. Fuji and the sea. At police headquarters they are checking all pay phones from which Mifune's house is visible (since the kidnapper said he could see it, and wondered why—when the police were there—the blinds were drawn)—they find three and we have already seen them do so. The kidnapper said it was hot—the police discover that one of them is in the sun at the hour the call came. It turns out the little boy was given ether to keep him quiet. The car model is identified and there is a glimpse of the police stopping a car. The police discover an abandoned car (seen) and its license number tallies with the number of a stolen car. The attendants on the freeway remember seeing a boy asleep in the back of a car— we see detectives talking with them; in the meantime the police have been trying to find a place where both Fuji and*

> *the sea are visible (and a short scene shows this). A detective in replaying the tapes hears the sound of a cable-train in the background. He starts to investigate: a short scene of his talking with train men, their identifying it. They find the house and the dead accomplices, they also find a note (seen in blow-up in the laboratory) saying they intend to spend the money unless they get more dope. In the meantime we know that the briefcase is still with the kidnapper and that it contains chemicals that color smoke if they are burned. Again a shortcut is used. The criminal sees a picture of the briefcase in the paper. Cut to the child having drawn a picture of the kidnapper. Cut to the children racing into the room to say some funny smoke is coming from a chimney.*

This last, as are all other successful clues, is accompanied by a fanfare on the sound track. And, like it, all of these tiny scenes are imbedded in the larger scene of policemen making separate reports to their superiors. While they explain we see them doing what they are talking about. Very often past and present are there at the same time, cause and effect are made practically one, a number of false leads are followed but, through elimination, the cops get warmer and warmer. One detail is piled on top of another, each one significant, some very witty. A cop looking through binoculars from a window is accompanied by a distant record playing a song the lyrics of which are: "I can see your lovely eyes;" when the police move in through the moonlight a radio plays *O sole mio*. This telescoping, and the technical brilliance of the exposition makes this section, about thirty minutes, the shortest half hour in all of Kurosawa's cinema.

Then the detectives decide to arrest, and in this climax of the hunt Kurosawa presents a kaleidoscope which must be compared with the night-town sequences of *Ikiru* for sheer visual exhilaration. One marvelous scene after another: the cops disguised as toughs in a Yokohama dance-hall; the villain walking through Chinatown, has glasses reflecting the lights; the head-cops in a car which is speckled with passing neons; a very exciting scene where the ruined Mifune is walking accidentally in the same neighborhood (looking at shoes in a store window) and the kidnapper, recognizing him, asks for a light and then looks curiously at him for a second. The hunt comes to an abrupt end when they snap the handcuffs on him at the deserted house overlooking the sea where they found the murdered couple. Then comes the coda and the confrontation.

In his depiction of contrasts Kurosawa follows Dante. Heaven is a measured place of muffled crisis where things as they are is insisted upon; hell is a chaos, wildly exciting, quite dangerous. The disguised cops move through this hell like demigods, or angels, always alert, always watching. Mifune moves through this world like Dante himself, oblivious even when confronted with the evil that has wrecked his life. Only the head detective, his brow furrowed, worries, invisible but watching over him, Virgil-like. The parallel need not be labored, there is no doubt that Kurosawa is surely on the side of the angels. In this film there is not the slightest sympathy for the villain nor for the world that is his. The police are true protectors, the villain is truly black. Morally, it would seem to be the most black and white of all of Kurosawa's films because its eventual ambiguity is not one of character.

# CHARACTERIZATION

Though there are many characterizations of others in the film (the wife is in kimono throughout except in the final scene at the house where, in Western dress, she faces eviction; each detective is given his own little quirk; the head detective is obviously and wholly benevolent), there are really only two fully-drawn characters: those of Gondo, the unfortunate; and Takeuchi, the bringer of misfortune.

Gondo is a completely ordinary man—he could be almost anyone. He has gotten where he is in the world through hard work, yet he has never sacrificed his integrity and this integrity is that of a workman who will not produce shoddy goods. This is fully established in the opening scene, a quarrel between him and the other directors of the shoe company based on just this point. Yet, at the same time, he has lived enough in the world to know how to take care of himself. When his son and the chauffeur's boy are playing outlaw and sheriff, Gondo calls out: "Running away from the sheriff won't help. Hide and then let him have it. Don't you run, let him run. It's kill or be killed . . . don't forget." This advice is precisely that which he himself is following in buying out the stock. It will ruin the other directors who are set on getting control themselves. He is therefore no better than they—though he has our sympathy because he has a kind of integrity which they do not. And this he shows, when, in the midst of his misfortunes, he sits down on the floor, calls for his tools—which he obviously has not used for years—and begins taking the leather briefcase apart to put in the smoke capsule. "In my day shoemakers made briefcases too. I never thought my days as an apprentice would be so valuable. Yet here I am, starting from scratch again." And he laughs—in the very face of his troubles. There is a cut to the train (the beginning scene in that sequence) where the head detective reinforces our own impressions with: "You know, I really admire that man."

He *is* admirable but as the film continues it becomes clear that this admirable quality is mainly that of his being able to tolerate the idea of beginning again, of his being willing to accept a meaningless disaster for which he could in no way be considered responsible, of his finding the strength to continue, his ability to believe in himself.

It is here that *High and Low* reveals itself as having the same ideological basis as the majority of Kurosawa's films. Like Watanabe in *Ikiru*, like the girl in *One Wonderful Sunday*, like the detective in *Stray Dog*, like the young hero of *Red Beard*—Gondo has the ability to believe and the will to continue.

The character of Takeuchi, the kidnapper, seems at first a complete contrast. It would seem that he is plain bad just as Gondo is plain good. Even the looks of the actors suggest this. Mifune is, of course, a good, even noble-looking man. On the other hand, Tsutomu Yamazaki (a stage actor whose first big film part this was) looks, at least in this part, untrustworthy, twisted, faintly repellent. This is the way the characters appear, but here we might remember Sanjuro's advice: You cannot tell what a person is like by how he looks.

Yamazaki certainly *acts* different from Mifune. He is compulsive, he is a man running away, and the police call him a maniac. While not that, he *is* one of life's dissatisfied. Unable to love, he finds pleasure —as he brags at the end of the film—in hating. This man, then, has chosen to be evil—just as the criminal in *Stray Dog* chose. And we remember Detective Shimura's words in that film: "Look, *my* knapsack and money were stolen too. I felt outraged. I knew that this was a dangerous point in my life. But what did I do? I chose this work." Evil, then, is merely the wrong choice at the moment of truth.

His choice of Gondo seems completely gratuitous. He has no motive other than the pleasure of hate, and that Gondo's house is so grand. Evil is non-selective and Gondo's first reaction is an outraged: "Why me?" When the kidnapper calls on the phone (always being careful to call him "*Mr.* Gondo" with an obsequiousness which cannot hide the joy he is feeling at the irony of his, finally the man in power, calling the other, the fallen, *Mr.*) Gondo's reaction is not anger so much as incomprehension.

We watch Gondo's attempt to escape from the consequences of the actions of the other. There is no reason why he should pay. It is that he cannot *not* do it. At first he refuses absolutely. Then he attempts to explain why he is refusing. Finally, he agrees to say he will pay. Next he agrees to take the money from the bank, but says he won't hand it over. It is only as he himself pushes it from the train window—in that one dazed second—that he realizes what has happened and says: "It is my life."

Both police and press think well of this action. They think it is socially desirable, civic-minded, even brave. He is a wonderful man, they tell each other. But his being thought a wonderful man will not get back his life for Mr. Gondo.

He, who has always taken full responsbility for his life (and prided himself in it) is suddenly no longer responsible for it. First, the kidnapper takes over his life and, second, the police take it over. These two things are equated in a curious and meaningful way. It is both kidnapper *and* police who make it impossible for him to work. The first has a certain power over him—if Gondo does as he says the boy may be returned; but the second has a like power—if he does what they say the money may be returned. In either event he can no longer do any work—and he apparently takes to wandering (an action which cannot have been habitual to him) and it is on one of these walks that he first, unknowingly, meets the criminal.

The world is indeed a fine place if things like this can happen to such a good-hearted man, such a well-intentioned man as Mr. Gondo. But (as Kurosawa never tires of pointing out) the world is just like this. It is indeed a hell (as we have been told in *Rashomon,* in *Record of a Living Being* in *The Lower Depths,* and now here). But it is not a private hell. We are all in it—so is the kidnapper.

He is a man to whom things have happened all of his life and so, just for this once, he decides to make something happen to someone else. He is "oppressed" and so he will oppress an "oppressor." There is something noble in his resolve in that it takes a kind of bravery and considerable courage. At least he is not going to sit back and let life batter him over the head. The flames of hell will not get him without a struggle. So he makes his plan.

However, the same thing happens to him that happens to Gondo. First, he becomes responsible—he must see his crime through to some kind of conclusion. Second, he too becomes responsible to the police. He might have been caught with the boy; now he might be caught with the money. We are much more familiar with this process in the bad man than we are in the good because so many stories and movies have shown us how one "evil" action leads to the next, and so on. Very rarely, however, have we been shown—and shown so clearly— that by the end the bad man has become thoroughly *subject* to those very actions through which he sought to free himself. He and Gondo have become rather alike—neither can work, both are given to wandering. They can be identified with each other.

# CAMERA

Reality is heightened in this film not so much through story, as in *Ikiru,* or form as in *Rashomon,* as through the eye itself. The references to seeing in the film are many and varied. The kidnapper can see into Gondo's house, the policemen, in turn, use binoculars to peep out; many in the cast wear glasses; the kidnapper wears dark glasses at night and their surface reflects what he sees; devices for seeing—still pictures, motion pictures, drawings, are constantly used; there are many mirrors in the picture—the wall mirror in the Yokohama dive, rear view mirrors in cars; there are all kinds of reflections, from reflections on water to reflections on the shiny surfaces of automobiles; a kind of paranoia is felt—someone is always *watching*—and in the confrontation scene it is reflections on a sheet of glass which give the film its final and profoundly ambiguous meaning.

Kurosawa's camera—never self-effacing—has almost never been so prominent. But, as always, it is completely to the point. Throughout the picture there is an insistence that the camera view-point be either high or low. The opening credits are from high above Yokohama; the kidnapper in his room is from below. Scenes in Gondo's house are taken from chest level. Scenes in the dope-dens are taken from a lower angle, around hip level. At the same time—particularly in the first half of the picture—there are many rising/falling shots which insist, accompanying risings and sittings of the actors, upon high and low. This kind of movement is particularly important in the first half because the scenes in themselves are static, as they must be if the second half is to have its full impact.

The way in which these static scenes were vivified is interesting. For the main set, Gondo's apartment was created twice—there were two major sets, identical. One was at the Toho studio, the other was overlooking Yokohama; in other words, Gondo's house was, in part, built. Scenes showing the family against daylight Yokohama were actually filmed there. The night scenes from ostensibly the same location were filmed from yet a third set which had a complete miniature set of Yokohama at night (the real one did not photograph well enough) outside the window. The main body of the first half (all scenes with the curtains drawn) was filmed at the Toho studio.

This set was made much like a stage with no proscenium—a room with the fourth wall missing. Kurosawa's cameras were outside this missing wall and tracks were laid in various positions. The camera itself was rarely taken into the set—close-ups being obtained through long-distance lenses.

For the morning scene mentioned above, the tracks were laid in an inverted V-shape with the two free ends meeting the corners of the set. On one track was a dolly with a camera equipped with long-distance lenses. On the other was another dolly with a small elevator attached. The third camera was hidden in the hallway leading from the far end of the room and was likewise equipped with a telescopic lense. The method of filming was something like that used in TV with different cameras using different lenses, changing position from time to time. The entire operation had been thoroughly practiced, the actors' movements had been worked out, the camera's movements (both dolly cameras moving continually, the elevator following the motions of the actors) and the cues for changing lenses—everything had been choreographed. The three cameras were run simultaneously and the take was repeated twice, which meant one hour of film for a ten minute scene. The sequence was then put together in the cutting room.

The effect is one of complete freedom within a very constricted area and the camera work alone is responsible for the fact that this half, though over an hour in length, seems so very much shorter. Yet this very restraint also assists the visual explosion of the train-sequence—one of the most exciting five minutes in Japanese film.

Here the camera is hand-held or it is bolted to the train floor to make it jump, or put into the cab of the engine, or held out of the window. Nine cameras were used for this sequence including the eight-millimeters which took the scenes later projected at the police headquarters. In the edited version the continuity is superb: one is never lost nor do any of the tiny reactions (Mifune's expression when he lets go the money) escape. At the same time the sense of crisis, of excitement is completely captured.

In the latter half of the film so much is happening that one has to look hard. The cops passing notes back and forth (the machinations of the police force would have delighted Dr. Mabuse); the crowded scenes in the dance-hall with only the flick of an eye to identify the fuzz; the fascinating juxtaposition of seeing what they did while they tell about doing it; the fantastic telephoto shots with people all jammed into a single plane; the bravura of throwing away breathtaking shots with Fuji in the distance. Just as the cops must remain completely alert, forever searching, so must the spectator.

At the same time the camera continuity is so swift that to lapse is to miss. An example of this is the way in which the kidnapper is finally identified. The kidnapper is looking through the newspapers again. The following is all one shot, the camera hand-held but rock-steady, shooting from a relatively short distance with a 75 mm. telescopic lens:

> *His face, extreme close-up looking at papers, looks startled, pan to paper, picture of briefcase; pan up to him, he drops paper, turns; door opens, extreme close-up, no telling what it is; he pulls things out of closet (it must have been the closet door); finally gets briefcase, holds it open, camera swings to see it just before it disappears into cardboard box; his hands in close-up, they find twine; pan to box, twine, up to enormous close-up of face, pan down to hand to show—for the first time, but only for a second, the cut on his hand which will eventually identify him.*

This shot of the most controlled brilliance and the most supernal difficulty lasts about 30 seconds.

> *Cut to Gondo's house. They are looking at the picture the child drew of the kidnapper and all notice that he has drawn one hand bandaged | cut. The boys run in and say to come look at the smoke | cut. Color shot (very brief) of police, family, Yokohama in distance, red smoke coming out of chimney. Fanfare on sound track.*
> *Cut to the bottom of the chimney, a policeman talking to the man who burns the refuse. Discovers that the briefcase came from an intern. Cut to the waiting room of the hospital. Cops are there. The kidnapper in his intern smock comes by. He stops on the stairway. They see the cut on his hand. They react. Fanfare.*

What the picture insists upon is the reality of what is happening but, at the same time, it is so extraordinarily concerned with the ways in which reality is counterfeited—mirrors, cameras, binoculars, even eyes—that it is almost equally concerned with illusion. The police are obviously trying to separate, for their own purposes, illusion from reality—that is what a police hunt is. As in *The Bad Sleep Well*, Kurosawa is here much concerned with illusion-making machines. In the former film there is the magical scene of the man looking at his own funeral service while listening to a tape which shows him how his

death was to have been contrived. In *High and Low,* too, the tape recorder is again used, as are films—ghost machines both.

That the picture is concerned not only with theory and practice but also with illusion and reality is wonderfully brought out—and the two are brought together—in the final scene, the confrontation. Yamazaki is in the death-cell and Mifune comes. Mifune is outside; Yamazaki is inside. They are separated by wire mesh and by a plate of heavy glass. Their conversation begins and the photographic method is, at first, the classic one-two shot: first a close-up of Mifune, then one of Yamazaki. But here we notice something strange. The close-ups of each are taken from the side of the glass opposite that on which he is sitting so that over each close-up is the reflection of the other. As their conversation continues, the set-ups move back further so that, for example, Mifune will be on one side of the screen and Yamazaki on the other but Mifune's reflection will appear in the middle. Over their talk the camera set-ups shift in such a way that the image of the one more and more precisely coincides with the other's reflection.

"If that is the way you feel, why did you send for me?" Mifune asks, and their images coincide. The tears in Mifune's eyes appear to be swimming in the dry eyes of the kidnapper.

In *Stray Dog* the cop and the robber roll fighting in the mud and at the end of the picture they are indistinguishable: cop and robber are one. At the end of *High and Low* something of the sort occurs but much more subtly. We know they are not one—they are good and evil; they are opposite poles. This is what we have been led to believe, this is what we *must* believe. Yet, here, slowly but inexorably, Kurosawa is showing us something entirely different. He is suggesting that, despite everything, good and evil are the same, that all men are equal.

"I am not afraid of going to hell," shouts the kidnapper but it is Mifune's reflection which seems to shout, just as it is the kidnapper's reflection which seems to weep. Good and evil are made to coincide; they are made identical. In *Stray Dog,* the men merely *look* alike. Here they are made to seem to be *giving* each other attributes of themselves. Precisely: they seem to be sharing an identity.

There is no longer any question of a hero or a villain, or heaven or hell, of high or low, of good or of bad. We have already seen that, since the kidnapping, they have come more and more to resemble each other. Having initially hated each other, they are now close to accepting each other.

Mifune, then, has truly had his sense of responsibility tested. He wants to be responsible to himself and make good shoes; his company directors disagree and so he feels right in trying to take over the company in order to continue making good shoes. When the boy is kidnapped a less central sense of responsibility is tested for he is asked to ruin himself for a reason he cannot accept. This, however, he does—and this already indicates how extraordinary he is. Now, at the very end, his sense of responsibility is given its most severe test—he is asked to take responsibility for the actions of the very man who has wronged him. And the indications are that he will.

Yamazaki is just as much a victim as Mifune is though it is more difficult to assess him because he falls into that convenient and meaningless category of "the victim of society." Actually, however, he falls victim to the actions of Mifune no less than Mifune falls victim to his. If Mifune had not made his grand house on the bluff none of this would have happened. You cannot realize yourself in this world without hurting something. Mifune wants to realize himself and builds the house which hurts the kidnapper; he, in turns, wants to realize himself, and takes the child which hurts Mifune.

There is one great difference, however. Yamazaki is going to die and he knows it. It is with horror, then, that he sees the awful alternative of going to heaven rather than to hell. Awful, because—accepting hell as hell—he has identified himself with it, acted as though he belonged there. If he goes to heaven what will become of *him.* Perhaps that is the reason he asked to see Mifune. He wanted to find hate in those eyes, he wanted this reassurance that he was evil, that he was at least this much, that he was at least something.

And the irony is that Mifune will not, cannot. It is no longer a question of compassion nor forgiveness. It has become interior. Mifune must accept responsibility for the criminal's action. It is easy enough to understand them (the cop in *Stray Dog* completely understood the criminal), it is a bit more difficult to accept them (though the hero of *The Bad Sleep Well* is very near that), but to accept these actions as your own, that is the most difficult of all.

And this—as Dostoevsky has pointed out—is necessary. The free man is he who accepts his own actions and accepts those of others as though they were his own. The reflections of the two men coincide and Yamazaki says: "You see, I'm concerned with the truth, no matter how ugly . . . " Which is just what Mifune is most concerned with at this very moment. He asks, and it is though he is asking himself: "Why are you so convinced that it is right that we hate each other?"

The question hangs, almost palpable, between the two men as one is led away, the iron shutter clangs shut, and one remains behind. After the screen darkens and the film ends, one may imagine Mifune still sitting there, the question before him, the question before us.

# Red Beard

"After finishing *Sanjuro*," Kurosawa has said, "I started looking around for something else to do and quite by accident picked up *Red Beard* by Shugoro Yamamoto [the author of the original of *Sanjuro*.] At first I thought that this would make a good script for Horikawa but as I wrote I got so interested that I knew that I would have to direct it myself.

"The script is quite different from the novel. One of the major characters, the young girl, is not even found in the book. While I was writing I kept remembering Dostoevsky and I tried to show the same thing that he showed in the character of Nelli in *The Insulted and Injured*.

"I had something special in mind when I made this film [he even issued a public statement that in it he 'wanted to push the confines of movie-making to their limits . . .'] because I wanted to make something that my audience would *want* to see it, something so magnificent that people would just have to see it. To do this we all worked harder than ever, tried to overlook no detail, were willing to undergo any hardship. It was really hard work [and the film took longer before the cameras than any other Japanese film including *Seven Samurai* —almost two years] and I got sick twice. Mifune and Kayama each got sick once. . . ."

## THE STORY

At the end of the Tokugawa period a young man, Yuzo Kayama (Yasumoto), returns to Edo after several years' study at the Dutch medical schools in Nagasaki. Told to make a formal call at the Koishikawa Public Clinic and pay his respects to its head, Toshiro Mifune (Kyojo Niidé, commonly called Red Beard), he learns that he is to stay there and work as an intern. Since he had hoped to be attached to the court medical staff and had certainly never considered working in a public clinic, the news is a great shock. He refuses, purposely breaks the hospital rules, will not wear a uniform, and further trespasses by lounging around a forbidden area, the small pavilion where a beautiful but insane patient (Kyoko Kagawa) is kept.

Her servant (Reiko Dan) accuses him of having (like a fellow-intern, Tatsuyoshi Ehara) a less than medical interest in her. Kayama refutes this, saying that he would like to treat such a case, that indeed he knows much more about medicine than Red Beard himself.

*Reiko :*    Then why not help the other patients.
*Kayama :*    Any doctor can help *them*.

Having thus revealed his high opinion of himself, he goes on to imply that, indeed, he is not interested in women as women. "I don't believe in them . . . I've suffered quite enough for believing in one," he says, referring to his fiancée who ran off with another man while he was in Nagasaki.

Nonetheless, when he is alone drinking in his room and the escaped mad girl appears, he allows himself to be seduced. She tells him her story, that she is not really insane, that she was sexually abused when

she was young, that it happened again and again and again. *They* won't believe her but he (who doesn't even wear a clinic uniform) might. And all the time she is skillfully preparing to murder him just as she did three other young men. In the midst of their embraces she has pressed her fingers against an artery in his neck causing him to faint, has already taken out her long, sharp hair-pin, when Red Beard comes in.

Later Red Beard says:

She just grazed your neck, you'll be well in a day or two, but if I'd come in any later, you'd be dead.... She was just born that way. I suppose you heard all about her childhood. Well, lots of other girls have had experiences like that. It's nothing.

This singularly hard-boiled observation impresses Kayama, particularly since his own gullibility has ended in what he chooses to see as his humiliation. Impressed, he begins to take an interest in the hospital. It is certainly different from what the court would be. It is over-crowded, under-staffed, and the poor are everywhere. It is just as Ehara described it at the beginning of the film:

It's terrible ... The patients are all slum people, they're full of fleas—they even smell bad. Being here makes you wonder why you ever wanted to become a doctor.

Among the poor is one old man (Kamatari Fujiwara) who is dying and Kayama is called in to watch over him. He is familiar with death only from medical books and watching the real thing is a horrifying experience. Afterwards he complains to another intern (Yoshio Tsuchiya):

Red Beard said I should watch carefully, that a man's last moments are very solemn. Solemn! I call it horrible. Did you think that that awful death was solemn?

*Tsuchiya:* The pain, the loneliness of death frighten me too, but Dr. Niidé, he looks at it differently. He looks into their hearts as well as their bodies ... I want to be like him someday.

The implication is that Mifune sees beyond the horror. More (as is seen in a scene following), he negates it. The dead man's daughter (Akemi Negishi) appears. She has had a very hard life, including bearing three children by her mother's lover. She wants, at least, to be assured that her father died peacefully.

*Akemi:* He wasn't in pain when he died, was he?
*Mifune:* Oh, no. He died quite peacefully.
*Kayama:* ...! (Startled, surprised at this lie.)
*Akemi:* It had to be that way, it just had to be! If not ... if not, then life would be just too unendurable.

But Kayama knows that he did indeed die in pain. Life then is unendurable?

Perhaps it need not be. This is suggested by another death. A very good, almost saintly man, Tsutomu Yamazaki (Sahachi), dies and his past is uncovered. He loved a girl (Miyuki Kuwano) but apparently lost her during an earthquake. Later he accidentally meets her again and discovers that she left him because:

We were too happy together. We were so happy, I became afraid. A girl like me didn't deserve it. I felt I'd be punished if it lasted. Then the earthquake came. I was right. It was a punishment; I'd had my whole life's share of happiness.

This very Japanese reasoning (the unendurability of living is called just punishment) and her death convince Yamazaki that it is only by living for others that one can live at all. He and Red Beard, an unknown wheelwright and a famous doctor, have both discovered the same thing. They overcome the facts of life by negating them, by refusing to believe in them. With a splendid stubbornness, both men act as though good really existed in this world—they create it .

All of this has its effect on Kayama. He puts on his uniform finally and goes around with the doctor on his calls. One of them is at the whore-house district. There they find a twelve-year-old, Terumi Niki (Otoyo), who is being beaten by the brothel mistress (Haruko Sugimura) because she will not "entertain" the callers.

After a spirited fight with the bouncers, Mifune takes her back to the clinic. She is very ill, physically, but—more seriously—she is spiritually near death. He tells Kayama that he is to cure her, that she is his first patient. And here occurs the intermission—after the first two hours of this three-hour film.

## CHARACTERIZATION

Like the hero of *Sanshiro Sugata,* like the detective in *Stray Dog,* and the shoe manufacturer in *High and Low,* the young doctor learns: *Red Beard* too is the story of an education. Kayama learns that medical theory (illusion) is different from a man dying (reality); that—as the picture later reveals—what he had always thought himself (upright, honest, hard-working) must now be reconciled with what he finds himself to also be (arrogant, selfish, insincere); and, the most important, that evil itself is the most humanly common thing in this world; that *good* is uncommon.

At the beginning his position is that of the hero in *High and Low*. He did nothing to merit exile in a public clinic, he has done nothing "wrong." And yet here he finds himself (like the manufacturer who must pay a ransom which will ruin him) unable to escape, unable to see in what way he *merits* this punishment. Put in a way that Kurosawa would not care for, one might say that he is, like all of us, born into an estate concerning which we were not consulted and for which we did not ask.

And, indeed, at first it seems very much like the hell that Kurosawa characters (in *Rashomon*, in *The Lower Depths*, in *High and Low*) are always talking about. It is very *bas-fond* (even some of the actors from the 1957 Gorky adaption—including Bokuzen Hidari—are again used) and, as in *Ikiru*, the talkative patient (played by the same actor, Atsushi Wataname) describes it and pronounces sentence on the doomed man—Kayama. The hospital stinks, they don't have enough food, they are not given good kimono, they are all sick, they will all die.

Yet, as the film progresses, we (along with Kayama) discover that this is all illusion. It is so horrible that indeed it "makes you wonder why you ever wanted to become a doctor." But the point is that you *are* a doctor. You are responsible both to and for these people.

Mifune (seen through the eyes and opinions of the fellow-intern) seems a monster and act likes one. When introduced to him, Kayama is met with a fanatical stare and an insulting silence. Good-hearted liberal Kayama hates him on sight.

Yet he might have remembered (from his appearance with Mifune in *Sanjuro*) the advice that a man is seldom what he appears to be and that a fine-looking, gracious man may indeed be the villain after all. Kayama is doubly fooled. The arrogant Mifune is revealed as a truly good man and Kayama comes to realize that he himself is, in his own words, "despicable."

Kayama does not begin to understand that the good need not be apparent until Mifune saves his life and prevents the mad girl from murdering him. He cries then and his tears are mainly those of self-pity; but if you finally pity and love yourself, you will end up pitying and loving others as well. He really begins to understand what this is all about only when he is put in a position much like that of Mifune himself, when he must save the girl.

The second part of the film begins with a series of very short scenes showing him caring for her and her progressive recovery. At one point she refuses to take her medicine, keeps hitting the spoon with her hand, splashing the liquid in his face. Mifune comes in and says that he will try. And so he does, again and again and again. His patience is supernal. She takes her medicine.

Kayama stares at this. He has just learned something: that patience and fortitude are invincible. This is a knowledge that Mifune has with other Kurosawa heros: with the detective in *Stay Dog*, who in the face of seeming impossibility continues to search for his pistol; with Watanabe in *Ikiru* who in the teeth of official indifference manages to push through the park for children which will become the ultimate goal in his search for meaning in his life. The girl has learned something too. She speaks for the first time and says:

Girl:      Why didn't he slap me?

Kayama:      For not taking your medicine? But, there *are* kind people in this world. You've just never met any before.

Girl:      You can't fool me. Mother told me . . . she said to watch out for people and never trust anyone. And she was right.

Kayama:      No, no. He's not like that. You know he isn't. Isn't that why you took your medicine? He wants to cure you.

Girl:      You too?

Kayama:      Of course, me too.

Girl:      (Suddenly hitting the bowl from which he has been trying to feed her, knocking it across the room, and breaking it.) Even now?

Kayama      (Begins to cry, picking up the pieces of the bowl.) You poor thing. You're really a nice girl. . . .

Like all of the "villains" in Kurosawa's films, she is "bad" only because she is afraid. Kindness, sympathy, understanding really terrify us. Prepared for the worst, armed with mistrust and suspicion, we can do nothing against disinterested good—except to try and belittle or destroy it. The girl, baffled by Mifune, turns on Kayama. She will be so bad that he will have to strike her—and therefore prove that he is not kind at all and that she was right in the first place. Only thus can she keep her world together. She is like the "villain" at the end of *High and Low* who is perfectly adjusted to the idea of going to hell after his execution, but—a sudden thought which shakes him with its

implications—what if it turned out that he was going to heaven?

The following morning she has disappeared. He finds her begging. After she had collected enough, she goes and buys something in a shop. He calls her name, she turns and drops it, breaking it—it was a bowl.

Kayama: And that was to replace what you broke? But why? Did I scold you for it? Did I? Did you think I did? If you did, I apologize. I am sorry. I am very sorry.

The bulwarks of pride and fear cannot stand this assault. This further understanding breaks her. She kneels in the dust and, for the first time, cries like the child that she is.

When someone breaks down and weeps in a Kurosawa picture (the girl in *Stray Dog*, Mifune in the uncut version of *The Bad Sleep Well*) recovery is in sight. But here complications enter. Kayama himself becomes ill. One of the reasons was that he sat up so much with her, but the real reason is that he is suddenly told how he happened to be placed in the clinic at all. (This is a plot point: his father was worried about him after he was jilted, talked with Mifune about it, and it was Mifune who suggested that hard work here would help.) Kayama is stunned and then, in light of these new facts, must look at his own actions.

Kayama: I'm no good at all. I'm selfish . . . I blamed [my fiancée] and yet it was I who almost let that mad girl kill me. I was vain of being a doctor just back from Nagasaki, I was too good for this clinic. I hated you, even despised you. I'm despicable . . . I'm conceited . . . I'm insincere. . . .

Mifune: You're tired.

One can appreciate the parallel. The girl breaks down; Kayama breaks down. Both admit being less than perfect—she in her "evil," he in his "good." Both finally admit to being human.

There is a further parallel. Kayama becomes very ill and it is now the girl who must nurse him. This is shown in a short series of very affecting scenes much like those which opened the second part of the picture. After recovering he goes off to see his mother (Kinuyo Tanaka) and she notices a change at once:

You don't really seem to have been ill . . . you just look a little leaner. You look like a man who's just had a bath.

He has indeed had a bath; he has had a baptism. (This is what Red Beard indicates when he says, about the illness: "Oh, he just saw a bit too much of the world at one time . . . a kind of growing-pains.")

Back at the clinic the girl has been distracted from her love for Kayama (and her jealousy of his fiancée's younger sister to whom he will eventually become married) by the sudden appearance of a little boy (Yoshitaka Zushi). He has been stealing from the rice-kettle and she refuses to catch him when she has the chance. This earns her the enmity of the kitchen-help until they and Kayama overhear a scene where the girl tells the little boy to stop stealing, that she will bring him the left-over rice every day. He has brought some candy to reward her for not giving him away and she refuses to take it. He wants to know why—because it was stolen? But then when he stole the rice she didn't say anything. Her answer does credit to Kayama's influence:

Stealing rice and stealing candy are two different things. You must not steal. It is better to be a beggar than a thief.

Much, much better, particularly if stealing is equated with the life of fearing, and begging with the life of trusting. It is very like the philosophy that opens and closes *Yojimbo*—that a long life living on gruel in the country is better than short life of living it up in the city.

When the little boy lies near death (he and his family have arranged a mass suicide, have all taken poison) he declares (somewhat like the dying Nakadai in *Yojimbo*): "I should have become a beggar, like you said."

Observing the parallels in this film (from Red Beard to Kayama to the girl to the boy) one sees that Kurosawa is, in effect, constructing a chain of good. The idea is a novel one. All of us believe in a chain of evil and are firmly convinced that bad begets bad. (Indeed, one Kurosawa film, *The Bad Sleep Well*, has shown us just that.) In *Red Beard*, however, the director is offering the proposition (startling, even alarming) that good also begets good.

One can see what Kurosawa has had the bravery to do in this film. He is suggesting that, like the hospital, the world in which we live may indeed be a hell but that good, after all, is just as infectious as evil. We so firmly believe that "evil begets evil" that its contrary is quite dazzling. To consider such a proposition, in a cynical age (and modern Japan is as cynical as anywhere), seems almost shameful. But this is why Kurosawa has made the movie.

Let us at once invoke the spirit of Dr. Kildare since he persists in hovering over this film. Let us also call upon John Wayne to fill out the Mifune role as "Big Red." This will be useful in demonstrating what the film is *not*. And this is necessary because this picture is the most open to misinterpretation of all Kurosawa's works.

It has already had more than its share. The director has been accused of making the most contrived tear-jerker since *One Wonderful Sunday*, of pushing do-goodism past even the limit of *The Quiet Duel*; it has been said that Kurosawa's famed humanism has been revealed as a weltering bathos into which even Ben Casey or *The Interns* would think twice before stepping. Doctor Toshiro Mifune and Doctor Lionel Barrymore have been equated.

Kurosawa's dilemma is rather similar to that of Dickens. Laconic realist though he is, he believes in the good; but the good is very difficult to dramatize. Difficult as it is, however, Dickens manages admirably in at least several novels. So does Griffith, a very Dickensian creator. In their best work, they affirm by refusing to sentimentalize —and that is what also Kurosawa does in this picture.

Dr. Red Beard, for example. He, like the doctor in *Drunken Angel*, is possessed by, consumed by, a rage for good. He will do anything to get at it, even—and again a parallel with *Drunken Angel*—things that he considers bad. When it appears that Akemi Negishi will be put into prison for trying to stab her husband, Mifune blackmails the magistrate by mentioning his knowledge of the magistrate's mistress. He is quite convinced of his badness in doing this.

*Mifune:* I'm abominable. Of course, it is true that the girl deserved to go free . . . still, I did hint. I did a cowardly thing. Yasumoto, from now on, if I am at any time arrogant, you just remind me of today.

Both Kayama and the master of the rooming-house (Eijiro Tono) smile at this. For Mifune to be so scrupulously blind to his own virtues is both touching and amusing. Still, he is at least not taken in by himself (as Kayama is until he learns better) and he is rarely taken in by anyone else. He has a professional sympathy but no other for the mad girl. When he says that what happened to her has also happened to any number of other young girls, he says much the same thing that Shimura says in *Stray Dog* when Mifune wants to excuse the criminal by saying that someone stole everything he had after the war and so he had no choice but crime. Shimura says that precisely the same thing happened to *him* but that he chose differently from the criminal. Mifune holds the girl responsible for her own hysteria; frightened, she *chose* to be hysterical. This is a hard-boiled line of reasoning indeed. If *Red Beard* were really a tear-jerker, insights such as this would only dry wet eyes.

Mifune is a brother to the doctor in *Drunken Angel*: the one railing against ignorance and the hospital; the other, against poverty and the sump. They are men possessed. The difference from the suave, knowledgeable Dr. Kildare with his crotchety bedside-manner is apparent. The latter cannot afford to hate illness; he makes his living from it. Red Beard's hate of disease is one of the reasons that he is in a public clinic—the lowest of medical positions. And he doesn't care. He does more than merely devote himself to the good; he devotes himself to a fight against bad.

This is why the picture is not sentimental. To simply feel for, sympathize with, weep over—this is sentimental because it is so ridiculously disproportionate to what is needed. But to gird the loins and go out and do battle, to hate so entirely that good is the result: this is something else.

And this then is the kind of man that Kayama will also become. Like Watanabe in *Ikiru*, the boy is given something to do, something to fling himself into, in which to find personal salvation. He *becomes* Red Beard, a thing which the other intern notices when, toward the end of the film, he says: "You know, you already talk just like Red Beard."

This kind of goodness has nothing weak nor even appealing about it. And it is the opposite of "being good," in the sense of obeying, or doing the expected, or even the rational. This is one of the most difficult of all lessons to learn: that the surface "good" is spurious. Kayama finally comes to understand. At the end of the film he is going to be married and has told the girl that he is going to stay on at the clinic. Mifune is furious because this means that the boy will refuse the chance to become the Shogun's doctor at the court. But Kayama has seen what the good really consists of. He is therefore "bad" and refuses to obey Mifune, just as at the beginning he refused to obey. But now he has come full circle and his reasons are entirely different. In the final scene of the film they are again in front of the clinic gate.

| *Mifune:* | You want me to shout at you? |
| *Kayama:* | Please do. I'll stay no matter what. |
| *Mifune:* | Who says so. |
| *Kayama:* | You did. You taught me the road to take and I'll take it. |
| *Mifune:* | You really over-estimate me. Have you forgotten [all the bad things I've done?] I do things like that. |
| *Kayama:* | I like that part of you. |
| *Mifune:* | You're a fool. |
| *Kayama:* | I owe it all to you. |
| *Mifune:* | Oh, you're young. That's why you talk like that. You'll regret it. |
| *Kayama:* | Then you'll give me your permission? |
| *Mifune:* | I'll repeat what I said. You'll regret it. |

This paradox is at the heart of many of Kurosawa's films. Sugata jumps into the pond and deaf to the seductions of the "proper way of behaving," of niceness, he stays there; the detective searching for his pistol is told that he is "crazy," and is upsetting the police department by his unreasonableness; the seven samurai in their efforts to build an army to hold off the bandits are not "nice" at all to the farmers; the hero of *Ikiru* is downright cruel (if you want to look at it that way) to his superiors in the local government. For this reason the Kurosawa hero (as in *The Bad Sleep Well*) must learn to be "bad" in order that he can become "good." He must unlearn what the world considers good in order to learn what he himself knows to be good.

This is what Kayama does in this film and what Mifune has done, presumably, before it started. The world is a hell only because it is a fraud and we who believe in it believe in an illusion. Just as much illusion, however, are the ideas of an absolute good or evil. We must decide what we think the good is and then act accordingly. The reason for this is not that we want to be nice, or well thought of: the reason is that only through enacting our idea of what is good can we realize ourselves, can we be consumed by the act of living. And this, as *Ikiru* has indicated, is the only thing that you can do if you happen to be a conscious human being.

We have travelled far from the world of *The Interns*—we are, in fact, very near that no-man's land that Camus speaks of so persuasively. In *Red Beard* Kurosawa presents us with such a mass of evidence, such a richness, such a complication, and such a challenge, that indeed one's initial reaction is *not* to believe.

That odd corollary that "good makes good," for example. It is dazzling only if we allow ourselves a like liberty of thought. But we who live in hell are so conditioned that we would much rather laugh than weep—for that seems the only alternative. If one prefers this, then the film may be called sentimental, but of course to do so is to miss its point—and through what Kurosawa considers moral cowardice. Red Beard rages that his poor are also poor in spirit—they want to die; Kurosawa rages that we are equally poor—that we desperately want to retreat before this vision of the personal "good" because of the responsibilities and hard work that an acceptance would insist upon. In this film (certainly his farthest out—even farther out than *High and Low*) he gambles—just as Dickens and Dostoevsky gamble. Using the commonest forms of compassion (that for a sick girl, a dying child, a dedicated doctor), he will force us into recognition that compassion is not enough. The film is both compassionate and hard-boiled—because Kurosawa's concern, like Red Beard's, is the opposite of indulgent. The film can carry its extraordinary weight of sentiment (including a happy ending) because it can carry us so far beyond the confines of our daily hells. The stake in Kurosawa's game is *us*—and he does everything he can to make us accept. One has a fleeting reminiscence of the girl in *One Wonderful Sunday* turning to the audience and pleading for, demanding acceptance. This 1965 picture is much more profound, personal, persuasive than the 1946 one, but the morality is the same. And so is the conclusion—if you accept yourself you are saved. Have courage enough to allow that you are moved, allow yourself respite from cynicism, from hate. Allow yourself to believe in yourself.

## TREATMENT

If you are to believe in yourself you must have the most incisive of insights, the clearest of visions. You must be entirely realistic about yourself and about the world you live in. Perhaps this is one of the reasons that all Kurosawa's films are strengthened by an abiding interest in the way things are, the way places look, the way people act, and why this film is his most realistic.

Not only is the look of the picture actual—a kind of meticulously detailed Tokugawa-period newsreel—but its structure is purposely amorphous, full of incident and detail, lacking in anything that one would usually call form. Indeed, as the précis indicates, the plot is as complicated as anything in Dickens, but there is no over-riding form. The film, to be sure, is vaguely cyclic. The first scene, the last scene before the intermission, and the last scene in the film all take place at the main gate of the hospital. But it would be quite impossible to schematize the plot and find any kind of imposed structure. Rather, as in the novels of Dickens, the film discloses through characterization and parallels of action. We have already discussed some of these. Let us look at a single simple example: the clinic uniform and the girl's kimono.

All the interns, the head doctor himself, wear a uniform. Kayama refuses. This becomes for him a symbol. Yet this refusal only gets him into trouble. During the operation scene he is advised to wear it lest he dirty his own clothes; he refuses and presumably gets his clothes very dirty indeed. The real reason that the mad girl picks him is because he does not wear a uniform, and therefore she "trusts" him. She does so precisely because he is apparently uncommitted. That uniform and commitment are the same is indicated by a scene which occurs directly after he has finally decided to wear the uniform. He steps outside the hospital and is at once stopped by a woman with a sick child. She recognizes the uniform and rushes up to him. His reaction is surprise and a rueful aside as he looks at the uniform: "... helping people?" It is as though he recognizes that he has now identified himself, has let himself in for frantic mothers and sick children for the rest of his life.

The young girl's offense in the whore-house is aggravated in that she rips up the kimono put on her to entice customers, and that is the ostensible reason she is being beaten. After she recovers there is some comment that she has nothing to wear. The sister of Kayama's fiancée notices this and, to reward her for looking after the young

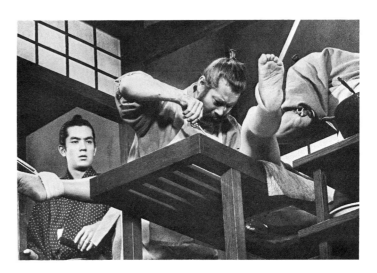

doctor when he was ill, she remakes one of her kimono (we saw her wearing it herself in an earlier scene) and gives it to the girl. Jealous of her obvious interest in Kayama, the child throws it in the mud. Later, however, when the whore-house madame returns to claim her, the first thing she does is to run and get the now-cleaned kimono and show it her saying that she is well cared for, look, she even has a nice kimono now, and that she will not return.

The parallel is obvious (much less so on the screen, separated as these uniform and kimono scenes are, and they are more subtle than I am here making them appear): the girl also commits herself. Both she and Kayama agree, in a way, to be what they are. They identify themselves.

This is, of course, what so many Kurosawa pictures are about: self-identification. The crisis occurs when the character finally agrees to define himself in his own eyes. Watanabe is not just a useless civil servant, he is a useful human being; the hero of *The Bad Sleep Well* is not an avenger, he is a good friend and husband; the actor in *The Lower Depths* is not a drunken sot, he is a good man who is going to find peace. He must predicate his present upon his past, upon what he has always been without recognizing it, and he must then act as he chooses.

If this is true, it might explain Kurosawa's singular interest in the past in this film. For the first time he becomes interested in what his people *were* and, unprecedentedly, he allows scenes which *explain* past actions. Consequently, his flash-backs in this picture are full, conventional looks into the past and not the literal flashes he has used (in all of his films except *Rashomon*) until now.

The first flash-back is in his "old" style. Mifune has just told the old man's daughter that her father died without pain. We see Kayama looking startled at this and then (with a burst of music) there is a five-second shot of the father's face as he lies dying in pain. This is the kind of flash-back we have seen in *Ikiru* and many other of the director's pictures. The next are real narrative flash-backs. These are segments of Tsutomu Yamazaki's story, conventionally cut into his telling it.

He and the girl meet when she gives him an umbrella to keep off the snow. (They meet on an immense set with full buildings, constructed in three dimensions, with real perspectives—all on the screen for just one minute.) Later, they meet by a field; again, they meet in Asakusa during a fair (hundreds of extras, a double-level set, seen on the screen for one minute); and, for the last time—a full ten-minute flash-back—in his room.

These are all scenes of explanation. If they were cut from the film they would not damage the continuity. What one would miss, however, would be an attitude which is new to Kurosawa—a new nostalgia for the past. Something like it was seen in the flash-backs in *Ikiru* but there the emphasis was upon the pain that remembering can cause. In *Red Beard,* we feel an almost Mizoguchi-like longing for the past.

For example, the extraordinary elegiac beauty of the scenes where they part at Asakusa. It is on a bridge, she is carrying a crying child on her back; the situation is painful for both of them. Kurosawa has chosen to shoot from very far away, using a long-distance lens. The result is that the close-ups appear two-dimensional. They are like something from an old romance, some illustrated cautionary tale. The man and woman seem very near each other, and yet, as they move, we see that they are separated. The lovely images comment upon the sweetness of the past, its impossibility of recapture. As the wife turns and begins her descent to the other side of the bridge, the child turns and looks at this man it has never seen and we suddenly realize that we too will never see these people again. Nostalgia strikes—and it is almost impossible to suggest how Kurosawa creates this pang. It is partly the fantastic beauty of the shot, partly the silence, and partly that these scenes are not necessary to the picture. We may enjoy them for their own sake. They do not forward plot, and so we are allowed the exquisite pleasure of a very strong but quite irrelevant sensation.

Sound is one of the senses (along with smell and taste) through which nostalgia is most strongly apprehended, perhaps because it is not often specific. When we see something reminiscent of the past, we "recognize" it; when we hear it, seldom; when we taste it, rarely. Kurosawa uses this fact brilliantly during these flash-back scenes.

He and she meet at a fair and he has bought a small basket of herbs to which a wind-bell is attached. At the beginning of the sequence Yamazaki turns and sees her and at the same time a breeze starts up. The hundreds of little bells at the herb-selling pavilion begin shrilling, an unearthly, sweet, and summer sound. Later, when he is leaving them by the bridge, the lonely tinkle of the single bell is heard. Still later, when she comes to see him, the basket is hanging just outside the door. We see its shadow and hear the sound of the bell as the wind teases it. After Yamazaki is dead, Kayama leaves his house. It is early morning and he is walking between a double row of houses. Suddenly he hears the sound of a tiny wind-bell. He turns and there, at the very end, far away, in front of one of the other houses, is a bell —just like the one we saw. He stops, remembering.

This is very like those aural ostinati that Kurosawa has long been fond of using in his films. One of the most spectacular is at the end of the picture. The little boy is dying and suddenly we hear the strangest of sounds—it is a long-drawn out, silvery echo; it is the name of the little boy, being called from an enormous distance. Everyone is startled because it sounds so entirely supernatural. Kayama goes to investigate and comes back to explain that the kitchen help are shouting down the well, there being a folk belief that all wells lead to the bottom of the earth and that the departing soul may be called back. We cut to the well itself and watch the weeping women gathered around it, shouting. There is an irrational beauty about the scene, and a hint of magic (very like that scene in *Los Olvidados* where the live dove is moved softly over the body of the sick woman) which is communicated through this odd, haunting sound, this rising and falling, this ostinato which is heard over the close-up of the dying child.

Other ostinati are also used. When the old man is dying, his eyes are open, his mouth is moving, and from his throat comes a rasping, straining, recurrent grunt, a blood-curdling sound, which quite curdles Kayama who has to stay there watching. Kurosawa has placed the camera rather low so that the moving, gasping, grunting mouth of the old man is always down at the corners of the frame. The sound is out of all proportion to the movement and, hence, our eyes—just as unwilling as those of Kayama—are drawn time and again to this moving mouth, which is precisely where we (and Kayama) do not want to look.

Sound, indeed, is perhaps more important in this film than in any of the director's others. For the first time he uses a stereophonic, four-directional system, which is spectacularly heard under the credits. During these the music pauses from time to time and we hear in the background the distant sounds of Edo, the call of a child or the cry of a fish-peddler, the slight rustle of wind in branches. We are presented from the first with this double level of sound. The upper (and louder) carries music and dialogue and effects. The lower (and softer) envelops the images in an extraordinarily complicated web of whispers and distant noises. The second level is, realistic as it sounds, rigorously controlled and contributes enormously to the feeling of realism which this film exudes. When the girl's fever rages and Kayama presses his hand against her forehead, we hear far in the distance the wooden clappers traditionally used to warn against fire. The far-away noises of the kitchen, someone (unidentified) walking in a distant corridor—these occur between lines of dialogue, creating three dimensions in sound, punctuating the dialogue.

The dialogue is also punctuated with music, in the secco-recitatif manner used in many of the later pictures, from *Yojimbo* on. The mad girl's recounting of her childhood is filled with pauses. In these we hear not only the minute sounds of the aged hospital building settling and creaking but also, as a part of this almost silent background, three very low alto flutes which always sound the same obsessive figure between the pauses.

One of the happiest uses of music in all Kurosawa occurs when the girl is tending Kayama. There has been a series of very short scenes (like those in the traveling scenes of *They Who Step on the Tiger's Tail*, Mifune trying to sleep in *Sanjuro*, etc.) showing her taking care of him and the last one of these has the following continuity:

*Kayama is delirious, perspiring. Hands place a wet cloth on his forehead. He opens his eyes. The girl bends down. They look at each other. She is afraid and moves away. Wipe to Kayama asleep. Hands take off the cloth. Tenderly she bends down and pushes his wet hair back into place. He opens his eyes. She stops. He closes his eyes. The hands return. Wipe to*

*Kayama asleep, close-up. He opens his eyes, alarmed. Cut back to show him watching her. She is wiping the floor in what seems at first the old, obsessive way that she had. Then he sees that the movement is different. She is really only wiping the floor, she is well. He closes his eyes. She stands up and begins wiping the window sills. He watches but when she turns toward him, closes his eyes so that she thinks him asleep. She opens the window. It is snowing. She reaches out and takes a double-handful of snow. Dissolve to her putting the snow into the water-bucket from which she moistens the towel for his forehead. She puts the cool towel on his forehead. He opens his eyes. They look at each other and then, slowly, he smiles. She stands up, half afraid, half pleased. She moves to the window and then, for the first time, she smiles. Cut to him, drowsy, almost asleep. She is sitting by the table, also almost asleep. Propped on one arm she is looking at one of his medical books. But her head drops again and again and he smiles at this. She nods. He smiles but his lids are heavy. Finally, her head slips to the table. With a smile still on his lips Kayama too falls asleep.*

The extraordinary beauty of this sequence is not easily described. It is entirely pantomime with only sound (the noise of water, the small sound of snow, the music) to support it. It is also the heart of the film, and what is so lovely is this growth of mutual feeling which we are witnessing, the dedicated care of the little girl, the loving playfulness of Kayama pretending to be asleep, the innocent trust of both. Again, one thinks of Dickens. It is rare that the good and the beautiful are shown us this clearly, this simply.

Much of the hushed beauty of this scene is contributed by the music. It begins when she opens the window and sees the snow, and it is a paraphrase of Haydn—the second movement of the *Surprise* Symphony. It is so transmuted that it is not recognizable at once, but the innocence and serenity of the original are quite apparent. It continues and supports the rest of the scene, ending only after both have fallen asleep. It is much more right for this scene than words can make apparent, and even its slightly old-fashioned, four-square air is apposite.

This is also true of the other music in the picture. The Brahms-like (*First Symphony*, last movement) major "theme" of the film is so right that it is almost impossible to imagine any other music. We first hear it during the titles, coming in strong all celli and glowing horns, under the name of the director; it appears again during one of Red Beard's scenes and we come to associate it with him. During the intermission (a real innovation since this five-minute break is a part of the film—the projector is left running, and the sound-track carries a full elaboration of the theme) and at the end (three minutes of music after the end title) the theme again appears, building—after the conclusion of the picture—into a really joyous Brahmsian finale with celli pizzicatti, purling woodwinds, divided strings, and horn calls.

It is quite impossible to think of this picture without thinking of

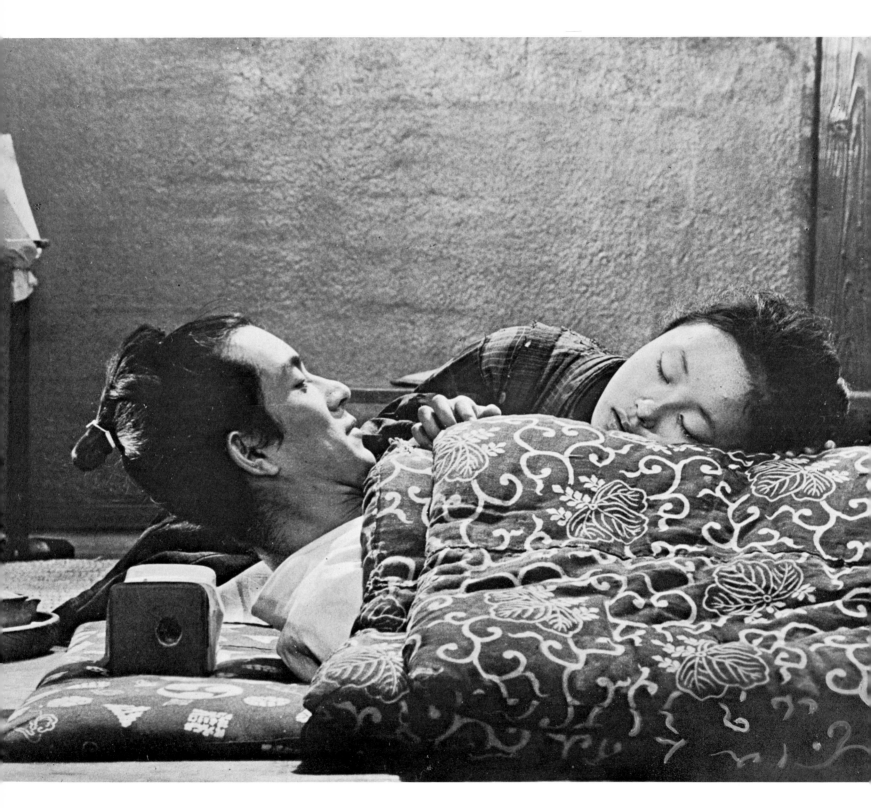

music. To describe the look of it one should speak of something burnished and glowing, like the body of a fine cello. If a single adjective were used I should think it would be: 'mellow.'

# PRODUCTION

This mellowness is contained within the look of the film itself. It has a patina, the way certain of Mizoguchi's films have a patina. This is the result of a like care for realistic detail. Kurosawa's efforts to achieve this are already legend in Japan. The main set was really an entire town with back alleys and side-streets (some of which were never filmed) which was so large that shots of just the roofs fill the whole wide screen during the credit titles.

All of the material used for the town was about as old as it is supposed to look. The tiled roofs were taken from buildings more than a century old; all of the lumber was from the oldest available farmhouses; costumes and props were all 'aged' for months before their appearance; the bedding (made in Tokugawa-period patterns) was really slept in for up to half a year before shooting. Making the main gate, which so figures in the film, occupied almost everyone. The wood was more than a hundred years old and both staff and director kept adding touches to make it look still older. (After the film was shot, the gate was re-erected at the entrance of the theater premiering the film and drew as great a crowd as the picture itself.)

Kurosawa used this magnificent set (so grand that tourist bus companies ran special tours during the two years of filming in order to show visitors its splendours) in a very telling way. The main street is seen for just one minute and its destruction was incorporated into the earthquake scenes; the scenes with the bridge are likewise short; so are those in the elaborately constructed paddy. The director, if one wants to look at it that way, completely wasted his multi-million-yen set.

The other way of looking at it is that in this way he used it to fullest advantage. By constricting three-fourths of the picture to interiors, and by using this magnificent set only several times, he brought a kind of life to the entire film which a single set—no matter its grandeur —could not. The opposite effect occurs in a picture such as *The Fall of the Roman Empire* where one feels: one more shot of that expensive forum and I'm going to scream. The *Red Beard* set is really real in part because it is so little emphasized. We see it casually, by accident, out of windows, behind the characters. It is never *used* and consequently creates that rich, varied, full and complicated life which we know surrounds the hospital.

This town is inhabited as well but we are rarely *shown* the people. Instead, when the characters leave the hospital or look out of the window, there they are. When the girl goes to beg on the bridge she does so against a fully realistic background of Tokugawa Japan. Vendors pass, fishermen fold their nets, a samurai stalks, a lady shops, and we sense them but do not *see* them because Kurosawa is focusing all of our attention upon the girl and upon Kayama. They too become this living background against which the story of the film is played.

This is very much like Mizoguchi. (Another example would be those fantastic scenes in Munk's *Pasazerka* where the most barbaric atrocities—dogs attacking naked prisoners—occur behind the main action, out of focus, thrown away, apparently to be noticed by the viewer no more than they are by the characters.) One believes in this reality precisely because it is not insisted upon.

Another Mizoguchi-like quality is Kurosawa's showing the impact that time has on his characters. *Sansho the Bailiff* and *The Life of Oharu* are about a single action (the kidnapping of children, a fall from grace at court) and the effect that this has upon a woman's character. More, however, Mizoguchi studies the effect that time itself has upon her. In *Sansho,* when mother and son are finally reunited (at least twenty-five years later) much of the pathos comes not from their initial separation but because, now, they are so very different that the separation has come to mean too little to them. *Red Beard* covers much less time (about half a year—the same as *Ikiru* or *Seven Samurai*) but the change is no less dramatic. Every one of the characters, except Red Beard himself, has undergone some dramatic change, all have had a spiritual crisis of some sort of another, and what was important to them at the beginning is of no importance at all at the end. Instead (and here the comparison with Mizoguchi does not extend) each has something new in his life.

Of all of the many production difficulties of *Red Beard* this demonstration of the effect of time was the most difficult to achieve. Kurosawa insisted that everyone change just half a year's worth, but the film was almost two years before the camera. Yuzo Kayama has said that the most difficult thing he has ever had to do in a film was this showing of six months change during two years of filming. Kayama is very young, very impressionable; he himself was rapidly changing, and not necessarily in the same directions as the hero. Further, due to illness, bad weather, financial problems, only the sections about the young girl were shot in chronological order. This meant that the young actor had to keep track of his presumed spiritual development at the same time that he was coping with his own. "It was simply back-breaking and if I had known what it was to be like I don't think I would have believed in myself enough to undertake it. But . . . it wasn't I who did it, you know. It was him. He made me do it. Somehow or other, I must have had it in me. At any rate, he got it out. I was astonished when I saw the fine cut of the picture. There I was, growing and changing, just like life itself."

The like development of the little girl caused Kurosawa much concern. "Terumi is really a very timid little girl, that's what she really is," Kurosawa has said. "I watched her every day on the set turning more and more into the character she was playing. I began to fear that even off the set she would go right on acting like her. Then one day when we were about half done I saw her playing around with some of the stage-hands on the lot. She was playing just like an ordinary little girl and I was quite relieved."

Many of her scenes caused difficulties. Kurosawa had decided that the character was probably epileptic and that therefore the white of her eyes ought to shine, somehow. (Here again, as in *The Quiet Duel* and *Drunken Angel,* the director's interest in if not knowledge of medicine is again indicated.) When she is first seen, she is kneeling in a darkened room and only her eyes are illuminated. "We tried everything. During these scenes we were doing well if we averaged a shot a day. Finally I had a little hole bored in the wall she was facing and put a light-man on the other side. He was holding a kind of flash-light torch that we invented and finally I got the light in her eyes properly."

Other difficulties concerned the dying of Tsutomu Yamazaki. "If he were going to die in a Western bed, that would be different and I could group people around him properly. But he was dying flat on his back on *tatami* and there seemed to be no way to get him lighted as I wanted and at the same time to compose the listeners around him." Devising the sequence as it appears on the screen took weeks of experiment.

"I finally decided that half of the problem was that he talked too much and that I had apparently conceived something with lots of silence in it. So I took away about two-thirds of his dialogue. That helped some." What helped the rest was discovering a place from which face, mouth, eyes, and listeners were all visible. In the finished scenes the camera appears to hover over the dying man, almost in full close-up. Actually, the camera was far away, flung onto a girder in the roof of the studio, shooting the scene with a 500 mm. lens.

Most of the picture was made using such extreme long-distance lenses. (The bridge scenes with Yamazaki and his wife were shot with a 750 mm. lens.) "The actors liked this fine, it got the camera far away from them, but that isn't why I did it this time. I did because I wanted to get that crowded, two-dimensional, slightly smoky effect that only a long-distance lens can give you."

(This constant use of long-distance lenses also accounts for a technical error in two scenes. The first is when Kayama and Reiko Dan are talking about not trusting women. Kurosawa shot it so that a tree-trunk comes in between them—the effect of the separating wall in *The Bad Sleep Well* and *Quiet Duel.* It looks as though Kayama is at the base of the tree. But the next shot is from the side, and now he is seen as at least twelve feet away from it. The second is when he is lying on the *tatami* and it looks as though the door through which the mad girl will enter is directly beside him. Again the next shot indicates just how much long-distance lenses foreshorten: he is across the room from it.

Concerning these two shots Kurosawa says: "Well, you learn something new all the time. I won't do *that* again.")

In addition to long-distance lenses Kurosawa again used his multiple-camera technique but limited it to only several scenes. During the big scene with Akemi Negishi he used five cameras running simultaneously. For the majority of the scenes he used two. And for many crucial scenes he contented himself with one. "Shooting this film was a different kind of experience for me," he has said. "*Seven Samurai* took a very long time to make too but for this film I wanted something even more dramatic and, well, active. There were lots of times when I had to control my own feelings and where I just sat and waited for something to happen." This something (in particular, nuances in the acting of Terumi Niki and Kayama) was something which he felt only the single camera could capture, just as in *Record of a Living Being* he threw out all alternate versions of Mifune kneeling before his family and chose only the single one taken by the 'main' camera in the 'conventional' camera position.

The single camera equipped with a long-distance lens has certainly contributed to the look of the picture but Kurosawa sees this look as different from what most critics, including myself, have seen. "There is a lot of talk about the look of this film and everyone is always telling me about its *sabi*. [*Sabi* is taken from the verb "to rust," and it implies what we mean when we say "patina," except that in Japanese there is an unavoidable connotation of the musty, the slightly old-fashioned.] It doesn't have *sabi* at all. It has freshness, vitality." In order to create this Kurosawa used a new highly sensitive film, which was also given special development, and a new kind of light which made his set even more blinding than it usually is. "Actually, though, it isn't the look that creates this vitality. It's the people. They did it all. You know me, so active and all. Well, in this film I just sat still and waited for them and sure enough, one by one, they got into the spirit of the film, they would do what I wanted voluntarily."

Like Dr. Mifune with his medicine, Kurosawa behaved with patience and fortitude to get what he wanted. What he wanted is indicated by what he did the first day of shooting. "I gathered everyone, cast and staff together, and I played them the last movement of Beethoven's *Ninth*—the "An die Freude" part, you know. I told them that this was the way that the audience was supposed to feel when it walked out of the theatre and it was up to them to create this feeling."

I wonder what would happen at, say, the MGM lot, if a director did this? What happened at the Toho lot was that everyone listened to Beethoven attentively, bought the record—Kurosawa favors the old Weingartner but will listen to the Bruno Walter—and came to work determined to do just what the director wanted.

(About the theme music, incidentally, Kurosawa disagrees: "No, you are wrong. It is not Brahms' *First*. It isn't Brahms at all. It is Beethoven—it is probably the *Ninth*. At least that is what I told Sato [the composer] I wanted and so that is probably what he tried to get. When he hears what he is supposed to do he just sighs and shakes his head and goes away and comes back with it after a while. Like in *Yojimbo*. I had seen some documentary about a bull-dozer and the sound impressed me very much. You ever heard a bull-dozer? No? Well, it makes a fine sound. And I reasoned that Mifune in the film was just like a bull-dozer and so he ought to have bull-dozer-like music. I told Sato and he sighed and came back with it. The Haydn was all my idea and I wish we'd used Haydn himself. The reason is that I put the sequence together and decided to start the music right where she opens the window and sees the snow and then continue it all through the scenes with Kayama and end it when they both fall asleep. That part of the score wasn't finished and so I put on a recording of the Haydn, the second movement, and played it along with the film to see what the effect was. Well, the effect was just fine but what really surprised me was that I had cut the sequence so that it came to an end precisely at the end of the Haydn. I must have heard that recording— it was the old Furtwängler one—so often that somewhere in the back of my head some kind of clock kept count. The Haydn and my sequence were not a second off. Things like that happen to me all the time.")

After *Red Beard* had opened, was still playing to packed houses (it may well turn out to be the director's most financially successful film), and was proving to be indeed just the kind of picture that people want to see, something "so magnificent that people would just have to see it," I told Kurosawa that I sensed that he had come to come sort of conclusion, some sort of resting place. He had pushed his style to what appeared to be its ultimate. At the same time he had continued and, it would seem, completed the theme which has been his through-out his entire film career. It might even be called the summation of his work because in *Red Beard* he had vindicated his humanism and his compassion, he had shown that only after the negative (evil) has been fully experienced can the positive, the good, joy itself, be seen as the power it still remains; that this wisdom was offered in a film filled with true sentiment, with the fact that in all of our glory, in all of our foolishness, we are—after all—human; further, that evil itself is merely human, after all, and that the good then lies in our realizing this and acting upon it.

Kurosawa listened to all of this patiently but when I was about to launch into examples, gently interrupted me with: "Well, I don't know much about all of that—there might be something in it. I don't know. What I do know is that every picture I've done has come out of something that has happened to me, has happened to me personally. A friend of mine had a son kidnapped and that kind of barbarism upset me so that I made *High and Low*. Since then I've gotten lots of letters, people accusing me of teaching people how to go about kid-napping children, but that's not what I meant. When it happened to him, it happened to me. Take gangsters, for example. They are stupid and they are dangerous, and I know it. So I make up Sanjuro and he goes around and defends innocent people. Look at our govern-ment. I don't think in any other country there is so thick a wall separating people from government officials and agencies. I go and make a film about it and they say I'm a Communist. But that isn't the point. The point is that something happens to me and I don't like it and I make a film.

"People always make so much out of my directing a movie. I wonder why. It is just me, only me. What do people find so special in all this? I'm like everyone else because I am making a personal statement. Look at *Red Beard*. I want people to come and see it because I want to show them Yasumoto [the young doctor] and I want them to remember him and I want them to try to be like him.

"But about something having ended . . . some sort of conclusion. Yes, I feel that myself very strongly. A cycle of some kind has con-cluded. Right now I am very tired and I need a rest badly. From now on I guess I'll be making a different kind of film. I don't know what it will be like. But I know the themes will be different and I guess I'll do it in a different manner. Right now I'm going to rest for half a year and then wait and see."

# Dodesukaden

## 1970

Red Beard marked the close of the major and most artistically significant part of Kurosawa's career. Five years passed before he made *Dodesukaden*, a low-budget, minor film that compares with Kurosawa's great works only as a shadow resembles substance. But the seeds of Kurosawa's decline as a film-maker were already apparent in *Red Beard*. With its all-knowing and wise Dr. Niidé (played by Toshiro Mifune) dispensing wisdom, *Red Beard*, even before the summarizations in *Dodesukaden*, included a final setting forth of the themes that had preoccupied Kurosawa throughout his career. In *Red Beard*, as in so many of his films (and *Seven Samurai* in particular), an older, more experienced man of samurai disposition initiates a young, promising disciple in basic truths. In *Red Beard* these pertain not merely to the rudiments of medicine, but to ethical imperatives, in particular the principles that good begets good and that the only life worth living involves aligning oneself with the suffering and the needy.

These precepts are already known to Dr. Niidé before the film opens; they are not revealed to him in the course of the action. As a result *Red Beard* contains a didactic quality absent from Kurosawa's finest works, films like *Ikiru*, which also treat social themes. In *Red Beard* there is for Kurosawa an unusual absence of conflict within the felt life of the film. And the wide-screen, grand-shot compositions and the virtuosity of Kurosawa's use of the telephoto lens function to conceal the film's failure to realize its point of view beyond the level of homiletic preaching. By 1965 Kurosawa seemed committed to the dangerous path of the artist who relies on a body of received truths that a master, as a surrogate for the director, imparts to an eager disciple.

In the five years that elapsed between *Red Beard* and *Dodesukaden* Kurosawa was involved in a series of abortive projects. He began work on a film about railroads, which was to have been shot in the United States, and signed a contract with Twentieth Century Fox to film the Japanese sequences of a flabby epic, *Tora! Tora! Tora!* The struggle to work on that film, complicated by the tampering of the American studio then headed by Darryl F. Zanuck, so utterly demoralized and exhausted

Kurosawa that he was finally driven to sabotage his own work. News leaked that Kurosawa was shooting scenes only to decide that the sets had to be another color and all the footage re-shot. His motive was clearly to provoke Fox into openly firing him and thus to avoid responsibility for contractual liability, through which he otherwise could be blamed for failure to live up to their agreement.

Kurosawa's involvement with Fox must be seen in light of his difficulties gaining financing from Toho or any other Japanese studio. Like their American counterparts, by the mid-sixties the Japanese companies were in search of blockbusters and increasingly unwilling to treat great artists any differently than the journeymen-directors who could be trusted to turn out several formula-films a year within limited budgets. Kurosawa sought American financing because film-making in Japan was closed to him.

Attracted by a *Life* magazine article about a railway accident in upstate New York, he wrote a script called *The Runaway Train*, to be shot in Rochester. Kurosawa traveled to the United States to hunt for locations and selected a spur from Syracuse to Albany for *The Runaway Train*. The film was to have been set in winter and would have been Kurosawa's first work in color, although he intended the film to appear as if it were in black and white by focusing solely on snow and earth (an effect he would later achieve in *Dersu Uzala*); the only actual "color" was to have been the lights of the railway signals. When bad weather necessitated a postponement of the shooting of *The Runaway Train*, Fox immediately invited Kurosawa to direct the Japanese sequences of *Tora! Tora! Tora!*

Actual shooting by Kurosawa on the Japanese half of *Tora! Tora! Tora!* occurred only during a few weeks of December 1968. By 1969 Kurosawa was no longer connected with *Tora! Tora! Tora!* Fox sought to blame him for their difficulties by arguing that he had resigned for "reasons of health," by which they meant mental health. To counter the assertion that he had abandoned the project because he was no longer capable of working on it, Kurosawa held several personal press-conferences to which he brought his own doctors to testify that he was perfectly fit, taking the position that he had been fired. Then his managing director, Tetsuro Aoyagi, resigned from Kurosawa Productions in a cloud of innuendo and mystery suggesting that in whatever conflict had ensued between Kurosawa and Fox, Aoyagi had sympathized and conspired with the studio.

Kurosawa repeatedly insisted that he had been forced out of the project against his wishes and fired, doubtless to clear himself of any further legal involvement. Doctors were called in by the other side to testify again that Kurosawa was exhausted and suffering from psychological disorders. And so it went. Associates of Kurosawa, inspired by Aoyagi, claimed that the director was deeply neurotic and difficult to work with, a clever ploy since this charge had been repeatedly brought against him throughout his career, though it was probably no truer for Kurosawa than for other equally fastidious and painstaking directors.

In retrospect it is clear that a project wherein a Japanese director such as Kurosawa would have to work under the demeaning conditions of

American studio production was doomed from the start. *Tora! Tora! Tora!*, as the final version of the film unmistakably reveals, was conceived as a box-office epic on a level with similar Hollywood war-films and deliberately lacking any artistic or intellectual interest.

Kurosawa had insisted on shooting the Japanese part of the film on his own terms, even if this meant personally absorbing a portion of the cost. He had planned to use the method of film-making that worked best for him, spending the first five days of a given week on rehearsals and shooting on the last two, in this way fulfilling a week's quota. Fox executives demanded a day-by-day shooting schedule on which they could check up and accused Kurosawa of violating their agreement. Yet among the lies Fox had told Kurosawa was that David Lean would direct the American sequences, a far cry from the director who had actually been chosen, Richard Fleischer. This deception was important to Kurosawa because Lean's presence would have meant that the film's two halves would be commensurate in aesthetic quality. No doubt Kurosawa also had hoped that Lean's demands of the studio could be made on behalf of them both.

In its structure, Kurosawa's script resembled the Japanese wartime film *The War at Sea from Hawaii to Malaya*, which at its climax includes the bombing of Pearl Harbor. The first half depicted exercises at Kagoshima in preparation for the attack on Pearl Harbor; the second half treated the attack itself. The script was re-written by the studio, something that had never happened to Kurosawa before and was certainly sufficient in itself to make him doubt the viability of participating in the project at all. By the time shooting began Kurosawa had probably decided to behave so eccentrically as to induce his release without the repercussions consequent upon his own initiative in breaking a contract. He decided to quit, but he was formally "fired." On the credits of the completed film, Kurosawa's name does not appear, nor was any of his footage used in the final cut.

The *Tora! Tora! Tora!* debacle consumed 1967 and 1968 for Kurosawa. And in general the years following *Red Beard* found him beset by production difficulties. Kurosawa's business affairs were then taken over by the capable Yoichi Matsue, who until *Kagemusha* had functioned for Kurosawa as the self-effacing disciple facilitating the work of the master, a real-life version of the pattern so frequently depicted in Kurosawa's films from *Stray Dog* and *Drunken Angel* to *Seven Samurai, Sanjuro,* and *Red Beard.* After five years of troubles, Kurosawa emerged with *Dodesukaden*, a gay little film whose title translates roughly as "clickety-clack," the sound of an approaching streetcar. The will to struggle with his art, as with those who finance movies, seems to have snapped in Kurosawa. In *Dodesukaden* he attempts little that is innovative and is content to play among themes he had developed seriously in his best works. The unpleasant experience with Fox, which had included a campaign of slander against him, clearly took its toll. *Dodesukaden's* lightness of tone therefore seems unexpected, and even more so because a year after its release Kurosawa would attempt suicide.

But *Dodesukaden's* sweetness and Kurosawa's refusal to treat the themes of pain and suffering in a dark and heavy manner was highly conscious. "Had I directed this film in a serious manner," said Kurosawa at the time, "it would have been unbearably depressing. 'Make it bright, light, endearing,' I told my staff." In the same mood Kurosawa next made a television film called *The Song of the Horse* (*Uma no Uta*), a lyrical documentary recalling *Horses* (*Uma*), the 1941 film on which he had worked as an assistant director and that had convinced everybody he would someday be a great director. As in *Dodesukaden* Kurosawa was returning in nostalgia to those moments of triumph when he had been most sure of himself as an artist.

# THE STORY

*Dodesukaden* is based on *The Town Without Seasons*, a collection of short stories by Shugoro Yamamoto, who was also responsible for the originals of *Sanjuro* and *Red Beard*. It is a film without a plot, comprising instead a series of episodes in the lives of a village of slum dwellers bound together by harsh and hopelessly dreary daily lives. The word *dodesukaden* was coined by Yamamoto in the original. It is significant that Kurosawa makes this term his title, for in so doing he abandons the normal onomatopoeic word for the sound of a trolley, *gatan goton*, for an imaginative fantasy word. "Dodesukaden" is shouted by a retarded boy named Rokkuchan who runs along the "streets" of this slum conducting a make-believe streetcar. Down the unpaved roads of the ghetto he travels, crying, "dodesukaden, dodesukaden," first as he starts up his "trolley" and then as he propels it along.

Rokkuchan is deluded in his belief that he is conducting a real streetcar. But his wish-fulfillment is different only in degree from the delusions of all the characters in the film, who can endure their pathetic circumstances only by buttressing themselves with unrealizable fantasies. In these dreams Kurosawa's characters present what life could and ought to be, even if they can do no more than imagine it. The artist himself, with an exalted vision of what life might be, sympathizes with them wholly.

A beggar constructs for his son an imaginary dream-house complete with swimming pool. Two young men get drunk and exchange wives, only to return to their original partners the next day blithely unaware of the difference. Shima, afflicted with an involuntary tic that throws his entire body into a convulsion without warning, must live with a domineering wife, a situation he renders tolerable by recalling with tenderness how she had stood by him when he was penniless. A man married to a promiscuous woman who has borne a passel of children, each by a different father, comforts his troubled charges by assuring them that if they feel him to be their father, then he is.

Hei, a tragic, decaying figure, is so traumatized by a single instance of adultery, a brief moment of abandon on the part of his wife, Ocho, that he allows the memory of her lapse to consume his entire existence, an embittering obsession that ensnares him in despair. Unable to forgive Ocho one essentially insignificant sexual encounter, he drives her to probable suicide with an accusatory silence he can no longer relinquish, although she actually loves him as much as he loves her. A girl named Kazuko, forced to labor day and night making crepe-paper flowers, is raped by the brutish, alcoholic husband of her aunt. Considering herself now all the more unworthy for having been violated, she stabs the delivery boy, the one person ever to show her kindness, out of the fantasy that only his death can prevent him from forgetting her.

And the whole group is presided over by Tamba, an old craftsman and beneficent spirit who understands and forgives all, a Kurosawa-surrogate who is able to assume sufficient distance to impart the wisdom of empathy. All must cope as they can. Tamba knows that there are times when the only healing response to the brutalities of everyday life is a renewal of compassion. Kurosawa has aptly described this character: "He has matured as an honest, good fellow throughout his life, and he has reached the position of the mature, experienced elder." His is the comforting presence in *Dodesukaden* of Kurosawa himself, who identifies with the devices, however bizarre, to which people are driven if they would endure. He values these pathetic, afflicted people for themselves with a love that is devoid of condescension. In each character Kurosawa locates a compelling claim to respect and dignity that grants the light and carefree tone of *Dodesukaden* an uplifting quality and validates the director's decision to present his characters as people above the slightest indulgence in self-pity.

# CHARACTERIZATION

In its treatment of human character *Dodesukaden* represents a departure in spirit from *The Bad Sleep Well*, *Yojimbo*, *Sanjuro*, *High and Low*, and

*Red Beard*, in short, from all the films made by Kurosawa after his contract with Toho terminated upon completion of *The Hidden Fortress*. Set in the present, *Dodesukaden* lacks the superman-samurai, that powerful figure at the center of all Kurosawa's films after 1960, even those not set in feudal times—a change greeted by many Japanese critics, from Tadao Sato to Midori Yajima, with relief. That Kurosawa no longer depended on a dominant figure—the leader often played by Toshiro Mifune and symbolizing an omnipotent ideal—marked his transcendence of a pattern that many had considered an elitist vision, one implying a necessary turn to the power of a superior individual with virtues so overwhelming that they take precedence over the suffering of the many. With *Dodesukaden* Kurosawa abandoned the glorification of supreme individuals and focused on the courage and endurance of the weak and the forgotten, revealing a sensibility we had begun to expect only from younger Japanese directors like Shohei Imamura.

In its handling of the concept of the hero *Dodesukaden* is similar to *The Lower Depths*. Both films were made on basically a single set and lack the old-fashioned, archetypal Kurosawa superman, that Mifune-like, powerful individual who can surmount the insurmountable. There is little opportunity for sword-slashing heroics in the midst of the abject poverty in which all the characters of *Dodesukaden* are enmeshed. For the first time since *Ikiru*, made in 1952, Mifune himself is absent from a Kurosawa film. Nor does Kurosawa include a figure like the old priest of *The Lower Depths*, who encourages his fellow slum denizens in the illusion that they will someday return to prosperity—a fantasy that leads directly to the death of the alcoholic actor, upon discovering he lacks the capacity within himself to return to his former life.

In *Dodesukaden* fantasy and delusion are seen by Kurosawa as part of the ailment, having nothing whatever to do with the cure, which is in any case beyond the power of the poor to effect within the given scheme of things. If under some circumstances only the madness of the unbridled imagination makes life endurable at all, the consequences of that absolute denial of reality which flows from the effort to withstand life's assault upon one's person will be psychosis and death. The beggar absorbed in his fantasized dream-house will cause his son to die painfully, so totally have his dreams of a better life overwhelmed his senses.

The vagaries of human behavior in *Dodesukaden* are rooted in social circumstances; Rokkuchan's insanity as a "trolley-crazy"—as he is called by passing children—is seen in terms of the decaying shack he shares with his heartbroken mother and the bleakness of their prospects. All they have is religion, and *Dodesukaden* is framed by scenes of mother and son chanting Buddhist prayers, portrayed by Kurosawa's camera as but one more fantasy through which besieged people maintain their hold on life. We are not told how or when Rokkuchan became unhinged. The pain of ex-

clusion from the rudiments of survival in a richly developed society, viewed by us in the shots of the beggar's dreams and in one scene of a busy Ginza street, is sufficient cause.

Tamba (played by Atsushi Watanabe), who comprehends that the strange behavior of his neighbors is as fixed and unchangeable as the circumstances of their impoverishment, approaches these people in the spirit of accepting them as they are, the one kindness he can bestow. He discusses seriously with Rokkuchan the intricacies of his imaginary streetcar. But although he never reproaches the boy, he refuses to encourage the ragged beggar in the illusion that his poisoned son can get well without a doctor. Kurosawa, lacking the fiery anger of Buñuel who in his sixties and seventies refused to accept the world's injustice as unchangeable, argues through the overview of Tamba that the best we can do in the

brutal, poisoned class-society of the present is ameliorate evil in small ways.

At the close of *High and Low*, Gondo, the shoe executive, can find nothing to say to his tormented antagonist, the intern who kidnapped a child out of the pain and fury of having to live in squalor and with his poverty in full view of those rich people like Gondo himself, whose luxurious mansion looks out arrogantly over the slums. It is a resounding moment, one of anguish that reverberates in subsequent films without ever being resolved. By *Dodesukaden* Kurosawa no longer finds redeeming grace even in small moments of social change, such as those overseen by Watanabe in *Ikiru*. In the seventies Kurosawa, *pace* Ozu, proceeds to define his hero as a man who has learned to accept in stoical resolve the pain of facing every day the consequences of life in an unjust society.

Tamba is the only fully realized character in *Dodesukaden*. Standing structurally and morally at the film's center, he earns Kurosawa's endorsement for having found the strength and wisdom to empathize with the most devastated, without the comfort of belief in what Kurosawa considers the chimera of social change. Tamba is able to place himself fully in the shoes of his confused, suffering neighbors, and this capacity renders him a hero. He never judges the people of his world but accepts and ministers to them.

On one depressing, rain-splashed day, so familiar in Kurosawa's films where extremes of weather echo and even inspire extremes of emotion otherwise constrained, a man becomes "crazy drunk." In unwitting mockery of the lost ability to revive Japan's former days of samurai glory—no less than such heroics in Kurosawa's own films—the drunk begins to swing a sword wildly and without coordination. The moment suggests at once terror, disarray, and loss of touch with reality. It is a brief but consummate suggestion of the futility of attempting to invoke the warrior values of Japan's feudal past in a present more closely approximated by the disintegration shown in *Dodesukaden*.

People cower behind their doors. The man has become a menace, but no one has the courage or the will to stop him. Uncontrollable rage, which flows from futility and frustration, is always close to the surface of life in the slums, a theme also explored in *The Lower Depths*. Out of his house marches Tamba under an umbrella, a matter-of-fact and practical man seemingly on an ordinary errand. He says but few words, which we are not permitted to hear, while the scene is kept in long-shot. The moment belongs to the two men alone and it is not for us to intrude. The sword-swinging drunk suddenly drops his weapon and hangs his head.

Kurosawa then repeats the incident in flash-back. Recovered and now bewildered by his experience, the man relates to a friend what transpired. Tamba had merely asked him if he were tired, and if so, whether he could help the man by assuming his place; ashamed, the man immediately took to his bed and slept off the alcohol which had fused his display. If there must be rage, someone truly sympathetic asks only if the pain can be shared, countering anger not by admonition, but by example. Such

burdens are, in any event, more than an individual can assume alone. They belong to us all, whether we perceive this or not. When the pain is felt by one, this individual acts, however erratically, as a surrogate for everyone in the community.

Tamba accepted the man on his own terms, recognizing, above all, the validity of his seeming madness. Kurosawa's attitude toward his characters in *Dodesukaden* is identical. The director gently embraces all the lowly orphans in his film, from Rokkuchan, who shouts "dodesukaden, dodesukaden," into the void, to Hei's wife, Ocho, who succumbed to the advances of a lover in a moment of passion, only to earn the relentless and finally self-immolating wrath of her husband. Like the drunk wielding his sword, Ocho simply had not been herself for the moment and yielded to impulse. Now, sharing her husband's judgment while yearning for his forgiveness, she says she had been a "wild beast." But if out of some death wish of his own Hei cannot forgive her, Kurosawa does.

Tamba, in pointed contrast, knowingly allows himself to be robbed one night by a thief, so well aware is he of how closely morality and character are bound up with the possession of or lack of property. He refuses to condemn people because they act out of need. Aware that there are worse fates than the loss of mere possessions, Tamba invites the man to return if ever again he finds himself short of money; by then Tamba will have saved up some more. When Tamba refuses to testify against the subsequently captured thief, the thief thinks him insane; but Tamba insists on covering for him, informing the police that he has never before seen the captured man.

No all-powerful samurai like Kambei in *Seven Samurai*, let alone the Mifune of superman prowess in *Yojimbo*, Tamba is a man whose strength proceeds from *mono no aware*—that sweet sense of the transitory quality of all earthly things, that peace that passeth understanding—which makes him closer in spirit to Ozu's wise characters than to Kurosawa's impatient heroes. It would be a savage justice indeed to punish this impoverished thief, for who lacking the means to survive would not steal? Tamba serves a higher justice by making implicit judgment on the injustice of the fact that a man needs to steal. This is why he urges the thief to return, should the need arise.

Tamba's attitude applies to all the slum's inhabitants and particularly to Hei, who ought to have forgiven his wife her transgression. Tamba is in tune with the needs of his friends, aware that life is "a diminished thing," in the words of Robert Frost. This mood, like the character of Tamba himself, marks *Dodesukaden* as a product of Kurosawa's later years. *Dodesukaden*, unlike *Ikiru*, *Seven Samurai*, or *Record of a Living Being*—angry films about the failure of people to do more to alter the terrible cruelty and unfairness of life in society—explores transcendence in a world impervious to change, in the spirit of Yeats' "Lapis Lazuli."

This nostalgic, contemplative and passive aspect of *Dodesukaden* emerges most fully in its central episode. An old man visits Tamba and begs him to provide an easy method of suicide. "Life is nothing but pain," the man laments, as it is for all the characters in this film. He sees no reason to go on living, a conclusion any of the people in *Dodesukaden* could reasonably reach. Both his sons were killed on the Chinese front during the Second World War, his wife died of an illness, and his house was burned to the ground in an air-raid. These disasters led him to neglect his business, leaving him pauperized as well as lonely.

In the face of all this, we assume that the poison he gratefully accepts is given to him by Tamba in kindness and pity. After ingesting it and while waiting for it to take effect, the man relaxes and begins to reminisce. His wife and sons continue to appear to him in his dreams, laughing and talking as if they were still alive. Tamba seizes the moment, acting here as a surrogate for Kurosawa, who searches his palette for the tones that will reveal startling loveliness in the lives of these abandoned people. "That happiness," Tamba points out, "is a part of your life. They are alive as long as you are alive."

The beauty of such memories filled with love can by itself sustain and validate life. Suddenly the mood shifts and the film takes a comic turn. The man, believing he has consumed poison when in fact Tamba had given him only a harmless digestive, begs Tamba for an antidote. Life is rich, as Kurosawa insists in *Dodesukaden* by exploring bleak lives that nonetheless contain a resilience and grandeur at first impossible for us to imagine. If hunger and filth characterize this man's physical existence, memories of his loved ones define his life as well. Unlike the insidious pilgrim of *The Lower Depths*, Tamba does not lie. He never deludes the man into thinking that his drapery business will flourish once again or even that his loneliness will abate. He argues only that the man's barren life is not without value.

A life of such heightened awareness as this man finally achieves is proposed in *Dodesukaden* as an alternative to despair, a theme we have met before in Kurosawa, though it was then joined to the hope that sufficiently powerful moral witness may in fact change the world. Such consciousness defined Nakajima, the protagonist of *Record of a Living Being*, who begs his family to escape a possible impending atomic attack on Japan by moving to Brazil. "I wonder who is mad, he or I?" the Tamba-figure of that film, Harada, asks himself. *Dodesukaden*'s fantasies, mirroring intense imagination driven by extremity to the border of delusion, more closely resemble the unrealizable dreams of the impoverished girl and boy of Kurosawa's early *One Wonderful Sunday*. These imaginings may sustain life, but they ultimately cannot lead the poor out of an existence that is all but unbearable.

For both the nostalgic Kurosawa of *Dodesukaden* and the young director of *One Wonderful Sunday* (made just after the war), the imagination as a value in itself offers moments morally superior to and more authentic than the brute facts of "real life." It bears the individual's felt experience that Kurosawa cherishes in all his films. The supreme value he places on the possibilities of the individual human being is what has made him seem so Western to Japanese critics more comfortable with the complacencies of the feudal ethos still pervading Japanese life. Never has Kurosawa subscribed to the philosophy so common in Japan whereby the individual must make himself subordinate to the group. His individualism, that abiding value whose implicit challenge to feudal notions of obeisance to authority accounts for Kurosawa's importance in revolutionizing Japanese culture after the war, reappears even in the summation of old themes as found in *Dodesukaden*. Treasuring the personal experience of the individual and valuing it for its own sake—all the more when people come into conflict with unjust authority—has always been a central feature of Kurosawa's finest works. *Dodesukaden* earns its place among these to the degree that this theme is primary here as well, even if the director no longer has faith in our capacity to implement our visions and thereby create a better world.

*Dodesukaden* insists that everyone's life contains enduring moments of redeeming dignity and value, experiences granting us satisfaction, but of which even those closest to us may remain unaware. Shima (played by Junzaburo Ban), the cripple with the nervous tic who is ridiculed by the local gossips, seems appallingly plagued by his shrewish wife, who struts through the film with a cigarette dangling from her lips, the caustic enemy of all. Shima's facial tic, beginning as a grimace and finishing as a near convulsion, appears inextricable from his bond to this sullen, abrasive wife. Kurosawa's approach to character in *Dodesukaden* is exemplified by the scene in which the unfortunate Shima brings three business colleagues home to dinner. In violation of propriety and of all the norms of hospitality and in a willful, unthinkable display of temper before strangers, Mrs. Shima rudely thrusts some fruit before her guests. She then announces that she is going out to take a bath and storms out of the house. There is silence. The youngest of Shima's friends—and hence for Kurosawa the person in closest touch with his own feelings, as children are those freest of hypocrisy for this director— is unable to restrain his emotions any longer; he is compelled to speak out against this outrageous humiliation and abuse of Shima by his wife. Kurosawa wryly mocks the easy moral indignation of those heroes of his own earlier films who so self-righteously rail against what they assume to be unmitigated injustice. The man passionately condemns his host's ungrateful, bad-mannered wife, seeking out of compassion, and at the risk of committing an impropriety of his own, to offer solace to his ill-used friend: "She doesn't deserve you . . . you're so good. I'm not blaming you . . . you should kick her out!"

Kurosawa, mellowed in *Dodesukaden*, reveals that it is all too easy to judge by externals. Only those involved in an experience can testify to its nature, for appearances very often deceive. The surfaces of reality say little of the complexity of consciousness: this truth, which Tamba taught his suicidal friend, is recapitulated in the vignette featuring Shima. Unexpectedly, Shima responds to the solicitude of his young friend with rage, both at the liberty taken and at the injustice rendered toward a wife whom in fact he values very highly. Shima replies in anger: "She might seem

worthless to you, but she means a lot to me. She stuck by me when we had nothing to eat." The friend can only beg forgiveness; like ourselves in the audience, he has misunderstood, confusing the apparent with the real. If Mrs. Shima is enclosed within her own irrational and indiscriminate anger, this doesn't alter her loyalty and stamina.

Shima is made noble in this anti-heroic little film because he retains respect for his own experience. The same insight is unfolded in another episode. The oldest son of the local whore is tormented because none of his brothers and sisters have the same father. He is filled with shame and self-loathing, exacerbated by the taunts of his middle-class schoolmates. His mother's current husband is a poor but kindly brush-maker, a craftsman who takes pride in his work (always a redeeming grace for Kurosawa); but he is father to none of these children. Yet it is he, another surrogate for Kurosawa, who guides them beyond their shame to personal happiness.

Worth is what we feel it to be; it is not based on an external judgment or on values that do not correspond to our needs. Truth emerges from being faithful to our own experience. "You are all dear to me," the brush maker tells his troubled children. "If you don't think I'm your dad, I'm not. . . . If you believe it, you are my son." His love for them is real and they are made to know it. Amidst the affection and laughter of their communal life, a moral order is restored, a code more humane and enduring than the arbitrary judgments of social convention.

To render love a reality is the condition of survival and redemption, whatever our situation and however harsh our lives, says Kurosawa in *Dodesukaden*. This theme applies both to the moral acts of the heroes of his earlier films and to the act of consciousness celebrated as an end in itself in *Dodesukaden*. The blasted tree outside Hei's door is an image of himself, a man withered and nearly dead because he cannot forgive Ocho's infidelity. "It's no longer a tree when it's dead," says Ocho. Hei is no longer a man because he has ceased to know how to love.

At times life becomes too painful for people to summon the energy to cherish what they have. Kurosawa does not blame the exploited girl Kasuko for stabbing her one friend, the delivery boy. Pregnant by her foster father, she would kill the boy rather than herself so that he would never forget her, a descent into irrationality brought on by her having been brutalized. But Kasuko never surrenders her capacity to love, her care for this boy; Kurosawa thus redeems her by having the boy recover and Kasuko regain her fragile hold on life.

With characters so beset by pain, Kurosawa nevertheless withstands any descent into the sentimental. The vivid colors reflect in themselves his sense that even for the most afflicted, life is worth living. But the people in *Dodesukaden*, downcast as they all are, still cause each other much pain. Despite the rich capacity for fantasy and heightened consciousness of these slum denizens, they each can see only the narrow vista of their own plight (Tamba is the one exception). This inability to see beyond our personal pain is Kurosawa's answer in *Dodesukaden* to the question cited earlier, which he has told us permeates all his films: "Why can't people be happier together?" The gossiping women who congregate at the communal water-pump fear the zombie-like Hei, ignorant of how his life has been maimed by his inability to cope with his wife's one lapse. They laugh at Shima and his tic and detest his bullying wife without knowing of the bond that unites them. They call the beggar who allows his son to die rather than get a doctor "proud," unaware that the distinction between fantasy and reality has snapped for this desolate man who paints magnificent houses for himself and his son on the canvas of his mind. Tamba merely says of him that he is "shy."

Men and women invariably misunderstand each other—a theme not surprising in Kurosawa, who at best approaches women in a spirit of

benevolent paternalism, demonstrating an ingrained feudal sensibility to which most Japanese males, intellectuals or not, are subject. A chorus bombards us with clichés about women from which the director is unable to distance himself: "All women are mysterious, age doesn't matter," "women are really devilish," "all women are the same." One of the mis-used drunken husbands compares, metaphorically, his wife's nagging to the pouring of a bag of sand on his head. The other, his crony, asks what it feels like. These two unhappy husbands, one dressed in red, the other in yellow, are the comic counterparts to the morose Hei. None can get along with women.

Women remain "the other" to all these men, at worst pathetic, at best a joke, like the perpetually pregnant whore, each of whose children has a different father. Exemplary men like Tamba remain at the forefront of Kurosawa's moral universe; the director's sense of character here as in his earlier films does not extend to the portrayal of women as the spiritual equals of men. They may be unjustly used and worthy of sympathy, like Ocho and Kasuko, but Kurosawa's women are without the strength or moral resonance of the fully worthy and remain subordinate and wanting.

As in many of Kurosawa's films, the acting is highly stylized, exempli-fied by the overdone grunting and posturing of the two drunken husbands in roles that would have been suitable for Mifune in his younger days. The characters become flat at moments, lacking psychological nuance, a flaw present at times in Kurosawa's earlier works as well, which are pre-occupied with moral dilemma and choice rather than with the workings of the psyche. In *Dodesukaden* his people are perceived solely in terms of their ruling passions, a method befitting the director's sense of the frag-mentary, stunted lives of the poor. Their own illusions have replaced the unbearable realities of the "objective" world.

Kurosawa sees retreats into fantasy such as the beggar's "construction" of a series of increasingly grand mansions for himself and his son as both heroic and desperate, a last resort in the attempt to survive. The refreshing and lyrical quality of *Dodesukaden* flows from Kurosawa's awe before the human capacity to withstand hardships of this magnitude while managing to extract pleasure from fleeting moments. The film's static quality, its most serious limitation, arises from the absence of any alternative to the never-ending dialectic of suffering and reverie in which its characters are en-snared.

# PRODUCTION

According to Kurosawa, the tension involved in the production of many of his other films did not surface during the making of *Dodesukaden*. Of his mood during shooting he has said, "as you can see from the snap-shots of me while working on the set, I was always smiling and never angry. I enjoyed it heartily." He states that he felt free of all obstacles and told his crew, "I want to make this one sunny, cheerful, light-hearted and charmingly pretty." These instructions were also imparted to composer Toru Takemitsu, who produced a lilting central motif in the manner of a folk-song, similar to Canadian song-writer Leonard Cohen's "Suzanne," written in the 1960's.

*Dodesukaden* was actually shot in a Tokyo dump; outdoor sets were constructed and houses built among the debris. The shacks and roads were dyed with a spray-gun to create the extraordinary pinks, golds, and greens that render *Dodesukaden* one of the most beautiful color films ever made in Japan. Kurosawa chose to shoot in standard 35 mm. so that the colors would be distinct and clear; cinemascope, which he had used from the time of *The Hidden Fortress* through *Red Beard*, would have lessened the immediacy of scenes such as that of the beggar and his son turning increasingly green from food poisoning before our eyes and crouched in an abandoned car, their only home. (By *Dersu Uzala* Kurosawa would feel comfortable enough with color film to shoot in 70 mm.) When it rained during production, a chemical reaction of the dye with the decaying junk in the city dump caused the ground to turn a variety of colors, to Kurosawa's delight.

The legendary Kurosawa rehearsals were omitted this time: the actors were instructed simply to behave spontaneously, to innovate, and to add to their roles extemporaneously. This too represented a departure for Kurosawa, who now employed a "one scene, one cut" method, in sharp contrast to the style of such films as *Rashomon*, with dazzling cuts in which some pieces are so short as to be barely discernible as separate shots. That he had to shoot in confined spaces probably influenced Kurosawa to cut in *Dodesukaden* much less frequently than he had in earlier films.

Departures such as the extremely long take in which Shima entertains his guests explain why *Dodesukaden* appears so different from Kurosawa's earlier work, irrespective of the use of color, and why its movement is slow and artificial, almost in the manner of filmed theater. The methods of production themselves establish *Dodesukaden* as a work completed in repose, a recapitulation of the central themes Kurosawa had treated earlier, granting *Dodesukaden* the quality of a summing-up as opposed to that of a venture into new territory. A dynamic method of filming would have demanded a leap forward in content. Kurosawa confined himself in *Dodesukaden* to insights previously digested, and the style, except for the inventive use of color, is placid, predictable, and static.

In preparation for *Dodesukaden* Kurosawa requested Japanese schoolchildren to send him drawings of streetcars to be pinned up on the walls of Rokkuchan's house. The finished paintings that appear in the film were actually done by Kurosawa's production staff, but were inspired by the two thousand pictures sent in by children. Such artifice in general defines the method chosen by Kurosawa in making this film. The sets are as unrealistic as the painted backdrops of Hollywood musicals of the 1940's. Even the acting was aided by technical means. The character Hei, played by

Hiroshi Akutagawa, was meant to be impassive, and Kurosawa instructed Akutagawa never once to blink his eyes. To shoot close-ups of his face, Kurosawa even put a transparent plastic bag over the actor's head so that light would not penetrate his eyes. Interestingly, the fact that only straight cuts link the shots of this film, without dissolves or the traditional Kurosawa wipes, adds a note of stark realism and works to prevent the slightest hint of sentimentality that might otherwise have crept into a film about the downtrodden.

# TREATMENT

One slum set of tin shacks splashed with the primary colors blue, yellow, and red contains all the action of *Dodesukaden*, with the exception of a single scene on the downtown streets of Tokyo, where the beggar's son solicits scraps from restaurants. As in *Drunken Angel*, *Stray Dog*, *The Lower Depths*, and *High and Low*, the slum conditions of people condemned to poverty limit their means of survival. *Dodesukaden*, like *Drunken Angel*, is set in a disease-breeding swamp that forms a class-barrier, separating the affluent well-dressed boys on their way to school from the lonely, crazed Rokkuchan. Singled out in close-up is a scrap of plastic fiercely buffeted by the wind, evocative of the helplessness of these people before the elements.

Yet slum life in *Dodesukaden* is painted not in the depressing grays of *The Lower Depths*, where the diagonal lines of the set and contrasts of black and white express the perpetual strife of people fraying each other's nerves under one roof. In *Dodesukaden* red and yellow predominante to convey both the intensity of life and the strength and tenacity of the poor. In seeming irony, iridescent greens, pinks, and frosty blue-grays are present when danger lurks, unexpected colors here carry Kurosawa's optimism and his belief in the capacity of his characters to surmount most obstacles to their survival. Shimmering gold bathes the set when Hei and Ocho act out their tragedy; if in other circumstances gold connotes something holy or transcendent, here Kurosawa employs it to heighten the sense of utter loss, the pain of abandonment and love withdrawn.

In its symbolic use of color, notably distinct from the far less imaginative uses in the last films of Ozu and Mizoguchi, *Dodesukaden* advances beyond the confines of visual naturalism. Violent colors, as if from the palette of Van Gogh, accompany Kurosawa's depiction of the oppression of his characters. These rich tones work in counterpoint, conveying a heightened expression of Kurosawa's awe of people who, possessing none of life's advantages, manage to extract from their daily existence humor, small joys, and sustaining memories.

The workers who come home drunk every night to nagging wives have no separate identities, robbed of individuality as they are by numbing drudgery. The wife of one is dressed in red, the other in yellow. One carries a red washbasin out to the water-pump each morning, the other a yellow. Rendered animal-like by the physical exhaustion of each day, the women are as indistinguishable as their men. But the reds and yellows that accompany them make triumphs of their eager, energetic attempts at gay abandon, even if these are facilitated by the saké bottle.

The multi-colored "children's" drawings of streetcars lining the walls of Rokkuchan's house are splendid and overpowering. Toward these projections of the "trolley-crazy's" pain, Kurosawa's camera is reverent; in a slow pan it reveals beauty where we would least expect to discover redeeming grace. The rainbow of colors, ranging from the intensely violent to the pastel, forms a paean to the capacity to endure and to the rich fantasy-lives of those rejected by the wealthy as dirty, drunk, and dangerous, or simply ignored like the young couple in *One Wonderful Sunday*, who might have been characters in *Dodesukaden*.

One of the most ironic uses of color occurs in Kurosawa's depiction of the life of Kazuko, the dependent of a parasitic foster father. Day and night she works to fashion crepe-paper flowers of blue, red, yellow, and pink—colors associated in these scenes with abuse and exploitation. Kazuko herself is dressed in dull gray and mauve, which expresses the barrenness of her neglected life. From slaving frantically for unending hours at her flower-making Kazuko has grown pale and thin, the color slowly bleached out of her face before our eyes until one day she collapses on a "field" of these multi-colored flowers, immobile in exhaustion and defeat. The image echoes the collapse of detective and criminal in *Stray Dog*, their identities indistinguishable as they fall together amid a profusion of wild flowers. Lying paralyzed by fatigue, Kazuko is raped by her foster father, crushing the now insidious red, pink, and yellow flowers that are as carelessly artificial as the life they simulate, the life that so destroys her.

Kurosawa's expressionistic use of color constantly reminds us that in the world of *Dodesukaden* joy and pain are inextricably entwined. If gold light bathes the tormented face of Ocho, gold represents by its unusual usage the inverted values through which her surrender to brief joy becomes the occasion for the denial of love. Equally, the bright yellow to which Kurosawa repeatedly returns expresses the primitive joy accessible to the most blighted, if only in the shout of a mad child crying "dodesukaden" into the wind. At times a cold blue light is introduced to convey the living death of slum life. It plays upon the faces of the beggar and his son, who is dying of food poisoning, and it colors the face of the unforgiving Hei as he lives out his days in the paralyzed perfection of absolute misery.

*Dodesukaden* allows but one scene outside its junkyard set. In night-time Tokyo, whose automobiles glisten iridescently, the beggar's son carries his pail to back doors of restaurant kitchens imploring the staff for the scraps from unfinished meals. The enormous automobiles dwarf the little urchin, a spatial contrast expressing Kurosawa's sense of two universes of experience: that of the city dwellers, with their material advantages, and that of those who live on the outskirts of the metropolis, who subsist on the periphery of social existence and on the edge of life itself.

Shocking pink and scarlet predominate in this scene, the artificial colors of Tokyo by night. They heighten the unspeakable callousness of the heavily rouged woman who refuses the boy the scraps from her restaurant as she spitefully tosses a pile of cigarette butts onto a plate of leftovers that the starving child coveted. A chef is kinder, as women once again prove themselves to be the morally inferior members of the species in the Kurosawa *oeuvre*.

Hoping to infuse his son's life with purpose and to offer him a vision of an existence worthy of human beings, the beggar constructs in fantasy a house of their dreams. Pictured as an enormous white structure of Western design, it becomes in the *mise-en-scène* one of Kurosawa's hymns to the fertility of the human imagination. For the beggar re-designs his creation constantly, adding the innovations of each phase of architectural history. He is linked in his imaginative delusion to the creative impulse in human existence itself, which Kurosawa suggests is our mad defense against the meanness of life. We view the house alternately with a Spanish and a rococo gate. Yellow suns and pink sunsets, painted backdrops of the imagination, contrast with the muddy roads and white sky of the slum—the world as it appears when its denizens fail to dream. If none of life's amenities are accessible to this beggar and his son, the past of world culture can fortify them. Out of his acquaintance with the history of architecture the beggar forges the creation of his dreams.

Kurosawa sanctions the redeeming necessity of fantasy while revealing the fragility of its tenure. He intercuts shots and sometimes stills of this house under construction. A quick cut accompanies the discarding of the Spanish gate for the rococo. The camera views the rococo gate first in long-shot, granting us a view in perspective. Then we are carried in by a zoom for a dazzling close-up view, much as the camera took us gradually into the peasant village at the beginning of *Seven Samurai* or under the

Rashomon gate, though in those scenes without the benefit of a zoom lens.

The little boy assents to all the architectural innovations, choosing to sustain this game with his father; he is played by an extraordinary young actor (Hiroyuki Kawase) who, Kurosawa has remarked, had "a certain mysterious air about him." The boy, far wiser than the man, pities his elder and feels only solidarity with him in his weakness. In this spirit he takes seriously the decision to "build" the house on a hill, in contrast to Japanese houses, which are constructed "in low places." Things Japanese are not glorified here by people for whom life in prosperous post-war Japan has brought only misery. Kurosawa cuts to a magnificent white mansion on a hill overlooking spacious green lawns. The image recalls the white house of Gondo in *High and Low* that stands above the city of Yokohama and haughtily overlooks its slums.

In *Dodesukaden* the house is first painted white, then pink, then a soft purple, a choice of color distinguishing it, says the beggar, from the houses of foreigners who "are tough and aggressive because they live in stone and concrete." Interestingly, the beggar judges all Japanese by himself: gentle, sensitive, passive, and incapable of doing injury to another—Kurosawa's definition of the nation at its best. In his very deprivation this beggar, in contrast to the people enjoying prosperity in a rampantly commercial Japan, embodies real Japanese virtue.

While their lives flicker, the beggar and his son fix on the image of a house that will never perish. The rococo gate is even painted red with an anti-corrosive, an ironic image of the stable and the permanent, which is available to these people only in their dreams. And they live in the rusting shell of a tiny car, one of the many thousands discarded, like themselves, on junk heaps and emblematic of the waste of human energy and potential in contemporary Japan.

Shots of this palatial house are intercut as a leit-motif throughout the film, expressing the pathos of slum life. When the boy dies because his dreamy father prevented him from boiling the rotting mackerel, although the chef who gave him this discard warned that he must, the dream explodes. The beggar loses the remaining shred of his sanity as he views the grave into which his son's ashes have been placed. Suddenly the father sees the grave as an enormous swimming pool, of which the little boy had dreamed.

His mind snaps. A gigantic swimming pool (the actual pool at Geihinkan in the Meguro section of Tokyo, made to look more extensive because the camera depicts only three of its sides) flashes onto the screen with the man behind it, his expression one of helpless despair. It is the first shot of the beggar's fantasies in which Kurosawa includes the man's physical presence, making complete the descent into madness. The beggar's absorption into the fantasy indicates that he has lost his ability to survive in the world as it is. Dreams no longer carry hope. They have, paradoxically, been assimilated into the reality they would defy because, by our full surrender to them, the hope of changing the real world is finally abandoned.

But even this tragedy is not treated sentimentally by Kurosawa. Father and son, exactly like the couple in *One Wonderful Sunday*, have at least known the joy of their vision, which their mutual assent made real. Given the logic of *Dodesukaden* the boy must die. Despite his invocation of the life of the imagination as beautiful and redeeming, Kurosawa argues that fantasy in the end can never compensate for misery or permanently alleviate unspeakable suffering. Yet the sad mood following the boy's death is soon broken by the gaiety of a flute as the chorus of women delightedly discovers that the two drunks have once again exchanged wives. Death is omnipresent, but so is the life-force that bubbles up again and again to prevent the days from being wholly joyless.

*Dodesukaden* is framed by scenes in the little house of Rokkuchan and his suffering mother. At the end, when a real trolley clangs past, we are reminded that Rokkuchan's particular choice of obsession stems in part from the fact that their house is situated practically on top of trolley tracks. At both beginning and end mother and son pray fervently before a statue of Buddha; Rokkuchan's aim— "to make my mother better"— indicates his complete innocence before his own plight. The idol is no different from any of the dreams, delusions, and fantasies we have met in this film.

No miracles are forthcoming. The camera returns, with the music at its loudest and most uplifting, to the brilliantly colored drawings of trolleys lining the walls of the shabby room. These splendid images become symbolic of man's transcendent imagination and of his exquisite value as a being whose magical fantasies and ability to survive in a world without hope, in Shugoro Yamamoto's "town without seasons," become miracles of their own.

# Dersu Uzala

On December 22, 1971, Kurosawa attempted suicide. That act might seem less shocking if it is understood to derive from the tradition of many great Japanese artists, such as the Nobel Prize-winning novelist Yasunari Kawabata, who perceived suicide as a logical culmination of a career that had drawn to its close. In Japanese culture death is viewed as part of the cycle of life and is valued in Buddhist philosophy as ultimate, comforting tranquility. Suicide, consequently, is considered a natural, logical, and permanently available response to experience and to the exhaustion of life's possibilities. It implies neither shame, nor trauma, nor defeat. For the artist who has reached sixty or more, self-inflicted death is regarded as a heroic act of homage to his art, an acknowledgment that with the diminution of his creative gifts, life should end as well since his art and his existence have been all but inseparable.

Given what appears to have been an unhappy domestic life, Kurosawa had become an artist totally dedicated to and consumed by his craft. Film creation had long been Kurosawa's *raison d'être*, taking precedence over emotional ties to family, which loom larger in the lives of less gifted and single-minded individuals. Feeling that he no longer was able to compose films of the clarity and brilliance that characterized his finest works, Kurosawa began to doubt the sufficiency of his powers. The trials of the preceding years may have led him to the decision to end his life, for some depletion of his skills is evident in *Dodesukaden*. His inability to work in Japan, followed by the disaster of *Tora! Tora! Tora!* contributed to Kurosawa's artistic and emotional exhaustion. Finding himself no longer "bankable" in his own country and hence left only with the option of once again subordinating himself to Hollywood Kurosawa became demoralized and depressed. The commercial failure of *Dodesukaden* in Japan heightened Kurosawa's sense of abandonment, completing the mood that preceded his attempted suicide. The abrupt surfacing of psychological distress, which he previously had been able to repress and sublimate through his art, was joined with an objectively barren reality. The decision to end his life no doubt flowed from this conjunction.

That Kurosawa survived the multiple razor slashes seems a miracle; equally astounding was the emergence of a new personality after his recovery. Throughout his long career Kurosawa had shunned the press and television, accusing critics of misunderstanding his work, and refusing to accept any obligation to elucidate his ideas. Kurosawa now, surprisingly, became an affable and familiar personality, granting interview after interview. In 1976 he even appeared on Japanese television in a commercial for Suntory whiskey (an act previously unthinkable): with Haydn's *Ninety-Fourth Symphony* (called *The Surprise*, appropriately enough) in the background, Kurosawa, wearing sunglasses, sits listening for at least twenty seconds. When the "surprise" comes on, he sips the whiskey and the scene fades out. In another scene Kurosawa is shown with a group of young people, presumably film buffs, talking, explaining, and laughing while, in voice-over, a narrator characterizes presumably both Kurosawa and the whiskey as "meticulous as the devil, bold as an angel." It seems incredibly incongruous for Kurosawa, who had scorned commercialism so unrelentingly—and nowhere more brilliantly than in the night-town sequence of *Ikiru*—to lend his persona and stature to the peddling of whiskey. It is as if his despair had been refined to a cynical surrender to a world he once challenged in disdain. Kurosawa seemed to be flaunting an ultimate alienation, asserting that he no longer considered it worth the effort to struggle; he appeared at home with his despair and with his loss of faith in the artist's ability to transcend the limitations of the present.

In his new persona, the artist resigned himself to giving up his exploration of the corruption he had always considered inherent in the social structure of post-war Japan. Yet the despair apparent in *Dodesukaden* became more fully present in the works and the public personality of Kurosawa. The looser, more relaxed personality may actually have concealed a hardening in Kurosawa, a determination to resist feeling deeply, whether in his work or in his life, perhaps because he had been profoundly hurt and betrayed by the Japanese film industry and by a public to which he had for years given his personal and creative all.

In August 1976 Kurosawa, who only a few years earlier had refused to meet even a director of the classic American cinema like King Vidor, spent several hours sharing observations with Harry Belafonte in the New Otani Hotel in Tokyo. (Kurosawa later said that while he was in Siberia filming *Dersu Uzala*, he listened every night to Belafonte's music, which hardly represents the culmination of Western musical culture; nor is it consonant with Kurosawa's established taste.) In their conversation Kurosawa expressed his fear that technological advance led to increasing alienation. The entire conversation as it was reported in the press is a parody of the great director who, in his prime, had stood aloof from any such trivialization of his views and had repeatedly refused to verbalize in clichés the wisdom he felt best able to represent visually through his film art.

After *Dodesukaden* Kurosawa found himself less capable than ever of raising the money necessary to direct a film in Japan. A shoestring budget had been provided for *Dodesukaden* by the "Yonki no Kai" (Club of the Four Knights), a company composed of Kurosawa, Masaki Kobayashi, Keisuke Kinoshita, and Kon Ichikawa, four of Japan's most distinguished directors of the older generation. Their first plan was for each of the four members to make one serious film in the hopes of independently rejuvenating a Japanese film industry increasingly preoccupied with pornos, *yakuza* (gangster) films, disaster epics, and light comedy.

Kurosawa was the first to begin, and when *Dodesukaden* proved a box-office disappointment, the entire enterprise foundered. Kurosawa's subsequent suicide attempt dispersed the short-lived "club." The failure of *Dodesukaden* also convinced Kurosawa that if he wished to continue making films, he would do better to produce the kind he did best: the epic on a grand scale. He would need three to four million dollars—a moderate budget by American standards, but still considered an outrageous sum by Japanese. But it is true that the wide screen and immense sets best suit the themes to which Kurosawa has returned.

It was in this spirit that in 1972 Kurosawa agreed to make a film financed almost entirely by the Soviet Union, not as a co-production with his old company, Toho, but as a Mosfilm enterprise with some participation by a new Japanese conglomerate called Nippon-Herald, which functioned as an investor. The entire project was part of the general courting of the Japanese by the Soviet leadership, which wished to share in the economic development of Siberia, a land rich in natural resources but still awaiting finance capital.

For his subject Kurosawa chose a work by the Russian soldier and explorer Vladimir Arseniev, whose accounts of his experiences charting the Russian-Manchurian border Kurosawa had read thirty years before. The Soviets had made a television film ten years earlier about Dersu Uzala, the aging hunter who helped Arseniev, but for Kurosawa this film was merely

a superficial adventure story that did not evoke the moral resonance of the central character.

But if *Dodesukaden* represented an interlude in Kurosawa's career—a fanciful, low-budget recapitualtion of all his early themes, as modest and unambitious in its use of the medium as in its essentially despairing look at human mistery—with *Dersu Uzala* the decline in Kurosawa's powers truly becomes apparent. In *Dodesukaden* Kurosawa used color in an expressionistic and brilliant manner to shield himself from subject matter with which he was no longer willing to engage in creative combat. A similar distancing of the artist from the world he depicts is accomplished in *Dersu Uzala* by means of the 70 mm., wide screen, so large that normal theaters cannot accommodate the film, and by six-track stereophonic sound, which surrounds the audience from rear and side speakers and envelops them in mood at the expense of substance.

Style had become an end in itself. Gone was Kurosawa's intervention in the pain his characters face in everyday life, which we still felt in *Dodesukaden*. Gone also, as in *Dodesukaden*, is any hope that human life may be made more bearable; the desire in Kurosawa's films to improve the human condition seems in retrospect to have been largely dependent on that superhuman, idealized figure, whose heroism is inaccessible to the main character here, Dersu Uzala, a hunter beset by the encroachments of progress and civilization. It is too late for a knowing elder to educate a younger man, because that instruction can no longer be put into practice in the world as it is: this feeling about present-day Japan Kurosawa transports to the Russia of the turn of the century.

Dostoevsky, his favorite Russian novelist, has in a strange manner asserted his influence anew in the older Kurosawa, and it is ironically fitting that the process should be completed in Kurosawa's Russian film, with its all-Russian cast and bleak Siberian landscapes. Were Dostoevsky only a nihilist, he would perhaps not have been so great a novelist, but the very eccentricity of his Slavophilism rescued him from a self-pitying abyss of hopelessness in the face of human suffering. In *Dersu Uzala* Kurosawa finds an ideology equivalent to Dostoevsky's Slavophilism in a pantheistic belief in the magnificence of nature and in an embarrassingly archaic, Rousseauesque adulation of the "natural man." But what worked for Dostoevsky proves disastrous for Kurosawa, because whatever his philosophical mood of the moment, the novelist, unlike Kurosawa, never sacrificed his deeply felt exploration of the seamy and the monstrous, the beautiful and the noble sides of human character; he never abandoned his interest in the ambiguities of the human travail.

It is true that Kurosawa has evident love for the simple power and dignity of Dersu, who lives in harmony with the rhythms of nature. But the contrast between the person at one with his surroundings and the world of industrialization, which Kurosawa depicts only in the abstract, is largely theoretical, rendering the work a sentimental journey. Kurosawa mourns the passing of the natural life. He is convinced that we can never recover the balance with nature enjoyed by men like Dersu. Such balance is irreconcilable with knowledge and our mastery of the forces of nature; progress and civilization are enemies of the nobility of men like Dersu. The movie illustrates this idea.

Kurosawa in fact appears to have lost all interest in the living human being beset by his own intransigence, balancing joy and sadness, and forced to face the depleted world as it is. And in abandoning a dynamic sense of character, Kurosawa has produced for the first time in his long and outstanding career a rather lifeless film. Its hollowness is barely concealed by the overwhelming screen size, the sound effects, and the elegiac musical motif mourning the death of that pure and good man of the earth, the Siberian hunter Dersu Uzala.

# THE STORY

*Dersu Uzala* has a very formal structure. It opens and closes with scenes after the death of the main character, then in the main body of the film flashes back to the days when Arseniev and Dersu Uzala explored the Ussuri region of Siberia. These explorations are treated in two distinct parts, separated in time by several years and on the screen by titles. A coda in the city, in which a distressed and aging Dersu attempts to live within "civilized" society and flees back to the wilderness where he is murdered, blends into the final framing sequence of Arseniev at the burial of his dearest friend.

The opening scene of *Dersu Uzala* takes place in 1910 in a new settlement in Siberia. Roads, lumber mills, and houses have destroyed the once-wild landscape. Here the explorer-soldier Vladimir Arseniev (played by Yuri Salomin) searches for the grave of his old friend Dersu, once more to pay his deepest homage to this now extinct, superior breed of man. The cedars between which he had been buried have been chopped down to make way for progress and Arseniev cannot even locate Dersu's grave. This incident represents the way that modern times have unfeelingly supplanted the more natural, harmonious world of the past, neither paying it proper respect nor absorbing any of its lessons.

The film then flashes back to 1902, with Arseniev leading a company of men exploring the Taiga region in the Ussuri territory. Part One is about the first meeting of Arseniev with Dersu (played by Maxim Munzuk), who leads the Russians skillfully through the untrammeled wilderness he knows and loves so well. It culminates in a magnificent blizzard scene, in which snow and ice suddenly close in on Dersu and Arseniev, who had gone out without the group because Arseniev wished to view a beautiful lake for himself instead of merely charting it.

Together they struggle to survive the snowstorm, guided only by Dersu's knowledge of his environment, the fruit of his oneness with the universe; he is a humble person who understands the insignificance of individuals before the power and majesty of nature. Until they meet Dersu, Arseniev and his cossacks are uncertain, fearful of strange sounds, and lacking any capacity to survive in the natural world. Without Dersu—who, with his quaint ways, seems at first barely human to these loutish products of the city and of "civilization"—they would truly be lost. At the end of the exploration Arseniev and Dersu part, to Arseniev's considerable sorrow.

Part Two opens in 1907. Arseniev and a band of men are back exploring the Ussuri. Once again they encounter Dersu. Arseniev is filled with delight and a sense of peace that he experiences only with his friend. The culminating adventure of Part Two involves the fording of rapids, a scene far less dramatic than the snowstorm of Part One and neither as frightening nor as well-photographed as a similar scene in the American

film *Deliverance*. The scene presages the decline of Dersu's powers: Arseniev and his group must this time rescue Dersu from being overtaken by the rapids, although they must rely on Dersu's own direction as he clings to a tree stump in the swirling waters.

Dersu is now in anguish because he has shot at a tiger, the creature he sees as the spiritual center of his universe, and believes he has thereby offended the balance of nature. According to Dersu, the tiger is sacred and must be left in peace; the human being who disturbs him will meet with disaster. Thus Dersu fears that Tanga, the Spirit of the Forest worshipped by the Gold people (the tribe of which Dersu is a member), will send another tiger after him. Shooting at the tiger, something Dersu knows better than to do, expresses a departure from his own natural impulses, a corrupting result of his association with Arseniev and the soldiers.

In fact, Dersu begins to lose his eyesight, a fatal circumstance for a person who lives by what he can hunt. To save him, and because he has never felt for a human being the love he bears Dersu Uzala, Arseniev invites him back to Khabarovsk to live with him in his warm, comfortable house. Kurosawa, in his desire to romanticize nature and disparage technological advance, permits certain incongruities. In the early twentieth century eyeglasses existed; that Arseniev does not entrust his friend to an eye doctor is anomalous given his eagerness to help Dersu. Kurosawa seems committed to disallowing even the most obvious benefits of science and organized human knowledge.

Within civilization, Dersu is like a caged animal, lacking all peace with himself, restless and discontent. Dressed in city clothes instead of the animal hides he had fashioned in the wilderness, he seems pathetic as he sits disconsolately on the floor before the fireplace, when he once sat before campfires in the wild. Idleness does not suit Dersu, who is now reduced to telling stories of his adventures to Arseniev's little son, who, inevitably, admires the guest enormously.

Dersu finds it difficult to accommodate himself to the restrictions of city life. The only way he knows how to clean his gun is to shoot it into the air, which is against the law. He objects when Arseniev's wife buys water from a vendor because water should be free; he calls the vendor a "bad man." Merchants who buy and sell, anything connected with commercialism or progress, is denounced by Kurosawa through the sage Dersu, a person who in his natural purity goes to light a fire, pitch a tent, and sleep in the park rather than in Arseniev's confining house. "I cannot breathe here," says Dersu, who is nearly arrested for cutting firewood in the park; wood too, says Dersu, should be free. The elements belong naturally to us all and, according to Dersu Uzala, should no more be conceived of as property than should ideas.

Finally Dersu begs the forgiveness of his beloved friend. "I cannot live in the city," he says. It hurts him to be so out of touch with nature. With the gift of Arseniev's high-powered rifle, which he needs in order to compensate for his failing eyesight, Dersu departs, only to be murdered for this valuable possession. A full shot of a telegram to Arseniev informs us that the civilized world of violence and brutality has claimed Dersu. His heart frozen, Arseniev identifies the body and Dersu is buried in the Taiga between two gigantic Siberian cedars on which, in elegiac homage, the snow falls. The music comes up loud and mournful, embodying the sentiments of the bereaved Arseniev. The chorus calls out "my gray-winged eagle, where have you gone?" and the reply rings back: "I am flying over the far mountains."

# CHARACTERIZATION

With *Dersu Uzala*, Kurosawa's interest in character and personality, in man as a struggling, developing being, vanishes. As he acknowledged in a memo affixed to the script of *Dersu Uzala* that was published in *Kinema Jumpo* magazine, his main subject was "the astonishingly beautiful, gigantic and awesome Great Nature of the Ussuri region of Russia." In disillusionment with the absence of spiritual progress in the Japan of his time, Kurosawa, like many Japanese, has lost faith in the capacity of people to make this a better world, to alleviate suffering and to eliminate injustice. Thus, in this story of the love between two men, Dersu and Arseniev, the landscape itself becomes the hero; all the director's feelings flow through his photography of the bleak, desolate, all-encompassing Siberian wilderness. The shot compositions resemble those magnificent landscapes of the Sung dynasty in China where mountains, rocks, and sky predominate, overwhelming the human beings who are so small that they are barely discernible.

The camera work of *Dersu Uzala* continually suggests that man is a weak and small creature, of little significance and of value only insofar as he is capable, like Dersu Uzala, of accepting submission to the powers of nature and merging with the elements. Arseniev's observation that "man is too small to face the vastness of nature" is a legacy of his friendship with Dersu.

The people of *Dersu Uzala* thus become papier-mâché figures whose characters are mere object lessons in Kurosawa's pantheism. They are not realized as sentient, complex human beings. *Dersu Uzala* is, like many Japanese films of the sixties and seventies, a polemic about the respective merits of the civilized and primitive. The characters are there to impart a lesson particularly acute for Japan—that industrialism and its attendant pollution have laid the homeland to waste. This "progress" has turned the lovely archipelago of Japan, where people traditionally lived in harmony with nature, into a smog-ridden, suppurating wasteland. Kurosawa had spoken after *Dodesukaden* of making a film about pollution. In *Dersu Uzala* he has essentially done that. Through the homely wisdom of Dersu Uzala the film asserts that we who have lost contact with nature and the physical world are as lost as Arseniev suddenly becomes, his compass

notwithstanding, in the face of the colossal blizzard. In reference to this film Kurosawa has elucidated his intentions:

> *The relationship between human beings and nature is getting worse and worse. . . . I wanted to have people all over the world know about this Soviet Asian character who lived in harmony with nature. . . . I think people should be more humble toward nature because we are a part of it and we must become harmonized with it. If nature is destroyed, human beings will be destroyed too. So we can learn a lot from Dersu.*

And there is, in fact, an undeniable sweetness in the character of Dersu Uzala. He stands as an ideal ethical figure, free of selfishness and corruption. To the bragging of Arseniev's soldiers who insist that they never miss a target because they are in the army, Dersu answers, "You shoot everything, leave for others nothing." He places rice, salt, and matches in an abandoned hut for wayfarers who may pass that way so that they will not die. Arseniev speaks for the director in his enchantment before Dersu's character: "I couldn't help admiring him. He was so wise . . . he was good-hearted, generous-minded . . . he could think of rendering kindness to a man he had never met nor ever would."

The physical appearance of Dersu Uzala itself represents a striking departure for Kurosawa. In his earlier works the pure, noble figure in touch with himself and his surroundings was always larger than life, a powerful specimen usually portrayed by Toshiro Mifune. Here, by contrast, the Russians—who are the physically powerful figures—are hapless, weak, and utterly inferior to Dersu. Yet Dersu is miniscule, a rotund elf of a man, almost like a forest fairy or one of the "little people" of Irish legend. Kurosawa appears to be contrasting the European alienation from nature through industrialization and commercialism with the natural life of an Asian tribesman. Hence the size of the Europeans connotes only clumsiness. Dersu's small appearance also runs counter to type for the traditional backwoodsman of the American West, figures like Davey Crockett or Paul Bunyan. It is an entirely positive corrective. When we first meet Dersu, he seems faintly ridiculous, the mountain dwarf in comparison to the tall, blonde, physically handsome Russians. But it is the Russians, forever testing their physical prowess, who are inept. Dersu is the small Asian who shows up the absurd pretensions of European superiority, he presents a different masculine image which suggests that absurd male bravado is infantile and utterly unrelated to competence and value.

Like the old man who comes to Tamba in *Dodesukaden* in search of an easy means to suicide, Dersu dreams of his dead loved ones. He burns all his possessions because in a dream his wife and children, who had died of smallpox, were cold and hungry. He too believes that as long as he is alive and loves them, they are alive as well. As Dersu describes an old Chinese whom they meet, he stands for Kurosawa: "He thinks and he dreams alone." Sad, misunderstood, and also alone, Dersu is a poignant figure, charming as he speaks to the elements as if they were people, instructing the fire to be quiet so the people can carry on a conversation. A kettle, the sun, the moon, wind, fire, and water are all worthy of respect for Dersu, and if Arseniev's troops at first laugh at this sage, it is no matter; they are the infidels, he the saint. Arseniev's son, Vova, is at once taken with Dersu as one innocent being responds to another. The final measure of Dersu's purity is his lack of acquaintance with anything connected with technology and human conquest. He had never seen a railroad and when he first observes the tracks, he says, "Me no understood, me now understand." Dersu remains unperturbed by the merchant who stole all the money he earned by hunting sable, because wealth means nothing to him. He can only remark, paraphrasing words Kurosawa has himself used, "Why are people like that?"

In keeping with this film's essential distance from the agonies of the human spirit in this century, Kurosawa openly admires some values that derive from feudal tradition in Japan. The noble command the unworthy. Dersu becomes even more admirable in the director's eyes when he asserts "rank," assumes leadership, and speaks quite harshly to the improperly acquiescent Russians, men softened by city living and incapable of surviving alone in the wilderness. An elitism pervades the film and suffuses the relationship between Dersu and Arseniev in a facile formula: Arseniev acknowledges that Dersu instinctively knows best about all things and is rewarded with the hunter's devotion. A real man takes charge of others and thus demonstrates his superiority, a militarist view toward which Kurosawa displays little irony, despite the fact that Dersu's harsh commands are at times faintly ridiculous to us no less than to the uninitiated buffoons accompanying Arseniev. But in paying so little attention to the nuances of character, Kurosawa fails to achieve for Dersu the authority he imagines his hero commands.

Arseniev himself, as played by Soviet actor Yuri Solomin, comes to us as a man with no psychology, no personal history, and no goals. He exists

for Kurosawa solely by virtue of his admiration for Dersu Uzala, a man worthy of Dersu's interest because Arseniev too will not let his men kill animals unless they need them for food. A product of the West, in this allegory Arseniev is present to be instructed in the secrets of human existence by the Asian Dersu. His blindness parallels that of many Japanese who fail to define the national identity in terms of the particular affinity to nature of the Japanese as an island people. Dersu is a "Gold" hunter—as distinct from being either Japanese, Korean, or Chinese—an Asian whose tribal name itself reflects the purity of his soul.

Like the best of Kurosawa's samurai, Dersu speaks little of his deepest feelings, conveying that "manly" stoicism Kurosawa has often admired. He is reserved and is typical of Kurosawa's heroes in his simplicity. He calls the sun "the greatest man," and the moon "the second greatest." Like a samurai, Dersu surrenders to a unity beyond the self, in which fire, water, and wind are more powerful than men. He and Arseniev are caught in the blizzard because Arseniev, mesmerized, cannot resist the fascination of the lake. Dersu, in tune with nature, knows that every passing moment renders more certain that they will be trapped by the life-menacing storm.

Dersu also feels an abiding compassion for others who have known pain and suffering, such as the old Chinese they meet along the way who Dersu alone knows has reconciled himself to a tragic life. Dersu respects the man's isolation and instructs his disciple to do likewise. When Arseniev would invite the old Chinese to join them at their fire, Dersu gently reproves him, explaining that it is important to the old man to be alone in order to feel and to reflect.

Thus, like any Kurosawa samurai, Dersu is superbly competent, attuned to nature, the weather, and the presence of other human beings in the wilderness. Above all he knows how to survive. He lives, as did the samurai at his best, purely by his own code, one not unlike *bushido* in its insistence on subordination of the individual to a transcendent ideal. Dersu would never verbalize such an idea, again in keeping with samurai manner; he simply embodies it.

In the script of *Dersu Uzala* these samurai-like attributes are awarded to an Asian of the area named Chen Pao: "The power of his personality," wrote Kurosawa, "is evidently the result of his intelligence, self-control and ability to make others obey his orders." But they are no less applicable to Dersu himself: he exhibits all these qualities in both the blizzard scene of Part One and the rapids sequence of Part Two; his manner in each evokes nothing so much as the heroic samurai of earlier Kurosawa films, in which the mood of nostalgia is accompanied by Kurosawa's regret at the fall of the samurai class. All that is left to us of value, Kurosawa implies, is what Dersu represents. The most moving moments of *Dersu Uzala* are those in which we feel all the more intensely for Dersu because we sense the precariousness of his tenure on this earth.

Although Arseniev's wife appears in the flat and unrealized Khabarovsk sequence late in the film, the only emotional relationship present is that between the two men. (It was no accident that in the script Kurosawa wrote in 1976 for a Japanese version of *King Lear*, called *Ran* [Chaos], the patriarch's daughters become sons.) In *Dersu Uzala* Arseniev and his wife behave like good friends; even in shots in the privacy of their home when no one else is present, they never once touch each other. Dersu and Arseniev, however, are openly demonstrative and have all the qualities of lovers. After surviving the all-night blizzard, they roll gleefully entwined on the ground, hugging and embracing each other in an outburst of passion. When by chance they meet again at the beginning of Part Two, they embrace once more. "I was feeling good," Arseniev says simply, "Dersu was with us."

That night, as the men sit around the campfire and sing, Dersu and Arseniev are placed together in the right-hand corner of the shot, bathed in gold light, like lovers reunited. They smile at each other in mutual understanding. The other men occupy the left side of the frame, cut off from the emotional circle by a diagonally placed log that bisects the screen, like a curtain delicately separating the two groups. It preserves the privacy of Dersu and Arseniev alone together after having been apart for so long.

Near the end of Part Two there is a picture-taking sequence in which Arseniev is very anxious to be photographed with Dersu. A montage sequence of stills follows. Their relationship is glorified as one beyond time, and as we view the photos we hear the song about Dersu that had been sung at the campfire. One after another the pictures preserve their ecstatic faces for us until the series ends with the two looking into each other's eyes in complete and unqualified admiration, though perhaps to our unintended embarrassment at witnessing so intimate a moment. Like civilization, progress, industrialization, and modernization, women are a negative force. In this idyll between Arseniev and Dersu women have no place; they remain superfluous beings incapable of the strong emotion and mutual understanding possible between men alone.

But, interestingly, Arseniev's men, also lesser beings, share none of the camaraderie that was so appealing in *Seven Samurai*. Gone for Kurosawa is even that fraternity, as if people no longer in touch with nature are equally alienated from spontaneous, comradely feeling. Only Dersu and his disciple Arseniev, two superior examples of manliness, are capable of love.

*Dersu Uzala* is set in the Ussuri region, the area of the ongoing Sino-Soviet border dispute. Much to the horror of Japanese Maoists and others, Kurosawa succumbs in an otherwise irrelevant sequence to a display of evident Soviet anti-Chinese propaganda. Animals that come to a stream to drink are found fallen into traps, to be starved and killed for their skins. We are told that "bad Chinese do that," just as these "bad Chinese" steal women and "murder all the men," a reference to money lenders of the area who, we learn, confiscate the wives and children of the debtors, whom they then bury alive. Such men, buried but still alive, are discovered by Dersu and Arseniev, who are enraged at the atrocity. The heroic Chen Pao,

a tribal Asian dedicated to fighting these Chinese, suddenly appears in all his strength and splendor. The Chinese of this area, one colonized by the Czar but originally Chinese territory, are thus portrayed as cruel and greedy predators who indiscriminately kill animals and men. This seems an attempt to justify both Czarist conquest and Soviet control of areas historically Chinese. Asians like Chen Pao and Dersu Uzala are shown to hate the Chinese and to welcome the Russians, as if the Chinese were the colonizers of this area when in fact the Russians are. The local tribes are to choose between exploitative Chinese and beneficent Russians; self-determination is, needless to say, never suggested as an option. Such moments of Soviet anti-Chinese propaganda remind us of the artistic limitations inherent in a Soviet-sponsored film. That *Dersu Uzala* won first prize at the 1975 Moscow Film Festival hardly compensates for this intrusion on the integrity of the film.

# TREATMENT

Just as landscape supplants character in *Dersu Uzala*, so imagery and color substitute completely for the quick cutting and restlessly moving camera of the earlier and best Kurosawa films. There are very few close-ups of the characters, and the camera is strangely reticent, moving only when the actors do, as when Arseniev rushes to embrace Dersu when they meet again at the beginning of Part Two. Kurosawa also uses fast tracking during the rapids sequence as the men run along the river bank in their attempt to rescue Dersu; here the movement of the camera expresses the urgency of rescuing such a valuable man. Kurosawa's habitual method of running more than one camera simultaneously is here retained; however, its purpose is no longer to focus on people in moral combat with their environment, but rather to locate what Kurosawa called "perfect objects to shoot" amidst the challenging Siberian landscape.

Thus *Dersu Uzala* is largely comprised of a series of static, though beautiful, shots of Siberia; it is as if we were viewing a slide show of splendid paintings, each more striking than the last, but ultimately leading nowhere. As in so many Japanese films, the railroad stands for raw technological progress and the decimation of the wilderness. In the last sequence as in the first, an unidentified train whistle implies where Kurosawa places the blame. The script is more explicit, labeling the "cold" railway a symbol of "the separation between the primitive and civilized worlds."

Yet *Dersu Uzala* contains some extraordinary images of the highest quality, including shots of a magnificent orange and black Siberian tiger brought from a zoo and photographed against a stark black background which makes the image appear, in the manner of William Blake, as if it existed outside of time and space. The image perfectly suits Dersu's sense of the tiger's supernatural meaning; it invokes awe, splendor, and the menace of nature. This symbolic value of the tiger is interpreted for us in a voice-over by Arseniev: "What Dersu calls 'amba' [tiger] . . . could it be the fear of unbearable solitude in the Taiga . . . a manifestation of the terror the wilds now held for him?" Kurosawa's use of the telephoto lens is at its best in these shots as the tiger twice slinks horizontally across the frame toward the camera and Dersu. In close-up the creature curls its lip in defiance and assertion of its prowess. In the best shot of the scene, Dersu and Arseniev are placed on each side with the tiger at the center. The success of the shot confirms André Bazin's insight that the integrity of an action is often broken by the cut and is realized only when all the elements can struggle together within the single shot. Later the tiger is silhouetted against Arseniev's tent. In the final close-up of the tiger, red light is superimposed, reflecting Dersu's awareness of the triumph the beast has wrought at his expense.

Equally magnificent is a montage of shots in which the bare branches of felled trees in Arseniev's camp appear as the arms of witches about to pull the men into the fire, recalling to Arseniev a painting he had once seen of the "Witches' Sabbath." In Part Two there is a parallel montage, which also depicts a night scene, accompanied by an eerie cacophony of noises as bells tinkle and rocks strike against the ice with the wind blowing more loudly than seems possible.

The blizzard sequence is the finest of all. Dersu and Arseniev are seen in long-shot as they attempt to locate the trail away from the lake, only to become lost. In a manner evocative of Monet, the camera stays on the scene as time passes and the day moves toward dusk. The colors change from blues to mauves and frosty purples and greens as Dersu and Arseniev hunt for the path to the dug-out. The two are shown in silhouette as they frantically cut the marsh grass in order to construct a shelter, on which their lives will depend, as the blizzard descends. Kurosawa cuts to a brilliant sun in an orange sky in contrast to the browns, grays, and blues of Dersu and Arseniev cutting grass as fast as they can. The sun begins to sink and is only one-quarter present when Arseniev falls over in exhaustion, leaving Dersu to complete the task alone.

The color and shot compositions of *Dersu Uzala* are extraordinary. A pond is filled with many-colored leaves. The autumn foliage is photographed three dimensionally in many shades of gold, tones that seem hitherto unknown to the human eye. Dusk is filled with mysteries of nature inaccessible to man. The richness of color as it permeates this desolate landscape indicates human smallness and insignificance before the power of the natural world. The men are dressed in browns and grays; nature, however, is ablaze with color.

In one overwhelming shot Dersu and Arseniev stand at the center with the sun to one side and the moon to the other, as if all of the nature were contained within the frame and the men were presented therein with whatever sustenance they required; there are no "civilizing" comforts alienating people from themselves and their own powers. In another scene they trudge along, the ground all gold and black; there is a deep tilt up to the bright sun, as deep as the stunning tilt in *Seven Samurai* during the ride preceding the raid on the bandits' den. In *Dersu Uzala* a full shot of the midnight sun hanging in a black sky expresses virtually by itself the meaning of the entire film. And when Dersu is finally rescued in the rapids scene, the water suddenly becomes very blue, as if delighting in his survival.

In still another wonderful shot Dersu sits forward performing the ceremonial ritual observance for his dead wife and children; the light plays upon his back in reds and blues as the moonlight divides his figure half in darkness, half in light. Images of fire punctuate *Dersu Uzala*, pinpoints of light in the darkness of the unknown territory of the Ussuri. Through the use of color alone Kurosawa conveys his personal perspective, finding meaning and pleasure only away from the sordid things of this world.

The shot compositions consistently place Arseniev as close to Dersu as possible. When his five loutish followers practice their marksmanship by

shooting at a bottle, Arseniev stands apart from them; when they play at blindman's buff like overgrown children, the more contemplative and serious Arseniev remains in his tent. In several shots Dersu and Arseniev stand side by side while the others are grouped around the campfire.

Sometimes the techniques suggest distilled versions of moments in earlier Kurosawa films. Some of his familiar camera work remains present, although unlike camera work in earlier films it does not illuminate a thematic personal struggle. The tilt up to the midnight sun is beautiful in itself but is finally static, paying homage once again to the magnificence of nature. Conflict arises only in the struggle between man and nature, as in the shots of Dersu and Arseniev cutting the marsh grass and rewarded when the darkened scenes of the raging storm give way to a sunny morning, nature all fresh and calm.

Much of the camera work of *Dersu Uzala* is thus concerned with merging man and nature, people and landscape, as if, as in the case of Dersu Uzala himself, these were truly one. Dersu is the film's hero by virtue of his ability to live in symbiosis with the natural world. In many frames we cannot even see the sky; the camera remains focused on the men as they trudge along, charting the unfamiliar. We perceive what the men themselves see—the earth itself, the uneven ground and the brambles that thwart them—rather than stunning panoramas that could only have been captured through a helicopter shot. From *Dersu Uzala* we tend to remember blood-red suns and silhouetted figures of men tentatively venturing forth on the land, or abstract shots like that in which Dersu and Arseniev look into the sun, a shot embodying Dersu's respect for the sun's power: "If he die one day, we all die."

Most unsatisfactory are the scenes—shot in a manner so uncharacteristic of Kurosawa—in Arseniev's Khabarovsk dwelling, where a confined Dersu unsuccessfully struggles with the shackles of civilized life. The shots look flat and barely two-dimensional; the rooms are small and without the contrasts of color that so enliven the outdoor scenes where Kurosawa is at his best. Arseniev and his wife, Anna, putter about from room to room. Their son sits like a puppet, enthralled by Dersu's tales. The entire sequence is faintly amateurish, which strongly suggests that Kurosawa left these scenes to be shot by his Russian assistant director. Even if this flatness was intentional and meant to express Dersu's discomfort in the stultifying city, it seems out of keeping with the rest of the *mise-en-scène*.

There are, however, some strikingly brilliant compositions even here. In one, the shot is bisected. On the right sit Dersu and little Vova on the floor against a light background, as Dersu gives the boy a bear tooth and the two communicate as only the pure and innocent can. On the left against a black ground are Arseniev and Anna, eavesdropping, shrouded in darkness even as they are alienated from nature. In another superb composition, Dersu occupies two-thirds of the shot, while Arseniev ascends the dark staircase almost in silhouette, only to return with a high-powered rifle, his final gift to Dersu.

The last shot of the film pictures only the makeshift grave of Dersu, with a stick marking the spot. The music comes on in choruses of homage making the ending so like the last moments of *Seven Samurai*, which conveyed the director's deep sorrow and nostalgia before the passing of a superior breed of men rendered obsolete by history. There we view only the four mounds of the dead samurai, mourned by the musical motif associated in that film with the warrior; likewise *Dersu Uzala* closes on the grave of the fallen hero, with the music a paean to his splendid character.

Kurosawa spent nearly four years on this project, two of which passed in grueling filming in the forty-below-zero Siberian weather. He referred to the making of this film as an "enormous military operation," and as always shot an enormous amount of film. But *Dersu Uzala* finally cost only about $4 million to make, a modest sum indeed given the exigencies of the filming.

Once again Kurosawa encountered post-production difficulties, although not in Japan, where *Dersu Uzala* did well (especially in Tokyo, where it played a respectable first run in a handsome Ginza theater). When twenty minutes were cut from this two hour and twenty minute film in Italy, Kurosawa angrily declared that the Soviets had lied in claiming that these cuts were made with his consent; he asserted that he would never again work with the Russians, who were guilty in his eyes of a lack of "sympathy for this great Soviet hero."

When a critic, absurdly, called the film a "Western"—a frequent and tiresome charge leveled not only against the Kurosawa *jidai-geki* (period-film), but also against many other Japanese films—Kurosawa replied, quite accurately, that in this film he was concerned with "the mystique of the Eastern world." Its theme of the devotion of an instinctive man to nature is indeed a very Japanese idea. One Japanese critic, Yikichi Shinada, has spoken of Kurosawa's arrival in *Dersu Uzala* at a new objectivity in which human beings exist as but one element in the universal scheme of things. This too is true. The most striking feature of *Dersu Uzala* may well be Kurosawa's newfound distance to be realized so much more magnificently in *Kagemusha*. The Kurosawa of *Dersu* and *Kagemusha* views men and nature in the calming perspective of the vastness of time. Aware of human alienation from the world, a scene of endless strife, he still seeks, if only in memory, the image of a unity between them.

# Kagemusha

During the five years following the completion of *Dersu Uzala* Kurosawa made no movies. The conditions within Japan that had forced him to make *Dersu Uzala* abroad continued and worsened. Toho, the company with which he had been longest associated, did not want to fund productions they knew would be expensive, nor did any of the other major companies. Costs had so risen in Japan that all the film companies wanted to be assured of large box-office returns from the beginning; but the earnings of both *Dodesukaden* and *Dersu Uzala* made large returns seem unlikely.

Though Kurosawa made no films during this period, he was not idle. He worked on the script for *Ran* (Chaos)—his version of *King Lear*—and on a project based on Poe's "Masque of the Red Death." He was also working with Masato Ide, a co-writer of the scenario for *Red Beard*, on the script that became *Kagemusha*. Of the three projects this last seemed the most likely to achieve completion. It would be a period-film, filled with action, like *Seven Samurai*; it would, like *The Throne of Blood*, continue the director's reflections on the nature of power and consequently war; yet, at the same time, it would be light—like *They Who Step on the Tiger's Tail* and *Yojimbo*, it would be an amusing film (it was written with the comic-actor Shintaro Katsu in mind) with serious implications. It is unlikely that Kurosawa thought of such parallels but, as the writing continued, he saw that the script was becoming more and more Kurosawa-like. When he and Ide were finished, they were convinced that they had drawn up a very interesting film.

However, Toho and the other major Japanese film companies were not convinced. Kurosawa went from door to door, as it were, only to be met with further refusals. There was no money in wealthy Japan for an expensive and problematical film of this sort. Nor were the Russians interested this time, even though *Dersu Uzala* had made money in Europe. *Kagemusha* would have to be made in Japan, and the Russian film industry, in effect the Russian government, had no experience in the foreign funding of films and no interest in pursuing such a project. Kurosawa himself had no money (and during this period he would do almost anything to make some: he even appeared in television commercials) and so filming was impossible. But he felt he could "make" the film in another form.

Having once been a commercial artist, he visualized every scene. Using conté crayon, gouache, water color, and *sumi*, he made hundreds of detailed drawings, planning the look of every shot and in the process de-

signing all the sets and costumes. Over the months the stacks of finished drawings grew and an ideal film—one that had never been photographed—emerged. Kurosawa says that during this period he was convinced that *Kagemusha* would never be made and that this vast series of drawings and paintings would be the only record of it. And in effect, they were to become the film.

One of the consequences was that when it was finally filmed *Kagemusha* was one of the most designed pictures ever made. Like *Ivan the Terrible* (a movie made under conditions somewhat similar to those surrounding Kurosawa's film), *Kagemusha* emerged with all its elements decided and coordinated in advance of the actual filming. After all, Kurosawa had intended the pictorial record to take the place of the unmade film.

In the meantime, however, he did not despair. His interest was kept alive in part by his work at the drawing table, and the pictures could also be used to interest and impress potential backers. In 1978 he went abroad, taking with him the translated script and his drawings. These he showed around the Continent, but to no avail. Then he went to America.

Here he found his backers. Francis Coppola and George Lucas, both successful film directors and both more than commonly interested in the films of other directors, had long admired Kurosawa. They thought of themselves as his students (Lucas said that the robot pair in *Star Wars* was based on the two peasants in *The Hidden Fortress*) and were shocked and distressed at Kurosawa's present plight. Since both had recently finished films that were commercially successful, they were in a good position to help Kurosawa. They approached Twentieth Century Fox (with whom Kurosawa had had the disastrous experience of *Tora! Tora! Tora!*) with a project for the partial funding of *Kagemusha*. The American company, in turn, approached Toho.

Toho, with the promise of a substantial amount of money ($1.5 million for all foreign rights for the finished film) decided that the project had become safe and agreed to cover the remainder of the costs. (The film eventually cost the equivalent of $6 million, making it the most expensive picture ever shot in Japan. It also grossed $10 million in the first-run circuit, making it one of the most financially successful Japanese films of 1980.) Kurosawa had finally found his backing and could begin the long-awaited production of *Kagemusha*.

# PRODUCTION

Of all the films of Kurosawa, the production of *Kagemusha* was the most disaster-ridden. That a film emerged at all is surprising; that it proved to be such a richly engrossing experience, such a Kurosawa-like entertainment, is evidence of the extraordinary will of the director.

Among the disasters was the sudden illness of Kazuo Miyagawa, the cameraman (perhaps Japan's finest), who had worked with Kurosawa on *Rashomon* and *Yojimbo*. They had already completed the elaborate color

tests required for this picture when Miyagawa's eyes began to fail due to diabetic complications. His place was taken by two cameramen—Takao Saito and Masaharu Ueda—and their work was supervised by Asakazu Nakai, a cameraman with whom Kurosawa had often worked.

Another disaster was the departure of Masaru Sato, the composer with whom Kurosawa had worked on most of his films since *Record of a Living Being*. Music was to play an important part in *Kagemusha* and Sato, a composer of note in his own right, had his own ideas. Kurosawa, as always, had *his* own. This time there was no accommodation. Sato left, giving "artistic incompatibility" as one of his reasons, and the finished film was scored by Shinichiro Ikebe, a composer who proved more tractable.

There were other disasters, some of them minor: Tatsuya Nakadai fell off his horse and was hospitalized; a typhoon interrupted production at a cost of $40 thousand a day. The major disaster, however, was the resignation—or firing—of the film's star.

Shinaro Katsu, known in the West mainly through his appearances as Zatoichi, the blind swordsman, was one of Japan's most popular actors. Though essentially a comedian, he was quite capable of serious drama, and brought to many films both his own dogged humanism and his own wry humor. *Kagemusha* had been written for him because both Kurosawa and Ide early thought that the main character—a distant cousin of Sanjuro in both *Yojimbo* and *Sanjuro*—could be played only by the lovable Katsu. Katsu, however, was not so lovable on the set. Here, for once, Kurosawa met with a determination as great and an ego as large as his own. What happened is now generally agreed upon, though there are various theories as to why it happened.

It occurred on the first day of shooting. Kurosawa, as usual, was using multiple cameras. Katsu arrived with his own television camera and his own crew. Kurosawa asked that Katsu's camera be removed because it would be within range of his own camera. Katsu said he needed it to document his performance to make certain he was doing a good job. Kurosawa said that he himself was the director and would tell Katsu whether he was doing a good job or not. Katsu said that as a responsible actor he must study his performance and therefore needed a television record. Kurosawa said that he was the director and what he said went. Katsu said that he was the star and ought to have his say. The conversation grew into an argument, grew more and more heated, and in the end Katsu quit or was fired, the conclusion depending on who is telling the story.

Both director and ex-star gave press interviews; both explained and defended their respective positions. Neither, however, explained why the break had occurred. Kurosawa and Katsu obviously needed each other. *Kagemusha* was written with Katsu in mind; Katsu himself entertained the ambition of becoming an international star, and this film would have been the ideal means to that end. The director later said that he realized that if Katsu was going to be this difficult on the first day of shooting, he would have grown quite impossible by the last day, that firing him was the only solution. Katsu gave no explanation as to why he was so difficult. It is possible that he engineered his own dismissal, that he was afraid of working for such a demanding director.

The result of the breakup between star and director nearly ruined the production. For a time it seemed once again that the film could not be made. There were searches for replacements and several candidates were found, but both Toho and Fox said that the actor had to be a star. This considerably narrowed the selection. Mifune would have been ideal (he had, after all, played the Sanjuro role in the earlier pictures) but he and Kurosawa had never mended fences broken during the filming of *Red Beard*, fifteen years before. More precisely, Kurosawa had for all those years refused to work again with Mifune.

This left but a single choice: Tatsuya Nakadai, a stage actor who had appeared in *Yojimbo*, *Sanjuro*, and *High and Low* and who, given the proper director and the proper film (notably Masaki Kobayashi and *Harakiri*), could turn in a very good screen performance. But Nakadai, though quite willing, was busy with stage performances, and the production of the film would have to accommodate itself to his schedule. This meant a wait of several months in an already tight schedule, but Kurosawa had no choice. He filled in the time by re-scouting locations and continuing to cast small parts in the picture.

Location scouting was a major project in *Kagemusha*—a picture set in sixteenth-century Japan, employing numerous castles and hundreds of extras and horses. In 1954 one could have shot a film like this almost anywhere in the country—all the locations for *Seven Samurai* were relatively close to Tokyo. By 1980, however, the entire country had so changed that such locations were not to be found. Highways, factories, and housing developments cover the lowlands, and even finding a stretch of land without high tension towers, electric lines, or television antennae is almost impossible. Consequently, finding a place to shoot the picture became a difficult and time-consuming process.

Kurosawa himself went to see all of the several dozen remaining castles. From these he selected a number and made various test shots, always shooting from a very low angle to avoid the modern clutter around their bastions. He then set out to find possible locations for the battle scenes. Finally he had to settle for the far northern island of Hokkaido, Japan's "frontier," the single place where nature in any large dimension remains.

The director's ideas for the casting of *Kagemusha* were innovative. His acting "unit," with Mifune at its head, had long broken up. Though

Kurosawa in this film used a number of actors he had formerly been associated with—Kamitari Fujiwara plays a small role, as does Takeshi Shimura (whose part, however, was cut from the international version of picture)—he mainly wanted to use new people. Thus, he chose actors with whom he had not formerly worked, including a number from the stage and from television. He also used amateurs, having long felt that with proper direction the non-professional can turn in the better performance. The important role of Tokugawa Ieyasu went to a complete amateur.

To obtain the number of extras needed for the film, Kurosawa had advertisements put into magazines and newpapers. The turnout was very large: thousands wanted to be in the new Kurosawa picture. From among these Kurosawa himself chose the hundreds he would use. Day after day he watched as these amateurs went through the simple drills arranged for them. The cast for *Kagemusha*, down to the last foot soldier, was hand-picked by the director.

When Nakadai became free, *Kagemusha* finally went into production. Despite this delay and the various other set-backs, Kurosawa and his staff managed to keep close to their tight and demanding schedule. The filming of the picture took in all about half a year. As usual, Kurosawa was rough-cutting the daily rushes and consequently was able to make the final cut of the film in just three weeks. The projected opening date of the picture was missed by only one week.

# THE STORY

The idea for *Kagemusha* came from a note in a history that Kurosawa was reading. Just as the idea for *Seven Samurai* was found when a history of sixteenth-century Japan mentioned that some peasants had hired samurai to defend them, so the idea for this new film was discovered when the director read that just before Japan's unification into a feudal state one of the lords, Takeda Shingen (1521–73), had apparently employed a double in order to confuse his enemies.

Before the unification Japan was ravaged by civil wars, and a number of independent war lords took advantage of these to advance their armies to the capital. Whoever ruled Kyoto, it was thought, would rule the country. The three major war lords, who controlled the various territories around the city, were Oda Nobunaga, Tokugawa Ieyasu, and Takeda Shingen. Their alliance, always uneasy, broke when Nobunaga and Ieyasu formed a new alliance against Shingen. In the resulting battles Takeda marched on one of Ieyasu's castles and he and his clan were exterminated. From this historical account and the footnote about Shingen's double, Ide and Kurosawa fashioned their film.

At the Takeda mansion it is already known that Ieyasu and Nobunaga have turned against Shingen. He (Tatsuya Nakadai) and his brother

Nobukado (Tsutomu Yamazaki) are conferring. Often in the past Nobukada has impersonated Shingen since they look somewhat alike. Now, however, he has found a condemned criminal (Tatsuya Nakadai in a double role) whose resemblance to the war lord is astonishing. Shingen wonders that a common thief could so closely resemble his august self. At this the thief suddenly speaks: "I stole only a few coins, a petty thief; you—you, you've killed hundreds, robbed whole domains, so who is worse, you or me?"

To this Shingen responds:

> I am as wicked as you believe. I am a scoundrel. I banished my father and killed my own son. I will do anything to rule over this land. War is everywhere and unless someone unifies the nation and reigns over it we will see more rivers of blood and more mountains of the dead.

Lord and double are thus confirmed in their identity. Not only do they look alike, they are also alike in that both are criminals. The lord, however, is criminal for a higher cause. This the double will come to realize. The opening scene of the film is the beginning of his education.

In the meantime the Takeda army has begun its siege of Noda Castle, one of the many belonging to Ieyasu. Shingen's advisors, Nobukada and Katsuyori (Shingen's son, played by Kenichi Hagiwara) hold council. Someone in Noda Castle has played the flute every night, a performance appreciated by the soldiers on both sides. Shingen decides that if the flute is not heard that night, the castle (now waterless since the aqueducts have been cut) will fall. He himself will sit on the ramparts and listen. That evening he is shot by a sniper from Noda Castle.

Both Ieyasu and Nobunaga learn of this and want to know if their rival is truly dead. Actually, Shingen has not yet died but is so badly wounded that his brother must continue to impersonate him in order to deceive these enemies. When Shingen finally expires the counselors are in a difficult position. News of the death, once known in their own camp, will reach the enemy.

At this point Nobukado brings forth the identical double, the condemned thief. They will thus deceive not only the enemy but also their own men. When the double, however, learns that his lord is dead, he refuses to continue with his part in the deception: "The lord is dead. I have no duty toward anyone else. . . . Suddenly all of this [impersonation] is meaningless."

The counselors remonstrate, but one of them finally says:

> He is right. He has nothing to do with the Takeda clan. It is selfish of us to make him solve our problems. The role is for someone who can die for the Takeda clan.

When he hears this (and again later when he fears that the spies of Nobunaga and Ieyasu will learn the truth), the double determines to help. He will go through with the impersonation. He had been impressed by the living lord, he wants to be like him, hence he will act like him. The education of the double continues—this is the first step toward the identification that will kill him but will also give a meaning to his life.

His is a very difficult assignment. He must fool not only the enemy but also everyone on the Takeda side who is associated with the lord. His first trial is Shingen's small grandson and heir. The boy at first flatly declares that this man is not his grandfather, but the double manages to convince him otherwise. The second trial comes when the double must meet the women of Shingen's harem, all of whom knew the lord intimately. He is ready to give up, indeed tells the women plainly that he is an impersonator. This, however, is taken as a witticism, and so once again the scheme is undetected.

As he continues his successful deception he becomes more and more like the late lord. And he comes to believe in his identity with the late lord. He believes that he truly is "The Mountain," as Shingen was known. The

reasons for this appellation are revealed by an attendant who, ostensibly instructing the little grandchild, also informs the double:

| | |
|---|---|
| *Attendant:* | You know the Master's banner. What do the letters mean? |
| *Grandchild:* | Swift as the wind, quiet as the forest, fierce as the fire, immovable as the mountain. |
| *Attendant:* | The lord is that mountain, both in battle and at home. He is steadfast, like a mountain. When his army moves, first come the horsemen, attacking as swiftly as the wind. Second, the lancers advance, quiet as the forest. Third, the cavalry raids, merciless as fire. And the lord is behind them always, immovable as a mountain. That is why our soldiers are strong. Immovable as a mountain. Our lord is this mountain. And that is why we call him The Mountain. |
| *Double:* | (*Who has been engrossed in this explanation*) Ah, I see. (*Then, recovering himself, turning to the grandson*) There, understand now, Takemaru? |

With the armies of both Nobunaga and Ieyasu advancing, the advisors hold a council of war. The double is carefully instructed in his role. All he has to do is endorse their views, thank them, and leave. He practices this role, but at the actual meeting Shingen's son Katsuyori (who knows well that the double is not his father but wants to enforce his rights as eldest son) turns directly to the impersonator and asks if he thinks they should attack or not. The double answers as he believes the dead lord would have: "Do not attack, do not move. A mountain does not move."

Furious, Katsuyori goes against the conclusions of the council and attacks Takatenjin Castle. The double and Shingen's forces follow and take part in the ensuing battle, which is won mainly through Shingen's supposed presence. The double sits through the battle like a mountain and his calm immobility inspires his men to victory.

The double is elated at his success, and in his efforts to truly become the late lord he attempts to ride a horse that only Shingen was ever able to ride. Though the double has misled the enemy, fooled Shingen's own men, and deceived the lord's grandson and wives, he cannot lie to the animal. He is thrown, and when he is examined for injuries two of Shingen's wives see that he does not have the familiar scars.

The secret is out. There is no longer any need for pretense. The Takeda soldiery now knows the truth, and shortly the spies of Nobunaga and Ieyasu will learn it. The double is given a small reward and is summarily dismissed. The counselors now realize that Lord Katsuyori is the master of the clan. He at once orders an attack, sends all his forces—wind, forest, fire—against those of Nobunaga and Ieyasu. Battalion after battalion is mowed down. The mountain has moved, says Nobunaga; Takeda will be no more, says Ieyasu.

Into this carnage wanders the double, witnessing with horror the destruction of those he had come to love, the ruin of everything he had learned to esteem. Retrieving a banner, the double advances into the line of fire and is shot. He turns, sees the clan flag floating in the river, tries to reach it, and dies.

# TREATMENT

As is apparent from the story, this film—like so many of Kurosawa's —is about reality and appearances, their differences and their eventual identity. Shingen's double must create the illusion of Shingen himself. He must, as he is often advised, "become" him. At the end of the film he has truly become him, and this he proves through his death.

We are prepared for the presentation of this theme by a pre-credit opening scene, a single shot that is six minutes long—the longest single shot in all of Kurosawa's films. In it, Shingen occupies the middle of the frame; his brother, dressed identically since he often impersonates the lord, is on the left; and the thief, dressed as the other two so that his resemblance to the lord will be demonstrated, is on the right. (Both Shingen and the double are played by Nakadai; the split-screen shot is extremely artful.) While the image shows the similarities between reality and illusion, the dialogue during this scene underlines the differences. In this opening scene Kurosawa states the theorem he will demonstrate in the course of the film and fore-shadows the results he will present at the end (the reality and illusion are one).

This major theme (reality/illusion, differences/similarities) is given in many variations throughout the picture. For example, when the double is taught what to reply at the final meeting of the council, he practices it for us and demonstrates what the illusion is; at the actual meeting, however, his "son" asks a direct question that makes the reality entirely different from the illusion. And after Shingen has been shot by the sniper, the real event is re-created (for the benefit of Ieyasu, but also for the benefit of the viewer) so as to illustrate how, through what "illusion," it was made real: we are shown the shooting, but this time a small pine tree is the target. This brief scene does nothing to further the story, to advance the plot; it is there precisely because it demonstrates the controlling theorem of the film. (During the editing of the international version of *Kagemusha* it was suggested that this scene be cut. Kurosawa was adamant in his refusal.)

At the same time that the differences between illusion and reality are being shown, their eventual identity is being stated. It begins when the double, reverting to his thieving habits, finds a large jar in the castle store-room. Believing it contains a treasure, he breaks it open and discovers instead the preserved and lacquered body of the dead Shingen. Illusion and reality are face to face. Caught in the act, the double is told that "this role is for someone who can die for the Takeda clan." He is thus dismissed, but having seen the reality of the death of the lord, he now begins to under-stand that he can really be Shingen. This meaning is underlined in the final shot of the sequence. The jar is large in the right foreground, the kneeling

double is small in the right background; he is staring at the cask and we know (from prior dialogue) what he is thinking. He is becoming one with the dead lord. In the next sequence we see him saying: "Make use of me. I want to be of some use to him."

The reasons for which the double must become the lord are given in a later scene where the late lord's brother, and former impersonator, is talking:

*Nobukado:* I know it is difficult. I was for a long time the lord's double. It was torture. It is not easy to so suppress yourself, to become another. Often I wanted to be myself, to be free. But now I think that this was selfish of me. Still, the shadow of a man can never desert that man. I was my brother's shadow. Now that I have lost him . . . it is as though I am nothing.

Later, after the double has been reinstated and is successfully continuing the impersonation, Nobukado says of him:

Even though he is tough, it must be torture. Yet, he is trying so hard. . . . It is because he saw the late lord once and was impressed. That last sight of our lord touched his heart. He is sincere by nature. I am sorry for him.

The double *is* sincere, probably, but his reasons for so completely taking on the persona of the late lord are different from what Nobukado believes. The impersonator does not simply want to be like the lord, he is trying to actually be him, a fact his death proves. The identity of illusion to reality is emerging. This can be seen in a shot where the double, having met Shingen's wives and having successfully (if inadvertently) convinced them that he is real, leaves the banquet room. As he passes we watch his shadow (the shot is from a low angle, the camera looking upward), and the shadow on the ceiling is that of the late lord himself.

Another indication of eventual identity (there are many in the film) is the creative use to which Kurosawa puts one of his directorial mannerisms. Characters in his films are often given habitual actions that serve as identification badges—the thief scratching himself in *The Lower Depths*, Sanjuro picking his teeth in *Yojimbo*. In *Kagemusha* the lord has a similar motion—stroking his moustache, slowly, reflectively, always on the right side. We see this often enough to associate it with the lord, and after he is dead we see the double cultivating the same mannerism. This gesture be-comes more and more his, and there comes a moment in the middle of the film when it has such a powerful, authentic effect that his attendants (who know that he is merely an impostor) are reduced to silence and tears: illusion has become reality.

Only we, the spectators, see this; others are kept in ignorance. At the end, indeed, no one in the film is alive to witness the final apotheosis of imper-sonator into lord, of the illusionary into the real. And during the process no one besides the audience is allowed to comprehend it—not even Nobukado and the rest of the counselors. Even less comprehending are the various spies used by Nobunaga and Ieyasu. They run about, speculating (like the

other choruses Kurosawa has used—the newspaper reporters in *The Bad Sleep Well*, for example), unable to tell illusion from reality, much less understand that they are identical.

(The only intelligence within the film that can distinguish illusion from reality is the horse. The grandchild instinctively told them apart but was soon seduced by adult reason. Two of the wives sensed discrepancies but were fooled by the more sophisticated assumption that a pleasantry was involved. Only the horse is not fooled. The animal—a very Kurosawa-like touch—simply *knows*. It knows that the impersonator is not the lord. However, it does not know, as we will, that the impersonator becomes him.)

Though Kurosawa often explores dichotomies—usually the appearance/reality dichotomy, as here—almost never has he treated his theme so rigorously or so fully resolved it as in *Kagemusha*. Though always a rigorous director, he has heretofore at least partially hidden his theme, usually in the interests of a realistic (that is, likely) presentation. In *Rashomon*, for example, the appearance/reality theme is more hinted at than shown; the film is also about a rape and a murder. In *Kagemusha*, the film is exclusively about the theme, it *is* the theme.

An indication of this is the way in which the scenes are shot, and also the way in which they are linked. Both are extraordinarily laconic. For example, after the double is thrown from the horse, the next scene illu-

210

strates in the simplest and most straightforward fashion what happens next. It is raining (and how often in Kurosawa's films has rain come to mean resolution) and the camera is on the low veranda from which it recorded the discovery of the double's identity. Now we see the double being led bareheaded through the rain, away from the camera, toward the gate. He is being dismissed. At the same time, the new heir, Katsuyori, shielded by a large umbrella, moves toward the camera, away from the gate. The scene reflects the theme in a double sense. The camera position must remind us of the disclosure of the double; and there he goes, out into the rain and the cold world, disclosed: there goes appearance, illusion. Coming toward us, assuming a new importance with every step, is the new reality—the new lord of the Takeda clan. Since this is accomplished only in one shot, within which all the necessary action occurs (without cutting), the effect is one of flat finality. The theme is being illustrated as much as is the story, and it occurs to us—or more precisely, we are shown—that they are identical.

Another example is the several sequences of small scenes that indicate and presage this debacle. Early in the picture we see the double successfully impersonating the lord. A small scene depicting his satisfaction is followed by a brief shot, apparently unmotivated, of the horse. Shortly thereafter is another scene in which the character of the horse, its difficult temperament, is discussed. The sequence shows that the prowess of the double is an illusion and presages (through the shot of the difficult horse) that reality will soon impinge on that illusion. Later in the film the double is in fact thrown by the horse. We do not see the actual fall. Instead we are shown a small commotion in the distance and then, in the next shot, the double being carried to the veranda, where the disclosure then takes place. This scene is followed by a shot of the horse, now in its stable, contentedly eating from its manger. Here we are shown the two elements of the previous sequence, but the effect is quite different. The fall was real and it resulted in disaster: cause and effect; illusion and appearance have vanished. When, in the next sequence the impostor is led through the rain out of the gate, illusion is symbolically expelled. (And we are prepared for the final turn of the theme: the battle sequence showing us that what we have here accepted as reality—as we have been led to accept it—is merely appearance; the double reveals himself as truly the lord.)

One of the reasons that the theme becomes so plainly the film—and that it is allowed to do so—is that in this picture Kurosawa is no longer interested in the realistic, the likely, the world of everyday appearances. As already noted, the production was from the beginning one of the most controlled. Costumes, sets, color—all were decided in advance of the filming and, I suspect, without too much regard for historical accuracy. The result is that, even more than in *The Throne of Blood*, Kurosawa presents us with an alternate world, one thought out in every detail, but having little contact with our own world. Again one thinks of *Ivan the Terrible*.

One also thinks of opera. The film is composed of arias, big set-pieces. It is not music-drama of a seamless quality, like Wagner; it is made of segments, like Verdi. The slow opening trio of the three principals is

followed by the fast stretto of the soldier coming to announce the cutting of the aqueducts, and this is followed by the first act's leisurely opening chorus of the counselors; and so forth. Tempo is used for contrast, slow alternates with fast: just before the first battle-piece is a sequence of serene beauty (the soldiers listening to the enemy flute recital), and after the fury of the final battle comes the extraordinary slow-motion coda of the carnage it has caused. Realism in its usual sense—that of being likely—is nowhere, with the correlation that there seems no likelihood, no way out, that things are somehow foreordained. As appearance slowly gives way to reality, that reality progressively takes on the aspect of fate (*La Forza del Destino*), of doom.

The construction of the film is economical and rigorous to a degree rare in cinema. As in a good opera libretto, everything is sacrificed to the theme; that is, all elements go into explicating and enriching the theme. That seems to be the single duty of the camera in this film. In *The Throne of Blood* the scene in which the cutting down of the forest fills the palace with birds is a "useless" but exhilarating passage; in *Kagemusha* the equally lyrical scene of the soldiers listening to the flute is made "useful" in a way that further closes the film and boxes it in, that contributes to its extraordinary economy, its single-mindedness, its exclusion of all that is not necessary.

The differences between *Kagemusha* and the preceding films are perhaps best exemplified by the final reel—the destruction of the Takeda clan. Compared with, for example, the final reel of *Seven Samurai*—a film made twenty-five years before—though there are some similarities (almost no dialogue, lots of action, the assumption that swords are good and guns are bad), it is the differences that impress. *Seven Samurai* is an intensely realistic film. Consequently, in the final battle sequence everything is shown.

Though there are a definite number of attacks and a definite number of repulsions, we quickly lose track of the number—we are not interested in it. Rather, we are carried away by sheer action. The camera seems to be everywhere, shooting everything. From this chaos is formed the final (empty) victory.

The final reel of *Kagemusha* is by comparison extremely structured. There are only a few camera positions, and the battle itself is made up of very few elements. First, there is the long line of the defenses of Nobunaga and Ieyasu, miles of posts behind which their gunners shoot, a palisade against the sea. Second, there is the plain in front of this from which the

Takeda army will attack. Third, there is the small hill where Katsuyori and the counselors sit and from which the attacks are signaled. These are the geographical centers of the sequence.

The way in which these are shown is equally restricted. Once the battle begins the enemy forces are never shown. We see only the long horizontal line of posts and the sporadic bursts of gun-fire. The enemy becomes as anonymous as does the German line in the sequence of the battle on ice in *Alexander Nevsky*, a film Kurosawa knew but had not thought particularly well of before *Kagemusha*. Katsuyori and the counselors are seen always from the same angle. The attacking waves of Takeda soldiery and cavalry are shown through dolly shots with an occasional close-up. The editing too is simplified. There is no fast cutting in the manner of *Seven Samurai*, and though scenes are not, of course, of equal length, they all seem to have the same value.

The battle sequence is a basic pattern of actions, namely:

1. The Takeda force enters the field. Details of its advance.
2. The enemy force (the row of posts in the distance); firing; bursts of smoke.
3. The reaction (alarm, dismay) of the Takeda post.

This pattern repeats three times, as each of the three groups of Takeda fighters enters the field. First are the horsemen, no longer swift as the wind—all are killed. Second are the lancers, no longer quiet as the forest—all are killed. Third is the cavalry, no longer merciless as fire—all are killed. Each attack has its own shot of the firing enemy; each has its shot of the Takeda counselors further confounded. In each of these latter shots we see the lord, the gesticulating Katsuyori, certainly no longer immobile as a mountain.

One of the qualities of this long final sequence is that since it is the enemy who is responsible for all the action, we see only the *reaction*. Even when the double himself comes on the scene to watch the slaughter, we see only his reaction. The effect is one of helplessness, a holocaust that must be endured, with no hope of action. The distant smoke-filled palisade is implacable. The Takeda forces are, precisely, doomed.

After this highly structured, even schematic sequence, comes a very long coda (the latter half of which was cut from the international version) consisting of details in slow-motion of the battlefield: writhing wounded horses, crawling soldiers, dead soldiers. Since we have seen nothing of the actual carnage until this point (we have only heard the screams of horses and soldiers during the palisade shots and inferred that men and animals were being slaughtered), the effect is considerable. We see—or rather, experience—the devastation for the first time. We have not believed in it (that is, it has not become real) until now. This then—and not the excite-

ment and glory of *Seven Samurai* (excepting the final sequence)—is the reality of war. Pain, death, annihilation.

*Kagemusha* alone, of all Kurosawa's films, holds out no hope. It is a self-conscious, noble, and hopeless picture. Heretofore if the hero kept on trying he would succeed; here he keeps on trying and fails. Adding to (and helping to create) this feeling is a closed, self-centered structure that states only its theorem—which is its essence—and has no room for useless but aerating scenes; a structure in which all the parts are driven to an inexorable end.

It is a very impressive film (despite the inadequacies: much bad acting from both the stage actors—including Nakadai—and the television actors, and an overly portentous score for which Kurosawa must take full blame), but one far removed from the original conception. The reasoned lightness of *Yojimbo* vanished along with Shintaro Katsu; we have instead the reasoned weight of *The Throne of Blood* pushed to an even higher pitch.

Though there are surprising, even diverting, scenes in the film (the beautiful scenes by the lake at Suwa Castle, for example, and the scene in which Nobunaga expresses his anger through a Noh poem), the feeling is mainly one of the inexorable. The picture is a supremely beautiful juggernaut, crushing its characters, eventually obliterating even itself. It is also (fittingly) the coldest of Kurosawa's films—many degrees lower even than *Record of a Living Being* and *The Throne of Blood*. The emotional deep-freeze manifest in this film is partially due to the great visual control exercized, partially to the miscast Nakadai, and partially to the rigidity of the script, with all emotions kept at a distance. In the main, however, perhaps the extraordinary coldness is due to the philosophical implication that all warmth is illusion; reality, eternity, and death are all cold.

*Kagemusha* emerges as an unsparingly bleak statement, a profoundly pessimistic view so powerfully imagined that for a time (until comforting illusion, once we are out of the theater, is sought) it is believed. Kurosawa's "humanism" has grown to include the true human condition.

# Ran

## 1985

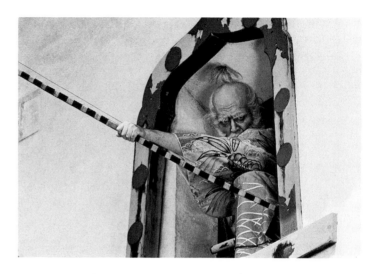

Again, there was a period of five years between films. After completing *Kagemusha,* Kurosawa returned to the script for *Ran,* on which he had been working for a decade. And, again, having completed it, he could find no money to make it. And so, once more, Kurosawa went looking for funds. It was going to be an expensive film to make (eventually it cost the equivalent of $12 million and took nearly a year to shoot), so money was difficult to find. Eventually, however, Masatoshi Hara (of Herald Ace Productions) agreed to provide part of the money and Serge Silberman (of Greenwich Film Productions) agreed to provide the rest.

The seventy-three-year-old Kurosawa, who had by this time almost lost hope of being able to make the film at all, announced himself particularly pleased because its production "would round out my life's work in film. I will put all of my remaining energy into it." When asked what his best film was, instead of answering "the next," as he usually did, Kurosawa simply said, *"Ran."*

Most of the preproduction work on the picture had long been done. As with *Kagemusha,* Kurosawa had had years to illustrate every action, color coordinate every detail. Again there were sheafs of drawings and piles of paintings for the art department to copy.

Production conditions were also much like those of *Kagemusha.* When this was remarked on, Kurosawa readily affirmed the similarity, even stating that while shooting *Kagemusha,* he had *Ran* in mind all along. However, though the earlier film may have been thought a "dry run," there were, he said, a number of differences. One that Kurosawa particularly mentioned was that if *Kagemusha* could be described as a series of events viewed by a single individual, then *Ran* would be a series of equally human events as viewed from heaven. The plot of this bird's-eye view was that of Shakespeare's *King Lear,* more or less Japanized by the addition of bits of Japanese history.

## THE STORY

After a successful boar hunt, the warlord Hidetora Ichimonji and his three sons and their guests—the neighboring lords Fujimaki and Ayabe—stop for a rest. The aged Hidetora, now seventy, falls asleep and has a frightening dream. This resolves him to take care of his affairs. He turns the main castle over to his eldest son, Taro, keeping for himself only a handful of retainers and the titles and forms of lordship. The second and third castles will go to his second and third sons, Jiro and Saburo.

He then gives them an object lesson in cooperation. Taking three arrows, he easily breaks each. But he then demonstrates that if one puts three arrows together, they cannot be broken. "You can break a single arrow," he tells his sons, "but not these held together. Just so, even if mishap befalls, if you stand together, this land remains secure."

Saburo, the youngest son, is disturbed that his father has so rashly given up his empire and does not trust his elder brothers. So he takes the bundle of arrows and breaks them over his knee. Hidetora, however, does not see this as proof of filial fidelity. He flies into a rage and banishes the loyal son.

Upon the return to the main castle, more quarrels break out. Lord Taro's wife, the Lady Kaede, leads her husband to complain about Hidetora's retainers and about the fact that he is not being allowed the proper titles and forms of lordship. Her motive for fomenting this disorder is that Hidetora murdered her father and brothers. And it was in this very castle that her mother committed suicide. When the discontented couple asks for a pledge—in blood—Hidetora angrily leaves the castle, determined to seek help from his second son.

Again, however, he is disappointed. Lord Jiro has already been instructed by his elder brother. He may welcome his father, but he cannot lodge his retainers. Jiro's wife, Sué, would have allowed Hidetora to stay, for in Buddhist fashion she has long forgiven Hidetora the violence he did her family, but she has no influence with her husband. So the aged warlord quits the second castle, once again furious, shouting that Jiro is no better than Taro and wishing them both ill.

At the third castle, they are allowed entry by the official in charge (for Lord Saburo, banished, is with Lord Fujimaki) because they have nowhere else to go. Indeed, they cannot even live in the villages since Lord Taro has by now officially banished Hidetora and warned the peasantry not to feed him or his party upon pain of death.

Shortly the armies of Taro and Jiro arrive at the third castle and a siege begins. It ends with the firing and destruction of the edifice and a battle during which most of the defenders are killed. In addition, Lord Taro also meets his end—murdered, it later turns out, by one of Jiro's agents.

The horrors of the destruction have rendered Hidetora mad, and he and his few remaining retainers, including his "fool," Kyoami, escape into the wilderness where they wander about until they find a small and seemingly abandoned hut. Here they discover a young blind man. This is Tsurumaru, the younger brother of the Lady Sué, blinded as a child by Hidetora, who also killed his father and burned

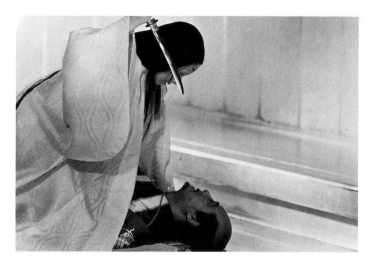

the family castle. Like his sister, Tsurumaru has embraced Buddhism and so forgives the warlord. He even plays his flute—his only remaining solace—to compensate for not being able to offer the wandering party proper hospitality.

Meanwhile, back at the first castle, Lord Jiro has come to announce the death of her lord to the widow. He is very shortly entangled by her wiles. She insists that he now take her for a wife, since he took her husband's life. He refuses, saying he already has a wife. She then demands the head of this unfortunate spouse, the Lady Sué.

In the meantime, Lord Saburo has come to the rescue of his homeless father. Lord Jiro, hearing of this, does not want to fight, but the Lady Kaede insists. Intent on her plan to kill all those who wronged her family, she insists that he murder his father and that to do so, he use his younger brother as unwitting guide.

Hidetora and Kyoami, now his sole retainer, have reached the remains of the Ozusa Castle, the ancestral home of Sué and Tsurumaru which the warlord himself burned years before. At the same time, Lord Ayabe sees this as a good time to take the land by force. There are thus three armies on the march: Lord Jiro's, Fujimaki's, led by Lord Saburo, and Ayabe's.

Saburo finds his father crazed, but the parent recovers his reason sufficiently to recognize his loyal son. During the retreat, however, Lord Saburo is shot and Hidetora again lapses into madness.

The Lady Sué is beheaded on Kaede's orders, but soon Kaede is herself stabbed to death by one of Jiro's loyal agents. During the tremendous battle that follows, Ayabe's men take the main castle and Jiro and his followers die.

Tsurumaru, alone, stands lost in the ruins of the castle as the daylight fades. The last word in the printed script of *Ran* is a single description: "Wretchedness."

And wretched those remaining are. *Ran* means, literally, "turmoil"

or "chaos," though when used as a suffix it can also mean "rebellion." It was perhaps a combination of these meanings that appealed to the director. He was filming a story about sons rebelling against their father, and he was illustrating a time when all social values were in a state of chaos.

The main inspiration for *Ran* was *King Lear,* and there are many similarities. Lear had three daughters, only the youngest of whom showed parental fidelity. Shakespeare has Gloucester; Kurosawa has Tsurumaru. Lear has his fool, and Hidetora has Kyoami; Cordelia dies, and so does Saburo. There are also a heath and complaints about both the cold and excessively noisy servants.

Though there are Japanese elements in the film (the incident of the three arrows, for example, is taken from a historical account), it is the Lear story that provides the narrative for the film. At the same time, however, this story—as with *Macbeth,* the basis for *The Throne of Blood*—is simplified, reduced to its single element, made into the vehicle for a single statement.

As the late critic Alan Booth has written: "The tragic force of Shakespeare's play is concentrated in the intense inward turmoil of Lear himself. It is symbolized dramatically by a storm and by an unhinged mind, and the effect of this turmoil, both on the man who experiences it on the stage and on the audience who experience it by proxy, is cathartic.

"Kurosawa's film, by contrast, is a parable of social behaviour: didactic, not cathartic. It leaves its audience, intentionally or not, with the feeling that they have had a moral truth neatly illustrated for them, but have themselves experienced none of the agony which racks the empathetic witness to *Lear.*"

This limited effect is certainly present in the film, but it is there because it is intended. As Booth adds, "If, finally, we are left immensely but comparatively unmoved by *Ran,* it is because *Lear* has taught us the potential in those stakes which Kurosawa chose not to play for."

Indeed, Kurosawa's concerns are quite different from those of Shakespeare in this film (close though they may have come in *The Throne of Blood*), and the means through which he realizes them are different. Empathy and catharsis are not Kurosawa's concerns. What he intends is something different.

"Kurosawa's greatness," the Shakespearean scholar Jan Kott has written, "lies in his capacity to reveal historical similarity and variance; to find a Shakespearean sense of doom in other, remote, and apparently alien historical places. . . . The further the 'other' setting is, the less likely it is that the image will match the text. It stops being an illustration and becomes its essence and its sign. . . . And here lies Kurosawa's genius and the singularity of his Shakespeare. The theater he makes use of is, of course, classic Japanese theater."

Kurosawa's "other" is the Noh drama, and *Lear* is seen through its accoutrements. The influence of this classical drama experienced in *The Throne of Blood* and in *Kagemusha* is even more visible in *Ran*. The visuals are often Noh-like. The costumes, for example, are, like those of the Noh, particularly and ostentatiously gorgeous. They are used as gesture—the many long-sleeved arm movements, the massive bulk, the bringing of custom into story, as when the Lady Kaede rips her kimono.

There is also much use of Noh-like hats, the strings of which tie tightly under the chin and make the face resemble a mask. Tsurumaru, with his long hair, is gotten up to resemble that classic Noh figure, the madwoman. And Hidetora's face turns into a Noh mask for the latter part of the picture. During the burning of the castle, each succeeding cut finds the makeup deepening until at the end the actor is "wearing" a known Noh mask, that of the old man who has, presumably, seen life.

Likewise, the sound track carries much that is Noh-like. There are the various stompings of the characters, there is the sound of the Lady Kaede's silks sliding across the polished wooden floors (a detail also noticed in *The Throne of Blood*), and there is the music.

The first thing we hear in the film is the Noh *fué,* that piercing, plaintive flute that we will later associate with Tsurumaru—a sound that will conclude the film as well and contribute much to its poignancy. There is also composer Toru Takemitsu's masterly pastiche of Noh music itself, the percussive sounds and—more—the irregular silences between them.

Also, the composition of the various scenes—their symmetry, assymmetry—are reminiscent of the Noh, a theater in which grouping is always formal. It is this formality of presentation common to all Noh dramas that informs the various compositions of *Ran*. The random-appearing compositions of earlier films are rarely seen, as indeed is "realistic" patterning of any kind. The acting is Noh-like in that it tends to be stately, formal, hieratic. There is, of course, much more passion (and much more overacting) than is common in the Noh, but there is, at the same time, a very Noh-like sense of presentation.

# TREATMENT

In the films following *Red Beard,* Kurosawa became increasingly interested in a presentation that was highly structured, even schematic, in that this structure became highly visible. The interest was not new. It had always been there but had been obscured by the director's greater interest in the realistic world, the world of appearances. *Sanjuro,* for example, may pick his teeth in *Yojimbo,* and this repeated detail indeed "structures" his personality, but this action is also accommodated by the realistic style of the film. One does not remark on it, or find it "unnatural." Hidetora, however, is himself but the accumulation of his various gestures, and there is nothing, no realistic context, to give them anything other than their nominal value. He becomes a visible idea rather than a believable person.

In the same way, though the structure of *Seven Samurai* (and other of the earlier films) may turn schematic (the map the samurai draw is seen as schema for subsequent action), the effect is softened and rendered less apparent by the realistic context. The map, for example, is there for the use of the samurai. It is only secondarily of any use to us.

In the later films, however, those made after *Red Beard,* the structure becomes more apparent and is less softened by any of the ordinary considerations of realism. Among these, *Ran* is the most apparently structured, the most openly schematic. This is seen in the opening sequence. The script describes the scene as "a three-forked road—two split to the right and to the left, toward the mountains on either side, . . . the other leads to the great expanse of the plain below." Just as there are three sons, three castles, three arrows, so there are three roads leading to the final three contending forces: the castles of Fujimaki, Ayabe, and Hidetora himself.

The warlords and their followers are in a subsequent scene seated in a circle. This is the first and last such composition we will see in this picture because what it symbolizes (and demonstrates), the quality of wholeness, completion, and, by extension, peace, will soon vanish from the film. This circle, soon to be broken, will never re-form. All further compositions must therefore be broken.

The form these compositions will take is presaged by the entertainment that Kyoami offers the seated party. It is a Kyogen song about a rabbit coming from afar. "From that far mountain," he sings, indicating those at one side, and "from those far mountains," indicating the other. The camera follows his gestures, and a precedent for opposing compositions is established.

Sure enough, when Saburo is banished and we see him on the road with Fujimaki, the composition consists of a pair, two horses and two men, each occupying its half of the screen, each facing away from the other. The composition is so arranged, so "unnatural" if you will, that it obviously exists to be read, and it can be read in only one way. Composition has become metaphor.

During the remainder of the film, there are so many of these metaphorical compositions that it would be wearying to list all of them. One might, however, describe the most powerful. Lord Taro and the Lady Kaede are visited by the irascible Hidetora. They are seated symmetrically on the left and the right side of the screen. In the middle is an empty mat. There is where Hidetora will sit. When he does so, we see that an obvious triangle has been formed. A triangle is a geometrical figure on its way to becoming a circle. Thus, if the fight had not continued, if Hidetora had not left his place and stormed out of the castle, peace and not war might have been one of the results.

Metaphor, one thing being described in terms of another, abounds in this film. The dialogue is full of it. Kyoami's song about the rabbit is understood (by Saburo, at any rate) as referring to the two neighboring mountain lords looking for something to eat on the plain below. Earlier, mentioning the recently slain boar, Taro wants to know if they are going to cook it. Hidetora glares at him and says, "That was an old boar. Its meat is tough—hardly edible." Then, revealing the metaphoric intent: "Just like me—Hidetora." Then, perhaps underlining a suspicion shortly to be revealed as valid: "Could you eat me?"

The script itself contains (rarely for a Kurosawa screenplay) many metaphors. The destruction-of-the-castle sequence is thick with them. A retainer staggers out "like someone running in a dream," the spear carriers rush "like an avalanche," Hidetora runs "like a madman," blood "runs like a river," and so on. There are also a large number of metaphorical actions. To mention but two, Hidetora loses his sword just when he loses his self (that is, becomes mad), and Jiro kicks the dead Taro's helmet aside as he is about to make love to the wife of the deceased.

In addition, all nature is regulated so that it may comment in a direct or a metaphorical manner on the domestic tragedy of Hidetora. A cut of the sun is followed at once by Hidetora, out under it, bleached to whiteness. Or bright sunlight is followed by dark fog, Hidetora lost in the midst of it. And there are more sunsets (representing the end of the world) in *Ran* than in any other film I can think of.

As Jan Kott has noted, the images of *Ran* indeed do not "illus-trate" the story. The film is not a realistic rendition or illustration of the Lear story, nor was it intended to be. Rather (again, Kott's terminology), the images become the "essence," the "sign." They do not illustrate the story, they *are* the story. And when these images might on their own enforce too much empathy, or too much illustration, they are subverted so that their true functions become paramount.

An example is the destruction of the castle and the massacre of its inhabitants. There is a vast amount of carnage, violence, spilled blood, and many startling details—arrow-spitted soldiers, a man holding his own severed arm, raped chambermaids. Lest, however, the sheer power of these small anecdotes detract from Kurosawa's grand theme, he undercuts them.

While the action is at its most furious, the music is at its grandest and its slowest. (Mahler's first symphony was the model the director insisted on.) The score makes a general comment on these particulars we are witnessing. And then, when the results of the carnage are viewed at length, all sound is suppressed—as though (another generalization) silence alone is fitting comment for such general misery. It is only with the report of the gun (which kills Taro) that sound is again permitted.

Kurosawa has previously used music (the "opposite" themes in *Drunken Angel,* for example) and silence (Watanabe's walk in the opening scenes of *Ikiru,* for example) in this manner but always with something specific in mind. Indeed, as we have seen, one of his qualities as a director has been an insistence on the specific rather than the general. Now, however, the grand overview that constitutes *Ran* demands a vast generalization. The Mahleresque music speaks of the misery of all people, the hopelessness of the human state. The following silence is no less eloquent a generalization. That this kind of open manipulation violates realistic canons can be seen as no criticism since Kurosawa has here so purposefully left realism (as one of many viable styles) far behind.

There is indeed in *Ran* very little pretense that we are seeing something "real," that any kind of reality other than the reality of the director's conscious intent is visible. We are to view not through the camera lens but through the inner eye of the creator. This extreme view is to become ours.

This is very near expressionism (in J. A. Cuddon's definition, an attempt "to avoid the representation of external reality and, instead, to present . . . a highly personal vision of the world"). And it is a style seen before in Kurosawa's earlier films: the short dream sequence in *Drunken Angel,* the long dream sequence in *Kagemusha.*

In *Ran,* the expressionist intent is so apparent that one thinks of that supreme expressionist form built on grand didactic generalities: the oratorio. *Ran* too has soloists, a chorus, and seems at times almost a concert performance rather than one fully staged. Its elevated subject aims to give not (only) pleasure but also instruction.

Like *Ivan the Terrible,* a film it much resembles, *Ran* can be seen as one long lesson.

It is a picture with a message, and this message is supported by didactic dialogue. Here is a sample from the end of the film. The bereaved Kyoami and Tango, a lord friendly to Saburo, are talking:

*Kyoami:* Oh, there is no Buddha in the world? Buddha, hear me. Are you so bored up in heaven that you enjoy watching men die down here? Is it amusing to hear them cry?

*Tango:* Enough! Do not slander the Buddha. It is he who is crying. Men—they are so stupid that they believe that survival depends upon killing. No, not even the Buddha can save us. Don't cry anymore. This is as it is. Men seek sorrow, not happiness. They prefer suffering to peace.

Since this is the last real dialogue in the film, it may stand as Kurosawa's "message." And we recognize it. It is the "people-are-no-damn-good" text that occurs in *Rashomon* and *The Bad Sleep Well* and other films. It has, however, been until now softened and qualified; note, for example, the end of *Rashomon* and its famously facile baby through which the film contrives an optimistic ending for itself. In *Ran,* there is no baby, and dialogue such as the above ensures a pessimistic ending. One can but ask oneself whether it is equally facile.

(It is interesting, if irrelevant, to read *Ran* as autobiography. Hidetora is seventy years old, and so was Kurosawa when he began writing the script. Also, like his hero, the director wandered many a heath in his efforts to find shelter—from Mosfilm to Twentieth Century-Fox. Too, like Hidetora/Lear, he experienced a number of serious emotional crises both before and during the filming. He lost two of his most valued assistants: Fumio Yano, his sound engineer, and Tatsu Kuze, the veteran expert of staged sword fights. In addition, Asakazu Nakai, his longtime cameraman, was seriously ill and would die several years later, in 1988. Finally, Kurosawa's wife, Kyo, suffering from terminal cancer, died during the shooting of the film, which was suspended for but one day for her funeral. There are many other similarities between director and his leading character. He may not have had anyone to whom to leave his empire, but he knew how to banish a filial son—Toshiro Mifune.)

In the final scene of the film, the blind Tsurumaru is wandering among the ruins of the castle, all alone in the last sunset. Having lost his flute, he now drops the religious scroll he is carrying. The camera moves in for a close-up. What it sees is described in the script as "the picture of Amitabha, torn in places. . . . [It] shines gold in the last light from the darkening sky. The face of the Amitabha looks sad."

Kurosawa himself described *Ran,* as we have seen, as a series of human events viewed from heaven. And so here we are at the end looking down upon the folly of men. The bleakness of *Kagemusha* is rendered even more bare; the coldness of that film has been reduced to near-freezing.

*Ran* is impressive. It intends to be, and it states that it intends to be. Its didactic message is that there is no hope and that life is indeed the tragedy we have sometimes suspected it of being. This is enough. We do not need to be freed of this truth (as, to an extent, we are in *Lear* because we are purged of emotions, having been made to experience them), because it is eternal and we must live with it forever. Consequently, we do not need to experience Hidetora's agony. All we need do is watch it.

We do not even need to believe in it. Indeed, we cannot. The film is too schematic for that, its elements too controlled. Also, since the director is not interested in believability, he allows—even indulges—where he had formerly forbidden. The overacting he allows, for example. Yet if one is not invited to believe in characters as real, if one is invited to see them as merely the signs of some quality, then the actor's skill, or lack of it, is beside the director's point.

*Ran* may thus be seen as a morality play—something one sees and learns from. It is also, as Kurosawa himself intimated, a final statement.

# Dreams

## 1990

After the completion of *Ran,* another five years were spent looking for financing for the next project. This time the money was once again found through the assistance of George Lucas and Francis Ford Coppola, and another admirer, Steven Spielberg. It was decided that Warner Brothers would fund the project.

The new film was a relatively recent idea. Kurosawa would write and direct a script consisting of nothing but dreams he had had during his life. He threw himself into this project with characteristic enthusiasm and drew a large number of pictures illustrating his ideas. There would be ten episodes in all, and Lucas's Industrial Light and Magic concern would engineer the many "visual effects."

The prospect of sitting and being told two hours' worth of a person's dreams is not, on the face of it, a pleasing one. One's dreams properly interest only oneself. They would therefore have to be told in a singularly interesting and engaging manner to interest the viewer as much as they manifestly did Kurosawa himself.

## THE STORIES

In the finished film there are eight episodes (more were envisioned, including one about flying that was later rejected as "unrealizable"). The first, in some ways the most successfully dreamlike of them all, finds the young Kurosawa being told not to go into the forest on this rainy day because this is when the foxes hold their wedding processions, and he must not look at them.

The director built in the studio an "almost exact replica" of his childhood home, and the nameplate on the gate reads, "Kurosawa." Before shooting he showed the actress playing his mother a number of photos of that lady and suggested ways in which she might resemble her.

Young Kurosawa does indeed see the forbidden procession, and when he returns home his mother tells him that the foxes have come in his absence and delivered a dagger with which he is to kill himself. If this is not to occur, he must go apologize to them. "And where are they to be found?" he wonders. "Under the rainbow, where they live," is the answer. The episode ends with a very pretty composite

shot—the child wandering off into a flower-strewn meadow under the arch of the perfect rainbow provided by Industrial Light and Magic.

The second episode finds the young Kurosawa a bit older. During the Hina Matsuri Festival (usually associated with cherry blossoms, though here with peach), he sees a strange young girl in the yard of his home. She is, it turns out, the spirit of the last peach tree in the orchard, all the others having been cut down for some reason.

Following her, he is led to the other ghosts of the lost trees, lords and ladies, dancers and musicians, all resplendent in the luxurious Heian period court costumes. Since he is "a good boy," they agree to dance for him. The sequence is very pretty. The camera slowly zooms back to show all fifty of the actors in four tiers of orchard, filling the frame with graceful movement, the little boy motionless at the bottom of the screen.

The third dream is about a known figure of folklore and one that

a child would presumably fear—the *yuki-onna* or snow-woman, famous for appearances in Lafcadio Hearn and in Kobayashi's *Kaidan*. She menaces the adolescent Kurosawa, lost on a climbing expedition in the mountains, and then vanishes.

Though this segment, like the rest, is noticeably studio-bound, it here becomes apparent that one of the pleasures of the picture is to be an unusually attentive sound track. Before the first line of dialogue, there are five minutes of beautifully contrived sound effects: grating ice, clanking equipment, the grunts and gasps of the climbers.

Equally interesting is the patterning of the snow, in many ways like the patterning of the rain in the first episode and the falling blossoms in the second. Also, there is almost no editing. One long scene of the panting mountaineers follows another, and when the snow-woman appears, the camera turns to slow motion. These few ingredients sustain the length of the episode, the dreamlike images rendered acceptable because they carry only their own weight.

From the fourth episode, however, it becomes apparent that recounting interesting dreams is to be only one of the concerns of the picture. Comment is going to be made. Here it takes the form of an antiwar anecdote. The dead soldiers of Officer Kurosawa's wartime regiment return, not knowing that they are dead. He must himself tell the sergeant (Yoshitaka Zushi, who played the trolley boy in *Dodesukaden*), and they then all march away.

Again, there is a fine sound track—in which footsteps inside the tunnel from which the soldiers appear and those outside it are brilliantly differentiated. Mountain echoes are exquisitely observed, and there is even the "empty" sound made by a snowy landscape.

In the fifth episode, both innocence and fancy retreat. The young Kurosawa is in a museum looking at a van Gogh. Then he walks through the frame and into "The Bridge at Arles."

In his biography Kurosawa wrote, "After looking at a monograph of Cézanne, I would step outside and the houses, streets and trees—everything—looked like a Cézanne painting. The same thing would happen when I looked at a book of van Gogh's paintings. . . . They changed the way the real world looked to me. It seemed completely different from the world I usually saw with my own eyes."

In *Dreams,* Kurosawa goes one step farther and puts the viewer inside the painting itself. We watch the young man walking through the sketches and then slipping and sliding along the heavy brush strokes of the painting—all accomplished through the wonders of Industrial Light and Magic. Like the sequence featuring animated impressionists in *An American in Paris,* the effect is one of grand kitsch. When Chopin begins, one would have thought that a kind of limit had been reached. But, no, the famous yellow cornfield is suddenly filled with animated crows.

*Dreams* was the first film that Kurosawa wrote all by himself. He formerly had associates writing with him to ensure that a strong script was the result. And to ensure as well, perhaps, that the director be kept from self-indulgence. There is no such presence in *Dreams,* and when his van Gogh observes, "I drive myself like a locomotive," there is a cut to a real locomotive, though such a machine plays no other part in the episode and only further lends its lonely wail to the final scene.

Indeed, ordinary questions of likelihood do not apply. The young Kurosawa steps into the frame and speaks French to the washerwomen of Arles. They tell him, in French, where the mad painter is to be found. Found, the painter (Martin Scorsese), addressed in French, answers in English.

Well, it is a dream, and so all things are possible. But it is also possible that Scorsese speaks no French, and it is also possible that Kurosawa thought it made no difference. Certainly the facts of van Gogh's life are not allowed to get in the way. The young director notices that the painter's ear is bandaged. "Are you all right?" he asks. "You appear to be injured." To which van Gogh replies, "This? Yesterday I was trying to complete a self-portrait. I just couldn't get the ear right. So I cut it off and threw it away."

The sixth episode was originally called "Red Fuji" and shows the mountain on fire, a number of nuclear reactors having exploded. Clouds are roiling, people are fleeing. If for an exhilarating moment or two it seems that Godzilla might appear, this is because, perhaps

for reasons of friendship, Kurosawa here retained the special-effects services of Ishiro Honda, the man responsible for the Toho monster-film look.

No such interest occurs, however. Among the flowing crowd is a mother and her gasping children. "And they told us that nuclear energy was safe," she cries. "Oh, how wrong they were." Then a man steps forward, announces that he was among those who so misled her, and steps off into the sea. At the end of the episode the young Kurosawa, the mother, and her two children are being menaced by clouds of colored smoke presumed to be clouds of radioactivity.

After *Dodesukaden,* Kurosawa had said that he wanted to make a film about nuclear pollution. *Dreams* is presumably it, since all the episodes from here to the end of the film treat this theme. But he had already made a much more powerful statement in *I Live in Fear.* Though this 1955 picture is not one of Kurosawa's strongest, it is nonetheless a powerfully imagined meditation on the dangers of nuclear power. By comparison, this episode is slight indeed.

The seventh episode finds the young Kurosawa wandering about a ruined landscape. He hears footsteps and learns that he is being followed by a hungry demon. In conversation he discovers that the demon was once human but that mass fallout (seen in the sixth episode) occurred and created monstrous mutations—giant dandelions and demons like himself. He leads Kurosawa to spy on the other demons in their misery and then says that he is hungry and is going to eat the young film director, who, in one of the few passages of dreamlike horror in the film, runs and runs.

After he had finished *Ran,* Kurosawa said that that picture was to be his final statement. In that case one wonders what he thought *Dreams* was. Was it also a statement, and if so, was it to be taken seriously? Other slight films, *Scandal,* for example, he has said were not to be taken seriously and one of them, *Those Who Make Tomorrow,* was to be forgotten completely.

Yet since Kurosawa is so parentally protective of the new product, it is difficult to guess how he regards *Dreams.* Usually, however, when he does not think well of a film and has not been drained by it, perhaps because it was too easy for him, he starts at once on some new project. In the case of *Dreams,* the film was no sooner in the can than he was already casting the next picture, having apparently written it during the filming of *Dreams* itself.

The eighth and final segment was originally to be called "The Village of Waterwheels," and here, if some of the earlier segments showed us the wicked world as it was, we are shown how it ought to be. We are in a fertile and watered plain, a place of waterwheels that reassuringly creak and splash. And here the children are polite and the adults are civil.

One of their number (the eighty-four-year-old Chishu Ryu made up to look one hundred four) explains everything. Man is destroying nature to make things more convenient, but convenience is not good. Here, however, in this watermill village, the people live naturally. He then gives a number of examples.

What the old man says is quite true. All of Kurosawa's statements in *Dreams* are true. One argues not with the statements but with the unconvincing way in which they are presented. Indeed, the problems that Kurosawa addresses are so complicated and so serious that his direct and simplistic statement both embarrasses and irritates.

The garrulous old person stops preaching eventually and then—magically—the picture returns to the dreamlike enchantment of the beginning. A joyous funeral procession is coming down the road. It is all music and movement and innocence—finding cause for content in death. One remembers the rice-planting song at the end of *Seven Samurai*, a celebration of the rightness of nature. This Kurosawa celebrates here by showing us rather than telling us about it and hence in these final moments returns to his picture a promised artistry.

*Dreams,* the work of an eighty-year-old man, might be compared to another picture by an aging director, Jean Renoir's *Le Petit Théâtre de Jean Renoir.* Though Kurosawa has never seen this film, there are many similarities: a lessening concern for the realist style, a predilection for the stage, a tendency to tell rather than to show, and an inclination to moralize.

The extent of Kurosawa's unconsidered indulgence is, as we have often seen, to be best detected in the use of something he loves very much—music. Here the depths of his affection and the shallowness of his musical culture become apparent. He was raised on a beloved 78-rpm record album, "The World's Best Classics," and he is faithful to the end.

In *Dreams* we not only have Chopin under the Dostoevsky of the paintbrush, we also find composer Ryoichi Ikebe forced to rewrite another old favorite, *Pictures at an Exhibition* (heard in the original in *No Regrets for Our Youth*) in order that the child may wander out under the rainbow to the beloved strains of "The Old Castle." And at the end, among the waterwheels and under the credits, we have yet another music chestnut. It is "In the Village" from the Ippolitov-Ivanov *Caucasian Sketches.*

Yet, when all of this is said, *Dreams* leaves behind a residue of beauty. It is beautiful despite itself because the beauty lies in the attitude of the director. This is indicated not only in the didactic intent but in the slowness of everything, in the amount of respect intended, and in the enormous and brazen sincerity of the work. That a director in 1990 could be this steadfast, this serious, this moral, and this hopeful is beautiful in its own right.

That *Dreams* is a most uneven film is evident. At the same time, there is nothing in it that the earlier pictures had not prepared us for. It is, in this sense, a summation.

# Rhapsody in August

## 1991

Like many directors, Kurosawa needs a rest after a major film but is impatient to get back to work after a minor one. Thus even before the completion of *Dreams,* he was deep into his next work.

Further, he already had funding for it. Shochiku, the company with which he had had such difficulties in the release of *The Idiot,* offered to finance this latest product. In addition, he had met the American actor Richard Gere while the latter was in Tokyo on a publicity tour. So he now had the money and the actor for the single part he had not as yet cast. The film was completed in a very short time, and the print was ready for viewing three months before the date Shochiku had scheduled for its release.

## THE STORY

The idea from which Kurosawa shaped his script came from the novel *In the Stew* by Kiyoko Murata, about an old woman who has difficulty distinguishing illusion from reality. Working alone on the script, Kurosawa departed further and further from the original and eventually produced a scenario very much in line with his own concerns.

The major concern, that which motived *I Live in Fear* and parts of *Dodesukaden* and *Dreams,* was nuclear destruction and the consequent pollution. For this reason the director moved the location of his story to Nagasaki and had the old woman's husband killed by the atomic bomb dropped by the Americans on that city.

The grandchildren are mollified when a visiting American relative visits and expresses concern. The old woman forgives all when he apologizes to her for the bombing. Nevertheless, at the end, crazed by a thunderstorm, the old woman believes that the destruction is about to begin again and runs through the rain, away from Nagasaki.

## TREATMENT

As in *Dreams,* the concern is shown in the most straightforward fashion. The grandchildren go to Nagasaki and one of them, Tami,

tells the other, "Underneath this beautiful Nagasaki there's another Nagasaki, ruined by the atomic bomb." When they visit the memorial park and little Shinichiro notices monuments from Czechoslovakia, Poland, Bulgaria, China, Cuba, and the USSR and says with surprise that there is none from America, Tami responds, "Naturally. It was Americans that *dropped* the bomb."

Commendable though it is to hear such straightforward talk in compromising modern Japan, it is not good artistic policy because it results in too simplistic a statement, one that is completely inadequate for its horrific subject. When Tami says, "We couldn't even guess how the A-bomb victims felt, . . . we never stopped to think," the effect is ludicrously weak.

The children think that their grandmother must consequently hate the United States, but she says she no longer does. "Nowadays I neither hate nor like America." This is because "the war was to blame." Which is true, but, after all, as Tami has reminded us, it was the United States that actually dropped the bomb. However, Kurosawa wants to make the viewer remember and then forgive. He himself, however, will not forgive those Japanese who turned to the United States for selfish reasons. When the children's parents come back from Hawaii, very pleased with their reception by wealthy relatives, one of the children wonders why they did not tell these people that grandfather had been killed by the A-bomb.

Young Tateo replies, "To put it nicely, it was consideration. To put it badly, it was calculation. To put it straight, it was that Hawaiian family's money." Nonetheless, the Americans prove to be of finer stuff. When the brother's son, Clark, learns that Grandfather was a bomb victim, his response is to come to Japan. When the family hears of this, they are upset because "Americans don't like to be reminded of the A-bomb."

Yet when Clark arrives, it is seen that he has come in contrition. He had not known what had occurred and now insists on being taken to the place of the grandfather's death, the school where he taught. Later there is a scene with the grandmother in which Clark apologizes in halting Japanese.

"We were wrong," he says. Grandmother gently forgives him, and little Shinichiro, spying, scampers to tell the others, "I feel like I just saw something real nice."

As a response to the realities of the bombing of Nagasaki, this is quite inadequate. Such an easy solution to a notoriously difficult issue is both sentimental and ludicrous. The effect becomes all the weaker when Kurosawa, illustrating nuclear fears, resorts to special effects—a great eye opening in the sky. This is something the literal cannot define.

Perhaps only indirection can suggest the scale of the atomic destruction of Hiroshima and Nagasaki. The events are too enormous, too catastrophic, and too cruel to be otherwise described. They can never be domesticated, or anthropomorphized, in the manner in which Kurosawa attempts. An example of the proper means to recapture the authentic horror of the event is seen in Shohei Imamura's *Black Rain,* a film that makes us feel the full terror of the destruction and the full horror of its results.

Kurosawa, however, has never practiced such indirection. He is far too sincere and straightforward for that. He attacks problems head-on, which is why such films as *Scandal* and *Dreams* are weak. When he is forced (often by the artistry of his fellow script writers) to approach his problem obliquely, as in *Ikiru* or *The Bad Sleep Well,* the resulting film is persuasive indeed.

In *Rhapsody in August,* however, Clark says, "Seeing these people here . . . I can feel that day in Nagasaki." Perhaps he can, but we can not, and his saying this does not help us to do so. Such an inadequate response can do nothing to illuminate the enormous fact to which it refers.

At the same time that the script is hindering the viewer, however, Kurosawa is also engaging us on an entirely different level, one far removed from political slogans, from mere dialogue, and from easy solutions. A paradigm of the method occurs fairly early in the picture. One of the grandmother's old friends visits and the children notice that the two old women do not talk with each other. There is a long, beautiful shot of the two old people facing each other, silent as the summer breeze blows the hanging screens. Though this is later explained by the grandmothers ("Some people keep silent when they are talking"), Kurosawa has already shown us that one image can be more meaningful than any number of words.

Indeed, the most memorable sections of the picture are those that remain "unexplained." The most powerful of these occurs during the memorial service (August 9) for the atom-bomb victims. Clark and little Shinichiro are listening to the sutras being chanted, when the little boy is distracted by the sight of a line of ants purposefully progressing into the woods. To the sound of the chanting, the camera leaves the humans and follows the insects. It is a breathtaking moment because it is unexpected, unprecedented, unexplained. Occurring in a film this contrived, it is as though a window has been suddenly opened and fresh air is pouring in.

(It was also one of Kurosawa's most difficult to film sequences. Ants were obtained from a Kyoto ant trainer—there are such in Japan—and brought to Gotemba where the sequence was being filmed. The ants balked, would not walk in a straight line, would not act at all. After many unsuccessful tries it was decided that the altitude might be wrong. Ants, full crew, Kurosawa, and all went to sea-level Kyoto, found a similar forest, and this time the ants behaved well, acting their parts with talent and assurance.)

We follow the ants deeper and deeper into the forest, into nature itself, and then watch them climb higher and higher. Into the frame comes one crimson petal, then another. It is a rose that the ants are climbing toward, a full-blown brilliantly red rose, while on the sound track the sutra still sounds.

It is a wonderful moment, precisely because it is unexplained. Any meaning is linked to a central concern, but the approach is entirely indirect and there are no words. Yet the moment is not arbitrary. It is linked to one of the major structural themes of the film, namely, the Schubert song "*Heidenröselein.*" The first music we hear in the picture (the opening credits are filled with natural sounds, not music) is this melody being picked out on an out-of-tune harmonium.

Tateo is going to fix the instrument. Like many another Kurosawa hero (Sanshiro Sugata, Sanjuro Tsubaki), he is going to try over and over until he gets it right. He is absolutely determined (*zettai ni*), as he says a number of times, and we see him working away at various points during the film.

We also hear the Schubert song at various times, picked out by him or sung by the children. The tune becomes a pleasant *leitmotiv* throughout the picture, in keeping with Kurosawa's known tastes in pop classical music and with the general well-bred niceness of the children. In the Goethe lyrics to the song, too, it is the heart of the rose that is apotheosized and it is toward this that the busy ants are, of course, progressing. Nevertheless, all of these references do not prepare us for the extraordinary apotheosis of Schubert and his rose which concludes the picture.

Grandmother, thinking that A-bomb day has again come, rushes out into the storm. Like some mad and misunderstood Lady Lear, she forces her way across the rainswept heath. The grandchildren and their parents race after her. There has been relatively little fast-cutting in the film, but now Kurosawa begins to establish a definite rhythm: shots of grandmother, shots of children and parents, one shot for each, becoming shorter and shorter as the sequence progresses.

(In place of fast-cutting Kurosawa in these later pictures more and more uses precise choreography of movement within a long-held scene, as in the battle sequences of *Ran* and the funeral procession in *Dreams*. Another example is the schoolyard sequence in *Rhapsody in August*. Here the choreography is especially controlled and confines itself to very few shots. The grandchildren arrive at the schoolyard, and in the background of the same scene is the taxi bringing Clark and their parents. While they are talking, schoolchildren enter from both sides and begin playing. Then, in the same scene, a small parade forms at the far rear of the schoolyard and begins to advance forward toward the camera. It is made up of the survivors, friends of the children who died at that school. They are now old and have come to wash and decorate the memorial to the dead. All of this makes good story sense, good action sense, good continuity sense, and good common sense. At the same time, it is patterned enough to make good aesthetic sense as well.)

In this final sequence of the film, the grandmother continues her flight, the shots alternate, the tempo picks up, and then suddenly the wind catches her umbrella and turns it inside out. When this occurs

there is a sudden silence. All the sounds of wind and rain and the calls of the children cease. Then within this sudden calm comes—like a vision from another world—the Schubert. But it is now transfigured, orchestrated and sung by a massed children's choir.

What makes one catch one's breath is the unexpected beauty of the music, its rightness, and the affirmation it suggests. In the original script, Kurosawa wrote of the indomitable nature of the old woman and how she runs into the storm as though into the heart of a red rose. And he wanted the Schubert to be intoned by a mighty pipe organ.

For me, this surprising sequence is another kind of affirmation, not counter to the director's but parallel to it. The innocence of the children's voices, the childlike quality of the Schubert melody, these suddenly remove all worries (Does Grandmother have Alzheimer's? Will she die?) and substitutes the certainty of innocence, beauty, survival. And after the didactic nature of so much of this film, the spontaneous outpouring of this final sequence with its vibrant multiplicity is both impressive and moving.

It is a moment of epiphany. Like Sanshiro in the pond, like Sanjuro walking into battle, like the joyous funeral parade in *Dreams*, it is an illumination, an elevation and celebration of the human.

# Madadayo

## 1993

The title of Kurosawa's 1993 film, *Madadayo*, is taken from one of the responses in the game of hide-and-seek. *Mo ii kai?* calls one child: Are you ready? And the answer is *Mada da yo:* Not yet. Thus, as in *Dreams* and *Rhapsody in August*, we are again in the world of children. At the same time, however, the title serves as an indication of larger and more mature concerns.

The picture is in the shape of a series of sketches, taken from the writings of Hyakken Uchida, a droll, eccentric, and much-beloved writer. It is structurally thus like *Dodesukaden*, which also derives from a collection of character sketches.

In this new film, however, the subject is a single character, a retired professor, and his relations with his wife, his cat, and his adoring former students. Though we may remember another wise and beloved teacher, the one in *No Regrets for Our Youth*, we are this time seeing academic retirement in the context of a comedy.

A parallel that suggests itself is that with the droll novel, *I Am a Cat*, by the nationally beloved Natsume Soseki, whose face graces Japan's thousand-yen bill. There are many resemblances in the Uchida (and hence in the Kurosawa): gatherings at the teacher's house, academic conversations filled with puns and learned allusions, elaborate jokes, a long-suffering wife, and in the plot a large role for the cat, an animal of which Kurosawa's professor is preternaturally fond and whose disappearance all but unmans him.

Behind the influence of Soseki's novel, however, stands the example of the *rakugo*, a popular entertainment that certainly informed both Soseki and Uchida. This is a storytelling form in which the narrator dramatizes various amusing domestic happenings.

In Kurosawa, these find the retired professor acting as *rakugo-ka*, and flashbacks often illustrate his droll tales. Thus he tells us about a horse warily passing a restaurant serving horsemeat, and sure enough, this is what we see. (The animal thus joins those other knowledgeable equines from *The Throne of Blood* and *Kagemusha*.)

Also, like *rakugo* monologues, the dialogue in the film is filled with puns, *oshari* (verbal playfulness), and the lowbrow kind of humor with which the form is associated. The professor, for example, quotes the famous opening of the *Hojoki*, the thirteenth-century classic by Kamo no Chomei. Since he himself has also retired to his own "ten-foot-square hut," the quote seems apt. "Ceaselessly the river flows, and yet the water is never the same," he intones, but it turns out that the reference is to his hearing someone the night before standing outside the door of his hut pissing.

All of these sallies are greeted with enthusiasm by his former students who eternally react and are in this sense the chorus—as were the newspapermen in *The Bad Sleep Well* or the courtiers in *Ran*. And it is they who arrange the birthday party with its wheeled-on cake for their old teacher (a perhaps conscious homage to the earlier film) and who worry about his failing health.

That he is failing is one of the themes of the film. In an earlier playful sequence we are given some indication of this concern. There is talk of the moon, and then we see the real moon and later a kind of pantomime in which the students use a large metal tray as the

moon and it becomes a halo behind the beloved professor's head. But, of course, all people with halos are, by definition, dead. And we are shown the seasons as they pass (and are treated to Vivaldi as we do), we watch the professor as he tries to cope with the years (like Kanji Watanabe in *Ikiru*, he is sick during the birthday party), and we are invited to find admirable his refusal to give in to death.

For this is the ultimate meaning of the title. *Madadayo* is a refusal of death itself. The teacher in this film is thus like Sanshiro clinging to the post in the middle of the lotus pond nearly fifty years before. Neither are going to give up. They are both going to keep on trying.

Though there are naturally many continuations and similarities among these later films of Kurosawa and those he made earlier, any comparison among them is beside the point. Like Jean Renoir before him, Kurosawa in his late pictures has been making a different kind of film. *Le Petit Théâtre de Jean Renoir* is a new departure and cannot be compared with *Le Regle de Jeu*. In the same way, *Madadayo* has few real points of correspondence with earlier films.

Not that former felicities of style are not visible. The opening shot is a bold long-held close-up of a school door, held to the limit, and speaking plainly to us of the later concerns of the films, including the final closed door of death itself. The linkage of sequences is as fluent as ever. A whole year passes in four little scenes, showing professor and wife in characteristic poses in their little house. World War II is encompassed with a single cut and a single sentence: "The house got burned down." Passage of time is also detailed: the willow tree next door grows up, the ruins across the road turn into a house, the students have grandchildren and it is they who bring in the birthday cake.

Also, the editing (though there is much less of it in these later pictures) retains its customary felicity. The songs and dances are beauti-

fully put together, and a fully described drinking party is edited with a fluency and grace that make it come quite alive.

The true concern in these later pictures, however, is ethical, and nothing captures this better than the single shot. There is no irony in the film since nothing is compared to anything else; all is straightforward presentation. Everything is apparent. It is right there, ready to be picked up, and it is this that gives the film a sententious tone, just as a lack of irony lends it a certain sentimentality.

(I wonder if Kurosawa remembered a sequence in a late Ozu picture, the hide-and-seek scenes in *The End of Summer*. There the grandfather, also about to die, plays the game with his grandchild and tricks the little boy into hiding so that he—*Mo ii kai?*—can walk out of the house to go and see his mistress. Here, of course, the irony is accomplished and there is no sentimentality at all.)

The film ends in a dream. Dreams in Kurosawa have played a continuing role, not only in *Dreams* itself but also in *Drunken Angel* and in *Kagemusha*. Here we see the professor dreaming of himself as a child, playing hide-and-seek in a country field. He starts to hide himself and then stops to look at the beauty of the summer clouds. The beauty of the clouds is disturbing because these are not the high summer images of, say, those in *Rhapsody in August*. Rather, these are Kurosawa clouds, the gesso swirls of his painting, as we remember them from his innumerable sketches and from the dream sequence in *Kagemusha*.

The hand of the director, like the hand of God, becomes plain. And this is an affecting image because it distracts the sleeping professor as a child (the living film director as the old professor) and he may this time fail to answer, *Mada da yo*.

# Method, Technique and Style

Kurosawa has said that he could not possibly define his own style, that he does not know what it consists of, that it never occurs to him to think of it. While quite ready to talk about lenses, or acting, or the best kind of camera-dolly, he is unwilling to discuss meaning or aesthetics. Once I asked what a certain scene was really about. He said: "Well, if I could answer that, it wouldn't have been necessary for me to have filmed the scene, would it?"

Perhaps the reason for his reluctance to talk about meaning, about aesthetics, is that they are not *real,* they have no visible actuality. Aesthetics presume a system, and style presumes an expression and a reflection of the man himself. Neither are of any interest compared to the *actuality* of the new film to be made, the new script to be written. A man concerned with his own style is a self-conscious man, and Kurosawa is self-contained. Each film is a direct expression of himself, it is true, but, far from wanting to trace parallels or seek comparisons among his pictures, he has an aversion against seeing himself as he was. Just as he insists that his heroes neglect their past and live continually in the present, so he himself is uninterested in anything that *has* happened to him. "A director always likes his current picture the best. If he doesn't, he cannot direct it," he once said, and because the present is of such importance, his attitude toward past accomplishments has been both neglectful and cavalier.

He is particularly distrustful of any discussion of aesthetics because he dislikes generalization. He finds it a very clumsy tool. The abstract statement is not true because it must try to handle life, and life—as his films up to the final few have indicated—should be shown subtly and delicately, and not handled at all. Theories, comparisons, generalizations, parallels, rules-of-thumb, these are destroyers of life and he refuses to use them.

Even in conversation he refuses the abstract. Shinobu Hashimoto, with whom he has written many of his best scripts, remembered: "When we first started working together, he told me: 'I want you to take in all of my good ideas . . . just like—like blotting paper.' If he had simply said I was to pay attention and absorb, it would have been an ordinary and serviceable expression. But he said 'just like blotting paper' and that is just like him. Everything he says is clear and particular and concrete. Everything that is meaningful and strong—that is Kurosawa. How much have I not learned from him about real and strong expression?"

The reason that Kurosawa so dislikes any writings about films ("I have never read a review of a film of mine which did not read false meanings into it") is that one writes about structure, about style, about invisibles; one must use words to describe an image meant to be seen, something that, precisely because it could not be put into words, became an image. One cannot be meaningful when writing or reading about something which is not even *there.*

Also, an act of criticism is an act of summing up. It takes into account the past but it rarely encompasses the present. It is not properly concerned with life. In the same way, discussion of a man's style is self-limiting in that it presumes that a man *is.* In Kurosawa's films—as we have seen—only the villains *are* something or other. The heroes are always, like Sugata, *becoming*; they live in the eternal present where, though history may indicate, it certainly does not define.

You cannot sum up a living person; you can only sum up the dead. It is easy to speak of a director's past films; it is difficult to speak of his continuing style. Kurosawa is profoundly disinterested in his own style because he is so alive. He is, on the other hand, quite ready to talk about methods, about techniques. These are tools. These are *real.*

## SCRIPT

I once asked Kurosawa which, of the three classical steps in film-making (scripting, shooting, editing) he considered most important. He answered: "Well, the editing is probably the most important, but if you don't have a good script, all the editing in the world won't help."

The script, then, is the most important—in that there is a "most." He usually thinks ahead two or three years and has a number of projects, things he eventually wants to make films about. Circumstances may force him to wait (both *Rashomon* and *Ran* had to wait for years) but the idea of the picture remains—partially on paper, mostly in his head—and is thought about.

The actual writing may take up to half a year and usually begins after the short vacation he habitually takes directly following the opening of his latest film. He gathers his script writers about (Shinobu Hashimoto, Hideo Oguni, Ryuzo Kikushima, Eijiro Hisaita, Masato Ide) and goes off to a hot-springs hotel or, more recently, begins work in his garden-house. They sit together around a large table, writing, comparing, correcting—a process that Hideo Oguni has described in relation to *Ikiru*—until everyone is satisfied. The most rapid and harmonious example of this form of group experience in screenwriting occurred with *Dodesukaden*. Kurosawa, Hideo Oguni, and Shinobu Hashimoto completed this script in one-third of the anticipated time. Kurosawa has joked about the manager of the hotel where the three had isolated themselves, who assumed, because of their unexpectedly early departure, that they were leaving because they found the place unsatisfactory; he began to ply them with his choicest cuisine.

Though the finished films never give any indication of who did what, all the ideas are subject to Kurosawa's final approval, and one may be certain that anything he does not want in the film will not get in. Creation by committee, as it were, has ruined many more films than it has helped, and in Japan (no less than in Hollywood) this is the usual result. Occasionally, however, combinations create excellence: Prévert and Carné, Nichols and Ford, Noda and Ozu, Wada and Ichikawa. Kurosawa has used the same five men for most of his films and has only scripted *Sanshiro Sugata* and the later films by himself. He has worked with these five both alone and in combination. A breakdown of their participation is:

| | |
|---|---|
| Eijiro Hisaita: | *No Regrets for Our Youth, The Idiot, The Bad Sleep Well.* |
| Ryuzo Kikushima: | *Stray Dog, Scandal, The Throne of Blood, The Hidden Fortress, The Bad Sleep Well, Yojimbo, Sanjuro, High and Low, Red Beard.* |
| Shinobu Hashimoto: | *Rashomon, Ikiru, Seven Samurai, Record of a Living Being, The Throne of Blood, The Hidden Fortress, The Bad Sleep Well, Dodesukaden.* |
| Hideo Oguni: | *Ikiru, Seven Samurai, Record of a Living Being, The Throne of Blood, The Lower Depths, The Hidden Fortress, The Bad Sleep Well, Sanjuro, High and Low, Red Beard, Dodesukaden, Ran.* |
| Masato Ide: | *Red Beard, Kagumusha, Ran.* |

An exception to this pattern occurred with *Dersu Uzala*. The idea for the project was Kurosawa's, but he worked on the script with a Russian, Yuri Nagibin, in place of his usual Japanese collaborators. From *Dreams* onward he wrote his scripts by himself.

Oguni has worked most often with Kurosawa and he was also the next-to-last to join him. The director has said that the best ideas for *Ikiru* came from him. In addition, he has done one film (*The Lower Depths*) in which he was the only co-author. Hashimoto was one of Japan's best scenarists (he did the screen play for Kobayashi's *Harakiri*) and he has also done one coauthored film—*Rashomon*. Kikushima has three times worked alone with the director: *Stray Dog, Scandal,* and *Yojimbo.* Hisaita has worked alone with Kurosawa twice, on *No Regrets for Our Youth* and *The Idiot*; and Ide twice, on *Red Beard* and *Kagemusha.*

Kurosawa's personal relationship to his writers is both intimate and strong. They, and a few actors, a few technicians, are the only friends he has. When writing the script they live together and even during the shooting one or more of the authors are usually around. Over the years they have come to agree on everything of any importance and, as far as the films are concerned, can be thought of as extensions of each other. Kurosawa thinks this way. "I do not trust myself to write a script alone. It is that simple. I need people who can give me perspective."

Once the story is decided upon (and it is always Kurosawa who decides), the writing begins. The director has told how character evolves in his discussions of *Ikiru* and *Scandal,* and how the other writers act as checks to each other, checking as it were on each other's honesty. In the act of writing, the form of the picture evolves. This form would seem to be accidental—there has never been any indication that any of them ever discussed something as abstract as "form"—but it is always present and, as we shall see, no matter the film the form is usually the same.

This is possible, even unavoidable, in that all Kurosawa films are about the same thing. In simplest terms, and shorn of all philosophy, his pictures are about character revelation. One of the reasons he has made so many suspense films either directly (*Stray Dog, The Bad Sleep Well, High and Low*) or indirectly (almost all the others, particularly *Rashomon* and *Ikiru,* with *Dodesukaden* and *Dersu Uzala* representing departures from this tendency) is that the suspense-story, like the detective-story, is about revelation. Kurosawa takes the "crime" (the unrealized life or the problem of choosing among evils) and works out a "solution." The solution is usually the hero himself and his character; this is what gives the film its final form.

Or forms, because Kurosawa has several favorites. One of them, for lack of any better name, I will call "sonata-form." The other (for the same reason) the "theme with variations." The latter is the simpler, and *Rashomon* is an example. So, however, is *One Wonderful Sunday;* so is *Ikiru;* and so is *Dodesukaden.* The sonata-form is more common in the later films and usually consists of (1) an introduction or prelude, which usually sounds the major theme, (2) a bridge, which is usually of major cinematic importance, (3) the main theme or *hauptsatz* (whether there is a *seitensatz* or not depends on the film), which is not as much a first "subject" as a complex of related ideas; it leads into (4) the development, of which it is also itself a part, and into (5) a recapitulation, which may be separate from the (often ironic) (6) coda. A breakdown of some of the films gives:

| | Introduction with Theme | Bridge | First Theme | Development |
|---|---|---|---|---|
| **Sanshiro Sugata** | opening scene, children's song | the judo fight | the jump into the pond | training for the fight |
| **They Who Step on the Tiger's Tail** | opening chorus | porter and monks | the scenes in the barrier-camp and the drama itself | |
| **Drunken Angel** | the two men meet and fight | the doctor at the sump | continuing relationship of the two men | |
| **The Quiet Duel** | the hospital camp | | the doctor and his girl | |
| **Stray Dog** | detective loses pistol | the search | the first murder and the chase | |
| **Scandal** | the meeting, photo taken | the publishing montage | the lawyer, his relations with hero and with his daughter | |
| **Seven Samurai** | the farmer's problem | search for the samurai | the various conflicts among samurai, bandits, and farmers | |
| **Record of a Living Being** | the dentist and his fears | reading of the report | the various conflicts between father and family | |
| **The Throne of Blood** | opening chorus, scenes with the king | lost in the forest, scenes with the witch | the conflicts concerning the hero's wife and the murders | |
| **The Hidden Fortress** | the farmers and the war | the revolt of the slaves | the farmers and the gold; the hero and his duty | |
| **The Bad Sleep Well** | the wedding sequence | the newspaper montage | the hero's conflict with duty, revenge, and love | |
| **Dersu Uzala** | Arseniev searching for the grave of Dersu (1910) | Title (1902) Arseniev and his company in the Taiga | the meeting with Dersu, scenes that reveal his character | Dersu and Arseniev in the blizzard sequence |

This sonata-form need not be insisted upon, but it is interesting that so many of the films exhibit the same pattern. Perhaps it is because these films are based on conflict in a way that ordinary pictures are not. Since the conflict is usually one of character rather than of situation, it naturally follows that a "recapitulation" (that is, a testing of the hero) would bring back to the film its own major idea in a new, different, or expanded form. The reason one may refer to the form as similar to first-movement sonata-form is that both are about conflict. Music has never found a better way of

| Second Theme | Recapitulation | Coda |
| --- | --- | --- |
| the hero and the girl | the fight with her father | scenes in the train |
| continuation of the drama itself with its disclosures | | the drunk scenes |
| the nurse and her problem | the fight with the boss | death scene and final scene by the sump |
| the doctor and the nurse | fight with villain | hospital, dedicated hero |
| hero and head detective | final fight | hospital scenes |
| hero and heroine | court-room scenes | final scene, last appearance of photo |
| love between girl and youngest samurai | the final battle and deaths | rice-planting, scene by the graves |
| | burning of the factory, incarceration of father | scenes in the asylum |
| continuation | lost in forest, witch, final battle | final chorus |
| the princess | the fight, the gold | the reward to the farmers |
| love for wife | kidnapping and final fight | press-conference, telephone call |
| renewed meeting with Dersu, the rescue from the rapids, the encounter with the tiger | Dersu attempts to live with Arseniev and his family in Khaborovsk | the telegram; Arseniev identifies the body of Dersu and witnesses his burial |

presenting conflict than through the sonata-form, and the fact that Kurosawa's pictures fall into a somewhat similar pattern is another example of its validity.

Another aspect of form seen in many of Kurosawa's pictures is that of the full circle, or the spiral, the return to the beginning with a difference, the cyclic. Some examples are:

| | BEGINNING | ENDING |
| --- | --- | --- |
| *Sanshiro Sugata* | the opening children's song and the lotus-pond | the opening song shown as true; references to the pond |
| *The Most Beautiful* | the factory, parade, military music | the factory, parade, military music |
| *Sugata II* | fight with the foreigner | final fight with the foreigner |
| *They Who Step on the Tiger's Tail* | journey through the forest | journey over the moor |
| *One Wonderful Sunday* | train station; cigarette butt; meeting | train station; cigarette butt; meeting following week |
| *Drunken Angel* | the sump | the sump |
| *The Quiet Duel* | doctor operating | doctor operating |
| *Scandal* | newspaper poster | newspaper poster |
| *Rashomon* | gate scenes | gate scenes |
| *Ikiru* | looking at watch | final close-up of clock |
| *The Throne of Blood* | fog, castle, chorus | fog, castle, chorus |
| *Yojimbo* | hero coming | hero going |
| *Sanjuro* | hero coming | hero going |
| *Red Beard* | the hospital gate | the hospital gate |
| *Dodesukaden* | the house of Rokkuchan in the morning | the house of Rokkuchan at night |
| *Dersu Uzala* | Arseniev searching for the grave of Dersu | Arseniev at the burial of Dersu |

The circle appears in various ways. The theme-and-variation form (seen in *Rashomon* and *Stray Dog*) leads us back to the beginning (with a difference), and within the films themselves circular forms are often seen. The triangle in *Rashomon* is visual and the composition enforces it; the horse in *The Throne of Blood* runs round and round in a circle; the farmers in *Seven Samurai* always gather in a circle, as do Arseniev and his company around their campfire in *Dersu Uzala*. The compositions of *Ran* consist largely of broken circles and unstable triangles. Circular images are stronger and more frequent in Kurosawa's films than they are in the pictures of most directors.

Likewise common is the form of the return. This is often inherent in the theme, since so many of Kurosawa's pictures are about the difference between theory and practice or the difference between illusion and reality. We see theory or illusion and then contrast and compare with practice or reality. This often has the effect of seeing the same thing twice (with enormous differences, of course), and this in turn creates the feeling of the return. In its simplest form this is seen in the many "practice" scenes that occur in Kurosawa's films. In *Sugata II* the teacher practices judo throws using a jug on a rope; these later become very real throws. During the practice he mentions one of Sugata's vices with every kick; during the fight Sugata—engaged in the real thing—discovers the reality of his own vices. In *Seven Samurai* Chiaki's wood-chopping (with its references to man-chopping) turns before our eyes into man-chopping during the film itself. In *Yojimbo* the practice with the knife (impaling dry leaves) becomes the real thing (impaling men). A variation on this motif, moving from reality to fantasy, occurs at the end of *Dodesukaden* when, with a cut, the flashing light of a real trolley becomes the lamp that Rokkuchan straps to his waist as he runs his imaginary streetcar at night. An example of the full return is also found in *Yojimbo*. The coward son returned home cries "mother" and she slaps him, and this is seen as funny; when he sees her killed he cries "mother" again and this is not so funny; when a swordsman drops his sword and dies shouting "mother," this extreme cliché from the period-film is given back all its horror and is extremely chilling, not funny in the slightest. A fine example of circular continuity is seen in *No Regrets for Our Youth*. A sequence opens with Fujita having a drink in a public bar. Some students are singing. This is followed by the dinner scene at the girl's home. She walks part of the way to the station with the guests—including Fujita. In the distance is a group of drunken students, obviously the same boys from the opening scene, still singing the same song. The next sequence opens with a title ("1938") and five years have passed. The opening scene is a group of young men going off to war. Though quite sober, they are singing the same song. The full return also defines the parameters of *Dersu Uzala*, where landscape reflects and merges with character. The two gigantic Siberian cedars between which Dersu Uzala was buried are missing from the opening scene but reappear in the final sequence when industrialization, if clearly imminent, has not yet engulfed the Taiga.

One could just as well see this as a process of metamorphosis, things changing with circumstances and yet, somehow, remaining the same; things viewed, as it were, from different angles, as though the director himself were circling around the object of his film.

Metamorphosis, the feeling for the circle, the sense of return, the recapitulation—all contribute to the form of the Kurosawa script and give the pattern of the picture. There are doubtless very personal reasons why this should be so, but another reason would be that Kurosawa is interested in the totality of a character, the totality of a situation. One of the few ways a narrative art may encompass a character is to circle the character, to reveal one facet after another, to return continually to what is already known, to contrast what we saw then with what we know now. The most revealing of psychological fiction (Proust, for example) continually circles and returns. Kurosawa's interest in character revelation insists upon a like movement—with the result of a like pattern.

# CAMERA

Kurosawa once said: "When I finally photograph something, it is merely to get something to edit," and among the elements of film-making it is the actual shooting that seems to command less interest for him, though neither less labor nor less concern.

"Before I decide how to photograph something, I first of all think about how to improve whatever it is I'm photographing. When that is done, then I think how it can best be photographed, from what angle, etc. And each technique I use necessarily differs according to whatever it is I'm taking a picture of." In order to capture the desired image, "I explain what I want in detail, not only to the cameraman but also to all other members of the staff. We all work together to get what I want—but whether I get it or not, that is my own responsibility." Kurosawa has never used a production designer. "It is always I who frame the shot, who design the movement—though I usually also take the advice of anyone who happens to have a better idea than I do."

Kurosawa's first and most important criterion for photographing is the apparent actuality of whatever is going to be photographed. He has been known to halt production because his long-distance lenses picked up nail-heads in a period-film set construction. Once he tore down an entire open set because the roof did not look real enough. Whole weeks were spent in aging the large *Red Beard* set, including the pouring of fifty years' worth of tea into the cups to be used, thus properly staining them. In order to create an extra-terrestrial feeling on the barren set of *Dodesukaden*, Kurosawa instructed his crew to pull out all grass growing amidst the debris of the junkyard where most of the film was shot; he even had them uproot small trees that had sprung up. Only inorganic materials were photographed, as befits a portrayal of the lives of those excluded from normal sustenance. In preparation for the scene in *Dersu Uzala* where Dersu instructs Arseniev to cut as much marsh grass as possible in order to erect a shelter against the oncoming blizzard, Kurosawa had actors Munzuk and Solomin spend ten days practicing the cutting of grass. Yuri Solomin has stated that when he finally collapsed in this scene in accordance with the script, his exhaustion was real.

The search for apparent actuality goes to extremes. In *Yojimbo,* Mifune practices impaling flying leaves with his knife, and Kurosawa got someone skilled enough to do just that. In *The Hidden Fortress,* the escaping party is shot at by soldiers and they dodge behind tree-trunks just in time, the bullets tearing at the bark. Kurosawa originally wanted the gunners to shoot at the actors—and just miss them—but that proved too dangerous. He resorted to the method of (1) photographing the actors dodging behind the trunk, (2) allowing them to retire, but not moving camera-position, (3) photographing the bullets raking the logs, (4) bringing back the actors, starting the camera, having them dash for the safety of the next log, etc.

At the spectacular conclusion of *The Throne of Blood,* however, such makeshift was not enough. He wanted arrows shot at Mifune. First he tried the two standard methods: (1) trick arrows planted in place spring up at the proper moment, (2) arrows already planted are pulled out with wire, the whole scene photographed backwards. These did not satisfy Kurosawa and so, after a conference with Mifune, he stationed real archers just out of camera range (about ten feet from the actor) and had them shoot real arrows, full force, point blank. The scene was carefully rehearsed with chalkmarks on the floor for Mifune to follow and was then photographed. Some of the arrows were designed to miss the moving Mifune by an inch, and missed him by just that much.

After the object to be photographed has thus been "improved" and made more real, Kurosawa is ready to decide how to photograph it. Though he accomplishes this in various ways, his considerations are usually: to do it in such a way that the meaning of the shot is enhanced, and/or in such a way that economy of action is created, and/or in such a way that the composition itself comments on the scene. If the meaning of the shot is "flight" or "chase," Kurosawa usually uses a dolly, believing that a fast scene should be shot "fast" with lots of trucking-shots cut together. On the other hand, a "slow" scene (for example, Mifune's change-of-mind scene in *The Bad Sleep Well,* Shima's encounter with his colleagues in *Dodesukaden,* and the opening scene of *Kagemusha*) is often shot in one long take with no cuts at all. If the scene is about "suspense," then Kurosawa will often use a pan (for example, the scene in *Stray Dog* where we think that Shimura's house is the home of a criminal, and then the camera pans to show us his happy family). If the scene is about "discovery," then he usually first shows the reaction (the faces of the cops in *High and Low*), followed by a cut or dolly or pan to the object (the dead bodies they discover).

This is by no means invariable and, in any event, is part of the equipment of most directors. The incisive way in which these techniques are used is very Kurosawa-like, however, as are the additions. One such would be the very fast dollies of the forest scenes from *The Throne of Blood,* where the foreground is continually obscured by bushes, tree-trunks, vines, etc., which alternately hide and expose the horsemen. The reason was that "I wanted to produce in the audience the same feeling that the characters have of being trapped." Very often, also, he will combine various techniques to create a new effect, and examples of this have been noted in the discussions of *Drunken Angel, Ikiru, Seven Samurai,* and other films.

Kurosawa is also interested in economy of action and sometimes will use a prop of some kind to obtain it. This prop may be as large as the single room in *The Lower Depths*—a great cage in which the camera may roam— or the junkyard "village" of *Dodesukaden,* or it may be as small as the electric fan in certain scenes of *Record of a Living Being* or the low table with the saké bottle in *Red Beard,* around which the camera set-ups are chosen. In *Dodesukaden* there are several examples of props used to comment on character. The crepe-paper flowers are used ironically in relation to the fate of Kazuko, who is raped while lying on them. The thirty-haired brushes counted by the brush-maker as he attempts to console his unhappy stepchildren represent the sole concrete, objective reality on which he can safely rely. The rags torn up by Hei both express how he earns his living and convey his frustration.

There is a fine example of the use of a small prop in *One Wonderful Sunday.* The boy and girl eat their cookies in a vacant lot in which a very large section of concrete sewer-pipe stands. They rest against it, they lean over it, she climbs into it—all in the most naturalistic way. At the same time the camera sees the pipe as a piece of sculpture. Details of it, different ways of seeing it, different set-ups emphasizing different parts of it—all hold the dialogue scenes together, create an economy of action. A more subtle example is the hay-rack in *Sanjuro.* The scene is the barn with the two rescued ladies and the boy samurai. First the camera is beside it, then in back of it, then under it—each of the many cuts containing a different portion of the rack itself, this visible structure, visibly holding these scenes together.

Sometimes economy is achieved by having multiple actions occur within the frame of a single scene. In *Scandal,* for example, the upper half of the screen shows the unwitting couple in their hotel window; the lower half has the photographers taking the incriminating photo. In the courtyard scene in *Red Beard,* the talking children are in the upper left-hand frame; the listening adults are in the lower right. Here, the composition of the scene comments directly on the action by explicating it. Usually, Kurosawa's compositions are more subtle, as in the metaphysically composed shot of Dersu and Arseniev situated with the sun on one side and the moon on the other in *Dersu Uzala.*

In both *The Quiet Duel* and *The Bad Sleep Well* a wall is used in the center of the frame, separating the lovers. In the second part of *Sugata* a standing pillar splits the screen, with the priest (*satori* achieved) on one side and Sugata (*satori* not yet achieved) on the other. In *Red Beard* a tree separates the girl who says she does not trust men from the young man who says he does not trust women. And in the campfire scene of *Dersu Uzala* near the beginning of Part Two, a diagonally placed tree bisects the shot, separating Dersu and Arseniev together in the lower right-hand corner of the frame from the group of singing soldiers at the left. The shot compositions of *Dersu Uzala* are frequently structured by such diagonals, depicting the conflict between two ways of life.

A favorite Kurosawa composition has two or more people carrying on a conversation while facing in different directions. *Yojimbo* is full of this; it is used to give the feeling of danger—both directions must be watched at once because the enemy is all around. Occasionally this composition is used (as it is in Antonioni's films) to indicate the difficulty of communication. In *The Quiet Duel,* when Mifune is trying to explain to Shimura, they face opposite directions. Richer and more complicated are those compositions that insist not only on the actors facing in different directions but also on various diagonals; the most famous example is the outdoor scene in *The Lower Depths.*

Kurosawa also uses other attributes of the camera to make his point. He has used slow-motion a number of times—two examples occur in *Seven Samurai*: the death of the madman at the beginning of the picture, and the death of the blustering samurai during the first fight with the swordsman.

Again, slow-motion is used for the advance of the forest in *The Throne of Blood,* and fast-motion is used for Mifune's fall down the stairs at the end of that film. And the long coda of *Kagemusha* (six minutes in the original version) achieves much of its power in that it is shot entirely in slow-motion. One remembers too the battle in *Ran* and the slow-motion finale of *Rhapsody in August.*

The special attributes of long-distance lenses are also used: to pile up images of night-time Yokohama at the end of *High and Low;* to throw images at the audience, as in the horse-fall in *Seven Samurai;* for humor, as when one of the bad men in *Yojimbo* carries Mifune in a tub and the lenses make his fat legs fatter, and his breathless trot appears to get him nowhere at all.

Kurosawa occasionally "stops the camera" by reprinting the same frame over and over again, as in the montage sequence in *The Bad Sleep Well.* Or he "stops" the actors and presents an actual but motionless scene (as in the end of the prize-fight in the second part of *Sugata*). Or he uses still photographs both as nostalgic evocation (*The Quiet Duel, Record of a Living Being, Ikiru, Dersu Uzala*) and because (as in *The Bad Sleep Well* and *High and Low*) a presented photograph in a film looks "realer than real."

Until *Dodesukaden* Kurosawa had never availed himself of color (except for the short scene in *High and Low*), and his reason, as one might expect, was that it was not "real" enough. "Color film isn't good enough to take Japanese colors . . . at present the degree of color transparency is too high. Japan's colors are all dull colors, dense colors, and if I did a color film I would want to bring this out. The film that got the prize . . . *The Gate of Hell*—those colors were exotic, not Japanese."

In *Dodesukaden, Dersu Uzala, Kagemusha, Ran,* and *Dreams,* Kurasawa's use of color is neither naturalistic nor exotic. *Dodesukaden's* bright and rich colors work in counterpoint to the apparent misery in which the characters live and by themselves suggest that even lives utterly barren materially may be enriched with compensating joys. In *Dersu Uzala* contrasts of gold and black invoke a mood suggesting the end of the world, an uprooting of all men from the face of the earth. Color conveys the director's sense that human beings no longer deserve to enjoy the fruitfulness of nature because they have been so profligate with her gifts. In *Kagemusha* the colors are muted (pale blues, thin greens) and become even more attenuated toward the end of the picture, as if to reflect the dilution of power, the waning of strength, the loss of vitality. In *Ran* color is used for identification, the various armies are color coordinated; in *Dreams* there seems to have been some intent to use a different color for each sequence.

In his color films as in those in black and white, Kurosawa continually emphasizes texture, and this concern is one of the things that gives his films the "Kurosawa look." To remember any of his films is, in part, to remember a texture: the sun-drenched whites and light grays of *Rashomon,* the coarse grain of *Record of a Living Being,* the blacks and dark grays of *Yojimbo.* In *The Bad Sleep Well* one remembers the texture of brocade (the wife's kimono) against polished wood and, eventually, raw concrete; in *The Throne of Blood,* pale white skin, dense white fog, the black texture of earth, the glint of black armor; in *Red Beard,* the mellowed sheen of old wood, the sunlit textures of human skin.

As we have seen in the discussion of *Rashomon,* Kurosawa's use of cinematic punctuation is entirely his own. He has found the wipe ideal for a change of scene that needs more than a cut; the fade is used only when a softening is desired; the dissolve usually means a great amount of time has passed (except in the dissolves at the end of *Rashomon* and those in *They Who Step on the Tiger's Tail,* where dissolves are used to show Benkei getting more and more drunk). The simple cut is most useful to him within the sequence itself. Punctuation is not a matter of deciding and letting the laboratory do the work. It is often in the script from the very first and is considered an integral part of the camera work of the picture.

Once all of the above have been more or less decided, Kurosawa is ready to shoot. He sometimes does so with three cameras running simultaneously, though this is by no means an invariable rule: many scenes in *Red Beard* used only one; the train sequence in *High and Low* used nine. In *Dodesukaden* Kurosawa had mobile and detachable sets constructed. He used two cameras but positioned the second only after the set had been taken apart, placing it, for example, where a wall had been earlier in the sequence. (The wall was actually removed at times after the first camera had begun running, to the occasional distress of the actors: at one point Junzaburo Ban tried, after the cameras had stopped running, to lean against a missing wall, not realizing that the set had been taken apart during shooting.) The cameras themselves are kept as light as possible. "They have to be," Takao Saito, one of Kurosawa's cameramen, has said. "The ordinary director, if he doesn't like the scene, moves the actors around, but Kurosawa moves the cameras. Ordinarily, the director sits next to the camera, but Kurosawa is always moving in and out among his two or three. He must walk about four times as much as other directors."

Another cameraman, Fukuzo Koizumi, has said: "Nowadays, he more and more goes in for long takes, three or more minutes, and lets the actors play naturally, and out of this he selects the best shots. Often the cameras will have long-focal-length lenses on them, one 350 mm. and the other 500 mm. [The standard is 50 to 75 mm.] What he really wants to get is the best possible shot." This search accounts, as we have seen in the discussion of *Record of a Living Being,* for the usual shooting ratio in the Kurosawa picture, which is 20 to 1 (i.e., one foot of film used for every twenty exposed)—a high ratio, about as high as Antonioni's, but by no means extravagant; certain TV films have been made at the ratio of 500 to 1.

Kurosawa's method of shooting causes lighting problems. Set and actors must be properly illuminated not for one camera viewpoint, but for three. In addition, telephoto lenses need more light than ordinary lenses. Ichiro Inohara, who usually lights the Kurosawa picture, has said: "We had to devise a special new tool—we call it the *yokan* reflector. Ordinarily, for outdoor daytime shooting we use silver-paper-covered boards, but these did not bounce light nearly far enough. Using long-distance lenses, we had to somehow light people three or four times further away than usual. Then we found that fine crinkled silver paper that *yokan* [Japanese bean-paste candy] comes in worked and so we use it.

"Kurosawa works on the principle that "everything seen on the screen is of equal importance" and this means that the camera must be stopped way down. We have to shoot at, say, f/22 on an ordinary f/4.5 scene. This means that even our day scenes need more light than most directors' night scenes."

With *Dodesukaden,* which for financial reasons Kurosawa shot at great speed, he continued shooting on cloudy days by painting shadows on the ground and found that colors actually reproduce best in cloudy weather. At times he would use floodlights with a variety of color filters attached. To create greater contrast on these cloudy days, he painted the shadowed areas a darker color and lighter areas a brighter shade.

Nasai Soeda, Kurosawa's still-man since *Drunken Angel,* has said: "The Kurosawa group never poses for stills. Instead, the still-man, staying near the camera, carrying all kinds of cameras himself, must shoot the moving actors from the same angle that they will later be viewed at on the screen. If you miss your chance just once, you rarely have the opportunity to take it over again. It is rather like being a newspaper cameraman. After everything is finished, Kurosawa looks through these hundreds of negatives and throws out all those he doesn't like.

"He doesn't know the meaning of the word 'compromise' and his search for the perfect extends all the way from the performances to my stills. This, of course, makes an endless succession of struggles and difficulties for his staff but, on the other hand, it opens up for all of us a whole world of creativity."

# ACTORS AND ACTING

Kurosawa, as he writes the script, often thinks of the actor who he knows will play it. In this he is like Ozu, who once said: "I could no more write, not knowing who the actor was to be than an artist could paint not knowing what color he was using." The personality of the actor colors the role and—like Antonioni, like Bergman—Kurosawa writes taking advantage of the characteristics he will be working with.

That Mifune is one kind of person, that Shimura is another—this affects the film even as it is being written. Since an actor is an actor he is able to counterfeit various emotions that are not his own, and Kurosawa is often in a position to distinguish actual characteristics within the actor and to encourage them, often at the expense of what the actor would have considered his own "interpretation." While the director is quite ready to let the actor take the lead (Mifune in *Drunken Angel*), usually he attempts to lead the actor into himself, to encourage responses that would be natural to the actor as a person.

Shimura has said: "The way we go about it is this. He has had the idea,

he has written the script, and then we have a reading, since the complete casting only occurs after the script is finished. After we've read it, we talk about it, and he will then correct lines or even whole scenes. Then we have a walk-through rehearsal; after that a make-up rehearsal; then a number of rehearsals with lights and camera positions; then lots of dress rehearsals, just like on the stage." Kurosawa may have whole weeks of "dress rehearsals" (as for *The Lower Depths*) or (for films after *Yojimbo*) he will light a cyclorama at the studio and have the entire film performed as a play, in full costume, over and over again while he, the sole audience, watches.

"Kurosawa," said Shimura, "never tells an actor how a thing should be done. Rather, he looks at the actor's interpretation and may then make suggestions such as: 'I don't think that's quite enough,' or 'How would this way be?' or 'Perhaps we'd better not do that.'"

As assistant director, Shiro Miroya, has said: "Kurosawa frequently says to new actors: 'OK, fine, but let's take it over again to make sure.' This relaxes them, and what always happens is that when he edits he chooses the one taken just to make sure. On the other hand, when it comes to veterans like Mifune or Shimura, he says almost nothing, gives hardly any direction. This is because, during rehearsals, they have been quite able to understand what he is after. It is really strange. Kurosawa, who can be a real demon at times when he'll scream out 'the rain isn't falling like I want it to,' or 'that damn wind isn't blowing the dust right,' is always so terribly gentle with actors."

Tsutomu Yamazaki (the criminal in *High and Low*) has said that in his first nine films no one paid any attention to him but that in his first Kurosawa film his acting was highly praised. "Yet, it isn't as though I'd myself done anything special. It was because I was working with Kurosawa. It is so easy to work with him, he spends time with you on your work . . . he treats his actors with such respect, he even listened to what *I* had to say. There wasn't much value in it, that's true, but he acted as though there were. I'd heard that the Kurosawa group was very severe, and that is true, but his kind of severity is the kind that gives you the true freedom necessary to act."

Seiji Miyaguchi, who has been in many Kurosawa films, from the second part of *Sugata* (where he played one of Sanshiro's fellow pupils) to *The Bad Sleep Well* (where he was the public prosecutor), said: "The man who made me as an actor is Kurosawa. . . . When he wanted me as the swordsman in *Seven Samurai* I couldn't even carry a sword, much less use one. (People tell me I was good in the role—but there was one scene I never could do: I was supposed to get on a horse and gallop away, and I couldn't do it; even went to riding school, and my behind got redder than any monkey's; finally we left the scene out.) During the shooting, which took a long time, over a year, I became friendly with him, got to know all of him, not just that strong side that makes some people call him 'the Emperor.' It was he, I now know, who created that performance for me. With pure skill he somehow got the very best out of me."

Tatsuya Nakadai (the villain of *Yojimbo* and *Sanjuro,* the head detective in *High and Low,* and the hero of *Kagemusha* and *Ran*) has said: "When you hear about the Kurosawa group, you . . . always hear that after dozens of rehearsals the actors' voices finally gave out, or that so-and-so had to fall off his horse dozens of times. Well, it is all true. Yet, one works for him with pleasure because one of the premises of our profession is to be as creative as we know how . . . and the danger is that we'll play it safe. I know that I can go off the rails in my creativity, can really create and at the same time can invalidate my role. Kurosawa is a great director and he never loses sight of what his film should become. He calls a lie a lie, and he cuts out what ought to be cut. . . . For this reason his very strength is an attraction and it is a proud pleasure to work with him."

Haruko Sugimura, one of Japan's finest stage-actresses, who plays the whorehouse madam in *Red Beard,* has said: "The first time I appeared in a Kurosawa film was *No Regrets for Our Youth.* [She played the mother of Susumu Fujita.] Since then thirteen years have passed and we have both gotten older, but I can't see that there has been any change at all in Kurosawa's way of directing. By which I mean to say that back then he had been a director for only two or three years, and yet even now he has preserved his vitality, unchanged during all of this time. . . . One of the things I find most characteristic of him is that he makes you accept *yourself* about one hundred and twenty percent—or perhaps it's just that he pulls about one hundred and twenty percent out of you.

"When we theater people play in films it is usually—to be brutally frank—in a bit-part. We don't bother to create a role, we merely play our type. With Kurosawa it is entirely different, he wrings what you are right out of you. Of course, this is difficult, but it is certainly good for an actor."

Kyoko Kagawa (the sister in *The Lower Depths,* the wife in *The Bad Sleep Well* and *High and Low,* the madwoman in *Red Beard,* the wife in *Madadayo*) has said: "It is only when I work with the Kurosawa group tht I feel fulfilled as an actress—and coupled with that is the feeling of relief that I know when I see that Kurosawa is satisfied and that the long cut is finally taken. It is very hard and very rewarding.

"I remember, during *The Bad Sleep Well,* there was a long shot, a love scene with Mifune, and I was to listen and then cry. After we had rehearsed it and were about to take it, Kurosawa came over to me and said: 'But I really want you to cry, you know.' This taught me that in his films it must be truth itself and not merely resemble truth. And he shows us this in other ways. Working with him, he pulls us along with his passion for his work, with his supreme individuality. . . . I'm always impressed by the way in which Kurosawa, being a man who is aware of the smallest things, sees into the states of mind of the actors and really takes wonderful care of us. He always shows us, in the very midst of work, how interesting, how pleasing, how meaningful it all is. After one of his pictures is over, you are exhausted, but at the same time you want more than anything else to be in the next one as well."

Takashi Shimura once said: "I've made twelve or thirteen films with him, and each one is something very like a revelation to me—not only about him, but about myself as well. Talking about actors' realizing themselves, when I am with Kurosawa . . . I realize myself best. And yet he never dictates. Rather, he *allows* you to do your best, and for him you do it." And Mifune has said: "There is nothing of note I have done without Kurosawa, and I am proud of none of my pictures but those which I have done with him."

Kurosawa's enormous sympathy and tact begin with the script and quite obviously extend through his treatment of his actors. For him, shooting a film is also a way of getting to know his actors, or getting to know them over again. For this reason he is fond of spending as much time with them as possible. "When you are directing," he has said, "you come to a point where you can no longer explain with words. Unless you can *see,* as an actor, what the director is trying to express simply by how he looks and acts himself, you are going to miss the finer points. When my cast and I are on location we always eat together, sleep in the same rooms, are constantly talking together. And you might say that *here* is where I direct.

"When I did *Rashomon* we all lived together in a little inn. We were a very small group and it was as though I was directing *Rashomon* every minute of the day and night. At times like this, you can talk everything over and get very close indeed.

"If you are working with someone for the first time, both sides get a bit shy—which is one of the reasons that I *like* to include new people, and is also one of the reasons I rarely let go of anyone I've once used. It isn't very good to simply use a person and then drop him.

"Of course, by and large, brand-new people tend to be good when they make their first appearances, but in a few years [working with various directors] they lose both their ability and their individuality. They turn into cute little things, only interested in themselves and that they are photographed flatteringly enough. Girls are most like this, but a lot of men are too. You make two or three films with some of them and anything that interested you at first just disappears. They become just like film actors. The ideal new person in my pictures has to have an individuality so strong that the studio won't be able to round off the edges.

"I remember Miki Odagiri [the girl in *Ikiru,* her only Kurosawa film]. She was a very funny girl, who had some highly interesting interpretive touches. She came from the stage, from the Haiyu-za [The Actor's Theatre]. Well now, she was one of the ones who could have gone on and done other things. She could even have become a romantic-lead-type actress if she wanted.

"About the actor's influence on me. Well, the older actors, those who are used to working with me, like Mifune and Shimura, they often advise me. Japanese directors are terribly prone to do everything by themselves and in their own way without really caring whether the actors understand or not. This is the reason why there are few actors who ever realize themselves. They become puppets for the director. I suppose that is why one actor may be terribly good with one director and quite poor with another."

Kurosawa here may have been thinking of Mifune, an actor little short of superlative in his Kurosawa appearances, but with other directors occasionally even worse than mediocre. Certainly, as Mifune himself has said, it is Kurosawa alone who draws his best from him. Mifune is in all of the major films from *Drunken Angel* to *Red Beard* except *Ikiru*. He is to Kurosawa what John Wayne was to John Ford, Max von Sydow to Ingmar Bergman; his fortune and career are linked with those of the director, even for the Japanese, who know him in the films of other directors; he is, in a special way, the supreme Kurosawa creation.

Under Kurosawa, Mifune's versatility is phenomenal. Compare him as the bandit in *Rashomon* (with Mori as the husband) and as the secretary in *The Bad Sleep Well* (with Mori as the president); compare his and Shimura's roles as cop and head detective in *Stray Dog* with their roles in *Seven Samurai*. It seems scarcely possible that the same actors are involved, so completely different, so utterly separate are the people they seem to be. Or remember Mifune as the old man in *Record of a Living Being*, followed by Mifune as the thief in *The Lower Depths*. The actor's range and versatility is astonishing. On the other hand, in the films of other directors, in *Samurai*, in *Rickshaw-man*, in the picture he himself directed, *The Legacy of the Five Hundred Thousand*, Mifune never once surprises, is always and eternally his own profile and nothing more. It is as though Kurosawa has been able to draw from Mifune something that even Mifune did not know he possessed.

Mifune may have received much from Kurosawa but he also gave a lot. Indeed, after his departure (occasioned in part by differences during *Red Beard*) the director's pictures were not the same and that sense of loss we feel in the later films, beginning with *Dodesukaden*, is in part the loss of Mifune and what he stood for.

Kurosawa did not use any of the members of his usual acting company in *Dodesukaden*. None of the familiar actors in his films appear, not even Shimura or Mifune. Only by eliminating the obvious star could he create a film without a hero, and for the first time Kurosawa fully encouraged the actors to innovate freely and to behave extemporaneously.

An even more striking departure occurred with *Dersu Uzala*, in which Kurosawa worked entirely with Soviet actors. Yet he seems to have employed the same methods he used in Japan. He chose Maxim Munzuk to play Dersu after sifting through photographs of twenty native Soviet Asian actors. Munzuk, who had been an actor in the Tuva National Theater, but had never before appeared in a film, did not meet with the approval of the Russians, no doubt because he did not look the part. But as Kurosawa has indicated, after many screen tests Munzuk proved to be "exactly Dersu Uzala," a small, ordinary-looking man perfectly suited to Kurosawa's theme: the coming obsolescence of the natural human being. Kurosawa had to stop the camera at points when Munzuk over-acted as a result of his theatrical training. But the final performance is as poignant as any in Kurosawa's work, a particular achievement given the fact that Kurosawa did not speak Russian and had to have his instructions conveyed through an interpreter.

In *Kagemusha* Kurosawa used a few of his regular actors (Nakadai, Yamazaki) but surrounded them with unknowns and amateurs. He had a whole

series of try-outs before filming began, even advertising in the newspapers for those interested to come and audition. Thousands did, and from these he chose the rest of the cast for his film.

Kurosawa extracts performances from his actors not only by (as Mifune once jokingly said) "telling [them] what not to do," but also by giving them things they *are* to do. He purposely takes advantage of something he has seen an actor do and makes it a motif: the walk in *Yojimbo*, the scratching of the stubbled chin in *Sanjuro*, the mussing up of the hair and scratching of the head (the character has dandruff) in *Scandal*, the peculiar sidewise stroking of the beard in *Red Beard*, the involuntary tic in *Dodesukaden*, the contemplative pipe-smoking of Dersu Uzala, the stroking of their moustaches by Takeda Shingen and his double in *Kagemusha*. By giving his actor a single attitude, something that identifies and illuminates, he creates a peg upon which the characterization may be hung. Not that Kurosawa always knows what it is going to be. Still, he knows more than the actor does and—more important—he knows his actors. He knows what kind of people they are, what possibilities they possess, better than they themselves do.

At the same time, in his later films, Kurosawa has obviously stopped thinking of any particular actor when he writes his script. Now actors are chosen because they conform to a type he has already imagined. One of the results has been a lowering of the acting level in his pictures: from overacting in *Ran* to the bad acting found in *Dreams, Rhapsody in August,* and *Madadayo.*

Since the Kurosawa film is about character, the actor and his interpretation, his abilities, become more important than in the ordinary picture. By giving the actor something to do, Kurosawa creates the state where the reassured actor may be advised. His method of patient coaxing, of slight but constant guidance, allows the desired characterization to appear, to grow, to bloom. And when it does, he is there with his cameras to record this new reality that he himself has nurtured.

# EDITING

As we have seen, Kurosawa says he shoots in order to get something to edit. Though what he shows must be important, and though he must show it in the best possible way, real life is created only in the editing room. "Among ourselves," Hiroshi Nezu, long Kurosawa's production chief, has said, "we think that he is Toho's best director, that he is Japan's best scenarist, and that he is the best editor in the world.

"He is most concerned with the 'flowing' quality which a film must have. Generally speaking, in an ordinary picture, the last scene may be taken on the first day of shooting—this is common procedure. With Kurosawa it is different. He follows the script, scene by scene, shooting chronologically. If you ask him, he'll say that it is to capture this flow and that otherwise he would not be able to edit properly. Certainly his ability to look at this flowing picture and then pick the precise place for the perfect cut is astonishing. The Kurosawa film flows *over* the cut, as it were."

The cut is usually invisible in the Kurosawa picture and the consequent "flow" of images is responsible for much of the impact of the film. He is like those composers (Stravinsky is an example) who never allow the bar line to sound. The flow of the music is natural, unforced, distinct, unique, and when one looks at the score one is surprised to find it is full of varied time signatures, changing rapidly from 3/8 to 5/16 to 10/8 to 2/4.

In the same way, when one holds a length of Kurosawa's film to the light, one is surprised at the number of cuts because, when viewing the film, one was not aware of them. Naoki Noborikawa—upon mentioning his surprise that what he had thought was one cut in *Rashomon* turned out to be, with repeated viewing, seven—has said that only Kurosawa could possibly put the Kurosawa footage together. "I once heard a very well-known film editor say: 'When I see anyone's exposed film I can usually establish in what kind of order it will be put together, but with Kurosawa's I simply have no idea.' Most people think that when the shooting is over the director's job is finished, and it all too often is. Not with Kurosawa, however. He shuts himself up in the editing room, week after week, he tries this and that, he experiments with various combinations and it is only after repeated polishings that life is finally breathed into this work—the kind of life he wants and that only editing can give."

Kurosawa's major editing innovations concern the amount of time an image remains on the screen, the continuity from one action to the next, and the placement of the cut. The ordinary way to cut a film is to wait until the necessary action or dialogue is concluded and then end the scene. A director like Ozu feels that this is being entirely too cavalier with the characters. His scenes will often continue past the necessary action or dialogue points, and we will continue to watch the characters after the plot-points are made. Kurosawa, sharing the same concern for character, also refuses to use his characters for purposes of plot; but his method is just the opposite of Ozu's. If an explanation is necessary, he will either cut back in time (*Ikiru, Red Beard, Dersu Uzala*) and show the necessary action, or he will show past and present at the same time (*The Most Beautiful, High and Low*), or he will interrupt the explanation and show its result (and this most usual method is seen in the many short-cuts that so tighten his films). He is particularly averse to any scene that would tend to explain a past action, to predicate itself in history, as it were. Kurosawa's premises are all in the future, and this is what makes them so suspenseful; one is always having to wait and see.

Just as he always cuts out business that gets a character from one place to another—that, for merely geographical reasons, has a character opening and closing doors, for instance—so is Kurosawa impatient with any shot that lasts too long for no good reason. His short scenes are often mere flashes. In *Seven Samurai* one of the shots showing a man pierced by an arrow is just twelve frames (one-half second) long. If you blink, you miss it. In *The Most Beautiful* the heroine falls asleep at her microscope, and there

is a flash of an American airplane, so quick it is almost not visible; but it wakes her up, and it startles the audience. Another example is during one of the fight scenes in *Sugata*. There was a cut showing the opponent flying through the air, having been thrown by Sanshiro. Kurosawa calculated its length and viewed it. Everyone said that it was tremendous. Kurosawa said it looked just like a kite. He halved it, then halved it again. The resulting flash is precisely what he wanted.

If there is good reason for a long scene, however, then the scene becomes very long indeed, even if nothing is happening in it. In *Dodesukaden*, the drinking scene in which Shima entertains his business colleagues consists of an extraordinarily long take. Kurosawa here refuses to cut because the surprise will flow from the action, rather than from the hand of the director. Shima's friends must become appropriately outraged at the inhospitable and rude behavior of his wife, and even go so far as to denounce her, before we learn that Shima, in fact, loves his wife very much. Even longer is the opening scene in *Kagemusha* where the hero, his confidant, and his double sit and talk. The content of the scene is pure explication; its length is justified because, like an introduction to the film, it fills the audience in on everything they will later need to know. Also it serves as a fine contrast to the violent action that follows. On the other hand, in the films after *Ran,* the long scene predominates for less apparent reasons.

Like most good editors, Kurosawa cuts on an action. If this is done the cut itself becomes less noticeable because one is watching something. While many directors observe this rule, the majority use it as a means of getting the camera closer or farther away. For example, a man lights a cigarette in long shot, and when he touches the match to the cigarette, the cut is made; then close-up, match at cigarette, the man inhales, etc. Kurosawa occasionally does this, but usually his action-cuts do not simply facilitate changes in distance; they mark changes of viewpoint. In *Sugata* there is an obscured cut that changes both viewpoint and scene. One scene ends on a dolly that passes very close to a black-uniformed guard. At least one frame is entirely filled with the black uniform. Here Kurosawa cuts and joins to the scene a new one, also a dolly, that begins from the black uniform of a bandsman—and we are in the hall waiting for the big judo bout to start.

Often, however, the change of viewpoint is observed within a single scene. In *They Who Step on the Tiger's Tail, Drunken Angel,* and *The Most Beautiful,* there occur characteristic examples of this cut—all concerned with one of the characters turning his head. In the last film, the heroine is sitting up in bed. The camera is in front of her. She is going to turn her head to one side to look out the window. She begins to turn; the cut occurs when the movement is half-completed; the camera is moved to her side; the action is completed; the light from the window (which we do not see) floods her face. In *Dodesukaden* a fine example of the same technique has the viewpoint change from that of one of the characters to the director himself. In the rape scene as Kazuko's foster father closes in on her, Kurosawa suddenly cuts to a high overhead shot, thereby distancing himself morally from the act; he then cuts away to spare us a view of the rape itself.

A much more involved example of change of viewpoint during action occurs in *The Bad Sleep Well*. Shirai, the company underling, has already seen the "ghost" of the man he thought dead; also an attempt has been made on his life; he is hysterical. The would-be murderer is still near; Shirai falls down. At that point an automobile drives up, and the subsequent camera set-ups are:

1. Shirai on the ground, a car backs into the frame, a door opens and a voice says: *Get in!*
2. A very short scene of the car turning and driving off.
3. Shirai in the front seat, seen from the front. The driver is revealed as Mifune. Shirai looks at him, then turns to look in the back seat.
4. Shirai completes the turn but the new set-up is from the back, in back of the "ghost," whom we did not know was in the car. Shirai looks and tries to scream, registers extreme fright, and collapses in the seat.

The economy of the editing is extreme. We do not, for example, see the door closing after the underling has gotten into the car, and 3–4 (above) are the only "connected" shots. These two shots (like those in *The Most Beautiful*) show the turning of a head and, more, both insist on our feeling what the character feels. We are shown the light from the window flooding the girl's face; we are shown the terror on the face of the man. *We* do not see the window itself; *we* do not see the "ghost."

The view is, in other words, subjective. Since Kurosawa's continual concern is with character, we who look at the film must look at the character himself. This is true of the writing of the script (the entire cinematic vocabulary is devoted to making us realize what it feels like to be Watanabe); it is true of the shooting itself (the "impressionistic" passages in *Rashomon,* for example, show us what the woodcutter is seeing); it is equally true of the editing. Perhaps even truer of the editing, because Kurosawa puts his film together in such a way that while it is unreeling before us (that is, ahead of us, since it proceeds at such speed that we are usually a bit unsure about a scene as we see it), we are continually placed in a position where the surprised reaction of the character must also be our own.

When Kurosawa says it is the editing that gives life to his films, he is saying that it is here that character is finally presented in full to the audience in terms of empathy, of identification, of emotion.

# SOUND AND MUSIC

"Ever since the silent film gave way to the talkie," says Kurosawa, "sound has interfered with the image—and at the same time this flood of sound has become largely meaningless. That is why the director must be very careful—because a motion picture must be the most effective combination of both image and sound. Cinematic sound is never merely accompaniment, never merely what the sound machine caught while you took the scene. Real sound does not merely add to the image, it multiplies it."

The reality of sound is of great importance to Kurosawa, though he oc-casionally uses "artificial" sound (for example, the oboe to simulate the train whistle in *One Wonderful Sunday*; the celesta to counterfeit the noise of the pin-ball machine in *Ikiru*). The sound of the thudding arrows in *The Throne of Blood* is the real sound of thudding arrows; the clash of swords is made by having men actually fight in front of the microphone to produce the peculiar scream of metal on metal. Wataru Konuma, Kurosawa's cur-rent soundman, has spoken of the difficulties inherent in "making horse-hoof sounds, because he makes us use real horses; we have to make them run and then record the sound."

The context of the sound is equally important, and some of Kurosawa's most magical effects have been achieved through an apparently irrational use of natural sound. The night-town sequence in *Ikiru* is heralded by the distant scream of a train-whistle; the scratchy recording of "La Paloma" is as hopelessly tawdry as the backstage of the girlie-show in *Stray Dog*; the claustrophobia of *The Throne of Blood* is heightened by the squeaks and skit-terings of the castle at night; the pathos of the thwarted love-story in *Red Beard* is greatly intensified by the melancholy tinkling of the wind bells; the reality of subjective fantasies in *Dodesukaden* is conveyed by the real sounds of the revving up of a streetcar that accompany Rokkuchan as he runs along shouting, "dodesukaden, dodesukaden."

The volume of the sound in Kurosawa is important. We must strain our ears to hear the ominous whisperings in *The Throne of Blood*; in the same way, recording the male dialogue, Kurosawa purposely cut out all the highs so that a series of startling barks and loud grunts makes up most of the talk. The banging of the tinker in *The Lower Depths* is much louder than the image seems to require; the same is true of the ice breaking at the begin-ning of the second part of *Dersu Uzala,* and the musical motif associated with the main character in that film is thunderously loud, particularly at its close. The sound of the electric fan in *Record of a Living Being* is as omi-nous, and almost as loud, as that of the airplane in a later scene. On the other hand, the sound caused by the many pounds of gold clinking in *The Hidden Fortress* is made as delicate as the sound of a triangle.

Reality, context, and volume are rigorously controlled in the Kurosawa sound track, and the result is a careful selection of what we know we hear and what we hear without realizing it. Music is used in somewhat the same way.

For Kurosawa, as for most directors, movie music means mood-music. Unlike many directors, however, he will often use music under the open-ing titles and then use it but sparingly throughout the film itself. This is true of the opening mambo (a slow mambo, but a mambo nonetheless) in *High and Low* and the rhumba in *The Bad Sleep Well*. It is particularly true in *Dodesukaden*, where music accompanies Rokkuchan at the beginning and end of the film, but is entirely absent from the individual episodes, which, without music, become even more stark and irrevocable. Often, how-ever, the opening music is also leit-motif. In *Ikiru* one of the themes of the opening music is the song that Watanabe will later sing; and both *Sanjuro* and *Yojimbo* use a theme that will later become associated with the hero.

Sometimes the music is also integral to the action of the film. The credit music for *The Most Beautiful* is a girls' chorus, and we later both see and hear his chorus; Mifune himself whistles a theme that is later much used in *The Bad Sleep Well*; most of the music in *The Lower Depths* is made by the cast; *Red Beard* practically has a "theme-song," as has *Dersu Uzala* (a leit-motif, first sung at the campfire by Arseniev's soldiers).

Usually, however, no matter how the music is used, it is only used when needed. Masaru Sato, through *Red Beard* Kurosawa's composer since the death of Hayasaka, has said: "There are many instances in his films where in the climactic scene no music whatever is used. He always says that music disturbs the more meaningful moments of a film."

Kurosawa tends to use music in two ways. One is to support the image and multiply its effect; the other is to combat the image and change its effect. An obvious example of the former is the use of fanfares—for instance, at the death of the daughter in *Scandal*, at the opening of the ruined-factory scenes in *The Bad Sleep Well*, at the final sections of *Sanjuro*, and at the discovery of each clue in *High and Low*. The earliest example is in the second part of *Sugata*, where Fujita suddenly makes up his mind, turns, faces the camera, smiles, and strides into combat—at which moment a brass fanfare is heard. The effect, seen at its most brilliant just before the final battle in *Yojimbo*, is exhilarating first because music supports an emotional moment, second because we realize that our attentlion is being called to this moment, and third because it is a surprise.

Music used to combat the image is psychologically the more interesting, and here Kurosawa often uses popular music (as did Weill, whom he so much admires). The children's song in *Sugata*, all innocence and beauty, is heard under the villains' cynical remarks; patriotic war-songs are heard under scenes of the girls' suffering in *The Most Beautiful*; Mussorgsky, triumphant, is heard under scenes of the girl's despair in *No Regrets for Our Youth*; the "Cuckoo Waltz" in *Drunken Angel* is heard, mindlessly optimistic, as accompaniment to Mifune's despair; the post-war popular hit "Happy Tokyo" is used in the painful hospital sequences of *The Quiet Duel*, and again during the more tense scenes in *Scandal*; it appears again, with many other cheap tunes-of-the-day, during the montage sequences of *Stray Dog*; cheerful Czerny is played by the unhappy girl in *The Idiot*; serene ceremonial music, the *gagaku*, is heard before the bickering gate scenes in *Rashomon*; happy festival-music is used just before the chilling final cut of *The Lower Depths*; the hero of *Ikiru*, in despair, sings an old-fashioned love-song; Wagner and Mendelssohn at their most assured accompany the anxieties of the wedding reception in *The Bad Sleep Well*; the motif associated with the sick Rokkuchan in *Dodesukaden* is entirely joyous, free of any sense of pain.

Both music and sound are given an attention comparatively rare in contemporary film. As with all the other elements of the motion picture, little is left to chance. The director is there choosing, guiding. "I am always struck by his understanding of music," Sato has said, "for this multiplying effect of music and image. He has an ear that can make entirely meaning-ful the combinations of melody, rhythm, and harmony on one hand, and the physical, the psychological, the *seen* on the other. . . . he has this great understanding, and before we start shooting he and I have the most thorough discussion as to what the score should be. And he always says the same thing: 'Now, let's not have any *mizuwari* [watered-down] music—all noise and no meaning.'"

# STYLE

Style is the individual. An artist's style is the artist. Throughout this book we have seen what Kurosawa is through what he has done. One cannot be more intimate than this. Yet, there is always a difference between what one does and what one looks and acts like, and in Kurosawa this difference is so extreme that even now he remains a "mystery" to those who look for profiles, for personal "close-ups," for "the man himself."

I remember that the *New York Times Magazine* once commissioned me to do a profile on Kurosawa. I did not one but three, each one different though similar, and each one was rejected because my subject was "not in focus," because the "idea" of Kurosawa did not emerge clearly enough, because I could not capture his essence in ten pages. Most of this inability was due to my lack of skill, but some of it was because Kurosawa is an extraordinarily complicated person. Generalizations fit him no more than they do his films. The only way to understand Kurosawa is to understand his pictures.

He is not at all interested in anyone's understanding him as a person. He has his family, friends, and drinking-companions; he has his relationships with the producers and the studio—this is quite enough personal understanding for him. Consequently he is not helpful in the slightest to anyone wanting to find out more about him than his films have already offered.

His physical features do not reveal much. He is tall, very tall for a Japanese, and his face centers around his nose. Flanked by large, generous ears, supported by a full, sensuous mouth, this nose—Kyoto-looking, traditionally aristocratic—indicates a sensitivity that is not suggested by the tall, lanky body and the big, capable, workman-like hands. Like many creators, he is not of a piece. He has a divided look: the face of a mystic, the body of a carpenter. Standing in the set, wearing the hat that is his single personal affectation, amid the ordinary furor and occasional chaos of movie-making, he is calm, patient, ruminative, sometimes softly smiling, or quietly indicating how things should be done—the personification of intellect. One might ascribe his demeanor to Oriental impassivity, were there any such thing. Rather, it is the knowing tranquility of a man under control. He already knows what he is going to do, and he knows how to do it. At the same time, however, his hands are always busy.

He plays with his hands; rather, it is as though they play with each other, expressing themselves rather than him. While he watches, friendly and impassive, his fingers are always busy with something or other, searching out something to do. When he directs, his hands are continually moving; hands that look as though they should be kneading clay or planing a board, creating gestures that cannot help but be plastic. Kurosawa literally shapes his film from the empty air. And when a lighter refuses to light or a ball-point pen to write, these hands, with the patience of Red Beard himself, will click the one or manipulate the other until it decides to.

Kurosawa's divided aspect is indicative of him as a person. He is a craftsman who works with ideas. One could carry the dichotomy further and introduce the heart-head schism. The former would then be concerned with "humanism" and Dostoevsky and would produce films such as *One Wonderful Sunday* and *Dodesukaden*; the latter would be all intellect and create films like *The Throne of Blood* and *Dersu Uzala*; somehow the two would occasionally come together and the result would be *Ikiru*.

Such a simplification is not untrue, but it leaves most of Kurosawa unaccounted for because, like most highly organized and complicated men, he is not accountable. Nor does he attempt to account for himself. "I am a director . . . that is all. I know myself well enough to know that if I ever lost my passion for films, then I myself would be lost. Film is what I am about.", A clue to the motive for his attempted suicide in 1971 may lie here.

About how he became what he is, he says: "I don't know—influences, I guess. From the very beginning I respected John Ford. I have always paid close attention to his films and they've influenced me, I think. I finally got to meet him. It was in a London hotel and I was having a quiet glass of wine. He came over and said 'Hey, Akira!'—bought a bottle of scotch and poured us out really stiff drinks. He'd remembered me from when he came here after the war with a group of Occupation people. In London he was very nice to me, sent me chrysanthemums [Japan's national flower] and treated me just like his own son. I liked him—he is so mature, and besides that he looks just like one of the cavalry generals in his own pictures.

"Other influences . . . well, the first film that really impressed me was *La roue* of Gance, and the pictures of Howard Hawks and George Stevens that I saw when I was young. [Elsewhere he has also mentioned Frank Capra and William Wyler as favorites.] And Antonioni. He's not influenced me but he is a very interesting director. . . . And, of course, Mizoguchi—of all Japanese directors I like him the best."

He is not so approving of Japanese films in general. "My liking Mizoguchi, it might be nostalgia—after all I *am* Japanese . . . and he creates a world which is purely Japanese . . . and he really cares about people. So do I. That's the thing about most Japanese films, they don't care anything about people. Then they go and call it artless simplicity or something and terribly Japanese. Well that certainly isn't my way. People abroad seem to like Japanese films right now, but I wouldn't count on it. Most Japanese pictures lack any real depth at all. Even programmers from abroad have depths which we don't approach. All Japanese culture has this thinness.

"I hear a lot about foreigners being able to understand my pictures so well, but I certainly never thought of them when I was making the films. Perhaps it is because I am making films for today's young Japanese that I should find a Western-looking format the most practical. In order for them to understand I have to translate, as it were. *Seven Samurai,* for example. Under Mifune's scenes I had Hayasaka put in a mambo. If purely Japanese music had been used I don't think the young people would have felt what that character was like, how much he resembled them. I really only make pictures for people in their twenties. They don't know anything about Japan or Japaneseness, not really. Oh, they will in time, but not now. Oh, I'm Japanese all right. I'm truly Japanese."

He is right. And despite the fact that he has become a director of international status, that the Japanese critics are always calling him "Western"; despite the fact that we of the West see his films without once remembering that the people are something so strange as "Japanese," one of the ways to define Kurosawa's style would be to insist upon this Japaneseness.

Kurosawa comes from samurai stock; his father was one of the last of the old military-educators. Whatever part heredity and environment may have played, Kurosawa himself embodies a number of these earlier qualities. In particular, in him is seen in a very pure form the old-fashioned virtue of compassionate steadfastness, complete moral honesty, inability to compromise, and action through belief—all of which come under that single much-maligned term: *bushido.*

Nowadays all one sees of it is in the *chambara* or the Kabuki, and in a very debased form indeed. It usually has to do with obligation, personal honor, self-sacrifice, and other uninteresting attributes. Originally, however, it was a code of ethics, based in part on Zen teachings, which in its finest form became a philosophy, part of which might be paraphrased (from one of the original teachings) as "if your mind is clean, orderly, likewise will your environment be clean, orderly." The follower of *bushido* could not blame environment for any lapse. He had to take full responsibility for wherever he was and for those with whom he was. Their state commented directly on his own. He was the center of his universe and if it was less than habitable then this was his own doing. Consequently early *bushido* had much to do with spiritual enlightenment, with an acute sensitivity to things as they are, and was of an innate practicality.

Another maxim of the time was: "Face both man and nature and learn." Thus the man adhering to *bushido* was a continual student in the face of the world and his test lay never in what he planned or thought but in what he did. If the *chambara* now has a large stock of heroes, it is because most heroes believe that a man is solely and entirely what he does. Consequently, the samurai who understood *bushido* was no sword-slinger. Action is far too precious to waste. Further, any action that could not in some way be corrected (a way of fighting, a way of thinking) was valueless. The reason was not, as might be thought, that perfection ought to be attained; rather, it was that *bushido* as a philosophy insisted on the fact that perfection was not only impossible, it was also a chimera, and a dangerous one at that. *Bushido* led nowhere, that is, it had no goal. It was just what the name implies, a way— a way of living, a process rather than a state. Therefore, anyone who thought himself past correction would be fraud, because in *bushido* one could never attain the status of an end-result, an accomplished thing. Accordingly, *bushido* could only be expressed through action, and the most profound of the samurai maxims was: "To know and to act are one and the same."

The application of *bushido* tenets to the films of Kurosawa is obvious. His heroes are always completely human in that they are corrigible. The Kurosawa fable shows that it is difficult indeed "to know"; but at the end of the picture the hero has come to learn that "to know and to act are one and the same." The Kurosawa villain is the man who thinks he knows, who thinks he is complete.

Perhaps nowhere more completely do these tenets of *bushido* define the Kurosawa hero than in *Dersu Uzala,* where Dersu himself is a living example of a person who embodies the maxim "face both man and nature and learn." He is, ironically, an isolated Siberian hunter and not a samurai; yet through Dersu Kurosawa has created a man who exemplifies the pure way of life in harmony with self and nature, in humble acknowledgment of man's smallness before the world. In having discovered the balance between the self and the demands of the environment, Dersu, although he carries no sword, is as ideal a warrior as Kambei of *Seven Samurai* himself. Like the samurai he cares nothing for material things, content to take from the world only what he requires for his own sustenance. His ethical code and his way of life are indeed identical.

Since the similarities between Kurosawa's heroes and Kurosawa himself are many, one may observe the old-fashioned virtues of *bushido* in the director himself—which is just what we have done throughout this book. With his ascetic face, his swordsman's hands, Kurosawa might be thought of as the last of the samurai.

In contemporary Japan, *bushido* is completely debased; the fury of the critics, to whom (in Japan more than elsewhere) compromise is a way of life, might be caused in part by Kurosawa's commitment to its virtues. At the same time, certainly, part of the success of *Seven Samurai, Yojimbo, Kagemusha,* and even the foreign-made *Dersu Uzala* with the Japanese audience is that these films present this ethic at a time when it is almost forgotten, yet still retains its part—however small—in the national character. When Kurosawa says he makes his films for the young people, he also says that he is bringing back to them a spiritual heritage that was once theirs. Like all creators, Kurosawa is a moralist; like all stylists, he usually manages to hide that fact superlatively well.

Thus, though Kurosawa's films appear to be of infinite variety, there is at the same time a unity, a completely responsible and ultimately serious attitude toward life that makes them, despite their seeming differences, all of a piece. And this totality is the totality of the man.

The basis of the Kurosawa style, as we have seen again and again throughout this book, is a search for reality and an inability to tolerate illusion. The Kurosawa character, like its creator, is possessed by a need to know things as they are, to know life as it is—though that knowledge necessarily includes suffering, since suffering is one of the ways through which one recognizes existence. Therefore reality is for Kurosawa a very different thing from what usually passes for it.

"There are people," he has said, "who criticize my work . . . and say it is not realistic. But I feel that merely copying the outward appearance of the world would not result in anything real—that is only copying. I think that to find what is real one must look very closely at one's world, to search for those things that contribute to this reality which one feels under the surface. These are few and one uses them to create. These are the core around which the world moves, the axis on which it turns. The novels of Dostoevsky, Tolstoy, and Turgenev show us what these things are. To be an artist means to search for, find, and look at these things; to be an artist means never to avert one's eyes."

In the films of Kurosawa one finds that these things include an awareness of oneself and of the world and an awareness of the fact that the world and the self do not, cannot, match. "I suppose all my films have a common theme. If I think about it though, the only theme I can think of is really a question: Why can't people be happier together?" To ask that question is to answer it—which is what Kurosawa has done in every one of his major films. People cannot be happier because they are people, *because* they are human.

Kurosawa is a philosopher who works in film and who affirms that in this weakness lies the essentially human quality. But, though weak, man can hope and through this can prevail. Samurai and robbers may be revealed as one and the same, but there are always the villagers who, after the great deeds are done, will plant the new rice with hope and confidence. Man must fight to retain hope in the midst of this hopeless world, and in this fight all men are brothers.

This is the central thesis of Kurosawa's films, most of which show the progress from despair to hope, and it is one of the reasons his films are so meaningful to the world. This thesis is also personal to the director, is an expression of himself as a man. "The director," he said, "really always makes his film for himself. . . . If he says he makes it for the public, he is lying. If the film is liked by the public and seems made for them, this is because their ideas are the same as the director's and not the other way around. He cannot make a picture different from his own ideas, from his own emotions—that is, he cannot make it and be honest about it. It is impossible for him to make a film below his own level; impossible that he make a picture which caters to public taste. Whatever level a picture is made on, that is the director's own philosophic, intellectual, emotional, artistic level."

# Filmography of Akira Kurosawa

The release dates given in this filmography refer to the opening date of the initial public release. The commonly used English title of each film is followed by the Japanese title and then, in order, alternative English titles, French titles, German titles. In preparing this filmography I am particularly indebted to the assistance of Uni Japan Film.

## Sanshiro Sugata

Sugata Sanshiro, 25 March, 1943
*Judo Saga / La légende de judo—I / Sanshiro Sugata.*

2,166 meters; 80 minutes. Re-released, 1952; negative in existence; prints in circulation. A Toho Production.

Produced by Keiji Matsuzaki. Scenario by Akira Kurosawa. After the novel by Tsuneo Tomita. Photographed by Akira Mimura. Art Direction by Masao Totsuka. Music by Seichi Suzuki. Edited by Toshio Goto and Akira Kurosawa.

| | |
|---|---|
| SUGATA | Susumu Fujita |
| SHOGORO YANO, *his teacher* | Denjiro Okoohi |
| HANSUKE MURAI | Takashi Shimura |
| SAYO, *his daughter* | Yukiko Todoroki |
| SABURO MOMMA, *the jujitsu teacher* | Yoshio Kosugi |
| OSUMI, *his daughter* | Ranko Hanai |
| GENNOSUKE HIGAKI | Ryunosuke Tsukigata |
| YOSHIMA DAN | Akitake Kono |
| YUJIRO TODA | Soshi Kiyokawa |
| KOHEI TSUZAKI | Kunio Mita |
| TORANOSUKI NIISEKI | Akira Nakamura |
| TSUNETAMI IIMURA | Sugisaku Aoyama |
| PRIEST | Kuninori Kodo |
| POLICE CHIEF | Ichiro Sugai |

## The Most Beautiful

Ichiban Utsukushiku, 13 April, 1944
*Most Beautifully / Le plus doux / Le plus beau / Am allerschönsten.*

2,324 meters; 85 minutes. Original negative in existence; prints in general circulation. A Toho Production.

Produced by Motohiko Ito. Scenario by Akira Kurosawa. Photographed by Joji Ohara. Art Direction by Teruaki Abe. Music by Seichi Suzuki.

| | |
|---|---|
| FACTORY PRODUCTION HEAD | Takashi Shimura |
| HIS ASSISTANT | Ichiro Sugai |
| GIRLS | Yoko Yaguchi |
| | Koyuri Tanima |
| | Takako Irie |
| | Toshiko Hattori |

## Sanshiro Sugata—Part Two

Zoku Sugata Sanshiro, 3 May, 1945
*Judo Saga—II / La légende de judo—II / Sugata Sanshiro Fortsetzung.*

2,268 meters; 83 minutes. No original negative, dupe-negative in existence; no prints in circulation. A Toho Production.

Produced by Motohiko Ito. Scenario by Akira Kurosawa. After the novel by Tsuneo Tomita. Photographed by Hiroshi Suzuki. Art Direction by Kazuo Kubo. Music by Seichi Suzuki.

| | |
|---|---|
| SUGATA | Susumu Fujita |
| SHOGORO | Denjiro Okochi |
| YOSHIMA DAN | Akitake Kono |
| GENNOSUKE | Ryunosuke Tsukigata |
| SAYO | Yukiko Todoroki |
| YUJIRO TODA | Soshi Kiyokawa |

## They Who Step on the Tiger's Tail

Tora no O o Fumu Otokotachi, August, 1945

*The Men Who Tread on the Tiger's Tail / Walkers on the Tiger's Tail / They Who Step on the Tail of the Tiger / Sur la queue du tigre / Les hommes qui marchèrent sur la queue du tigre / Die Männer, die dem Tiger auf den Schwanz traten / Die Tigerfährte.*

1,575 meters; 58 minutes. Released: 24 April, 1952. Original negative in existence; prints in circulation. A Toho Production.

Produced by Motohiko Ito. Scenario by Akira Kurosawa. After the Kabuki *Kanjincho.* Photographed by Takeo Ito. Art Direction by Kazuo Kubo. Music by Tadashi Hattori.

| | |
|---|---|
| BENKEI | Denjiro Okochi |
| TOGASHI | Susumu Fujita |
| KAMEI | Masayuki Mori |
| KATAOKA | Takashi Shimura |
| ISE | Aritake Kono |
| SURUGA | Yoshio Kosugi |
| HIDACHIBO | Dekao Yoko |
| YOSHITSUNE | Hanshiro Iwai |
| PORTER | Kenichi Enomoto |

## Those Who Make Tomorrow

Asu o Tsukuru Hitobito, 2 May, 1946

*Ceux qui font l'avenir / Ceux qui bâtissent l'avenir / Erbauer des Morgens.*

2,250 meters; 81 minutes. Original negative in existence; no prints in existence. A Toho Production.

Produced by Ryo Takei, Sojiro Motoki, Keiji Matsuzaki, and Tomoyuki Tanaka. Scenario by Yusaku Yamagata and Kajiro Yamamoto. Photographed by Takeo Ito, Mitsui Miura, and Taiichi Kankura. Directed by Kajiro Yamamoto, Hideo Sekigawa, and Akira Kurosawa.

| | |
|---|---|
| FATHER | Kenji Susukida |
| MOTHER | Chieko Takehisa |
| ELDER SISTER | Chieko Nakakita |
| YOUNGER SISTER | Mitsue Tachibana |
| CHAUFFEUR | Masayuki Mori |
| HIS WIFE | Sumie Tsubaki |
| LIGHTMAN | Ichiro Chiba |
| DIRECTOR | Hyo Kitazawa |
| ACTRESS | Itoko Kono |
| THEATER MANAGER | Takashi Shimura |
| SECTION CHIEF | Masao Shimizu |
| DANCING GIRLS | Yuriko Hamada |
| | Sayuri Tanima |

## No Regrets for Our Youth

Waga Seishun ni Kuinashi, 29 October, 1946

*No Regrets for My Youth / Je ne regrette rien de ma jeunesse / Je ne regrette pas ma jeunesse / Kein Bedauern fur meine Jugend.*

3,024 meters; 110 minutes. Original negative in existence; prints in circulation. A Toho Production.

Produced by Keiji Matsuzaki. Scenario by Eijiro Hisaita and Akira Kurosawa. Photographed by Asakazu Nakai. Art Direction by Keiji Kitagawa. Music by Tadashi Hattori.

| | |
|---|---|
| YAGIHARA | Denjiro Okochi |
| HIS WIFE | Eiko Miyoshi |
| YUKIE, *his daughter* | Setsuko Hara |
| NOGE | Susumu Fujita |
| HIS FATHER | Kuninori Kodo |
| HIS MOTHER | Haruko Sugimura |
| ITOKAWA | Aritake Kono |
| POLICE COMMISSIONER | Takashi Shimura |

# One Wonderful Sunday

Subarashiki Nichiyobi, 25 June, 1947

*Wonderful Sunday / Un merveilleux dimanche / Ein wunderschöner Sonntag.*

2,950 meters; 108 minutes. Original negative in existence; no prints in circulation. A Toho Production.

Produced by Sojiro Motogi. Scenario by Keinosuke Uegusa and Akira Kurosawa. Photographed by Asakazu Nakai. Art Direction by Kazuo Kubo. Music by Tadashi Hattori.

| | |
|---|---|
| YUZO | Isao Numasaki |
| MASAKO | Chieko Nakakita |
| YAMIYA, *the black-marketeer* | Ichiro Sugai |
| SONO, *his mistress* | Midori Ariyama |
| BAR-OWNER | Masao Shimizu |

# Drunken Angel

Yoidore Tenshi, 27 April, 1948

*A Drunken Angel / L'Ange ivre / Der trunkene Engel.*

2,690 meters; 98 minutes. Original unreleased version: 4,105 meters; 150 minutes. Original negative of cut version in existence; no prints of uncut version in existence; cut prints in general circulation. A Toho Production.

Produced by Sojiro Motoki. Scenario by Keinosuke Uegusa and Akira Kurosawa. Photographed by Takeo Ito. Art Direction by So Matsuyama. Lighting by Kinzo Yoshizawa. Music by Fumio Hayasaka.

| | |
|---|---|
| SANADA, *the doctor* | Takashi Shimura |
| MATSUNAGA, *the gangster* | Toshiro Mifune |
| OKADA, *the gang-boss* | Reisaburo Yamamoto |
| MIYO, *the nurse* | Chieko Nakakita |
| NANAE, *Matsunaga's mistress* | Michiyo Kogure |
| GIN, *the bar girl* | Noriko Sengoku |
| TAKAHAMA, *the doctor's friend* | Eitaro Shindo |
| THE OLD SERVANT | Choko Iida |

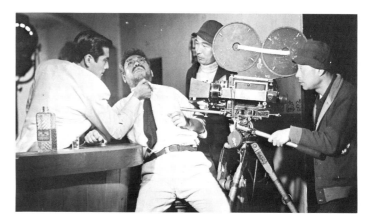

# The Quiet Duel

Shizukanaru Ketto, 13 March, 1949

*A Silent Duel / Le duel silencieux / Das stumme Duel.*

2,591 meters; 95 minutes. Original negative in existence; prints in circulation. A Daiei Production.

Produced by Sojiro Motogi and Hisao Ichikawa. Scenario by Senkichi Taniguchi and Akira Kurosawa. After a play by Kazuo Kikuta. Photographed by Shoichi Aisaka. Art Direction by Koichi Imai. Music by Akira Ifukube.

| | |
|---|---|
| KYOJI FUJISAKI | Toshiro Mifune |
| KONOSUIE FUJISAKI, *his father* | Takashi Shimura |
| MISAO MATSUMOTO, *Kyoji's girl-friend* | Miki Sanjo |
| SUSUMU NAKADA | Kenjiro Uemura |
| TAKIKO NAKADA, *his wife* | Chieko Nakakita |
| RUI MINEGISHI, *the nurse* | Noriko Sengoku |

## Stray Dog

Nora Inu, 17 October, 1949
*Le chien enragé / Ein herrenloser Hund.*

3,342 meters; 122 minutes. Original negative in existence; prints in general circulation. A Shintoho Production; acquired by Toho in 1959.

Produced by Sojiro Motogi. Scenario by Ryuzo Kikushima and Akira Kurosawa. Photographed by Asakazu Nakai. Art Direction by So Matsuyama. Music by Fumio Hayasaka.

| | |
|---|---|
| MURAKAMI, *the detective* | Toshiro Mifune |
| SATO, *the head-detective* | Takashi Shimura |
| YURO, *the criminal* | Ko Kimura |
| HARUMI, *his girl* | Keiko Awaji |
| HONDO, *the suspect* | Reisaburo Yamamoto |
| GIRL | Noriko Sengoku |

## Scandal

Shubun, 30 April, 1950
*Scandale / Skandal.*

2,860 meters; 104 minutes. Original negative in existence; prints in circulation. A Shochiku Production.

Produced by Takashi Koide. Scenario by Ryuzo Kikushima and Akira Kurosawa. Photographed by Toshio Ubukata. Art Direction by Tatsuo Hamada. Music by Fumio Hayasaka.

| | |
|---|---|
| ICHIRO AOYE | Toshiro Mifune |
| MIYAKO SAIGO | Yoshiko Yamaguchi |
| HIRUTA, *the lawyer* | Takashi Shimura |
| MASAKO, *his daughter* | Yoko Katsuragi |
| SUMIE, *Aoye's model* | Noriko Sengoku |
| HORI, *the publisher* | Eitaro Ozawa |
| DRUNK | Bokuzen Hidari |
| FARMER | Kuninori Kodo |

## Rashomon

Rashomon, 25 August, 1950
*Rashomon / Rashomon*

2,406 meters; 88 minutes. Dupe-negative in existence; prints in circulation. A Daiei Production.

Produced by Jingo Minoru (later titles: Produced by Masaichi Nagata). Scenario by Shinobu Hashimoto and Akira Kurosawa. After two stories by Ryunosuke Akutagawa. Photographed by Kazuo Miyagawa. Art Direction by So Matsuyama. Music by Fumio Hayasaka.

| | |
|---|---|
| TAJOMARU, *the bandit* | Toshiro Mifune |
| TAKEHIRO, *the samurai* | Masayuki Mori |
| MASAGO, *his wife* | Machiko Kyo |
| THE WOODCUTTER | Takashi Shimura |
| THE PRIEST | Minoru Chiaki |
| THE COMMONER | Kichijiro Ueda |
| THE POLICE-AGENT | Daisuke Kato |
| THE MEDIUM | Fumiko Homma |

## The Idiot

Hakuchi, 23 May, 1951
*L'Idiot / Der Idiot.*

Original unreleased version: 265 minutes—no prints extant. Original released version: 4,543 meters; 166 minutes. Cut negative in existence; cut prints available. A Shochiku Production.

Produced by Takashi Koide. Scenario by Eijiro Hisaita and Akira Kurosawa. After the novel of Dostoevsky. Photographed by Toshio Ubukata. Art Direction by So Matsuyama. Music by Fumio Hayasaka.

| | |
|---|---|
| KAMEDA | Masayuki Mori |
| AKAMA | Toshiro Mifune |
| TAEKO | Setsuko Hara |
| ONO | Takashi Shimura |
| AYAKO, *his daughter* | Yoshiko Kuga |

| | |
|---|---|
| DEPUTY MAYOR | Nobuo Nakamura |
| CITY ASSEMBLYMAN | Kazuo Abe |
| DOCTOR | Masao Shimizu |
| INTERN | Ko Kimura |
| PATIENT | Atsushi Watanabe |
| NOVELIST | Yunosuke Ito |
| HOSTESS | Yatsuko Tanami |
| NEWSPAPERMAN | Fuyuki Murakami |
| GANG-BOSS | Seiji Miyaguchi |
| GANG-MEMBER | Daisuke Kato |
| HOUSEWIVES | Kin Sugai |
| | Eiko Miyoshi |
| | Fumiko Homma |
| POLICEMAN | Ichiro Chiba |

## Ikiru

Living, 9 October, 1952
*To Live / Doomed / Vivre / Vivre enfin un seul jour / Leben!*

3,918 meters; 143 minutes. Original negative destroyed; several dupe-negatives in existence; prints in circulation. A Toho Production.

Produced by Shojiro Motoki. Scenario by Shinobu Hashimoto, Hideo Oguni, and Akira Kurosawa. Photographed by Asakazu Nakai. Art Direction by So Matsuyama. Lighting by Shigeru Mori. Sound Recording by Fumio Yanoguchi. Music by Fumio Hayasaka.

| | |
|---|---|
| KANJI WATANABE, *Chief, Citizens' Section* | Takashi Shimura |
| MITSUO WATANABE, *his son* | Nobuo Kaneko |
| KAZUE WATANABE, *Mitsuo's wife* | Kyoko Seki |
| KIICHI WATANABE, *Kanji's elder brother* | Makoto Kobori |
| TATSU WATANABE, *Kiichi's wife* | Kumeko Urabe |
| THE MAID | Yoshie Minami |
| TOYO ODAGIRI, *the girl in Watanabe's office* | Miki Odagiri |
| ONO, *sub-section chief* | Kamatari Fujiwara |
| SAITO, *subordinate clerk* | Minosuke Yamada |
| SAKAI, *assistant* | Haruo Tanaka |
| OHARA, *assistant* | Bokuzen Hidari |
| KIMURA, *assistant* | Shinichi Himori |

## Seven Samurai

Shichinin no Samurai, 26 April, 1954

*The Magnificent Seven / Les sept samouraïs / Die sieben Samurai.*

207 minutes. Original negative in existence; 16 mm. TV print of uncut version in existence; prints in circulation. A Toho Production.

Produced by Shojiro Motoki. Scenario by Shinobu Hashimoto, Hideo Oguni, and Akira Kurosawa. Photographed by Asakazu Nakai. Lighting by Shigero Mori. Art Direction by So Matsuyama. Art Consultation by Seison Maeda and Kohei Ezaki. Fencing Direction by Yoshio Sugino. Archery Direction by Ienori Kaneko and Shigeru Endo. Sound Recording by Fumio Yanoguchi. Music by Fumio Hayasaka. Assistant Director—Hiromichi Horikawa.

| | |
|---|---|
| KAMBEI, *leader of the samurai* | Takashi Shimura |
| KIKUCHIYO | Toshiro Mifune |
| GOROBEI | Yoshio Inaba |
| KYUZO | Seiji Miyaguchi |
| HEIHACHI | Minoru Chiaki |
| SHICHIROJI | Daisuke Kato |
| KATSUSHIRO | Ko Kimura |
| MANZO | Kamatari Fujiwara |
| GISAKU | Kuninori Kodo |
| YOHEI | Bokuzen Hidari |
| MOSUKE | Yoshio Kosugi |
| RIKICHI | Yoshio Tsuchiya |
| GOSAKU | Keiji Sakakida |

| | |
|---|---|
| PEASANTS | Jiro Kumagai |
| | Haruko Toyama |
| | Tsuneo Katagiri |
| | Yasuhisa Tsutsumi |
| SHINO, *Manzo's daughter* | Keiko Tsushima |
| GRANDFATHER | Toranosuke Ogawa |
| HUSBAND | Yu Akitsu |
| WIFE | Noriko Sengoku |
| MASTERLESS SAMURAI | Gen Shimizu |
| COOLIE | Jun Tatari |
| VENDOR | Atsushi Watanabe |
| MINSTREL | Sojin Kamiyama |
| BANDITS | Kichijiro Ueda |
| | Shimpei Takagi |
| | Akira Tani |
| | Haruo Nakajima |
| | Takashi Narita |
| | Senkichi Omura |
| | Shuno Takahara |
| | Masanobu Okubo |

## Record of a Living Being

Ikimono no Kiroku, 22 November, 1955

*I Live in Fear / What the Birds Knew / Chronique d'un être vivant / Vivre dans la peur / Notes d'un être vivant / Si les oiseaux savaient / Bilanz eines Lebens / Ein Leben in Angst.*

3,103 meters; 113 minutes. Export version: 2,838 meters; 104 minutes. Original negative extant; prints of export version in circulation. A Toho Production.

Produced by Shojiro Motoki. Scenario by Shinobu Hashimoto, Hideo Oguni, and Akira Kurosawa. Photographed by Asakazu Nakai. Lighting by Kuichiro Kishida. Art Direction by Yoshiro Muraki. Sound Recording by Fumio Yanoguchi. Music by Fumio Hayasaka—completed by Masaru Sato.

| | |
|---|---|
| KIICHI NAKAJIMA | Toshiro Mifune |
| TOYO, *his wife* | Eiko Miyoshi |
| ICHIRO, *his first son* | Yutaka Sada |
| JIRO, *his second son* | Minoru Chiaki |
| YOSHI, *his first daughter* | Haruko Togo |

| | |
|---|---|
| SUÉ, *his second daughter* | Kyoko Aoyama |
| KIICHI'S FIRST MISTRESS | Kiyomi Mizunoya |
| TAEKO, *her daughter* | Saoko Yonemura |
| ASAKO, *his present mistress* | Akemi Negishi |
| HER FATHER | Kichijiro Ueda |
| YAMAZAKI, *Yoshi's husband* | Masao Shimizu |
| KIMIE, *Ichiro's wife* | Noriko Sengoku |
| RYOICHI, *Nakajima's son by a former mistress* | Yoichi Tachikawa |
| HARADA, *member of the family court* | Takashi Shimura |
| SUSUMU, *his son* | Kazuo Kato |
| THE OLD MAN FROM BRAZIL | Eijiro Tono |
| ARAKI, *the judge* | Ken Mitsuda |
| HORI, *the lawyer* | Toranosuke Ogawa |
| OKAMOTO | Kamatari Fujiwara |
| PSYCHIATRIST | Nobuo Nakamura |

## The Throne of Blood

Kumonosu-jo, 15 January, 1957

*The Castle of the Spider's Web / Cobweb Castle / Kumonosu-Djo / Le chateau de l'araignée / Le trône sanglant / Macbeth / Das Schloss im Spinnennetz.*

3,006 meters; 110 minutes. Original negative in existence; prints in circulation. A Toho Production.

Produced by Shojiro Motoki and Akira Kurosawa. Scenario by Shinobu Hashimoto, Ryuzo Kikushima, Hideo Oguni, and Akira Kurosawa. After Shakespeare's *Macbeth*. Photographed by Asakazu Nakai. Art Direction by Yoshiro Muraki and Kohei Ezaki. Sound Recording by Fumio Yanoguchi. Music by Masaru Sato.

| | |
|---|---|
| TAKETOKI WASHIZU | Toshiro Mifune |
| ASAJI, *his wife* | Isuzu Yamada |
| YOSHIAKI MIKI, *his friend* | Minoru Chiaki |
| YOSHITERU, *Miki's son* | Akira Kubo |
| KUNIHARU TSUZUKI | Takamaru Sasaki |
| KUNIMARU, *Kuniharu's son* | Yoichi Tachikawa |
| NORIYASU ODAGURA | Takashi Shimura |
| WITCH | Chieko Naniwa |

## The Lower Depths

Donzoko, 17 September, 1957
*Les bas-fonds / Nachtasyl.*

3,744 meters; 137 minutes. Original negative in existence; prints in circulation. A Toho Production.

Produced by Shojiro Motoki and Akira Kurosawa. Scenario by Hideo Oguni and Akira Kurosawa. Based on Gorky's play. Photographed by Kazuo Yamasaki. Art Direction by Yoshiro Muraki. Music by Masaru Sato.

Produced by Masumi Fujimoto and Akira Kurosawa. Scenario by Shinobu Hashimoto, Ryuzo Kikushima, Hideo Oguni, and Akira Kurosawa. Photographed by Kazuo Yamasaki (widescreen). Lighting by Ichiro Inohara. Art Direction by Yoshiro Muraki and Kohei Ezaki. Sound Recording by Fumio Yanoguchi. Music by Masaru Sato.

| SUTEKICHI, *the thief* | Toshiro Mifune |
|---|---|
| OSUGI, *the landlady* | Isuzu Yamada |
| ROKUBEI, *her husband* | Ganjiro Nakamura |
| OKAYO, *her sister* | Kyoko Kagawa |
| KAHEI, *the priest* | Bokuzen Hidari |
| THE EX-SAMURAI | Minoru Chiaki |
| THE ACTOR | Kamatari Fujiwara |
| TOMEKICHI, *the tinker* | Eijiro Tono |
| ASA, *his wife* | Eiko Miyoshi |
| OSEN, *the prostitute* | Akemi Negishi |
| YOSHISABURO, *the gambler* | Koji Mitsui |
| OTAKI | Nijiko Kiyokawa |
| TATSU | Haruo Tanaka |
| POLICE AGENT | Kichijiro Ueda |

| GENERAL ROKUROTA MAKABE | Toshiro Mifune |
|---|---|
| THE PRINCESS YUKIHIME | Misa Uehara |
| GENERAL IZUMI NAGAKURA | Takashi Shimura |
| GENERAL HYOE TADOKORO | Susumu Fujita |
| LADY-IN-WAITING | Eiko Miyoshi |
| TAHEI | Minoru Chiaki |
| MATAKISHI | Kamatari Fujiwara |
| GIRL | Toshiko Higuchi |
| SLAVER | Kichijiro Ueda |
| SOLDIER | Koji Mitsui |

# The Hidden Fortress

Kakushi Toride no San-Akunin, 28 December, 1958

*Three Bad Men in a Hidden Fortress / Trois salauds dans une forteresse cachée / La forteresse cachée / Die verborgene Festung.*

Original version: 3,802 meters; 139 minutes. Export version: 3,453 meters; 126 minutes. Original negative extant; prints in circulation. A Toho Production.

# The Bad Sleep Well

Warui Yatsu Hodo Yoku Nemuru, 4 September, 1960

*The Worse You Are the Better You Sleep / The Rose in the Mud / Les salauds dorment en paix / Les salauds se portent bien / Die Verworfenen schlafen gut / Die Bösen schlafen gut.*

Original version: 4,123 meters: 151 minutes. Export version: 3,700 meters; 135 minutes. Original negative extant; prints in circulation. A Kurosawa Films Production. Distributed by Toho.

Produced by Tomoyuki Tanaka and Akira Kurosawa. Scenario by Shinobu Hashimoto, Hideo Oguni, Ryuzo Kikushima, Eijiro Hisa-ita, and Akira Kurosawa. Photographed by Yuzuru Aizawa (wide-screen). Art Direction by Yoshiro Muraki. Lighting by Ichiro Inohara. Sound Recording by Fumio Yanoguchi and Hisashi Shimogawa. Music by Masaru Sato.

| | |
|---|---|
| KOICHI NISHI, *secretary to Iwabuchi* | Toshiro Mifune |
| ITAKURA, *his friend* | Takeshi Kato |
| IWABUCHI, *the president* | Masayuki Mori |
| MORIYAMA, *administrative officer* | Takashi Shimura |
| SHIRAI, *contract officer* | Akira Nishimura |
| WADA, *accountant* | Kamatari Fujiwara |
| MIURA, *accountant* | Gen Shimizu |
| KIEKO, *Iwabuchi's daughter* | Kyoko Kagawa |
| TATSUO, *Iwabuchi's son* | Tatsuya Mihashi |
| KANEKO | Kyu Sazanka |
| NONAKA, *public prosecutor* | Chishu Ryu |
| OKAKURA | Seiji Miyaguchi |
| LAWYER | Nobuo Nakamura |
| COMMISSIONER | Susumu Fujita |
| JOURNALIST | Koji Mitsui |

# Yojimbo

Yojimbo, 25 April, 1961
*The Bodyguard / Le garde du corps / Die Leibwache.*

3,025 meters; 110 minutes. Original negative in existence; prints in general circulation. A Kurosawa Films Production. Distributed by Toho.

Produced by Tomoyuki Tanaka and Ryuzo Kikushima. Scenario by Ryuzo Kikushima and Akira Kurosawa. Photographed by Kazuo Miyagawa (widescreen). Art Direction by Yoshiro Muraki. Lighting by Choshiro Ishii. Sound Recording by Hisashi Shimonaga and Choshichiro Mikami. Music by Masaru Sato.

| | |
|---|---|
| SANJURO KUWABATAKE | Toshiro Mifune |
| GONJI, *the saké-seller* | Eijiro Tono |
| TAZAEMON, *the silk merchant* | Kamatari Fujiwara |
| TOKUEMON, *the saké merchant* | Takashi Shimura |
| SEIBEI, *Tazaemon's henchman* | Seizaburo Kawazu |
| ORIN, *Seibei's wife* | Isuzu Yamada |
| YOICHIRO, *their son* | Hiroshi Tachikawa |
| USHITORA, *Tokuemon's henchman* | Kyu Sazanka |
| UNOSUKE, *Ushitora's younger brother* | Tatsuya Nakadai |
| INOKICHI, *Ushitora's brother* | Daisuke Kato |
| HANSUKE | Ikio Sawamura |
| KUMA | Akira Nishimura |
| KOHEI, *a farmer* | Yoshio Tsuchiya |
| NUI, *his wife* | Yoko Tsukasa |
| HOMMA, *the ex-yojimbo* | Susumu Fujita |

# Sanjuro

Tsubaki Sanjuro, 1 January, 1962
*Sanjuro / Sanjuro*

2,685 meters; 96 minutes. Original negative in existence; prints in circulation. A Kurosawa Films Production. Distributed by Toho.

Produced by Tomoyuki Tanaka and Ryuzo Kikushima. Scenario by Ryuzo Kikushima, Hideo Oguni, and Akira Kurosawa. After the novel by Shugoro Yamamoto. Photographed by Fukuzo Koizumi (widescreen). Art Direction by Yoshiro Muraki. Lighting by Ichiro Inohara. Sound Recording by Wataru Konuma and Hisashi Shimonaga. Music by Masaru Sato. Advisor on Swordplay—Ryu Kuze.

| | |
|---|---|
| SANJURO TSUBAKI | Toshiro Mifune |
| HANBEI MUROTO | Tatsuya Nakadai |
| IIRO IZAKA, *leader of the samurai* | Yuzo Kayama |
| SAMURAI | Akihiko Hirata |
| | Kunie Tanaka |
| | Hiroshi Tachikawa |
| | Tatsuhiko Hari |
| | Tatsuyoshi Ehara |
| | Kenzo Matsui |
| | Yoshio Tsuchiya |
| | Akira Kubo |
| KUROFUJI | Takashi Shimura |
| TAKEBAYASHI | Kamatari Fujiwara |
| KIKUI | Masao Shimizu |
| MUTSUTA | Yunosuke Ito |
| HIS WIFE | Takako Irie |
| CHIDORI, *his daughter* | Reiko Dan |
| THE SPY | Keiju Kobayashi |

# High and Low

Tengoku to Jigoku, 1 March, 1963
*Heaven and Hell / The Ransom / Le paradis et l'enfer / Entre le ciel et l'enfer / Zwischen Himmel und Hölle.*

3,924 meters; 143 minutes. Original negative in existence; prints in circulation. A Kurosawa Films Production. Distributed by Toho.

Produced by Tomoyuki Tanaka and Ryuzo Kikushima. Scenario by Ryuzo Kikushima, Hideo Oguni, and Akira Kurosawa. After the novel *King's Ransom* by Ed McBain (Evan Hunter). Photographed by Asakazu Nakai (widescreen). Art Direction by Yoshiro Muraki. Lighting by Ichiro Inohara. Sound Recording by Hisahi Shimonaga. Music by Masaru Sato.

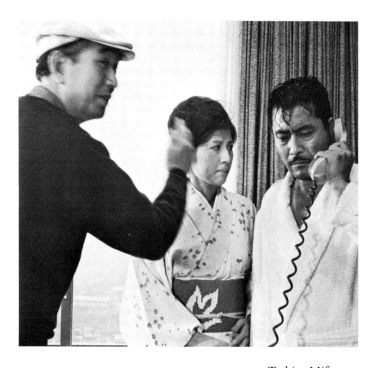

| | |
|---|---|
| KINGO GONDO | Toshiro Mifune |
| REIKO, *his wife* | Kyoko Kagawa |
| KAWANISHI, *her brother* | Tatsuya Mihashi |
| AOKI, *the chauffeur* | Yutaka Sada |
| INSPECTOR TOKURO | Tatsuya Nakadai |
| DIRECTOR | Takashi Shimura |
| COMMISSIONER | Susumu Fujita |
| DETECTIVE TAGUCHI | Kenjiro Ishiyama |
| DETECTIVE ARAI | Ko Kimura |
| DETECTIVE NAKAO | Takeshi Kato |
| DETECTIVE MURATA | Yoshio Tsuchiyama |
| DETECTIVE SHIMADA | Hiroshi Unayama |
| NEWSPAPERMAN | Koji Mitsui |
| GINJI TAKEUCHI, *the kidnapper* | Tsutomu Yamazaki |

# Red Beard

*Akahige*, 3 April, 1965
*Barbe rouge / Rotbart.*

5,069 meters; 185 minutes. Original negative in existence; prints in circulation. A Kurosawa Films Production. Distributed by Toho.

Produced by Ryuzo Kikushima and Tomoyuki Tanaka. Scenario by Ryuzo Kikushima, Hideo Oguni, Masato Ide, and Akira Kurosawa. After the novel by Shugoro Yamamoto. Photographed by Asakazu Nakai and Takao Saito (widescreen). Art Direction by Yoshiro Muraki. Lighting by Hiromitsu Mori. Sound Recording by Shin Watarai (four-track). Music by Masaru Sato.

| | |
|---|---|
| KYOJIO NIIDE (AKAHIGE) | Toshiro Mifune |
| NOBORU YASUMOTO | Yuzo Kayama |
| HANDAYU MORI | Yoshio Tsuchiya |
| GENZO TSUGAWA | Tatsuyoshi Ehara |
| OSUGI | Reiko Dan |
| THE MAD WOMAN | Kyoko Kagawa |
| ROKUSUKE | Kamatari Fujiwara |
| OKUNI | Akemi Negishi |
| SAHACHI | Tsutomu Yamazaki |
| ONAKA | Miyuki Kuwano |
| GOHEIJI | Eijiro Tono |
| TOKUBEI IZUMIYA | Takashi Shimura |
| OTOYO | Terumi Niki |
| KIN | Haruko Sugimura |
| MASAE | Yoko Naito |
| HER FATHER | Ken Mitsuda |
| NOBORU'S MOTHER | Kinuyo Tanaka |
| NOBORU'S FATHER | Chishu Ryu |
| CHOJI | Yoshitaka Zushi |

## Dodesukaden

Dodesukaden, 15 October, 1970

244 minutes. Original negative in existence; prints in circulation. A Yonki no Kai/Toho Production. Distributed by Toho.

Produced by Yoichi Matsue. Scenario by Akira Kurosawa, Hideo Oguni, Shinobu Hashimoto. After stories by Shugoro Yamamoto. Photographed by Takao Saito (standard screen / Eastmancolor). Art Direction by Yoshiro and Shinobu Muraki. Sound Recording by Fumio Yamaguchi. Music by Toru Takemitsu.

| ROKKUCHAN | Yoshitaka Zushi |
| *His mother* | Kin Sugai |
| SHIMA | Junzaburo Ban |
| *His wife* | Kiyoko Tange |
| *His guests* | Michiko Hino |
| | Tape Shimokawa |
| | Keishi Furuyama |
| MASUDA | Hisashi Igawa |
| *His wife* | Hideko Okiyama |
| KAWAGUCHI | Kunie Tanaka |
| *His wife* | Jitsuko Yoshimura |

| RYO | Shinsuke Minami |
| *His wife* | Yoko Kusunoki |
| *His children* | Toshiyuki Tonomura |
| | Miika Oshida |
| | Satoshi Hasegawa |
| | Kumiko Ono |
| | Tatsuhiko Yagishita |
| KYOTA | Tatsuo Matsumura |
| *His wife* | Tsuji Imura |
| *His step-daughter* | Tomoko Yamazaki |
| OKABE | Masahiko Kametani |
| BEGGAR | Noboru Mitani |
| *His son* | Hiroyuki Kawase |
| HEI | Hiroshi Akutagawa |
| *Ocho, his wife* | Tomoko Naraoka |
| TAMBA | Atsushi Watanabe |
| KUMAMBA | Jerry Fujio |
| THIEF | Sanji Kojima |
| VEGETABLE MAN | Masahiko Tanimura |
| PAINTER | Kazuo Kato |
| GIRL | Akemi Negishi |
| BAR GIRL | Michiko Araki |
| COOK | Shoichi Kuwayama |
| OLD MAN | Kamatari Fujiwara |

## Dersu Uzala

Derusu Usara, 2 August, 1975

3,900 meters; 141 minutes. Original negative in existence; prints in circulation. A Mosfilm Production. Distributed (in Japan) by Herald Eiga.

Produced by Nikolai Sizov and Yoichi Matsue. Scenario by Akira Kurosawa and Yuri Nagibin. After the novelization by Vladimir Arseniev. Photographed by Asakazu Nakai, Yuri Gantman, and Fiodor Dobronravov. Art Direction by Yuri Raksha. Music by Isaac Schwalz. Associate Direction: Teruyo Nogami, Vladimir Vasiliev. Production Manager: Karlen Agadjanov. Interpreter: Lev Korshikov.

| ARSENIEV | Yuri Salomin |
| DERSU | Maxim Munzuk |
| JAN BAO | Schemeikl Chokmorov |
| TURTWIGIN | Vladimir Klemena |
| MRS. ARSENIEV | Svetlana Danielchenka |

mancolor) by Takao Saito and Masaharu Ueda. Photography Supervised by Kazuo Miyagawa and Asakazu Nakai. Art Direction by Yoshiro Muraki. Music by Shinichiro Ikebe. International Version Producers: Francis Coppola and George Lucas.

| | |
|---|---|
| SHINGEN TAKEDA | Tatsuya Nakadai |
| HIS DOUBLE (the *Kagemusha*) | Tatsuya Nakadai |
| NOBUKADO TAKEDA | Tsutomu Yamazaki |
| KATSUYORI TAKEDA | Kenichi Hagiwara |
| TAKEMARU TAKEDA | Kota Yui |
| MASAKAGE YAMAGATA | Hideji Otaki |
| NOBUHARU BABA | Hideo Murata |
| MASATOYO NATIO | Takayuki Shiho |
| MASANOBU KOSAKA | Shuhei Sugimori |
| MASATANE HARA | Noboru Shimizu |
| KATSUSUKE ATOBE | Koji Shimizu |
| NOBUSHIGE OYAMADA | Sen Yamamoto |
| NOBUNAGA ODA | Daisuke Ryu |
| IEYASU TOKUGAWA | Masayuki Yui |
| RANMARU MORI | Yasuhito Yamanaka |
| GYOBU TAGUCHI | Takashi Shimura |
| OYUNOKATA | Mitsuko Baisho |
| OTSUYANOKATA | Kaori Momoi |
| NODA CASTLE SOLDIER | Akihiko Sugizaki |
| KUGUTSUSHI | Toshiaki Tanabe |
| SALT VENDOR | Yoshimitsu Yamaguchi |
| MONK | Takashi Ebata |
| TAKEMARU'S NURSE | Kumeko Otowa |
| DOCTOR | Kamatari Fujiwara |

## Kagemusha

Kagemusha, 23 April, 1980
(*The Shadow Warrior*)

5,012 meters; 179 minutes. Original negative in existence. International version: 162 minutes; prints in circulation. A Kurosawa Films/Toho Production.

Produced by Akira Kurosawa and Tomoyuki Tanaka. Assistant Producer: Teruyo Nogami. Production Coordinator: Ishio Honda. Production Advisers: Shinobu Hashimoto and Takao Saito. Written by Akira Kurosawa and Masato Ide. Photographed (Panavision, East-

## Ran

160 minutes. Original negative in existence; prints in circulation. A Franco-Japanese coproduction for Greenway Film Production/ Herald Ace, Int./Nippon Herald Films, Inc.

Produced by Masato Hara and Serge Silberman. Executive Producer: Katsumi Furukawa. Production Managers: Teruyo Nogami, Seikichi Iizumi, Satoru Iizeki, Takashi Ohashi. General Production Manager: Ully Pickardt. Production Coordinator: Hisao Kurosawa. Written by Akira Kurosawa, Hideo Oguni, Masato Ide. Photographed (Eastmancolor) by Takao Saito and Masaharu Ueda in collaboration with Asakazu Nakai. Art Direction by Yoshiro and Shinobu Muraki. Costumes by Emi Wada. Music by Toru Takemitsu. Director Counselor: Ishiro Honda. Directed by Akira Kurosawa.

| | |
|---|---|
| HIDETORA ICHIMONJI | Tatsuya Nakadao |
| TARO | Akira Terao |
| JIRO | Jimpachi Nezu |
| SABURO | Daisuke Ryu |
| KAEDE | Mieko Harada |
| SUÉ | Yoshiko Miyazaki |
| TANGO | Masayuki Yui |
| IKOMA | Kazuo Kato |
| FUJIMAKI | Hitoshi Ueki |
| AYABE | Jun Tazaki |
| OGURA | Norio Matsui |
| KUROGANE | Hisashi Igawa |
| SHINANE | Kenji Kodama |
| NAGANUMA | Toshiya Ito |
| HATAKEYAMA | Takeshi Kato |
| TSURUMARU | Takeshi Nomura |
| KYOAMI | Peitah |

## Dreams

120 minutes. Original negative in existence; prints in circulation. A Warner Brothers Production. A Steven Spielberg presentation.

Produced by Hisao Kurosawa and Mike Y. Inoue. Production Manager: Teruyo Nogami. Associate Producers: Allan H. Liebert, Seikichi Iizumi. Photographed (Eastmancolor) by Takao Saito and Masaharu Ueda. Creative Consultant: Ishiro Honda. Art Directors: Yoshiro Muraki, Akira Sakuragi. Costumes by Emi Wada. Music by Shinichiro Ikebe. (Also, music by Chopin and Ippolitov-Ivanov.) Visual effects by Industrial Light and Magic. Other effects by Sony PCL, Tokyo, and Den Film-Effects, Tokyo. Written and directed by Akira Kurosawa.

With: Akira Terao, Mitsuko Baisho, Toshie Negishi, Mieko Hara, Mitsunori Isaki, Toshihiko Nakano, Yoshitaka Zushi, Hisashi Igawa, Chosuke Ikariya, Chishu Ryu, and Martin Scorsese.

# Rhapsody in August
Hachigatsu no Kyoshikoku, 6 May, 1991

100 minutes. Original negative in existence; prints in circulation. A Kurosawa Production presented by Feature Film Enterprises II and Shochiku Film.

Produced by Toru Okuyama and Hisao Kurosawa, with Yoshie Inoue and Seikichi Iizumi. Photographed by Takao Saito and Masaharu Ueda. Associate Director: Ishiro Honda. Art Director: Yoshiro Muraki. Lighting: Takeji Sano. Recording: Kenichi Benitani. Costumes: Kazuko Kurosawa. Music by Shinichiro Ikebe. (Also music from Schubert and Vivaldi.) After the novel by Kiyoko Murata. Written and directed by Akira Kurosawa.

| | |
|---|---|
| GRANDMOTHER KANE | Sachiko Murase |
| TADAO, *Kané's son* | Hisashi Igawa |
| MACHIKO, *his wife* | Narumi Kayashim |
| TAMI, *his daughter* | Tomoko Otakara |
| SHINJIRO, *his son* | Mitsunori Isaki |
| YOSHIE, *Kané's daughter* | Toshie Negishi |
| NOBORU, *her husband* | Choichiro Kawarasaki |
| TATEO, *her son* | Hidetaka Yoshioka |
| MINAKO, *her daughter* | Mie Suzuki |
| CLARK, *Kané's nephew* | Richard Gere |

# Madadayo
Madâ dâ yo, 17 April, 1993

134 minutes. Original negative in existence; prints in circulation. A Daiei/Dentsu Production/Kurosawa Productions Film.

Produced by Yasuyoshi Tokuma, Gohei Kogure, Yo Yamamoto, Yuzo Irie, and Hisao Kurosawa. Based on works by Hyakken Uchida. Photographed by Takao Saito and Masaharu Ueda. Art Direction by Yoshiro Muraki. Lighting by Takeji Sano. Sound Recording by Hideo Nishizaki. Costumes by Kazuko Kurosawa. Music: Vivaldi, arranged by Shinichiro Ikebe. Written and directed by Akira Kurosawa.

| | |
|---|---|
| THE PROFESSOR | Tatsuo Matsumura |
| *his wife* | Kyoko Kagawa |
| TAKAYAMA | Hisashi Igawa |
| AMAKI | Joji Tokoro |
| KIRIYAMA | Masayuki Yui |
| SAWAMURA | Akira Terao |
| PRIEST KAMEYAMA | Asei Kobayashi |
| DOCTOR KOBAYASHI | Take Klusaka |

## Kurosawa Scripts Filmed by Other Directors

**Uma** (Horses.) Script by Kurosawa and Kajiro Yamamoto. Directed by Yamamoto in 1941.

**Seishun no Kiryu** (Currents of Youth.) Directed by Osamu Fushimizi in 1942.

**Tsubasa no Gaika** (A Triumph of Wings.) Directed by Satsuo Yamamoto in 1942.

**Dohyosai** (Wrestling-Ring Festival.) Directed by Santaro Marune in 1944.

**Appare Isshin Tasuke**. (Brava, Tasuke Isshin!) Directed by Kiyoshi Saeki in 1945.

**Hatsukoi** (First Love.) A section of the omnibus film, *Yotsu no Koi no Monogatari* (Four Love Stories.) Directed by Shiro Toyoda in 1947.

**Ginrei no Hate** (To the End of the Silver Mountains.) Script by Kurosawa and Kajiro Yamamoto. Directed by Senkichi Taniguchi in 1947.

**Shozo** (The Portrait.) Directed by Keisuke Kinoshita in 1948.

**Jigoku no Kifujin** (The Lady from Hell.) Directed by Yotoyoshi Oda in 1949.

**Jakoman to Tetsu** (Jakoman and Tetsu.) Directed by Senkichi Taniguchi in 1949. Remade by Kinju Fukasaku in 1964.

**Akatsuki no Dasso** (Escape at Dawn.) Directed by Senkichi Taniguchi in 1950.

**Jiruba Tetsu** (Tetsu 'Jilba'.) Directed by Isamu Kosugi in 1950.

**Tateshi Danpei** (Fencing Master.) Directed by Masahiro Makino in 1950.

**Ai to Nikushime no Kanata** (Beyond Love and Hate.) Directed by Senkichi Taniguchi in 1951.

**Kedamono no Yado** (The Den of Beasts.) Directed by Tatsuyasu Osone in 1951.

**Ketto Kagiya no Tsuji** (The Duel at the Key-Maker's Corner.) Directed by Issei Mori in 1951.

**Sugata Sanshiro**. Remade under its original title by Shigeo Tanaka in 1955. Again remade under its original title by Seiichiro Uchikawa, edited by Akira Kurosawa, 1965.

**Tekichu Odan Sanbyaku Ri** (Three Hundred Miles through Enemy Lines.) Directed by Issei Mori in 1957.

**Sengoku Guntoden** (The Saga of the Vagabond.) Written after the original of Sadao Yamanaka. Directed by Toshio Sugie in 1960.

**Shichinin no Samurai**. Remade as *The Magnificent Seven*, directed by John Sturges in 1961.

**Rashomon**. Remade as *The Outrage*, directed by Martin Ritt in 1964.

**Yojimbo**. Remade in pirated version as *Per un pugno di dollari* by Sergio Leone in 1964.

**Runaway Train**. Directed by Andrei Konchalovsky in 1985.

## Kurosawa's Unfilmed Scripts

**Daruma-dera no Doitsujin** (A German at the Daruma Temple.)

**Shizukanari** (All Is Quiet.)

**Yuki** (Snow.)

**Mori no Senichiya** (A Thousand and One Nights in the Forest.)

**Jajauma Monogatari** (The Story of a Bad Horse.)

**Dokkoi kono Yari** (The Lifted Spear.)

# A Selective Bibliography

Few of the writings listed in this bibliography are cited in the present book. The purpose of the following list is to suggest the best of Kurosawa criticism. In writing, however, I did make much use of three publications: the undated Toho mimeographed 'autobiography' of Kurosawa, and the two *Kinema Jumpo* volumes devoted to the director. All three are in Japanese and are the sources of some of the quotes from Kurosawa and others. The remainder of the quotes are from conversations with the director, with those about him, with actors, with technicians, with friends.

"Akira Kurosawa." *Études cinématographiques,* nos. 30–31, 1964.

Anderson, Joseph L. "Japanese Swordfighters and American Gunfighters." *Cinema Journal* 12, no. 2, 1973.

Anderson, Joseph L., and Loren Hoekzen. "The Spaces Between: American Criticism of Japanese Film." *Wide Angle* 1, no. 4, 1977.

Anderson, Joseph L., and Donald Richie. *The Japanese Film: Art and Industry.* Charles E. Tuttle Co., Tokyo, 1959. Grove Press, New York, 1960. Feltinelli Editore, Milano, 1961. Revised edition, Princeton University Press, 1982.

Arbeitsgemeinschaft für Filmfragen an der Universität zu Köln. *Der Japanische Film. I—Akira Kurosawa—Dokumentation.* University of Cologne, 1962.

Bachmann, Dieter, ed. "Akira Kurosawa: Mit den Augen des Ostens." Zurich; *Du: Die Zeitschrift der Kultur.* Heft nr. 8, 1990.

Bock, Audie. *Japanese Film Directors.* Kodansha International, San Francisco, 1985.

Boyd, David. "*Rashomon*: From Akutagawa to Kurosawa." *Literature/Film Quarterly* 15, no. 3, 1987.

British Film Institute. *A Light in the Japanese Window.* Programme brochure for the National Film Theatre's Japanese Week. London, British Film Institute, 1959.

———— *Orient: A Survey of Films.* London, British Film Institute, 1959.

Burch, Noel. "Approaching Japanese Film." In *Cinema and Language.* Ed. Stephen Heath and Patricia Mellencamp. University Publications of America, Frederick, Md., 1983.

————. *To the Distant Observer: Form and Meaning in the Japanese Cinema.* Rev. and ed. Annette Michelson. University of California Press, Berkeley, 1979.

Buruma, Ian. "Japan's Emperor of Film." *New York Times Magazine,* October 29, 1989.

*Cinéma '55.* No. 6. June–July, 1955. Paris. *Le cinéma japonais.*

Cinémathèque française. *Initiation au cinéma japonais.* Cinémathèque française, Paris, 1963.

Chang, Joseph S. "*Kagemusha* and the *Chushingura* Motif." *East-West Film Journal* 3, no. 2, June 1989.

Chang, Kevin K. W., ed. *Kurosawa: Perceptions on Life, An Anthology of Essays.* Honolulu Academy of Arts, Honolulu, 1991.

Daney, Serge. "Un ours en plus (*Dersu Uzala*)." *Cahiers du Cinéma,* no. 274, March 1977.

Decaux, Emmanuel, and Bruno Villien. "Entretien avec Akira Kurosawa." *Cinématographe,* no. 88, 1983.

Desser, David. "Kurosawa's Eastern 'Western': *Sanjuro* and the Influence of *Shane*." *Film Criticism* 8, no. 1, Fall 1983.

———. *The Samurai Films of Akira Kurosawa*. UMI Research Press, Ann Arbor, 1983.

Erens, Patricia. *Akira Kurosawa: A Guide to References and Resources*. G. K. Hall & Co., Boston, 1979.

*Etudes cinématographiques*. Nos. 30–31, 1964. Paris. *Akira Kurosawa*.

Ezratty, Sacha. *Kurosawa*. Editions Universitaires, Paris, 1964.

Falk, Ray. "Interview with Kurosawa." *New York Times*, June 1, 1952.

*Film Journal*. No. 11, October, 1958. Melbourne. *The Japanese Cinema*.

Goodwin, James. *Akira Kurosawa and Intertextual Cinema*. Johns Hopkins University Press, Baltimore, 1994.

Govaers, Hiroko, ed. *Le Cinéma japonais de ses origines à nos jours*. La Cinémathèque Française, Paris, 1984.

Grilli, Peter. "Kurosawa Directs a Cinematic *Lear*." *New York Times*, December 15, 1985.

———. "The Old Man and the Scene: Notes on the Making of *Ran*." *Film Comment* 21, no. 5, 1985.

Giuglaris, Shinobu et Marcel. *Le cinéma japonais*. Editions du Cerf, Paris, 1956.

High, Peter B. "Kurosawa: Dread and Loathing in Siberia: A Study of Script Revisions for *Dersu Uzala*." Unpublished paper.

Iwata Shigetoshi. "Kurosawa's Descent into Self-Indulgence." Tokyo. *Japan Echo*, Vol. XVIII, no. 3, 1991.

Japan Film Center. *Kurosawa: A Retrospective*. Japan Society, New York, 1981.

Kawamoto Saburo. "An Interview with Kurosawa Akira," Tokyo. *Japan Echo*, Vol. XVIII, no. 3, 1991.

*Kinema Jumpo*. No. 338, March 25, 1963. Tokyo. *Akira Kurosawa*. (In Japanese.)

———. Special Issue no. 10, September 5, 1964, Tokyo. *Two Japanese: Kurosawa and Mifune*. (In Japanese.)

Kott, Jan. "The Edo Lear." Trans. Lillian Vallee. *New York Review of Books*, April 24, 1986.

Kurosawa, Akira. *Complete Works of Akira Kurosawa*. (In Japanese and English.) Trans. Kimi Aida and Don Kenny. Tokyo: Kinema Jumpo Sha, 1971. Volumes published: 1, *Dodesukaden*; 2, *Sugata Sanshiro / No Regrets for Our Youth*; 3, *One Wonderful Sunday / Drunken Angel*; 4, *Quiet Duel / Stray Dog*; 6, *The Idiot / Ikiru*; 9, *The Hidden Fortress / The Bad Sleep Well*. Volumes 5, 7, 8, and 10 not issued; series discontinued.

———. *Ikiru*. Trans. Donald Richie. Simon & Schuster, New York, 1969. Reprinted in Howard Hibbett, ed., *Contemporary Japanese Literature: An Anthology of Fiction, Film, and Other Writing Since 1945*. Alfred Knopf, New York, 1977. Reprinted Faber & Faber, London, 1992.

*Kagemusha*. In Japanese, with foreword by Kurosawa. Includes 110 plates, drawings, and designs for the film. Kodansha International, Tokyo, 1980.

———. *Ran*. Trans. Tadashi Shishido. Shambhala, Boston, 1986.

———. *Rashomon*. Ed. and trans. Donald Richie. Grove, New York, 1969.

———. *Seven Samurai*. Trans. Donald Richie. Lorrimer, London. Faber and Faber, London, 1992.

———. *Something Like an Autobiography*. Trans. Audie E. Bock. Vintage, New York, 1983.

———. The Throne of Blood. Trans. Hisae Niki. Faber & Faber, London, 1992.

McDonald, Keiko I. *Cinema East: A Critical Study of Major Japanese Films*. Fairleigh Dickinson University Press, Rutherford, N.J., 1983.

Mellen, Joan. "The Epic Cinema of Kurosawa." *Take One* 3, no. 4, 1971.

Mellen, Joan. *Voices from the Japanese Cinema*. Liveright, New York, 1975.

———. *The Waves at Genji's Door: Japan Through Its Cinema.* Pantheon, New York, 1976.

Mesnil, M. "Visite à l'empereur du Japon." *Cinéma,* 103, 1966.

Mitchell, Greg. "Kurosawa in Winter." American Film, April, Washington, D.C., 1982.

Miyagawa, Kazuo. "My Life as a Cameraman: Yesterday–Today–Tomorrow." Trans. Linda Ehrlich and Akiko Shibagaki. *Post Script* 11, no. 1, 1991.

Niogret, Hubert. *Kurosawa.* Editions Payot et Rivages, Paris, 1995.

Nolletti, Arthur, and David Desser, eds. *Reframing Japanese Cinema: Authorship, Genre, History.* Indiana University Press, Bloomington, 1992.

Powers, John. "Kurosawa: An Audience with the Emperor." Trans. Audie Bock. *L.A. Weekly,* April 4, 1986.

Prince, Stephen. *The Warrior's Camera: The Cinema of Akira Kurosawa.* Princeton University Press, Princeton, 1991.

Raison, Bertrand, and Serge Toubiana, eds. *Le Livre de Ran.* Cahiers du Cinéma/Seuil, Paris, 1985.

*Revue internationale du cinéma.* No. 14. *Regards sur le cinéma japonais,* 1960.

Richie, Donald. "Dostoevsky with a Japanese Camera." In Lewis Jacobs, ed. *The Emergence of Film Art.* Hopkinson & Blake, New York, 1969.

———, ed. *Focus on Rashomon.* Prentice-Hall, Englewood Cliffs, N.J., 1972.

———. *Japanese Cinema: Film Style and National Character.* Doubleday, Garden City, N.Y., 1971.

——— "Kurosawa on Kurosawa." *Sight and Sound,* Spring–Summer and Fall–Winter, 1964.

———. "A Personal Record." *Film Quarterly* 14, no. 1, 1960.

———. "Viewing Japanese Film: Some Considerations." *East-West Film Journal* 1, no. 1, 1986.

———. *Japanese Cinema: An Introduction.* Oxford University Press, Hong Kong, 1990.

Ross, Lillian. "Profiles: Kurosawa Frames." *New Yorker,* December 21, 1981.

Roud, Richard, ed. *Cinema: A Critical Dictionary.* 2 vols. Viking Press, New York, 1980.

Sadoul, Georges. "Entretien avec Akira Kurosawa." *Cinéma,* no. 92, 1965.

Sato, Tadao. *Currents in Japanese Cinema.* Trans. Gregory Barrett. Kodansha International, Tokyo, 1982.

———. "The World of Akira Kurosawa." Trans. Goro Iiri. *The Study of the History of Cinema* (Tokyo), no. 1, 1973; no. 2, 1973; no. 3, 1974.

Seltzer, Alex. "Seeing Through the Eyes of the Audience." *Film Comment,* May–June, 1993.

Seton, Marie. "Akira Kurosawa: des classiques russes et anglais pour faire réfléchir les japonais." *Radio-cinéma-télévision,* no. 417, 1955.

Shirai, Yoshio, Hayao Shibata, and Koichi Yamada. "'L'Empereur': entretien avec Kurosawa Akira." *Cahiers du Cinéma,* no. 182, 1966.

Svensson, Arne. *Screen Series: Japan.* A. S. Barnes, New York, 1971.

Tada, Michitaro. "The Destiny of Samurai Films." *East-West Film Journal* 1, no. 1, 1986.

Tessier, Max. "Propos d'Akira Kurosawa." *Revue du Cinéma,* no. 408, 1985.

Toho, Publications Section, Tokyo. *Akira Kurosawa.* (In Japanese.) No date—ca. 1960.

Yakir, Dan. "The Warrior Returns." *Film Comment* 16, no. 6, 1980.

Yu, Beoncheon. *Akutagawa: An Introduction.* Wayne State University Press, Detroit, 1972.

Zambrano, Ana Laura. "*Throne of Blood:* Kurosawa's *Macbeth,*" *Literature/Film Quarterly* 2, no. 3, 1974.

# Index

# List of Plates